I & II SAMUEL

THE OLD TESTAMENT LIBRARY

A. Graeme Auld

I & II Samuel

A Commentary

WJK
WESTMINSTER
JOHN KNOX PRESS
LOUISVILLE • KENTUCKY

First edition
Published by Westminster John Knox Press
Louisville, Kentucky

11 12 13 14 15 16 17 18 19 20—10 9 8 7 6 5 4 3 2 1

Book design by Jennifer K. Cox

Library of Congress Cataloging-in-Publication Data

Auld, A. Graeme.
I & II Samuel : a commentary / A. Graeme Auld.—1st ed.
p. cm.—(The Old Testament library)
Includes bibliographical references (p.).
ISBN 978-0-664-22105-8 (alk. paper)
1. Bible. O.T. Samuel—Commentaries. I. Title. II. Title: I and II Samuel. III. Title: First & Second Samuel.
BS1325.53.A95 2011
222'.4077—dc23

2011023669

PRINTED IN THE UNITED STATES OF AMERICA

♾ The paper used in this publication meets the minimum requirements of the American National Standard for Information Sciences—Permanence of Paper for Printed Library Materials, ANSI Z39.48-1992.

Westminster John Knox Press advocates the responsible use of our natural resources. The text paper of this book is made from 30% postconsumer waste.

for Sylvia:

best friend, wife,
and fellow lover
of Jerusalem

The habit of perusing periodical works may be properly added to Averroës' catalogue of Anti-Mnemonics, or weakeners of the memory.

—Coleridge

Never use epigraphs—they kill the mystery in the work!

—Adli

(with apologies to Orhan Pamuk)

CONTENTS

ACKNOWLEDGMENTS

I have appreciated the support—often challenging support—of colleagues associated with Westminster John Knox and the Old Testament Library. Jon L. Berquist invited me to undertake a project that has allowed me to develop at much greater length proposals about the development of the books of Samuel (and Kings)—proposals that have still to persuade many of my academic colleagues. David L. Petersen and S. David Garber have in turn given my work very careful scrutiny, and contributed greatly to its accuracy and clarity. Any blemishes that remain are entirely my responsibility.

ABBREVIATIONS

A (= LXX[A])	Codex Alexandrinus
AB	Anchor Bible
abs.	absolute
abstr.	abstract (term)
adj.	adjective
Akk.	Akkadian
aor.	aorist
Arab.	Arabic
art.	article
B (= LXX[B])	Codex Vaticanus
BA	*Bible d'Alexandrie*. Vol. 9.1, *Premier livre des règnes*. Translation and notes by Bernard Grillet and Michel Lestienne. Paris: Cerf, 1997.
BDB	Brown, F., S.R. Driver, and C. A. Briggs. *A Hebrew and English Lexicon of the Old Testament.* Oxford: Oxford University Press, 1907
BETL	Bibliotheca ephemeridum theologicarum lovaniensium
BHL	*Biblia Hebraica Leningradensia*
BHS	*Biblia Hebraica Stuttgartensia*
BTH	Book of Two Houses (house of David and house of Yahweh)
BWANT	Beiträge zur Wissenschaft vom Alten und Neuen Testament
BZAW	Beihefte zur Zeitschrift für die alttestamentliche Wissenschaft
c.	century
CAT	Commentaire de l'Ancien Testament
CEV	Contemporary English Version
ch(s).	chapter(s)
CL	Codex Leningradensis
cst.	construct
DCH	*Dictionary of Classical Hebrew*. Edited by D. J. A. Clines. Sheffield, 1993–
DJD	Discoveries in the Judaean Desert 17
Ébib	Études bibliques

f.	feminine
FAT	Forschungen zum Alten Testament
FOTL	Forms of the Old Testament Literature
FP	Former Prophets
FRLANT	Forschungen zur Religion und Literatur des Alten und Neuen Testaments
Gk.	Greek language
GT (= B + LT)	Greek Text
HRCS	*Concordance to the Septuagint.* Compiled by Edwin Hatch and Henry A. Redpath. 2d ed. 3 vols. in 2. Grand Rapids: Baker Books, 1998.
HB	Hebrew Bible
Heb.	Hebrew language
ICC	International Critical Commentary
impf.	imperfect
inf.	infinitive
Índice	*Índice griego-hebreo del texto antioqueno en los libros históricos.* Vols. 1–2. Compiled by Natalio Fernández Marcos, Mª Victoria Spottorno Díaz-Caro, and José Manuel Cañas Reíllo. Madrid: Instituto de Filología del CSIC, 2005.
JBL	*Journal of Biblical Literature*
JSOT	*Journal for the Study of the Old Testament*
JSOT Sup	Journal for the Study of the Old Testament: Supplement
K	Kethib (*kĕtîb*), "[what is] written"
KAT	Kommentar zum Alten Testament
KBL	Koehler, L., and W. Baumgartner. *Lexicon in Veteris Testamenti libros.* 2d ed. Leiden, 1958
KHC	Kurzer Hand-Commentar zum Alten Testament
LHBOTS	Library of Hebrew Bible / Old Testament Studies
lit.	literally
LSJ	Liddell, H. G., R. Scott, H. S. Jones, et al. *A Greek-English Lexicon.* 9th ed. with revised supplement. Oxford, 1996
LT (= LXX^{L})	Lucianic Text
LXX	Septuagint
m.	masculine
Mand.	Mandelkern, S. *Veteris Testamenti concordantiae hebraicae atque chaldaicae, etc.* 9th ed. Jerusalem and Tel Aviv: Schocken, 1971
MS(S)	manuscript(s)
MT	Masoretic Text of the Hebrew Bible
NETS	*A New Translation of the Septuagint and the Other Greek Translations Traditionally Included under That Title.* Edited

	by Albert Pietersma and Benjamin G. Wright. New York and Oxford: Oxford University Press, 2007. http://ccat.sas.upenn.edu/nets.
NRSV	New Revised Standard Version
obj.	object
OG	Old Greek
OL	Old Latin
OT	Old Testament
OtSt	Oudtestamentische Studiën
pass.	passive
pf.	perfect
pl.	plural
prep.	preposition
ptc.	participle
Q	Qere (*qĕrê*), "[what is to be] read"
RB	*Revue biblique*
RSV	Revised Standard Version
subj.	subject
sg.	singular
SOTSMS	Society for Old Testament Studies Monograph Series
STDJ	Studies on the Texts of the Desert of Judah
suf.	suffix
Syr.	Syriac
Tg.	Targum
Vulg.	Vulgate
vb.	verb
VS(S)	version(s)
VT	*Vetus Testamentum*
VTSup	Vetus Testamentum Supplements
v./vv.	verse/verses
WBC	Word Biblical Commentary
ZAH	*Zeitschrift für Althebräistik*
ZAW	*Zeitschrift für die alttestamentliche Wissenschaft*

BIBLIOGRAPHY

This commentary makes no attempt at thorough documented interaction with other studies on Samuel and related topics. The relevant secondary literature is vast; here I simply note the texts and tools that have been used in the preparation of this translation and commentary, and two other sorts of material that have been explicitly cited: classic and standard commentaries; and some newer studies unavailable to (or at least unused in) recent larger commentaries. I comment on a larger selection in "1 and 2 Samuel," in *Oxford Bibliographies Online: Biblical Studies*, edited by Christopher Matthews (New York: Oxford University Press, online in 2011).

Texts

Aleppo Codex (*Keter Aram-Zoba*). Jerusalem: Ben Zvi Institute, 2007. www.aleppocodex.org.

Biblia Hebraica Leningradensia. Edited by Aron Dotan. Peabody, MA: Hendrickson, 2001.

Bibliorum sacrorum Graecorum Codex Vaticanus B. Rome: Istituto Poligrafico e Zecca dello Stato, 1999.

The Leningrad Codex: A Facsimile Edition. Edited by David Noel Freedman et al. Grand Rapids: Eerdmans; Leiden: Brill, 1998.

The Old Testament in Greek. Vol. 2, Pt. 1, *I and II Samuel*. Edited by Alan E. Brooke, Norman McLean, and Henry St. John Thackeray. London: Cambridge University Press, 1927.

El texto antioqueno de la Biblia griega. Vol. 1, *1–2 Samuel*. Edited by Natalio Fernández Marcos and José Ramón Busto Saiz. Madrid: Instituto de Filología del CSIC, 1989.

Qumran Cave 4. Vol. 12, *1–2 Samuel*. Edited by Frank M. Cross, Donald W. Parry, Richard J. Saley, and Eugene Ulrich. DJD 17. Oxford: Clarendon, 2005.

Tools

A Greek-English Lexicon. With a revised supplement. Compiled by Henry G. Liddell, Robert Scott, H. S. Jones, et al. Oxford: Clarendon, 1996.

Concordance to the Septuagint. Compiled by Edwin Hatch and Henry A. Redpath. 2d ed. 1998. Grand Rapids: Baker Books, 1998.

Índice griego-hebreo del texto antioqueno en los libros históricos. Vols. 1–2. Compiled by Natalio Fernández Marcos, Mª Victoria Spottorno Díaz-Caro, and José Manuel Cañas Reíllo. Madrid: Instituto de Filología del CSIC, 2005.

Veteris Testamenti Concordantiae hebraicae atque chaldaicae, etc. Compiled by Solomon Mandelkern. 9th ed. Jerusalem and Tel Aviv: Schocken, 1971.

Commentaries

Cited by author, plus volume number if needed

Alter, Robert. *The David Story: A Translation with Commentary of 1 and 2 Samuel*. New York: Norton, 1999.

Bar-Efrat, Shimʿon. *Das erste Buch Samuel: Ein narratologisch-philologischer Kommentar*. BWANT 176. Stuttgart: Kohlhammer, 2007.

———. *Das zweite Buch Samuel: Ein narratologisch-philologischer Kommentar*. BWANT 181. Stuttgart: Kohlhammer, 2009.

Budde, Karl. *Die Bücher Samuel*. KHC 8. Tübingen and Leipzig: Mohr (Siebeck), 1902.

Campbell, Antony F. *1 Samuel*. FOTL 7. Grand Rapids: Eerdmans, 2003.

———. *2 Samuel*. FOTL 8. Grand Rapids: Eerdmans, 2005.

Caquot, André, and Philippe de Robert. *Les livres de Samuel*. CAT 6. Geneva: Labor et Fides, 1994.

Dhorme, Paul. *Les livres de Samuel*. Ébib. Paris: Gabalda, 1910.

Driver, Samuel R. *Notes on the Hebrew Text of the Books of Samuel*. Oxford: Clarendon, 1890.

Grillet, Bernard, and Michel Lestienne. *La Bible d'Alexandrie*. Vol. 9.1, *Premier livre des Règnes*. Paris: Cerf, 1997.

Jobling, David. *1 Samuel*. Berit Olam. Collegeville, MN: Liturgical Press, 1998.

Klein, Ralph W. *1 Samuel*. WBC 10. Waco, TX: Word Books, 1983.

McCarter, P. Kyle. *1 Samuel*. AB 9. New York: Doubleday, 1980.

———. *2 Samuel*. AB 10. New York: Doubleday, 1984.

Stoebe, Hans J. *Das erste Buch Samuelis*. KAT 8/1. Gütersloh: Gerd Mohn, 1973.

———. *Das zweite Buch Samuelis*. KAT 8/2. Gütersloh: Gerd Mohn, 1994.

Wellhausen, Julius. *Der Text der Bücher Samuelis*. Göttingen: Vandenhoeck & Ruprecht, 1871.

Monographs and Articles

Cited by author, plus date if needed

Adam, Klaus-Peter. 2009. "1 Sam 28: A Comment on Saul's Destiny from a Late Prophetic Point of View." *RB* 116:27–43.

———. 2010. "Saul as a Tragic Hero: Greek Drama and Its Influence on Hebrew Scripture in 1 Samuel 14,24–46 (10,8; 13,7–13A; 10,17–27)." Pages 123–83 in *For and Against David*. Edited by Graeme Auld and Erik Eynikel. BETL 232. Leuven: Peeters.

Auld, Graeme. 2002. "Bearing the Burden of David's Guilt." Pages 69–81 in *Vergegenwärtigung des Alten Testaments. Beiträge zur biblischen Hermeneutik*. Edited by Christoph Bultmann, Walter Dietrich, and Christoph Levin. Göttingen: Vandenhoeck & Ruprecht.

———. 2004. *Samuel at the Threshold: Selected Works of Graeme Auld*. SOTSMS. Aldershot: Ashgate.

———. 2010a. "Response: Kings Resisting Privilege." Pages 135–41 in *Soundings in Kings: Perspectives and Methods in Contemporary Scholarship*. Edited by Mark Leuchter and Klaus-Peter Adam. Minneapolis: Fortress.

———. 2010b. "Synoptic David: The View from Chronicles." Pages 115–26 in *Raising Up a Faithful Exegete: Essays in Honor of Richard D. Nelson*. Edited by K. L. Noll and Brooks Schramm. Winona Lake, IN: Eisenbrauns.

———. 2011a. "Reading Genesis after Samuel." In *The Pentateuch: International Perspectives on Current Research*. Edited by Thomas Dozeman, Konrad Schmid, and Baruch Schwartz. FAT 78. Tübingen: Mohr Siebeck.

———. 2011b. "Reading Joshua after Samuel." In *On Stone and Scroll*. Edited by James Aitken, K. J. Dell, and B. A. Mastin. BZAW 420. Berlin: de Gruyter.

———. In press. "David's Census: Some Textual and Literary Links." In *Textual Criticism and Dead Sea Scrolls Studies in Honour of Julio Trebolle Barrera*. Edited by Andrés Piquer Otero and Pablo Torijano Morales. Journal for the Study of Judaism Supplement. Leiden: Brill.

Auld, Graeme, and Erik Eynikel, eds. 2010. *For and Against David: Story and History in the Book of Samuel*. BETL 232. Leuven: Peeters.

Avioz, Michael. 2005. *Nathan's Oracle (2 Samuel 7) and Its Interpreters*. Bible in History. Bern: Peter Lang.

Barthélemy, Dominique, David W. Gooding, Johan Lust, and Emanuel Tov. 1986. *The Story of David and Goliath. Textual and Literary Criticism*. Orbis biblicus et orientalis 73. Fribourg: Éditions Universitaires; Göttingen: Vandenhoeck & Ruprecht.

Campbell, Antony F. 2010. "2 Samuel 21–24: The Enigma Factor." Pages 347–58 in *For and Against David*. Edited by Graeme Auld and Erik Eynikel. BETL 232. Leuven: Peeters.

Chankin-Gould, J. D'ror, et al. 2008. "The Sanctified 'Adulteress' and Her Circumstantial Clause: Bathsheba's Bath and Self-Consecration in 2 Samuel 11." *JSOT* 32:339–52.

Couffignal, Robert. 2009. "Le Roi, le Prophète et la nécromancie." *ZAW* 121:19–30.

Dietrich, Walter. 2010. "Die Überführung der Lade nach Jerusalem: Geschichten und Geschichte." Pages 235–53 in *For and Against David*. Edited by Graeme Auld and Erik Eynikel. BETL 232. Leuven: Peeters.

Eschelbach, Michael A. 2005. *Has Joab Foiled David? A Literary Study of the Importance of Joab's Character in Relation to David*. Studies in Biblical Literature 76. New York: Peter Lang.

Esler, Philip F. 2005. "The Role of Hannah in 1 Samuel 1:1–2:21: Understanding a Biblical Narrative in Its Ancient Context." Pages 15–36 in vol. 2 of *Kontexte der Schrift*. Edited by W. Stegemann. Stuttgart: Kohlhammer.

Fincke, Andrew. 2001. *The Samuel Scroll from Qumran: 4QSam(a) Restored and Compared to the Septuagint and 4QSam(c)*. STDJ 43. Leiden: Brill.

Fokkelman, Jan P. 1981–93. *Narrative Art and Poetry in the Books of Samuel: A Full Interpretation Based on Structural and Stylistic Analysis*. 4 vols. Assen: Van Gorcum.

———. 2001. *Reading Biblical Poetry: An Introductory Guide*. Louisville, KY: Westminster John Knox Press.

———. 2010. "The Samuel Composition as a Book of Life and Death: Structural, Generic and Numerical Forms of Perfection." Pages 15–46 in *For and Against David*. Edited by Graeme Auld and Erik Eynikel. BETL 232. Leuven: Peeters.

Fox, Everett. 1999. *Give Us a King: Samuel, Saul, and David; A New Translation of Samuel I and II*. New York: Schocken.

Frolov, Serge. 2004. *The Turn of the Cycle: 1 Samuel 1–8 in Synchronic and Diachronic Perspectives*. BZAW 342. Berlin and New York: Walter de Gruyter.

Garr, W. Randall. 2008. "The Medial Demonstratives *hlzh, hlzw,* and *hlz*." *JSOT* 32:383–89.

Gibson, John C. L. 1994. *Davidson's Introductory Hebrew Grammar: Syntax*. Edinburgh: T&T Clark.

Gosse, Bernard. 2008. *L'influence du livre des* Proverbes *sur les rédactions bibliques à l'époque Perse*. Supplément à Transeuphratène 14. Paris: Gabalda.

Green, Barbara. 2003a. *How Are the Mighty Fallen? A Dialogical Study of King Saul in 1 Samuel*. JSOT Sup 365. London and New York: Sheffield Academic Press.

———. 2003b. *King Saul's Asking*. Interfaces. Collegeville, MN: Liturgical Press.

Herbert, Edward D. 1994. "2 Samuel V 6: An Interpretative Crux Reconsidered in the Light of 4QSam[a]." *VT* 44:340–48.

———. 1997. *Reconstructing Biblical Dead Sea Scrolls: A New Method Applied to the Reconstruction of 4QSam[a]*. Leiden: Brill.

Ho, Craig Y. S. 1995. "Conjectures and Refutations: Is 1 Samuel XXXI 1–13 Really the Source of 1 Chronicles X 1–12?" *VT* 45:82–106.

Holm-Nielsen, Svend. 1993. "Did Joab Climb 'Warren's Shaft'?" Pages 38–49 in *History and Traditions of Early Israel: Studies Presented to Eduard Nielsen.* Edited by André Lemaire and Benedikt Otzen. VTSup 50. Leiden: E. J. Brill.

Kaminsky, Carol M. 2008. "Beautiful Women or 'False Judgment'? Interpreting Genesis 6.2 in the Context of the Primeval History." *JSOT* 32:457–73.

Kim, Sun-Jong. 2009. "Les limites de l'omniscience du narrateur dans 1 Sm 15." *RB* 116:15–26.

Klein, Ralph W. 2006. *1 Chronicles: A Commentary*. Hermeneia. Minneapolis: Fortress Press.

Knoppers, Gary N. 2004. *1 Chronicles*. AB 12–12A. New York: Doubleday.

Kratz, Reinhard G. 2005. *The Composition of the Narrative Books of the Old Testament*. Translated by John Bowden. London: T&T Clark.

McKane, William. 1986. *Jeremiah.* Vol. 1. ICC. Edinburgh: T&T Clark.

McKenzie, Steven L. 2000. *King David: A Biography*. Oxford: Oxford University Press.

Milgrom, Jacob. 2001. *Leviticus 23–27*. AB 3B. New York: Doubleday.

Pamuk, Orhan. 2001. *My Name Is Red*. Translated by Erdağ M. Göknar. London: Faber & Faber.

Polzin, Robert. 1989. *Samuel and the Deuteronomist: 1 Samuel.* Part 2 of *A Literary Study of the Deuteronomic History*. Bloomington: Indiana University Press.

———. 1993. *David and the Deuteronomist: 2 Samuel.* Part 3 of *A Literary Study of the Deuteronomic History*. Bloomington: Indiana University Press.

Rezetko, Robert. 2007. *Source and Revision in the Narratives of David's Transfer of the Ark: Text, Language, and Story in 2 Samuel 6 and 1 Chronicles 13, 15–16*. LHBOTS 470. New York and London: T&T Clark.

Rudnig, Thilo Alexander. 2010. "'Ausser in der Sache mit Uria, dem Hithiter' (1 Reg 15,5): Jahwes und Davids Gerechtigkeit in 2 Sam 10–12." Pages 273–92 in *For and Against David*. Edited by Graeme Auld and Erik Eynikel. BETL 232. Leuven: Peeters.

Sasson, Jack M. 1979. *Ruth: A New Translation with a Philological Commentary and a Formalist-Folklorist Interpretation.* Baltimore: Johns Hopkins University Press.

Schenker, Adrian. 2006. "Die Verheissung Natans in 2 Sam 7 in der Septuaginta: Wie erklären sich die Differenzen zwischen Massoretischen Text und

LXX, und was bedeuten sie für die messianische Würde des davidischen Hauses in der LXX?" Pages 177–92 in *The Septuagint and Messianism*. Edited by Michael A. Knibb. BETL 195. Leuven: Leuven University Press.

Schipper, J. 2005. "'Significant Resonances' with Mephibosheth in 2 Kings 25:27–30: A Response to Donald F. Murray." *JBL* 124:521–29.

———. 2006. *Disability Studies and the Hebrew Bible: Figuring Mephibosheth in the David Story*. LHBOTS 441. New York: T&T Clark.

———. 2010. "Hezekiah, Manasseh, and Dynastic or Transgenerational Punishment." Pages 81–105 in *Soundings in Kings: Perspectives and Methods in Contemporary Scholarship*. Edited by Mark Leuchter and Klaus-Peter Adam. Minneapolis: Fortress.

Smend, Rudolf. 1966. *Jahwekrieg und Stämmebund: Erwägungen zur ältesten Geschichte Israels*. 2d ed. FRLANT 84. Göttingen: Vandenhoeck & Ruprecht.

Stevens, Marty E. 2006. *Temples, Tithes, and Taxes: The Temple and the Economic Life of Ancient Israel.* Peabody, MA: Hendrickson.

Tov, Emanuel. 1999. "Different Editions of the Song of Hannah and of Its Narrative Framework." Pages 433–55 in *The Greek and Hebrew Bible: Collected Essays on the Septuagint*. VTSup 72. Leiden: E. J. Brill.

Trebolle Barrera, Julio. 1989. *Centena in libros Samuelis et Regum: Variantes textuales y composición literaria en los libros de Samuel y Reyes*. Madrid: Instituto de Filología del CSIC.

Vermeylen, Jacques. 2000. *La loi du plus fort: Histoire de la rédaction des récits davidiques de 1 Samuel 8 à 1 Rois 2*. BETL 154. Leuven: Peeters.

Williamson, Hugh G. M. 1981. "'We are yours, O David.' The Setting and Purpose of 1 Chronicles xii 1–23." Pages 164–76 in *Remembering All The Way . . . : A Collection of Old Testament Studies Published on the Occasion of the Fortieth Anniversary of Oudtestamentisch Werkgezelschap in Nederland*. By B. Albrektson et al. OtSt 21. Leiden: E. J. Brill.

Willi-Plein, Ina. 2002–3. "Anmerkungen zur Frage der Herkunft des Terafim." *ZAH* 15/16:172–75.

Zakovitch, Yair. 2008. "'And the Lord sent Moses and Aaron.'" Pages 191–99 in *Birkat Shalom: Studies in the Bible, Ancient Near Eastern Literature, and Post-biblical Judaism Presented to Shalom M. Paul on the Occasion of His Seventieth Birthday*. Edited by Chaim Cohen et al. Vol. 1. Winona Lake, IN: Eisenbrauns.

Zwickel, Wolfgang. 1994. "Dagons abgeschlagener Kopf (1 Samuel V 3–4)." *VT* 44:239–49.

INTRODUCTION

The Book of David

This book is about David; it brings the first king of Israel and his reign in Jerusalem a larger place in the Hebrew Bible story than any other figure. Moses may be mentioned on more pages, but much less is told us about him: his character is much less fully explored. We find David presented and re-presented with and against a very large supporting cast:

- David's predecessor and rival King Saul, his daughter Michal, who becomes David's wife, and Saul's son Jonathan, who becomes David's friend
- Saul's Edomite henchman Doeg; Nabal, Saul's double; and Abigail, wife of that Fool, who later becomes one of David's wives
- David's general Joab with brothers Abishai and Asahel, killed by Saul's general Abner
- David's daughter Tamar, with her half brother Amnon, who rapes her; and with her full brother Absalom, who avenges her and then becomes rival to David
- David's loyal soldier Uriah, and his wife, Bathsheba, who becomes one of David's wives
- Philistines (both foes and friends) from Gath: Goliath, King Achish, and Ittai
- Abiathar and Zadok, the priests
- Nathan the prophet and Gad, David's seer; crafty counselors, such as Ahithophel, Hushai, and the (unnamed) wise woman from Tekoa

And this already long list has not mentioned David's father and brothers, many named warriors, the kings of Ammon and Moab, generous hosts in troubled times such as Barzillai, survivors of Saul's family and some of their retainers, and many anonymous groups—nor the much smaller cast we meet in the opening chapters before David comes on stage: Eli the old priest and his wicked sons; the Philistine lords; and Hannah with her husband, Elkanah; the rival wife, Peninnah; and Hannah's son, Samuel—who himself leads Israel before he anoints Saul as king forever, judges Saul and anoints David in his place, and anticipates Elijah, Elisha, and Jeremiah.

This book is about David: all the other personalities are there so that we may see and know David better; but the book is called 1–2 Samuel, or 1–2 Kingdoms (or Reigns). The ancient titles and divisions of the biblical narrative books mask the dominance in the text itself of this one figure. David has one royal predecessor and thirty-nine successors as kings of Israel or kings in Jerusalem. Yet the story of David takes up more than half the space occupied in the books of Samuel and Kings by all these other forty taken together. He occupies more than a third of the pages of what the ancient Greek Bible calls the four books of "Kingdoms," or "Reigns," and some three-quarters of the first two—better known as 1–2 Samuel. (Thus 1 Kingdoms equals 1 Samuel, 4 Kingdoms equals 2 Kings, and so on.) These could be called "the books of David." And yet the familiar titles, "1–2 Samuel" and "1–2 Kings," or "1–4 Kingdoms," are not simply ancient: they also reflect important aspects of the contents. In an important sense, all four books belong together: several elements within the opening chapters of 1 Kingdoms deliberately anticipate the end of 4 Kingdoms. As for Samuel, he not only dominates the first half of 1 Samuel, but he also has an important role to play beyond the grave; Samuel anticipates not only Elijah and Elisha at the heart of 1–2 Kings (they like he, and not the kings of the moment, wield real authority in their time), but also the prophetic tradition that outlives the kings.

The books of Samuel invite us into a fascinating world. No other biblical books in such detail take us into the lives of their principal characters and their families. The stories about them have charmed and puzzled their readers in equal measure over more than two thousand years—and have led to the writing of a huge number of commentaries and other studies. The story of the ancient written texts of Samuel, and their family relationships, is hardly less interesting than the story in them. Recent years have seen easier access to the great manuscripts that are our prime witnesses to the books of Samuel; and such access has led to greater understanding of how ancient books were produced.

Few readers have the privilege themselves to handle such manuscripts in Jerusalem, Rome, or Saint Petersburg. But high-quality photographic reproductions are now available of the fragments in Jerusalem of Hebrew manuscripts of Samuel found in caves near the Dead Sea, dating back some two thousand years. And one of these manuscripts (listed anonymously as 4Q51, or more familiarly as 4QSam^a), though fragmentary, is better preserved than almost any other biblical manuscript from Qumran. Then the Vatican celebrations of the second Christian millennium included the 1999 publication of a magnificent photographic edition of (probably) the most important biblical manuscript in the Vatican Library: a copy of the Bible in Greek made some 1,600 years ago. And a photographic facsimile of similar quality had just been published (1998) of what is still widely called Codex Leningradensis, one of the two oldest and most prestigious copies of the complete Hebrew Bible, some 1,000 years old. Then the Aleppo Codex, now in Jerusalem (and slightly older, though no longer complete) is freely available online. We need no longer depend exclusively on other scholars' reports of these manuscripts: we can see for ourselves how the ancient scribes arranged their pages, how they wrote, and how they were corrected; after seeing the evidence, we can ask our own questions. But first: a fuller account of the contents.

Reading Samuel from Beginning to End

The first book of Samuel opens in hope and despair (1 Sam 1–8). The stories of his birth and of his vision when he was still a lad identify Samuel as a figure of promise. And this portrait of expectation is heightened against a background of foul behavior by Eli's priestly family and the loss of the divine ark to the Philistines. The narrative attests to the return of the ark, a success under Samuel, but protests too about his sons, leading to confrontation and dire warnings from the old leader about his people's request for a king. The next quarter (chs. 9–15) reports the moves that lead to the choice of Saul as king. Though Saul does remain a key character throughout 1 Samuel, there is also a sense in which his short reign is appropriately dispatched in only two chapters (13–14); by the end of this portion, Yahweh has repented ever having made him king, and Samuel has left Saul in grief, never to see him again this side of the grave. The second half of this long book is a much more leisurely account of the rise of David: also anointed by Samuel; victorious over a Philistine giant; in increasingly complicated relationships with Saul, his daughters, and his eldest son Jonathan; and sometimes a refugee among the Philistines. This narrative comes to an interim climax with Saul's life in David's hands (ch. 24) and the death of Samuel. However, opportunity is taken to explore some of its themes a second time, before it ends (ch. 31) with Saul dead after battle with the old enemy; and with David at a conveniently safe distance to the south, neither implicated in his death nor able to save him from it.

The second book of Samuel tells the story of David as king. The first four chapters show him dealing with the inheritance of Saul: first publicly lamenting Saul and Jonathan; then, from his base in Hebron in the heartland of Judah, struggling with the late king's family and supporters. It is in Hebron that Israel's leaders anoint him as king; but he moves quickly north to take Jerusalem and establish himself there, to defeat the Philistines, and to bring the ark to his new capital (chs. 5–6). Nathan prophesies two houses (ch. 7): a royal dynasty to spring from David, and a house for the Deity's name, to be built by David's son. Victories for David in Syria and Transjordan follow (chs. 8; 10); the last of these, in Ammon, provides the background for David's elimination of Bathsheba's husband, Nathan's parable of condemnation, and the eventual birth of Solomon (chs. 11–12). Eight chapters follow, reporting strife within the royal house: the rape of David's daughter Tamar by her half brother Amnon; rebellion by Tamar's brother Absalom, driving his father from his capital; and a final, painful return of David to Jerusalem. It is typically ironic that these disruptive chapters should have a leading character whose name (Absalom) may be understood as "my father is peace." A final well-structured unit (chs. 21–24) starts by returning to the topic of relations between David and Saul and the Philistines. At its heart are two poems embodying the royal ideology. The book concludes with David's failing Yahweh's test over taking a census of the people.

Samuel in Two Main Forms?

We have access to two main forms of the ancient Hebrew book(s) of Samuel. The first of these forms is the more familiar, and the more easily described. As already mentioned, the 1,000-year-old Aleppo Codex can be inspected online, and the Codex Leningradensis can be inspected in a photographic edition; the text of the latter has also been conveniently transcribed in a printed edition: *Biblia Hebraica Leningradensia* (2001), although with some alteration of the paragraphing. In practice, it is this latter codex that is widely described as "the Masoretic Text" (MT). This traditional Jewish text ("Masorah" means tradition) is available in a multitude of manuscripts; these do differ from each other, though only in the tiniest details. The two earliest complete manuscripts we possess were copied (around 1000 C.E.) only a few centuries after this form of the text had been completed. Only after making these qualifications can we say that we "have" the Hebrew text, as standardized by the Masoretes (MT), available to us.

The other ancient Hebrew form of Samuel (if it is only one) is rather harder to assess, but the main facts are easily stated. We do not have it in anything like its pristine state; but we have four substantial witnesses to it: two in Hebrew and two in Greek. The fragments from the Dead Sea caves represent only some 10 percent of the text; but they are the oldest evidence we have. The other Hebrew evidence is preserved in 1 Chronicles; that alternative biblical history shares the equivalent of about eight chapters of the fifty-five in 1–2 Samuel, but the wording of the shared material is often significantly different from the MT of Samuel. The only complete version of this other ancient Hebrew book of Samuel is the Old Greek (OG) or Septuagint (LXX) version—the earliest translation of biblical books into another language. And the other vital Greek testimony is provided in the first-century C.E. *Jewish Antiquities*, by Flavius Josephus—the account of his people's past prepared for his new Roman masters by the former Jewish general. Of these four witnesses, the only complete one is a translation into Greek; 1 Chronicles shares no more than 15 percent of Samuel; and 4QSam[a] is evidence for no more than 10 percent of the text. But the crucial fact is that when these four witnesses do overlap, they are more like each other than any of them is to the traditional Jewish text (MT).

The commonest conclusion drawn from this evidence is that the Chronicler, the Septuagint translator, and Josephus all worked from a version of Samuel rather like 4QSam[a] had been, when still complete. There are several striking agreements between 4QSam[a] and 1 Chronicles, against Samuel MT. And the many agreements between either or both of these Hebrew witnesses and the Old Greek (OG) version confirm the judgment that its translators had provided a quite literal rendering of the Hebrew from which they worked. This group of four witnesses could be compared to siblings, or at least to first cousins—while the MT is related to them more distantly. We shall also review evidence that MT is a younger, more recent form of the text. When we compare it with the OG (the only other witness to the whole book), we find two main sorts of difference: accidental loss and separate development. Broadly, where the MT is shorter, the reason is often accidental damage; and where the MT is different or longer, that is reckoned as scribal decision within one tradition or another. That is the conclusion most commonly drawn from these various bits of evidence. But we have to be careful not to overemphasize the significance of 4QSam[a]. It does contain some surprisingly independent elements of its own; and so it may be safer to characterize it as a descendent of the Hebrew text used by the OG and the Chronicler.

More on the Ancient Texts of Samuel

We have already noted (in the previous section) that there were two ancient groups of texts or text families for the books of Samuel. The translation below presents together the best complete example of each group or family.

1. Not much more needs to be said at this stage about the Masoretic Text (MT). The fully vocalized or "pointed" version of the traditional Jewish text (in the form we find it in the Aleppo and Leningrad codices copied around 1000 C.E.) may not have been completed till the seventh century C.E. That was when early Islam was spreading to the east and south of the Mediterranean. But this form of the older consonantal text was probably substantially complete around the beginning of the Common (or Christian) Era, by the time the second Jerusalem temple was destroyed (70 C.E.). This "Proto-Masoretic Text" in unvocalized Hebrew is reflected in three ancient witnesses in other languages. The Aramaic Targums (Tg.) are based on paraphrases of the sacred text used in synagogues where Hebrew was no longer familiar. The Syriac (Eastern Aramaic) Bible (Syr.) was prepared for early Christian communities eastward from the

Mediterranean. And what came much later to be recognized as the Latin Vulgate (Vulg.) was translated in Bethlehem by Jerome, who learned his Hebrew there from local rabbis.

2. Only one of the fragmentary Hebrew Samuel manuscripts found by the Dead Sea has been mentioned so far. Much more of the text of 4QSam[a] has been preserved than of the other three manuscripts; the fact 4QSam[a] overlaps more with distinctive readings in 1 Chronicles and Josephus gives it added interest and importance. But evidence from each of the others will also be noted in the commentary: 1QSam (1Q7); 4QSam[b] (4Q52); and 4QSam[c] (4Q53).

3. The story of the alternative text family is more complex, and also perhaps more interesting, because in the end this did not become the standard text. We reviewed ("Samuel in Two Main Forms?") the fourfold evidence that makes us suspect that the "Old Greek" (OG) or Septuagint (LXX) was witness to a version of Samuel older than the Proto-Masoretic one. But two factors make evaluating this exactly more difficult. First Chronicles and Josephus only provide evidence for parts of 1–2 Samuel—and that is even truer of the fragmentary Qumran evidence. Then, though the ancient Greek biblical manuscripts are complete, they are far from uniform. For most of 1–2 Samuel, or more properly 1–2 Kingdoms, the best witness to the Old Greek translation (OG) is Codex Vaticanus (B). But starting from 2 Sam 10:1 or 11:2 the text copied in B had been substantially revised toward the emerging Proto-Masoretic Text. From that point, therefore, B loses much of its value as evidence of a text different from and probably earlier than MT; and we take the "Lucianic" text (LT) as our best evidence for OG. The LT is a less pristine witness than unrevised B (B at its best), but a better witness than revised B. However, LT is not the name of a single ancient codex (like B); it is the reconstructed ancestor of five interrelated "Lucianic" witnesses. Why they are called this need not concern us here. The Greek text translated below is B in 1 Sam 1–2 Sam 9, and LT in 2 Sam 10–24. But both these Greek texts will be reviewed throughout the commentary. Where B and LT agree, the abbreviation GT is used. It is the Lucianic text that continues 2 Kingdoms beyond the census story, and as far as the death of David (1 Kgs 2:10–12). Quite often these readings differ from those in the widely used *Septuaginta*, edited by Rahlfs.[1]

The OG has important daughter versions in other languages (Armenian, Georgian, Coptic, and Ethiopic). But only one of these is occasionally mentioned below. The Latin translation of the Old Testament in popular and widespread use (*vulgata*) in the Western church was made from Greek. Jerome's translation from the Hebrew was almost a thousand years old before it officially supplanted what then became known as the Old Latin (OL). In the provocative but

1. *Septuaginta. Id est Vetus Testamentum graece iuxta LXX interpretes*, ed. Alfred Rahlfs (Stuttgart: Württembergische Bibelanstalt, 1935).

illuminating formulation of Julio Trebolle Barrera, the Old Latin is sometimes witness to an older Greek and thereby witness to the oldest Hebrew.

Translating and Presenting the Books of Samuel

This volume is intended as a study of the traditional text of Samuel. The translation and the way the translation is displayed on the pages below have three main aims:

1. The first is to offer some indication of how the text is presented in the most widely recognized witness to the Masoretic Text (the so-called Leningrad Codex). Following a tradition that reaches back at least as far as the Dead Sea Scrolls, both the methods and the purposes of "paragraphing" in this codex were rather different from modern ones. It is easier to state what the methods were; and it is important to note that these differ in one important respect from the familiar printed editions, which are based on this ancient codex. *BHL,* like *BHS* before it, marks only two types of division: major or "open" (*pĕtûḥôt*) divisions in the text (as in modern paragraphing), where the new paragraph is started on a fresh line (the end of the previous line being left "open"); and minor or "closed" (*sĕtûmôt*) divisions, marked by leaving a larger than normal space within a line between sentence-end and next sentence-start. This twofold division is based on halakic rules from a date later than the codex.

Except in the case of the Song of David (see below on 2 Sam 22), the text of Samuel in both ancient codices is presented in pages of three columns, and therefore in quite short lines. Their scribes were clearly operating with not two but three categories of text divider. The most important divisions were marked by leaving a complete line blank. And in the three cases in Samuel where a line is left blank at the top or bottom of a column, we find the letter *pê* (פ for *pĕtûḥâ*) in the middle of the blank line. Less important divisions were marked by a move to the beginning of the next line. However, later Jewish tradition and our printed editions of MT have collapsed this distinction into a single category of *pĕtûḥôt*.

In the Aleppo Codex, there are forty-nine such major *pĕtûḥôt* dividers, and thirty are in Codex Leningradensis (CL); but they share only fourteen: before 1 Sam 3:11; 4:1; 5:1; 10:17; 17:1; 18:17; 28:3; 2 Sam 3:6; 4:1; 6:1; 14:18; 15:7; 17:14; 22:1. The further blanks in the Aleppo Codex occur before 1 Sam 3:1; 4:18; 7:5; 8:7, 22; 10:1; 11:1; 12:6; 13:1; 14:19b, 49; 15:10, 16; 16:12b; 17:12, 17; 19:11; 20:1, 27b; 21:1, 6; 24:17; 26:10, 25; 29:1; 2 Sam 2:8; 5:1, 11; 8:1; 12:1; 14:28; 15:10; 23:1; 24:11b, 18. The further sixteen in the CL precede 1 Sam 2:11; 3:19; 9:1; 10:25; 13:15; 14:17, 36; 18:25; 25:1; 30:26; 2 Sam 3:31; 5:17; 10:1; 13:34; 14:8; 20:20. These ancient divisions within the text often do not correspond to what most modern readers perceive as the start or finish of major sense units or paragraphs. Equally, they do not at all correspond to the familiar chapter divisions, which originated in medieval copies of the Latin Bible. Often what starts a fresh (sub)paragraph is a speech or action of an influential character, such as God or the king, as if the extra space before it is being used to draw attention to the imminence of a significant comment or intervention. However, the blank lines in the codex do indicate a clear strategy for reading the book (see further below at the end "Writing Samuel"). This translation and commentary do not imitate the ancient practice but do draw attention to it. The 31 major sections are determined by the 30 blank lines in CL. The sections into which these are divided follow the *pĕtûḥôt*, the next major divisions of MT. And the presence of *sĕtûmôt* within a larger masoretic "paragraph" is noted by the insertion of a blank line in the translation and in the commentary below.

2. The next aim is to use the printed layout to give some sense of how Hebrew works to readers who may have little knowledge of Hebrew. Each new clause begins on a fresh line (and most clauses are short enough also to end on that line). If the new clause is formally subordinate to the preceding one (most often either introduced by the relative marker *ʾšr* [as in 1 Sam 1:27], or headed by an explanatory infinitive [1:3, 12, 21, 26]), its start is indented. And the start of direct speech is also indented. But there is one consistent exception to these rules. Direct speech is often immediately preceded by the Hebrew infinitive *lēʾmōr* (rendered "saying"), which resumes a previous verb or phrase implying speaking. However, for reasons of space, this particular explanatory infinitive is not given its own line. Such visual display of the text permits ready appreciation of several stylistic features. At a glance we can see when the narrative is galloping on, using only verb after verb; when a clause is unusually long; and when we are dealing with speech within speech (each embedded speech is shown further indented on the page). And we can also more readily notice rhetorical patterns of repetition or balance.

3. A third aspect of the translation invites attention to what is distinctive in the traditional Masoretic Text by means of comparison: by setting it side by side with the Old Greek—the only complete extant version of the alternative ancient Hebrew text (discussed above). The translation is presented in normal (roman) type where the versions agree; where they disagree, readings of GT[2] are shown *in italics* and the variant MT's readings within square brackets: [certain]. In cases of larger divergence, the two texts are translated in full, Greek on the left and Hebrew on the right. Uncertain or supplied text is enclosed in rounded brackets: {became servant}. Textual notes will explain how each version has been reconstructed from the primary manuscript evidence available to us. Versification follows English versions; variant verse numbers in MT (and GT) are supplied in parentheses or brackets following the English reference numbers.

For two reasons, the translation offered is deliberately literal rather than idiomatic. The rhetoric of biblical Hebrew prose makes much greater use of

2. Often supported by 4QSam[a].

repetition than does idiomatic modern English. Translating Hebrew terms as constantly as possible is intended to help the reader become sensitive to these unfamiliar repetitive rhetorical dynamics. I contrast the literal, word-for-word rendering offered below with translation into more idiomatic English—"idiomatic" rather than "literary." Literary assessment may be more a matter of taste; however, part of the power of some poetry consists in its challenge to contemporary prose idiom. The merits of literal translation from biblical Hebrew have been well described by Alter, and also by Fox, whose translation is modeled on Buber's German version. I also try to render MT as it is, even where that text is quite problematic and almost certainly "wrong."

There is also ancient precedent for such translation, not just in English in the King James (or Authorized) Version of 1611, but also in the most ancient translation known to us—the Old Greek (OG), often called the Septuagint (LXX), made in the closing centuries B.C.E. And that leads to the second reason for offering a literal rendering here: literal translation of both MT and OG makes it easier for us to compare these early texts of Samuel—another of our priorities. The aim of my rendering of the Greek needs to be distinguished from *A New English Translation of the Septuagint* (2007) in one important respect. When *NETS* aims to preserve "the 'translationese' character of Septuagint Greek" (xiv), its purpose is to aid the modern English reader to share what the ancient Greek reader would have perceived as rather stilted Greek. My concern is less with the ancient reader of OG, and more with the translators of OG, and how their literalistic and stilted renderings give us access to the Hebrew text in the form in which they read it.

Writing Samuel: From End to Beginning

The books of Samuel are a work of creative genius—not by one great author, but by several. But, though we read them from beginning to end, we have to understand that they were composed from end to beginning—and I mean this in at least two senses. The one is that the story of David is pregnant with the whole succeeding story of monarchy in Israel and Jerusalem: it is told as the first part of what follows—written to help explain it. The other is that we can still identify the single major source of the David story—and since this only told the story of David from the time that he became king, it has determined the shape of 2 Samuel more obviously than of 1 Samuel. The authors of our whole book, as well as adding detail to this inherited story of David as king, also created 1 Samuel as a wholly fresh introduction.

First Chronicles has already been mentioned above ("Samuel in Two Main Forms?") as one of the witnesses to the alternative ancient Hebrew text of the books of Samuel. The central chapters (10–21) of that book also give us closer access than the parallel material in Samuel to a more pristine form of the older

David story, which has been developed separately in each book. In the same way, 1–2 Kings and 2 Chronicles have been separately expanded from the material they share on the kings in Jerusalem from Solomon till the fall of the city. The Book of Two Houses (BTH) is the name I give to that whole older story of the house of David and the house of Yahweh, from the death of Saul till the fall of Jerusalem.

The order of the shared material appears to have been changed more in Samuel than in Chronicles. It is harder to make a relative judgment about wording because of the greater textual fluidity—that is, the larger amount of rewriting—within the Samuel tradition: how much rewriting of the old source was part and parcel of the creation of the books of Samuel, and how much was due to rewriting the books of Samuel? The following table provides a synoptic overview of this source material.

1 Chronicles	**Topic**	**2 Samuel**
10:1–12	Death of Saul and his sons	(1 Sam) 31:1–13
11:1–3	Israel makes David king	5:1–3
11:4–9	David acquires Jerusalem	5:6–10
11:10–41a	David's heroes	23:8–39
13:1–14	David brings ark to Obed-edom's house	6:1–11
14:1–7	David is established in Jerusalem	5:11–16
14:8–17	David defeats Philistines in Rephaim	5:17–25
15:1–16:3; 16:43	David brings the ark to Jerusalem	6:12–20a
17	Nathan and David	7
18	Various victories	8
19	David, Joab, and Ammon	10
20:1–3	Joab, David, and Rabbah	11:1; 12:26, 30–31
20:4–8	David's heroes and Philistine giants	21:18–22
21	Census, plague, site for sacrifice	24

One certain and one possible exception need to be admitted to the rule that the Chronicles text is normally shorter. The Chronicler's version of David's bringing the ark to Jerusalem has been much more extensively rewritten than is the norm elsewhere; and hence, for this topic, the shorter 2 Sam 6:12–20a will undoubtedly be much closer to the source. More open to debate is whether (with Chronicles) the shared source had David start to bring the ark toward Jerusalem before the completion of his establishment there, or only after his successes against the Philistines. Discussion will be found in the commentary.

The authors of 2 Samuel worked from—and to a great extent they were bound by—this older source. They reworded it modestly, but a little more freely than the Chronicler normally did; and they added several blocks of new material, both larger and smaller.

Source	**New**	**Source topic**	**New topic**
(1 Sam) 31		Death of Saul and sons	
(2 Sam)	1–4		David and the Saulides
5–8		David, king in Jerusalem	
	9		David and Mephibosheth
10		David and Ammon	
11:1; 12:26, 30–31		Joab, David, and Rabbah	
	11:2–12:25		David and Bathsheba
	13–20		David and civil war
	21:1–14		David, Saul, and Gibeon
	21:15–17		David and a Philist. giant
21:18–22		3 heroes and Philist. giants	
	22		Song of David
	23:1–7		Last words of David
23:8–39		David's heroes	
24		David and the census	

Only one major block of material was moved to a wholly different position: the list of David's heroes (plus just a few of their exploits)—from 2 Sam 5 (after the taking of Jerusalem) to the end of the book, just before the census. One positive reason for this had been to help construct a balanced coda to the book (2 Sam 21–24), to place material about David's heroes both before and after the two poems at its heart. A more negative purpose may have been to emphasize David's own role in Jerusalem by delaying details of his many supporters.

When writing 1 Samuel, the authors were no less indebted to their source; but they related to it differently. Many storytellers or novelists explain how they start each tale with a situation, or with a couple of characters intersecting—and they let that situation or these characters develop and take them where they will. But 1 Samuel is essentially a prequel to the story of David as king: the authors do not start with a fresh beginning, but are working toward a given end. They expand and expound in Samuel in seemingly more authentic detail what is reported in summary form in BTH (David's house did survive for hundreds of years—Saul's did not). Much of 1 Samuel was no doubt written by the same authors as those who extended the first (David) part of BTH to produce 2 Samuel. Their extended story of the interconnected houses of David and Saul dominates no less than three-quarters of the two books of Samuel. And according to this fresh presentation, David was a problem for Saul from early in the first king's reign, just as Saul's surviving family (for not all of them died with him) and part of Saul's legacy would haunt King David to the end.

The facts with which the authors of 1–2 Samuel had to deal—not necessarily historical facts, but certainly textual facts—are these: Saul, king of Israel, was killed in battle with Philistines. He was not succeeded by his sons, but by his former, and popular, army commander, David. This David captured Jerusalem, brought the ark to Jerusalem from the borderlands between Israel and Philistines, and was promised by his God a sure royal house and firmly established throne. Against this view of BTH, it is often urged that the death of Saul is an odd place to start the story that follows. But a death is where most royal reigns begin; and the story finishes with a removal (to Babylon)—which eloquently poses the question, Is the royal line finished or not?

First Samuel puts all of these textual facts in a new context. By reconstructing what must have gone before, it answers many of the questions left open in its source. If anointed David started a long royal line, why has that not been true of anointed Saul? Did David have anything to do with Saul's death? What was the relationship between Saul and David? How did David—and Saul too—become aware of the divine will? Why was the ark where it was, when David had it brought to Jerusalem? What had any or all of these issues to do with the subsequent fate of the houses of Yahweh and David in Babylonian times?

The following two examples, one from each book of Samuel, nicely illustrate the interplay of source (BTH) and imagination that our authors exhibit.

1. The attention of one author had been caught by the strange opening of the report on the campaign against Rabbat-Ammon (preserved in 1 Chr 20:1 and OG, but provocatively modified in the Masoretic Text of 2 Sam 11:1): "And it came to be at the turn of the year, at the time when kings 'go out,' and David sent Joab, and his servants with him, and all Israel . . ." Why did Joab "go out" when it was time for kings to be going out? our author asked himself. Why not

King David himself? What was David doing at the time? In a splendid yet awful answer, this author wrote 2 Sam 11:2–12:25, the tale of David and Bathsheba, Uriah the Hittite, Nathan the prophet, guilt and forgiveness, and the death of a child and the birth of a future king.

2. The attention of the same or another author had been caught by some brief notes in the source about several of David's heroes killing individual Philistine giants. One of them was called El-Hanan from Bethlehem, and he finished off Goliath from Gath (2 Sam 21:19). I share the long-standing hunch that we have in this brief note the kernel of the much more famous story that our author has attributed to David, and set at the very beginning of his career (1 Sam 17). Whether or not El-Hanan and David were alternative names for one and the same hero from Bethlehem is less important. More significant is how we answer the question whether great narratives in Samuel did grow from such modest seeds.

It seems likely that the first draft of what became 1 Samuel should be looked for within its central half (1 Sam 9:1–25:1). The story of Saul's becoming king and quickly being rejected by Samuel on Yahweh's behalf (chs. 9–15), and the story of the meeting of Saul and David and their worsening relationship (chs. 16–24)—these give a first answer to many of the questions we face when we read the account in BTH of the death of Saul and Israel's choice of David to succeed him.

The first and last quarters of 1 Samuel have the character of supplements to this core. First Samuel 25–30 recapitulates several themes from 1 Sam 21–24—David and Achish of Gath, Saul in David's power, and the death and burial of Samuel. If the preceding chapters already indicate that David was moving south, away from Saul's final confrontation with the Philistines, these final chapters prove David's alibi and establish his innocence of any complicity in Saul's death. They also anticipate key themes of 2 Sam 1–4: David's handling of the Amalekites, and his successful cultivation of the leaders of Judah around Hebron. And 1 Sam 1–8 introduces Samuel, the "man of God" whom Saul had been advised to consult on a domestic matter, but who anointed him king (1 Sam 9–10). This fresh introduction insists that Samuel is no mere clairvoyant, but a mover and shaker of kings. Frolov has also advanced the case that 1 Sam 1–8 was a fresh introduction to a story of Saul and David that had once started with 1 Sam 9: his view is that these opening chapters were a substantial and subversive insert into the primary biblical narrative stretching from Genesis to Kings. While not all points of Frolov's closely argued case carry equal conviction, it is attractive on several counts to recognize the arrival of Saul on the scene in 1 Sam 9 as the beginning of a major section of the book, and work backward with the consequences.

The final chapters of 1 Samuel repeat and redevelop themes from the central core of this book; the opening chapters offer a fresh anticipation of others. But at the same time a linked rewriting of the central section (chs. 9–24) was being undertaken. The long narrative in 1 Sam 15 about Saul's failure to complete putting the Amalekites to the "ban" includes a further declaration by Samuel (one was already issued in 13:13–14) that Saul's kingship is rejected; and this story of failure also compares unfavorably with the way David will deal with these ancestral foes (1 Sam 30; 2 Sam 1). And Saul's second encounter with a band of prophets (1 Sam 19:18–24) not only directs our attention back to the first such encounter (10:10–13) and explores puzzles in that shorter scene; it also demonstrates the king's same lack of power over Samuel that we will witness just before his end, even when he resorts to the black arts (1 Sam 28). There are other elements of apparent duplication within the central core of 1 Samuel, over the election of Saul (chs. 9–11) and his recruitment of David (16–17). Then, just as some of the duplicates within 1 Sam 9–24 link up neatly with themes in the later block at the end (1 Sam 25–30), so too Samuel's evaluation of the institution of kingship in 1 Sam 12 has several links with the devastating critique at the end of the similarly later block at the beginning (1 Sam 1–8). The ends of chapters 8, 16, and 24 are marked by blank lines in CL. (The remaining blanks will be noted in the introduction to each major section.)

My thesis that the earliest identifiable origins of the stories of Saul and David are to be found in the few chapters that the later books of Samuel and Chronicles share has been presented in other studies and will not be argued again here, ahead of our reading of the text. Many aspects of it will be explored and furthered and tested in our reading of the text; some thematic implications will be reviewed at the end of this volume. But the development of the books of Samuel did not end with the large expansion that included the new introduction in 1 Sam 1–8. That substantial revision had produced an account of kingship in general and of David in particular more critical than its predecessors. The older and more positive tradition, maintained in Psalms and Chronicles, was powerfully reinstated with the addition of four strategically placed and mutually reinforcing poems: the Song of Hannah (1 Sam 2:1–10), David's lament over Saul and Jonathan (2 Sam 1:19–27), the Song of David (2 Sam 22), and David's last words (2 Sam 23:1–7).

Samuel in the Bible: Two Canonical Contexts

These books became perceived, or have been received, differently in the Jewish (Hebrew) Scriptures from (what became) Christian (Greek) Scriptures. Jewish tradition recognizes just four narrative books as the Former Prophets: Joshua, Judges, Samuel, and Kings—with the latter two of these further subdivided as 1 and 2 Samuel, and 1 and 2 Kings (exactly as in standard English Bibles). Other narratives such as Ruth and Esther, Ezra and Nehemiah, and 1 and 2 Chronicles, were preserved in a separate Hebrew Bible collection called Writings. However, early biblical codices in Greek copied Joshua to Kings as simply the first among this much larger narrative of "historical" group of books (as in standard English Bibles).

Ancient Greek tradition agreed with Hebrew tradition over the names Joshua and Judges. We have already noted, however, that it treated 1–2 Samuel and 1–2 Kings together as 1–4 Kingdoms. We could suggest that Hebrew tradition emphasized the prophetic role of Samuel by naming his book(s) separately from Kings among the Former Prophets; and that Greek tradition underscored his role in anointing Saul and David, Israel's first two kings, whose story alone occupies the first half of 1–4 Kingdoms.

The other related matter is just where our book ends. Samuel–Kings, or 1–4 Kingdoms, are divided into four sections—but differently. The divisions between 1 and 2 Samuel and between 1 and 2 Kings do correspond to those between 1 and 2 Kingdoms and 3 and 4 Kingdoms. Second Samuel comes to an end before David dies. However, in one family of ancient Greek manuscripts (see below on LT), the division between 2 and 3 Kingdoms comes sixty-five verses later in the total story—after rather than before the deathbed scenes where the transfer of power from David to Solomon is reported (1 Kings 1:1–2:12). In these manuscripts, in other words, 2 Kingdoms (like 1 Chronicles) does not come to its end until David is dead.

Samuel as Part of a Larger History of Israel's Origins

Many scholars now describe the books from Genesis through to Kings (the combined Torah and Former Prophets of the Hebrew Bible) as a Primary History, which they contrast with the Bible's Secondary History in 1–2 Chronicles and Ezra–Nehemiah. Even more widespread is the view that the books Joshua to Kings, or Deuteronomy to Kings, constitute a Deuteronomistic History—and this includes two main related judgments: that these books were written as a connected and coherent narrative, and that the norms by which the narrator assesses what he reports are closely related to the standards proclaimed in the core of the book of Deuteronomy. And third, some scholars link these two views, holding that the first draft of the narrative in Genesis–Numbers was also Deuteronomistic—which would mean that there was already a first draft of a primary history, from creation to Jerusalem's fall, before the books from Genesis to Numbers were completed.

Whether or not it is through Deuteronomistic spectacles that they read the books of Samuel and Kings, all who ponder them have to cope with tensions or fault lines relating to the institution of kingship. They find enthusiasm and critique; they find promise and rejection; and there are those who read these as oppositions that had always coexisted, and others who detect an earlier and more positive history, overwritten by disappointed opponents. Martin Noth was the twentieth-century father of this Deuteronomistic History (DH) hypothesis. He located the single Deuteronomist among the disappointed exiles of the mid-sixth century B.C.E., but recognized that much of the source material first assembled in DH had been more positive about monarchy. Many scholars (especially in the English-speaking world) have followed the alternative view proposed by Frank Moore Cross: that a first and more positive draft of Deuteronomy to Kings (DH^1) was written before the fall of Jerusalem in order to endorse and promote the reform by a king of Jerusalem, Josiah; and this was rewritten (DH^2) in the disappointment of exile. The thesis that undergirds this commentary—and is being tested in this commentary—accepts what is common to Noth and Cross and a broad consensus of scholarship: that the books of Samuel and Kings as a whole are more disappointed in the institution of kingship than much of the individual materials they contain. But it differs in several important ways: it reckons with much less written source material available to the authors, and much more creative writing done by them; it holds that the most extensive source was the Book of Two Houses; and it notices that that source quietly implies more criticism of the Davidic house than Cross's DH^1.

The most detailed critique of any king in BTH was of Manasseh (2 Kgs 21:1–9, 17–18). The authors of Kings reinforce this (21:10–16) and link the collapse of Jerusalem explicitly to Manasseh's misdeeds (23:26–27; 24:3–4). However, they also relate Hezekiah (2 Kgs 20) to the deportation (24:13–17), without mentioning him again by name, despite maintaining the introduction they had inherited from BTH: "[Hezekiah] did what was right in the eyes of Yahweh, just as his father David had done." (2 Kgs 18:3).[3] And they also add much discreditable material about even proverbially wise Solomon (esp. 1 Kgs 11). The authors of Samuel have much more scope for a revision downward of the BTH reputation of David, father of the dynasty.

The books of Samuel look forward—over and beyond the whole story of kingship in Israel and Jerusalem. There may be some minor differences of emphasis between Samuel and Kings, yet essentially these books belong together as a single history of monarchy. Yet to a much more limited degree, the books of Samuel look backward in time. There are a few brief references to what we know as the exodus traditions, both the deliverance from Egypt (1 Sam 2:27; 10:18; 12:6, 8) and the associated plagues on Pharaoh and his people (4:8; 6:6). The oldest such reference (2 Sam 7:6–7, BTH) talks first about Yahweh's bringing Israel out, and then an intervening period during which Yahweh and his ark moved about, residing in temporary accommodation. This past is always reported, not by the narrator, but by characters in the story. On Yahweh's behalf, Nathan (2 Sam 7:6–7), Samuel (1 Sam 10:18; 12:6, 8), and an unnamed "man of God" (1 Sam 2:27) transmit the memory of the

3. See Schipper (2010) and the response in Auld (2010a).

deliverance; and the Philistine enemy is fully aware of how Israel's God had plagued Egypt (1 Sam 4:8; 6:6).

Only in the most detailed of these few backward references (1 Sam 12:8–11) does Samuel talk of Israel as being settled "in this place" after their fathers were brought out of Egypt. But Samuel surprisingly credits Moses and Aaron with leadership under Yahweh during the settlement, not just during the liberation from Egypt. Some characters we know from the book of Judges are mentioned next (12:9–11), though in different order from that book. Yet there is complete silence in the books of Samuel about the leadership of Joshua. This is all the more puzzling because, to a much greater degree than Samuel in his book, Joshua is integral to every part of the book that bears his name. That seems to render implausible the widespread view that Joshua to Kings were composed together, from beginning to end, as a connected history. In the commentary, some assessment will be offered of the many links between the books of Samuel and Joshua and Judges, including some clusters of links. If 1 Samuel was already a freshly drafted preface to an older history of King David and his successors (BTH), we should perhaps reckon that Joshua (and Judges too) were still more recent accounts of still earlier stages in the nation's story.

COMMENTARY

1 Samuel 1–8
A Fresh Introduction

It has already been suggested that all of 1 Samuel but the final chapter was written in stages as a new preface to the story of the house of David in 2 Samuel–2 Kings. Its main source in the Book of Two Houses had simply opened by reporting the death of Saul (1 Sam 31). One of these stages (still a major section of the book) had opened with the arrival on the scene of Saul in 1 Sam 9. The addition of 1 Sam 1–8 had come still later; and in these chapters several very important themes are introduced. The Codex Leningradensis has a blank line before 9:1, and the Aleppo Codex has one just a sentence earlier.

The first section ends the story of Hannah with her song, although she continues to play a role in 1 Sam 2. The second begins (2:11) with the ministry of Samuel under Eli and ends (3:10) with his hearing the divine call. The third reports Yahweh's informing Samuel of the fate of Eli. And the fourth reports the loss of the ark and the death of Eli. After this, all of 1 Sam 5–8 is to be read together.[1] Chapters 5–7 demonstrate Yahweh's power, and his preparedness to save Israel. Chapter 8 documents Israel's rejection of his kingship in favor of human kingship.

The contrast between the young Samuel and Eli's wicked sons (chs. 1–2) prepares us for the first rejection from office of an established family line. The call of Samuel (ch. 3) does more than legitimate a major character of this book: it also foreshadows the whole following story of prophecy in the Hebrew Bible. Similarly the account of the ark of God in enemy hands (chs. 4–6) both brings on stage the Philistine, one of Israel's archetypal foes, and foreshadows its eventual loss to the Babylonians. Samuel enjoys success in leadership against

1. Codex Leningradensis leaves lines blank close to the familiar chapter divisions in 1–4. We find these after 2:10 and 3:1, and at the ends of chs. 3 and 4. Chapter 3 is further divided after vv. 10 and 18; but there is no further blank till the end of ch. 8.

the Philistines (ch. 7)—but only briefly, for the controversial question of kingship is quickly raised (ch. 8).

1 Samuel 1:1–2:10 Hannah's Story

The introductions to Samuel (1:1–2) and Saul (9:1–3) both start in similar terms. We are presented with the family tree of their fathers and told of a problem to be solved. If 1:1–2 was written first, then 9:1–3 signals a new stage by repeating familiar motifs. Equally, if we grant that the first stage in extending forward BTH's story of (Davidic) kingship had been to offer a fuller account of the earlier king (Saul), who in BTH had merely died without royal successor from his family, Saul's arrival on the scene (9:1–3) may have been drafted first and in turn provided a model for Samuel's appearance (1:1–2).[2]

Comparing chapters 1 and 9 quickly leads to an important contrast. Each does start with a genealogy and a problem to solve—a problem moreover that will be rehearsed before the Deity's representative, Eli or Samuel. However, while Kish's son Saul is quickly on the scene in chapter 9, searching for his father's lost animals, the trouble in chapter 1 is whether Samuel's mother can have a child at all. Partly because this issue is handled in such detail, and partly because in any case Samuel is often not the principal character in chapters 1–8, it is wise to characterize the opening section (1 Sam 1:1–2:10, or even 2:21) simply as Hannah's story, not the story of Samuel's birth.

As Hannah's story opens formally with her husband's genealogy, we become quickly aware of distinctive family traits it shares with other biblical stories. The unusual phrase *wyhy hywm*, which opens the action in 1 Sam 1:4, is repeated in 14:1 and then, three times each, in only two further contexts in the HB: in another woman's story with a man of God within Samuel–Kings (2 Kgs 4:8, 11, 18), and in the prologue to Job (1:6, 13; 2:1). Hannah's husband's claim that he is better for her than ten sons (1:8) resonates with the words of Naomi's neighbors, who tell her that Ruth is more for her than seven sons (Ruth 4:15), as does the description of Hannah as *mārat nāpeš* (10) with Mara (Ruth 1:20), the name Naomi thinks more appropriate for herself. Samson's childless mother is told (Judg 13:5) that "no razor should come on his head" (1:11). And Hannah's story continues, like the first half of Jonah's story ends, with a psalm—and both stories include mention of sacrifice and vows. All of these significant links are common to both ancient texts of Samuel; and we shall observe in more detail below how some of them were further developed in one text or the other. The

2. Whichever way we argue this point, and quite apart from Frolov's arguments at the micro-level for 1 Sam 1–8 as a well-balanced composition, his probing of the tensions between the attitudes to monarchy in 1 Sam 8 and 1 Sam 9–12 makes it unwise to perpetuate the consensus description of chs. 8–12 as an integrated introduction to monarchy.

end of Hannah's story (2:18–21) is reported within the account of the fall of Eli's house, to be discussed in our second main section.[3]

1 Samuel 1:1–28

1 There was a [certain] man from Ramathaim *Zipha* [Zuphim] from Mount Ephraim,
and his name was Elkanah son of *Yerahme-el* [Yeroham[a]] son of Elihu son of Tohu son of *Ziph of Ephraim* [Zuph[b] an Ephrathite[c]].
2 And he had two wives:
one's name was Hannah, and the name of the second was Peninnah;
and Peninnah had children, but Hannah had no children.
3 And *the* [that[a]] man went up from time to time from his town *from Armathaim*
to offer obeisance
and to sacrifice to *Lord* Yahweh of hosts at Shiloh;
and there *Eli and his two sons* [the two sons of Eli], Hophni and Phinehas, were priests of Yahweh.
4 And the[a] day came
and Elkanah sacrificed;
and he would give to Peninnah his wife and to all her sons [and her daughters] portions.
5 But to Hannah he would give[a] one choice[b] portion,
for Hannah he loved,
though Yahweh had closed her womb.
6 And her enemy[a] would vex her with utter vexation
in order to enrage her,
for Yahweh had closed about her womb.
7 And so he would do year on year:
as often as she went up to Yahweh's house,
so they vexed her;
and she wept
and would not eat.
8 And Elkanah her husband said to her,
"Hannah, why do you weep
and why do you not eat
and why are your thoughts bad?
Am I not better for you than ten sons?"

3. In the translations, where ancient texts disagree, readings in *italics* are from the Greek Text (GT), and readings from the Masoretic Text (MT) are within square brackets. In double columns, GT is translated on the left and MT on the right. Uncertain or supplied text is within rounded brackets.

9 And Hannah got up
after [she] *they* had eaten at Shiloh [and after drinking[a]];
and Eli the priest was *sitting*[b] on the seat by the doorposts of the temple of Yahweh.
10 And she was bitter in spirit;
and she prayed [against] *toward*[a] Yahweh
[and wept] and wept.
11 And she vowed a vow,
and said,
"Yahweh of hosts,[a]
if you really do look on the affliction of your maidservant
and remember me
[and do not forget[b] your maidservant]
and give your maidservant male seed,
I will give him [to Yahweh all the days of his life[c]],
and a razor will not come on his head."
12 And it came to be
when she continued long
praying before Yahweh,
and Eli was minding her mouth.
13 And [Hannah,] she was speaking in her heart
(only her lips were moving, but her voice could not be heard);
and Eli reckoned her as a drunk.
14 And Eli*'s lad*[a] said to her,
"How long will you make yourself drunk?
Get rid of your wine from you,
and come away from before Yahweh.
15 And Hannah answered
and said,
"No, my lord, I am *a bad-day woman* [a woman hard of spirit]:
wine and strong drink I have not drunk;
but I have poured out my soul before Yahweh.
16 Do not put your maidservant *to* [before] a worthless woman;
for out of the abundance of my complaint [and my vexation] I have [spoken] *been stretched* up to here."
17 And Eli answered
and said,
"Go in peace.
And the God of Israel—may he grant *every* [the] asking
you have asked of him.'
18 And she said,
"[May] your maid [find] *found* favor in your eyes."

And the woman went on her way,
and came to her lodging,
and she ate *with her husband*
and drank;
and her face, *it* [she] no longer *fell* [had it[a]].

19 And they rose early in the morning
and did obeisance before Yahweh
and *went on their way*[a] [returned]
and *Elkanah* [they] came to *his* [their] house in *Ramathaim* [Ramah];
and [Elkanah] knew Hannah his wife;
and Yahweh remembered her.

20 *And she conceived*
And it came to be at the turn of the days
and [Hannah conceived
and] she bore a son;
and she called his name Samuel,
and she said
"For of Yahweh *God of Hosts*[a] I asked him."

21 And the man Elkanah went up and all his house
to sacrifice *at Shiloh* to Yahweh the periodic sacrifice and his vow
and all the tithes of his land.[a]

22 But Hannah did not go up,
for she said to her husband,
"Till[a] the lad is weaned,
and I bring him
and he appears to the face of Yahweh
and he stays there forever."

23 And Elkanah her husband said to her,
"Do what seems good to you.
Stay
till you wean him.
But let Yahweh establish *what proceeds from your mouth*[a]
[his word]."
And the woman stayed
and nursed her son
till she weaned him.[4]

24 And she went up with him
to Shiloh[a]
with a three-year-old calf

24 And she brought him up with her
as she weaned him
with three cattle

4. Throughout the book, unless otherwise labeled, the left column is GT and the right column is MT.

	and loaves[b]	
	and an ephah of flour and a skin of wine	and one ephah of flour and a skin of wine
	and entered the house of Yahweh at Shiloh	and had him enter the house of Yahweh at Shiloh
	and the lad with them.	and the lad {became servant}.
	And they brought him before Yahweh,	
	and his father slaughtered the sacrifice	
	which he made from time to time to Yahweh.	
	And he brought the lad,	
25	and he slaughtered[a] the ox	25 And they slaughtered the ox
	and Hannah the mother of the lad brought {him} to Eli.	And they brought the lad to Eli.

26 And she said,
"May it please my lord,
as my lord lives,
I am the woman stationed by you [then],
praying to Yahweh.
27 For[a] this lad I prayed;
and Yahweh granted me the asking
which I asked of him.
28 And I too *lend him to* [have let him be asked of] Yahweh:
all the days that he *lives* [is], *a loan* [asked (*šāʾûl*)] for Yahweh."
[And they did obeisance there to Yahweh.[a]]

1a. Here *yrḥmʾl* and *yrḥm* are simply the full and abbreviated forms of the same name.

b. Codex B offers "in Naseib," which retroverts to *bnṣyb*, while MT has *bnṣwp*. This is further if different testimony to the place name being *ṣyp* (as in Chronicles) not *ṣwp*, as MT (and codex A and LT) here and in 9:5. Here, and throughout this book, "(Codex) B" refers to what the first scribe wrote. For that scribe, and presumably also the still earlier translator, Gk. *ei* in transliterated names corresponded to Heb. vocalic *y*. By far the commonest example is king *Daueid,* because the translator had used a Heb. MS which wrote *dwyd*, as in the Qumran scrolls of Samuel and as in 1 Chronicles, and not *dwd* as in MT Samuel. B was later "corrected" by deleting every *e* from such instances of *ei*. Rahlfs's edition (see p. 6, n. 1) uses the adjusted spelling, so losing important evidence.

c. Here *ʾprty* is used as the adj. for *ʾprym*, and so there is no material difference between the readings; but it is ambiguous, as it also corresponds to *ʾprth* in Judah, as in Ruth 1:2; 4:11.

3a. Not only is "that" plus in MT, and "from Armathaim" a plus in B, but the word order also is different: MT specifies place before time. On Eli and his sons, see below.

4a. Translating with MT. The Gk. *hēmera* is not articulated (not preceded by "the"). Loss of one *ēta* (η) between two others is eminently possible. Yet it is remarkable that, though unarticulated *wyhy ywm* is never attested in HB, there is a similar lack of a Gk. art. in all four other instances in Kingdoms (1.14:1; 4.4:8, 11, 18).

5a. An aor. in B corresponds to *ytn* here, as also to *wntn* (in v. 4).

b. Apart from the two minuses over against B as tabulated below, the main problem in MT is the obscure *'pym*, which is best understood, not as a description of Hannah's one portion, but as a corruption of *'ps*.

B	MT
wlḥnh ytn mnh 'ḥt	*wlḥnh ytn mnh 'ḥt*
ky 'yn lh yld	
'ps ky 't ḥnh 'hb	*'pym ky 't ḥnh 'hb*
'lqnh mz't	
wyhwh sgr b'd rḥmh	*wyhwh sgr rḥmh*

6a. The table below offers a retroversion of OL and LT alongside the text of MT. Trebolle Barrera has argued that LT is the fullest representative of the conflation of alternative versions of the same material, one of which can still be inspected in OL. As is clear from the parallel renderings above, B lacks the opening two lines of LT, while MT retains only some of the redundant material. Apart from the different number of clauses in each version, the main difference between MT and B/OL is over their understanding of *ṣrth*. Both understandings are at least as old as LT. MT and the first portion of LT take *ṣrh* as the f. (unique in HB) of *ṣr* (adversary, oppressor) from *ṣrr* II. Yet *thlipsin* B and the 2d portion of LT, with *tristitiam* OL, read it as the much commoner abstr. from *ṣrr* I (misery, distress), although nowhere in HB is that attested with prep. *k*-. Perhaps alternative understandings of this key word led to explanatory divergences in the surrounding text, and these were then conflated.

OL	LT	MT
wk'sth	*wk'sth ṣrth*	*wk'sth ṣrth*
gm k's b'bwr hr'mh	*gm k's b'bwr hr'mh*	*gm k's b'bwr hr'mh*
	ky l' ntn lh yhwh yld	
	kṣrth	
wtk's kṣrth	*wkk's ṣrth*	
	wtk's 'l z't	
	ky sgr yhwh b'd rḥmh	*ky sgr yhwh b'd rḥmh*
	lblty tt lh yld	

9a. Although LT attests first *w'ḥry šth* (MT) and then *wttyṣb lpny yhwh* (B), it may be that both are secondary and LT is a conflate text. Certainly neither can be a corruption of the other. See further below.

b. The shorter text of B is possible; but MT supported by LT is more natural.

10a. Here *pros* (GT) may attest *'l* (read by some HB MSS). However, *'l* (MT), though more striking in the context of prayer, does develop the theme of Hannah's bitterness. Twice *htpll 'l* occurs in Chron (II.30:18; 32:20), but in neither case does *'l* introduce the Deity.

11a. As in v. 3, B attests a fuller divine title than MT.

b. Since the conjunction of "remember" and "not forget" is attested nowhere else in FP but is found in Deut 8:18–19 and 9:7, MT's plus may be secondary here.

c. Often B is presented as an expansive rebuilding of MT; but see further below.

14a. Almost exclusively in the following paragraphs, *naʿar* refers to Samuel; but "the priest" has a servant "lad" in 2:13, 15.

18a. Over against MT's puzzling *hyw-lh*, GT attests *nplw*.

19a. The GT attests *wylkw ldrkm*, pl. of the expression just used of Hannah alone (18).

20a. As frequently in GT, the divine title is fuller; indeed LT not only agrees with B, but also adds *pantokratoros* (a 2d rendering of *ṣĕbāʾôt*).

21a. The GT's plus at the end could revert to *wĕkol-maʿśar ʾarṣô* (cf. Lev 27:30) or . . . *ʾadmātô* (cf. Neh 10:38).

22a. The first line of its 2d column ends at *ʿd ʾšr* ("till"); and so, though much more is extant here, 4QSam[a] cannot be cited in favor of either B or MT. LT is fuller: "I shall not go up till the lad's going up with me, when I wean him; and he will appear. . . ."

23a. Here 4QSam[a] does attest GT's "what proceeds from your mouth." See comment.

24a. The words *[w]tʿl ʾwtw šylh kʾšr* (4QSam[a]) may be rendered either "[and] she went up with him to Shiloh as" (starting as B) or "and she brought him up to Shiloh" (starting as MT). 4QSam[a] attests both the place name (B) and the [beginning of the] relative clause (MT).

b. Here 4QSam[a] *mšlš wlḥm ʾḥd* ("3-year-old and one loaf") is close to B; before the preceding *bqr* in 4QSam[a], *pr bn* is widely reconstructed as *pr bn bqr*, which is widely used in sacrificial texts in the Pentateuch. This supposes that an original *bpr<u>bnbqr</u>mšlš* had accidentally lost the underlined letters, so becoming *bprmšlš*, which had been "corrected" to MT's *bĕpārîm šĕlōšâ*.

25a. Like B, 4QSam[a] has a sg. subj. with "slaughtered." Following *kyriō* (Yahweh), LT has "and they brought the lad and slaughtered the ox, and Hannah the mother of the lad approached Eli." Like B, this may attest *wtbʾ*, which can be read as *qal* (LT) or *hipʿil* (B).

27a. Here Gk. *hyper* does not render *ʾl* lit. but catches its sense.

28a. In this verse 4QSam[a] is longer than both B and MT. After the 2d "Yahweh," it reads . . . *hw šm wtšthw*, which Fincke reconstructs as "[and she left] him there and did obeisance [to Yahweh]." Here B could have suffered accidental loss between two instances of the divine name. The pl. subj. (MT) of "did obeisance" requires specification of the sg. subj. of "said" before the song in 2:1. Here B is more likely to be original here (so DJD); Fincke is unwise to follow MT with *wttpll ḥnh*.

[1–3] Readers have divided the opening verses of Samuel differently. Most have recognized a break after v. 11, for which there is ancient testimony in the complete line break in 4QSam[a]. However, the paragraphs of B end at the close of 1:8 and 1:19, and a few words before the end of the longer Greek text at 1:24. The opening verses introduce us to place and people, but say nothing of period (unlike the opening words of Ruth: "In the days that the judges judged"). The many readers who simply read on from the book we call Judges may notice no lack. But if we proceed backward from "And Philistines were warring on Israel" (1 Sam 31:1) to recognize first "And there was a man of Benjamin" (1 Sam 9:1) and then "And there was a man from Ramathaim (the Twin Heights)" (1 Sam

1:1) as a pair of fresh introductions, we will note that each anticipates the same lack of time frame as had characterized the opening of BTH. The MT has almost certainly added *ʾḥd* to bring this story into closer alignment with (v. 2 of) Judg 13.

Names: Exactly why Samuel's town, elsewhere *hrmh* (sg.), is introduced in this dual form (unique here in MT, although GT uses "Armathaim" throughout) is a puzzle; but it does draw attention to its meaning. If it were not for the clear statement in the opening verse that this Ramathaim was in the hill country of Ephraim, it would be attractive in light of 7:16–17 to place it in proximity to Mizpah: the Ramah that was fortified against Jerusalem by Baasha, then destroyed by Asa, with its stones used to rebuild Mizpah and Geba to the north as border forts against Israel (1 Kgs 15:22, BTH).

The genealogy from Elkanah back to Ziph is found also in 1 Chr 6:34–35 (19–20) as part of a longer tree in which some of the names appear more than once. There too Elkanah's father is given as Yeroham, but his father as Eli-el, whose own father is spelled *twḥ* rather than *tḥw*. While *ṣyp* is the K(ethib), the Q(ere) is *ṣwp*. Since the Hebrew letters *wāw* and *yôd* were easily confused, a move between *ṣwp* and *ṣyp* could have been accidental. On the other hand, since *ṣyp* is attested in Heb. in 1 Chr 6:20, it may be more likely that MT, possibly influenced by the following *m-* ("from"), has adjusted *ṣyp m-* to *ṣwpym m-*, playing on the participle *ṣwpym*, from *ṣph* ("scout"), so suggesting that the family's place of origin was already pregnant with special "seeing."

"God has [be]gotten" (*ʾel-qānâ*) is a striking name for a man who has not achieved a child with the wife he loves, but "Favor" (*ḥannâ*) is unsurprising for his first (v. 2) and loved (v. 5) wife. "Peninnah" remains opaque, though it has been interpreted as "pearl[s]." She is not the elder, like Leah, although she is the first to have children, like Hagar (who was not a full wife). Peninnah has children but is neither loved nor hated.

Phinehas (*p[y]nḥs*) is well-known in HB as a priestly name, but Eli and Hophni are unique to this story in its wider ramifications: *ḥpny* shares all of its consonants with *pynḥs* and is not found outside 1 Sam 1–4; *ʿēlî* and *pînḥās* do appear again in 14:3 as Yahweh's priests in Shiloh, and "the house of Eli" is used in 1 Sam 3:14 and 1 Kgs 2:27. The name *ʿly* can be understood as cognate with *ʿlh* ("Highest"), which some see as an alternative form of Elyon (see below on 2:10). However, since his sons are described (2:12) as "sons of no use" (*bĕnê bĕlîyāʿal*), it is quite as possible that our author plays on this "high" name as if *ʿly* has been [mis]created out of *yʿl* ("use/benefit"). In GT the introduction (v. 3b) to the priestly family at Shiloh ("Eli and his two sons") seems more straightforward. The MT instead mentions Eli not as priest, but only as the father of his sons. We might suppose that he himself is no longer officiating, and yet Hannah will shortly find him in the temple. Were the sons seeking to replace their old father, rather like Absalom would make himself available to hear appeals (2 Sam 15:1–6)?

[4–9] The verbs at the heart of this section require attention to an issue skated over in our preliminary translation. The simple English past tense we used can embrace both punctual and habitual action. But this masks the situation in much of this section (esp. vv. 3–7), although it is handled differently in MT and GT. The GT does recognize the habitual in this extended portrayal of the situation by using the (frequentative) imperfect at beginning (v. 3) and end (7), although (punctual) aorists in between (vv. 4–6). The MT opens its depiction of what goes on year after year with the *w-qṭl*: "and that man would go up"; and many of the verbs in vv. 4b–7 are either *w-qṭl* or simple *yqṭl* (connected or unconnected frequentatives): "he would give [2x]; . . . she would vex [2x]; . . . he would do." But at two points the situation is more complex. Fokkelman (1981–93, 4) attractively suggests that, with the double *w-yqṭl* of regular narrative (beginning of v. 4b), the reader is led to expect action at last, after what has been a remarkably leisurely start to this book—since the normal canons of crisp Hebrew storytelling lead readers to expect action. But they are immediately teased with further background: "And she wept and would not eat" (v. 7b), with the brief return to the punctual immediately interrupted by a further simple *yqṭl*. This proposal has occasioned much discussion. Possibly influenced by GT, many readers have sought to discount the masoretic pointing and read the *w-* of *wtbkh* as a simple copulative (v. 7; Frolov 61). But it may be preferable to read Hannah's weeping and refusal to eat as the next stage in the long-interrupted (vv. 4b–7a) narrative after her husband's sacrifice (4a).

Three verbs that are key to this introduction also anticipate terms that play a distinctive role in BTH. This gives important early support to the view that Samuel (and Kings) do not simply adopt BTH as a principal source. Their relationship with it is much richer than that: they explore it as a primary text, both adopting and adapting its thought world. Hannah is vexed by her rival (vv. [6,] 7, 16), like Yahweh by wicked king Manasseh in BTH (2 Kgs 21:6; 22:17) and by almost every king of northern Israel in the rest of Kings. Hannah weeps (vv. 7, 8, 10), as the prophetess Huldah commends good king Josiah for having done (2 Kgs 22:19). And Hannah prays to Yahweh in his temple[5] (vv. 10, 12, 26, 27), which only David and Solomon are reported in BTH as doing, though in the rest of Samuel–Kings prophets also pray: Samuel (3x), the man of God from Judah (1 Kgs 13), and Elisha (3x). We have to conclude that Hannah is not simply Samuel's mother-to-be: as a key figure in her own right, she already prefigures royal, prophetic, and even divine experience. See further below on her song.

[10] Not every detail reported of Hannah enjoys the same positive connections. The woman who prays to Yahweh and weeps is described as embittered: bitterness has taken root in, or at least entered, her inmost spirit. The narrator has not drawn this term from BTH, but it will be used twice more in Samuel:

5. Does talk of a *hykl* ("temple") in 1 Sam 1:9 and 3:3 contradict 2 Sam 7:6?

embittered men are one of the three groups that gather under David's leadership at the cave of Adullam (1 Sam 22:2); Hushai warns Absalom (2 Sam 17:8) that his father and his men are not only mighty but embittered as well, "like a bear robbed of her cubs in the field." In similar vein, the unscrupulous Danites threaten Micah that he may fall into the hands of *mārê nepeš* if he keeps up his protests (Judg 18:25). We find closely related phrases four times in the poetry of Job: "the bitter in spirit, who long for death, but it comes not" (3:20–21 RSV alt.); "I will not restrain my mouth; . . . I will complain in the bitterness of my spirit" (7:11 RSV alt.; cf. 10:1); while 21:25 talks of the one who "dies in bitterness of spirit, never having tasted of good" (RSV alt.).

Advice said to have been taught by a mother (Prov 31:3–7) links several of these themes from Samuel and Job—women, kings, drink, bitterness, and forgetting:

> Give not your strength to women,
>   your ways to those who destroy kings.
> It is not for kings, O Lemuel,
>   it is not for kings to drink wine
>   or for rulers to desire strong drink;
> lest they drink and forget what has been decreed
>   and pervert the rights of all the afflicted.
> Give strong drink to him who is perishing,
>   and wine to those in bitterness of spirit;
> let them drink and forget their poverty,
>   and remember their misery no more. (RSV alt.)

A further example of Hannah's prefiguring key themes of the books of Samuel is absent from MT: the GT has this feisty woman leave the family feast (v. 9) and "take her stand" before Yahweh. This term *htyṣb* is not used in BTH, but it is found a further ten times in Samuel and is even used once of Yahweh before Samuel (3:10)! But we are reminded particularly of the sons of God, including the testing satan, "taking their stand" before Yahweh (Job 1:6; 2:1). That story too is punctuated by "and the day came" (1:6, 13; 2:1); and that story also features eating and drinking at a family feast (1:13). If B and LT share taking one's stand before Yahweh with the opening of Job, MT and LT share drinking in addition to eating at the feast. Whether or not original to the story of Hannah, the fact that "and after drinking" is separated from the mention of eating "at Shiloh" emphasizes this feature and brings into fresh relief the discussion between Hannah and Eli over whether she has been drinking (vv. 13–15).

Hannah, as the first main character of the books of Samuel (and Kings), emphasizes a key difference between these books and their major source, or their reference text. In BTH, women have a tiny role: the foreign Queen of Sheba, the usurping queen Athaliah, and the prophetess Huldah. Samuel and

Kings have many more characters who remind us of Ruth and Esther, and may belong to similar late-biblical storytelling. Particularly striking within these are the connections between Ruth, David's ancestress, and Hannah, mother of Samuel and prototypical of the prophetic line. Links with Jonah too have already been noted. The OG reading of *ṣrh* as "distress" not only links with the opening of his psalm or prayer (2:3) but also anticipates 1 Sam 10:19; 26:24; and 2 Sam 4:9.

[11] It is widely held that the substantial plus in Hannah's vow marks a secondary adjustment of (in this case, original) MT toward the instructions received by Samson's mother in Judg 13:4–7. However, two arguments tell for the priority of OG here: it is almost certain that mention of wine and strong drink was part of 4QSam[a] (DJD; Fincke); and "till the day of his death" (OG) is used in BTH (2 Kgs 15:5//2 Chr 26:21) as well as 1 Sam 15:35 and Judg 13:7—on the other hand, "all the days of his life" (MT) is the commoner expression in the Samuel–Kings pluses (1 Sam 7:15; 1 Kgs 5:1; 11:34; 15:5–6; 2 Kgs 25:29–30 [= Jer 52:33–34]), but is never attested in BTH. That there should be "no razor on the head" is shared only with Judg 13:5; 16:17; and the pairing "wine and strong drink" is found outside Judg 13 and 1 Sam 1 only three times: the priests should abstain when entering the tent of meeting (Lev 10:9); a nazirite should abstain (Num 6:3); and the people as a whole had abstained over forty years in the desert (Deut 29:6 [5]).

Despite the seemingly impossibly heavy freight of expectation and interconnection that she incarnates, this opening scene finds Hannah in the most natural of domestic situations. Irked by the fecundity of her junior and rival, and perhaps even by her husband's fair-handed recognition of the two sections of his household, she cannot bear to hear Elkanah protest, during their celebration by the sanctuary, that he is better for her than even ten sons. She takes herself to the temple and challenges the Deity with a solemn vow: if he will give her one son, she will give him back forever.

[12–14] It is just how she prays that brings Hannah to the attention of Eli. The phrase *hrbh* plus infinitive is used once in BTH (2 Kgs 21:6//2 Chr 33:6); but does it describe the abundance or the continuity of Manasseh's evildoing (cf. Amos 4:4 on sinning at Gilgal, and Ezra 10:13)? The expression is used of the avenger's destroying overmuch (2 Sam 14:11) and of the national leadership indulging too much in *maʿal* (2 Chr 36:14). Overabundant giving seems to be the theme of Exod 36:5. But is it of abundant or of continuous forgiving that Isa 55:7 and Ps 78:38 speak?

Codex B marks vv. 12–18 as a separate portion. However, one obvious difference between B and MT that spans the first two portions requires that we consider them together: MT reports drinking in connection with Hannah in v. 9, but B not till v. 18. In each case specification of location ("in Shiloh" [9] and "with her husband" [18]) separates "drink" from "eat"; but delaying this paired term is not uncommon in itself. Drinking does not have to be specified alongside eating for it to be assumed to be part of the meal. However, the fact that B mentions it first in v. 18, after Hannah's denial (15) of having drunk wine or strong drink, does suggest that we should take her words and the narrator's at face value. The MT faces its readers with more questions. Eli may have jumped to an everyday conclusion when he saw her state. Drinking was common at such a feast and has occurred in her husband's party. Has Hannah drunk at the feast? If so, does she make a false disclaimer to Eli, or do her words simply intend to give the impression that she has not drunk as much as to make her drunk—the only extended pouring out she has done was of her "soul"? The MT is, superficially at least, the more difficult text. However, its mention of "drinking" is stated in a rare instance of an infinitive absolute, *šātōh* following "after" (v. 9); this does not specify the drinking as hers. Of course, the narrator may have used Eli's lack of perception as an early indication that he is old (2:22) and unable to see well (3:2). If so, MT develops this further with the suggestion (1:3) that he is no longer the principal officiating priest.

[15–16] The first element in Hannah's response to the charge of being in a drunken state is presented quite differently in B and MT. Here B's *qšt-ywm* finds a parallel only in Job 30:25: "Did I not weep for the hard-of-day? Was not my soul grieved for the poor?" There is no exact parallel to M's *qšt-rwḥ* (v. 15); yet insofar as "spirit" may be regarded as a part of the body, it may be similar to "hard-of-face," "hard-of-heart" (Ezek 2:4; 3:7), and "hard-of-neck" (Exod 32:9; 33:3, 5; 34:9; Deut 9:6, 13). "No, sir, I am an obstinate woman" seems to be a more accurate rendition of MT than the French ecumenical "I am not, sir, an obstinate woman" (*BA* 133).

The narrator has described her as embittered (v. 10), and she has described herself as obstinate or at least in hard times (15). Yet Hannah insists (16) that she not be taken for a *bat-bĕlîyāʿal* ("daughter of no use"). Many "sons of no use" follow her through 1 Samuel: Eli's sons (2:12); those who refuse to acknowledge the new king, Saul (10:27); the preeminently foolish Nabal (25:17, 25). But when we come to "every evil and no-use man" of the men who went with David (30:22), we remember two things: when David's band was formed at Adullam (22:1–2), one of the groups who had joined him were called *mārê nepeš* ("embittered"); and the thugs responsible for the scandal at Gibeah, called *bĕnê-bĕlîyaʿal* in Judg 19:22 and 20:13, seem little different from the *mārê nepeš* (18:25) with whom the Danites had just threatened Micah. Hannah herself might not accept the narrator's *mārat nepeš* (v. 10) as a fair description of her; she insists that she is no *bat-bĕlîyāʿal* (though the one may readily develop into the other).

[17–18] Eli dismisses Hannah with the words *lky lšlwm*, which will be echoed by Jonathan to David (20:13, 42) and David to Abigail (25:35). It is not clear how far *lšlwm* differs in sense from *bšlwm* with verbs of motion (29:7; 2 Sam

3:21, 22, 23; 15:9, 27; 19:25, 31). "Find favor [*ḥēn*] in someone's eyes" (v. 18) is a relatively common expression in Samuel,[6] but it is particularly apt for someone named *ḥannâ*. It is used 13 times in Genesis;[7] 6 times in Exod 33–34 alone;[8] in Num 11:11, 15; 32:5; Deut 24:1; Judg 6:17; Ruth 2:2, 10, 13; and Esth 5:8; 7:3; 8:5. The idiom is never found in BTH and may be an instance of later biblical usage. The fact that Hannah here, like Ruth in Ruth 2:13, also describes herself as "your maid" (*šipḥātkā*) marks another significant link with that book. Hannah's name may also hint at another feature of her story. She is more often subject of the verb "pray" (*htpll*) than any other character in HB; a near equivalent of *pll hitpaʿel* is *ḥnn hitpaʿel*.[9]

[19–20] The GT suggests an immediate link between Elkanah's arrival home and his intimacy with Hannah and similarly juxtaposes more immediately Yahweh's remembering and Hannah's conceiving; it is the birth rather than the conception that awaits "the circuit of the days." The exact phrase is found nowhere else in HB, but *tqwpt hšnh* (the circuit of the year) is used in Exod 34:22 and 2 Chr 24:23, referring to the (autumnal) equinox at year-end. The interplay between Hannah, Elkanah, and Yahweh deserves close attention. From the time she departs from the family feast to confront her God in his temple, Hannah's independence is notable. It is she who names Samuel (v. 20); but exactly what is she claiming when she explains this? That she does the naming because it was she who did the asking? That the El suffix in his name relates to his being asked of Yahweh? That the name *šmwʾl* has a close relation to being asked (*šʾwl*), all of whose consonants it shares? Or any or all of these together?

[21–25] The attention moves immediately to Elkanah and his whole house, who must offer up not only the due sacrifice but also the appropriate return on his or his household's vow (the suffix on *nidrô* could refer to either). Two comments are necessary. "The sacrifice of the days" (*zebaḥ hayyāmîm*) is an expression used only in 1 Samuel. If the opening chapters represent a further extension of the book, then 1:21 and 2:19 may depend on the sacrifice said to claim David's attendance in 20:6. Then we learn from Num 30 that a married woman's vow was only valid when endorsed by her husband. Yet Hannah's independence is quickly restated (v. 22): Elkanah's *whole* house does not on this occasion include her. The reason she gives may not have convinced her husband: those who do what is right in their own eyes (v. 23) are not always approved of! He does not insist on her joining him on pilgrimage; but he caps his acquiescence in her plans with a wish that has been preserved differently in our two main texts: "May Yahweh establish his word / what comes out of your

6. See 1 Sam 1:18; 16:22; 20:3, 29; 25:8; 27:5; 2 Sam 14:22; 15:25; 16:4.
7. See Gen 6:8; 18:3; 19:19; 30:27; 32:5 (6); 33:8, 10, 15; 34:11; 39:4; 47:25, 29; 50:4.
8. See Exod 33:12, 13 (2x), 16, 17; 34:9.
9. Oral communication from Marc Zvi Brettler.

mouth." Both the idiom and who has done the speaking are different; parallels can be quoted on both sides. Where *hēqîm* is used of "establishing" something spoken by oneself, it is always a question of Yahweh's fidelity to what he has spoken (10x).[10] Even where doer and speaker are different, the words are either Yahweh's or are at least claimed to be his: Yahweh through Samuel blames Saul for not establishing his (Yahweh's) words (1 Sam 15:11), while Saul immediately claims that he done so (15:13); Isaiah sings of Yahweh's confirming the words of his servant (44:26); and Jeremiah wishes success to the words of his opponents (28:6), although he has doubts.

In one way, all of the above makes MT the more expected text. And yet the divine word is normally (always?) spoken through a prophetic intermediary. It has, therefore, worried many commentators that they cannot identify the occasion for speaking the word in question, unless Elkanah is wishing that, in Samuel, Yahweh will confirm what Moses had promised (Deut 18:15, 18): to "establish" (the same word: *yāqîm*!) a prophet like him. Of course, this solution is more readily available to those who hold that Samuel was originally part of a composition that continued from, or was at least indebted to, the book of Deuteronomy. However, this long-range solution is not necessary: good sense can be made of the alternative text within its immediate context. Indeed, the secondary adjustments to produce MT may have been made precisely to effect a link between Elkanah's words and Mosaic Torah. The text in 4QSam[a] and GT is open to different levels of explanation. On the surface, Elkanah's words may suggest either one of two things: (1) He appears to have lost control of his wife. He has earlier showed his preparedness to endorse her vow. But now it has to be down to Yahweh to keep her to what she has just said. (2) (a variant of 1) Elkanah is quite as distrusting of what his wife says as was Jeremiah of his opponents (Jer 28:6, cited above), but he does grudgingly hope that Yahweh will achieve what he thinks is unlikely. And yet (3) at a deeper level, of which he is unconscious, and only readers who know the wider tradition detect, Elkanah may also be recognizing Hannah as "prophetic," as the medium of the divine word. As we also know, what she herself has promised concerning the son she requested of Yahweh (1:11) is similar to what a "messenger of Yahweh" had intimated to Samson's mother-to-be (Judg 13:5).

[26–28] Although the terms GT uses in Hannah's declaration are rare (*kichrō* in v. 27 is a variant of *kichrēmi*; and the related noun is *chrēsis*), their meaning ("lend/loan") is clearly established. By contrast, MT's *š'l* ("ask") is a common Hebrew word, but its use in this passage is remarkable. Some facts and figures help to set the context. Verbal forms of *š'l* are found 30 times in 1 Samuel (MT), and 31 times in the remainder of Samuel–Kings, but of these only 6 times in

10. Deut 9:5; 1 Sam 3:12; 2 Sam 7:25 (= 1 Chr 17:23); 1 Kgs 2:4; 8:20 (= 2 Chr 6:10); 1 Kgs 12:15 (= 2 Chr 10:15); Jer 29:10; Ps 119:38; Dan 9:12; Neh 9:8.

BTH.[11] It is an important term for Samuel–Kings as a whole, but is most densely used in 1 Samuel, much of which is the story of Saul/*Shāʾûl* ("Asked")—and most often of all in the opening chapter (5x). More historically minded critics used to argue that a birth-and-naming story more suited to Saul, and originally told about the first king, had been displaced onto Samuel. And we have agreed that an earlier version of the book had begun with 1 Sam 9. Yet, within the architecture of 1 Samuel, it is sufficient to notice that the people's asking for a king has been anticipated by Hannah's asking for a child.

"Request" (*šĕʾēlâ*) in v. 27 is found almost as often in Esther (6x) as in all the rest of HB (7x), and four of these other instances are in Samuel–Kings.[12] These requests are pleas to a monarch, and here and in Ps 106 to the divine monarch; the unique case where Gideon makes a plea to his people (Judg 8:24) simply underscores the rhetoric of his refusal to be their king. The term *šʾl* in *hipʿil* (v. 28) has a parallel only in Exod 12:35–36: "The sons of Israel—they did as Moses said and asked of the Egyptians. . . . And Yahweh—he put the people's favor in the eyes of the Egyptians, and they 'permitted being asked of them.'" Admittedly the consonantal text (*wyšʾlwm*) could also be read as *qal*: "and they asked them"; in an unpointed text, it is not clear who are "they" and who "them" at each stage in the transaction; and the *hipʿil* pointing may have been influenced by 1 Sam 1:28, which can only be read this way. Be that as it may, it remains most likely that GT's word choice here in 1 Kgdms 1 depends on *echrēsan* in Exod 12:36. That said, we need to suppose neither that GT here represents a different text from MT in this matter, nor that *šʾl hipʿil* did mean "lend." We are not dealing here with regular commercial language, but with a forced yet suggestive extension of a common word, and so a clumsy translation is not inappropriate.

And yet, although the Hebrew terminology does not appear to come from the regular world of commerce, the Greek translation has quite a lot to commend it. Temples in the ancient world did serve as "safe deposits" and functioned in other ways like our banks. And Hannah is involved in a transaction with the Deity that involves what to her is a very valuable deposit.[13]

On the evidence we have seen so far, the narrative of the books of Samuel develops entirely naturally out of itself. Two wives in one household, one without children and one with, is a recipe for bitterness and even strife. It is remarkably apt that the first major textual problem relates to a conflicted situation. The trouble between Peninnah and Hannah is partly mirrored, and therefore also partly obscured, in the conflict between MT and GT over the details of that problem—it is quite likely that each text was developed out of different readings (in v. 6) of the same word *ṣrh*: "rival wife" (MT) and "trouble" (GT). The

11. See 2 Sam 5:19, 23; 8:10; 1 Kgs 3:5, 11; 10:13.

12. See Judg 8:24; 1 Sam 1:27; 2:20; 1 Kgs 2:16, 20; Ps 106:15; Job 6:8.

13. See the discussion in Stevens 164–66.

priests are introduced as soon as Elkanah's regular pilgrimage is mentioned. Conflict made more acute during the celebrations in the environs of the temple takes Hannah to the temple itself. Mention of Eli's sons along with their father at the outset leads us to expect that learning more of them will not be long delayed, since they play no part in the opening scenes. The central installation at the pilgrim center of Shiloh is called a temple (1:9); at its second mention (3:3) we are told that the divine ark was there; and ark and Eli's sons are leading characters in the episode that introduces us to the Philistines. Similarly, in this opening chapter all the talk of asking signals the arrival of Saul (*Šāʾûl*) after an even greater narrative delay. And yet what happens develops no more naturally out of itself than childbirth occurs to a childless woman. Many impulses to the action come from words spoken in the name of Yahweh by priest or prophet.

We have already noticed some links between the contexts of the songs of Jonah and Hannah. On this, in 2:1 MT's plus "and Hannah prayed" (*wttpll ḥnh*) reinforces this connection, as we see in the opening words of Jonah 2:2.

1 Samuel 2:1–10

1 And [Hannah prayed
and] she said:
My heart has exulted in Yahweh.
My horn is exalted in [Yahweh[a]] *my God.*
My mouth is wide against [my] enemies.
[Yes,[b]] I take pleasure in your deliverance.
2 *For*[a] Holy there is not like Yahweh.

	And there is none righteous like our god.		For there is not but you.
	There is none holy besides you.		And there is no rock like our God.
3	Do not boast[a] and do not speak high things;	3	Do not multiply speaking "Height, height";
	let not boasting come out of your mouth.		let not forwardness come out of your mouth.
	For a God of knowledge is Yahweh;		For a God of knowledge is Yahweh;
	and a God preparing his pursuits.		And by him[b] acts are measured.
4	The bow of the mighty has become weak;	4	The bow of the mighty—they're shattered;
	and the weak have girt on strength.		those fallen backward girt on strength.

5 Those full of bread have diminished.
And the weak have forsaken the land.
Because the barren has borne seven,
and she many in children has weakened.
6 Yahew brings death
and makes alive,
brings down to Sheol
and raises up.
7 Yahweh makes poor
and makes rich,
brings low,
and sets on high.
8 Raises from earth the needy,
from refuse sets the poor on high,
making him sit with powerful nations,
allotting them a seat of honor.
9 Granting prayer to him who prays,
and he blessed the years of the just.
For not by power is a man mighty.[a]
10 Yahweh makes weak his opponent;
Yahweh is holy.
Let not the wise boast in his wisdom;
and let not the powerful boast in his power;
and let not the wealthy boast in his wealth;
but rather in this let the boaster

5 The sated—for bread they're hired.
And the hungry are fat with food.
The barren has borne seven,
And she many in sons mourns.
6 Yahweh brings death
and makes alive,
brings down to Sheol
and raises up.
7 Yahweh makes poor
and makes rich,
brings low,
also sets on high.
8 Raises from dust the needy,
from refuse sets the poor on high,
making him sit with the noble
allotting them a seat of honor.
For Yahweh's are the straits of the earth;
and he has set on them the world.
9 The feet of his loyal one(s) he will mind;
the wicked in darkness will become silent;
for not by power is a man mighty.
10 Yahweh, his opponent will be shattered;

boast—
understanding and knowing Yahweh,
and doing justice and righteousness
in the midst of the earth.
Yahweh went up[a] to the heavens
and thundered;
he[b] it is will judge the ends of
the earth.
And he gives strength to those who
reign over us,
and will exalt the horn of his
anointed.

against him[a] in the heavens
he will thunder.
Yahweh will judge the ends
of the earth,
and will give strength to
his king,[c]
and exalt the horn of his
anointed.

1a. The MT in Samuel often reads "Yahweh" where GT or a parallel in Chronicles reads "God."

b. Two variants in v. 2 also concern the presence or absence of *ky*.

2a. The opening "For" is attested in 4QSam[a]: [*k*]*y*ʾ. If we compare only GT and MT, it appears that stichs 2 and 3 have been reversed in one or other. Equally *ṣdyq*, suggested by "Just" (GT), is not dissimilar (in Heb. characters) to *ṣwr* (MT). However, all four lines appear to be attested by 4QSam[a]. Either all are original, or 4QSam[a] preserves the complete conflation of alternate variants (so McCarter). If the latter, then both GT and MT have preserved only one (different) two-line stich from a variant.

3a. "Boast" (GT) appears to be a free rendering.

b. The translation follows Q in MT (*wĕlô*). The K *wl*ʾ ("and not") attests the same consonants as *w*ʾ*l*, "and God" (GT); and that suggests that MT's Q (*lw*, "his") is subsequent to the consonantal reversal, and that GT's "El" is to be preferred.

9a. Here B can count as a literal rendering of MT, with *dynatos* as a verbless predicate corresponding to *ygbr*. The longer LT ("for a powerful man is not strong by his own strength") results from an inner-Greek decision to recognize *ENIΣXY*[*E*]*I* as first vb. and then prep.+noun.

10a. "Against him" (*ʿlw* or *ʿlyw*) has the same consonants as "[and] he has gone up" (*wyʿl*) = the same consonants as at the end of v. 6. Fokkelman (4:130 n.160) adds his vote to those who would restore the divine title *ʿly* or *ʿlywn* here ("the Highest"). From this perspective, GT may have offered a double reading of *ʿly*: as part of the vb. "go up," and as a divine subj. "Lord."

b. The emphatic "he" (*hw*ʾ) sounds similar to *yhw* (an alternate for *yhwh*).

c. "Our kings" (*mlkynw*) start and finish like "his king" (*mlkw*).

[1–5] Hannah's song calls for interpretation in several different contexts. Set near the beginning of the books of Samuel, it corresponds both to the song of David (2 Sam 22) and to David's last words (23:1–7). The narrator is not quite finished with Hannah, any more than with David later; and yet their songs both have a summative function. In Hannah's case, though she does continue to play a role in 1 Sam 2:19, she does not speak again. Like the songs of two other women, Miriam (Exod 15) and Deborah (Judg 5), there is a prophetic context: the other two are explicitly called "prophetess," and we have noted how both Hannah and her story prefigure other prophets and the narratives about them. Perhaps the close links between the main plus in GT (v. 10) and Jer 9:22–23 represent an extension of this feature. The precise setting differs in MT from GT and 4QSam[a]. Tov has argued sensibly that GT and 4QSam[a] are more consistent and original in their presentation of the events before and after Hannah's song: MT has shifted actions of Hannah to her husband, Elkanah. It is GT that preserves the original opening of the song. Unlike MT, the GT makes no paragraph break before the beginning of the song.

There are several connections with the language of the Psalms. "Horn" is subj. of *rûm* in Ps 112:9 and also in the royal Ps 89:17, 24 (18, 25). The mouth open wide against enemies is reminiscent of Ps 81:11. But other links (e.g., v. 5, *ʾumlālâ*, "withered," in Jer 15:9) are with poetry in the prophetic books; while, within the poetry of HB, Deut 32:39 offers the closest parallel to Yahweh as the one who brings both death and life (v. 6). Many individual words and situations are shared with Ps 113 (most of 2:8 is identical to Ps 113:7–8a; and "happiness" and sons for the barren recur).[14] Although there is little stock psalmic phraseology in Hannah's song, there are many links in situation and individual wording, not only with Ps 18 = 2 Sam 22, but also with David's lament over Saul and Jonathan (2 Sam 1). Polzin (1989: 33–34) characterizes Hannah's song as "a proleptic summary of David's final hymn," listing echoes of the latter in all but two verses (3, 5) of the former. Yet quite as significant are the many links with key themes of the main prose narrative: Saul and Goliath are both "tall"; and Samuel is warned against such an external characteristic when choosing Saul's successor. In Kings *gĕbûrâ* "refers exclusively to royal power or might" (35), while in Samuel both Saul and David are called *gĕbārîm*. And in light of the closing phrase, Polzin nicely asks if it is not significant that David and Solomon will both be anointed with oil from a horn, but Saul and Jehu only from a phial.[15]

[6–10] Fokkelman has contributed a lengthy and probing treatment of the poem (1981–93, 4:73–111), but without an explicit word on the several variants in GT or 4QSam[a]. He helps readers savor the microartistry of the poet. The following are a small sample of his observations: the phonetic balance of *śĕbēʿîm* and *rĕʿēbîm* (v. 5); the shared sounds but semantic contrast of *rʿbym* and *rbt* (5); the phonetic suggestiveness (7–8) of "bringing low" (*mšpyl*) then raising "from the refuse" (*mʾšpt*).

The final element of v. 8 (MT) is found also in 4QSam[a]. Tov finds that the addition here of a theme already found in v. 10 is intended to stress the universal

14. The language of high and lowly—*gbh* (1 Sam 2:3 and Ps 113:5) and *špl* (2:7 and 113:6)—is also shared, but differently used.

15. Gosse (218–19) notes significant links between 1 Sam 2:1 and 2 Sam 22:51; 1 Sam 2:2 and 2 Sam 22:32; 1 Sam 2:7–8 and 2 Sam 22:28.

power of God. He argues that the earlier text of vv. 8–9 had consisted only of 8ab and 9b, and that 4QSam[a] is a hybrid of additions in MT and GT. The opening two lines of 9a in MT (supported by 4QSam[a]) offer a theological interpretation of the song, while the corresponding lines in GT accommodate the song to Hannah's own situation.

In Fincke's reconstruction, there is a fourth boast, beyond the three shared by B, LT, and Jer 9. The fragmentary evidence of 4QSam[a], plus the fact that B and LT are identical neither with each other nor with Jer 9, demonstrates that the longer Gk. text did have a Heb. original. Be that as it may, the major plus appears inappropriately placed between the original components of the conclusion as preserved in MT.

Hannah's song beautifully recapitulates and reinforces a feature we noted in the opening paragraph of her story. Just as she is quite naturally herself there, so too her song, while it could be sung by many a worshiper, fits perfectly the situation of the long barren who has now borne many, and of the hungry who has now eaten—and, no less, the situation of the elite priests who have lorded it over worshipers but will have their comeuppance (Esler). Equally, just as she (while being herself) also prefigures significant royal and prophetic characteristics, so in her song she can be heard as foreshadowing important moments of the story of Israel's kings as it is told in Samuel and Kings.

Frolov recognizes all this yet argues a more nuanced reading of this song as the culmination of Hannah's whole story, yet within the more restricted context of a fresh preface in 1 Sam 1–8 to the story of Israel's kings. To read the poem as theological commentary on the books of Samuel as a whole is to miss the intimate relationship between poem and previous story (95). The occasion of the singing is the presentation of her son in the temple, by which time Hannah's independent fortunes are on the wane: her bargain with Yahweh is concluded, and her son is handed over. Following MT's different and shorter text in v. 11, he deduces that Hannah has disappeared again without trace into Elkanah's household. The relationship between her triumphant cry "My horn is exalted in Yahweh" (2:1) and her final assertion that "He would exalt the horn of his anointed one" (2:10) has often been noted. Frolov asks (97): "What will happen to Yhwh's anointed one once his 'horn' has been exalted. Will it remain in that position indefinitely or promptly fall, like that of Hannah?" And yet, even in MT, Hannah hardly disappears without trace back into Elkanah's house: she not only continues to provide cloaks for her growing firstborn, but also bears her husband five more children as well (2:19–21).

1 Samuel 2:11–3:10 Samuel between Eli and Yahweh

The next large block of text is punctuated by two thrice-repeated, though lightly varied, statements about Samuel. The one reports but does not further describe his service before Yahweh (2:11, 18; 3:1). The other reports his growth, or increasing greatness (2:21, 26; 3:19). From four of these notes, B appears to take a lead and opens new paragraphs at 2:11 (following its plus), 18; 3:1, 19. Fincke notes clear evidence of paragraphing in 4QSam[a] at 2:11b, 18; and 3:1; but not at 3:19. The second note about Samuel's service (2:18) is followed by the final report about Hannah. It may be that the account of the wickedness of Eli's house (within 2:12–36), which precedes and explains the loss of the ark (chs. 4–6), was originally told without reference to Samuel or his mother. The beginning of this older tale has been overlaid with the end of the story of Hannah.

1 Samuel 2:11–3:3

11 And she left him there facing Yahweh. And she went to Ramathaim	11 Elkanah went to Ramathaim to his house.[a]

And the lad was serving *in face of*[b] Yahweh, facing [cf. v.17] Eli the priest.

12 But the sons of Eli *the priest* were sons of uselessness:
they did not know Yahweh.

13 and[a] the right of the priests from the people[b] everyone sacrificing	13 As for the rule of the priest with the people[b] every man sacrificing a sacrifice

the priest's lad would come
as he was cooking the flesh,
and the trident fork in his hand.

14 And he would strike in the *great* pot [or in the kettle[a]] or in the cauldron or in the pan—
everything the fork brought up the priest would take of it.
So they would do to all Israel
those coming *to sacrifice* [there] at Shiloh.[b]

15 Even before they made the fat smoke,
the priest's lad would come
and say to the man sacrificing:
"Give flesh
to roast for the priest—
and *I* [he] will not take from you boiled flesh *from the pot*[, but 'living'[a]]."

16 And the man said to him,[a]
"The fat should be properly burned as usual—
and take for yourself *of all*
as your soul desires."

And he would say [to him],
"*No*, you will give now.
And if not, I *shall* take it by force."
17 And the sin of the lads was very great in the sight of Yahweh
[cf. v. 11],
because the*y* [men[a]] were contemptuous of the offering to Yahweh.
18 But Samuel became servant in face of[a] Yahweh;
a lad girt[b] with an ephod of linen.[c]
19 And a small robe did his mother make for him
and brought it up to him from time to time
when she came up with her husband
to offer the periodic sacrifice.
20 And Eli [would] bless*ed* Elkanah and his wife,
[and would] say*ing*,
"May Yahweh *pay back*[a] [put down] for you seed from this woman
against the asking
which *you*[b] [was] asked of Yahweh";
and the[y] *man*[c] would go to his place.
21 [Yes,[a]] *And* Yahweh noted Hannah,
and she [conceived
and] bore[b] a further three sons and two daughters.
And the lad Samuel grew great [with] *before* Yahweh.
22 Now Eli grew very old;[a]

	and he heard what his sons were doing to the sons of Israel.		and he heard[b] everything[c] that his sons were doing to all Israel:
			that they were lying with the women assembling at the opening of the appointed tent.[d]
23	And he said to them, "Why do you do a thing like this,	23	And he said to them, "Why do you do things like these,
	that I am hearing		that I am hearing—your deeds,[a] evil—
	from all the people of Yahweh.		from all the people—these.
24	No, sons. For the report I am hearing is not good. Do not do thus—for the reports I am hearing are not good:[b]	24	No, [my[a]] sons. For the report I am hearing is not good:

a people not serving God.[c] making the people of Yahweh transgress.[c]

25 If a man sins *utterly* against a man,
[a God[a] may mediate] *they will pray* for him *to Yahweh.*
But
if against Yahweh *he* [a man] sins,
who will intercede for him?"
But they would not listen to the voice of their father,[b]
for Yahweh was *utterly*[c] pleased
to *destroy them* [put them to death[d]].
26 But the lad Samuel was growing [greater[a] and] better [both] with Yahweh and with men.

27 And there came a man of God to Eli,
and said [to him]:
"Thus has Yahweh said,
'Did I not[a] actually reveal myself to the house of your father
when they were in Egypt, *slaves* of the house of Pharaoh:
28 choosing *the house of your father* [him[a]] from all the staffs of Israel
for myself as priest,
to raise offerings over my altar,
to burn incense,
to bear an ephod [before me];
and I gave your father's house all the [fire] offerings of Israel's sons
for food.
29 Why do you[a] [all] despise/kick against my sacrifice and my offering
with shameless eye
[which I have commanded {as} refuge[b]];
and have you honored your sons more than me,
taking yourself a blessing [fattening yourselves[c]]
from the first of every offering of Israel *before me* [of my people[d]]?'
30 Therefore, utterance of Yahweh, God of Israel,
'I [surely[a]] said,
"Your house and the house of your father will go about before me forever."
But now, utterance of Yahweh,
"It would profane me—
surely those who honor me will I honor,
and those who despise me will be slighted."
31 Look times are coming
when I will chop down your *seed* [right arm[a]]
and the *seed* [right arm] of your father's house[,

lest there be an elder in your house.
32 And you will look on {a rival in the residence}
in all that he makes Israel prosper;[a]]
and there will not be an elder in *my* [your] house for all time.
33 And a man will I not cut off [of you] from my altar,
wearing out[a] *his* [your] eyes
and [sicken] your soul *dropping off*;
but all *that remains*[b] [the larger part] of your house shall [die] *fall by the sword of* men.
34 And this is the sign for you which will come to[a] *these* your two sons,
to Hophni and Phinehas:
in one day both of them will die.
35 And I shall establish for myself a faithful priest:

who all in my heart and in my soul shall do.	as[a] my heart and soul desire he shall act.

And I shall build for him a faithful house
and he will go to and fro before my anointed for all time.
36 And everyone
who is left in [your] house
will come
to do obeisance to him for a piece of silver [or a scrap of food[a]];
[and will] say*ing*,
"*Cast*[b] [Attach] me [please] to one of *your* [the] priesthoods,
to eat [a piece of] food.'"'"

3:1 The lad Samuel was ministering to Yahweh before Eli *the* priest.[a]
And the word of Yahweh was precious in those days:
there was no vision [broken] *expanding*[b] through.

2 And it came to be on that day—
And Eli was lying in his place,
and his eyes had begun to be dim:[a]
he could not see,
3 and the lamp of God was not yet extinguished,
and Samuel was lying in the temple [of Yahweh[a]]
where the ark of god was—

11a. Both B and MT may have supposed that Hannah and Elkanah are traveling together back to his/their home in Rama, but each focuses our attention on different aspects of such a totality; and it takes LT to put them together: "And they left him before Yahweh there, and did homage to Yahweh, and departed for Ramah for their home." None of this verse is preserved in 4QSam[a].

b. Here B (but not LT) attests not *ʾt-yhwh* (MT) but *ʾt-pny yhwh*.

13a. A principal difference between GT and MT concerns sentence division: in GT, the priestly due is a 2d obj. of "not knowing" (v. 12). While otherwise identical to B, the LT adds *ēn* ("was") after "making a sacrifice," which has the effect of detaching the opening words of v. 13 from the end of 12, as in MT.

b. The GT retroverts to *hkhn mʾt-hʿm*; MT's *hkhn(y)m ʾt-hʿm* has arisen from wrong division of these consonants.

14a. Presumably either *hgdwl* presupposed by GT or MT's *ʾwbdwd* is a corruption, though hardly simple, of the other.

b. The LT reads "at Shiloh" after "all Israel."

15a. The GT and MT offer real alternative texts. GT's "from the pot" is straightforward, and probably translates *mhkywr*, with which the more puzzling MT *ky ʾm-ḥy* shares 3 consonants. MT spells out the implications of not accepting what has been boiled. The opposition here of boiled and *ḥāy* (lit., "living") is found only in this one instance in HB and I am not persuaded that it is sufficient to justify the unique sense of "raw." It seems quite as possible that MT's reading has caught the impudence of the lads!

16a. Immediately before the opening words of v. 17, 4QSam[a] has a more extended text. This starts very similar to MT and GT:

4QSam[a]	**GT**	**MT**
And the man responded *and* said	And the man said (the one sacrificing)	And the man said
to the priest's lad,	to him,	to him,
"Let the priest burn	"Let there be burned	"Let them wholly burn
as usual the fat, and take for yourself of all that your spirit desires."	as usual the fat, and take for yourself of all that your spirit desires."	as usual the fat, and take for yourself as your spirit desires."
And he said, "No, for now you will give and	And he said, "No, for now you will give and if not,	And he said to him, "For now you will give, and if not,
I shall take by force."	I shall take by force."	I shall take by force."

Most of the differences between these three texts can be put down to explanatory expansion of a shorter original. The opening pluses in 4QSam[a] and GT remove any possible ambiguity over who is speaking to whom. There are two linguistic puzzles about MT: nowhere else in HB is a finite form of *qṭr* strengthened by an inf. abs.; and it is anomalous to have a finite *hipʿil* strengthened by a *piʿel* inf. *yqṭr* is read as active (4QSam[a] and MT); and the pass. in GT could reflect either a *puʿal* reading or idiomatic rendering of an impersonal subj. "No" is the correct reading, as recognized in the Q of MT. And 4QSam[a]'s shorter reading at the end is surprising and correspondingly effective: it is under duress that you-giving-me-taking is happening. But 4QSam[a] continues with material more like vv. 13–14 in MT and GT (and might give indirect support to the sentence division there adopted in B):

4QSam[a]	GT	MT
as the flesh is being cooked;	as the flesh is being	as the flesh is being cooked,
and take the trident fork {in	cooked, and the trident	and the trident fork in his
your hand and . . . strike}	fork in his hand.	hand.
. . . in the pot or in {the pan	And he would strike in	And he would strike in
	the *great* pot . . . or in the	the pot [or in the kettle] or
all} that the fork would	cauldron or in the pan—	in the cauldron or in the
bring up and	all that the fork would	pan—all that the fork would
take whether bad or good—	bring up the priest would	bring up the priest would
apart from the . . . right leg	take of it.	take of it.

We have to suppose either a major repetition within the Qumran scroll, or that it read the constituent elements of this paragraph in a different order from MT and GT.

17a. Here "the men" (MT's plus) introduces a fresh term into the list of characters—see below.

18a. Fincke sensibly supposes *lpny* (a literal retroversion from GT's *enōpion*) for *ʾt-pny* (MT and DJD); GT's earlier *tō prosōpō* (v. 11) had presupposed *ʾt-pny*.

b. The pass. ptc. *periezōsmenon* (GT) agrees with *ḥgwr* (MT), while *ḥwgr* (4QSam[a]) is act. (as MT in 1 Kgs 20:11; 2 Kgs 3:21).

c. Here 4QSam[a] does read *bd*. B does not translate what it has read, but transcribes it as *ʾpwd br*—has the scribe misread *d* as *r*, or did its underlying text intend "pure ephod"? The sentence in LT concludes simply with *ephoud*, which may be original.

20a. The term *yšlm* (4QSam[a] not *yśm* MT) is the expected correlate of *apotinein* (GT). MT no doubt suffered accidental loss of a letter. Given the consonants they share, payment (*šlm*) against a request (*šʾl*) is aptly described.

b. As in 1:28, GT's translation does not attest a basically different text. In place of MT's puzzling *šʾl* (rendered impersonally above), 4QSam[a] attests the hipf. (*hšʾl[h]*), as in 1:28.

c. The GT unusually pays more attention here to Elkanah.

21a. Only the initial letter distinguishes the opening *kypqd* (MT) from *wypqd* (4QSam[a] and GT).

b. Here B's text agrees with 4QSam[a]; that suggests that LT has conflated the alternatives: "and she conceived again and bore." The final clause in 4QSam[a] starts *wygdl šm* and supports GT against MT toward its end: *lpny y* . . . DJD conjectures *wygdl šm šmwʾl lpny yhwh*; however, Fincke retains *hnʿr* between *šm* and *šmwʾl*.

22a. After "very old," 4QSam[a] adds that Eli was 90 years of age (cf. 98 at his death in 4:15).

b. This is *wĕqāṭal* for simple past (as in B), or perhaps "and he was hearing."

c. Here B agrees with 4QSam[a]; the MT has added *kl* before *ʾšr* and has replaced *bny* with *kl* before "Israel."

d. The 4QSam[a] has no space for MT's long specification of the crimes of Eli's sons; but typically LT does offer a translation.

23a. Here 4QSam[a] does attest at least *dbry* . . . after "hearing," like MT; for the earlier [*kdbrym hʾl*]*h*, DJD and Fincke follow MT.

24a. The term *bny* (4QSam[a]) supports MT against *tekna* (GT), which retroverts to *bnym*.

b. Here 4QSam[a] and B share a doublet not found in MT or (unusually) LT.

c. Fincke's conjecture *mʿbwd ʿm yhwh* presumably draws together three pieces of evidence: (i) 4QSam[a]'s *mʿb...* (ii) B's *tou mē douleuein laon theō*; and (iii) MT's concluding *ʿm-yhwh*. In light of Isa. 43:23–24, which talks also of sacrificial offering, I would have proposed rather *mʿbydym (ʿm) yhwh*—"making (the people of) Yahweh serve." However, DJD reads the first word as *mʿbr[ym]*.

25a. MT is unlikely: *ʾlyhwh* (4QSam[a]) may have corrupted into *ʾlhym*.

b. "[The voice] of their father" (MT and GT) is not attested in 4QSam[a], which has no space between *qwl ky'*.

c. The phrase *boulomenos ebouleto* in the final clause of both B and LT achieves a neat balance with their opening *hamart(an)ōn hamartē*; however, MT does not read an inf. abs. at beginning or end, although 4QSam[a] does have *ḥṭwʾ* before what DJD and Fincke conjecture as *yḥṭʾ*.

d. Nowhere else in OT does *diaphtheirai* correspond to *hmyt*: as the underlying text we should expect *lhšmydm* rather than *lhmytm*.

26a. Here *wgdl* (MT and LT) is not preserved in 4QSam[a], but the space in its line appears to attest it. A literal retroversion from B hardly works in Hebrew.

27a. It is difficult to justify the question posed in *hnglh*: the interrogative *h-* may be a dittograph of the end of *yhwh*.

28a. The *ʾtw* rather than *bw* after *bḥr* is unusual and possibly late. Its use in 1 Kgs 11:34 and 2 Chr 7:16 are both pluses to BTH; it is also used in Ps 78:68 (but not in 67 or 70).

29a. The vb. *epeblepsas* (GT) renders *tbyṭ* (4QSam[a]). This *hipʿil* of *nbṭ* is, however, used just below, within the long MT plus in vv. 31b–32a. *tbʿṭw* (MT) is attested elsewhere only in Deut 32:15.

b. There is no help from 4QSam[a] over the substantial divergence between *ʾšr ṣwyty mʿwn* (MT) and *anaidei ophthalmō* (read by LT as well as B), although the final *ʿwn* and *ʿyn* are easily confused. Elsewhere in OT, *anaidēs* is used to render forms of *ʿz* (strong, strength) with "face" (5x) and "spirit" (1x); the only connection between *ʿzz* and *ʿyn* is where wisdom talks of the Creator's "making strong the eyes/fountains of the deep" (Prov 8:28).

c. The phrase *lhbryʾkm* (MT) is longer than either *(l)hbrtk* (4QSam[a]) or *lhbrk* (GT); the suf. *-k* (sg.) is expected in context rather than *-km* (pl.)—the final *m* duplicates the opening of the next word. Each text supposes a different vb.: MT has the unique instance in HB of a vb. related to the adj. *bryʾ* ("fat"); 4QSam[a] offers a first instance of *brh* ("eat") found only in Samuel (3x *qal* and 2x further in *hipʿil*, as here); and GT renders the straightforward *nipʿal* of *brk* (bless).

d. Here *lʿmy* (MT) and *lpny* (both B and LT) are variants.

30a. The force of the inf. abs. plus in MT is illustrated in Judg 15:2, where Samson's father-in-law claims he had made a declaration that Samson had fully divorced his daughter.

31a. The terms "seed" and "arm" are alternative readings of *zrʿ*.

32a. 4QSam[a] does not attest MT's long plus in vv. 31b–32a; but LT does. The LT does not render MT's 31b in the same place; but does render 32a, and represents 31a in its fuller 32b: "and there shall not be an elder in your house, and there shall not be of you an elder in my house all the days." However, MT's repetition of 31b at 32b would be a significant indicator that 31a was a supplement, even without the negative evidence of B and 4QSam[a].

33a. Though *eklipein* may be transitive, and so a good rendering of the *pi'el lklwt*, it is as often intransitive, and that appears to have influenced the less literal choice of *katarrein* for *l'dyb*.

b. Here as in v. 36, *perisseuein* may attest *nwtr* (remain over); *kl-hnwtr* is regularly attested, while *kl-mrbyt* (MT) is unique.

34a. The MT reads *'l* before "your two sons," but GT attests *'l*; then while MT repeats *'l* before Hophni, *toutous* in GT attests *'lh*; the sole *l* in 4QSam[a] could be part of either.

35a. Against *k'šr* (MT) the GT appears to retrovert to *'šr kl-'šr*, and this longer text is reconstructed in DJD for 4QSam[a].

36a. "And one bread" (LT and OL) gives broad support to *wkkr lḥm* (MT); but at the end of the verse both agree with B. The phrase *kkr lḥm* was an element of the provisions given by David to each person in Israel on the ark's arrival in Jerusalem (1 Chr 16:3; 2 Sam 6:19 uses *ḥlt lḥm*, more at home in priestly texts).

b. Here *pararripson* (GT) is followed by *proice* (OL). It is used in the pass. to render the unique verbal form *hstwpp* (Ps 84:10 [11]), "be at the threshold/be a doorkeeper." In a causative verbal form, this would make good sense here. However, *spḥ hitpa'el* is used in 1 Sam 26:19.

3:1a. As at 1:3, GT gives Eli the title "priest," or MT takes it away.

b. The act. ptc. *diastellousa* suggests *prṣ*: Wellhausen notes that, following *ḥzwn*, an *n* could as easily have been added as lost. The GT has the sense of "expanding" or "distinctive."

2a. Here *barynesthai*, lit., "to be weighed down," can mean "to be weary."

3a. With B, here 4QSam[a] may lack *yhwh*, and it appears to have no room for the following *'šr šm 'rwn 'lhym*.

[11–17] Discussion of this paragraph must seek to answer two possibly related questions: Where are the minor (sentence) divisions, and how many characters are featured? To start with the second: both our texts (not just GT) describe Eli as "the priest" (v. 11), and have a "lad" in front of him who is in some sense "serving Yahweh" (11), and then useless sons who "know not Yahweh" (12). Following this summary introduction, the larger part of the paragraph concerns the kind of attention suffered by worshipers at the hands of the priest's "lad" (vv. 13, 15) or "lads" (17). In all four verses, GT renders *na'ar* by *paidarion*. It is at the end that our texts differ (possibly) significantly: MT specifies those contemptuous of Yahweh as "the men." When reading GT, I suspect that it is more satisfactory not to multiply characters, but take the "lads" of the main paragraph as one and the same as Eli's "sons." We are given no reason to suspect that the priest is as bad as his "lads" make him out to be. On this reading, the plural "lads" at the end of this portion will refer not to a generality of sinful priestly servants, but to Eli's two sons. On the other hand, those who render "lad" as "servant" may suppose that the "priest" whom his servant quotes to the worshiper is one of Eli's worthless sons. This reading is easier in MT, where "the men" at the end of the portion who are the source of the sin are identical with Eli's no-good sons at the beginning.

As to the first question, the Yahweh (*ʾt-yhwh*) Samuel serves is in some sense coordinate with Eli (*ʾt-pny ʿly*). Similarly the uselessness of Eli's sons is related to their not knowing Yahweh. The rather "clumsy balance" of 11b–12 may also suggest that while Samuel's service of Yahweh is in the full face of Eli, his sons' ignorance of Yahweh is manifested in actions behind his back. Overwhelmingly in HB, the verb *šrt* refers to priestly "service." The only use of the verb in BTH (1 Kgs 8:11) is in line with this, together with all five instances in Deuteronomy[16] and 2 Kgs 25:14. But there are exceptions: Joseph's service in Egypt (Gen 39:4; 40:4), Abishag's to David (1 Kgs 1:4, 15), and Elisha's to Elijah (1 Kgs 19:21) were not priestly; and the nominal *mšrt* is normally used of a personal assistant, whether of Moses, Amnon, Solomon, or Elisha. It may be that the nature of Samuel's "service" is left deliberately unclear. See further on the next paragraph (vv. 18–21).

The interpretation of the next phrase (reading the text supposedly underlying GT) *mšpṭ* (*hkhn mʾt hʿm*) (v. 13) as "(priestly) due (from the people)" has long been deduced from the similarly stated Deut 18:3. Here GT's genitive phrase *pantos tou thyontos* (v. 13) is as clearly appositional as is *mʾt zbḥy hzbḥ* after *mʾt hʿm* in Deut 18:3, and may well show awareness of GT in that verse; but if so, GT has not adopted *krisis* for *mšpṭ*, but used *dikaiōma* (followed by OL *iustificationem*). Indeed neither GT nor MT appears to have understood the original import of this phrase. In treating ignorance of sacrificial law as an instance of ignorance of Yahweh, GT offers an entirely credible reading of the same wording as MT has preserved. But it is much less clear what was intended in MT's division of these words. Let us take the three main puzzles in reverse order: (1) When separated from *ʾt hʿm* by the *athnach* (pause mark), "every man offering a sacrifice" is less likely to be appositional to it and more likely to represent the protasis of a conditional sentence. (2) In the absence of a relevant preceding verb, *ʾt-* will mean "with." (3) Having lost the close connection with "the people" stated in the original *mʾt-*, now *mšpṭ* will bear the sense of "customary behavior," as in 1 Sam 8:9, 11 of the future king (as opposed to 10:25, which intends the rules for the kingdom). In the comment that closes this paragraph (v. 17), "offering" seems simply a nonspecific name for what "every man" was "sacrificing" (13, 15).

[18–21] After the scandals relating to Eli's family (vv. 12–17), we resume (18) almost where we started (11b); however, this time Eli is not mentioned

16. See Deut 10:8; 17:12; 18:5, 7; 21:5.

immediately after Yahweh, and it is Yahweh's own "face" that is specified. We are reminded that Samuel too is a "lad." The ephod with which he is girded is worn or borne almost always by priests;[17] but we shall find David wearing it when bringing the ark to Jerusalem (2 Sam 6:14, BTH). We may wonder whether this youngster's distinctive uniform anticipates a priestly role or a royal (or at least leadership) role. The topic of dress is immediately developed in the final scene, in which his mother appears (vv. 19–21). The little "robe" she makes for him is worn alike by princes and priests (indeed Exod 28:31 talks of "the robe for the ephod"). And, just as he himself had been "brought up" (1:24–25 in both GT and MT) to the sanctuary—the same verb as is also used of offering certain sacrifices there—so too his mother "brings up" this garment "periodically" (the same term as is used for the "periodic" sacrifice).

Eli's blessing (v. 20) is of both parents, but it is the father whom he addresses. Yet it is Hannah whom Yahweh "notes" or "counts" (*pqd*), just as earlier he had "remembered" her (1:19). Just once more *pqd* is used of Yahweh in HB prior to conception and birth—there by the mother of the nation, Sarah (Gen 21:1). Hannah's five further children are compensation for the one for whom she asked and immediately gave away. But though numbered, they remain unnamed, and attention quickly returns to Samuel (v. 21). We are told of his growth; and this could be a relatively trivial comment about a youngster growing up. Yet recognizing a further anticipation of David in BTH (2 Sam 5:10), and this time of Solomon too (1 Kgs 10:23), GT narrows the implication to the growth of his reputation and renders *gdl* by "was magnified" (*emegalynthē*). The preposition *ʿm* (MT, "with") is often used to express being in company with or at home with. The GT's "before" (*enōpion*) either attests *lpny* or offers a more cautious rendering. The next time "and he grew" (*wygdl*) appears in the text (3:19), it is followed immediately by *šmwʾl*, but on that occasion Yahweh is said to be "with him."

[22–25] Twice now (vv. 18, 21b) the relationship between Samuel and Yahweh has been restated without mention of Eli (contrast 11b); now the focus returns to him and his sons. Just as the troubles in Elkanah's household were described in frequentative verbal forms (1:4b–7a), so too *wĕšāmaʿ* and *yaʿăśûn* (2:22) describe repeated hearing and doing. The MT not only underscores the *comprehensiveness* of both by adding "all" (*kl*) twice, but also supplies a scandalous example. The combination of terms it uses is unique to Exod 38:8 (itself apparently one of the latest elements added to the book of Exodus). The role of the women at the entrance to the sanctuary (Exod 38:8) is already far from clear. When the MT plus at the end of 2:22 has Eli's sons lying with such women, the context suggests they were abusing them rather than availing themselves of cultic prostitutes. The broad sense of vv. 23–24 is clear and is common to both

17. See 1 Sam 2:28; 21:9 (10); 22:18; 23:6, 9; 30:7.

texts—I assume secondary supplementation in each—at least until the final phrase (see detailed textual notes). Comparing GT and MT in v. 24 suggests that GT has conflated two versions of Eli's words, one singular and the other plural; however, GT's version corresponds to 4QSam[a], and so either the conflation is early or else MT has lost or deleted Eli's emphatic repetition.

The culmination of the old man's words to his sons is particularly interesting. One may conceive of a remedy for sins by one human against another, but what of human sins against Yahweh? It may have to remain unclear just how distinct in sense are the very rare *piʿel* of *pll* and the much commoner *hitpaʿel*. But what is beyond dispute is that one of those few other occurrences of the *piʿel* relates to another Phinehas, who took a stand and interposed himself to stay a plague in the desert (Ps 106:28–30) like Moses before him (106:19–23). How does Eli's warning relate to the report in the psalm? Is he suggesting a general rule? In that case, he may be unwilling to see the success of Phinehas in the wilderness situation as a precedent. Or is he sketching an issue that is particularly acute for priests? If this time it is Phinehas the priest (with Hophni) who is leading the sin against Yahweh, then there is no intermediary to intercede. We cannot be sure, because he is (simply!) asking a question. There is ambiguity in the question. Is Eli challenging his sons to identify an intercessor competent in their case? Or is he rhetorically suggesting that there is none such? His question will reverberate throughout both books of Samuel.

The narrator explains the refusal of Eli's sons to heed his warning in terms with interesting resonance. Around half of all the occurrences in HB of *ḥāpēṣ* ("be pleased") have Yahweh as their subject. Talk of Yahweh being "pleased to put to death"' is used only once more in HB. Manoah's wife scorns his fear of the consequences of having seen God: "If Yahweh had been pleased to put us to death, he would not have accepted . . . [offerings] . . . at our hands, or shown us all these things" (Judg 13:23). And yet presumably Yahweh had accepted offerings at the hands of Eli's sons. This echo is further explored in vv. 27–36.

[26] Completing the frame around Eli's rebuke is a more expansive version of v. 21b. Samuel is "titled" the same way: "the lad Samuel." He is not simply increasing, but increasing more and more (the idiomatic use of *hlk* before another verb, which seems to have been missed in GT's rendering), and also becoming better, with humans as well as with Yahweh. As the fate of the house of Eli becomes ever more obviously sealed, Samuel's reputation grows and grows. If there was any doubt whether the house of Eli sinned against only humans or also against Yahweh, there is no doubt regarding Samuel's relations with both.

[27–36] If the story of Hannah resonates with much that is to follow in the books of Samuel (and Kings), this is no less true of the story of Eli and his house. At the most obvious level, the story of a chosen line that will die, father and sons, during a war between Israel and Philistines, and a rival growing up among them with increasingly positive reputation, anticipates the demise of the house of Saul and the rise of David. What is less obvious—and correspondingly more interesting—is how far the story of Eli, no less than the story of Saul and their houses, bears on the fate of David and his house. I shall argue more fully at the end of this commentary that there are important "gaps" in the haunting and puzzling story of Yahweh's inciting David to have his people counted (2 Sam 24). I find that each of the (not many) narratives earlier in 1–2 Samuel that anticipates the talk there at the end of "sin," "guilt," and "folly" is probing these "gaps."

There is no passage in the rest of Samuel–Kings that uses so many stock elements of developed prophetic narrative so close together as 2:27–36. "Man of God" (v. 27), "thus has Yahweh said" (27), and "utterance of Yahweh" (2x in v. 30) are all found in BTH[18] and then here and there throughout Samuel–Kings. "Behold, days are coming" is repeated only in 2 Kgs 20:17. David says "it would profane me" once in BTH (2 Sam 23:17); but this expression is attributed to Yahweh nowhere in HB.[19] An accumulation like this is without parallel and calls for explanation. Is the narrator concerned to introduce readers quickly to a wide selection of prophetic terminology, or to portray the language of this man of God as "over the top"? Does it require a manifold guarantee of prophetically mediated authority to dispossess a priestly line that extends back to the constitution of the people itself? If we add "And this is the sign for you" (v. 34), which is found twice in 2 Kgs 18–20 and then only in Exod 3:12 and 1 Sam 14:10, it is only in the narrative about Isaiah and Hezekiah shared by 2 Kgs 18–20 and Isa 36–39 that the majority of these features of our portion recur.[20]

Yet some of the influence on this passage may be more local. "Sign" is not the only term shared with an episode in ch. 14. The emphatic *niglōh* of the Deity's being uncovered or revealed (27) is repeated in the equally prophetic 3:7, 21 but is uncommon elsewhere in HB (only Gen 35:7 and Isa 22:14). Yet it is used twice (14:8, 11) in close proximity to "sign," where Jonathan and his armor-bearer take a lonely and dangerous but successful initiative when they disclose themselves to a Philistine garrison. Divine disclosure may be equally risky but may also lead to success. "Signs" recur in only one more portion of Samuel: promised by Samuel to Saul as they conclude their first meeting (10:7, 9). Belonging in Egypt to "the house of Pharaoh" (v. 27) is the first of a very small cluster of portions of 1 Samuel that make reference to the traditions of

18. See *ʾyš-hʾlhym* in 1 Kgs 12:22; *kh ʾmr yhwh* in 2 Sam 7:5, 8; 24:12; 1 Kgs 12:24; 22:11; 2 Kgs 22:15, 16, 18; *nʾm yhwh* in 2 Kgs 22:19.

19. The closest approximation appears to be Job 34:10: "It would profane El to do evil, and Shaddai to do wrong." Appropriately for our context, 34:11 continues: "For as a man works he will repay him."

20. See *nʾm yhwh* (2 Kgs 19:33), *kh ʾmr yhwh* (19:6, 20, 32; 20:1, 5), *hnh ymym bʾym* (20:17), *zh-lk hʾwt* (19:29; 20:9).

Israel's earlier servitude and deliverance from Egypt (the others are 4:8; 6:6; 10:18; and 12:6, 8).

Both occurrences of *mʿwn* are peculiar to MT and unlikely to be original. Indeed *ṣwyty mʿwn* (v. 29) and *ṣr mʿwn* (32) might be doublets. The word occurs nowhere else in Samuel; and there may have been influence from a text such as Ps 71:3: *hyh ly lṣwr mʿwn* ("be to me a rock abode").[21]

The question raised at the beginning of this previous comment, how far the fate of the house of Eli bears not just on the house of Saul but also the house of David, receives a partial answer toward the end of this portion. The descriptions of the house of Eli being chosen "from all the staffs/tribes of Israel" (v. 28) to "go about" (30) align it with the divine choice of David and Jerusalem in the foundation document; for these phrases are a stock theme of BTH, as in 2 Sam 7:7; 1 Kgs 8:16; 14:21; 2 Kgs 21:7. The nonspecific "offerings" (twice in v. 29) is repeated from v. 17, though here paired with the standard noun "sacrifices." And "forever" (2:30) is used more densely in 2 Sam 7 than elsewhere in the narrative books of HB. Hannah was the first to use the expression "forever" in Samuel (1:22): her presentation of her son, once weaned, would be full and final. Here (2:30) the man of God bears Yahweh's report that, Yahweh's own declaration concerning Eli's father's house notwithstanding, that house will be cut off. This threatened demise of the house of Eli must threaten the house of David. Talk in Deuteronomy (18:5) of the choice of Levi "from all the staffs/tribes of Israel" will be a further anticipation of the theme (the passages are clearly related); and the same holds true for the "fire offerings" (v. 28)[22] that, apart from here and Deut 18:1, are mentioned only in Josh 13:14 outside the books Exodus–Numbers—and only here are called "the fire offerings of Israel's sons" rather than "of Yahweh." There is no need to derive vv. 28 and 35 here from Deuteronomy.[23]

[3:1] The whole paragraph about the wickedness of Eli's house has been interspersed with brief reminders of young Samuel's development. And it nears its end with another (3:1a). The added comment (v. 1b) looks both backward and forward, noting that a substantial oracle such as 2:27–36 was both rare and precious in these days and prefiguring Samuel's vision. In pointing forward to the young lad's call, it also anticipates language from BTH: "word of Yahweh" and "vision." And the other instances of "precious" (*yāqār*) in all of biblical narrative relate to David, Solomon, Hezekiah, and the temple.[24]

21. Unless we should read *lṣwr-mʿwz* (a rock stronghold), as in Ps 31:3 (the two psalms have almost identical openings).

22. McCarter queries the rendering.

23. It is arguable that the wider Deuteronomic theme of the choice or election of Israel as a whole was also a development backward from the choice of David and Jerusalem.

24. See 2 Sam 12:30 (= 1 Chr 20:2) and 1 Kgs 10:2, 10, 11 (= 2 Chr 9:1, 9, 10) in BTH; and also 1 Kgs 5:17 (31); 7:9–11; 2 Chr 3:6; 32:27.

The opening words of 3:1 link with what has gone before and offer a third summary statement of Samuel's service. Unlike 2:11, 18, the MT and GT are agreed that Samuel's service is now (directly) to Yahweh. It is hard not to detect a double meaning in "before Eli": formally Samuel may still be in Eli's sight and under his direction, but now he has the real precedence (as will be the case of David over Saul in much of 1 Samuel). It is in this context that Yahweh's word (*dābār*) is first mentioned in this book, if one discounts the MT variant in 1:23; and it is used again in 3:7. It is as rare or prized as the gemstone in a royal crown (2 Sam 12:30) or an exquisitely decorated temple or palace. The fact that the verb *yqr* is used just twice in Samuel offers striking confirmation of our previous remark: both relate precisely to David and Saul. The first talks of David's reputation as prized when he begins to demonstrate greater success than Saul (1 Sam 18:30); and then Saul states his relief in finding that his life is precious in David's estimate (26:21).

The final element of this interesting verse is the most puzzling: "there was no 'broken-through' vision." The term *prṣ*, like *ḥāzôn* ("vision"), is at home in BTH. It features in and also explains two names in the David story: Baal-Perazim (2 Sam 5:20) and Perez-Uzzah (6:8). Very suitably to the present visionary context, both these refer to divine irruptions. In 2 Kgs 14:13, it is a matter of Jehoash of Israel breaking through (or down) the wall of Jerusalem to a length of 200 meters; and in similar terms, Prov 25:28 talks of "a city broken into—no wall" (*ʿîr pĕrûṣâ ʾên ḥômâ*).[25] Do the two statements of 3:1b together suggest that "word" is all the more prized where vision has not broken through?

[3:2–3] The final subparagraph includes significant anticipations of key terms from the synoptic (BTH) chapters about David and Solomon. (a) Eli lies down in his "place" (v. 2), as will Samuel (v. 9); and *māqôm* is used of the "place" where the divine ark belongs,[26] the "place" to which prayer should be directed,[27] and of the "places" where a divine breakthrough, or *pereṣ*, has occurred.[28] (b) Only in the account of the dedication of Solomon's temple does HB associate temple (*hêkāl*) and ark (*ʾărôn*), as in v. 3. It also repeats a feature of the opening of the book: it gives a great deal of background (vv. 2–3) before the action starts. We are told a good deal about the divine word before it is first spoken. In 3:1, Eli is mentioned after Samuel, and the absence of vision after prized word; but in what follows they are suggestively developed together: there was an expectation that incubation in sanctuary precincts could lead to

25. Proverbs 29:18 also uses *ʾēn-ḥāzôn* with the assonant verb *prʿ*, also *nipʿal*: "With no vision, a people is set loose."

26. See 2 Sam 6:17; cf. 1 Kgs 8:6, 7.

27. See 1 Kgs 8:29, 30, 35

28. See 2 Sam 5:20; 6:8

visionary experience, but Eli's capacity for sight (of all sorts?) was reduced. He shared this incapacity with Isaac (Gen 27:1), who could be tricked out of a blessing by one of his sons, but not with Moses (Deut 34:7), who remained clear-sighted till the day of his death. Two further uses of this relatively rare word lead us to wonder whether Eli is suffering from "vexation" (Job 17:7) or is being punished as a wicked shepherd (Zech 11:17). In any case, the problem is not that the lamp of God has gone out. The noun *nēr* (v. 3) recurs in Samuel only at the end, where David is Israel's light (2 Sam 21:17), and Yahweh is David's (2 Sam 22:29); that leaves the reader here wondering whether the divine lamp is more than simply a temple lantern.

1 Samuel 3:4–10

4 And Yahweh called [to Samuel[a]]
"*Samuel, Samuel,*"
and he said
"I'm here."
5 And he ran to Eli,
and said
"I'm here;
surely you called me."
And he said,
"I did not call.
Go back,
lie down."
6 And Yahweh went on
to call again,
"Samuel."
And Samuel got up
and went to Eli
and said,
"I'm here;
surely you called me."
And he said,
"I did not call *you,* my son;[a]
go back,
lie down."
7 And Samuel did not yet know *God* [Yahweh],
and the word of Yahweh had not yet been revealed to him.
8 And Yahweh went on
to call Samuel a third time;
and he got up

and went to Eli
and said,
"I'm here,
surely you called me."
And Eli perceived
that Yahweh was calling to the lad.
9 And *he* [Eli] said [to Samuel],
"Go back,[a]
lie down, *my child.*
And
if he calls to you,
you will say,
"Speak[, Yahweh].
Surely your servant is listening."
And Samuel went
and lay down in his place.
10 And Yahweh came
and stationed himself,
and called him as from time to time[,
"Samuel, Samuel"].
And Samuel said,
"Speak.
Surely your servant is listening."

4a. After "called," B attests *šmwʾlšmwʾl*, while MT's *ʾlšmwʾl* is without the opening 3 letters. Here 4QSam[a] appears to attest *šm-* immediately after the final *-h* of *yhwh*. Although the textual tradition is somewhat more uniform in this portion, there is considerable variation over the name Samuel, when it is repeated, and when it is spoken in direct speech.

6a. In MT and LT, "my son" immediately follows "I did not call."

9a. While Eli starts his speech with *lk*, B repeats *šwb* (v. 6)—under the influence of the following *škb*? GT follows *škb* with *teknon* (< *bny*, as in v. 6, "my son").

[4–10] The start of a fresh masoretic paragraph does correspond to the main thrust of this portion. However, the rendering of the end of the previous section suggests that the main statement already began at *wyhy bywm hhwʾ* (3:2a), only to be immediately interrupted with further introductory details (vv. 2b–3). The narrative here does have a leisurely start. However, in light of all the above, we must also recognize it as a whole part of a grand introduction—an overture. This paragraph again anticipates key terms from the synoptic (BTH) chapters about David and Solomon. (a) Samuel like Eli (v. 2) lies down in his "place" (v. 9). (b) In BTH, "knowledge" related to Yahweh (v. 7) is a remarkably rare commodity, associated only with David[29] and possibly Solomon. (c) Samuel is taught to respond to Yahweh as his "servant" (vv. 9–10); that expression is particularly densely used in the synoptic chapters, which include the prayers of David (2 Sam 7 [12x]) and Solomon (1 Kgs 8:23–53 [11x]), and then once in David's plea to Yahweh for forgiveness after his census (2 Sam 24:10).

Samuel's sleeping position is defined in relation to the divine ark, which is quite material and soon itself to be endangered. It is all the more striking, after reading three times of Samuel's ministering (in some sense) to or before Yahweh, to be told (v. 7) that he did not know Yahweh, that Yahweh's word had not been uncovered. Eli understands what is happening to Samuel before Samuel himself does (vv. 8–9). The following clause is quite remarkable, whichever of two ways it is understood. Several biblical characters "take their stand before Yahweh"; but nowhere else in HB is Yahweh said to take a position before a human. It is unclear whether "as from time to time" covers Yahweh's position at each call, or simply suggests that, having taken up this special position, Yahweh now calls as each previous time.

1 Samuel 3:11–18 Samuel Speaks Yahweh's Word to Eli

11 And Yahweh said to Samuel:
"Look—
I am doing [something[a]] *my words* in Israel:
the two ears of anyone who hears it will tingle.
12 On that day I will establish [to[a]] *against* Eli everything
I have spoken to his house, from start to finish.
13 And I [will declare] *have declared*[a] to him
that I am judging his house forever in the perversit[y]*ies*
of his sons [that he has known[b]]—
for his sons are cursing *God*[c] [themselves],
and he has not rebuked them.
14 Therefore I have sworn to the house of Eli,
'The perversity of the house of Eli
shall not be atoned by [sacrifice or by offering] *incense*[a] *or by sacrifices* forever.'"
15 And Samuel lay down till the morning,
and he rose early in the morning,[a]
and he opened the doors of the house of Yahweh.
Now Samuel was afraid
to declare the vision to Eli.

29. See 2 Sam 5:12; 7:20, 21—and possibly 1 Kgs 3:7 (but the parallel with 2 Chr 1:10–12 is not precise).

16 And Eli [called Samuel,[a]
and he] said *to Samuel*,
"Samuel, my son."
And he said,
"I'm here."
17 And he said,
"What is the word
which [he spoke] *was spoken*[a] to you?
Please do not hide it from me.
So may God do to you
[and so may he continue],
if you conceal from me a word from all the word*s*
spoken [which he spoke] to you."
18 And Samuel declared [to him] all the words
and did not hide them from him.
And *he* [Eli] said,
"He is Yahweh:
what seems good to him he will do."

11a. The GT attests not *dbr* (MT) but the pl. *dbry*, perhaps influenced by the implicit pl. in "everything/all" (v. 12).

12a. Corresponding to the first *'l*, GT has *epi*, attesting *'l*; to the 2d, B has *eis* but LT *kai epi*. See below.

13a. GT reads the *w-* as simple copula, taking *hgdty* as coordinate with the immediately previous *dbrty* (B renders by pf. and LT by aor.). It remains unclear whether MT reads *whgdty* as coordinate with *'qym* early in the previous verse, or like GT.

b. It is not easy to explain either *b'wn 'šr-yd'* (MT) or *b'wnwt bnyw* (GT) as a corruption of the other, or as separate expansions of an earlier *b'wn*. Neither adds significantly to what follows, where the sons' misbehavior is specified and the nonintervention of their father presumes his knowledge.

c. Here *lhm* seems a much less probable reading than *'lhym*, attested in GT.

14a. In 1–4 Kingdoms, *thysia* is often used, and corresponds to both *zebaḥ* and *minḥâ*. In 1 Kingdoms it corresponds to *zebaḥ* 13x (1:21; 2:19; 6:15; 9:12, 13; 10:8; 11:15; 15:22 [2x]; 16:3, 5; 20:6, 29), and to *minḥâ* 5x (2:17, 29 [2x]; 3:14; 26:19). The stock rendering for *qĕṭōret* is *thymiama*, and the verbs also correspond throughout HB/OT, including 2:16, 28 above. But in 2:29 and 3:14, the only verses in which *zebaḥ* and *minḥâ* are paired, it is *thymiama* that corresponds to *zebaḥ*.

15a. The similar-looking *wyškm bbqr* attested in GT but not in MT after *wyškb šmw'l 'd-hbqr* may result from an alternative Hebrew text; but it also anticipates Samuel's early start in 15:12, when he is due to confront Saul. Whether MT preserves the original short text is less easy to decide (Trebolle Barrera 48).

16a. Both MT and B attest "Samuel" twice in this sentence, but typically in different places. Here MT and GT do agree over *bĕnî/teknon*.

17a. *dbr* is read as *puʿal* 2x in HB and LXX (Ps 87:3; Song 8:8), and also 2x by GT here.

[11–12] Both CL and the Aleppo Codex have a blank line before 3:11. This paragraph continues the several anticipations of BTH: (a) Yahweh makes a declaration (v. 13) to Samuel about Eli, just as to Nathan about David (2 Sam 7:11); and this is the only instance of *higgîd* in BTH. The following statement (v. 15) that Samuel was "afraid to declare [the sight]" goes on to link a further distinctive word: David "fears" Yahweh when Yahweh breaks out on Uzzah (2 Sam 6:9). (b) The "guilt" (*ʿăwôn*) of Eli's house (v. 14) uses a term drawn from the synoptic account of David's census (2 Sam 24:10). (c) Eli's response that Yahweh will do what "is good in his eyes" (v. 18) uses words of David in a synoptic text (2 Sam 10:12).[30]

It is also true that there is hardly an item in the whole range of HB terminology relating to vision and prophecy that is not deployed in ch. 3 or the preceding speech of "the man of God": here "the word of Yahweh" (vv. 1, 7); "vision," *ḥāzôn* (1); "on that day" (2, 12); "see," *rʾh* (2); "vision," *marʾâ* (15)—only "revealed" (*niglâ*, v. 21) is repeated from 2:27. And the key term at the end of the opening verse (*ḥāzôn*, v. 1) could have stood in the previous list as well; for the only other instances in Samuel–Kings of this (Aramaic?) term for "vision" and "seer" are in the synoptic narratives relating to David: 2 Sam 7:17; 24:11.

Tingling ears resulting from hearing about divine action (v. 11) is a theme shared only in Jer 19:3 and 2 Kgs 21:12. In the other two passages the introduction reads *hinĕnî mēbîʾ rāʿâ ʿal-* ("see, I am bringing ill against"), with "this place" as the target in Jer 19 and "Jerusalem and Judah" in 2 Kgs 21. However, the "something" that Yahweh is "doing" here is more generally "within Israel." The links between the three passages are far from fortuitous. Apart from Ps 99:6, Jeremiah (15:1) is the only nonnarrative book in HB to mention Samuel; and precisely this passage goes on to mention Manasseh (15:4), the subject of 2 Kgs 21. Then in BTH it is Manasseh who causes Yahweh vexation (2 Kgs 21:6; 22:17); and we noted earlier how this is anticipated in the behavior of Peninnah to Samuel's mother, Hannah. These opening chapters of Samuel already have the demise of David's line in their sights.

"Establishing" (*hēqîm*, *hipʿil* of *qûm*) normally has positive connotations throughout HB, and in Samuel too—its previous objects were "the poor from the dust" (2:8), "a faithful priest" (2:35), and (only in MT) "his word" (1:23), However, here the implications of the last of these are made explicit to Eli's cost (v. 12). "Against Eli" (GT) is the more straightforward statement; but "toward Eli" (MT) underscores the unexpected menace following *ʾāqîm*. It is uncommon for LT to have readings different from B and MT (or a combination of both). Here

30. David will use the phrase once more, in 2 Sam 15:26.

LT's "and against his house" extends the threat from Eli to his house, while B and MT insist that Eli too will suffer the threats spoken to his house—and that appears to fit more naturally with the following verse, which charges the sons with the prior offense.

[13–15] Yahweh's decision is solemnly stated (v. 13) and then restated (14). In both cases, it is against the house of Eli that judgment is given; and in both cases this decision is "forever": the very term used in Yahweh's original promise to Eli's father's house (2:30) is now employed in its judgment. "Judging" (*šōpēṭ*), when not a neutral term, more often appears in HB to bear a sense favorable to its object, such as "vindicate." And *ekdikō* (GT) normally corresponds to *nāqam* or *pāqad*. But it corresponds to *šāpaṭ* in some interesting contexts: saviors on Mount Zion, judging the mountain of Esau (Obad 21), and several judgments hostile to Israel in Ezekiel.[31] The most interesting parallel is Jehu's judging the house of Ahab (2 Chr 22:8), which may preserve the original wording of BTH.[32] I have found no other biblical context that combines "judge" and "forever." "Slighting God" is summarily prohibited in Exod 22:28, with a cautionary tale told in Lev 24:10–16 about a man who did so. The term that expresses Eli's nonresponse (*khh, piʿel*, v. 13) is unique in HB and appears to have no connection with "dim" (3:2)—*nouthetein* (G) corresponds in Job to *yāsar* ("discipline") and *bîn* ("understand").

After the focus on the charge (v. 13), we might expect a statement of sentence. Yet Yahweh's sworn declaration (v. 14), repeating "house of Eli" (twice) and "forever," announces instead (as normally understood) that the guilt cannot be atoned by cultic means. Just as the fateful behavior of the sons (*mĕqalĕlîm*, v. 13) resonates with *ûbōzay yēqāllû* (end of 2:30), so also Yahweh confirms to Samuel the truth of what Eli has warned his sons (2:25). How does this story bear on the fate of the future house of David? In one respect, quite directly: solemn oaths in favor of a house can be revoked in light of the behavior of future sons. And in another respect, our earlier question remains unanswered: Is it as priests or as any Israelites that the house of Eli is denied cultic remedy for behavior as grave as theirs? There is an alternative rendering of Yahweh's oath, which sees the preposition *bĕ-* as introducing specification of the perversity rather than the means of expiation: "The perversity of the house of Eli in the matter of [whatever offerings] shall not be expiated forever" (v. 14).

[16–18] The scene has opened with Samuel going to Eli when Yahweh calls; it closes with his answering Eli's own call (v. 16). As if to underscore a link already noticed, Eli requires a straight answer from Samuel in terms to be repeated only once in the books of Samuel: where David addresses the

31. See Ezek 7:3, 27; 16:38; 20:4; 23:24, 45.

32. Elsewhere I have argued that it was from the short passage preserved in 2 Chr 22:7–9 that the longer narrative of 2 Kgs 9–10 was developed.

wise woman of Tekoa (2 Sam 14:18). And the double insistence (v. 17) on no concealment is reinforced by an oath used more by David[33] than any other leader,[34] and attributed to his ancestress in the only instance reported outside Samuel–Kings.[35] The old man has known enough to remonstrate with his sons (2:23–25); he has heard from a man of God (2:27–36). Now, with the matter confirmed by a Samuel understandably fearful (3:15), he states that it is the divine prerogative to do whatever seems good (v. 18). Is he now accepting what he knows to be appropriate? Or, in noting that there is a divine prerogative, is he hoping that it may yet be exercised in mercy?[36]

1 Samuel 3:19–21 Samuel's Reputation

19 And Samuel grew up,
and Yahweh was with him,
and [he did not let] *there did not* fall[a] any of his words to the ground.
20 And all Israel knew from Dan to Beer-sheba
that Samuel was established as prophet of Yahweh.
21 And Yahweh continued
to let himself be seen[a] at Shiloh,
for Yahweh revealed himself to Samuel
and Samuel trusted
he had become prophet of Yahweh for all Israel
from the ends of the earth and up to the ends.[b]
And Eli was very elderly,
and his sons were continually on the move,
and their way was evil before Yahweh[c] [at Shiloh in the word of Yahweh].

19a. The MT has the *hip'il* form *hippîl*, while GT attests *nāpal* as *qal.*

21a. The LT adds "to him" after "seen."

b. The closest parallel to "from . . . ends" appears to be Gen 47:21, where pl. *akrōn* is also used: normally in this phrase the sg. *akrou* renders *qṣh* in *mqṣh h'rṣ 'd-qṣh h'rṣ.*

c. The large plus in GT retroverts to something like *wy'mn šmw'l lhywt nby' lyhwh lkl-yśr'l mqṣh h'rṣ 'd-qṣh. w'ly zqn m'd wylkw bnyw hlwk wtr' drkm lpny yhwh.* It has support in OL; however, Fincke finds no place for this plus in his reconstruction, and DJD is silent on the matter.

33. See 1 Sam 25:22; 2 Sam 3:35; 19:13 (14).

34. Saul (1 Sam 14:44); Jonathan (20:13); Abner (2 Sam 3:9); Solomon (1 Kgs 2:23); and the king of Israel (2 Kgs 6:31).

35. Ruth 1:17.

36. The same question may be asked of David's words at the end of the book (2 Sam 24:14).

[19–21] Samuel's position: despite his now-acknowledged status, Samuel will be wholly absent from the next portion of the narrative. Almost every phrase (in vv. 19–21a at least) is drawn from BTH; but what is most noticeable is an absence: now that he is "established," Samuel is no longer a "lad."[37] Both earlier summary statements of Samuel's developing stature (2:21, 26) have mentioned Yahweh in the evaluation ("before Yahweh" or "with Yahweh"). But this third statement of his growing greatness is even more closely modeled on what was said about David in BTH after his capture of Jerusalem (2 Sam 5:10), and adds unequivocally that "Yahweh was with" Samuel. The next statement even trumps what is said about David in that same context. There David himself was conscious that Yahweh had established him as king over Israel (5:12); here "all Israel" recognizes Samuel as "established prophet of Yahweh." The BTH has Jehoshaphat ask the king of Israel for "a prophet of Yahweh" when he has found the counsel of four hundred prophets unsatisfactory (1 Kgs 22:7). And "established" (*neʾĕmān*) comes from the same narrative as so much else in 1 Sam 2–3.[38] The end of the David story in BTH furnishes our earliest attested instance of "all Israel" defined as "from Dan to Beer-sheba" (2 Sam 24:2);[39] and the accounts of Solomon's two visions (1 Kgs 3:5; 9:2), the language of Yahweh's "letting himself be seen." The sole exception is the clause that MT and GT transmit differently: MT's *npl hipʿil* with *dābār* as obj. is unique in HB; and even *npl* as *qal*, attested in GT, finds a near parallel only in Josh 21:45; 23:14.

What follows no longer adapts language from BTH. The clause that MT and GT share aligns Samuel with Eli's father's house: like them when first chosen (2:27), he has received a decisive revelation from Yahweh. The shorter MT goes on to emphasize that Shiloh is the locus of revelation to Samuel, as it has been of Eli's priesthood, and insist that divine revelation and Yahweh's "letting himself be seen" were to be understood not visually but verbally (*bidĕbar yhwh*). It is not easy to decide whether to describe longer GT as development or simply restatement of part of the shared text. If the first sentence was drafted as restatement (and "from one end of the land to the other end" looks like a rephrasing of "from Dan to Beer-sheba" [v. 20]), we might suppose that *wyʾmn* (hypothetical antecedent of GT) was *nipʿal* like *neʾĕmān* before it. However, GT rendered it as *hipʿil*, so portraying Samuel as passing the test that Isaiah put to "the house of David" (Isa 7:9b): *ʾim lōʾ taʾămînû kî lōʾ tēʾāmēnû* ("if you will not believe/trust, you will certainly not be established"). In what he adds about Eli's

37. This description of Samuel has been offered repeatedly in 2:11, 18, 21, 26; 3:1, 8.

38. Earlier in the Samuel version (2 Sam 7:16) and later in Chronicles (1 Chr 17:23, 24); but almost certainly rooted in a narrative whose language has been adjusted in both Samuel and Chronicles.

39. Repeated in 2 Sam 3:10; 17:11; 24:15; 1 Kgs 4:25 (5:5).

sons, the author of the text underlying GT appears to recognize the influence of 2 Sam 5:10 (*wayyēlek dāwīd hālôk wĕgādôl*).

1 Samuel 4:1–22 The Ark Lost and Eli Dead

1 Samuel 4:1–17

1 [And the word of Samuel was for all Israel.[a]]
And *it happened in those days*
and Philistines were assembling for war on Israel;[b]
and Israel went out to meet *them* [Philistines[c]] for battle;
and they camped at the Stone[d] *of* [the] Help,
and *the* Philistines camped at Apheq.
2 And *the* Philistines drew up
 to meet Israel,
and the battle *turned* [let be[a]];
and Israel was smitten before *the* Philistines;
and they struck down in the line in the field about four thousand men.
3 And the people came to the camp,
and the elders of Israel said,
 "Why has Yahweh smitten us today before *the* Philistines?
 Let us take to ourselves from Shiloh the ark of *our God*
 [the covenant of Yahweh[a]],
 and let him come *from* [in] our midst
 and save *you* [us] from the hand of our enemies."
4 And the people sent to Shiloh
and took from there the ark [of the covenant] of Yahweh [of hosts]
 who rules {enthroned} the cherubim;
and the two sons of Eli were [there] with the ark [of the covenant
of the Deity]—
 Hophni and Phinehas.
5 And it came to be
 as the ark [of the covenant] of Yahweh came to the camp
and all Israel roared a great roar
and the land was in a stir.
6 And *the* Philistines heard [the sound of[a]] the roar,
and said,
 "What is [the sound of] this great roar in the camp of the Hebrews?"
And they knew
 that the ark of Yahweh had come to the camp.
7 And the Philistines were afraid;
and [for[a]] they said,

"*These gods have*[b] [A god has] come *to them* into the camp."
And they said,
"Woe to us;
deliver us, Lord[c], *today;*
for something like this has not happened yesterday
or the day before.
8 Woe to us.
Who will deliver us from the hand of these mighty gods?
These are the very gods
who struck Egypt with every blow *and* in the desert.
9 Take courage and become men, [Philistines,
lest you serve the Hebrews
as they have served you:
you must become men[a]]
and fight *them*."
10 And *they* [Philistines] fought *them*
and Israel was smitten
and they fled each to his tent;
and the blow was very great,
and there fell of Israel thirty thousand foot.
11 And the ark of God was taken;
and the two sons of Eli died, Hophni and Phinehas.
12 And a *Jaminite* man[a] [of Benjamin] ran from the line
and came to Shiloh on that day,
clothes torn and soil on his head.
13 And he came—
and there was Eli
sitting on the throne [by the side of the way] *by the gate*,
watching closely *the way*;
for his heart had became terrified on account of the ark of the Deity.
And the man came
to make a report in the city,[a]
and the [whole] city cried out.
14 And Eli heard the sound of the cry,[a]
and he said,
"What is the [sound of this stir] *cry of this sound*[b]?"
And the man hurried
and came
and made announcement to Eli.
15 And Eli was ninety[-eight] years old;
and his *eyes were* [eye was] set
and he [was not able to] *did not* see.

And Eli said to the men standing by him,
"What is the sound of this din?"
16 And the man *made speed,*
approached Eli,
and said to *him* [Eli],
"It is I who have come from the line;
and I—I've fled from the line today."
And he said,
"What was the word, my son?"
17 And the [news-bringer] *lad* answered
and said,
"*The man of* Israel has fled before *the* Philistines;
and [also,] there has been a great blow on the people;
[and also,] your two sons are dead, Hophni and Phinehas;
and the ark of the Deity has been taken."

1a. Here *šmwʾl* and *lkl-yśrʾl* are shared by the shorter MT and the longer text attested by GT at the end of the previous paragraph (3:19–21).

b. The plus in GT that attributes the initiative to the Philistines is stated in terms very similar to 28:1a.

c. The pl. gentilic "Philistines" is almost always without article in MT, although with article not only in GT but also in 4QSam[a].

d. The term *ʾeben* without art. is reflected in *Abenezer* (GT), and is expected; *hʾbn hʿzr* (MT) seems wrong.

2a. Here *klinein* (GT) corresponds regularly to *nṭh*; *wtṭš* (MT) may have corrupted from *wtṭh*.

3a. Typically MT is fuller than B in references to the ark, as also in vv. 4–5. But LT is conflate.

6a. *qwl htrwʿh* (vv. 6–7 MT) is unique in HB. The addition of *qwl* may have been influenced by the fuller *btrwʿh wbqwl šwpr* ("with a roar and with a sound of a trumpet") in 2 Sam 6:15 (BTH).

7a. Only the initial letter differentiates *wyʾmrw* (GT) from *ky ʾmrw*—the same phenomenon occurred with *pqd* in 2:21.

b. In place of *bʾ ʾlhym* (MT), B may retrovert to *bʾw ʾlhym ʾlh ʾlyhm*, and LT to *bʾw ʾlhyhm ʾlh ʾlyhm*.

c. "Lord, deliver us" would retrovert to *ʾdwny hṣylnw*, which shares all the consonants of *ʾwy lnw* ("Woe is us"). It is less desperate than the related clause in v. 8.

9a. The fact that MT's plus is clearly attested in 4QSam[a] proves that the shorter text of B has resulted from haplography, whether in Greek or in the Hebrew text before the translator; however, the letters preserved do not include "Hebrews."[40]

12a. The GT appears to have read *ʾyš ymyny*, as (MT too) in 1 Sam 9:1; 2 Sam 20:1.

40. In fact no other verse attesting "Hebrews" in MT of Samuel is preserved in the Qumran manuscripts.

13a. Here B places "in the city" and "to make a report" in reverse order.
14a. The terms *ṣʿq* and *zʿq* are alternative spellings.
b. Here B retroverts to *mh ṣʿqt hqwl hzh*, which seems an unlikely combination.

[1] Both CL and the Aleppo Codex have a blank line before 4:1. Philistine initiative (GT) gives easier sense to Israel's going out "to meet" them. It would also demonstrate close correspondence between this first mention of Philistines in 1 Samuel and what may have been the opening words of BTH (31:1), where Philistines are fighting with Israel. Typical of HB as a whole, the Philistines do not play a large part in BTH: Saul falls to them (1 Sam 31), and David fights a successful early campaign against them (2 Sam 5:17–25; cf. 8:1), but they are not mentioned again. Yet out of this success of David and failure of Saul in their major source, the books of Samuel create a major theme—with Philistines mentioned more in 1 Samuel alone than in all the rest of HB together. Philistines gather against Israel at an Aphek in 29:1 also: whether the same place or different is unclear—since *ʾāpaq* means "be strong" and *ʾāpîq* a "water channel," the name is unremarkable. "Help Stone" recurs only in 5:1 and 7:12 (where it is explained).

[2] The key statement about Israel's being worsted is often mistranslated. The Hebrew does not say that they were "defeated by" their Philistine foes, but that they were "smitten before" them. The narrator uses the verb *ngp*, which suggests a divinely inflicted "blow" or plague. Throughout the Bible, Yahweh is most frequently the subject of active parts of this verb and can often be assumed to be the unspoken agent when the verb is passive. In its own terms, the narrative opens with the suggestion that Israel was defeated by Yahweh, and that Philistines followed this up with a slaughter of the defeated foe. This is exactly how Israel's own elders understand the situation (v. 3).

[3–4] The ark is a further theme found at just two points in BTH: David brings it into Jerusalem after his capture of the city (2 Sam 6); then Solomon installs it in the innermost sanctum of his new temple (1 Kgs 8). There is no further mention of it in the royal story, whether in BTH or in the successor books of Kings.[41] The ark too plays a larger role in 1 Samuel (a role now intertwined with the Philistines), as it does when the book of Joshua reports Israel's crossing the Jordan. In neither case can we have any confidence that this extrapolation backward in time from the data in BTH is historically valuable. As the ark developed its prehistory with the passage of time, it also developed more elaborate titles. Throughout Samuel we shall detect a greater preference in MT than in B for elaborate titles. Thus B varies (vv. 3–5) between attesting "the ark," "the ark of our God," "the ark of Yahweh ruling the cherubim,"[42]

41. Thus 2 Kgs 24–25 specify many individual objects removed from Jerusalem during the Babylonian sack, but never mention the ark.
42. For a fuller discussion of this phrase, see below on 2 Sam 6:2.

and "the ark of Yahweh"—but never includes "the covenant" (4x in MT). See further below, on 2 Sam 6:2.

[5–10] The narrator describes a struggle between Israel and Philistines. While Israel call their opponents Philistines, the Philistines talk of their foes (vv. 6, 9) as Hebrews (*ʿibrîm*). There has been a huge discussion about the background to this term: whether it refers principally to a social class or an ethnic group; and how it relates to the terms *ʿapiru* and *ḫabiru* found in documents from the ancient Near East. At this first of several mentions in Samuel of Hebrews, I restrict myself to the following few remarks. (a) Both in the stories of Joseph and the dealings with Pharaoh before the departure from Egypt, "Hebrew" is a term used by the Egyptians[43]—and by members of the emergent Israel of themselves only when they are addressing Egyptians.[44] The Philistines here are speaking like Egyptians in Genesis and Exodus. (b) There are laws in Exodus and Deuteronomy (mentioned in Jer 34) about the treatment of a "Hebrew slave" (*ʿebed ʿibĕry*).[45] The Philistines exhort each other to behave like men (v. 9), precisely lest they become slaves to these "Hebrews." (c) Jonah's self-description as a "Hebrew" is much closer to familiar modern usage—and comes from a late-biblical text (Jonah 1:9), with which we have seen several links in the opening of Samuel.[46]

There is no consultation of God before his ark is taken into the battlefield. However, many in Israel participate in the decision: the elders propose it (v. 3), the people go to collect the ark (4), and Eli's two sons are with it (4). The Philistines are said to be afraid (v. 7) at the novelty of defeat—when they conclude their lament with "yesterday or the day before," they use an idiom that will recur frequently in the books of Samuel.[47] However, they respond by boosting their morale (v. 9). They fight, and Israel is smitten—but it is left unsaid (v. 10) whether the blow was inflicted on Israel by Philistines or Yahweh (if indeed that is an proper distinction).

The Philistines are presented as showing awareness of Israel's traditions of its earlier history (v. 8, as again in 6:6), like Rahab and the Gibeonites (Josh 2 and 9) and the king of Ammon (Judg 11). They speak in the plural about the god[s] represented in the ark (or do they mean the cherubim?), as Jeroboam would (1 Kgs 12:28) about what the golden calves represented at Bethel and Dan.[48] But their version of their opponents' history was rather mixed up (v. 8)—

43. See Gen 39:14, 17; 41:12; 43:32; Exod 1:15, 16; 2:6, 11, 13.

44. As in Gen 40:15; Exod 1:19; 2:7; 3:18; 5:3; 7:16; 9:1, 13; 10:3.

45. See Exod 21:2; Deut 15:12; Jer 34:9, 14.

46. Yet the Greek text of Jonah does not read "Hebrew," but "servant of the Lord" (as if it had read not *ʿbry*, but *ʿbd yhwh*).

47. As in 1 Sam 4:7; 10:11; 14:21; 19:7; 21:6—cf. also 2 Sam 3:17; 5:2 (BTH).

48. In discussing the implications of 1 Kgs 12 and its correlate in Exod 32, it is often suggested that bull-calf images, long before they became branded as idolatrous, were already unacceptable as

or perhaps we should simply say that, like the account of the king of Ammon in Judg 11, it was different from what became the classical biblical version.

[11] The first sentence of B's new paragraph (v. 11) has been attributed by many more recent editors to the end of the battle report. The capture of the ark is the main topic of the paragraph, stated at beginning and end; however, as with the smiting of Israel (v. 10), this fact is stated in the *nipʿal*, passive, with no agent credited (see further below on 5:1). The GT adheres to the word order in MT, reversing the opening words *waʾărôn ʾĕlōhîm nilqāḥ* (v. 11) in the closing *kî nilqāḥ ʾărôn hāʾĕlōhîm* (22). Though the verb "take" is one of the commonest in the language, its passive is remarkably rare: the five occurrences in this paragraph (vv. 11, 17, 19, 21, 22) make up half of the total in HB. The passive again suggests divine agency: one of the remaining instances is Elijah's being "taken" into heaven (2 Kgs 2:10).

[12–17] As for Hophni and Phinehas, they are simply "with" the ark as it is removed from Shiloh; and quite as simply as its taking is described, so is their death—the narrator does not pause to tell us the manner of their death (v. 17). His sons are physically "with" the ark in the field of battle, and their father's heart has gone out with it (v. 13). It is on hearing of *its* loss, rather than of *their* death, that he falls from his ceremonial seat. We are reminded (v. 15) that Eli does not see (cf. 3:2). The messenger (4:17) is simply a "lad" in GT; however, in that the demise of Eli and his sons foreshadows that of Saul and his sons, MT's more precise *mĕbaśśēr* ("bringer of news"—often good news, but not in this case) nicely anticipates 1 Sam 31:9 (BTH).

1 Samuel 4:18–22

18 And it came to be
at his mentioning the ark of the Deity,
and he fell off his throne backward by the side[a] of the gate,
and his skull was shattered,
and he died;
for the man was old and weighty;
and he [had judged] *was judging*[b] Israel *twenty* [forty] years.
19 And his daughter-in-law, wife of Phinehas, was pregnant near term.
And she heard the report about the taking of the ark of the Deity,
and her brother-in-law had died and her husband;
and she crouched down
and gave birth,
for her pains came suddenly over her.

---

being rival bases or pedestals for the Deity to the ark-plus-cherubim throne in the Jerusalem temple. Here even that sacred object is miscalled by the Philistines.

20 And at *her time she died* [the time of her death],
and the women standing near her said,
"Don't be afraid,
for a son you have borne."
And she did not answer
and did not give[a] her attention.
21 And she called the lad *Woe Barchaboth*[a] [Ichabod, saying,
"Glory has gone from Israel"],
because of [the taking of] the ark of the Deity
and because of her father-in-law and her husband.
22 And *they* [she] said,
"Glory has gone from Israel,
because taken has been the ark of the Deity."

18a. In GT *echomenos* frequently corresponds as here to a prep. expression with *yd*; the next instance (19:3), however, with Jonathan standing close to his father, shows that "clinging to" is not be taken lit.

b. *ekrinen* (impf.) may have read *špṭ* as ptc., not pf. (MT).

20a. The vb. *šît* takes *lēb* as obj. in Prov 27:23. GT will have read the same text as MT but has made "heart" the subj. of its sentence.

21a. Regarding the lad's name, B and MT are closer than first appears. Thus MT has read the first element as *ʾy* ("where" or "not"), but GT as *ʾwy* ("woe"). Here GT interposes *bar* between the other two elements; this is hardly the Aramaic for "son of," but may (*BA* 170) be a truncated element of some form of Gk. *barys* ("heavy"). *Ouai Bar Iōchabēl* in LT seems typically conflate.

[18–22] The MT opens a new paragraph at v. 18. Although its choice of place is different from B, it agrees with B over spotlighting the divine ark. It is hearing of its fate—not his sons'—that brings Eli's death. Exactly which part of Eli's anatomy was broken as he dies is not clear. Here *mapreqet* (MT) is unique in HB; it is explained variously as "neck" or "skull'; however, GT uses *nōtos* ("back"). Shiloh and the family of Eli will be mentioned only once more in the books of Samuel (1 Sam 14:3, 18).

Phinehas's pregnant wife immediately goes into labor and dies while giving birth. Being told she has a son proves no help; but she is able to name him. Several themes of the opening chapters of the book are woven together in the final sentences of this paragraph, so serving to underline the close association of Eli and ark. Different forms of the word *kbd* are employed to document the linkage. First of all *kābôd* means "glory," and Yahweh's glory is closely related to his ark. The last words of the episode in BTH about Solomon's bringing the ark into the new temple (1 Kgs 8:1–11) are that now "the glory of Yahweh filled the temple." The short passage in Ps 78 telling of Yahweh's rejecting Israel at Shiloh speaks of his delivering "his glory to the hand of the foe" (v. 61). The version in MT (v. 21) of the name of the newborn (with its explanation repeated in v. 22) shares this tradition by linking *kābôd* with *ʾy*. And the prefix may be interpreted as "where?" or "not": "where is the glory?" or "no glory." Despite being conflate, the final element of LT's version of the name may preserve important evidence of an alternative reading—*KABHΛ* may preserve an original *KABHΔ* (note similarity of the final Greek letters)—which understands *kbd* as "weighty"; and this is exactly the description (v. 18) of the boy's dying grandfather. The first and last elements of both B and LT suggest *ʾwy kbd*, "alas weighty one." If we reduce both readings (MT and GT) to the minimal consonants, the resulting *ʾykbd* would be ambiguous, neatly comprising references to both Eli and the ark, over which his heart has fretted. In similar two-word brevity (*mĕkabbĕday ʾăkabbēd*), the man of God had deftly promised (2:30) honor to those who honor God (and his ark). Eli's formal seat (1:9; 4:13, 18) was close to the proper "place" of the ark (3:3); and Hannah's song brings the two nouns into close relationship when it talks (2:8) of Yahweh's allotting "a seat of honor" (*kissēʾ kābôd*).

1 Samuel 5:1–8:22 Yahweh's Power Displayed; Israel's Rejection

Both CL and the Aleppo Codex have a blank line before 5:1. Aleppo further divides chs. 5–8 at 7:5 and 8:7.

1 Samuel 5:1–7:1

1 And Philistines—they took the ark of God.
And they brought it from the Stone of Help to Ashdod.
2 And Philistines took the ark of [God] *Yahweh*
and brought it to the house of Dagon,
and set it up beside Dagon.
3 And the Ashdodites rose early the next day,
and entered the house of Dagon
and look: Dagon
fallen [before him[a]] *on his face* on the ground, before the ark of [Yahweh] *God.*
And they [took] *raised*[b] Dagon
and put him back in his place.
And the hand of Yahweh was heavy toward the Ashdodites
and he tortured them;
and he struck them on their seats: Ashdod and its territory.[c]
4 And they rose early in the morning of the next day,
and look: Dagon
fallen before him on the ground, before the ark of *the covenant of* Yahweh,[a]

and Dagon's head and the two soles of his hands cut off [toward the threshold]
each upon the foreparts amapheth,
and both palms of his hands fallen on the threshold;[b]
only Dagon*'s trunk*[c] was left [upon him[d]].

5 On account of this the priests of Dagon and all the comers to the house of Dagon do not tread on the threshold of Dagon at Ashdod to this day
because stepping over they step over.[a]

6 And the hand of Yahweh was heavy toward the Ashdodites
and he [devastated] *brought on*[a] them;
[and he struck them with swellings: Ashdod and its territory;]
and it caused them a boiling into the ships,
and amid their land "mice" grew up;
and there was a great confusion of death in the city.[b]

7 And the men of Ashdod saw that it was so,
and they said,
"The ark of the god of Israel shall not live with us,
for his hand is hard against us and against Dagon our god."

8 And they sent
and gathered all the lords of *the* Philistines to them,
and they said,
"What shall we do to the ark of the god of Israel?"
And [they] *the Gittites* said,
"[To Gath] the ark of the god [of Israel] should move round *to us*."
And they moved round the ark of the god [of Israel[a]] *to Gath.*[b]

9 And it came to be
after they moved it round,
and the hand of Yahweh was in the city: very great commotion.
And he struck the men of the city from least to greatest,
and [swellings burst out on them] *he struck them on their seats*
and the Gittites made for themselves seats.[a]

10 And they dispatched the ark of the god to [Ekron] *Ashkelon*,
and the [Ekronites] *Ashkelonites* cried out, saying,
"[They have] *Why have you* moved round to me the ark of the god of Israel
to bring [me] *us* to death and [my] *our* people."

11 And they sent
and gathered all the lords of *the* Philistines,
and they said,

"Send away the ark of the god of Israel
and let it [turn to] *sit in* its place
and it will not bring [me] *us* or [my] *our* people to death;
for there has been *confusion* [death-commotion] in all the city,
very heavy:

as the ark of the god of Israel entered there."	very heavy[a] has been the hand of the god[b] there."

12 And the [men] *living*
who did not die
were struck [with swellings] *on their seats*;
and the cry of the city went up to heaven.
6:1 And the ark [of Yahweh] was in the field of *the* Philistines
seven months,
and their land teemed with "mice."[a]
2 And *the* Philistines called the*ir* priests and diviners *and* charmers,[a] saying,[b]
"What shall we do to the ark of Yahweh?
Make known to us
by what means may we send it away to its place."
3 And they said,
"If [they] *you*[a] are sending away the ark of *the covenant of*[b] the god
the Lord[b] of Israel,
do not send it away empty-handed:
you must in fact return to it a guilt-offering.[c]
Then you will be healed
and it will *be redeemed for*[d] [become known to] you.
Why will his hand not turn from you?"
4 And they said,
"What is the guilt offering that we should return to it?"
And they said,
"*As* The number of the lords of *the* Philistines—five [tumors] *seats*
of gold,

	{and five "mice" of gold;}
for it is one plague for you and for your rulers and for the people,	for it is one plague {for them all and for your lords.
5	5 And you shall make your images of tumors and}
and golden "mice": image of your "mice" that are destroying the land,	image{s} of "mice" that are destroying the land,

and you will give honor to the god of Israel.
Perhaps[a] he will ease/lighten his hand from you and from your gods
and from your land.

6 And why should you make your hearts heavy,
as Egypt and Pharaoh made their hearts heavy?
Is it not so—
  just as he had made sport with them
  and they sent them away,
  and they went—
7 now then, take
and make one new cart and two [suckling] *first-bearing* cows *without the young*
[on which a yoke has not been laid],
and bind the cows to the cart,
and turn back home their young from following them.
8 And take the ark [of Yahweh[a]]
and put it on the cart,
and the objects of gold
[which] you must return to it as a guilt offering
you should put in the container[b] beside it;
and send it away
and let it go.
9 And you will see:
  if by way of its territory it ascends—to Beth Shemesh—
then he himself has done to us this great ill.
And if not,
then we will know
  it was not his hand that reached us:
  it was chance that happened to us."
10 And the [men] *Philistines* did so,
and they took two milking cows
and they bound them to the cart,
and their young they detained at home.
11 And they put the ark [of Yahweh] on the cart,
and the container and the golden "mice" [and the images of their tumors].
12 And they set the cows straight on the way, on the way to Beth Shemesh:
  on one highway they walked[, going[a] and lowing] *and toiled*,
  and they did not turn to right or left.
And the lords of *the* Philistines were walking behind [them] *it* to the border of Beth Shemesh.
13 And Beth Shemesh were harvesting the wheat harvest in the valley
  and they raised their eyes
  and saw the ark *of Yahweh*
  and they were glad to [see] *meet*[a] it.

14 And the cart—it came to the field of Joshua of Beth Shemesh
and stood still there;
and *they raised up* there *beside it* [there was] a great stone,
and they chopped up the wood of the cart
and the cows they offered up as a whole burnt offering to Yahweh.

15 And the Levites—they brought [down] *up* the ark of Yahweh and the container
which was with it
in which were the objects of gold,
and they placed them on the great stone.
And the men of Beth Shemesh—they offered up whole burnt offerings
and [sacrificed] sacrifices[a] on that day to Yahweh.
16 And the five lords of *the* Philistines—they saw,
and they returned to [Ekron] *Ashkelon* on that day.

17 And these are the golden tumors[a]
that the Philistines returned as a guilt-offering to Yahweh:
of Ashdod, one;
of Gaza, one;
of Ashkelon, one;
of Gath, one;
of Ekron, one
18 and the golden mice to the number of all the cities of the Philistines,
of the five lords,
from fortified city to village of the [peasantry[a]] *Perizzite*—
and as far as the great [Abel] *Stone*
on which they set to rest the ark of *the covenant*[b] *of* Yahweh,
[to this day] in the field of Joshua of Beth Shemesh.
19 And [he struck down some of] *the sons of Jechoniah*
were not pleased with the men of Beth Shemesh
because they had seen[a] [in] the ark of Yahweh;
and he struck down of the people seventy men and fifty thousand men;
and the people were in mourning
because Yahweh had inflicted on the people a *very* great blow.
20 And the men of Beth Shemesh said,
"Who could [stand] *pass*[a] before [Yahweh[b]] this holy *one* [God]?
And to whom will [he] *the ark of Yahweh* go up from us?"

21 And they sent messengers to the inhabitants of Kiriath-jearim, saying,
"*The* Philistines have returned the ark of Yahweh.
Come down,
and take it up to yourselves."

7:1 And the men of Kiriath-jearim came
and brought up the ark of Yahweh,
and brought it to the house of Abinadab [in Gibeah] *on the hill.*[a]
And Eleazar his son they consecrated
to keep the ark of *the covenant of* Yahweh.

3a. GT retroverts to *ʿl pnyw*, often used after "fall" to express formal prostration; there the suf. refers clearly to Dagon. MT's *lpnyw* is ambiguous: if the reference is to Dagon, the expression could suggest simple collapse rather than worship; but I have translated it as referring to making obeisance to Yahweh, anticipating the fuller "before the ark of Yahweh."

b. GT's *kai ēgeiran* represents *wyqymw* rather than *wyqḥw* (MT).

c. Here B, but not LT, reports the torture by swellings at the end of v. 3 rather than after v. 5.

4a. Broadly, both MT and GT repeat their different descriptions (v. 3) of the fallen Dagon. Unusually, it is GT here, not MT, that has added "covenant" to the description of the ark.

b. It must be nearly certain that B has conflated two renderings of MT's text about Dagon's separated parts. The first uses *ichnos* (more common in Gk. for the sole of the foot) for *kp*, which Hebrew uses for both sole and palm, and *hmptn* is both translated in GT as "the foreparts" and then transliterated from Heb. In the second, GT uses *karpos* (including the consonants of *kp*); "fallen" corresponds only freely to "cut off," but it has already been used twice in the shared context (vv. 3–4). LT is similar to B but offers "feet" after "soles" and *tōn stathmōn* (instead of *amapheth*) after *epi ta emprosthia*. In both cases, these appear to be sensible editorial "corrections" of a text whose strangeness had been due to conflation.

c. GT as well as versions closer to MT include a noun specifying the part of Dagon that was not removed: body (Tg.), trunk (Vulg.), backbone (GT).

d. Logic in seeing Dagon as referent of the suf. in MT's plus *ʿlyw* can hardly be defended; but the alternative is worse: that the reference is to the threshold (which only his severed parts had reached).

5a. GT's plus *hoti hyperbainontes hyperbainousin* apparently represents Hebrew idiom and may retrovert to *ky dlwg ydlgw*. The term *dlg* is used of "leaping over a wall" by God's help (2 Sam 22:30); and Zeph 1:9 includes *kl-hdwlg ʿl-hmptn* ("everyone jumping over the threshold") in a long list of officials whose behavior is being noted for punishment.

6a. GT's *kai epēgagen autois* might render *wyby' lhm*, but would normally require a direct obj.

b. LT is a conflate text: first it reports the devastation, as in MT, and then what happened in the ships, as in B.

8a. With MT, 4QSam[a] includes "Israel."

b. Here 4QSam[a] supports GT in reading *gt* after *yśr'l*.

9a. It is not easy to retrovert the last clause in B; and there are further pluses in LT.

11a. In GT, "very heavy" refers back to "confusion"; but in MT, *kbdh* is a vb. with "hand" as subj.[49]

49. The phrasing of v. 11b in MT is *ky-hyth mhwmt-mwt bkl-hʿyr/kbdh m'd yd h'lhym šm,* while B retroverts to *ky-hyth mhwmh bkl-hʿyr kbdh m'd/kbw' 'rwn 'lhy yśr'l šm.*

b. The GT has "the ark of the god of Israel," but MT "the hand of God." The phrase *yd yhwh* occurs in 1 Sam 5:6, 9; 7:13; 12:15; 2 Sam 24:14. *yd h'lhym* is found in Eccl 2:24; 9:1; 2 Chr 30:12 (cf. also Exod 8:19 [15]; Dan 5:5, 24).

6:1a. Both LT and B mention "mice" again here, before they are first mentioned in MT; but here 4QSam[a] = MT.

2a. Here LT also includes *epaoidous* ("charmers," who bring an "ode" to the problem in hand) as a third group of religious consultants. The Gk. OT uses this term to render *ḥarṭummîm* (Exod 7–8) and *yiddĕʿōnîm* (Lev 19–20; 2 Chr 33:6). Since the latter is cognate with the following vb. *hôdīʿunû*, it is the more likely to have stood in the text underlying GT, whether original there or secondary.

b. Before *l'mr*, 4QSam[a] attests *wlmʿwnnym* ("and to the augurs"), which Fincke takes as a fourth member of the series; it figures with other members of this list in Deut 18:10–11, 14 and 2 Kgs 21:6 (= 2 Chr 33:6).

3a. MT reads a pl. ptc. with subj. unstated, and so impersonal. GT's *hymeis* attests *'tm*, which could easily have been omitted from *mšlḥym'tm't-'rwn*.

b. Unusually, GT has added to the titles of the ark. Is it deliberate mockery of these foreign experts to have them reverse the normal order in *theou kyriou*?

c. Here and in vv. 4, 8, 17, GT inappropriately uses *basanos* ("touchstone") for *'šm* ("guilt offering"), apparently influenced by its choice (appropriate in 5:6) of the related vb. *ebasanisen* to render *yšmm*.

d. GT's *kai exilasthēsetai* is an exact rendering of *wnkpr* (4QSam[a]); for the idiom see Num 35:33. MT's *wnwdʿ* makes good but quite different sense.

5a. Here 4QSam[a] reads not *'wly* (MT), but *lw*.

8a. Fincke takes a lone *h* above [']*šm* in the line below as evidence of *yhwh* following *'rwn*.

b. The Heb. *'argaz* is used only in this chapter (vv. 8, 11, 15); and in each case this unusual noun is both translated (by *thema*—"deposit[ory]") in GT and then transliterated.

12a. MT uses inf. abs. *hlk* to resume *hlkw* before continuing with a 2d inf. abs. (*w-gʿw*, from *gʿh*). GT simply uses two coordinate impfs.; in B the 2d (*ekopiōn*) attests not *gʿh* but *ygʿ*, but in LT as in MT the cattle "low" as they walk, rather than "toil."

13a. GT attests *lqr't*, one letter more than *lr't* (MT).

15a. LT supports MT; B may have lost *ethysan* before *thysias*, or its underlying text *yzbḥw* before *zbḥym*.

17a. The MT (K) introduces a new noun for the golden objects (*ṭḥry* for the earlier *ʿply*): there is no corresponding change in GT, and in any case *ṭḥry* has been Q for *ʿply* throughout chs. 5–6, and in Deut 28:27.

18a. Deut 3:5 differentiates similarly between *ʿrym bṣrt* (here *ʿyr mbṣr*) and *ʿry hprzy* (here *kpr hprzy*). GT's transcription uses the commoner (gentilic) *pĕrizzî*; only in these 2 verses does HB make a distinction and vocalize *pĕrazî*.

b. Here and in 7:1, it is GT that attests the fuller *'rwn bryt yhwh*.

19a. The Syr. *dḥlw* ("feared") attests not *r'w* (MT) but *yr'w*.

20a. B's *dielthein* is frequently used in the Gk. OT, most often corresponding to *ʿbr* and nowhere else to *ʿmd*. LT (*parastēnai*) reads as MT.

b. Yahweh appears in this verse in both MT and B, but at different points. LT has *kyriou* at both points—4QSam[a] agrees with it over *yhwh hqdwš hzh*; but Fincke finds no space for a 2d *yhwh* after *'rwn*.

7:1a. Rightly or wrongly, GT does not recognize *bgbʿh* as a place name.

[1–5] The opening clause signals a fresh human initiative: the new subject is placed emphatically at the start; and "take" is now an active verb again. Philistines now "take" the ark, as Israel had done (4:3–4). And when the narrator says "they set it up" (v. 2), he anticipates a term used in Samuel–Kings only in 2 Sam 6:17 (BTH), where David would set up the ark in a tent he had prepared for it. Yahweh's allowing the ark to be taken was one thing; Israel or Philistines daring to take it was another.

There is no significant divergence between MT and GT in the opening clauses; however, different accounts may be offered about the repetition of much of v. 1 in v. 2. The substantial repetition may betray "from the Help Stone to Ashdod" as a secondary attempt at precision, with the preceding words recapitulated after the insertion. Or it may have been deliberate from the outset to suggest a move of the ark in two stages, first to Ashdod and then into the temple, as would happen later in Jerusalem.

In vv. 2–3, B and MT each have "ark of God" and "ark of Yahweh" once; but LT has "God" in both verses, which may preserve the earlier reading. Each element rendered above in v. 3a, as far as "look," is found in LT: if a conflation of MT and B, it reads very well; and so it may be that both MT and B have suffered loss. The ark does not belong in the "place" (v. 3) to which fallen Dagon should be restored, but in its own place to which it should be returned (5:11; 6:2). Outside this narrative (5:2–8), HB mentions Dagon (and his house) only as the place where Samson contrived his end in Gaza (Judg 16:23), and where Saul's head was brought (1 Chr 10:10, but not its parallel in 1 Sam 31:10—see below). He was a weather-god, who gave his name to grain (*dāgān*), rather like Roman Ceres to cereal.

[6–8] During the previous struggle, the Philistines had called their opponents "Hebrews" and had remarked on the arrival of the ark in Israel's camp by speaking of a god or gods. Faced with an unwelcome power in their own midst, they speak throughout this chapter (more respectfully) of "the ark of the God of Israel" (vv. 7, 8 [2x], 10, 11), and complain (7) of the hardness of his hand against them. In the ark stories, the divine "hand" is frequently featured (4:8; 5:6, 7, 9; 6:3, 5, 9 [11]). All the more appropriately, part of the damage done to Dagon at his fall (5:4) is the cutting off of his hands.

The excavation of many torsos of divine statues of the Persian and Hellenistic periods, together with narratives in the books of the Maccabees, and the change from "ark of God" (vv. 1–2) to "ark of Yahweh" (3–4), have suggested to Zwickel that 5:3–4 be placed as late as the second half of the second century B.C.E. The etiological note about jumping across the threshold (v. 5) may not have been an original part of vv. 3–4 (240), but presumably depended on it. The change in designation of the ark does not have full text-critical support (see above). However, the plus in B does anticipate at the beginning of v. 3 the talk of Yahweh's hand, which appears first in other versions only in v. 6.

The narrator calls Yahweh's hand "heavy" (v. 6), making use again of the term *kbd* played on in ch. 4. The Ashdodites themselves experience it as "hard" (v. 7). This specific connection appears unique in HB, although elsewhere neck, face, spirit, and heart can all be "hard," as well as work, words, answers, and visions. The links with "work" and "answer" are prefigured in 1 Kgs 12:4, 13 (BTH).

[9–12] There are two principal differences between GT and MT in this chapter. The GT repeatedly (3x) reads Ashkelon for Ekron in MT (v. 10). Since 4QSam[a] clearly preserves the middle three letters of *ʿqrwn*, it appears that the alteration was made deliberately within the Greek tradition (and hence not before 2d c. B.C.E.). In Kingdoms, as in most of the OT, *plštym* (unlike the names of most other peoples) was not transliterated but translated as *allophyloi*, or "foreigners" (lit., "of another tribe"). Maccabees (1 Macc 10:88–89) and Josephus tell of the transfer of Ekron to Jonathan between 147 and 145 B.C.E., from which time it was no longer a foreign city. Ashkelon maintained its independence and became a more suitable stopping place for the ark among "the foreigners" (*BA* 106).

Then GT includes mention of "mice"[50] among the afflictions of Ashdod, while MT makes no reference to them till the proposals in the next chapter for remedial measures. Against MT is the reader's surprise that half of the proposed remedy bears no obvious relation to the problem as described. Against GT is the fact of considerable variation between B and LT in this chapter, and between each and MT. Both B and LT report this element of the plague at the same point (v. 6); and yet, if the "mice" are a secondary element here, LT may simply have added "mice" to the attack on "their seats" while B anticipated talk of "their seats" at a point that seems too early in the narrative (end of v. 3). There is no fragment of 4QSam[a] to which appeal may be made between 4:13 and 5:8. It is possible that this textual difference preserves evidence of the development of the materials in chs. 5–6 (see further below).

Simply moving the ark to another Philistine city has proved of no use. The Ekronites too have suffered death. Their proposal is sensibly worded: the ark should be dispatched so that it may return (not dispatched and returned) to its "place"—and that word is also neutral. It may refer simply to a locality; but it is frequently used in HB for a "sanctuary" or "shrine," as in 3:2, 9 above. The sentence that opens ch. 6 is in the middle of a subparagraph of MT; and it is far from clear whether it looks forward or backward. Is it intended to inform us that the preceding events have transpired over a seven-month period? Or are we to suppose that it takes a further seven months before the urgent plea from Ekron about their troublesome booty is acted on? The fact that priests are among the experts consulted, along with diviners (6:2), tends to underscore that we should understand the "place" (5:11) as a sacred one.

50. See comment on chap. 6.

[6:1–3] When practitioners within Israel are being talked about, "diviners" is always a pejorative term—perhaps because they were reckoned as foreign imports. It may be part of Israel's stereotyping of Philistines that they could not be expected to have had the services of "prophets" or "seers," but simply of "diviners." The question put to these priests and diviners is quite limited: not whether to send the ark away, not whether to send a gift with it, but simply what gift to send. The experts agree (6:3) that, if it is being sent (and on that prior question they offer no comment), then it should not go empty-handed: a guilt offering should accompany it. But now, as experts tend to do when invited late and asked too limited a question, they begin to offer more detailed comment: if they do send a guilt offering with the ark, they should receive not only healing, but also ransom (so GT) or knowledge (MT).

Much of the comment on this whole episode has been based on the assumption that the plague is associated with rodents. It appears that, in the ancient eastern Mediterranean world, people were fully aware that plague was spread by rodents, often carried by ships and reported as particularly prevalent in coastal ports. However, I have put "mice" in quotation marks throughout, because it is not at all clear what was intended by HB *'kbr* or GT *mys*. In ancient Greek, *mys* comprised all small rodents—mice, rats, ermine, gerbils, and so forth; but the literal sense also included "muscle" and "mussel" (both derived from *musculum*, diminutive of Latin *mus*); and strangest of all, it can refer to the largest of beasts: the whale. Though *'kbr* may not represent that whole range, it seems it at least comprises rodents and muscles—in particular here: anal muscles.

[4–6] In the unusual case of 6:4–5, there appears to be a need for more general comment aware of the textual complexities before any solution to the puzzles is proposed. In B, the phrase "for it is one plague" could have either or both of two functions: (a) "One" may explain the preceding "five." Although events in only three cities have been mentioned in the text so far (ch. 5), these are illustrative of the totality of Philistia, which is traditionally represented as a Pentapolis. It is one problem for all five cities, and all five should be represented together in the hoped-for solution. (b) "One" may relate more directly to the words that follow: Philistia's social groups are all suffering the one problem, lords and people alike. "For it is one plague" can bear two senses in MT also. As in B it can relate to what follows: it is the same for greatest as for least. But if it is a comment on what precedes, it is more natural in MT to relate "one" not to "five" but to the tumors-and-"mice": these are one plague, and not two.

Two details make it difficult to have confidence in the text following "one plague." Though B and MT are so different, they are making much the same point; and *archontas* ("rulers") is the only instance in 1 Samuel where *srnym* (the special term for the Philistine leadership) is not represented in B by (the Persian term) "satraps." Perhaps B's supplement (betrayed by tell-tale *archontas*) was a response to an earlier supplement made to the tradition represented in MT.

A second point to note is that, somewhat as in the previous section, where the "mice" appeared only in GT but not at all in MT, here they appear at different points in B and MT. The LT largely supported B in ch. 5. Here it offers a text longer than either B or MT: "As the number of the satraps of the foreigners, make five golden seats, image of your seats, because the plague is in you and your rulers and in the people. And five golden 'mice' you must make, image of your 'mice' that are destroying your land." The LT follows B in using *archontes* for the second *srnym*; however, it has a second *en* before "the people." The LT follows MT in including a verb of instruction; however, it uses *poiēsate* not once but twice. In one respect, 4QSam[a] supports the shorter text of B, in that it reads *ʿply zhb ky-mgph ʾḥt* together: "golden swellings for it is one plague."

What then are golden swellings in the shape of "mice," which represent a destructive plague? Our choice has to be between seeing B and MT as having suffered different losses from a longer neater original, such as we find in LT; or as differently supplemented from a shorter original—with LT conflating the results of both processes of supplementation. I suspect that the "original" response of the Philistine diviners read simply as follows: *mspr srny plštym ḥmšh ʿply zhb ky-mgph ʾḥt lklm ṣlm ʿkbrykm hmšḥytym . . .*—"The number of the lords of Philistines, five golden swellings—for it is one plague for them all—the image[s][51] of your "mice" that are destroying . . ."

From ancient times, this whole plague episode has been understood, whether rightly or wrongly, as scatological. In MT, *ʿplym* is not given its proper vocalization; instead, it is supplied with the vowels of the word for hemorrhoids. Even if *ʿplym* did not originally specify an anal disorder, these "swellings" may have been a euphemism for "buttocks." The GT may have understood them so; for it renders throughout by "seats" (*edras*). In its reference to the same tradition, Ps 78 speaks of Yahweh's striking his enemies "behind."[52]

The relationship between the words for honor and weight are played on again in vv. 5–6, as indeed the opposition of *kbd* and *qll*.[53] It is appropriate at several levels that the religious experts speak of "giving *kbwd* to Yahweh": *kbwd* commonly means "a present" as well as "glory"; and if made from gold, a present bringing honor that consists of models made from this most precious of metals is also *kbd* (heavy). But this is not the only wordplay. "Make mischief" (*htʿll*, v. 6) is the first of several terms sharing the consonants *ʿ* + *l*; and it has immediate resonance in two directions—the dying Saul will worry that the Philistines will abuse him (1 Sam 31:4, BTH); and this same rare verb is

51. Here 4QSam[a] has the pl. cst.: *ṣlmy*.

52. See *ʾḥwr* in Ps 78:66. We have noted several other links with this psalm.

53. The only other passage in HB in which *hql* (*hipʿil* of *qll*) is linked with *kbd* is in BTH (1 Kgs 12:4, 9, 10//2 Chr 10:4, 9, 10), where *ʿl* ("yoke") is also part of the context (see immediately below here). And we noted on 5:7 above that *qšh* (hard) provides a further unusual link with that passage.

used to describe Yahweh's abuse of the Egyptians (Exod 10:2).[54] The next two refer to the cows, which are not only "suckling" (*ʿlwt*, vv. 7, 10)[55] but will also be bound to the "cart" (*ʿglh*, 7, 8, 10) to which they will be yoked. Since it is not attested in B, we cannot be confident that "on whom a yoke has not gone up" (*ʾšr lʾ-ʿlh ʿlyhm ʿl*, v. 7) was original or a secondary extension to the play.[56]

[7–12] Like their colleagues in the battlefield (4:7–8), the religious experts are familiar with Israel's early traditions (6:6): the Philistines should not replicate Pharaoh's mistakes. However, when they warn their compatriots against making their hearts "heavy," they use the *piʿel* theme of *kbd*, and not the *hipʿil*, as in Exod 8:15, 32 (11, 28); 9:34 (and 10:1). Their test for whether Yahweh is in fact intimately associated with the ark is ingenious. If milking cattle, just separated from their calves, drag the cart without guidance toward Israelite territory, then it was Yahweh who caused the Philistine troubles (6:7–9). The alternative is equally interesting: if it was not Yahweh, then it was "chance"—or perhaps we should call it "fate," for in the books of Samuel, it seems always to be malign. And yet we should reckon with the likelihood that the narrator does not want his hearers to acquiesce in the alternative propounded by the Philistine diviners. The next character in this book to talk of chance is Saul (20:26): "chance" is his first response to a situation we readers know was of David's making—and Yahweh's?

[13–16] The cattle do head straight for Beth-shemesh, where the ark is greeted by the harvesters. The "large stone" on which the ark is laid (6:14, 18) may be a euphemism for an earlier altar or standing stone. The dutiful cows become a burnt offering. The Israelite population there do not share David's later scruples (2 Sam 24:24) about not using for an offering what he had not paid for. But there are casualties among the people because of divine displeasure. The ancient texts give quite different reasons: either one clan did not join in the celebrations (GT), or some people looked into the ark (MT). The upshot is that the Israelite people of Beth-shemesh, not unlike the Philistines of Ashdod and Gath, want to be rid of it. After severe losses, they pose two questions: Who can stand before Yahweh? To whom will "he" go from here? Their emissaries

54. The same verb is used of his donkey's mischief with Balaam (Num 22:29); of the mistreatment in Gibeah of the Levite's concubine (Judg 19:25); and of King Zedekiah's fear of mistreatment (Jer 38:19).

55. This ptc., always pl., occurs also in Gen 33:13; Isa 40:11; Ps 78:71.

56. This exact phrase appears only once more in HB, in the law relating to the red heifer (Num 19:2). Here MT has the support of LT, which also represents B's distinctive *aneu tōn teknōn* but with *tetegmenōn* instead of *teknōn*. The fact that B and LT differ over the final element suggests that they are translating differently from the same or only slightly divergent HB text: *[m]blʿdy hyldym* (B) and *[m]blʿdy hylwdym* (LT). Yet two admissions must be entered: elsewhere in 1–4 Kingdoms, *teknon* always renders Heb. *bn* (as here at the ends of vv. 7, 10); and vv. 7, 10 already sufficiently state the content.

are sufficiently economical with the truth that their neighbors in Kiriath-jearim come and relieve them of their holy burden. Its new host consecrates his son as its priest. The ark is not mentioned again till 2 Sam 6.

Changing perspectives are a feature of the return of the ark to Israel. The sequence of narrative verbs concludes with the cattle making straight for Beth-shemesh (6:12a). And an ordered miscellany of perspectives follows:

The lords of Philistines focus on the rear of the ark (6:12b).
Beth-shemesh are happy to have their harvesting interrupted (v. 13).
The procession arrives and becomes a sacrifice (v. 14).
The Levites deal with the ark (v. 15a).
The men of Beth-shemesh offer sacrifice (v. 15b).
The lords of Philistines observe and leave satisfied (v. 16).

The public sacrifice (holocausts and other "sacrifices")[57] offered by the men of Beth-shemesh anticipates that offered by David (2 Sam 6:17–18) once the ark is in Jerusalem. However, sudden mention of "the Levites" is a surprise (1 Sam 6:15): they are not mentioned in Josephus's version of the episode. No part for them will be reported in the onward move of the ark to Jerusalem (2 Sam 6, BTH), and they reappear in Samuel only once (2 Sam 15:24–29), again as porters for the ark when it is removed from Jerusalem and then returned. Much of 1 Sam 6:15 repeats content from verses nearby; its concluding words link "on that day" from the end of v. 16 with "for Yahweh" from the end of v. 14. These Levites appear only at the return of the ark; and there may be an implicit claim that, since they have had no involvement, they bear no blame for its loss. If we recognize v. 15a as a later addition to the text, the original context had been no less balanced:

The lords of Philistines focus on the rear of the ark (6:12b).
Beth-shemesh are happy to have their harvesting interrupted (v. 13).
The procession arrives and becomes a sacrifice (v. 14).
The men of Beth-shemesh offer sacrifice (v. 15b).
The lords of Philistines observe and leave satisfied (v. 16).

[17–18] There is no principal verb in 6:18. The conclusion of the Philistine part of the story (vv. 17–18) is apparently one single sentence. Verse 18 opens with "and"; this connective is formally ambiguous: what follows is most often additional, but it may be explanatory. In strict grammatical terms, the question must remain open whether the content of v. 18 restates 17 or adds to it, whether the golden "mice" represent the swellings or are additional to them. These opening chapters of Samuel have offered no information about the contents of this

57. The older[?] term *šĕlāmîm* is never used in these opening 8 chapters.

"ark." In sending their own container with five golden votive objects back with it, the Philistines may have supposed that the ark contained something similar. Their own container will be placed solemnly alongside it on the "great stone" in strange parody of what should happen to the scroll recording Moses' words (Deut 31:24–26).

[6:19–7:1] The lords of the Philistines may have been content; but the end of the story springs a new surprise, with many casualties in Beth-shemesh. The ark's presence is no less destructive to Israel now than it had been to Philistines (ch. 5) or indeed Israel (ch. 4). Despite their early pleasure (6:13) and their cultic response (v. 15b), the people of Beth-shemesh are soon in despair and seeking, like the people of Ashdod before them, to off-load the ark to another place (19b–21). When they appeal for advice, Philistines now speak of the ark as Yahweh's (6:2); however, their religious experts continue to use the language of ch. 5—"the ark of the god of Israel" (6:3). In v. 8 the textual tradition is divided: simply "the ark" (GT), and "the ark of Yahweh" (MT).

Although Israel and Philistines are in opposing camps, it is interesting how many similarities there are in the narrator's depiction of each, and how few important distinctions. Beth-shemesh is little different from Ashdod in its reaction to disaster relating to the presence of the ark there. Just as events in three of their cities are held to be significant for every Philistine, so what happens in Beth-shemesh puts the whole house of Israel in a state of mourning. Philistine "priests" are identified by using the regular Hebrew *khnym* (5:5; 6:2). Although the other Philistine advisers are termed "diviners" (*qsmym*), and this term is only mentioned pejoratively elsewhere in HB, the advice they give appears sound.[58]

Then, although there is no question of Philistines as having "prophets" or "seers," this by no means implies that Philistines do not "see." After the disaster in the temple of Dagon, the Ashdodites simply "saw that it was so" (5:7): the text does not need to use the phrase "see and know," which is not infrequent in 1 Samuel.[59] Similarly, their experts promise (6:9) that when the people "see" how the cattle-cart-ark combination fares,[60] they will be able to deduce who has been responsible for the calamities. And finally, closure is achieved for the Philistine lords after this catastrophic series of events when they simply "see" the arrival of the ark in Beth-shemesh (6:16), and having seen, they depart. What the folk of Beth-shemesh first see is also straightforward (6:13). But their next looking motivates the death of large numbers (6:19). Here MT, but apparently not GT, has a significant change in idiom, using *r'h b'rwn* rather than the

58. See 1 Sam 15:23; 28:8; Num 22:7; 23:23; Deut 18:10, 14; Josh 13:22; 2 Kgs 17:17; Isa 3:2; 44:25; Jer 14:14; 27:9; 29:8; Ezek 13:6, 9, 23; 21:21, 23, 29 (26, 28, 34); 22:28; Mic 3:6–7, 11; Zech 10:2; Prov 16:10.

59. See 1 Sam 14:38; 23:22–23; 24:11 (12); 25:17; 26:12.

60. The whole procession is understood by these diviners as a sort of divinatory instrument.

earlier and more straightforward *r'h 't-h'rwn* ("see the ark"). As explained by Driver (45–46), *r'h b-* means not "look into" but "look at/upon" with interest or pleasure. It is far from clear why this is so wicked. And our question simply anticipates the puzzle in the parent text (2 Sam 6:6–11): the fatal divine displeasure with Uzzah who (simply?) steadies the ark when the oxen pulling its new cart stumble. The house of Abinadab is known from the main source on the ark (2 Sam 6:3, BTH); but there his sons are called Uzzah and "Ahio" (or Uzzah and "his brother"). The name of the unfortunate Uzzah (*ʿzh*) does share key consonants with Eleazar (*'lʿzr*) in this verse (and we may usefully recall a later king of Judah named both Azariah and Uzziah). Eleazar is a much more familiar priestly name: one Eleazar was not only son and successor of Aaron, but even (according to Num 26:60–61) brother of Nadab and Abihu, whose names together make up Abinadab.

Within the whole context of Samuel–Kings, these opening chapters cast a long shadow. Yahweh's letting his ark be taken can be seen as a foretaste of Yahweh's letting his temple or "house" in Jerusalem be taken by the Babylonians. If so, then its return unaided may serve to warn exilic Israel against initiatives taken by themselves for its return. In the more local context of a narrative about the ark's loss immediately after Samuel's call, it may be that once prophecy was established, the ark became dispensable. Certainly the book of Jeremiah invites its readers not to expect an ark after the exile (3:14–18).

1 Samuel 7:2–4

2 And it came to be from the day of the ark's settling at Kiriath-jearim
and the days multiplied
and it was twenty years;
and the whole house of Israel [were in mourning[a]] *looked attentively*
after Yahweh.[b]

3 And Samuel said to the whole house of Israel, saying,
"If with your whole heart you are turning to Yahweh,
put aside the gods of the foreign land from your midst and the [Ashtaroth] Asheroth;[a]
and make steadfast your hearts[b] toward Yahweh
and serve him alone,
that he may save you from the hand of *the* Philistines."
4 And the sons of Israel put aside the Baals[a] and the Ashtaroth,[b]
and they served Yahweh alone.

2a. Unique to this verse is *nhh* as *nipʿal*, and a *qal* form occurs only 2x in HB. *Nipʿal* can refer to the deliberate or self-conscious practice of the action described by the *qal*.

Since 6 of the 9 occurrences of the *qal* and the related noun *nhy* are in Amos and Jeremiah, and both have close links in this chapter, it seems unwise to look for an alternative meaning. However, two main options have been proposed: "follow" (cf. Arab. *nahā[y]*); and "turn" (cf. Akk. *nêʾu*). Here *epeblepsen* (B) has not been explained as a rendering of a consonantal cluster at all similar to *wynhw* (MT) and may therefore be a guess. Also, *epestrepsen* (LT) may be an alteration of B, influenced by *epestrepsate* (v. 3).

b. The LT adds "in peace" at end (*en eirēnē*).

3a. Throughout the Gk. OT *alsos/ē* is the stock correspondent to *ʾšrh/ym/wt*.

b. "Heart" is obj. of *hkyn* in Pss 10:17; 78:8; Job 11:13; and 1 Chr 29:18; 2 Chr 12:14; 19:3; 20:33; 30:19. This will correspond to "heart" as subj. of *nkwn* in Pss 57:7–8 (8–9); 78:37; 108:1 (2); 112:7.

4a. For *hbʿlym* (MT), B uses the f. art. (*tas*) with *Baaleim*, and LT neuter (*ta*).

b. Unique in the Gk. OT, the combination *ta alsē Astarōth* (GT) first translates *ʾšrwt* and then transliterates *ʿštrwt*.

[2] Fokkelman notes nicely how few words suffice to suggest not simply that there has occurred a considerable lapse of time, but also how quickly one day becomes many—and soon many days are twenty years. The Yahweh whom the people are in mourning "after" is the Yahweh they know they have lost much earlier with his ark, the Yahweh who has killed as many Israelites as Philistines, the Holy One "before" whom the people of Beth-shemesh were aware they could not stand (or pass).

[3] "The gods of the foreign land" (*ʾlhy hnkr*, v. 3) are found elsewhere in HB; most commonly, as here, they are the object of "turn aside."[61] But their mention here in the books of Samuel appears unmotivated and comes as a surprise. Hannah has been blamed for drunkenness, and the sons of Eli for several sorts of misbehavior. But even if Yahweh's people have fallen short of his standards, there has been no whisper of disloyalty to Yahweh. Israel has been worsted by its Philistine neighbors, but no religious motivation is offered in the text for this defeat—not even the generalized introduction to several episodes in the book of Judges, "the people of Israel continued to do evil in the eyes of Yahweh." We have to consider two options. Either we suppose that the people have resorted to these foreign gods in the (supposed) absence of Yahweh with his ark; or we recognize the alien hand of a later editor, making connections here with a wider biblical theme.

[4] When Samuel next speaks to Israel, it is after summoning them to Mizpah (7:5). In addition to an absence of religious motivation, no context, or at least no corresponding locality, is specified for what precedes (vv. 3–4). These verses look like an editorial insertion from a very late biblical period. "Setting the heart," though used in Ps 10:17, is an expression known elsewhere only in Chronicles (1 Chr 29:18; 2 Chr 12:14; 19:3; 20:33; 30:19). Ashtoreth or

61. See Gen 35:2; Josh 24:23; Judg 10:16; 1 Sam 7:3; 2 Chr 14:3 (2); 33:15.

Ashtaroth are warned against in Judg 2:13; 10:6; 1 Sam 7:3, 4; 12:10; 1 Kgs 11:5, 33; 2 Kgs 23:13. (They are also mentioned in 1 Sam 31:10, but not in 1 Chr 10:9.) Such editors are often associated with the "Deuteronomists"; yet not one of these expressions is found in Deuteronomy. "Return with your whole heart" is commended in Joel 2:12—and we never find "with all your heart" in Deuteronomy without the immediate addition of "and with all your soul."

1 Samuel 7:5–17

5 And Samuel said,
"Gather all Israel to Mizpah,
and I shall pray about[a] you to Yahweh."[b]
6 And they gathered to Mizpah,
and they drew water
and poured it before Yahweh *on the ground*
and they fasted on that day
and they said there,
"We have sinned against Yahweh."
And Samuel judged[a] the sons of Israel at Mizpah.
7 And *the* Philistines heard
that *all* the sons of Israel had gathered themselves to Mizpah,
and the lords of *the* Philistines went up [toward] *against* Israel;
and the sons of Israel heard
and were afraid of *the* Philistines.
8 And the sons of Israel said to Samuel,
"Do not be mute for us,
not crying to Yahweh *your*[a] God,
that he may save us from the hand of the Philistines."
9 And Samuel took one milk lamb
and offered it up as a [whole[a]] burnt offering *with the whole people* to Yahweh;
and Samuel cried to Yahweh about Israel
and Yahweh answered him.
10 And Samuel was offering up the burnt offering
and *the* Philistines had approached
to do battle with Israel.
And Yahweh thundered with a great voice on that day over *the* Philistines
and discomfited[a] them
and they were smitten before Israel.
11 And the men of Israel went out from Mizpah
and pursued *the* Philistines,

and they struck them down as far as below Beth Kar.
12 And Samuel took one stone
and set it up between Mizpah and the [Tooth] *Ancient*
and called its name Stone of Help;[a]
and he said
"Up to this point Yahweh has helped us."
13 And the Philistines were humbled,[a]
and they did not continue further
coming into the territory of Israel,
and the hand of Yahweh was on the[b] Philistines all the days of Samuel.
14 And the cities
that *the* Philistines had taken from *the sons of* Israel
returned to Israel, from Ekron to [Gath[a]] *Azob*,
and their territory Israel did save from the hand of *the* Philistines;
and there was peace between Israel and the Amorite.
15 And Samuel judged[a] Israel all the days of his life.
16 And he would walk from year to year
and go round Bethel and Gilgal and Mizpah
and would judge Israel, *in* all these places.[a]
17 And his return was to [Ramah] *Armathaim*
for his house was there,
and there he judged Israel,
and he built there an altar to Yahweh.

5a. *peri* (B) and *hyper* (LT) are both more precise than *bʿd* (MT).

b. At the end LT adds *kai euērestoun autō*; the idiom corresponds to *hthlk lpny* 9x in Gk. OT. It is a GT plus also in Judg 10:16, in a passage with several links to 1 Sam 7:3–4.

6a. Here *dikazein* corresponds to *špṭ* in 7:6, 15, 16, 17; 8:5, 6, 20; 12:7; 24:12, 15 (13, 16); but *ekdikein* in 3:13; and *krinein* in 4:18 (as in the book of Judges and in Ruth 1:1), which appears to correspond in sense with this verse. In classical Greek, *dikazein* is more strictly juridical.

8a. For GT, Yahweh is Samuel's God. The LT adds "for us" to the people's request.

9a. Here *klyl* appears redundant after *ʿwlh*; Psalm 51:19 (21) has them linked: *ʿwlh wklyl*. The GT plus will retrovert to *ʾt-kl-hʿm*.

10a. Either *synechythēsan* (GT) is a free rendering of *wyhmm* (*qal* in MT), or GT has read it as *puʿal*.

12a. GT first transliterates and then translates *ʾbn hʿzr*. LT adds *mou* after *boēthou*.

13a. The GT's *etapeinōsen* may attest *wyknʿ* (*hipʿil*), rather than *nipʿal wyknʿw* (MT).

b. Unusual in this verse, *pělištîm* bears the article.

14a. The LT follows MT's Gath rather than the otherwise unknown Azob (B).

15a. Here LT has *ekrine*, but in vv. 6, 16, 17 it has *edikaze* with B.

16a. Is *hēgiasmenois* (GT) an interpretation of *mqwmwt* (MT), or a rendering of *mqdšym*? For GT, the three sites provide the locus of Samuel's judging; in MT they appear to represent (at least part of) its obj. If MT is secondary here, this may have motivated its alteration to *mqwmwt*: this pl. is used in Amos 4:6 in a complaint about Bethel and Gilgal; and has pejorative cultic association in Deut 12:2; 2 Chr 33:19.

[5–6] Verses 3–4 are only the first of the several puzzles within this short ch. 7. To suggest that "and Samuel said" (v. 3) is a secondary anticipation of the same words in v. 5 simply postpones questions relating to his reappearance there. The earlier report of his "vision" had ended in talk of his further development, of his establishment and recognition as prophet of Yahweh, and of an ongoing significance for Shiloh (3:19–21). And yet, in chs. 4–6 when the narrative goes on to tell of momentous events for Israel and an important symbol of its God over a considerable period, during all of it there is not a mention of this established prophet. And here he is now, gathering all Israel neither to Shiloh nor to Kiriath-jearim, where the ark has long been housed, but to Mizpah. And this location is not simply specified in passing: it is emphasized (4x in vv. 5–7). The stress on the name (*mṣph*) is among the significant marks of correspondence between ch. 4, where Yahweh gave victory to the Philistines, and ch. 7, where he gives victory to Israel. This place to which Samuel gathers his people recalls the action of Eli (4:13) "watching closely" (*mṣph*) for news from the field.

Mizpah fits into a much larger series of overlapping patterns. It becomes significant again at the very end of the royal story, as the Babylonian administrative center for Judah after the fall of Jerusalem. After another national collapse, and a second loss of the ark, the center of restoration is somewhere other than the expected national sanctuary. Then we noted (on 1:1) that Mizpah and Ramah (7:17) feature together with Geba of Benjamin in BTH (1 Kgs 15:22). The story told there of defense works undertaken by Asa of Judah against Baasha of Israel is mentioned in Jeremiah (41:9), within a portion of the book that refers to Ramah (40:1) and events largely located at Mizpah (14x in chs. 40–41). Furthermore, in this section of the book of Jeremiah (37:3; 42:2, 4, 20) we find the prophet requested to "pray about" his people. We have already noticed that Samuel is mentioned in the book of Jeremiah (15:1). And several features of the presentation of both do overlap: the reports of an inaugural vision when a "lad," and the role of the divine "word" within that vision. We must ask (even if we cannot answer), In what form were traditions relating to Samuel available to the authors of Jeremiah? How far is Jeremiah presented as a second Samuel? Or how far, in the books of Samuel, is Samuel presented as anticipatory of Jeremiah?

When his people ask Jeremiah to pray about them, the context makes clear that their request is for guidance about the future: the prayer is to be divinatory rather than intercessory. The all-too-brief report of Samuel's praying for his people (7:5–6) does not easily yield up its meaning. They do not approach him;

he takes the initiative: they should gather, and he will pray. The Samuel who makes this proposal is the son of his mother: she is subject of the verb "pray" more often than any other character in HB. But while she prayed "against," "before," and "to" Yahweh, and "toward" (attaining) "this lad," his offer is to pray "about" (or "for") them.

Yet, when they gather at his request at Mizpah, they do not endorse his offer of prayer about them, but embark on what appears to be a penitence ritual; and he responds by "judging" them. They fast, and they confess that they have sinned against Yahweh. And the water, which they draw and then pour out before Yahweh,[62] may not just be a solemn offering as they approach Yahweh, but may also signify that their fast is a major one, involving abstinence from water as well as food (Jonah 3:7). It seems as if, in response to Samuel, the people are acting out their own answer to Eli's question (2:25) as to whether anyone can pray for the one who has sinned against Yahweh. They had so sinned, and prayer could hardly be effective. Samuel's judging them is also an acted response. From one perspective it ranks Samuel alongside Eli, who had "judged Israel" for a substantial period (4:18). But it has extra menace: it also recalls part of the content of his own inaugural vision (3:13), that Yahweh would forever be "judging" Eli's house because he did not restrain his sons.[63]

[7–11] When the Philistines hear of the assembly at Mizpah (and take it for a muster against themselves), the people now ask Samuel not to remain silent (7–8). With another catastrophe in prospect, they require him not to "pray about" them but to "cry out" for their deliverance. The people speak as if they have advance knowledge of the (ironic?) lament that Yahweh has Jeremiah voice on behalf of Judah (Jer 14:7–9)—an earlier part of the very portion (14:1–15:4) within which Samuel is named (15:1):

> Though our iniquities testify against us, act, Yahweh, for your name's sake;
> For our backslidings are many, we have sinned against you.
> O hope of Israel, its savior in time of trouble,
> Why should you be like a stranger in the land,
> Like a wayfarer who turns aside to tarry for the night?
> Why should you be like a man confused, like a hero who cannot save?
> Yet you, O Yahweh, are in the midst of us, and we are called by your name.
> Leave us not.

Bethel and Gilgal appear together with Mizpah (7:16) in only one other biblical context (1 Sam 10). The fact that they appear there in the same relative

62. The only other water drawn and then poured out in Samuel is what David wants from the spring in Bethlehem (2 Sam 23:16).

63. To describe the statement of Samuel's judging Israel as "appended by a Deuteronomistic hand to incorporate the career of Samuel into the succession of 'judges' who ruled Israel between Joshua and Saul" (McCarter 1:145) is to lose its force.

order (vv. 3, 8, 17), and report Samuel as moving in that order between them, makes it likely that the author of 1 Sam 7 has generalized from this report in ch. 10 (and esp. so, if 1 Sam 1–8 is a new preface to what once started in 1 Sam 9). Samuel places his sons as judges in Beer-sheba (8:2): this has already appeared (3:20) as the southern border point of the land; and yet, so soon after Bethel and Gilgal (7:16), the connection of all three with Amos 5:4–6 is to be strongly suspected.

[12–17] McCarter (1:150) is sensibly reluctant to detect long-standing traditions about Samuel in this chapter. He notes instead four general anticipations of 2 Sam 5–8: battle reports (1 Sam 7:7–11; 2 Sam 5:17–25); recovery of captured land (1 Sam 7:14a; 2 Sam 8:1); administration of justice (1 Sam 7:15; 2 Sam 8:15); and the pacification of the land (1 Sam 7:14b; 2 Sam 8). However, still more of this chapter appears to depend on such patterning. Beyond the role of the priests of the house of Eli at Yahweh's altar (1 Sam 2:28, 33), an altar is mentioned only three more times in the books of Samuel. Just as David builds an altar on the ground bought from the Jebusite in Jerusalem (2 Sam 24:18, 21, 25), shortly before he is succeeded by Solomon, so Samuel (1 Sam 7:17) builds an altar shortly before the anointing of Saul; and so does Saul (14:35), before the anointing of David. Then also in this chapter, the distinct separation of the role of the stone (7:12), which is simply a memorial, between talk of sacrifice (vv. 9–10) and of building an altar (v. 17) may imply unfavorable comment on the role of the great stone as (at least temporary) altar for Saul in 14:33–35.

Second Samuel 7:11 neither names nor suggests the remit of the "judges" (*špṭym*) who preceded David. In the consensus approach to the books of the Former Prophets (the so-called Deuteronomistic History), this is taken as an obvious summary reference back to the heroes of the book of Judges. However, another account of the matter is equally possible. When 1 Samuel ascribes a judging role to Eli (4:18) and Samuel (4x in ch. 7), it is not necessary to understand these figures as continuing in the tradition of the leaders reported in the book of Judges: they may simply be identified as precursors of David. Similarly, Judg 10:6–16 may have drawn expansively on 1 Sam 7:3–4, rather than vice versa.

The Amorite (v. 14) is mentioned again in Samuel only in 2 Sam 21:2, where the Gibeonites are described as being *mytr h'mry*. Similarly, BTH includes them in the list of those pressed into service by Solomon: *kl-h'm hnwtr mn-*. . . (1 Kgs 9:20 has Amorite at the head of the list before Hittite; 2 Chr 8:7 has these in reverse order). Talk of Yahweh's hand on the Philistines in the time of Samuel (7:13) resumes a theme of 5:6, 9. Elsewhere in Samuel "the hand of Yahweh" is part of a threat against Israel (12:15); and the phrase is used in BTH by David (2 Sam 24:14), as he chooses punishment by plague or famine, rather than defeat in war.

1 Samuel 8:1–3

1 And it came to be
as Samuel grew old,
and he made his sons judges for Israel.
2 And *these are* the name*s* of his *sons*[a]
the firstborn [son] was Joel,
and the name of his second son was Abijah:
judges in Beer-sheba.
3 But his sons did not walk in his way[s];
and they turned aside after a cut[a]
and took presents
and turned judgment*s*[b] aside.

2a. The GT has apparently read *w'lh šmwt bnyw hbkwr . . .*

3a. Commonly rendered "gain," *bṣ'* does lit. mean "cut." The LT's *pleonexia* ("advantage," "undue gain") is a closer translation than *synteleia* (B). However, *synteleia* is sometimes explained in terms of *collatio* (forced "contribution" for the ruler); and "collation" has been used to render *bṣ'* in a savage critique of the misrule of Israel's princes (Ezek 22:12).

b. In 1 Kingdoms 2:13; 8:3, 9, 11; 10:25; 27:11; 30:25, *dikaiōma* is the stock rendering of *mšpṭ*, but only here in pl.

[1–3] The hereditary principle was already alive in Israel, but not well. Samuel has installed his sons as judges, just as earlier Eli had installed his sons as priests. And in each case the succession was a failure.

1 Samuel 8:4–6

4 And all the elders of Israel gathered,
and came to Samuel at Ramah.
5 And they said to him,
"Look here,
you have become old,[a]
and your sons—they have not walked in your ways.
Make[b] for us a king
to judge us like all the nations."[c]
6 And the word was bad in the eyes[a] of Samuel,
as they said,
"Give us a king
to judge us."[b]
And Samuel prayed to Yahweh.

5a. In HB, *ʾth zqnt* is said only to Samuel and Joshua (Josh 13:1). And apart from Joshua (Josh 23:2) and Samuel (1 Sam 12:2), only Sarah (Gen 18:13) says *ʾny zqnty* in HB.

b. The vb. *śym* is used with *mlk* as obj. in 10:19 and Deut 17:14–15. But it is only with Deut 17:14–15 that there are links in 1 Sam 8—and not in the wider promises and threats.

c. In HB, *kkl-hgwym* appears to be unique to Deut 17:14 and 1 Sam 8:5, 20. The comparison is not offered in (the possibly prior) 10:19.

6a. The closest comparisons to *wyrʿ hdbr bʿyny* are 1 Sam 18:8; 2 Sam 12:1 (11:27) with Gen 21:11 and 1 Chr 21:7.

b. The LT repeats "like all the nations."

[4–6] "The elders of Israel" (*zqny yśrʾl*) play a role in BTH only twice, but at key points: over the anointing of David (2 Sam 5:3) and bringing the ark into the new temple (1 Kgs 8:1).[64] It is often noted as somewhat ironic that it is the elders who approach Samuel with the message that he has become old. But that may be to misunderstand their words: their concern is not that he has aged like themselves, but that he has appointed his sons and they are misbehaving in their judging. If the elders are inconsistent, it is more in showing no awareness that kings tend to be succeeded by their sons, even when that is not constitutionally required. We might think that Israel has all the essentials of monarchy already. It seems that what is important to the elders is that their ruler should now bear the same title as those of other peoples. Nothing is said about the king's sons or who will succeed him.

1 Samuel 8:7–21

7 And Yahweh said to Samuel,
"Listen to the voice of the people
in all they say to you.
For not you have they rejected,
but me they have rejected
from being king over them
8 just like all the deeds they have done
since I brought them up from Egypt and up to this day—
and they have abandoned me
and served other gods.[a]
So they are doing to you too.
9 And now, listen to their voice.
However, you must bear solemn witness[a] to them

64. Elsewhere in Samuel–Kings only in 1 Sam 4:3; 8:4; 2 Sam 3:17 (anticipating 5:3); 17:4, 15. The context is always counsel.

and declare to them[b] the judgment of the king
who will be king over them."

10 And Samuel said all the word[s[a]] of Yahweh to the people
who were asking of him a king.

11 And he said,
"This will be the judgment of the king who will be king over you:
Your sons he will take
and will put them in his chariotry and on his horses
and they will run[a] in front of his chariotry,
12 and make for himself leaders of thousands and leaders of *hundreds* [fifties]:
to [plough his ploughing[a]
and to] reap his reaping
and *to gather his gathering*
and to make objects for war and objects for chariotry.
13 And your daughters he will take: for perfumers and for cooks[a] and for bakers.[b]
14 And your fields and vineyards and olives—the good ones—
he will take,
and give to his servants.
15 And your seeds[a] and your vineyards he will tithe[b]
and give to his officers and his servants.
16 And your servants, male and female, and your *cattle* [young folk—the good ones—]
and your goods and asses he will take,
and [make[a]] *tithe* for his service.
17 And your flock he will tithe;
and you yourselves will become his servants.
18 And you will cry on that day away from[a] your king
whom you have chosen[b] for yourselves,
and Yahweh will not answer you on that day,
because you chose for yourselves a king."
19 And the people refused
to listen to [the voice of[a]] Samuel;
and they said *to him*:[b]
"No! Assuredly there will be a king over us.
20 And we too shall become like all the nations.
And our king shall judge us,
and shall go out before us
and shall fight our battles."[a]

21 And Samuel listened to all the words of the people,
and he spoke them in the ears[a] of Yahweh.

8a. The LT adds "which they themselves make, and worshiped them."

9a. Only here in Samuel is *h'd* used; and it is strengthened with inf. abs. only here and Gen 43:3; Jer 11:7. It seems to be used only (mainly?) in later texts.

b. Here 4QSam[a] reads *'*[*t*] between *lhm* and *mšpṭ*.

10a. The LT is pl. like MT.

11a. . . . *m lpny mr* . . . supports *kai protrechontas* (GT) as rendering *wrṣym* (4QSam[a]) for *wrṣw* (MT).

12a. Here 4QSam[a] supports the mention of plowing before harvesting (MT). The GT has two paired expressions relating to harvest and ingathering: *trygan* corresponds to *bṣr* in Lev 25:11; Deut 24:21; Judg 9:27; and *trygētos* renders *bṣyr* in Lev 26:5; Judg 8:2; but the Heb. noun and vb. are never attested together (and that is true also of *'sp* and *'syp*).

13a. Only in 9:23, 24 is *ṭbḥ* ("cook") used in HB; the f. *ṭbḥh* is hapax.

b. The vb. *'ph* is found in 1 Sam 28:24.

15a. Here pl. *zr'ym* is hapax.

b. Here *'śr* as *qal* is unique to 1 Sam 8:15, 17; but *pi'el* and *hip'il* are found in Gen 28:22; Deut 14:22; 26:12; Neh 10:38, 39.

16a. For *w'śh* (MT), 4QSam[a] has pl. *w'św*, but GT attests *w'śr*.

18a. In Samuel–Kings *mlpny* is used only in 1 Sam 8:18; 18:12; 21:7; 2 Sam 7:15 (different in 1 Chr 17); 1 Kgs 8:25, 54; 21:29; 2 Kgs 5:27; 6:32.

b. The LT's *ēretisasthe* will also render (the earlier) *bḥrtm*; but *ētēsasthe* retroverts to *š'ltm* as in 10 above and 12:17, 19.

19a. LT = MT. The MT may have omitted *lw* before *l'*.

20a. The vb. *nlḥm* is construed with *mlḥmwt yhwh* in 1 Sam 25:28 (MT) and 18:17 (MT's plus); but the only precise parallel is 2 Chr 32:8. The term *l'zrnw*, of Yahweh as helping his people, is part of this same verse (2 Chr 32:8). Outside Isaiah (5x), Psalms (7x), and Chronicles (5x), and the Song of Moses (Deut 32:38), this occurs only in 1 Sam 7:12.

21a. (Speaking) "in the ears of Yahweh" has parallels only in Num 11:1, 18 (complaining, weeping).

[7–9] "A king to judge us" (v. 11) resumes the theme of the preceding paragraph (vv. 5–6). Nathan's words to David on behalf of Yahweh were that his reign would lead to Israel's living in their own place, being disturbed no more, no longer afflicted by violent men as they had still been under the previous "judges" (2 Sam 7:10). Anticipating the terminology in 2 Sam 7, this paragraph takes "judging" to be the given form of rule before "reigning." The verb "judge" (*špṭ*) is remarkably uncommon in BTH: found there only in 2 Sam 7:11; 1 Kgs 8:32; 2 Kgs 15:5—and possibly 1 Kgs 3:9. How different are Samuel's words to his people on behalf of the same Yahweh: the "judging" (*mšpṭ*) of the king, far from guaranteeing their freedom, will enslave them (11–18); and they will "cry out" not to their king but in fruitless appeal against him.

Yahweh's brief explanation of the situation to Samuel (vv. 7–9) is a mixture of the familiar and unfamiliar. "Reject" is most at home in the books of the Latter Prophets and (other) poetry[65]—it is never used in BTH or in Deuteronomy. On the other hand, "abandoning Yahweh" and "serving other gods" (v. 8) are part of the core language of BTH (1 Kgs 9:6, 9; 2 Kgs 22:17). We also meet "abandon [Yahweh]" in 1 Sam 12:10; 1 Kgs 11:33; 2 Kgs 21:22; and "serving other gods" recurs in 1 Sam 26:19 and frequently in Kings.[66]

[10] The fact that Samuel reports Yahweh's *whole* response to his people asking for a king is stated clearly before the details of the response are set out.

[11–18] The focus of Samuel's response is solely on the burden of a growing establishment. Once all the individual specialists detailed in verses 11b–17a are in the king's service, the people themselves are too (17b)! As documented in the notes above, some of the details in Samuel's speech (vv. 11–18) are much less common in HB, although "cook" and "baker" (13) do anticipate terms in 1 Sam 9 and 28. His climax (v. 18) develops further the themes of being in mourning "after" Yahweh, "before" whom they could not stand (6:20; 7:2), and "crying out" to Yahweh for deliverance (7:8–9). When they realize the full extent of what they have let themselves in for, they will "cry out" ("to Yahweh" is not specified here) *mlpny* their king, but (the rejected) Yahweh will not answer. The unusual *mlpny* ("away from") is the negative of *lpny* ("before"), without being its opposite (*ʾḥry*, "after"). Similarly "chosen" (v. 18) is the positive counterpart of "rejected" (v. 7).

[19–21] There seems no reason to suppose that the narrator intends any distance between Samuel's views and Yahweh's views of the judgments a king will make—not, at least, while these are being reported. It would be wrong to say that the people refuse the analysis laid out by Samuel. He warns that what they call "judging" is going to involve considerable loss of independence as they are enlisted in the king's service. They respond that the judging they expect of their king will be positive. When they say he would lead them, they are accepting implicitly that they would be enlisted as Samuel has said—but they add defiantly that it would be their battles which he would fight.

The end of this paragraph leaves the reader pondering how far the people are satisfied that their cause has been advanced. When they say, "There will be a king," do they expect that they will be taking the initiative, like their elders would later approach David in Hebron? Or are they repeating their demand (v. 5b) that Samuel should do something about it?

65. Isaiah (9x), Jeremiah (10x), Ezekiel (6x), Hosea (2x), Amos (2x), Psalms (7x, including 78:59, 67), Job (11x), Lamentations (2x). Elsewhere it is found only in Lev 26 (3x); Num 11:20; 14:31; Judg 9:38; and a few contexts in Samuel–Kings: 1 Sam 8:7; 10:19; 15:23, (2x), 26 (2x); 16:1, 7; 2 Kgs 17:15–16, 20; 23:27.

66. First Kings 11:4, 10; 14:9; 2 Kgs 5:17; 17:7, 35, 37, 38.

1 Samuel 8:22

22 And Yahweh said to Samuel,
“Listen to their voice,
and ‘king’ for them a king.”
And Samuel said to the men of Israel,
“Go[a] each to his city.”

22a. Here *apotrechein* (GT) is the stock rendering of *hlk* before “to his city/tent/place.”

The sharpest interpretive puzzle comes in this brief culmination of 1 Sam 5–8. The terms of Yahweh’s response leave open both possibilities envisaged in the previous paragraph. Yahweh charges Samuel with taking appropriate action, but notes significantly if quietly that this will be done “for them.” Samuel’s response is somewhat opaque. Sending each to his “city” is unusual:[67] the more normal idiom uses his “tent[s]” or his “house” or his “place.” The more important observation is that we would expect this formula to mark the (successful) end of a story. Here, however, we have to ask, Is Samuel playing for time? Or is he even refusing to take the divine instruction forward?

Excursus 1: Afterword on 1 Samuel 1–8

One way of reading the blank, or (completely) open, lines in the CL transcription of Samuel is that they underline or emphasize the immediately preceding statement. From that perspective, five main points are made in this first quarter of 1 Samuel: (1) Yahweh will give strength to and exalt his anointed king (2:10). (2) Samuel is already serving Yahweh, before Eli, at a time when communication from Yahweh is rare (3:1). (3) Yahweh’s call of Samuel is not “one-off,” but Yahweh’s revelation (*glh*, in one sense) through Samuel at Shiloh continues (3:21). (4) Glory is exiled (*glh*, in another sense) from Israel when God’s ark is taken (4:22). And (5) Yahweh commands Samuel to listen to Israel and king them a king (8:22). The scribe in the Aleppo Codex has left a blank line before this sentence, not after it.

67. The expression *ʾyš lʿyrw* is used only in Ezra 2:1; Neh 7:6—cf. *ʾyš ʾl-ʿyrw* in 1 Kgs 22:36 (Kgs plus).

1 Samuel 9–16
Two Kings Anointed by Samuel

The middle half of 1 Samuel takes us into a very different world from the first quarter. First Samuel 1–8 has set in a wide context the complete novelty of kingship to Israel. The principal features of the social and religious landscape, which that introduction has depicted, are prophecy, priesthood, a temple, the ark of Yahweh symbolizing his presence, and Philistines as Israel's rivals in the land. Successes and failures, both in battle and in divine-human communication, have been reported. The introduction of kingship into this mix is portrayed as Israel's choice. In 1 Samuel 9–16 we move from why it was done to how it was done; and the request itself—the "asking"—seems to be the problem. The larger part of this portion reports a false start: the appointment of a king whose very name means "asked for." He is rejected (13:8–14; 15:10–35) almost as soon as installed; and this second quarter of 1 Samuel ends with the anointing of a new king, whose line will last. The lengthy return in 1 Sam 15 to the theme of Saul's rejection as king, already more briefly stated in 1 Sam 13, is a typical demonstration of recurring elements in 1 Samuel.

Much of the story of Saul is an account of a prototype of David, and the connections start at the beginning. There are several links between the two almost neighboring reports of anointing by Samuel in 1 Sam 9–10 and 16. Each follows sacrifice and an invitation, and each results from Yahweh's choice (10:24//16:8–10). Saul is from the least of the tribes, and David the youngest of his brothers. Saul is anointed in secret, and David is anointed in the company of only his father and brothers. There are several musicians among the group through whom Saul is caught up in the spirit, and it is through David's music that the bad effects on Saul of an evil spirit are dispelled.

But some connections between Saul and David are from further afield. The theme of Saul as *nāgîd*, or "designate" (1 Sam 9:16; 10:1; 13:14), anticipates the David of 2 Sam 5:2 and 7:8 (BTH)—and also of 1 Sam 25:30 and 2 Sam 6:21—but not the early chapters about David.[1] And there are contrasts as well as similarities. The verb "make king" (*himlîk*) is never used with David as its object, though of Saul as many as five times with three different subjects:

1. Others who are *nāgîd* are Solomon (1 Kgs 1:35), Jeroboam (14:7), and Baasha (16:2).

Samuel (1 Sam 8:22; 12:1); the people, as in the case of Jeroboam (1 Sam 11:15; cf. 1 Kgs 12:20); and Yahweh (1 Sam 15:11, 35). Moreover, although never himself "made king," David is said to have made Solomon king (1 Kgs 1:47). The locus of Saul's kingship in 1 Sam 10:1 is the divine *nḥlh*, which in Samuel means the land (and its people?). It will reappear in four emotive contexts beyond 1 Sam 9–24 (1 Sam 26:19; 2 Sam 14:16; 20:19; 21:3).

1 Samuel 9:1–10:16 Saul Anointed by Samuel

1 Samuel 9:1–27

1 And [there was] a man from *the sons of* Benjamin,
and his name was Kish son of Abiel son of Zeror son of Bekhorat son of Aphiah son of a Yemini man, a mighty man of valor.
2 And he had a son
and his name was Saul, choice and good;
there was not a man of the sons of Israel better than he;
from his shoulder and upward he was higher than all the [people] *land*.
3 And the asses wandered—of Kish, Saul's father;
and Kish said to Saul his son,
"Be sure to take with you one from the lads,
and be up
and off:
search for the asses."
4 And [he] *they* passed through the hill country of Ephraim,
and [he] *they* passed through the land of *Selcha* [Shalishah],
and they did not find.
And they passed through the land of [jackals] *Easakem*
and there was nothing;
and [he] *they* passed through the land of [Yemini] *Iakeim*
and they did not find.
5 These came into the [land of] Zuph;
and Saul—he said to his lad
who was with him,
"Come
and let us go back,
in case my father leaves off the asses
and becomes concerned for us."
6 And [he] *the lad* said to him,
"Take good note,[a]
there is a man of God in this town,
and the man is honored:

everything he says comes.
And now let us go[b] [there]:
[perhaps] *and* he will tell us our way
on which we have been walking."
7 And Saul said[a] to his lad *who was with him*,
"And suppose we go—
and what will we bring to the man *of God*?
For the food has gone from our vessels
and there is no present
to bring to the man of God;
and what do we have?"
8 And the lad continued
to answer Saul,
and said,
"Look—a quarter shekel of silver:
it happens to be in my hand,
and [I] *you* will give it to the man of God
and he will show us our way."
9 *And* formerly in Israel this is what the man said
as he went to consult [a] God:
"Come
and let us go to the seer."

For the prophet the people	For the prophet today
would formerly call the seer.	would formerly be called the seer.

10 And Saul said to his lad,
"[Your] *the* word is good.
Come,
let us go."
And they went to the town
where the man of God was.
11 They were going up the ascent to the city
and they found maids coming out
to draw water.
And they said to them,
"Is the seer here?"
12 And they answered them
and said,
"He is—right there in front of you.
[Hurry] now,
[for today] *because of the day*[a] he has come to the town
because there is a seasonal sacrifice for the people at the high place.

13 As you enter the town, so you will find him *in the town*
before he goes up to the high place
to eat.
For the people will not eat
till he comes,
for he himself will bless the sacrifice—
afterward those invited will eat.
And now go up;
for [him—] this very day[a] you will find him."
14 And they went up to the town.
They were entering into the town and look: Samuel [was coming] *came* out
to meet them,
to go up to the high place.

15 Now Yahweh had uncovered Samuel's ear one day before Saul's coming, saying,
16 "About this time tomorrow I will send you a man from the land of Benjamin,
and you will anoint him as leader over my people Israel,
and he will save my people from the hand of the Philistines.
For I have seen *the humiliation of*[a] my people,
for their cry has come to me."
17 Now Samuel—he saw Saul,
and Yahweh answered him:
"Note the man
of whom I said to you,
'This one will [refrain from] *rule in*[a] my people.'"
18 And Saul approached Samuel in the middle of the [gate] town,[a]
and said,
"Tell [me] please
wherever the seer's house is."
19 And Samuel answered Saul
and said,
"I am *he*[a] [the seer]—
go up before me to the high place,
and you will eat[b] with me today,
and I will send you off in the morning,
and everything in your heart I will tell you.
20 But on your asses wandering now three days—set not your heart on them,
for they have been found.

And for whom is [all] the desire of Israel?
Surely it is for you and [all] your father's house."

21 And Saul answered
and said,
"Surely I am son of a Yemini *man*,
of the small[est of the] staff[s] of Israel,[a]
and my family is more slight than all the families of the staff of Benjamin—
and why have you spoken to me a word like this?"

22 And Samuel took Saul and his lad
and brought them to the hall,
and he gave them *there* a place at the head of the invitees
—[and these were] some thirty men.
23 And Samuel said to the cook,
"Give the portion
which I gave you,
about which[a] I spoke to you,

"Put it beside you."

OL	B	4QSam[a]	MT
24 And[a] the cook lifted up	24 And the cook lifted up	24 [And the cook lifted up]	24 And the cook lifted up
	the thigh bone	the upper leg	the leg and raised it up
and placed it before Saul,	and placed it before Saul,	and placed [it before Saul,	and placed it before Saul,
and Saul ate			
and Samuel said,	and Samuel said to Saul,	and said,	and said,
"Note what is left;	"Note what is left;	"Note what is left;	"Note what is left;
place it in front of you;	place it in front of you;	place it in front of you;	place it in front of you;
and eat	and eat	eat	eat
because	because	because it is	because
for	for	for	for
a testimony	a testimony	the festival]	the festival
it is placed for you;	it is placed for you;	place it for yourself,"	it is kept for you,"
		saying,	saying,

beyond the others pluck it."	beyond the others snip it."		"The people I have called."
And Saul ate with Samuel on that day.	And Saul ate with Samuel on that day.		And Saul ate[a] with Samuel on that day.

25 And [they] *he* went down from the high place to the town,
and *they spread for*[a] [he spoke with] Saul on the roof.
26 And *he slept* [they rose early]
and it came to be
as the day star was rising,
and Samuel called Saul to the roof, saying,
"Come up
and I will send you off."
And Saul went up,
and the two of them went out, he and Samuel, outside.
27 They were going down to the edge of the town,
and Samuel said to Saul,
"Say to your lad
that he should pass on before us,"
[and he passed on,]
"and you stand still right now
and [I will let you] hear the word of God."

6a. In Samuel–Kings, *hnh* strengthened by *nʾ* is often found in a broadly prophetic context—1 Sam 9:6; 16:15; 2 Sam 13:24; 14:21; 1 Kgs 20:31; 22:13 (the parallel in 2 Chr 18 uses only *hnh*); 2 Kgs 2:16, 19; 4:9; 5:15; 6:1. The expression is found also in Judg 13:3; 19:9; and in Genesis (8x); Job (4x); but apparently never in the books of the Latter Prophets.

b. Here DJD 59 conjectures the similar *ʾlyw* (to him) before *ʾwly* (perhaps).

7a. The MT is shorter than GT, but 4QSam[a] shorter than both: *whnh* follows immediately on *šʾwl*.

12a. Here *dia tēn hēmeran* (G) renders *khywm*, as in v. 13.

13a. Normally *khywm* is construed with *hzh*, and rendered "as at this day" (Gen 39:11; Deut 6:24; Jer 44:22; Ezra 9:7, 15; Neh 9:10). It is alone as here in Neh 5:11.

16a. The GT attests *ʿny* before *ʿmy*.

17a. If GT has the sense of MT, then *ʿṣr b-* had a unique sense in this passage (and in 10:1, from which it was accidentally omitted). If, however, *ʿṣr b-* is used as in Job 4:2; 12:15; 29:9, then it could point forward to Saul's hiding himself (10:21–23). Then GT's *arxei*, if the translator's guess, may be influenced by the sound of *yʿṣr*.

18a. The GT attests not *hšʿr* but *hʿyr*. The first two letters are not preserved in 4QSam[a], and the third only partially. In deciding between . . . *ʿr* and . . . *yr*, DJD 61 reports that under magnification the traces of the penultimate letter conform better to GT's *y* than to MT's *ʿ*.

19a. Here "the seer" renders MT's *hr'h*; GT's "he" renders *hw'*, of which 4QSam[a] preserves the final -'.

b. Here *w'kltm*—sg. in GT, as in the whole context.

21a. It is not clear how far B and LT are rendering freely, and how far their text differs from MT (4QSam[a] is not extant here).

23a. Here GT = MT; but 4QSam[a] reads *kdbr* before *'šr*.

24a. In this verse, MT, 4QSam[a], B, and OL all differ. Trebolle Barrera argues (65–66) that the OL's doubling "and Saul ate" points to the secondary nature of the material in between: the insert itself provides two distinct explanations, the first introduced by "note" (*hnh*) and the second by "because" (*ky*). It appears that 4QSam[a] attests both [*ś*]*ym lk* ("place for you") like GT for *šmwr lk* ("kept for you") in MT, and MT's "saying" after it. If *mw'd* is original, then GT has had difficulty with translating it here as elsewhere.

25a. The GT may attest *rbd* (cf. only Prov 7:16), rather than *dbr* (MT).

[1–2] The story of Saul and the lost asses begins like a folktale. No time and no national background is suggested. Location is provided instead by a reasonably extended genealogy within the people and area of Benjamin. The culmination of this family line, the characters in the story to be told, are a father, who is more than simply a man of substance; and his son, who is not merely "choice and good" but better than any other son of Israel and taller than all the people.

Kish is portrayed as more than the current representative of his family line: *ḥāyil* encompasses both power and wealth. To be a powerful and wealthy man (*'îš ḥāyil*) is remarkable enough; but Saul's father is *gibbôr ḥāyil*: a powerful and wealthy hero. He will have championed the family's interests. And his son is set fair to follow him: *bāḥûr* is the first thing said of him, and it resonates in different ways. First of all, the word has two different senses: it can mean either "young man" or "chosen." The distinction between the two is "not always certain" (*DCH* 2:134); and that uncertainty is played on here. Saul as "a young man and a good one" would be expected to "practice warfare" (1 Kgs 12:21//2 Chr 11:1) and so be ready to follow in the military steps of his father. Saul as "chosen and good" looks forward, not backward; for the narrator goes on to offer one comparison and suggest another: he is not only good, but better than other sons of Israel; he is not only choice, but notable as such within a chosen people of Israel. When David is produced before Samuel (1 Sam 16:12), he is described as "good-looking." In Saul's case, though we are asked to remark on his height, what is good about him is not restricted to his appearance.[2]

There are several such notes in Samuel on the personal appearance of characters: Eliab (1 Sam 16:6–7); David (16:12; 17:42); Abigail (25:3); Tamar I (2 Sam 13:1); Absalom (14:25, 26); Tamar II (14:27); and an Egyptian (23:21). Indeed, if we add Abishag (1 Kgs 1:3, 4) and Adonijah (1:6), from the closely related opening of Kings, there are around as many such references in Samuel

2. Compare Kaminsky, esp. 462–64.

(broadly defined) as in all the rest of HB together: Sarai, Rachel, and Joseph (Gen 12:11, 14; 29:17; 39:6); Moses (Exod 2:2); Esther (Esth 2:2, 3, 7); Job's daughters (Job 42:15); the Shullamite (Song 1:5, 15, 16; 4:1, 7; 6:4); and Daniel and his three colleagues (Dan 1:4). Rezetko (46) notes that only Saul and Absalom among these are described as the most handsome "in all Israel'; and it is only their descriptions that focus on their shoulders upward. It might also be suggested, on the basis of the listings above, that such interest in striking appearance is a feature of later HB texts.

All of these comments are appropriate and are part of reading the opening of 1 Sam 9 as a new beginning; and so it may once have been. But the description of Saul as *bāḥûr wāṭôb* (v. 2) also has a backward reference in 1 Samuel as we know it. "Good" is not a much-used word in Samuel; so its three occurrences in this chapter stand out. But it is also used twice in the immediately previous warning over the malign implications of having a king: he will take from you your "good fields and orchards and olives" (8:14)—and even more strikingly "your young folks—the good ones" (8:16).[3] As for "choice," of good quality, that ambiguous term neatly and awkwardly reminds us that the house of now-rejected Eli had once been "chosen" by Yahweh (2:28). And of course Saul's very name reminds us that Samuel has been "asked for" by his mother.

[3] The straying of the family asses may not have been an everyday event, but in itself it is an unremarkable matter. What seems more noteworthy, after the narrator's hyperbolic introduction, is what we can glean from the scenes that follow about Saul's character or experience. He is sent off by his father and told to take with him "one from the lads" (deliberately translated quite literally because of the unhelpful and somewhat pejorative English overtones of "one of the lads"): *naʿar* is a term of status rather than age. It is used throughout the narrative books of HB, but much more densely in the books of Samuel than in any other, yet never in BTH. However young or old this servant is, he is not specifically assigned to him by his father, but is simply one of the retainers to be chosen by Saul. We shall find "one from the lads" recurring in the books of Samuel (1 Sam 9:3; 16:18; 25:14; 26:22; 2 Sam 1:15; 2:21): and the phrase is found nowhere else in HB. The final element in Saul's father's instructions is also the first instance in the book of Samuel of one of its most characteristic verbs: "seek" (*bqš*).[4] Though used throughout the HB, we find it as often in Samuel alone as in all the rest of Genesis to Kings together.

[4–8] Our estimate of Saul is complicated by variation between our texts. In MT, it is Saul in the singular who is sent to look for the asses; it is "he" who

3. In MT at least—GT has "cattle."

4. The instructions given by Kish (*qyš*) start with monosyllables opening with the same letter: "take" (*qḥ*) and "be up" (*qwm*), and conclude with this significant verb, which is also assonant with *qyš*.

passes through various areas in search of them;[5] however, it is "they" who are twice reported as not finding them. In MT, Saul does the leading, but the servant is implicated in the lack of success. The Greek tradition is (surprisingly) uniform in reading plural forms throughout: once recruited, the "lad" receives the father's instructions with the son, and it is a joint expedition that follows. Whichever of these texts has been more original in vv. 3b–4, once they come into Zuph, the fifth specified area, Saul proposes returning home, concerned—or using as his excuse—that his father will now be more worried about their loss than about his lost asses; and his "lad" counters his proposal with local knowledge about a "man of God" (vv. 5–6). Saul again provides a reason—or excuse—for not doing this: nothing to offer the man of God (v. 7); but his companion again trumps him with a piece of silver in his hand (8); and Saul now confirms (10) that what the lad has said is "good." The silver quarter-shekel produced as appropriate payment almost certainly fixes the date of the story in the Persian or Hellenistic period.

[9–10] Yet, before Saul's confirmation, there is a pause (v. 9), seemingly occasioned by the humor in what Saul has just said (7): "What 'shall-we-bring' (*nābîʾ*) to the man; . . . there's nothing 'to-bring' (*lĕhābîʾ*) to the man of God." In Hebrew, the word "shall-we-bring" looks and sounds exactly the same as the common word "prophet" (*nābîʾ*). Corresponding wordplay in English would be "the prophet is in it for profit" or "the prophet motive." "Prophet" means "We shall bring": we cannot consult one empty-handed. There has been a great deal of discussion of this explanation (v. 9), which is often seen as being "out of place" in one sense or another: whether simply at the wrong position within the chapter, or whether altogether secondary and not from the original narrator. Whether original and correctly placed or not, what is certain about this note is that it is quite as allusive as Saul's jest. The old phrase "go to the man of God" has never been used in so many words, but it has been lying just under the surface of each of the three previous verses (6–8). Now it has disappeared in two directions. The whole phrase has become "go to consult God" (v. 9); and the intermediary himself is now called not "man of God" but "seer"—or (the term that started this whole detour by being just hinted at) "prophet." It is hard to deny that this note would be more logically placed after v. 11 rather than after v. 8: the divine intermediary is still "the man of God" in v. 10, and it is only as they ask directions of the women coming to draw water that they first speak of him as "the seer." But it can also be accurately claimed that v. 9 is just halfway between the two terms, *nābîʾ* and "seer," whose relationship it explains. And it is also true that, within 1 Sam 9–16, it is only in ch. 9 that any of these titles (man of God, seer, prophet) is applied to Samuel; he is not named as the man in question until 9:14. We should read 1 Sam 9 as making sense without what now goes before it in chs. 1–8.

5. The MT has "they" at the beginning of 4b.

We find the combination "formerly in Israel" only once more in HB, where it marks another interesting link between the early chapters of 1 Samuel and the book of Ruth (4:7). "Formerly" on its own is, hardly surprisingly, given its meaning as a mark of later biblical literature. It is found in some clusters, in late books or later additions to books: 3x in Deut 2 (10, 12, 20); 3x in Joshua (11:10; 14:15; 15:15); 3x in Judg 1 (10, 11, 23) and 1x in 3:2; in Neh 13:5; and 3x in Chronicles (1 Chr 4:40; 9:20; and 2 Chr 9:11).[6] In the last of these passages, Chronicles reads the more distant "formerly," while the parallel passage in 1 Kgs 10:12 has "to this day." But this is its only occurrence in the books of Samuel.

[11–14] It is only on a second reading of Samuel–Kings that we can possibly become aware that this second scene marks the start of an interesting pattern. There are three accounts of failed royal investitures close to the beginnings of kingship in Israel. Saul, Absalom (2 Sam 15), and Adonijah (1 Kgs 1) all become king in the context of a large ceremonial meal, following a sacrifice to which guests have been invited. The only "guests" (*qĕruʾîm*) who appear anywhere in Samuel–Kings are those invited to precisely these three occasions. When Adonijah takes all but one of his brothers and almost all of Jerusalem's leading figures to En-rogel (1 Kgs 1:9–10), they may well have known what they were about. By contrast, those whom Absalom brings in a tryst to Hebron for his celebratory sacrifice go with him in all innocence (2 Sam 15:11). And those waiting for Samuel to bless the sacrifice may never even have come to know that Samuel is to anoint Saul secretly next morning (10:1). And yet the alert reader of the whole royal narrative can hardly miss the narrator's warning. Guests mentioned alongside sacrifice and banquet: a reign that starts like this is bound to fail.

Adonijah and Absalom organize their own investitures as king; Absalom's guests are unaware why they have been invited to Hebron. But in Saul's case, even he is taken unawares—and Samuel is given only one day's notice of what he should do. The narrator describes his tip-off from Yahweh (v. 15) in very significant language. It is drawn from BTH, where David claims to have been notified of Yahweh's decision to build a house[hold] for him (2 Sam 7:27); and it is more loosely adumbrated in the report of the vision of the young Samuel himself (1 Sam 3:7, 21). The divine speech too (v. 16) uses further terms from the same context. The report in BTH of David's beginnings as king of Israel also uses "anoint" (2 Sam 5:3); "leader" (5:2; 7:8); and "my people" (5:2; 7:7). David's first "external" campaign too is against the Philistines (in 2 Sam 5 [BTH], and also in 1 Sam 17).

[15–17] One significant element of the divine advice to Samuel is not drawn from BTH. Yahweh highlights to Samuel what the narrator has foregrounded for

6. The only other relevant references are Ps 102:25 (26) and Job 42:11; in Jer 7:24 and Job 17:6, *lpnym* means spatially "in front," not temporally "before."

his readers (9:1), that the man in question is from Benjamin. In fact "the land of Benjamin" occurs in the books of Samuel only at beginning and very end (2 Sam 21:14) of the story of Saul. The phrase itself is commonest in the book of Jeremiah; and we have seen that that book has several links with Samuel. Jeremiah also comes from a town in Benjamin (Jer 1:1) and has property there (32:8; 37:12). And "the land of Benjamin" is one of several districts of which a greater Judah is composed, and to which future livelihood is promised in Jer 17:26; 32:44; 33:13. People in postexilic Yehud who were familiar with the book of Jeremiah and turned to the books of Samuel would not have thought of Saul as coming from a people or land different from David, only from a different part of it.

Seeing and hearing have equal prominence at the head of this section. Yahweh has uncovered the ear of Samuel, because he (Yahweh) has "seen" his people, whose cry has come to him. We are immediately told that Samuel "saw" Saul, and Yahweh "answered" him. Here at least, Yahweh's and Samuel's eyes and ears are focused on the same things. Their senses are as one.

What follows is a linguistic puzzle. "This one will 'rule' in my people" (GT) gives the expected conclusion. And yet the basic and commonest sense of *ʿṣr* appears to be "restrain/hold back." Since the related *ʿṣrt* is used of an "assembly," the verb may mean "muster (the troops)." "The people" provide an important but flexible backdrop throughout this whole introduction of Saul (and Samuel). Saul is taller (v. 2) than all the people (than anyone in Israel). The people (around Zuph) have a *zebaḥ* (sacrifice) *hayyôm* (today) at the high place (v. 12). The people (around Zuph? anywhere?) will not eat till the seer blesses the *zebaḥ* (v. 13). "The people (invited) have I called" (v. 24). Interest in the people as Yahweh's is at its most concentrated in vv. 16–17: "You will anoint him . . . over my people, . . . and he will save my people; . . . for I have seen my people, . . . and this one will muster among my people." Mention of "the people" in all of vv. 12, 13, and 24 (MT at least), encourages us to recognize *zebaḥ hayyôm* (v. 12), *zebaḥ* (v. 13), and *mwʿd* (v. 24) as three expressions for one and the same festival sacrifice (see further on 13:11 below).

[18–20] Samuel's words (in v. 19) confirm that Saul's installation is being presented in Davidic phrases: apart from 1 Sam 14:7 (later in the Saul narrative), "all that is in your heart" occurs in all the rest of HB only in 2 Sam 7:3 (BTH). The words are the same; and yet it is not entirely clear what they mean here. Nathan gives David carte blanche, promising that Yahweh is with him; Jonathan's armor-bearer gives him carte blanche, promising that he will be with him whatever he does. However, here it is not a matter of Saul's "doing" anything, but rather of Saul's "being informed." Equally it is not a simple matter of being told what is at the top of his mind, what is his main concern of the moment; for Samuel tells Saul immediately that his father's asses have been found, and he goes on to foreshadow (v. 20) the declaration he has promised for the next day. "The desire of Israel" is a unique phrase. The related verb *ḥmd* is used negatively at the end of the Ten Commandments, and precisely with "house" as its object. Samuel informs—or warns—Saul that there is one house that all Israel "covets" or "desires." He does not add the words "to supply them with a king"; but it is clear that Saul has understood at least part of what he has been told. In his reply, he replaces Samuel's expression "father's house" (i.e., extended family) not just by clan but also by the ambiguous term that encompasses both "tribe" and "scepter."

[21] David and Jonathan are given encouragement to do as they wish. However, it appears that Saul has to have his deepest wishes explained for him. It seems that there has been a further dimension to the earlier words of his servant lad (v. 6), that the man of God will tell them their path on which they have been walking. Saul now understands enough to protest that he is from the most junior family of the smallest tribe in Israel (v. 21). He accepts in his self-description the Benjamite label the narrator had already attached to him (vv. 1, 4).

[22–27] By the following morning (v. 27b), what Samuel is to "let Saul hear" is not simply his own innermost thoughts but a divine word (and "word of God," not here "word of Yahweh," may anticipate the original wording of 2 Sam 7:4 and of BTH, cf. 1 Chron 17:3 with 2 Sam 7:4). There appear to be only two parallels to the other element in this phrase: only Deut 4:10 and Jer 18:2 present Yahweh as "let[ting] you hear my words."

1 Samuel 10:1–16

1 And Samuel took the flask[a] of oil
and poured it on his head
and kissed him.
And he said,
"Has not Yahweh surely anointed you
as leader over his people, over Israel? | over his holding, as leader?
And you will rule within the people of Yahweh,
and it is you will save it from the hand of its enemies round about.
2 *And this is the sign for you*
that Yahweh has anointed you over his inheritance as leader:[a]
When you walk today from me,
you will find two men by the tomb*s* of Rachel
in the [territory] *hill country* of Benjamin [at Zelzah[b]] *leaping greatly*;
and they will say to you,
"The asses
which you went to look for
have been found.
And look: your father has abandoned the "word[s]" of the asses

and has worried for you, saying,
'What shall I do for my son?'"
3 And you shall move from there and beyond,[a]
and you shall come to the oak of Tabor[b]
and three men will find you there
going up to the God at Bethel:
one carrying three goats,
and one carrying three rounds of bread,
and one carrying a skin of wine.
4 And they shall ask for peace for you
and will give you two[a] loaves,
and you will take it from their hand.
5 After that you will come to the Hill of the God
where the Philistine post[s are] is[a];
and may it be
as you come there to the town,
you encounter a "line"[b] of prophets
coming down from the high place—
and in front of them a zither and a tambourine and a flute and a lyre,
and themselves acting the prophet.
6 And the spirit of Yahweh settle on you
and you act the prophet with them,
and you be turned into another man.
7 And it shall come to be,
when these signs come to you,
do [yourself][a]
what comes to your hand,
for the Deity is with you.
8 And you will go down before [me to Gilgal] *Gilead*—
and look: I am coming down to you
to offer up holocausts and *shĕlāmîm*-sacrifices.
Seven days shall you wait
till I come to you,
and I shall tell you
what you will do."
9 And it came to be
as he turned his shoulder to go[a] from Samuel,
and the [a] God turned over to him another heart,
and all these signs came in that day.

10 And they came *from* there to Gibeah,
and there was in fact a "line" of prophets

to meet him,
and a divine spirit leaped on him,
and he acted the prophet among them.
11 And there was everyone who knew him from former days
and they saw,
and there he was [with] the prophets [acting the prophet[a]];
and the people said, each to his fellow,
"Whatever has happened to the son of Kish?
Is Saul too of the prophets?"
12 And a man answered from there,
"And who is *his* [their] father?"[a]
Accordingly it became a saying,[b]
"Is Saul too of the prophets?"
13 And he stopped acting the prophet
and he came to the high place.
14 And Saul's kinsman said to him and to his lad,
"Where did you go?"
And [he] *they* said,
"To look for the asses,
and we saw
that they were not there,
and we came[a] to Samuel."
15 And the kinsman [of Saul] said *to Saul*,
"Pray tell me
what Samuel said to you."[a]
16 And Saul said to his kinsman,
"What he in fact related to *me* [us] was
that the asses had been found"—
but the talk of the kingship he did not relate to him[,
what Samuel had said.[a]]

1a. The term *pak* is used again in HB only in 2 Kgs 9:1, 3 (the anointing of Jehu). The GT's *phakos* may have been selected for assonance.

1–2a. A classic instance of major textual loss from MT, where the eye of a scribe has jumped from *mšyḥ yhwh* (v. 1) to *mšyḥ yhwh* (v. 2). DJD presents no fragments between 9:24 and 10:3; Fincke, however, finds no place for this material in his reconstruction of 4QSam[a].

2b. The term *ṣlṣḥ* (MT) is otherwise unknown. GT retroverts to *ṣlḥym m'd*. LT adds *mesēmbrias* after "Beniamin": Driver reads LT's "noon" as an interpretation of *bṣl ṣḥ* (yet "in bright shadow" seems a contradiction in terms); a more literal retroversion would yield *bṣhrym*, which may provide independent testimony to the cluster of Hebrew consonants that yielded *allomenous* (*ṣlḥym*). (Is there a connection with B's Selcha in 9:4?)

3a. The phrase "and beyond" (*whlʾh*) is used within FP only in 1 Samuel (10:3; 18:9; 20:22, 37).

b. Here *tēs eklektēs* (LT) retroverts to *bāḥûr* for *tābôr* (MT and B).

4a. For *šty* before *lḥm* (MT), *aparchas* (LT) may attest *rʾšyt* or *trwmt* or *tnwpt*; 4QSam[a] reads . . . *wpwt lḥm*; and B has the numeral *dyo* before *aparchas*.

5a. Both B and LT conflate the translation and transliteration of *nṣyb plštym*; MT has pl. *nṣby*.

b. The GT's *choros* normally renders a nominal form from *ḥwl*. Nowhere else does *ḥbl* refer to a "line" of men: its metaphorical usage is normally for a piece of territory, measured by line.

7a. The GT does not represent a second *lk* after *ʿśh*.

9a. The idiom *hpk X l-Y* normally means to turn *X* into *Y*, such as dawn into dusk or the Nile into blood.

11a. Here 4QSam[a] reads *hitpaʿel*, not *nipʿal*: [*nbyʾ*]*ym mt*[*nbʾ*].

12a. Like MT here, 4QSam[a] reads "their father."

b. Often *mšl* is not a compliment, as in its only use in BTH: "a saying and a byword" (1 Kgs 9:7).

14a. Here 4QSam[a] has the (apparently) cohortative form *wnbwʾh*.

15a. The pronoun "you" is pl. in MT, but sg. in GT.

16a. With MT here, 4QSam[a] does read *ʾšr ʾmr* at end.

[1–9] If sacrifice, banquet, and guests put Saul into the unpropitious company of Absalom and Adonijah, being anointed from a vial (*pak*) of oil has Saul anticipate one of the revolutionary kings of the future northern Israel: Jehu (2 Kgs 9:1, 3). By contrast, it will be from a horn (*qeren*) that David (1 Sam 16:1, 13) and Solomon (1 Kgs 1:39) will both be anointed. Where the older BTH reported the anointing of David (2 Sam 5:3, 17), Jehu (2 Chr 22:7), and Jehoash (2 Kgs 11:12), it made no mention of what contained the oil: that refinement was imported by later authors of Samuel–Kings. Kissing is also unknown to BTH.[7] In Samuel–Kings it is the senior who kisses the junior party (Samuel here; David in 2 Sam 14:33; 19:39 [40]; Absalom in 2 Sam 15:5; and presumably Joab also in 2 Sam 20:9, as he approaches Amasa to kill him). And, in the only possible exception, David and Jonathan kiss in a context that emphasizes mutuality (1 Sam 20:41).

The much longer GT text in 10:1–2 includes (virtual) repetition of content from 9:16: "as leader over his people, over Israel." If the shorter text of MT ("over his holding, as leader") is more original, the modified repetition is an example of recapitulation after an insert. If the longer text is more original, then a copyist's eye has jumped from one instance of "Yahweh has anointed you" to the next. Apart from what is repeated, the longer text has three additional elements. "You will rule within the people of Yahweh" and "You will save [my

7. It is found 11x in Genesis, 8x in Samuel–Kings, and 13x in the rest of HB.

people] from the hand of its enemies round about" are both developments of what Yahweh has said to Samuel (9:17). The "enemies round about" is a theme shared with 12:11 and 14:47. "This is the sign for you" does commonly introduce signs; and the use of the singular in this promise, when in fact three signs follow, does have a ring of authenticity. Whether reported once (MT) or twice (GT), one of the most interesting elements of these opening verses is Samuel's statement that it is Yahweh who has anointed Saul. Yahweh has asked Samuel to anoint him. Has any distinction between Yahweh and his trusted intermediary been elided? Or are Samuel and Yahweh both trying to shift the responsibility to the other for anointing Saul as king? What Yahweh's "holding" means is discussed below (on 2 Sam 20:1).

The (first) sign promised by Samuel confirms quite literally the expectation of Saul's "lad," that the man of God will tell them the way on which they have been "walking" (9:6): as they "walk" on from him, the two men they meet will tell them that the asses they have "walked" to look for are found; and they will confirm Saul's expectation at an earlier stage of their walk, that his father will now be more worried about his son than his asses. The coming to pass of the next sign, of simple provision for life (vv. 3–4), is not separately reported; we are simply told (v. 9) that all these signs "came." The third sign, however, the meeting with the prophets, is quite fully reported (vv. 10–14).

Yet, before that happens, the final words of Samuel's speech to Saul (vv. 7–8) give the reader pause. If we consider all the words "Do what comes to your hand, for the Deity is with you" (v. 7) as a single unit, then they are at least limited, if not actually subverted, by the following "Go down before me to Gilgal . . . and wait, . . . and I shall tell you what you will do" (v. 8). Is Saul really offered the freedom to do what seems right to him to do, once he has been empowered by the divine spirit? Or despite whatever experience he might have of the divine spirit, is he to remain subject to Samuel's guidance? Perhaps we should see a difference between doing "what is on your heart" and doing "what your hand finds": the first allows independence of aim, but the second permits only choice of means. The king will have some choice over how things are done, depending on what his hand finds at the time; but the prophet will generally be around to make the overarching divine will plain. And is it general guidance that is in mind, or specific instructions about the conduct of the various sacrifices?

There is also ambiguity in what Samuel says (v. 8). An alternative punctuation makes this clear: "And you will go down before me to Gilgal (and note that I am going down to you), to offer up . . ." Putting this reading of Samuel's instruction together with what the young women have told him earlier (9:13), Saul could suppose that he will be responsible for offering the sacrifices, and Samuel for the blessing, without which those present would not take part in the associated feast (see further on 13:11 below).

[10–16] The encounter between Saul and the prophets is promised for "Gibeah of the Deity" (v. 5): possibly a location different from "Gibeah of Saul" and possibly the place we know also as "Gibeon," at whose great *bāmâ* Solomon would have his first vision (1 Kgs 3:3–15, BTH). This portion of 1 Samuel is remarkable for using "God" or "the Deity" in several expressions where Yahweh is more common, and all the remarkable because MT and GT agree on the reading in every case—and also 4QSam[a], in the two relevant readings preserved (vv. 9 and 10): "word of God" (9:27); "Gibeah of God" (10:5); "for God is with you" (10:7); "God turned him another heart" (10:9); and "the spirit of God" (10:10). I have argued (1994: 144–46) that expressions in Judges and Samuel like "ark of God" and "inquire of God" may be more original than the standardized "ark of Yahweh" and "inquire of Yahweh."

It is not said explicitly in so many words, but it is suggested that there is a musical component in Saul's new companions' "acting the prophet." Everyone who has known him for some time is surprised at what they now see: Saul's being caught up among the prophets. The way in which this is described breaks a pattern that we shall find established several times in the books of Samuel, with "know" and "see" closely linked. Here they have already known something—or better, someone—for a long time, but what they now see is different from what they have long known. Can they believe what they are seeing? Do they have to make a reassessment?

What has happened to Kish's son? Is he now among the prophets? Has he now joined the prophets? Someone answers this question with a question (v. 12), and it is over the exact terms of this question that the tradition divides. The MT has him ask, "Who is *their* father?" "They" indicates the prophets; but what is the intended answer? Does the question imply that people do not know who is in control of such a band? Or does it simply hint that Samuel (or God) is their patron? If so, then in the light of Yahweh's putting on seventy elders some of the spirit that had previously rested only on Moses (Num 11:16–17),[8] we shall suppose that this patronage is being extended to Saul. The question in GT ("Who is *his* father?") is no less tricky. Saul has just been called "son of Kish" (v. 11), and so the question may be a slighting one—like father, like son, both insignificant; yet the point of the question may also be to suggest that it is no longer his biological father that has power over Saul now. When Saul stops "prophesying," he continues on to the "high place," which the prophets have just left.

At the high place, he meets not his father but his uncle. The uncle asks not just Saul where they have walked, but the servant too. Saul's answer ("We saw . . . and we came to Samuel") plays with words with whose double meanings we

8. Later in the same scene (11:24–25), the elders who have received some of the divine spirit are said to "prophesy," just as Saul does here (10:10).

are already familiar from 9:7, 9, 11. Samuel is the "seer" (9:9, 11); then "and we came" (*wnbw*ʾ) is just one letter different from "and we brought" (*wnby*ʾ)—and these two letters are often confused. Whether or not the uncle is similarly aware of the double meanings, he wants to know what Samuel has said. And now Saul is content to prevaricate with a half-truth: he makes no mention of kingship. It is not enough to ask what connection is being stated between prophecy and kingship. We need to know the relationship between Samuel, Saul, and the prophets; and the textual tradition divides at a significant point.

We have to ask how far the one narrative in BTH, which tells of a king of Israel and a large group of prophets (1 Kgs 22), bears on the interpretation of this story. If the manner of Saul's anointing anticipates that of Jehu (see above on 10:1), perhaps he is being ranged here along with Ahab also. Perhaps the relationship between Micaiah and the four hundred prophets impinges on how we should understand Samuel and this band of prophets. First Kings 22 appears to share with most of the material in the book of Jeremiah a low estimate of prophets in the plural, even where these are prophets of Yahweh. Second Kings 2–10 takes a more benign view of the prophetic groups with which Elisha is associated. At what point within such a spectrum in the books of Kings does our story belong? It gives the appearance of being one element in a positive start to Saul's kingship. It is the third in a triad of signs, and the first two have been benign. It is Yahweh's spirit that is to come on Saul (v. 6), and not simply any divine force; and talk of being turned into another man is immediately followed by the assurance that the Deity is with him (v. 7). It is not a matter of Dr. Jekyll turning into the sinister Mr. Hyde. The first two signs have served to reassure Saul about Samuel's credentials. The third appears to be more than just the culmination of the series: it also effects a change in Saul. In the story of Micaiah (1 Kgs 22), a spirit from the divine court empowers him for a successful (lying) mission. Here, although Saul's experience within the prophetic group is similarly temporary, the change this brought him lasts longer. We should reconsider his encounter afterward with his uncle. Is it obvious to someone who has known him that something important has happened to Saul? If "Where did you go?" and "What did Samuel say to you?" are framed as more polite alternatives to "What has happened to you?" Saul is not prepared to give anything away.

None of these suggestions has included attention to the fact that Samuel advises Saul that he will meet the prophets close to a Philistine post. It may be that the behavior of Saul with the prophets that puzzles us is also intended to mislead the garrison: to suggest that Philistines have nothing to fear from the local young man, Saul—if any change has come over him, it is simply that he has become another mad prophet. We should recall that when David later comes under suspicion in Philistine Gath, he will pass himself off as mad (1 Sam 21:12–15).

1 Samuel 10:17–24 Saul Chosen by Lot before Samuel

The CL and Aleppo Codex share a major break at 10:17.

1 Samuel 10:17–18a

17 And Samuel called out the people to Yahweh at Mizpah.
18a And he said to the sons[a] of Israel:

18a. Here 4QSam[a] reads not just *bny* (GT) but *kwl bn*[*y*]—"all the sons."

[17–18a] In Samuel's dealings with Saul, he has anointed a surprised young man as king on Yahweh's behalf, and he has promised him a prophetic experience that has transmitted to him life-changing divine spirit. As he now convokes a popular assembly in neighboring Mizpah, he changes tack and crossly blames the people for rejecting the God who has successfully led them, and for requiring that a king be set over them.

1 Samuel 10:18b–24

18b "This is what Yahweh, God of Israel, has said:
'I for my part brought up *the sons of* Israel from Egypt,
and I saved you from the hand of *Pharaoh king of* Egypt
and from [the hand of] all the king[dom]s
that were oppressing you.
19 And you on your side today have rejected your God,
who himself is your savior from all your distresses and hardships,
and you have said [to him],
"*No.* A king you must set over us."
Now then take your positions before Yahweh by your staffs
and by your [thousands] tribes.'"[a]
20 And Samuel brought near all the staffs of Israel,
and the staff of Benjamin was taken.
21 And he brought near the staff of Benjamin by its families,[a]
and the family of the Matrites was taken,
and they brought near the family of the Matrites by individuals,
and Saul son of Kish was taken;
and *he* [they[b]] looked for him
and he was not found.
22 And [they] *Samuel* asked further of Yahweh,
"Did [one more] *the* man come here?"
And Yahweh said,

"Look—he is hidden by the implements."
23 And [they] *he* ran
and took him from there,
and he took his position among the people,
and he was higher than all the people from his shoulder and upward.
24 And Samuel said to all the people,
"Have you seen
whom Yahweh has chosen *for* himself,[a]
for there is no one like him in all *of you*[b] [the people]?"
And all the people *knew it*[c] [shouted]
and said,
"Life to the king."

19a. Here *phylas* (B) looks like a second rendering of *šbṭym*; it also shares letters with *ʾlpym*.

21a. Again B uses *phylē* for the noun following *šbṭ*, in this case *mšpḥh*.

b. Earlier in this verse there was a shift from Samuel to an impersonal "they" as the subj. of the actions. The MT continues with "they," while GT ("he") apparently returns to Samuel.

24a. Here GT has read *lw*, not *bw* (MT).

b. The GT attests not *bkl-hʿm* (MT) but *bklkm*.

c. Here GT attests not *wyrʿw* but *wydʿw*.

[18b–24] This fourth recollection in 1 Samuel of the "exodus" theme (v. 18) is at the same time an ironic anticipation of the scene at Mizpah, following the fall of Jerusalem and the deportation of many of the leaders to Babylon. On that occasion, a group of Judeans decides to go in the opposite direction, precisely to Egypt, for fear of the Chaldeans (2 Kgs 25:22–26; the story is told at greater length in Jer 40–44).

The call to present themselves before Yahweh (v. 19) is preparatory to identifying the new king by lot. We should at least notice that the same procedure is used to identify Jonathan in 1 Sam 14 as a culprit (and Achan in Josh 7)! The precise process of selection, from all Israel, to Benjamin, to the Matrite family, to Saul, is unclear: Saul was "taken" without being physically there: he had gone off to hide. Reluctance is often seen as one of the qualifications for office; but we are given no indication whether Saul's hiding himself is demonstrating commendable modesty or a flaw in character. Be that as it may, once he is found and collected, he "takes his position" (v. 23) among the people: the same verb was used of the people before Yahweh (v. 19).

Many scholars have long read this story as an account quite distinct from what we have read in 9:1–10:16 of Saul's beginnings as king. But in the narrative of 1 Samuel as it stands, the Saul who hides away as the process unfolds is a Saul who has already been anointed (even if in secret), has already been granted a series of confirmatory signs, and has already been empowered by the divine spirit. Gideon, in Judg 6–7, presents a picture of similar reluctance despite all attempts at divine reassurance—see further on ch. 13 below. And, to add to the oddity, Saul has been able to crouch unseen among the implements or large storage pots despite being taller than all the people by a head. The people have wanted a king. In presenting Saul to the people (v. 24), Samuel the "seer" asks his people whether they have "seen" Yahweh's choice; and Saul is duly acclaimed. In the books of Samuel, it is only in connection with kings that Yahweh exercises "choice" (1 Sam 10:24; 16:8–10; 2 Sam 6:21). First Kings 8:16, 44, 48 and 2 Kgs 21:7 (all derived from BTH) talk of the divine choice of Jerusalem as well as of David. Just as their acclamation follows their perception of the situation, so the sight and sound of the Hebrew "and they whooped" (*wyrʿw*) echoes the sight and sound of "and they saw" (*wyrʾw*). In the alternative text attested in Greek, "and they knew" (*wydʿw*) after "and they saw" anticipates the close link between "know" and "see" often found in Samuel.[9] Samuel goes on to use an expression that will be used only once again in Samuel (1 Sam 21:9 [10]): "there is none like . . ." There David speaks of the sword of Goliath and seems to be offering a straightforward appraisal of (size and) quality. But Goliath's sword was also used to cut off his own head. What will Saul do to those who acquire him (as their king)?

1 Samuel 10:25–13:14 From Acclamation by the People to Rejection by Yahweh

1 Samuel 10:25–27

25 And Samuel stated to the people the judging of the king[ship],
and he wrote it in a document
and set it to rest before Yahweh;
and Samuel dispatched the whole people,
and it went each to his house.[a]
26 And Saul too went to his house, to Gibeah;
and with [him] *Saul* went the sons of the Force[a]
whose heart God touched.
27[a] But the worthless lads, they said,
"How will this one save us?"
And they scorned him
and they did not bring him an offering.
[And he was as a silent one.[b]]

25a. Here 4QSam[a] ends: "and they went each to his place."

9. See 1 Sam 12:17; 14:38; 24:11 (12); 25:17; 2 Sam 24:13; also 1 Kgs 20:7; 2 Kgs 5:7.

26a. Here 4QSam[a] like B has *bny* before *hḥyl.* Both MT and B are unusual: *hḥyl* does not normally refer on its own to the army; then, while the Gk. "son of power" is better known, "sons of powers" here is unique.

27a. In 4QSam[a] a space within the line is left between vv. 26 and 27.

b. For *kmḥryš* (MT) B attests *kmw ḥwdš*. The LT attests first MT and then B. The much more extensive text in 4QSam[a] reads *kmw ḥwdš* and is attested in B, but with an additional paragraph before it (see below)!

[25–27] Samuel now tells the people (not Saul) what is involved in kingship, writes it down, and places his record of his explanation "before Yahweh" (v. 25, just as in v. 19). Moses follows an analogous procedure (Deut 31:24–26): the completed *tôrâ* is written down and placed alongside the ark, which already contains the text of the covenant. Not just a record, but a solemn record; and if the analogy is at all complete, then Samuel's record too will be available as a witness against the people. If so, it is not spelled out: the witnesses whom Samuel will shortly invoke against his people are Yahweh and his anointed (12:5).

The people have acclaimed their new king; and yet it is Samuel who sends them all home—all, including Saul, who has clearly not yet taken command. And this narrative ends with a divided response to Saul: some follow him home, while others scoff. The distinction offered is focused on two groups of "sons': *bny hḥyl* and *bny blyʿl*. The "sons of Valor" (which renders what may have been the original text of v. 26) have had their hearts touched by God, and they attach themselves to Saul. But the "sons of Useless" (v. 27) do not hear, and in fact cannot have heard Samuel's words at the secret anointing—and might not have trusted them in any case: their reaction is to deny that "this fellow" can save them. The core of Saul's army is favorably contrasted here with the sort of ruffians who later gather round David at his base in the cave of Adullam (22:2). Some of the latter are *mry npš*; and we noticed already, in our discussion of Hannah, that the *bt-blyʿl* (1:16) and the *mrt npš* (1:10) are easily confused. That these rascals bring Saul no present suggests that the others have brought presents.

One group scorning Saul as he goes to his home, after the people have been dispatched following an important national event, anticipates an important moment in the older David story (BTH) and suggests a further contrast between Saul and David. Saul's daughter Michal scorns David as he dances before the ark when it is being brought into Jerusalem—only inwardly ("in her heart") in the shorter BTH (2 Sam 6:16), but then quite explicitly to David as he goes home to bless his house (6:20b, a plus in Samuel).

The transition between chs. 10 (after the word "offering" [*minḥâ*]) and 11 is achieved in remarkably different ways in the main textual traditions:

1. The MT's *wyhy kmḥryš*, "and he was as one holding silence," is read most naturally as the conclusion of ch. 10, and is in fact followed in MT by a major pause.

2. Then B attests *wyhy kmw ḥdš*, "and it was about a month," which makes a better introduction to ch. 11, as the paragraphing in B recognizes.

3. Typically conflate, LT attests first MT and then B.

4. In 4QSam[a] we see the most extensive text, occupying much of lines 5–8 of a more than usually substantial fragment. Here 4QSam[a] sets 10:27a (down to "offering") after a substantial space in the middle of line 3, so marking it as a short unit quite distinct from what precedes. Then v. 27a on lines 3–4 is followed by a line break, showing that v. 27a is also to be read as quite distinct from what follows. The line break is followed in turn by four lines of text; of these, three and a half are wholly additional to MT or GT, and the second half of line 8 contains the start of 11:1b (here with line numbers):

5. And Nahash, king of the sons of Ammon, he harried the sons of Gad and the sons of Reuben with force and he gouged out their every

6. right eye, and he made it a reproach upon Israel; and there was not left a man of the sons of Israel who were a[cross the Jordan]

7. of whom Nahash king of the sons of Ammon did not gouge out his every right eye, [but in fact] seven thousand men

And it was about a month, and Nashash the Ammonite went up and encamped against Jabesh.

8. [escaped from the hand of] the sons of Ammon and came to Jabesh of Gilead. And all the men of Jabesh said to Nahash . . .

The text of the scroll looks like the above. I have used small type to keep to the four lines of the original. The scribe made a mistake when writing line 8, and omitted a sentence after the 1st mention of Jabesh. Realizing the mistake, he made it good in small writing above the line. The Hebrew words that correspond to 11:1a in B ("And it was about a month, and Nahash the Ammonite went up and encamped against Jabesh") are inserted between the ends of lines 7 and 8 (that is, above the words corresponding to the beginning of 11:1b). However, the editors of DJD insist that this supralinear half-line between the first and second halves of line 8 is in the hand of the original scribe of 4QSam[a].[10] This short paragraph in 4QSam[a] is also part of Josephus's report, although there the elapse of a month is mentioned at the beginning and not the end of the relevant paragraph.

Although the "extra" paragraph has been adopted as "original" into the main text of the NRSV, it appears to me that the varied placing of the time reference (which is also part of the B text), before (in Josephus) and after (in 4QSam[a]), indicates that the "extra" material is a late addition to Samuel. Two other features tell against its originality, though not decisively: Nahash is twice "king of the sons of Ammon," while in 11:2 (like 11:1a) he is "the Ammonite"; and Gad and Reuben feature nowhere else in the books of Samuel.[11]

10. "In copying the text, the scribe committed haplography owing to homoioteleuton in line 9, his eye skipping from *ybš* to *ybyš*." (DJD 66)

11. Reuben never; and Gad only in 1 Sam 13:7 ("to the land of Gad and Gilead"). The order Gad and Reuben is found in very late texts such as Num 32.

1 Samuel 11:1–15

1 And *it was about a month*[a]
and Nahash *the Ammonite* went up
and camped against Jabesh-gilead;
and all the men of Jabesh said to Nahash the Ammonite,
"Make for us a covenant,
that we may serve you."
2 And Nahash the Ammonite said to them,
"In this {manner} I shall make for you *a covenant*:
in gouging out[a] your every right eye;
and I shall make [it] a reproach upon [all] Israel."
3 And the [elders] *men* of Jabesh said to him,
"Let us alone seven days
that we may send messengers in all the territory of Israel;
and
if no one is saving us
we shall come out to you."[a]
4 And the messengers came to Gibeah of Saul,
and they spoke the words in the ears of the people,
and all the people raised their voice and wept.
5 And Saul was to be seen coming after the [cattle] *morning*[a] from the field;
and Saul said,
"What's with the people
that they should weep?"
And they recounted to him the words of the [men] *sons* of Jabesh.
6 And a divine spirit leaped on Saul
at his hearing these words,
and his anger *at them* waxed very hot.
7 And he took [a yoke of] *two* cattle
and sundered[a] [it] *them*,
and dispatched into all the territory of Israel by hand of [the] messengers, saying,
"Whoever is not coming out after Saul and after Samuel—
thus shall be done to his cattle."
And the fear of Yahweh [fell] *came* on the people *Israel*,
and they [came out] *shouted* as one man.
8 And [he] *Abiezek* counted them in [Bezeq] *Bama*,
[and] *all* the men of Israel [were three] *six* hundred thousand,
and the men of Judah [thirty] *seventy*[a] thousand.
9 And he [they] said to the messengers
who were coming,

"Thus shall you say to the men of Jabesh [Gilead]:
'Tomorrow [there shall be] deliverance for you,[a] at the heat of the sun.'"
And the messengers came *to the city*
and reported to the men of Jabesh,
and they were glad.
10 And the men of Jabesh said *to Nahash the Ammonite*:
"Tomorrow we shall come out to you,
and you shall do for us
whatever is good in your eyes."

11 And it came to be on the morrow
and Saul set the people *into* three heads.
And they came into the midst of the camp at the dawn watch,
and they struck down *the sons of* Ammon till the heat of the day;
and [there were] those left over
[and they] scattered,
and there were not left of them two together.
12 And the people said to Samuel,
"Who is the one who is saying,
'[Is it] Saul will *not* be king over us[?]'?[a]
Produce the men
that we may put them to death."
13 And [Saul] *Samuel* said:
"Let not any man be put to death on this day,
because today Yahweh has achieved deliverance in Israel."

14 And Samuel said to the people,
"[Come and] let us go to Gilgal,
that we may make new there the kingship."
15 And all the people went to Gilgal;
and [they kinged Saul] *Samuel anointed Saul as king* there before Yahweh at Gilgal;
and they sacrificed there *shĕlāmîm and* sacrifices before Yahweh;
and [Saul] *Samuel* was happy[a] [there[b]] and all [the men of] Israel, exceedingly.[c]

1a. Here LT attests *ymym* after *ḥdš*.

2a. Judges 16:21 also uses *nqr* for the removal of Samson's eyes.

3a. "You" is pl. in GT, but sg. in MT.

5a. The same consonants *bqr* are differently read in MT and B. The LT reflects both readings.

7a. In Judg 19:29 *ntḥ* is used for dismembering the concubine's body, and likewise for sacrificial victims in 1 Kgs 18.

8a. Here GT's higher total of 70,000 is supported by 4QSam[a].

9a. The message to Jabesh-gilead is differently reported:

MT:	*mḥr thyh-lkm tšwʿh*
B:	*mḥr lkm htšwʿh*
LT:	*mḥr lkm thyh htšwʿh*
4QSam[a]:	*myhwh htš*

DJD invites us to note the graphic similarity in Hebrew of *myhwh* and *thyh*, and proposes that the addition of *myhwh* here anticipates *yhwh tšwʿh* in v. 13.

12a. The question as rendered above is not marked in MT; but we may compare *hʾth tbnh* in 2 Sam 7:5 (MT) where B attests *lʾ ʾth tbnh* (as read in 1 Chr 17:4).

15a. Twice *śmḥ* ("was happy") is used in this chapter (vv. 9, 15), also in two poems (1 Sam 2:1; 2 Sam 1:20) and twice in proximity to "see" (1 Sam 6:13; 19:5). In two of these contexts (19:5 as in 11:9), the occasion is a *tšwʿh* ("deliverance") that Yahweh has "done."

b. The MT's *šm šʾwl* shares the letters of *šmwʾl* (attested by GT) but for the repetition of a single *š*.

c. At the end *ʿd-mʾd* (the text confirmed by GT) may be a late usage. It is found only in Gen 27:33, 34; 1 Sam 11:15; 25:36; 2 Sam 2:17; 1 Kgs 1:4; Isa 64:9, 12 (8, 11); Pss 38:6, 8 (7, 9); 119:8, 43, 51, 107; Lam 5:22; Dan 8:8; 11:25.

[1–3] On our working assumption that 1 Samuel is a fresh prologue to an expansion of the Book of Two Houses, the main part of this chapter anticipates the story of David and the new king Hanun of the Ammonites, which begins in 2 Sam 10. Hanun is introduced there (10:2) as "son of Nahash." David speaks at the outset of practicing *ḥesed* toward his Transjordanian neighbor. However, after the humiliation of his envoys, he launches a campaign against the Ammonites and their capital, which (may have) concluded in some brutality. Our story provides some background.

Here Nahash the Ammonite takes a hostile initiative against a city of Israel in Gilead, one of his Transjordanian neighbors. They are prepared to submit, to become his servants, but they seek formal terms. On being told that one of the terms of the treaty (*bĕrît*) will be the gouging out of all their right eyes in order to make a cause of reproach against Israel (like son, like father), they seek respite for a week in case Israel can save this eastern outpost. All the other talk in the books of Samuel of "treaty" or "covenant" is connected with David's becoming king and lacks any mention of cruel or hostile terms. Is this episode intended to mark a contrast? Or is it a timely warning of the dangers of making oneself over to a king as his servants or slaves?

Two significant word choices should be mentioned. Nahash seeks to cause Israel "reproach" (*ḥerpâ*)—what his immediate victims ask him in response is the similar-sounding "Let us alone" (*herep lānû*). Then *bĕrît* (the term for the relational structure) and *ḥesed* (the term for the relational behavior) are nouns that overlap and are sometimes paired: both require or imply loyalty. We may wonder whether the grant of their plea was part of the chivalry of the times, or whether it simply confirms that Snake (*nāḥāš*)[12] has his sights on all Israel and not simply on a single outlying city.

[4] There is no suggestion that the envoys from Jabesh come first or specially to Gibeah because that is where they would find Saul, though this Gibeah is first called "Gibeah of Saul" here. We may rather suppose that it is simply one appropriate stop on their weeklong tour of all Israel for support. As recently as 10:5, Gibeah was called "Gibeah of God," or "hill of God," and Saul has encountered a band of prophets there.

[5–8] The effect on Saul of hearing what has caused his people to weep reminds us of Samson, for Judg 14:19 is the one other biblical verse that links the onset of the divine spirit and the anger of its recipient. Saul's anger at the prospect of some of his people being grossly mistreated anticipates David's.[13] The envoys' message is now to be reinforced with tokens of Saul's threat against the oxen of any in Israel who do not come out after Saul and Samuel. Saul is here giving the orders and is empowered by the divine spirit, but he still invokes the name of Samuel, who has so recently sent all the people to their homes. The resultant "dread" (*paḥad*) has a divine aura (v. 7),[14] and Yahweh's people come out as "one" (*'eḥād*). The next sentence plays still further with these words: "counted" (*pāqad*) also sounds very similar to "dread" (*paḥad*); and "one" (*'eḥād*) people, when counted (*pāqad*), becomes two large totals. In almost every case where such totals are given, we find that the details differ between MT and GT, or between Samuel–Kings and Chronicles. A separate reckoning of the people as Israel *plus Judah* seems without motive in the immediate context; and we shall meet it just once more in 1 Samuel (15:4). In both cases it is a matter of Saul's numbering his mustered forces; and the reason for dividing the count in each passage will be literary: that is how David's census team would bring him the results of their survey of the whole people (2 Sam 24:9, BTH). Put another way, 1 Sam 11 was written with an eye on 2 Sam 24 as well as on 2 Sam 10; and our interpretation must take account of this.[15]

12. This Hebrew name could also suggest "bronze" or "diviner"; but "snake" appears to be the most appropriate to this story.

13. See 2 Sam 6:8; 12:5; 13:21.

14. The phrase *pḥd-yhwh* is otherwise found only in Isa 2 (3x) and 2 Chr 14:14 (13); 17:10; 19:7; and *pḥd 'lhym* in 2 Chr 20:29.

15. There are only a few instances of *pqd* with Saul or David as subj., and always with *h'm* as the implied obj. In 1 Sam 13:15; 14:17; and 2 Sam 18:1, "the people" is limited to "those [found] with him"; and the total is not divided. In 1 Sam 11:8; 15:4; and 2 Sam 24:1–9, the numbers are much larger and a separate total for Judah is provided. In the books of Samuel, we find Israel and

[9–10] Though we have four versions of the brief message sent back to Jabesh in Gilead (v. 9), only the fragmentary version of 4QSam[a] is materially different from the others: it already promises what the other versions only claim after the event—that Yahweh will be responsible for their deliverance. The men of Jabesh are sufficiently pleased by what they hear that they send "Snake" an insolently ambiguous reply: "Tomorrow we shall come out to you, and you will do to us what you think best."

[11–13] What actually happens the next day is reported in a separate subparagraph. The introductory time phrase is used also in 1 Sam 31:8 (BTH) and in 18:10. In the event there is no mention of Jabesh coming out, but only of Saul's three-pronged assault on Ammon. Israel as a whole has instead come out as "one man" (v. 7), though with three "heads" (11a). By contrast, and as a result of Israel's attack, no Ammonite was left together with another (v. 11b): Ammon, in another nice and even related wordplay, is not only not *ʾîš ʾeḥād* (one man) but not even *šĕnayim yaḥad* (two together).

The doubters of 10:27 have received their answer but escape their comeuppance. If the weeping (11:4) reminds us of Judg 2:4; 20:23, 26; 21:2; and the divine spirit (v. 6) recalls Jephthah and Samson in the same book; the escape of these of no use (v. 13) contrasts with the treatment Gideon meted out to the leaders of Succoth and Penuel who fearfully refused to help him. Success is its own vindication. The people seek Samuel's agreement for putting to death those who have questioned Saul's kingship. Here B has Samuel himself reply to the question asked him; but in MT and LT Saul is the one who interrupts with the declaration that no one should be put to death on the day that Yahweh has wrought deliverance in Israel. David will show similar magnanimity to critics in victory (2 Sam 19:23). Whether it is Samuel or Saul who gives the diplomatic answer, the point is the same: since after all it was Yahweh who was the deliverer, the question whether Saul can save is irrelevant. The doubters have questioned his kingship; he has ascribed the victory to Yahweh: the result is a formal and united fresh start to his kingship—and as ch. 11 nears its end, Israel's unity is no longer marred by discontented mutterers.

[14–15] With the military business finished, with Saul's tactics successful, and with the people satisfied over Saul's kingly credentials, Samuel now in a final subparagraph proposes to the people that they repair to Gilgal and there "inaugurate" or "renew" the kingship. The verb "make new" can mean either; and our choice here may be affected by two other decisions: how this chapter relates to chs. 9–10; and whether to follow the text of MT or of GT in the next sentence.

Judah in parallel in 1 Sam 11:8; 15:4; 2 Sam 2:10; 3:10; 5:5; 19:40–43 (41–44); 20:2; 24:1, 9; and Judah separate in 1 Sam 22:5; 23:23; 27:6, 10; 30:16, 26; 2 Sam 1:18; 2:1, 4, 7, 11; 19:11, 14, 16 (12, 15, 17); 20:4, 5.

Has Saul already become king before this point in the narrative? He has been given—and has had some understanding of—a heavy hint by the seer he went to consult about something else (9:20–21). He has received special attention at a banquet (9:23–24). He has been anointed by the great Samuel (10:1–2) and given a series of positive signs (10:2–6). And yet, through all this, the "king" word (*melek*) has not been used, whether as noun or verb. The first time we meet that term (since ch. 8 at least) is in a note by the narrator, which makes an interesting claim and disclaimer at the same time (10:16): it was in fact about kingship that Samuel has spoken to Saul, even if the word itself has not been used; but Saul has said nothing about this matter to his uncle. At this point Samuel moves to the public arena: the people have asked for a king (10:19), and he should now be selected by lot. The same reluctant Saul is identified and acclaimed (10:24).

If Saul has been presented with a series of convergent indicators, we readers—and perhaps Samuel too—are now being assured that Saul should be king. What Samuel has received in a divine revelation is confirmed by the process of the sacred lot. And yet Saul simply goes home as part of the general dismissal (10:25–26), albeit accompanied now by some good men and true. He has been identified as (future?) king. But is he now king? Is it as king, or at least king-designate, that he has the authority to instill divine dread into his people (11:5–7)? Or is decisive leadership in a time of nationally perceived need a sufficient explanation of his success against Ammon? Perhaps that is the wrong way to pose the question. If the first of three frames (9:1–10:16) *talks* kingship without using the word (until its very end), then the third (11:11) may *walk* kingship—similarly without the word till 11:12. Though it is only toward their close that these two outer frames of 1 Sam 9–11 use the word "king," they do share earlier the distinctive talk of Yahweh's spirit leaping on Saul. The stimulus is quite different in each case: in the one case it is induced by meeting a prophetic band and sharing group behavior with them, which has been stimulated or at least accompanied by music. In the other it is induced by rage or manifested itself as rage at news of an impending atrocity.

Saul has been anointed and divinely selected, and he has successfully led his people within the context of a divine deliverance. But is Saul already king? David will be both anointed and successful, and will be several times acclaimed as more successful than Saul, before he himself becomes king. There may be protesters (11:12); but are they protesting against his kingship in the present, or against a future that they fear is already set? It seems to be thoroughly appropriate, after all that has been said, that the verb "make new" (see further below on 11:14) is also ambiguous. What the supporters of Saul say (v. 12) could be a diplomatic protest against Samuel himself; for he has made plain (10:19) that he considers the request for a king to amount to a rejection of Yahweh. Since their question has been stated in general terms, it can also be answered in general terms, whether by Samuel himself (GT) or by Saul (MT): no one should die on such a day.

There is heavy emphasis on place in the report of Samuel's next proposal and the people's response. Gilgal is named three times in 11:14–15 and reinforced as often in GT by the word "there"—and once more in MT. In MT (v. 15) it is the people who make Saul king. The echoes are less than flattering: on the only other two occasions on which "the sons of Israel" are subject of "made king," the object is Jeroboam (1 Kgs 12:20; 2 Kgs 17:21). The GT has it that, after all the people went to Gilgal, "Samuel anointed Saul there as king before Yahweh." The Hebrew that this renders is sufficiently different from MT to make accidental corruption unlikely. A deliberate change has been made in one direction or the other. Of course, although the words are different, the reality envisaged in both versions may have been the same: that Samuel performed the sacred action at the people's urging.[16] And yet we readers are already familiar with something approaching both expressions. We know that Samuel has already been instructed to king a king (still unnamed) for Israel (8:22), and that he has already anointed Saul as designated leader (*nāgîd*) in secret (9:16; 10:1). Is anointing a king not a once-for-all act? Is it sensible that what has been done already in secret (to reassure Saul) is now repeated (to reassure the people)? Or if kingship can be "renewed," was reanointing part of the associated ceremonial? There are also two accounts of David's being anointed: one by Samuel within his family circle, long before he succeeds Saul (1 Sam 16); and one by "the elders of Israel" once "all the tribes of Israel" have approached him after Saul's death (also after Samuel's death) and in recognition of the fact that David is already a proven commander of Israel (2 Sam 5:1–3). As on that occasion, this "kinging" of Saul is carried out "before Yahweh." Only the public anointing of David has been part of the older narrative in BTH. It is the author of Samuel who has furnished accounts for both Saul and David of earlier private designation as king, accompanied by anointing.

This short subparagraph ends in great rejoicing (v. 15); and that in turn has two textual echoes. It recapitulates the immediate, if preliminary, joy of the men of Jabesh when they hear that help is on the way (11:9). At that earlier stage, only a part of Israel is happy; now it is the turn of all Israel to be not only happy, but very happy. But it also anticipates a number of situations in Kings: the installation of Solomon (1 Kgs 1:40, 45); his dedication of the temple (1 Kgs 8:66); and the anointing of Joash after the interregnum of Athaliah (2 Kgs 11:14, 20). The latter two were original elements of BTH; and the dedication of the temple also includes sacrifice.

The relationship between this short chapter and those around it is rather complex. If we read the beginning of the chapter with GT and 4QSam[a], the

16. Accordingly, Fokkelman's description of the LXX reading as "catastrophic" (1981–93, 4:485 n. 6) is gross overreaction.

gap of a month or so ties this report to the end of ch. 10. Equally the scoundrels who refuse to recognize Saul at the end of ch. 10 seem to be referred to in 11:12–13. On the other hand, the empowerment of Saul by divine spirit (11:6) may resume his experience of the spirit in 10:6, which was to give him discernment over what actions to undertake (v. 7). It is easier to view ch. 11 as a more original sequel to 9:1–10:16 if we follow MT at the transition between 10:27 and 11:1 ("as one keeping silent" is intrinsically the more difficult reading in 10:27). And yet, even if the explicit "month" is removed from our consideration, the timescale required for the Jabesh-Ammon-Saul story seems impossible within the seven days' wait at Gilgal prescribed by Samuel in 10:8 and to which 13:8–14 reverts. Neither the supposition of many critics that ch. 11 could be historically reliable, and therefore early, nor the fact that it draws on BTH, requires us to believe that it belongs to the same compositional layer as 9:1–10:16 + chs. 13–14. The third subparagraph has transitional status: it marks both an end and a beginning. Fokkelman is right to insist that it is an integral part of ch. 12; but wrong, I think, to fault the medieval chapter division. Adding a diachronic dimension to thorough synchronic reading of the sort he champions enables even richer results. I suspect that these two verses had been drafted as the culmination of ch. 11, before they provided an opportunity to draft ch. 12.

1 Samuel 12:1–5

1 And Samuel said to all Israel:
"Look! I listened to your voice,
in all that you said to me;
and I kinged a king over you.
2 Well then, look! The king is going about before you.
And I, I have become old
and [hoary] *shall sit*;
and my sons, look—they are with you;
and I, I have gone about before you from my youth[a] till this day.
3 Look at me.
Respond concerning me before Yahweh and before his anointed.
Whose ox have I taken?
And whose ass have I taken?
Whom have I oppressed?
Whom have I crushed?
And from whose hand have I taken a bribe
and [covered my eyes with it] *sandal*?[a]
Respond[b] *concerning me*,
and I shall return it to you."

4 And they said *to Samuel*:
"You have not *wronged us*[a]
and you have not oppressed us,
and you have not crushed us,
and you have not taken anything from any man's hand."
5 And [he] *Samuel* said to the[m] *people*:
"Yahweh is witness against you,
and his anointed is witness *today in* this day,
that you have not found anything in my hand."
And they said:[a]
"Witness."

2a. The term *nʿry* either resumes chs. 1–3 or provides an opportunity for their later composition. Samuel–Kings mention the youth of only four characters, and all in speech: by Samuel here, Goliath (1 Sam 17:33), Joab (2 Sam 19:7 [8]), and Obadiah (1 Kgs 18:12).

3a. Here B reads not *ʾʿlym* ("I covered," MT) but either *nʿlym* or *nʿl* ("sandals" or "sandal").

b. In B "respond" attests *ʿnw* for MT's *ʿyny* ("my eye").

4a. Here B renders *ʿšq* as in v. 3, but *rṣṣ* differently; its opening *ēdikēsas* may be a blander alternative rendering of *ʿšq*.

5a. At the end of the verse, "said" has sg. subj. in MT, as also in LT, where "the people" is specified.

[1–5] Samuel cites Yahweh and his anointed together as witnesses in his own defense. After the great happiness reported at the assembly at Gilgal, we might have expected a note about the dismissal of all present to their homes (as in 10:25—and 2 Sam 6:19 or 1 Kgs 8:66). Instead, we are treated to two dialogues between Samuel and his people, one short (12:1–5) and the other lengthy (vv. 6–25). These are regularly stated to be pure Deuteronomistic creation, the only outstanding question being to which stage of Deuteronomistic composition they should be assigned. Polzin (1989) restates this position in a fresh way, with his claim that in this chapter we hear the character Samuel and the author speaking as one. Whatever the truth of that observation, the compositions appear to be anything but Deuteronomistic: the evidence against that is well reviewed by Campbell (1:120–24). Instead, there are echoes of different biblical texts, blended into a major, well-structured composition. Many of the seeming allusions in this eclectic text are to poetic (including "prophetic") books. Our quest for an adequate overview must attend both to the whole and to comparisons with similar compositions.

If we focus on the main character, we see an interesting set of moves designed to play down the implications of the fact that Samuel has been instrumental in making Saul king. If that fact is admitted in a single clause (v. 1b),

Samuel's preemptive self-justification has already been launched in a double clause: "I listened to your voice, in all that you said to me" (v. 1a). Samuel has been merely the people's instrument. No response is invited from the people; but instead Samuel launches a wider defense of his general integrity as leader. With Yahweh and his newly anointed called as witnesses in Samuel's defense, the people meekly confirm that no evidence has been found that Samuel has received any material benefit from his leadership (vv. 4, 5b). Yahweh has been cited as witness (vv. 3a, 5a); and Samuel now moves to recall some of the relevant past, which includes Moses and Aaron and the exodus from Egypt (v. 6).

What Samuel has to say about the new king, his own sons, and himself (v. 2) does not give up its meaning easily. Four features of his wording appear significant.

- The king is now going about in front of the people, while he himself (Samuel) has become old.
- While Saul is described as "in front of" the people, Samuel's sons are "with" the people.
- Despite his age, Samuel is still going about in front of the people, as he has always done since his youth.
- "Going about in front of" (*hthlk lpny*) has interesting echoes both earlier and later in the book.

"Going about" has been used in only one previous portion of Samuel: in the speech of the man of God about the house of Eli. The house of Eli had received a solemn declaration from Yahweh that they would "go about in front of" him forever (2:30), but they had proved unworthy. In their place, Yahweh would raise for himself an established priest and would build for himself an established house that would "go about in front of" his anointed one. Those in a public role who forfeit respect may find themselves removed from office. Samuel appears to be claiming an ongoing role before the Lord's anointed. He is far from having been completely supplanted. Without his help, the new anointed of the Lord might turn out to be as unworthy as Eli. But this same verb will be used of David going about in the southern desert areas, protecting or plundering as he chooses (chs. 23–30)—and of David's going about on his roof and seeing a beautiful woman (2 Sam 11:2).

The texts with most echoes in vv. 1–5 are Amos, Micah, and Ps 2. Although the pairing "oppress/crush" is found also in Deut 28:33 and Hos 5:11, as well as in Amos 4:1, it is only in Amos 5:12 that "take a bribe" is also used. Then "sandal" (in v. 3), if original, provides a link to Amos 2:6; 8:6. With "hide my eyes," compare Isa 1:15. Micah 1:2 invokes Yahweh "as witness against you"

(1 Sam 12:5); and Mic 6:1–5 not only mentions Gilgal (1 Sam 11:14–15), but also talks of Moses and Aaron,[17] and provides the only other instance in HB of "speak up about" (*ʿnh b-* [Mic. 6:3; 1 Sam 12:3]), and one of only two others of "Yahweh's right acts" (*ṣdqwt yhwh*), mentioned only a couple of verses later (Mic 6:5; 1 Sam 12:7). Then Yahweh and his anointed (v. 5) feature together as opposed by kings of the earth in Ps 2:2.

1 Samuel 12:6–25

6 And Samuel said to the people, *saying*,
"[It] *Witness* is Yahweh
who [acted with] *made* Moses and Aaron,
and who brought up [y]our fathers from [the land of] Egypt.
7 Well then, present yourselves
and [let me enter into judgment with] *I shall judge*[a] you before Yahweh,
and I shall report to you all Yahweh's right act[s]
that he did [with] *among* you and [with] *among* your fathers—
8 how Jacob [and his sons] came to Egypt
[and Egypt ill-treated them];
and [y]our[a] fathers cried to Yahweh,
and Yahweh sent Moses and Aaron,
and they brought your fathers out of Egypt,
and let them settle in this place;
9 and they forgot Yahweh their God,
and he made them over into the hand of Sisera, leader of the army of *Jabesh king of* Hazor,
and into the hand of the Philistines,
and into the hand of the king of Moab,
and [they] *he* fought with them.
10 And they cried to Yahweh,
and they said:
'We have sinned;
for we have abandoned Yahweh
and served the Baalim and the [Ashtaroth] *groves*.[a]
Well then, deliver us from the hand of our enemies,
and we shall serve you.'
11 And Yahweh sent [Jerub-baal] *Jeroboam*, and [Bedan] *Barak*, and Jephthah, and Samuel,

17. Only a few passages outside the Pentateuch do so: Josh 24:5; Pss 99:6–9; 105:26; 106:16.

and delivered you from the hand of your enemies all around,
and you lived securely.
12 And you saw
that Nahash, king of the sons of Ammon, came against you,
and you said [to me]:
'No—but a king shall rule over us'
while it is Yahweh your god who is your king.
13 Well then, look at the king
whom you have chosen, [for whom you have asked[a]]—
and look! Yahweh has set over you a king.
14 If you fear Yahweh
and serve him
and listen to his voice
and do not respond stubbornly to Yahweh's voice/mouth,
[then] *and* both you and the king
who has become king over you
will be *following* behind[a] Yahweh your God.
15 But if you do not listen to Yahweh's voice,
and rebel against Yahweh's mouth,
the hand of Yahweh shall be on you and on your [fathers] *king*.
16 Even now present yourselves
and see this great thing
that Yahweh[a] is doing in your eyes.
17 Is it not wheat harvest today?
I shall call to Yahweh,
that he may give voices and rain.
And know
and see
that your evil is great
that you have done in Yahweh's eyes,
asking for yourselves a king."

18 And Samuel called to Yahweh,
and Yahweh gave roars and rain on that day;
and all the people were very afraid[a] of Yahweh and of Samuel.
19 And all the people said to Samuel:
"Pray for your servants to Yahweh your God,
and let us not die.
For we have added to all our sins evil
in asking for ourselves a king."

20 And Samuel said to the people:

"Do not be afraid.
You for your part have done all this evil.
However, do not turn from after Yahweh,
and serve Yahweh with all your heart.
21 And you must not turn [except] after the 'chaotic,'[a]
which are of no use
and will not deliver,
because they are chaotic.
22 For Yahweh will not forsake his people, on account of his great name;
for Yahweh is willing
to make you as a people for himself.
23 And me too—heaven prevent me
from sinning against Yahweh,
from ceasing to pray for you,
and I shall serve Yahweh,
and I shall instruct you in the way of the good and the straight.
24 Nevertheless fear Yahweh
and serve him with trust and with all your heart,
for [see] *you saw*
what great things he has done with you!
25 And if evil is what you are set on doing,
both you and your king will be [removed] *added*."

7a. The MT vocalizes *ʾšpṭh* as *nipʿal* (*nšpṭ* is construed with a following *ʾt-* also in Jer 2:35; Ezek 20:35, 36; Prov 29:9); but GT attests the commoner *qal*.

8a. Here 4QSam[a] also has "your fathers" (MT).

10a. Compare 7:3–4; GT has again read *ʾšrwt* ("groves"), not *ʿštrwt*.

13a. Trebolle Barrera (68–69) argues for the greater originality of "for whom you have asked" (MT plus) over "whom you have chosen."

14a. Both B and MT are unusual here. B continues the conditional, and offers no main clause, but does represent the normal Hebrew idiom "go after" (= follow). MT lacks the expected participle *hlkym* ("going").

16a. In B "that Yahweh" is represented by *ho ho kyrios* ("that the Yahweh"): this first instance in Kingdoms of articulated *kyrios* in nom. may have been to avoid misreading the relative pronoun. The LT removes the problem by a change in word order.

18a. Here in B and 4QSam[a], "feared" is pl., but sg. in MT and LT.

21a. The GT interprets *tōhû* (cf. Gen 1:2) as "the things that are nothing."

[6–17] Now that Samuel has been cleared (vv. 4–5), he cites Yahweh as sole witness in a case that involves people and their king together. After a résumé of the people's history (vv. 6–11), which culminates in the recent Nahash episode (v. 12), a further double *hnh* (v. 13a, 13b; cf. 1, 3 above) focuses attention on their choice to be ruled by a king and Yahweh's appointment of that king. A brief reminiscence of the ancient deliverance from Egypt (v. 6) is developed (7–12) in ways that are partly traditional and partly surprising. "And now present yourselves . . . before Yahweh" (v. 7) resumes 10:19. This subparagraph concludes (vv. 16–17) by returning to the opening words of v. 7. This could be the sort of recapitulatory device that betrays the insertion of new material in vv. 7–15.[18] After brief mention of Moses, Aaron, and the Exodus (v. 6), Samuel may have moved immediately, in an earlier and shorter version of his speech, to promise a spectacular out-of-season storm (vv. 16–17), in terms that recall one of the plagues in Egypt.[19] We might prefer to say "see and know," putting the evidence of our eyes before the conclusion we draw from that evidence; but "know and see" (v. 17) is characteristic of the books of Samuel. Yet it needs to be recognized that the first mention of Moses and Aaron (v. 6) is striking: the Greek translation "who made Moses and Aaron" catches the natural way of reading the Hebrew—natural at least until the following verse guides one away from "made" toward the less common "acted with."[20]

The theme of Samuel's case against his people (v. 7), *ṣdqwt yhwh* ("right acts," MT), is found elsewhere only in Judg 5:11 (where they are celebrated) and Mic 6:5 (again in the context of divine complaint over the people's lack of response). The exodus (here in line with normative tradition) has been preceded by Jacob's arrival in Egypt; more unusually, it has been followed by Moses and Aaron's settling the fathers "in this place" (v. 8b)—quite apart from the idea of Moses and Aaron as presiding over the settlement, the phrase "settle *X* in this place" is unique within HB.[21] The fathers had "forgotten" Yahweh, as in the opening of the first deliverer story in Judges (3:7)—and this is a stock theme of the Psalms, but also Deuteronomy (6:12; 8:11, 14, 19; 32:18). Yahweh "sold them" (v. 9) into the hands of three enemies: in Judges, Yahweh does "sell" Israel into the hands of Sisera (4:2) and the Philistines (10:7), and they also have trouble with Eglon, king of Moab (3:12–30), although it is only in the previous section (3:7–11, about Othniel) that the book of Judges also uses "sell." After these three foes had fought with them, they had confessed their "sin" and asked for help (1 Sam 12:10), and Yahweh had sent four leaders and had delivered them (v. 11). Their confession (v. 10) makes a first mention of "sin" since 7:6 and resumes "abandon" (derived from BTH [1 Kgs 9:9; 2 Kgs 22:17]) from 8:8.

18. This is argued by Trebolle Barrera 66–68 (also see the repetition of much of v. 6b in 8).

19. If so, the new insert will have repeated Moses, Aaron, and the exodus in v. 8b from 6b; and Yahweh's "voice" (14–15) immediately precedes Yahweh's "voices" (17–18). The beginning and end of vv. 7–15 have clear links with the text just before and after.

20. Zakovitch has proposed that v. 6 originally identified Yahweh as God of creation and of exodus: in Hebrew, "[who made] heaven and earth" shares many letters with "[who made] Moses and Aaron"—*'t-hšmym w't-h'rṣ* and *'t-mšh w't-'hrn*.

21. Even "settle *X*" in a specific locality or city is uncommon enough: 1 Sam 30:21; 2 Kgs 17:6, 24, 26; Ezek 26:20; 2 Chr 8:2.

The four deliverers do not quite correspond either with the situations into which Israel had been sold (v. 9) or with the order of events in the book of Judges. Even if "Barak" of the OG and Syriac translations is more original than the "Bedan" of the familiar Hebrew, he appears in Judges before and not after Jerub-baal. At the end of the short list of four deliverers, LT again is more in line with familiar tradition when it reports Yahweh's sending Samson, while MT and B surprise us with Samuel listing his own name in fourth place. Strangest of all, Samuel goes on to reframe (v. 12) the account we have just read of the Nahash episode: Israel has not followed Saul's spontaneous lead (as ch. 11 has told the story); it has requested a king, although Yahweh is their king. They now have this king: Yahweh has set over them the one they (not Yahweh) have chosen, the one they have asked for (12:13). The people's choice resumes 8:18, while their asking resumes not only 8:10 but also the whole issue of Hannah's asking for a son.[22] It would be possible for them and their king to serve Yahweh (12:14); but if not, they would experience again the weight of Yahweh's hand (v. 15).

Samuel recalls several themes, or variants of them, that we find in earlier portions of 1 Samuel. "Deliver" (*hṣyl*, v. 11) has been used with Yahweh as subject in 7:3 and 10:18; and with other subjects in 4:8; 7:14.[23] "Securely" (*lbṭḥ*) is much commoner, although the only other case of *bṭḥ* with *yšb* occurs in Deut 12:10. Trebolle Barrera (68–69) argues for the greater originality of "for whom you have asked" (v. 13, MT plus) over "whom you have chosen." The phrase *(h)mrh ʾt-py* (14–15) is rare, found elsewhere only in Num 20:24; 27:14; Deut 1:26, 43; 9:23; 1 Kgs 13:21, 26; Lam 1:18, 20 (all relatively late contexts). However, although some of the names mentioned by Samuel are reported also in Judges, nothing at all corresponds to the stories of Israel's settlement in its land as reported in the book of Joshua. We shall see several striking examples in the following chapters of language and motif shared between Samuel and Joshua, but no evidence in Samuel of knowledge about the Joshua story. If there was influence, it seems to have been in the opposite direction.

[18–19] Confronted by the demonstration of Yahweh's power and Samuel's influence, the fearful people admit their sin over requesting a king and ask for Samuel's intercession.

[20–25] Samuel's closing speech explores and develops the themes "fear," "sin," "prayer," and "evil" (vv. 20–25). Though the closing verbs in MT and GT are opposite in literal sense (MT representing the *nipʿal* of *sph*, "sweep away," and GT of *ʾsp*, "gather"), both threaten death (in GT expressed by being gathered [to one's ancestors]). A similar textual issue recurs in 26:10; 27:1.[24]

22. See 1 Sam 1:17, 20, 27, 28; 2:20 (here, Elkanah and his wife).

23. The verb *hwšyʿ* ("save") was used in 4:3; 7:8; 9:16; 10:27; 11:3—with divine subj. in 7:8.

24. But only in 12:25 can MT's consonants (*tspw*) be reread as a defectively spelled form based on either *ysp* or *ʾsp*.

From Samuel's pleading his cause to the people, with Yahweh and "his anointed" as witnesses, we have moved to Yahweh and Samuel being jointly feared by the people and a threat of a fate that they and "their king" will share. One theme is constant: whether Samuel refers to the king as Yahweh's anointed or as the people's king, Samuel disclaims any share in Saul—even in his opening admission that he has "kinged the king," he insists that he was simply listening to his people's voice. After that start, the composition moves to a dialogue confirming Samuel's innocence. With that achieved by argument, the next stage in Samuel's case is advanced by display. The mere fact of a terrible storm as late as wheat harvest (in May) is proof positive that something is badly out of kilter; and since Samuel's closeness to Yahweh is part of the demonstration, the people readily assent to his claim that that "something" has been their request for a king. Samuel concludes by claiming an ongoing role: if he continues to pray, he will be able to instruct them, for true service of Yahweh is still possible for them. But if they are bent on serious evil, then so much the worse for them and their king: it appears that Samuel expects to be exempt.

In our discussion of 12:1–5, we noted that the texts most echoed in the paragraph are Amos, Micah, and Ps 2. Psalm 2:2 also includes the verb *htyṣb* ("present oneself," vv. 7, 16). "Voices and rain" (17–18) are a unique combination; but the displaying and withholding of weather phenomena link this passage with 1 Kgs 8:35–36 (BTH) together with Exod 9 and 1 Kgs 17–18; and locate Samuel between Moses and Elijah. Yahweh's thundering "voices" accompany a plague of hail in Exod 9:13–35. That storm affects the earlier crops of barley and flax, but not the later crops of wheat and spelt (vv. 31–32); and it is intended (v. 30) to produce "fear" of Yahweh. This storm is timed precisely at wheat harvest; and the people fear not only Yahweh but also Samuel (1 Sam 12:18b). The latter point makes a further link with Exodus, this time the culmination of the wonder at the sea, where "the people feared Yahweh, and they believed in Yahweh and in his servant Moses" (Exod 14:31); and it also resonates with believing "in Yahweh . . . and his prophets" (2 Chr 20:20).[25] Then several elements within 1 Kgs 8:35–36 reappear, though in fresh combinations, in 1 Sam 12:19–25. In the new text the problem is rain too much and too late, rather than no rain; but the people do acknowledge their sin (v. 19), and there is mention of Yahweh's "name" (v. 22). And there is now specific mention of mediation: the people ask Samuel to pray for them to Yahweh (v. 19); and Samuel (v. 23) undertakes Yahweh's role of "teaching them the good way" (1 Kgs 8:36).

It is Samuel's final statement that most gives an impression of drafting by a "Deuteronomistic" author. "Fear" describes an appropriate attitude to Yahweh in 1 Kgs 8:40, 43 (BTH). It is more widely used in Samuel–Kings to identify or

25. All the more important that Trebolle Barrera (69) notes that *m'd* ("very") *follows* Yahweh in 1 Sam 12:18 LT, which may suggest that "and Samuel" is a secondary addition.

distinguish those fearing Yahweh or from those fearing other gods. But it is in Deut 6–10 that "fear" and "serve" are most often juxtaposed, so that each comes almost to define the other as the appropriate attitude to Yahweh. Moreover, "in truth, with all your heart" (1 Sam 12:24) anticipates three passages in Kings (1 Kgs 2:4; 3:6; 2 Kgs 20:3), which describe proper kingly behavior before Yahweh. "In truth" (*beʾĕmet*) is never used in Deuteronomy. But "serve" (*ʿbd*) is construed with "in truth" once more in HB (Josh 24:14). "Heaven prevent me from ..." (*ḥlylh ly mn*) is drawn from BTH (2 Sam 23:17//1 Chr 11:19). It is used 7 times more in Samuel, together with 3 times in Genesis, 2 times in Job, and 2 times in Joshua: the close parallel in Josh 24:16 is one of these. Two links close together in Josh 24:14, 16 encourage some scholars to diagnose "Deuteronomism"; but it may be more appropriate to notice a series of local links between Joshua and Samuel. The closing verse (1 Sam 12:25) ends by explicitly linking king and people; and at the beginning of this sentence, the reinforcement of the verb "do evil" with the noun "evil" resumes the theme that the final evil has been the request for a king (v. 19).

The connections with vv. 7–12 are rather different. "Yahweh's righteous acts" (following MT's pl.) represent a further link with Mic 6:5. The idea is quite novel that Moses and Aaron have anything to do with the settlement of the people (1 Sam 12:8), except insofar as the settlement was enabled by what they did at an earlier stage. Some elements in 1 Sam 12:9–11 appear also in the book of Judges, including the admission of sin (v. 10) in Judg 10:10, 15. But it is not easy to decide whether these three verses are a sketch for the book of Judges, or an idiosyncratic précis of it. And the words attributed to the people in response to Nahash (v. 12) do not exactly map onto 11:12b, whether in MT or GT.

Whether an original part of the composition or not, 12:12–15 unpack further implications of "make new the kingdom" (11:14), as Fokkelman (1981–93, 4) has nicely shown. The ambiguity in that phrase is not simply whether Saul is already king or only qualified to be king (with his kingly rule starting as reported in 1 Sam 13), but also whose kingship is being "made new." "The" kingship could be Saul's or Yahweh's—or both. Whether Samuel likes it or not, Saul is now (to be) king. This fact of human kingship within Israel is a novelty; and its implications need to be explored. Yahweh has been, and still is, king over Israel; and the implications of that fact for the new king require explication. Saul will assume at least some of the functions of Samuel. Will he inherit any of the responsibilities of Yahweh? The people have asked for Saul and chosen Saul, and Yahweh their king (v. 12) has set him over them (v. 13).

The alternatives (vv. 14–15) may be set out too briefly to answer the question definitively; but they give a strong indication that the new king will simply be one of Yahweh's subjects, mentioned in both verses *after* the rest of his people. There are two reasons for pausing over the word "after" or "behind" (v. 14). Less important is its form: MT reads *ʾḥr* (normally the adverb) for the expected

ʾḥry (normally the preposition). More important is the ambiguity: if the "after" is temporal, then a jibe may be intended against the new king who is ruling over them "after" (replacing) Yahweh; but if they are obediently "behind" Yahweh (as opposed to confronting him to his face), then GT will have captured the sense even if it has misread the text.

If human kingship is being inaugurated, divine kingship is being renewed—and without diminishment. Responding stubbornly to Yahweh's "mouth" (vv. 14–15) is a stock phrase with powerful associations. In Numbers it is used of the people's rebellion at the waters of Meribah, which would cost Aaron (20:24) and Moses (27:14) their deaths outside the promised land. The refusal of the people to proceed directly into that land from Kadesh (Deut 1:26, 43; 9:23) costs them forty years of wandering. Similar rebellion leads to the fall of Jerusalem (Lam 1:18, 20). And the refusal of a man of God from Judah to adhere to clear divine instructions has him mauled by a lion (1 Kgs 13:21, 26). The parallels, and especially the first and last, appear as threatening to Samuel as to his people—yet not as he chooses to use the phrase.

The earlier part of the argument is structured with a high density of emphatic markers: *hinnēh* ("look") is clustered in 1–3 (4x in MT and 5x in GT); and there is a further pair in v. 13, which we can expand. "Take note that I listened to you. Take note of the result: the king ranging back and forth in your sight, while I am old and grey (yet take note of my sons!). And take note of me, who have ranged back and forth in your sight throughout my long life. The persons for inspection and comparison are all patently in the public domain; there is nothing secret or hidden about them. Everything is known: and is there a single thing wrong about me? About my sons, yes; about the new king, no comment yet; but about me, absolutely not." When Samuel comes to invite similar inspection of the new king they have asked for, he immediately asks them to note (v. 13) that this king is Yahweh's appointee (not theirs).

And there is repeated use of *wĕʿattâ* ("and now" or "well then"): 2, 7, 10, 13, 16 (more emphatic *gam-ʿattâ* in MT and LT). Time after time, Samuel challenges his people to consider the implications of what he is saying. He has listened to them: "well then." Yahweh, their ancient deliverer, is witness: "well then." They have demanded a king: "well then." Yahweh's hand will be upon them and their king: "well then." The frequent reinforcement of the pattern in Samuel's words simply points up the (insolent) contrast in what (he says) the people have said (v. 10): "we have sinned; . . . well then, deliver us and we will serve you."

Another aspect of the argument, especially near its beginning and end, is exploration by repetition of further key terms. (1) We have already noticed that both the new king and Samuel move around in the public gaze (v. 2). (2) The divine power on public display results in mortal fear (vv. 18–19). In response, Samuel urges the people *not* to be afraid *but* to serve Yahweh without deviation

(v. 20); and yet, within a few words (v. 24), he is urging them to fear Yahweh *and* serve him: not fear as terror this time, but fear as reverence, and service (whatever else). (3) The people's "Pray for us because we have sinned in asking (Yahweh) for something wrong" (v. 19 recast) receives Samuel's response: "For me, not praying for you would be sin" (v. 23). Yet, if fear can mean different things, so too can prayer. Asking Samuel to "pray" for them lest they die seems not much different from "asking" Yahweh for a king for themselves (v. 19): both are requests for a favor. However, Samuel envisages "praying" for them that will result in instructing them in the way that is good and straight (v. 23). This is not a plea against sentence, but a request for direction toward a path that is less hazardous. If the people use a strong term (sin) for what they have *committed*, Samuel cleverly adopts it for what he must *not omit* to do. And he thereby protects his role as their instructor, which will continue into the new regime.

1 Samuel 13:1–14

[1 Aged . . . was Saul at his becoming king;
and two years did he rule over Israel.]
2 And Saul chose for himself three thousand from *the men of* Israel;
and there were with Saul two thousand at Michmas[a] and on the Hill of Beth-El,
and a thousand there were with Jonathan at Gibeah/Hill of Benjamin;
and the rest of the people he sent away, each to his tent[s].
3 And Jonathan struck the garrison of the Philistines
which was at Geba,
and the Philistines heard.
Now Saul sounded the trumpet in the whole land, saying,
"[Let the Hebrews hear] *The slaves have rebelled.*"[a]
4 And all Israel—they heard say:
"Saul has struck the prefect of the Philistines.
Israel has moreover become [smelly] *ashamed* among the Philistines."
And the people were called out after Saul to Gilgal.
5 And the Philistines, they assembled
to fight with Israel:
thirty thousand chariots and six thousand horsemen, and a people like the sand that is by the seaside for number;
and they went up
and encamped at Michmas east of[a] Beth-[Awen] *Horon.*
6 And the men of Israel, they saw
that they were in distress,
[for the people was hard pressed] *so as unable to proceed;*[a]

and the people hid themselves in the caves and in the thickets and in the rocks and in the clefts and in the cisterns.

7 And [Hebrews] *the crossers* crossed the Jordan to the land of Gad and Gilead.
And Saul, he was still at Gilgal;
and all the people—they trembled after him.
8 And he waited seven days[a] for the [festival] *witness*[b]
as Samuel *said*;
but Samuel did not come to Gilgal,
and the people scattered[c] from him.
9 And Saul said:
"Bring near to me [the]
that I may make holocaust and [the] *shĕlāmîm*."
And he offered up the holocaust.
10 And it came to be as he was completing offering up the holocaust,
and [look] Samuel is coming,
and Saul went out
to meet him,
to bless[a] him.
11 And Samuel said:
"What have you done?"
And Saul said:
"Because I saw
that the people had scattered from me.
And you—you had not come [by the seasonal festival[a]]
as you appointed in the witness of the days.
And the Philistines, they were gathering at Michmas.
12 And I said,
'Now the Philistines will come down to me at Gilgal,
and Yahweh's face I have not [appeased] *wanted*.'"[a]
And I collected myself,[b]
and I offered up the holocaust."

13 And Samuel said to Saul:
"You have been foolish.
You have not kept [the] *my* command [of Yahweh your God]
which [he] *Yahweh* commanded you.
[For] *As* now Yahweh has established your kingdom [toward] *over* Israel forever.
14 And now your kingdom, it shall not stand.
Yahweh has sought out for himself a man like his heart;
and Yahweh [has] *shall* command[ed] him as leader over his people,

because you have not kept
what Yahweh commanded you."

2a. There is confusion within MSS of MT between *mkmś* and *mkmš*.

3a. In the narrative books, *athetein* is most often correlated with *pšʿ*, which shares two consonants with MT *šmʿ*.

5a. Here *qidmat* ("east of") is used, as in Gen 2:14; 4:16; Ezek 39:11, in place of the more common *miqqedem*, used in Josh 7:2 to plot Ai in relation to Bethel (which may be an alternative name for Beth-awen, in MT).

6a. Again, as over the place name (v. 2), there is confusion over how to read the (same) final consonant of the vb.: as *ngś* (MT) or *ngš* (GT). Here B would retrovert to *mhngšw*, for *ky ngś hʿm* (MT)—inf. *nipʿal* is attested at Qumran, but not in HB.

8a. Trebolle Barrera (69–70) suggests that LT preserves the full evidence of a double reading, and that the originally shorter text was "And he waited seven days for the appointment, and Saul said 'Samuel has not come to Gilgal.'"

b. In 1 Kingdoms (5x), *martyrion* is the sole correspondent to *mwʿd*: 2:22; 9:24; 13:8, 11; 20:35.

c. Here *pwṣ hipʿil* is used intransitively, in the same sense as *npṣ qal* in v. 11.

10a. Did Saul "bless" Samuel (after officiating at sacrifice), or simply "greet" him? The vb. *brk* is used 5x in 2 Sam 6–8 (BTH—6:11, 18, 20; 7:29; 8:10), and also in 1 Sam 2:20; 9:13; 13:10; 25:14; 2 Sam 6:12; 13:25; 14:22; 19:39 (40); 21:3.

11a. The variant expressions in MT and B represent rather more similar Hebrew phrases than the renderings above suggest. The MT is briefer: *lmwʿd hymym*; B might retrovert to *kmdd lʿd hymym*.

12a. The vb. *ḥlh piʿel* is always construed with *ʾt-pny yhwh* or the equivalent. Most of the contexts are late: 1 Kgs 13:6; Zech 7:2; 8:21, 22; Mal 1:9; Dan 9:13. The LXX frequently uses *deisthai* for *ḥlh* and hence may not represent a different underlying text.

b. The noun *ʾpyq*, cognate with this reflexive vb., is used of a water channel.

[1–2] Despite the textual uncertainty at the beginning of this chapter (the opening verse is absent from GT and strange in MT), the report of military leadership by Saul against the Philistines represents good narrative continuity with the campaign against Ammon (11:1–13) or, more probably, the opening Saul report (9:1–10:16)—and thereby may offer further evidence that "making the kingdom new" at Gilgal (11:14–12:25, or at least 12:1–25) was a later addition, if not all of chs. 11–12. Saul's selection of three thousand men (v. 2) could be from the much larger numbers mustered for the Ammonite struggle (11:8); if so, the dismissal of the rest might have been expected after the success against Ammon. Be that as it may, "the rest of the people" is derived from the report of the Ammon campaign in 2 Sam 10:10 (BTH). The selection of such a small force is only the first of several links with the story of Gideon (Judg 7:2–8), which also uses the rare phrase *yeter hā-ʿām* (7:6). Note also the people skulking in caves (1 Sam 13:6; Judg 6:2); the fear (*ḥrd*) of the people (1 Sam 13:7) and Trembling Spring (*ʿên ḥărōd* in Judg 7:1). We could add from ch. 10 the number of confirmatory "signs" offered by Samuel (2–6); and the "hero" hiding by the baggage (22), rather like Gideon's beating out wheat in a winepress (Judg 6:11).

Both parts of the opening verse supplied in MT are odd. The first part begins the regular age formula but supplies no number; then the two years offered in the second for the length of Saul's reign seem impossibly short, though they are powerfully suggestive of impermanence. It is not only at the beginning that there is variation between the texts of MT and GT. In most cases, it is a matter of different readings of the same or very similar consonants. The differences are of little (and mostly local) interpretive significance. However, if GT has failed to recognize—or even suppressed mention of—"Hebrews" twice (vv. 3, 7), or if MT has read them when they were not there, that affects our understanding of wider relationships within this book. The issue recurs in 14:21 and (differently) in 29:3.

[3–7] It is Jonathan who secures the victory (v. 3), but Saul who is identified as victor around the country (v. 4). The narrator does not introduce us here to Saul's eldest son and presumptive heir; but all readers who know the main source (1 Sam 31, BTH) know well who Jonathan is. The names Geba (*gbʿ*), Gibeah (*gbʿh*), and Gibeon (*gbʿwn*) constitute a notorious set of puzzles. "Gibeah of God" is described (10:5) as the location of a Philistine post. Is it the same place as "Gibeah of Benjamin" (13:2), where Jonathan starts his action against the Philistines? And is that Gibeah the same place or a different one from the Geba whose Philistine post Jonathan overwhelms? Do Jonathan's "thousand" gather under the very noses of the hostile garrison, or do they gather in a neighboring location before moving against the post in Geba? Whatever the details, tweaking the end of the Philistine tail means trouble. Now Israel stinks to their overlords, and they want to remove the source of the odious smell; so Israel is summoned to Gilgal. The Philistines gather in overwhelming force: "innumerable as the sand by the sea" is used in the Bible either in promises to Israel of its growth (Gen 22:17; 1 Kgs 4:29 [5:9]), or (as also in Josh 11:4 and Judg 7:12) to underscore the odds against Israel. There are similar formulations in 2 Sam 17:11; 1 Kgs 4:20. The extended statement of Philistine numbers (v. 5) with the sand by the sea as its climax is nicely complemented by the list of hiding places to which the people of Israel have taken themselves.

Given the several repetitions and near repetitions in these episodes concerning Saul, we may wonder just who has called out the people "after Saul." He himself has called out Israel "after Saul and after Samuel" against Ammon (11:7), still deferring to Samuel, or indeed still recognizing Samuel's leadership? Saul is content to have his son's victory described as his own (vv. 3–4a). With his (?) kingdom "made new," is he now ready to muster a force without reference to Samuel? Or with Yahweh's (?) kingdom renewed, and with Samuel having wrested back the initiative, should we detect Samuel's authority behind the passive verb (v. 4b) mustering Israel behind Saul at the shrine at Gilgal?

Jonathan may have won a skirmish against a Philistine outpost; but he has provoked a reaction from which his people are to suffer greatly. Key language in the report of this first campaign between Saul and the Philistines is drawn from BTH: the Philistines gathering together to fight (v. 5) anticipates 2 Sam 23:9, 11, as well as Aram gathering in 2 Sam 10:15; and the defeated side, which takes to flight or concealment, is identified by the collective "man of Israel," as in an earlier version of 1 Sam 31:1, 7 (see below). The BTH vocabulary reservoir has also supplied (from 2 Sam 10:6) "become smelly" in 1 Sam 13:4. The Philistine's "gathering" is repeated in 13:11 and 17:1, while "the man of Israel" reappears in the same contexts: 14:22, 24; 17:2, 19, 24, 25.

[8–12] Saul waits seven days for the *môʿēd* (v. 8); he complains, when questioned by Samuel, that the latter has not arrived for the *môʿēd hayyāmîm* (v. 11). The translation above understands these terms as an extension of the series *zebaḥ hayyôm* (9:12), *zebaḥ* (9:13), and *môʿēd* (9:24) examined above. However *môʿēd* is rendered into English, the "appointed meeting" to which it refers is the seasonal celebratory gathering of the people, not a private engagement between two individuals (as between David and Jonathan in 20:35). The sacrifices that Saul begins to offer (vv. 9–12) are those that Samuel has indicated in 10:8. Holocausts, or "wholly burnt" offerings, together with *šĕlāmîm* are a comprehensive pairing. They were inspired here by two scenes within the David story in BTH: the arrival of the ark in Jerusalem (2 Sam 6:17–18) and the acquisition of ground in Jerusalem for an altar (2 Sam 24:22–25). The same pair of public sacrificial offerings, but with the second called simply "sacrifices" rather than *šĕlāmîm*, has celebrated the return of the ark from Philistine captivity (1 Sam 6:14–15). The beginning of Saul's kingship in the context of renewed Philistine pressure provides the occasion here. However well or badly Saul has understood Samuel's instructions (see on 10:8 above), he seems to have exceeded them when he goes out to "bless" Samuel (13:10). However, what Samuel blames Saul for is not having waited for him (as "the people" would have expected?). Even if Samuel's "seven days," when uttered, have been intended to mean 168 hours, the more important part of his earlier command has been to wait for instructions.

[13–14] The main interpretive and theological issues in the chapter are at vv. 13–14; and they are associated with major translational problems in these verses. The key problem in translating and understanding the logic of the argument here is the double use of *ʿattâ*.[26] The basic sense of *ʿattâ* is temporal, "now" or "at this time" (derived from *ʿēt*, "time"). But it is often used rhetorically, and even logically, as "now" and "then" are in English, to introduce the main point of an argument: "And now . . ." or "Well then . . . (all these things being the

26. We find *kî ʿattâ* used in Gen 22:12; 26:22; 29:32; 31:42; 43:10; Exod 9:15; Num 22:29, 33; 1 Sam 13:13; 14:30; 2 Sam 16:11; 18:3; Isa 49:19; Hos 5:3; 10:3; Mic 4:10; 5:3; Zech 9:8; Job 3:13; 4:5; 6:3, 21; 7:21; 8:6; 13:19; 14:16; Dan 10:11.

case), the conclusion follows. . . ." Polzin (1989) reads and renders vv. 13–14 as follows: "You have acted foolishly; would that (*lûʾ*) you had kept the commandment of the LORD. For then (*kî ʿattâ*) the LORD would have established your kingship over Israel forever. But now your kingship shall not be established." And McCarter has: "If you had been careful of the appointment that Yahweh, your god, gave you, then he would have established your kingship over Israel forever! But now your kingship will not endure!" However, I suspect that, in modern terms, Saul is told that he has been appointed with tenure, that Yahweh has established his position forever, but he (Saul) has demonstrated he is not up to the job, and so he will be dismissed.

Samuel's charge that Saul "has been foolish" (*skl*) recurs in Samuel, in the *nipʿal*, only once: in David's admission of guilt in 2 Sam 24:10 (BTH);[27] and the punishment for David's folly on that occasion underscores the seriousness of the situation here.[28] Comparison and contrast with David is operative at several different levels—at least four.

1. David realizes his own folly: Samuel has to point out Saul's—it is only much later, toward the end of his struggle with David (26:21), that Saul expresses such a realization in his own words (but with a self-serving modification).

2. Samuel spells out the implications of Saul's folly in several expressions drawn from the ideology in BTH of David and his royal line. The linkage of "establish" (*hēkîn*) and "kingdom" (*mamlâkâ*) anticipates the promises to David in 2 Sam 5:12; 7:12. "Forever" (*ʿad-ʿôlām*) will be used as many as eight times in 2 Sam 7:16–29. "Rise" (*qûm*) provides another anticipation of the Davidic royal ideology: it is part of the promise to Solomon in 1 Kgs 9:5 (BTH): "And I shall raise the throne of your kingdom"; and it is an element in the name of Jeho-iakim ("Yahweh will raise"), one of David's last reigning descendants. Even more poignantly, the verb "establish" is part of the name of Jehoiakim's son, exiled to Babylon—King Jeho-iachin: "Yahweh will establish." The long line that had been David's could have been Saul's. Saul would lose his kingdom; but he did still reign till his death. The prediction presumably means that his family would not continue after him.

3. Samuel's declaration operates to limit our expectations of "forever" promises elsewhere in this book: not only in the words of Nathan and David taken over from BTH (8x in 2 Sam 7), but also Jonathan's desperate triple mention of the eternal covenant between David and himself (1 Sam 20:15, 23, 42). Samuel here applies to a king the rule already proclaimed by an unnamed man of God to a priest (2:30): "forever" is conditional on behavior.

27. The Chronicler uses *nskl* just once more, too, apart from the parallel in 1 Chr 21:8 (BTH): to reinforce the verdict on Asa in 2 Chr 16:9.

28. Also, *skl* is found in 1 Sam 26:21 (*hipʿil*) and 2 Sam 15:31 (*piʿel*).

4. Jerusalem's last kings embody the disjunction between their fate and the royal ideology proclaimed in their names. This contrast has been even more starkly apparent within the shorter compass of the Book of Two Houses.

The statement that "Yahweh has sought out for himself a man like his heart" (1 Sam 13:14) is open to different interpretations: a. it may offer an implied comparison—"a man [whose heart is] like his heart"; b. remembering that *lbb* in Hebrew is more cerebral than "heart" in English, it may mean "a man of his choice" (cf. *ʾt-kl ʾšr hyh ʿm-lbbh* in 1 Kgs 10:2//2 Chr 9:1). In an even closer portion of BTH (2 Sam 7:21//1 Chr 17:19), *klbk* ("as your heart") follows and reinforces "for the sake of your word," and will amount to "as your pleasure." In the light of what Jonathan's armor-bearer says to him in 1 Sam 14:7, we may fairly hear the suggestion that Yahweh, being Yahweh, is perfectly free to make his choices and change his mind. A further ambiguity is over "*your mamlākâ*" (13b, 14a). Saul must have been left wondering whether it refers to his own rule as king, or to his whole royal dynasty.

There seems to be no strong reason for considering this short subparagraph as additional to its context. If we remove vv. 13–14, then the remainder of the story has Samuel turn on his heel wordlessly when he has heard Saul's (inadequate) answer to his briefest of questions ("What have you done?"). An unspoken response might have communicated very effectively, but it would have been uncharacteristic of Samuel. Then, since several items of his response are drawn from the royal ideology already in BTH, there is no question of a later writer importing external terminology. The high price demanded so much earlier in Saul's career for his folly (someone after Yahweh's own heart already sought out as his successor), leaves a question over the divine attitude to David's folly. To develop the analogy with modern employment terms, Saul is told remarkably early in his probationary period that he has been appointed to a post with tenure, but has already demonstrated he is not up to the job.

1 Samuel 13:15–14:16 Saul, Jonathan, and the Philistines

1 Samuel 13:15–14:12a

15 And Samuel rose,
and went up from Gilgal *on his way*;
and the remainder of the people went up after Saul for a meeting behind the people of war,
they arriving from Gilgal to Gibeah of Benjamin
and Saul numbered the people, those found with him, some six hundred men.
16 And Saul and Jonathan his son and the people [that was] *and*[a] *those* found with them were sitting/living at Geba[b] of Benjamin *and were* weeping.[c]

And the Philistines, they camped at Michmash.
17 And the destroyer came out of the [camp] *field* of the Philistines: three heads.
The one head [turned to] *was looking on* the Ophrah road, to the land of Shual[a] {fox? jackal?}.
And the one head [turned to] *was looking on* the Beth-Horon road.
18 And the one head [turned to] *was looking on* the [border] *Gibeah*[a] road,
which looks down on [the valley of the hyenas toward the desert] *Gai tēn Samein.*[b]

19 And an artisan *in iron* was not found in all the land of Israel,
because the Philistines said:
"Lest the Hebrews make sword or spear."
20 And all Israel came down to *the land of* the Philistines
to [sharpen] *forge* each his [plowshare[a]] *sickle* and his [mattock] *implement* and his axe and his [goad] *scythe.*
21 And the crop[a] was ready to harvest; and the implements were
three shekels for the tooth; and for the axe
and for the scythe the substance was the same.

21 And the impost would be pym
for the goads/plowshares and the blades
and for the trident and the axes,
and to set the goad.

22 And [on a day] *it came to be in the days*[a] of *the* battle *of Michmash*
there was not found sword or spear in the hand of all the people
who were with Saul and with Jonathan,
and it was found for Saul and for Jonathan his son.
23 And *from*[a] the Philistine post *there* went out [to] *in* the Michmas*h* pass.

14:1 And the day came to be
and Jonathan son of Saul said to his lad, his armor-bearer:
"Come and let us cross to the Philistine garrison
that is across here."[a]
But his father he did not tell.
2 Now Saul was staying at the edge of Gibeah, under the pomegranate which is at [Migron] *Magon*;
and the people who were with him were some six hundred men.
3 And Ahijah son of Ahitub brother of [Ichabod] *Iochabel* son of Phinehas son of [Eli] *Levi* priest of [Yahweh] *the Deity* at Shiloh was w/bearing the ephod.

And the people, they did not know
that Jonathan had gone.
4 And [between] *amid* the crossing[s]
which Jonathan sought to cross against the Philistine garrison,
there were the tooth of rock across from here and the tooth of rock across from there;
and the name of the one was Gleaming/Miry (Bazes),
and the name of the other was Thorny (Sennaar).
5 And the one [tooth] *way* was [a pillar] on the north opposite Michmas[h],
and the other way was on the south opposite Geba.

6 And Jonathan said to his lad, his armor-bearer,
"Come and let us cross to the garrison of these uncircumcised.
Perhaps Yahweh will act for us;
for there is no impediment for Yahweh in saving by many or by few."
7 And his armor-bearer said to him,
"Do everything that [is in] your heart *turns to*. [Turn!]
Here am I with you, as your heart *is my heart*."

8 And Jonathan said:
"Look, we are crossing to the men,
and we shall [disclose ourselves] *roll down*[a] to them.
9 If what they say to us is
'Stay still till we [reach] *tell* you,'
we shall stand in our place
and we shall not go up to them.
10 And if what they say to us is
'Come up to us,'
we shall go up
for Yahweh has given them into our hand,
[and] this is the sign for us."
11 And the two of them [disclosed themselves] *entered* to the Philistine garrison;
and *the* Philistines said:
"Look, *the* Hebrews are coming out of the*ir* holes
where they hid themselves."
12 And the men of the garrison answered Jonathan and his armor-bearer and said,
"Come up to us,
and let us have you know [something] *a word*."

16a. Here B distinguishes between "the people" and "those found with them'; but LT like MT equates them.

b. The MT apparently distinguishes between *gbʿt* of Benjamin (15) and *gbʿ* of Benjamin here; B apparently distinguishes between *Gabaa* (v. 15) and *Gabee* (v. 16); LT transcribes *Gabaa* in both verses, but also interposes *bounon* (the stock rendering in GT of *gbʿh*) between *Gabaa* and *Beniamin* in v. 15. In the longer text of GT, we do not know where Samuel goes "on his way" from Gilgal; but in MT it appears that he goes to Gibeah, while Saul and his party are at Geba.

c. Here GT's "and were weeping" will retrovert to *wbkym*, which could also have been rendered "and Bochim," an alternative name for Bethel (Judg 2:1).

17a. The GT transliterates *šwʿl* as *Sōgal*. The fox (*šwʿl*) is mentioned in Judg 15:4; Ezek 13:4; Ps 63:10 (11); Song 2:15; Lam 5:18; Neh 4:3 (3:35).

18a. *Gabee* (B) and *tēn Gabaa* (LT) attest *gbʿh* or *hgbʿh* for *hgbwl* (MT).

b. Here B has *Samein* and LT has *Sabain* for *hṣbʿym* (MT)—*ṣbʿ* (dyed stuff) is attested only in Judg 5:30.

20a. The first (plowshare) and fourth (goad) items share the same Hebrew consonants (*mḥrštw*), but are vocalized differently. Cook has argued that these Hebrew homonyms have different proto-Semitic roots: *ḥrt** ("plow") and *ḥrš* ("craft").

21a. Instead of *pṣyrh* (MT), GT attests either *bṣyr* or *qṣyr* (as in 8:12).

22a. The GT is part of the report of the battle of Michmash, while MT describes a general situation. Trebolle Barrera (70–71) argues that vv. 19–21 are secondary, and that MT has altered v. 22 to make it part of the parenthesis.

23a. Either GT has read *mmṣb* for *mṣb* (MT), or the translator was unwilling to personify "post."

14:1a. The term *hlz* is an occasional equivalent to the regular *zh* ("this").

8a. Reading a form of *gll* (as in Jer 51:25) rather than of *glh*.

[15–18] This principal paragraph in MT is divided into five subparagraphs (13:15–18, 19–23; 14:1–5, 6–7, 8–12a). The second of these and much of the third do not advance the action but do provide background information. However, the third (14:1–5), fourth (vv. 6–7), and fifth (vv. 8–12a) combine to force the keyword *ʿbr* ("cross") before our attention.

By "rising" or "standing up" (13:15), Samuel himself now does and embodies what he has just said (v. 14) Saul's kingdom will not do. The geographical connection—that Saul and his people also return like Samuel from Gilgal by the Jordan to the hill country of Benjamin—has to be assumed in MT; but it is stated in GT and may have been lost from an earlier Hebrew text by an easy copyist's mistake (the eye jumping from one Gilgal to the next). In GT's long plus, "meeting" is used absolutely. This usage is unique not just in Kingdoms but in all the translated OT; however, it is found four times in Maccabees. Philistines are still in nearby Michmash; and they now use against Saul (v. 17) the same "three-headed" tactic that he has used against Nahash of Ammon (11:11). To reinforce the already-noted parallel between Saul's "folly" (13:13) and David's

(2 Sam 24:10), this three-company thrust is called a "destroyer" (*mašḥît*)—like the divine agent in 2 Sam 24:16–17. After the routes taken by the three companies of Philistine raiders have been described (1 Sam 13:17–18), the expected battle report is delayed for a preliminary account of the technological imbalance between Israel and Philistines.

[19–23] Weapons are simply farmers' tools with a few adjustments: spears can become pruning hooks and then spears again, and swords become the blades of a plough—just as farmers themselves become soldiers (after the harvest, when kings lead out their armies to war). But such alterations, just like regular sharpening, require technical skill that is said to be a Philistine monopoly. The Philistines are content to sharpen tools for the appropriate fee (vv. 20–21), but they keep to themselves the skills of their trade to prevent Israel's tools from becoming weapons turned against them (v. 19). This information heightens the expectation of success for the "three-headed destroyer," so that the exploits of Jonathan and his lad are all the more surprising. Contrary to the expectations of some scholars, who know they are dealing here with a narrative that purports to tell of a period in which we know that iron began to be used in the ancient Near East (hence "Iron I"), there is no indication in this text that it is the new iron technology that separates Philistines from Israel. Iron (*barzel*) is rarely mentioned in Samuel–Kings. It has made only two appearances in BTH: iron tools mentioned at the end of David's victory at Ammonite Rabbah (2 Sam 12:31), and the "iron horns" worn by the prophet Zedekiah (1 Kgs 22:11). And we find talk of iron more often in nonsynoptic portions of Chronicles (9x)[29] than of Samuel–Kings (6x).[30] However, the *pym* (v. 21), equivalent to two-thirds of a shekel, is often stated to be evidence that this report has originated close to the period that it reports: the one securely dated and inscribed example of this weight belongs to the early monarchic period.

[14:1–5] Jonathan proposes to his armor-bearer action against a Philistine position (14:1); and the report begun by this challenge is interrupted immediately and at length (vv. 2–5) before being resumed and repeated in 14:6. The proposal will build on Jonathan's earlier success—only his "thousand" have been reported victorious at Geba, but neither of Saul's two thousand (13:2–3). The introduction to this fresh exploit of Jonathan offers several contrasts between father and son (1–3). Jonathan has one lad, while his father has reduced his force to some six hundred men; Jonathan's one lad bears/wears (*nōśēʾ*) his armor (v. 1), while a priest in Saul's entourage bears/wears (*nōśēʾ*) the ephod (v. 3); Jonathan has half of the metal weapons available to Israel (13:22); and

29. See 1 Chr 22:3, 14, 16; 29:2 (2x), 7; 2 Chr 2:7, 14 (6, 13); 24:12.
30. See 1 Sam 17:7; 2 Sam 23:7; 1 Kgs 6:7; 8:51; 2 Kgs 6:5, 6.

despite the availability of the divinatory ephod, Saul and his men are unaware that Jonathan and his lad have slipped away.

[6–7] Jonathan is already a more kingly figure than his father. He has a confidence in Yahweh (v. 6) equal to his name ("Yahweh has granted"); and when he repeats his call to his armor-bearer, he manifests a soldier's coarse scorn for his opponents. When he dubs the Philistines "the uncircumcised" in the first words the author puts in his mouth, he anticipates his dying father (31:4) in the first—and also last—words ascribed to him in BTH; and he thereby introduces a theme that we find in the books of Samuel clustered near the beginning (1 Sam 14:6; 17:26, 36; 18:25, 27) and the end (1 Sam 31:4; 2 Sam 1:20; 3:14) of Saul's story. We have already noticed (on 1 Sam 13:5–6) how this narrator models himself on the language of BTH. The readiness of Jonathan's armor-bearer to follow his master's heart's wish (14:7) echoes what Samuel has explained about Yahweh's expectation of Saul's successor (13:14). Would that Saul shared Yahweh's heart.

[8–12a] Jonathan responds to his lad's readiness to follow, using the most hard-worked word in this whole passage: "we're 'crossing' (*ʿbrym*) . . ." (vv. 1, 6, 8); and the Philistines, as if they have half overheard them, pick up the same consonants (only differently vocalized) and talk about these "Hebrews" emerging from their caves (v. 11). Jonathan says that he will take one of the possible answers of the Philistines as a sign from Yahweh. Such signs are not a part of BTH, and are featured only near the beginning (1 Sam 2:34; 10:7, 9; 14:10) and the end (2 Kgs 19:29; 20:8, 9) of Samuel–Kings. In every other case, the sign is promised to someone else ("to you") by a man of God, or Samuel, or Isaiah. In this case, talk of the sign starts with Jonathan himself, and it is promised "to ourselves." I suspect that his wager is of the "Heads I win, tails you lose" variety. Jonathan knows the Philistines to be completely confident on their rocky outpost: if the Hebrew slaves have come to turn themselves in, they should wait below; if they have more mischievous intent, they were welcome to attempt a contest against impossible odds after an impossible ascent. We have just been reminded of the Philistine technical superiority (13:19–22). Jonathan is set on achieving such a surprise, and his lad is with him 100 percent. In any case, when the enemy post responds with words they intend as a taunt against fugitives emerging from their hiding places (14:11–12; cf. 13:6), tantamount to "We'll show you a thing [*dābār*] or two," Jonathan takes as the promised sign the "word" (*dābār*) that for them was a threat: "Yahweh has put them in Israel's power."

1 Samuel 14:12b–16

12b And Jonathan said to his armor-bearer,
"Come up behind me,

for Yahweh has given them into the hand of Israel."
13 And Jonathan went up on his hands and on his feet,
and his armor-bearer behind him;
and they [fell] *looked attentively* facing Jonathan,
and he struck them
and his armor-bearer was dealing death behind him.
14 And the first strike
that Jonathan struck, and his armor-bearer,
was some twenty men [in about half a furrow of an acre of field[a]] *by missiles and pebbles of the field.*
15 And there was trembling in the camp, *and* in [the] field, and [in] all the people.
[The] *Those in* post and the destroyer trembled as well
and they were not willing to act;
and the earth shook,
and it came to be as divine trembling.
16 And the scouts of Saul in Gibeah of Benjamin saw;
and look: the [horde] *camp*[a] [melted and went] *was troubled hither* and thither.[b]

14a. Here MT's *kbḥṣy mʿnh ṣmd śdh* is difficult: *mʿnh* is read as "furrow" in Ps 129:3 (K); and what a pair (*ṣmd*) of oxen plow in a day is taken to be an acre. However, GT may have read *wbḥṣym wbʾbny hśdh* (both with arrows and with stones of the field)—*DCH* 5:409. Or there could have been confusion between *ṣmd* and *ṣwr*.

16a. The GT represents *hmḥnh* rather then *hhmwn* (MT).

b. Instead of MT's difficult *wylk whlm*, GT appears to have read *hlm whlm*. Perhaps both became corrupted from the straightforward *wylk hlm whlm* ("and went hither and thither").

[12b–16] After so much preparatory talk (vv. 6–12a), Jonathan's instructions to his lad are brief (12b), and the action is reported at lightning speed (13). Jonathan scrambles hands-and-feet to the top, his armor-bearer behind; and—in even fewer words—he fells the enemy in front, for his lad to dispatch behind. The GT reports the "weapons" they used on some twenty victims; the variant in MT defines the space in which this "harvest" took place. The spreading effect of Jonathan's lightning strike on different groups of Philistines is told at greater leisure, as it comes to embrace even the (elite?) "destroyer" force—and even the ground itself, which suffered a colossal shaking (v. 15). If MT has "all the people" (of Israel) "trembling after" Saul in the previous episode (13:7), now the boot is on the other foot. Saul's lookouts can see that the Philistines are in turmoil.

1 Samuel 14:17–35 Saul's Curse

1 Samuel 14:17–19a

17 And Saul said to the people who were with him,
"Be sure to count
and see
who went away from us."
And they counted,
and saw
that Jonathan and his armor-bearer were not *found.*
18 And Saul said to Ahijah,
"Bring near the [ark of the Deity] *ephod.*"

For he it was b/wore the ephod on that day before[a] Israel.	For the ark of the Deity came to be on that day—and the sons of Israel.

19 And it came to be, [as long] as Saul spoke to the priest,
and the thronging that was in the Philistine camp . . .
and it was getting larger and larger.

18a. The difference in Hebrew between "and the sons of" (*wbny*, MT) and "before" (*lpny*, GT) is easier to explain than between ark and ephod.

[17–19a] We have already seen how Jonathan's opening words to his armor-bearer (v. 1) are resumed with a small but significant alteration (v. 6). The opening of this paragraph (vv. 17–18) takes us back to Saul, his people, and Ahijah the priest—to the material reported in a parenthesis (vv. 2–3). We are told there that the "people" with Saul are six hundred men. Saul, assuming that some of his own people are the cause of the commotion, has a count taken to see who is not with him: a further numbering now will elicit just who is missing. Readers who know the troubling story at the end of the books of Samuel of David's count of his people may wonder at the abandon—and at least apparent impunity—with which Saul numbers his people time after time (11:8; 13:15; 14:17; 15:4).

The MT and the GT differ over the next of Saul's instructions: whether Ahijah the priest is asked to produce the divine ark (MT) or the ephod (GT)—and 4QSam[a] is not extant here. When first introduced, Ahijah is wearing or bearing an ephod; but the mention then (v. 3) of his three immediate ancestors recalls the story of the ark (chs. 4–6). Exactly what passes between king and priest (vv. 18–19) is not easy to decide. The MT's version of Saul's orders is the only mention of the ark between its return to Israel (7:1–2) and its transfer to Jerusalem by David (2 Sam 6). On the other hand, an ephod also features in that story (2 Sam 6:14), worn by David, who was himself officiating at the transfer. Here, as in the ark narratives, along with confusion on the ground and din in the air, there is also uncertainty over the text—and possibly even gaps in the narrative line. Whatever the disagreements between our witnesses to the ancient text, the confusion among the Philistines has been caused solely by Jonathan's surprise attack.

1 Samuel 14:19b–35

19b And Saul said to the priest,
"Take in your hand."
20 And Saul [was called out] *went up* and the whole people that was with him,
and they came to the battle,
and found each man's sword against his fellow, a very great commotion.
21 And the [Hebrews] *slaves who* were with the Philistines as normal,
who went up [with them] into the camp [round about]
turned round they too
to be with Israel,
who were with Saul and Jonathan.
22 And every man of Israel,
those hiding themselves in the hill country of Ephraim,
heard that Philistines had fled,
and they too stayed close after them in the battle.
23 And Yahweh on that day saved Israel.
And, as for the battle, it passed [Beth-Awen] *the Bamoth*;
and all the people were with Saul, some ten thousand of men;
and the battle was scattered into every city in the hill country of Ephraim.[a]

24 And Saul, he had acted ignorantly in great ignorance on that day,	**24** And the men of Israel, they had been hard-pressed,[a] on that day,

and [Saul] put a curse[b] on the people, saying,
"Cursed be the man who eats food till evening
and I take vengeance on my enemies."
And the whole people did not taste food.

25 And the whole land breakfasted, and Iaal was an apiary thicket on the surface of the ground.	**25** And the whole land had come into the thicket, and there was honey on the surface of the ground.

26 And the people came to the [thicket/comb] *apiary*,
and look, there was [a trail[a] of honey] *a speaker walking*;
but no one let his hand reach[b] his mouth,
for the people were afraid of the oath.

27 Now Jonathan did not hear
when his father made the people swear;
and he directed the end of the staff
that was in his hand
and dipped it in the comb of the honey,
and he brought his hand back to his mouth
and his eyes [lightened[a]] *looked up*.
28 And a man responded from the people,
and said:
"Your father put an oath—yes, an oath—on the people, saying,
'Cursed be the man[a] who eats food today.'
And the people was weary."[b]
29 And Jonathan *knew and* said:
"My father has [troubled[a]] *changed* the land.
See for sure
that my eyes have lightened
because I have tasted this little honey.[b]
30 All the more then, had the people eaten—yes, eaten—today[a] from the booty of their enemies
which they found;
for now *the* striking on the Philistines has [not] been greater."[b]
31 And [they] *he*[a] struck the Philistines on that day from Michmas[h] to Ayyalon;
and the people was extremely weary.
32 And the people went by night[a] to the booty;
and they took sheep and cattle and young cattle
and slaughtered them on the ground,
and the people ate on top of the blood.
33 And they reported to Saul, saying,
"Look, the people are sinning against Yahweh
in eating on top of the blood."
And he said:
"[You have acted treacherously;] *In Gettaim*[a] roll to me [today] *here*[b] a great stone."
34 And Saul said:
"Scatter[a] among the people
and say to them,
'Bring near to me each his ox and each his sheep,
and slaughter them on this
and eat,
and do not sin against Yahweh

in eating on top of the blood.'"
And all the people brought near each [his ox by] *what was in* his hand at night,
and they slaughtered them there.
35 And Saul built *there* an altar to Yahweh.
This he began—building an altar to Yahweh.

23a. The *BA* (257–58) proposes that GT found this large plus in the underlying text; against Wellhausen, it claims that MT could not have omitted it by accident.

24a. The textual divergence at the beginning of this verse is probably related to what has gone before. Wellhausen, followed by many, including McCarter, retroverted GT to *wšʾwl šgh šggh gdwlh bywm hhwʾ*; and DJD 72 demonstrates how the position of [*w*]*š*ʾ[*wl*], attested in 4QSam^a, renders this reconstruction plausible. Although the texts are very different in sense, the confusion may have started from the same simple misreading that we noted at 13:2, 6 above. In unpointed Hebrew, no distinction is made between *ś* and *š*; and this increases the possibility of confusion between *yśrʾl* (Israel) and *šʾwl* (Saul), which share three consonants, and between *ngś* ("be hard pressed") and *šgg* ("act ignorantly"), which share two (though in reverse order).

b. Elsewhere *ʾlh hipʿil* is used only in 1 Kgs 8:31 (BTH, //2 Chr 6:22). The GT's *arasthai* renders *ʾlh* as *qal* also in Judg 17:2. The GT appears to have a double rendering of *wyʾl*: *agnoein* is used in Num 12:11 to render *yʾl nipʿal* (act foolishly).

26a. The term *hlk* appears as a noun only once more in HB (2 Sam 12:4), where it appears to be personal: a "walker" (as GT takes it here); and GT's "speak" appears to have read *dbr* rather than *dbš* ("honey").

b. Since in v. 27 *wyšb* precedes "his hand to his mouth," and since GT uses the same vb. in both verses, *mśyg* (MT) should be seen as a corruption of *mšyb*.

27a. The MT (K) has "and his eyes saw," as rendered by GT. The verbs *rʾh* and *ʾwr* are side by side in v. 29; Q here requires *wtʾrnh*.

28a. Here 4QSam^a reads *hʾdm* (cf. *anthrōpos* in GT) for *hʾyš* (Fincke 88). The MT reads *ʾrwr hʾyš* in Josh 6:26; 1 Sam 14:24, 28; Jer 11:3; 20:15—and never *ʾrwr hʾdm*. In each case GT has *epikataratos ho anthrōpos*. Frequently *anthrōpos* corresponds to *ʾyš* in 1 Samuel (MT); but there may also have been a shift in Hebrew usage.

b. This *wyʿp* is from *ʿyp*, not the commoner *ʿwp*. It is not clear whether the observation about the weariness of the people is spoken by their representative or added by the narrator (as in v. 31 below).

29a. This is the unique instance in Samuel of *ʿkr*. Here DJD 73–74 reads *ʿkwr* before a gap in the MS (while admitting that only the damaged initial ʿ is at all clear) and supposes that 4QSam^a has read the emphatic *ʿkwr ʿkr* and not the simple *ʿkr* as in MT (see also Fincke 89). The GT gives no support to reconstructing emphatic duplication. Nowhere else in the Bible is *ʿkr* correlated with the ambiguous *apallassein* (see further below).

b. In 4QSam^a, as in GT, "honey" (*dbš*) bears the article.

30a. Here 4QSam^a lacks *hywm* before *hʿm*.

b. The GT, like 4QSam^a, has *rbh hmkh* for *rbth mkh* (MT).

31a. The GT, like 4QSam^a, opens with a sg. vb.

32a. Caquot and de Robert accept the K here, taking it as a homophone of the common *ʿśh*, and cognate with *ʿśh* in Arabic. The Q is *wyʿṭ*. Polzin suggests that the vb. may be *ʿwp*, "the people flew on the booty." See the full note in Fincke 89–90.

33a. The GT has *bgtym* for *bgdtm* (MT).

b. The GT's "here" supposes *hlwm* for MT's *hywm* ("today").

34a. Here 4QSam[a] has *npṣw* for *pṣw* (MT).

[19b–24] Two related terms provide the keynotes for the troubled situation of the Philistines: *hāmôn* (v. 19, repeated from 16), related to *hāmâ*, means a throng, both a crowd and the noise and confusion associated with it; and *mĕhûmâ* (v. 20), related to *hûm* (also cognate with *hāmâ*), means a tumult. Each word has been anticipated in the earlier ark narratives: *hāmôn* is the thronging battle din that Eli can hear at a distance (4:14), and *mĕhûmâ* (5:9, 11) refers to the great and deadly panic in the Philistine cities. These two nouns and their related verbs will not reappear in either book of Samuel. However, 1 Sam 7:10 (in the immediate context of 1 Sam 4–6) and 2 Sam 22:15 (= Ps 18:14 [15]) use yet a third cognate verb: *wyhmm* from *hmm*.

The Philistine turmoil, in turn, allows different groups of Israelites—"they too" (*gam-hēmmâ*)—to rally to their people's cause (v. 22). Each of vv. 21 and 22 focuses on a different category. Those who have been in regular Philistine service in their army camp are best placed to turn immediately to Saul and Jonathan (v. 21). Then all those in hiding in the central highlands (GT goes as far as to say "all Israel in hiding" [v. 22]) joined in on the battle. It seems best to suppose that Saul is seeking a divine ruling over whether to involve himself and his army in what is going on. We may also suppose that the replacement of ephod by ark in MT has been influenced by the renewed cluster of nouns for noise and confusion.

All of the above seem sensible comments; and yet it remains obscure just how the elements of v. 19 relate to each other and to the opening of v. 20: (1) While Saul is speaking to the priest, the confused din in the Philistine camp is becoming greater and greater. (2) Saul tells the priest to "take in" (*ʾsp*) his hand. (3) Saul and everyone with him is called out to the battle. The first question is whether the increasingly noisy confusion from the battle makes the discussion between king and priest more or less necessary: does it require greater clarification, or is a Philistine rout becoming more and more obvious? The commotion on the field is nicely reflected in some textual confusion between the reports of it in MT and GT.

"Take in" and "hand" are both very common words, but nowhere else in HB are they connected. We cannot deduce with any certainty, because of the unique terms in which Saul's instruction is couched, whether the priest is to do what he has been summoned to do, or to stop doing it. However, since "gather" or "collect" (the more normal sense of the verb) is more likely to imply "retract" or "withdraw," we may suppose that Saul was seeking to bring these proceedings to a close. On the other hand, the fact that Saul—and not just his people—is "called out" (v. 20) to the battle suggests that the decision is not his own, but a divine summons mediated by the priest. Has a cautious Saul been protracting the consultation till it becomes obvious how things stand? To add, even if only minimally, to the confusion of the scene, MT and GT are again (14:21, as in 13:3, 7) at variance over whether to read *hʿbrym* ("the Hebrews," MT) or *hʿbdym* ("the slaves," GT).

It is only at the end of Judges[31] and in 1 Samuel[32] that GT simply transliterates the Hebrew *ʾēpôd* (as in 1 Sam 14:3). The preferred rendering in the Greek Pentateuch and elsewhere is *epōmis* ("tunic"), a word that is probably a reasonably fair rendering and also starts with letters sounding similar to the Hebrew. However, David is said to wear a *stolē* ("robe") in 2 Sam 6:14//1 Chr 15:27; and two other translations are used once each.[33] When formally dressed, the high priest wears an ephod, and the ephod is a divinatory device. Some scholars hold these distinct, while others see them as one and the same. It seems clear, at least, that the divinatory ephod is normally carried (or worn?—*nāśāʾ* can mean either), and was presumably operated by a priest, as here, or priest substitute. Resort to transliteration at least more or less guarantees that the translator has found exactly this Hebrew word in his text.

Jonathan has told his lad it matters little to Yahweh whether he "saves" by many or by few (1 Sam 14:6). They have started the assault on the Philistines as a twosome and have become many; but it is still Yahweh who saves Israel on that day (v. 23a). At this point B marks not just a verse break but also the start of a major new paragraph (vv. 23b–35). Which town the battle passes (v. 23b) is a matter of divided testimony: The MT has Beth-Awen, a near neighbor of or alternate name for Beth-El; GT has Bamoth, perhaps the locality at or near Gibeon (2 Chr 1:3). In the longer text of GT, the battle itself "became dispersed" into every town in the hill country of Ephraim. This phrase reappears in the report of Absalom's rout (2 Sam 18:8), there too immediately before mention of a thicket (*yaʿar*).

Both (very different) texts of the beginning of v. 24 open with the subject of the sentence, not the verb, thus marking a disjunction in the narrative. It is natural grammatically to read what follows in both versions as a flashback. Saul has more than one reason for being suspicious of his son. Although it has been trumpeted abroad as a victory in Saul's own name (13:3–4), the success at Geba has been Jonathan's—and even worse, it has led to a large-scale Philistine reprisal. And he has been informed by Samuel that Yahweh has already

31. Judges 17:5; 18:14, 17, 18, 20.
32. First Samuel 2:18, 28; 14:3; 22:18; 23:6, 9; 30:7 (2x).
33. Exodus 28:27; Hos 3:4.

identified his successor—is he to be replaced by the impetuous Jonathan? It might still be a forced reading to suppose that Saul only utters his curse once he knows that his son is missing, and hence out of earshot. But even if the curse was spoken before Jonathan's disappearance (on another rash expedition?) is known, Saul has reason for dissatisfaction with him. However, it is effective storytelling when both king and reader learn at the same time that the most successful agent of the king's vengeance on his enemies may be in unwitting breach of a royal oath. The opening words of MT return to the rare expression in 13:6, of Israel being "hard-pressed," the population dispersed and in hiding (repeated as recently as v. 22), and the fighters facing overwhelming odds. What will be said about Jonathan is similarly disjunctive (v. 27). The issue is whether Jonathan has not "heard" or has not "hearkened" at the time of his father's curse. If he has not been there to hear, hearkening hardly comes into question.

The text of our narrative preserved in Greek draws explicit attention to one of the issues for the interpreter: whether Saul is unaware that Jonathan has not heard his oath, and indeed whether Jonathan is unaware that Saul has uttered it. In the text attested here by GT, whether more original or not, the narrator anticipates at an early stage what Saul only belatedly becomes aware of: the narrator has taken the opportunity early in the story of Saul to evaluate his mistaken action by using a (normally cultic) term that Saul will find appropriate to use of himself only toward the end.

Neither *šgh šggh* ("lapsed a lapse") nor *šggh gdwlh* ("a great lapse") is precisely replicated in HB. However, the verb *šgh* is used once (more) in Samuel (1 Sam 26:21); there Saul is not being talked about, but he is talking of himself. And there again the verb is intensified, this time by "very." But Wellhausen's retroversion of 14:24a, which DJD is able to correlate with the sketchy evidence in 4QSam[a], is particularly apt. The cognate Greek verb (*agnoein*) and noun (*agnoia*) are only combined in one other passage of HB, where the corresponding Hebrew verb and noun are *šgg* and *šggh*. In itself, the match between Greek and Hebrew terms is less than ideal. However, the context in Lev 5:17–19 is of inadvertent error; and the Greek translators of the "historical" books were influenced by the rendering of relevant portions of the Pentateuch.

[25–30] The MT does not divide vv. 25–35. A fully satisfactory account of the first episode may be unattainable; however, it is at least possible to describe some of the complexities:

- In MT, v. 26a largely repeats what we have read in v. 25, about all the land/people entering a *yaʿar* and finding honey there.
- In GT, "all the people" (with Saul) are distinct from "all the land": the people are refraining from food, while the (rest of the) land breakfasts.

- In addition to the common *y'r*, meaning "forest" or "thicket," there is a rare homonym that means something like or something related to "honey" (Song 5:1).
- Its unique cognate *y'rh* (perhaps "honeycomb") is connected with the regular term for honey in v. 27.
- Whether or not there is deliberate play on the two senses of *ya'ar*, there is a conflict of readings at the end of v. 27: MT requires that we read *wt'rnh* as "shone"; GT uses "looked up" to translate the same consonants as are preserved in MT, but with the middle two transposed (*wtr'nh*).
- The GT's *apēllachen* (v. 29) is ambiguous: "has made away with" would offer a fair rendering of *'ākar* ("destroy/injure"), while "has delivered" would represent a polite euphemism.

The *qal* form of MT's verb *'ûr* ("shine/be light") is very rare in HB. "Eyes" are its subject only in 1 Sam 14:27, 29; the three further instances are in 1 Sam 29:10; Isa 60:1; and Prov 4:18. The *nip'al* is even less common: 2 Sam 2:32 along with Ps 76:4 (5) and Job 33:30. The GT does recognize the forms of this verb *'ûr* in 1 Sam 29:10 and 2 Sam 2:32, both of which refer to the "lightening" that occurs at dawn; and GT does agree with the consonantal text of MT in 14:27 (see above). However, it is likely that forms of *'ûr* were original to both verses. The wordplay in "tasted" (*ṭ'm*) a "piece" (*m'ṭ*) almost guarantees that the previous clause in 14:29 had read "See [*r'w*] that my eyes shone [*'rw*]." The significance of "shone" may be clarified by two of the few passages in which the (causative) *hip'il* of this verb takes "eyes" as its object: "For our God to lighten our eyes and to grant us a little reviving in our slavery" (Ezra 9:8) and "Lighten my eyes, lest I sleep the sleep of death" (Ps 13:3 [4]). In both cases, the eyes shining or becoming light are a sign of revival and recovery. The food has done Jonathan good; and the wider army would also have benefited. The MT uses *r'w* ("see") and *'rw* ("shone") side by side in v. 29; but GT has only "see" and "seen."

The wordplay goes still further. When one of the bystanders tells Jonathan about his father's oath, this is introduced as a response (v. 28)—in this case, a response not to something said to him, but to something he has seen. He has seen the "lightening" (*'ûr*) of the prince's eyes and is immediately reminded of the king's "curse" (*'rr*). In an unvocalized text, the consonants *wt'rnh* (v. 27) can be read either "and they shone" or "and they were cursed." No wonder that the one suggested or recalled the other. Jonathan's own following comment (v. 29) continues the spirit of wordplay, but redirects attention away from "shine"/"curse" toward "shine" (*'rw*)/'see" (*r'w*). The danger of the curse is restated in the verb *'ākar*—and that "dire trouble" is something Saul has brought on the land, not on himself. For Jonathan, at least in his public response, eating the honey has improved his own situation, but being inhibited from eating has worsened the national situation.

Jonathan was not only ignorant of his father's curse, but also scathing about the folly of it once he heard of it. Saul may have wanted to impose some military discipline on a growing band of escaping slaves, while Jonathan knew that an army marches on its stomach. In any case, Jonathan has been fighting for longer in the day than Saul and his men: a rule that has served to keep them in order is rash when applied to him. The term he uses of his father's action is far from diplomatic. Often *ʿākar* is rendered "trouble," but that is hardly a strong enough term for the danger caused to Jacob when two of his sons avenged the rape of their sister Dinah (Gen 34:30), or to Israel by Achar/n (Josh 7:25), or to Jephthah (at least as he stated the matter) by his daughter (Judg 11:35). It is dangerous folly on that scale that Saul shares, and accordingly the whole land is in hazard. Yet Jonathan does not appear to consider himself under threat from his father's curse: his eyes have improved as a result of eating honey, and Israel might have fought better if they had eaten something.

[31–35] The following episode is read in two competing ways. The one accepts the interpretation made explicit in GT, while the other believes that something more sinister is at stake. When night comes, Saul's people are free from the terms of his curse. They now slaughter animals looted from their enemies, as Jonathan has wished they would have done earlier. The focus of critical attention is on the Hebrew phrase *ʾākal ʿal-haddām*, literally, "eat upon/over the blood." The GT translates this "eat *with* the blood," and understands the sin against Yahweh to consist in a breach of the food laws: meat should only be eaten from an animal slaughtered in such a way that all its blood has been drained from it (and slaughter on a stone assists the draining process). The other interpretation takes off by comparing this scene with the instruction in Lev 19:26—"You shall not eat upon the blood. You shall not practice augury or divination"—and understands that eating over the blood, especially at night, represents a form of communication with the forces of the underworld. That is what Saul seeks to block; and such a reading makes Saul's later desperate turn (ch. 28) to a woman who can call Samuel back from that lower world all the more poignant.[34]

Two readings can also be offered of the relationship between the great stone (v. 33) and the altar (v. 35). The latter verse may provide a delayed clarification that the great stone ordered by Saul is actually an altar. Alternatively, it may intend that we understand that Saul goes on to build a proper altar, after his temporary expedient of the great stone. Either way, Saul here takes his place as altar builder between Samuel (7:17) and David (2 Sam 24). This will be the first altar built by Saul, and indeed any king of Israel. According to Bar-Efrat

34. The specific terms used in Lev 19:26 for illicit divination (*nḥš* and *ʿwnn*) appear next to those driven out by Saul (*ʾwb* and *ydʿny*) in the comprehensive list of diviners in 2 Kgs 21:6 (BTH).

(2007: 206), David Kimchi (1160–1235) comments that that altar was the first of the altars that Saul built.

1 Samuel 14:36–16:23 Saul Rejected, David Anointed

1 Samuel 14:36–15:9

36 And Saul said:
"Let us go down after the Philistines by night,
and let us plunder among them till the light of morning,
and we shall not leave among them any man."
And they said:
"All that is good in your eyes, do."

And the priest said:
"Let us draw near hither to the Deity."
37 And Saul asked of the Deity:
"Shall I go down after Philistines?
Will you give them into the hand of Israel?"
But he did not answer him on that day.
38 And Saul said:
"[Come] *Bring* near here, all corners[a] of the people,
and know
and see
whereby this sin came about today.
39 For, as Yahweh lives, the one who saves Israel,
even if [it exists in] *he answers against*[a] Jonathan my son,
he will die the death."
And no one was answering him of all the people.
40 And he said to all Israel:
"You—you shall be [across there,[a] one] *for servitude*;
and I and Jonathan my son—we shall be [across there, one] *for servitude*."
And the people said to Saul:
"What is good in your eyes, do."

41 And Saul said [to] Yahweh, God of Israel,
"*Why is it you did not answer your servant today?*
Is it in me or in Jonathan my son that the wrong is?
Yahweh, God of Israel, give 'manifests';
And
if it says this,

surely give to your people Israel,
surely give 'whole'";
and Jonathan was taken and Saul,
and the people went out.
42 And Saul said,
"Cast between me and Jonathan my son.
And whomever Yahweh takes, let him die."
And the people said to Saul,
"The matter is not so."[a]
And Saul prevailed over the people,
and they cast between him and Jonathan his son.
And Jonathan was taken.
43 And Saul said to Jonathan,
"Declare to me what you have done."
And Jonathan declared to him
and said,
"I tasted, just tasted, with the end of the staff
that was in my hand,
a little honey.
I am before you.
I should die."
44 And Saul said,
"So may God do *to me*
and so may he continue—
if Jonathan does not surely die."
45 And the people said to Saul,
"Shall Jonathan die,
who has performed this great deliverance in Israel?
[It is unthinkable![a]]
As Yahweh lives, there shall not fall to the ground from the hair of his head,
for it is [with] *the people*[b] *of* God that [he] has performed this day."
And the people [ransomed] *prayed for* Jonathan *on that day*,
and he did not die.

46 And Saul went up from following *the* Philistines;
and *the* Philistines went to their place.
47 As for Saul, he took the kingship[a] over Israel;
and he fought round about with all his enemies: with Moab, and with the sons of Ammon, and with *the sons of* Edom,
and with Baitheor, and with the king[s] of Zobah,[b] and with the Philistines, and everywhere he turned he would [bring ill[c]] *be saved.*

48 And he acted valiantly
and struck Amalek;
and he delivered Israel from the hand of their plunderer[s].[a]

49 And the sons of Saul were Jonathan and Ishvi[a] and Malkishua;
and as for the name of his two daughters,
the name of the firstborn was Merab and the name of the younger was Michal.[b]
50 And the name of Saul's wife was Ahinoam daughter of Ahimaaz.
And the name of his army chief was Abiner, son of Ner, uncle of Saul.
51 And Kish father of Saul and Ner father of Abner were *son of Iamein*[a] son of Abiel.

52 And the battle against the Philistines was strong all the days of Saul;
and Saul saw every heroic fellow and every man of valor
and gathered him to himself.

15:1 And Samuel said to Saul:
"Me Yahweh sent
to anoint you king [over his people,] over Israel.[a]
Now then, listen to the voice of Yahweh['s words].

2 This is what Yahweh of hosts has said:
'*Now* I have taken account of what Amalek has done to Israel,
[what he set for him] *how he met him*[a] on the way,
at his going up from Egypt.
3 Now go
and strike down Amalek

and Iereim and everything that is his	and make *ḥērem*[a] everything that is his

and you shall not preserve him
and you shall destroy him,
and you shall not have pity toward them;
and put to death from man to woman, from weaned and to suckling,
from ox and to sheep, from camel and to ass.'"

4 And Saul let the people hear,
and he counted them in [Telaim] *Gilgal* [two] *four* hundred thousand of foot,
and [ten] *thirty* thousand—the men of Judah.
5 And Saul came to the cit[y]*ies*[a] of Amalek,

and lay in wait[b] in the watercourse.
6 And Saul said to the Kenites:
"Come,
turn aside,
[come down] from the midst of the Amalekites,
lest I gather you with them.
And you yourselves acted loyally with all the sons of Israel
at their going up from Egypt."
And the Kenites turned aside from the midst of the Amalekites.
7 And Saul struck Amalek from Havila as one goes to *Ash*Shur
which is opposite Egypt.
8 And he took Agag king of Amalek alive,
but all the people he [made *ḥērem*] *killed*[a] by sword's mouth.
9 And Saul had pity, and the people, on Agag *alive*,
and on the best of the flock and the herd and the [fatlings] *eatables*,
and on the [young[a]] *vineyards* and on everything good;
and [they were] *he was* not willing
to [make them *ḥērem*] *destroy*[b] *them*;
but all the work despised and rejected, that they did [make *ḥērem*] *destroy*.

38a. Here "corners" (B) is a very literal rendering; *pnwt* is used similarly with "the people" in Judg 20:2, and may refer to prominent members of the community rather than representatives of all sections. The LT has *phylas* (tribes).

39a. The GT has *yʿnh* for MT's *yšnw*. We see *yšnw* once again in 1 Sam 23:23,[35] there too in close proximity to "know and see" (23:22).

40a. The MT's *lʿbr* is attested only once more (1 Kgs 7:20), while *lʿbd* (underlying GT) is unique, although pl. "as servants" is common. Since GT is very literal, we can assume that it did not know the plus *ʾḥd* (2x) in MT.

42a. "The word is not this" (B) has rendered the underlying text overliterally.

45a. To the thought of Jonathan's dying with Saul's consent, MT has the people make the same response (*ḥālîlâ*, "It is unthinkable") as Jonathan will make when David tells him (20:2) his father is set on killing him.

b. Here GT has read *ʿm* as *ʿam* ("people") rather than *ʿim* ("with"). See further below.

47a. Here B renders alternate Hebrew texts: *elachen tou basileuein* represents *lkd hmlwkh*, while *kataklēroutai ergon* represents *lkd mlʾkh*; LT conflates and simplifies.

b. Here 4QSam[a], like GT, has "king of Zobah" (sg.).

c. The final vb. as reconstructed in 4QSam[a] is "save," as in GT, but active (*ywšyʿ*), not pass. MT's *yršyʿ* may be a misreading of the 2d consonant, no less polemical than the alteration of "save" from active to pass. in GT. Klein appears to defend MT.

35. And only 2x more, in Deut 29:14; Esth 3:8—and with 2d pers. suffixes in Gen 24:42, 49; 43:4; Deut 13:4; Judg 6:36.

48a. Here *šsyw* (4QSam[a]) is pl., as in GT. The MT's sg. may refer to David.

49a. For *yšwy* (MT), LT has *Iessiou* (< *yšyw*?) and B *Iessioul*, which Fincke (91) explains as a corruption of the nickname *yšy'wd* ("another Jesse"). He reports that the space in 4QSam[a] requires a longer name—he "restores" Aminadab from 1 Sam 31:2 (GT).

b. Here 4QSam[a] gives Saul's daughter's name as *mkl*—i.e., neither *mykl* (MT) nor *mlkl* (B).

51a. "Son of Iamein" in B represents *bnymyn*, i.e., Benjamin (LT has "son of Iabin").

1a. The LT also reads "over his people," but after "over Israel," not before. The different placing of this plus suggests that it is a secondary adjustment toward the (otherwise unique) 9:16. Both 1 Sam 15:17 and 2 Sam 12:7 follow the shorter "anoint . . . over Israel" of 2 Sam 5:3, 17 (BTH).

2a. The GT *apantan* ("meet") normally corresponds to *pg'*; but MT has *śm* ("place") here.

3a. "Make *ḥērem*" is analogous to B's *IEREIM* (here and in v. 8), which has been understood as a proper name but had been intended as transcribing a form of the Hebrew *hḥrym*, although not the exact form found in MT. Later in the verse, B then translates *hḥrym* by *anathematizein*. On the rendering of this list of commands, *BA* (271) has a full note.

5a. In Hebrew, "city of" and "cities of" differ only in the order of the letters: *'yr* (MT) and *'ry* (GT). Amalek's towns are otherwise unknown and are puzzling in terms of a mobile, bedouin-like people.

b. The GT's *kai enēdreusen* probably represents *wy'rb*, of which the (unique *hip'il* form of) MT's *wyrb* is a defective spelling, not a form of *ryb* ("strive").

8a. Here (contrast v. 3), following *IEREIM*, B renders the sense with the common vb. "kill."

9a. The MT's *krym* may be more appropriate for a nomadic context than *krmym* (GT).

b. Now "destroy" is a third rendering in GT for *hḥrym*.

[36a] Saul now proposes a different use of the night: plundering the Philistines till morning light. His people are ready for him to do what he thinks best.

[36b–40] And—there is no indicator in the Hebrew or Greek text of a "but"—the priest calls for a confirmatory approach to the Deity. One wonders whether the priest has been wanting to have a formal consultation with the Deity since being asked to "gather" or "take in" his hand (v. 19). Saul puts his question in terms that closely anticipate those used by David in BTH (2 Sam 5:19; cf. 5:23), also concerning an assault on the Philistines. In 2 Sam 5:19, Yahweh simply says to David, "Go up. . . ." However, David has not proposed leaving no one alive. Here no response—and that is not the same as a negative response—comes to Saul's question; and he interprets that silence as the result of a "sin." But is this presumed sin (v. 38) the same sin as the irregular slaughter (vv. 31–33) that he has supposed he has put an end to by providing a stone altar (vv. 34–35), or something else?

The theme of divine response (*ʿnh*, v. 37) is uncommon in Samuel (and Kings)[36] and thus all the more significant where it does occur. It is mentioned three times in 1 Sam 7–9. Samuel cries to Yahweh following sacrifice and is answered (7:9); Samuel looks on Saul and is answered (9:17); and between these two instances, Samuel warns the people that they will appeal to Yahweh against their king but will receive no answer (8:18). However, as things turn out, the first person in the narrative to lack divine response is Saul: this is noted near both beginning (14:37) and end (28:6, 15) of his reign.[37] As for the people, the answers they give and the answers they fail to give are also significant in this story. One of the people answers Jonathan's unspoken query about what has happened to him (14:28); but no one from his people answers Saul when he announces the method by which he is to identify the sin that has blocked his access to divine response (14:39)—his people are already all too well aware (14:28).

Saul summons his chiefs "hither" (v. 38), as the priest has earlier proposed approaching "hither" to God (v. 36).[38] Despite superficial similarity with the invitation in Judg 20:7, Saul's chiefs are being invited not to provide answers but to witness the divine answer. "Know and see" is a combination that we shall find recurring in the books of Samuel, but in different contexts. Here the seeing and knowing are simply the two aspects of the one act of recognition. The authority of the promised demonstration is underscored when Saul pronounces—in an oath by Yahweh's very life!—that even Jonathan, his son and heir, will die if guilty: no answering protest comes from those present (v. 39). However, his statement of the situation is open to different readings. Is stating the extreme case a neutral indication that no favor will be shown, that everyone's life is on the line? Why then is his own life not stated as the extreme case? Or does he already know that Jonathan has eaten and has deplored his father's curse? And is he content to be rid of a son who takes matters into his own hands, however successfully? Does he wonder whether Jonathan is the one whom Yahweh has already selected to replace him (13:14)? Is it for such reasons that he needs his leaders to witness the divine response?

[41–45] Be all that as it may, the same public process before God by which his own kingship has been recognized (10:20–22)[39] now identifies Jonathan as

36. "Answer" was never used in BTH with a divine subject; and the only two instances in Chronicles are within a plus at the end of the Chronicler's version of David's census (1 Chr 21:26, 28), where the divine response to David is noted following sacrifice at the new altar—like Samuel (1 Sam 7:9), and unlike Saul (14:37).

37. See below on 1 Sam 23:2–4 for David's contrasting receipt of a divine response.

38. The term *hălōm* is relatively rare. In Gen 16:13 and Exod 3:5, the presence of the Deity is suggested, as in v. 36; but Judg 18:3 and Ruth 2:14 involve simple invitations; and Judg 20:7 reports a summons seeking answers.

39. Significantly, though Saul has then been identified by lot, he is in hiding, and Samuel needs to ask whether someone else has not come "hither" (*hălōm*, 10:22).

having a statement to make (vv. 42–43). Like Achar/n (Josh 7:20), Jonathan admits what he has done. Resuming and also expanding his earlier, more private admission (v. 29), he declares that he has tasted—no more than tasted—a little honey, such as could be picked up with the end of his staff; and like Jephthah's daughter (Judg 11:36) he consents to his fate (v. 43). He has done what the people as a whole have not done (v. 24b). Having noticed in the forest that tasting a little honey has done him good, he now admits to the very little he has done and presents himself for death. Only at this point do the people intervene.

No one else in all of HB utters Jonathan's last words in this scene: *hinĕnî ʾāmût*. Bar-Efrat (1:209) renders "I am ready to die," directing our attention to David's words in 2 Sam 15:26 ("If he says, 'I take no pleasure in you,' here I am, let him do to me what seems good to him" [NRSV]). The comparison is particularly apt because the royal judge does proceed to pass sentence—a decision for death that is fortified by a second oath (14:44, resuming v. 39). Jonathan states that he is ready to die, and this may in a real sense be true. But in accepting his fate, is he also challenging it? By stressing how minimal his action has been, is he also drawing attention to the lack of any proportionality in the fate he is accepting? Nevertheless, the people enter the proceedings, pleading for recognition of a different imbalance.

Jonathan has said to his armor-bearer that Yahweh can "save" by many or by few (v. 6). The narrator has reported the result of the battle as Yahweh's "saving" Israel (v. 23). Saul has sworn before his leaders in the name of Yahweh, who "saves" Israel (v. 39). But his people insist that it is Jonathan (the name means "Yahweh has granted") who "has achieved this great 'saving' today"—and add that it is with God that he has achieved it (v. 45). Their protestation is skillfully worded: they anticipate reports in BTH (2 Sam 23:10, 12) of David's heroes "performing salvation" by striking down Philistines; but they also recall the occasion on which Saul has declared that not even a scoundrel should be put to death on a day when Yahweh has "performed salvation" in Israel (1 Sam 11:13). The people trump Saul's oath (*ḥy-yhwh*, 14:39) by prefacing *ḥlylh* to their own *ḥy-yhwh* (v. 45). He should not die: he is redeemed by the people. Perhaps the people agree with what Jonathan has said about the stupidity of his father's curse (vv. 29–30): if the people had been allowed to eat in the course of the day, more of the enemy would have been killed.

There are several connections between this narrative and elements of Josh 6–8. Joshua warns the people (6:18) of the danger of meddling with the devoted booty; and also utters a curse on anyone who would rebuild Jericho (6:26). An unexpected reverse (7:2–6) indicates a sacral problem; and the malefactor is identified by lot. The verb *ʿākar* ("trouble"), a principal theme of Josh 7, is used once in 1 Sam 14:29—but by Jonathan, who blames his father and not himself for the grievous trouble to the land. However, despite these correspondences, there is nothing in 1 Sam 14 that indicates knowledge of Joshua. Given the absence throughout Samuel of any explicit reference to any portion of the book of Joshua, we must suppose that Joshua has drawn on Samuel rather than the other way round.

[46–48] While MT indicates a minor paragraph break after v. 45, the first hand in B transcribes vv. 41–48 as a single unit. That invites us to read Saul's breaking off his pursuit of the Philistines as a response to the lack of divine and perhaps popular support. The following summary of Saul's military leadership (vv. 47–48) anticipates almost exactly what BTH reports about David (2 Sam 8:12): the same foes in a slightly different order:

David in 2 Sam 8:12	**Saul in 1 Sam 14:47–48**
Edom, Moab, the Ammonites, the Philistines, Amalek, Zobah	Moab, the Ammonites, Edom, Zobah, the Philistines, Amalek

The pairings Moab/Ammonites and Philistines/Amalek are maintained. And then, by pairing David's first and last[40] enemies at the center, space is provided at the end (v. 48) to expand on Saul's "valiant" actions against Amalek. Although *ḥayil* is attributed to Saul's father (9:1), and although Saul gathers to himself men who exhibit *ḥayil* (14:52), it is only in connection with his strike against Amalek that this quality is reported of himself; hence, it appears that this summary statement endorses his behavior to the Amalekites; and it is against such a backdrop that the following chapter (15), with its different judgment, must be assessed.

[49–51] Family information follows.

[52] If we already know from the principal source (1 Sam 31, BTH) that Saul will be killed in battle with Philistines, we are now told in this first interim conclusion that fighting with them is strenuous all his days—yet also that Saul relies on others: this may look forward to his recruitment of David.

[15:1–3] The earlier major systematic reflection (1 Sam 12) took the form of a dialogue between Samuel and people, which had as its topic the institution of kingship as such. The name of the first king was not mentioned but may have been hinted at (12:17, 19)[41] by the repetition of the verb "ask" (*šā'al*). This second major theological reflection also includes substantial dialogue, this time with *Šā'ûl* himself. While 1 Sam 12 developed out of the existing campaign narrative in ch. 11, the dialogue in 1 Sam 15 is set within a fresh narrative created for the purpose. Many important constituents of 1 Samuel appear (at least) twice; and this chapter offers not only a second major reflection on (Saul's) kingship, but also provides a further account to 1 Sam 13 of his rejection as king. But why Amalek? And why *ḥērem*?

40. Although part of 2 Sam 8:12, Zobah is not listed in the otherwise identical 1 Chr 18:11 and hence may not have been original at this point to BTH.

41. And v. 13 in MT.

A fresh author has returned to the summary account of Saul's generalship cited above (14:47–48) and compared it with the wider context of its source (the summary in 2 Sam 8:11–12 of David's actions). Within the confines of a short summary, special mention has been made of Saul's acting with valor in striking down Amalek and delivering Israel from those who have been plundering them (v. 48). But David, in one respect at least, has done still better: he has dedicated to Yahweh gold and silver booty taken from these same enemies (including the Amalekites). The author of 1 Sam 15 draws two observations from comparing the two summary reports. First, Saul's striking down the Amalekites may be specially noted in 14:48, but the task cannot have been completed; for in that case David would not have needed to fight with them again. Then the author found no record of what Saul had done with the spoils from any of his campaigns. The deduction from these two observations was that Saul's Amalekite campaign, already specifically mentioned in summary, would repay still closer attention. Amalek should finally pay for the trouble they caused Israel after the exodus from Egypt. The story of that bitter conflict (Exod 17:8–16) ends in all-too-typical angry inconsistencies: it is to be solemnly recorded in writing that Amalek is to be utterly erased (17:14), and war is to continue with Amalek from generation to generation (17:16)!

Samuel's opening gambit (15:1) involves two interesting moves: his own role (in anointing Saul) is mentioned before Yahweh's; and yet Yahweh is claimed as the instigator—"It was me whom Yahweh sent." Does he, in drawing attention to his own role, make us wonder whether what he next attributes to Yahweh is really spoken at his own behest?

Yahweh has "taken account of" (*pqd*) the behavior of Amalek at the time of the exodus (v. 2), as Saul would "take a count of" (*pqd*) his people before moving against Amalek (v. 4). Throughout HB, and especially in the Latter Prophets,[42] Yahweh is quite the commonest subject of the verb *pqd*—but in the books of Samuel only in 1 Sam 2:21 (where Hannah is the object) and here in 15:2. In 1 Samuel, it is Saul who is the noted tally-keeper.[43] As already in 11:8, so here too Saul counts Judah separately. And here, as in the intervening 13:15, his main force is called not "Israel" but "the people."

Samuel instructs Saul to "strike down Amalek" (15:3; exactly the phrase used in 14:48)—and "make *hērem*" everything that is theirs—and not spare them—and put to death everything living, both human and animal. Different extended phrases are found in HB denoting totality. The final phrase is lightly adapted from the slaughter of the priests at Nob (22:17–19).[44] "Spare" (*ḥml*)

42. Jeremiah, 34x; Book of the Twelve, 12x.

43. First Samuel 11:8; 13:15; 14:17; 15:4; 20:6. David takes a count only in 2 Sam 18:1; 24:2.

44. Notice links between 1 Sam 11 and 15 (do they share an author after all?): separate counting of Judah; use of *hmyt*; use of *hrp*.

is uncommon in narrative yet rather more common in (later) prophecy. In narrative it is used of Pharaoh's daughter toward the infant Moses (Exod 2:6), the people of Ziph toward Saul (1 Sam 23:21), and David toward Saul's son Mephibosheth (2 Sam 21:7). We find it only once in Deuteronomy (13:8 [9]), in a list of synonyms for the mercy that should not be shown even to a close relative who urges following a god other than Yahweh. This is one of only three biblical narratives in which this verb is repeated (1 Sam 15:3, 9, 15); hence it is to be understood as prominent and important within the text. One of the others is also in Samuel (2 Sam 12:4, 6); and the other occurs at the end of Chronicles (2 Chron 36:15, 17).

[4] Saul's "count" of his people (1 Sam 15:4) uses again (previously 11:8; 13:15) one of the key terms of David's fateful census (*pqd*) reported in 2 Sam 24. That also produced a separate tally for Israel and Judah. The GT places the count at the well-known Gilgal, which is clearly the location of the majority of ch. 15 (vv. 12, 21, 33), but in v. 4 MT reads *baṭṭĕlāʾîm*. This is widely rendered "in Telaim" and understood to be the same place (in southern Judah) as is called Telem in Josh 15:24. Be that as it may, spelled Telaim it suggests "lambs," whether gathered in a shepherd's arms (Isa 40:11) or offered in sacrifice (1 Sam 7:9). These two versions also differ over the totals, both the grand total for all Israel and the subtotal for Judah (11:8; 15:4).

[5–9] The Kenites are given the opportunity to "turn" from amid the Amalekites on the basis of their earlier supportive "loyalty" toward Israel on the occasion of their "going up" from Egypt (v. 6). These key terms play an interesting variation on one of the themes of 2 Sam 7 (BTH). There Yahweh has caused Israel's "going up" from Egypt (7:6); and there Yahweh has promised that he will not "turn" his "loyalty" (7:15). Here, precisely on the basis of unwavering loyalty, the Kenites should be given the opportunity to turn away in time. We shall meet the Kenites twice again in 1 Samuel (27:10; 30:29). In another (negative) correspondence, Saul's campaign against Amalek takes him toward that same Egypt (15:7) from which his ancestors have been delivered (v. 6). Shur belongs to the wilderness area south of Judah and east of Egypt, associated especially with Abraham and Ishmael in Gen 16:7; 20:1; 25:18—and the third of these passages associates Shur with Havilah in exactly the terms we find here. Kenites and Amalekites belong to Israel's foundational narratives. With the exception of Ps 83, there is no explicit mention of them in the biblical story after David. As plotters against Israel (vv. 6–7 [7–8]), that psalm lists six nations whose continuing relevance is well attested (Edom, Moab, Gebal, Ammon, Philistia, and Tyre), and in among them three nations who feature only in stories about ancient times (Ishmaelites, Hagrites, and Amalek).

"Make *ḥērem*" calls for more detailed discussion. Even a brief description of the textual evidence has demonstrated some of the difficulties associated with the noun *ḥērem* (v. 21), and the related causative verb (vv. 3, 8, 9 [2x], 15, 18, 20). If we can assume that the Greek translator did find each of these instances of *ḥērem* in the Hebrew text before him, then all but the first two are rendered simply "destroy" ("destruction" in v. 21). In v. 3, GT gives every impression of being overloaded: the larger part of two attempts to render the whole command have been preserved, including three approaches to this difficult term: transliteration, literal translation, and free translation; the first recurs in v. 8 side by side with "kill" (which renders "put to death," not "make *ḥerem*" in v. 3); but from v. 9 only the third option is followed ("destroy"). Although we cannot be certain in each case (esp. in v. 8), the Greek evidence largely confirms our Hebrew text on this point. Within FP, *ḥrm* is used by far the most often in Joshua.[45] We also find it once each at beginning and end of Judges (1:17; 21:11); only here in Samuel; and three times in Kings (first and third in BTH contexts): 1 Kgs 9:21;[46] 20:42; 2 Kgs 19:11.[47]

It is clear that the verb has the broad sense of "kill-and-destroy-utterly." But it is the ultimate source of this whole chapter (2 Sam 8:11) that provides an entry point to a fuller understanding of what the term means and why it is used here: the booty that David plunders from his several foes he has "consecrated" (*hiqdîš*) to Yahweh. Only the final chapter of Leviticus within the Hebrew Bible links words related to "holy" (*qdš*) to *ḥērem*: "everything that is *ḥērem* is utterly holy [holy of holies] to Yahweh" (Lev 27:28b). Thus *ḥērem* is the limiting instance of consecration. Other persons or animals or objects that have been consecrated to the Deity ("made holy" and deposited in the sanctuary) can be redeemed for a fifth of their value; but nothing devoted as *ḥērem* can ever be redeemed. The implication for persons or animals of being "unredeemably consecrated" is death. David is said to have added captured metals to the gifted ones that he has consecrated to Yahweh. In this context, it would have been irrelevant to state what David does with captured humans and animals. But Samuel in 1 Sam 15, speaking for Yahweh, takes advantage of this silence and lays on Saul, created so largely in David's own image, an impossible task: the "final solution" of the Amalekite problem—impossible, because the narrator's source knows that they will still be around for David to fight!

The rights and wrongs in this narrative turn on the issue of "sparing." The instruction to Saul includes the command not to spare the Amalekites (v. 3); but the report of the campaign concludes with king and people sparing king Agag and the best of the animals suitable for sacrifice, "unwilling" to make

45. Verb 14x and noun 10x.

46. But 2 Chr 8:8 uses *klh pi'el*.

47. The accounts of Hezekiah in Kings and Chronicles diverge widely but share important elements.

them *ḥērem* (v. 9). Saul leads his people in the "sparing"; and MT goes on to report them all (pl.) unwilling to destroy the choice elements, while GT blames Saul (sg.) only. We will meet "spare" and "despise" (v. 9) together again only once, in 2 Sam 12 ("spare" in vv. 4, 6; "despise" in v. 9); and "Yahweh's word" features in both these prophetic stories.

I have suggested that this narrative "takes off from" a number of other texts that include the summary accounts of the wars of David and Saul against surrounding nations (2 Sam 8:11–12; 1 Sam 14:47–48) and David's count of his people (2 Sam 24). A further text that may underlie it is the extended account of a campaign by Ben-hadad of Damascus against Samaria in the time of Ahab (1 Kgs 20). The king of Israel is encouraged and advised by prophet (vv. 13, 22) and man of God (v. 28). There is a great slaughter of Aramaean troops, but Ben-hadad is spared. One of the "sons of the prophets," himself encouraged by the grisly fate of a colleague who did not act on a command presented to him as a divine instruction, traps Ahab by an acted-out parable and then reports Yahweh's announcement of his punishment for letting go free "my *ḥērem* man" (v. 42).[48] In this Ahab story it is only at the very end that the "prophetic party" makes the divine purpose for Ben-hadad explicit. In 1 Sam 15 it is explicit from the outset that (all) Amalek should be devoted as *ḥērem*. Two principal reasons encourage me to see Saul being compared with Ahab, rather than Ahab with Saul. One is that a relatively isolated phrase in the Ahab story, "my *ḥērem* man," has become a major theme in the story of Saul. The other is that Ben-hadad's staff advises him that the kings of Israel are known for exemplifying *ḥesed*; and that term is much more securely anchored in the traditions about David (and Solomon)[49] rather than Saul.[50]

In respect of treating *ḥērem* as a major theme, this story of Saul, Samuel, and Amalek must be compared with the story of Jericho in the book of Joshua. While it is noted more briefly elsewhere in Joshua that other towns and all life in them are "made *ḥērem*," it is only in the wider Jericho story and here that biblical narrative explores the totality of destruction implied in *ḥērem*, in each passage by featuring an exception. Here Saul is blamed for exempting Agag and prime animals. There, and somewhat paradoxically, Rahab and her family are exempted from the complete destruction of their town, while Achan and his family pay the ultimate price for retaining some booty from Jericho. The importance of Gilgal in the wider context of both narratives serves only to encourage closer comparison.

48. The nearest parallel is found in Isa 34:5, where Edom is described as "my *ḥērem* people."

49. See 2 Sam 10:2 (BTH), plus 2 Sam 2:5, 6; 3:8; 9:1, 3, 7; 1 Kgs 2:7.

50. It has to be admitted that Saul exhibits *ḥesed* to the Kenites, in response to how they had earlier treated Israel (15:6); but it is hard to see how the Aramaeans could usefully press that analogy to their own benefit.

1 Samuel 15:10–35

10 And the word of Yahweh came to Samuel, saying,
11 "I regret that I kinged Saul as king,
for he has turned from following me
and my words he has not established."
And Samuel blazed
and called out to Yahweh all the night.
12 And Samuel rose early
and went to meet Saul in the morning;
and it was reported to Samuel, saying,
"Saul has come to the Carmel;
and he [is in fact erecting] *has erected* for himself a [monument] hand."[a]
And he turned around[, and crossed over,] *the chariot*[b]
and went down to Gilgal *to Saul*,
and look, he was offering up burnt offering to Yahweh the first of the booty he brought from Amalek.[c]
13 And Samuel came to Saul,
and Saul said to him:
"You are blessed of Yahweh.
I have established [Yahweh's word] *what Yahweh said.*"[a]
14 And Samuel said:
"And what is the sound of this flock in my ears,
and the sound of the herd
which I am hearing?"
15 And Saul said:
"From Amalek I brought them,
on which the people had pity:
the best of the flock and the herd
in order to sacrifice to Yahweh your God—
and the remainder [we] *I* have [made ḥērem] *destroyed.*"[a]

16 And Samuel said to Saul:
"Desist
and let me report to you
what Yahweh spoke to me at night."
And he said to him:
"Speak."

17 And Samuel said *to Saul*:
"Surely, [even if] you are small in [your own] *his* eyes
you are head of the staff[s] of *the tribe*[a] *of* Israel,

and Yahweh has anointed you king over Israel.
18 And Yahweh has sent you on a way,
and has said [to you],
'Go and [make ḥerem] *destroy; you will take up*[a] the sinners (Amalek) *to me*
and do battle with them
till finishing them off.'[b]
19 But why have you not listened to Yahweh's voice
and [grasped for] *started to put down on* the booty,
and have done evil in Yahweh's eyes?"

20 And Saul said to Samuel:
"Because I listened to Yahweh's voice;
and I went on the way
on which Yahweh sent me,
and I brought Agag king of Amalek,
and Amalek I have [made ḥerem] *destroyed.*
21 And the people took of the booty flock and herd the first of the [ḥerem] *destruction*,
[to sacrifice to] *before* Yahweh[a] [y]our God at Gilgal."
22 And Samuel said:
"Is there pleasure for Yahweh in burnt offerings and sacrifices
as in listening to Yahweh's voice?
In fact listening is [better than] *beyond good* sacrifice,
paying attention than the fat of rams.
23 [Surely the sin of divination is rebellion;
and nothingness and teraphim are urgency.]
For augury is sin; bitterness and trouble urge on healing.[a]
Because you have rejected Yahweh's word,
he [has rejected] *will reject*[b] you
from being king *over* Israel."[c]

24 And Saul said to Samuel:
"I have sinned,
for I have transgressed Yahweh's mouth and your word[s],
for I feared the people
and listened to their voice.
25 Well then, be sure to lift my sin;
and return with me
that I may prostrate myself to Yahweh *your God.*"
26 And Samuel said to Saul,
"I shall not return with you;

for you have rejected Yahweh's word,
and Yahweh *has rejected* [will reject] you from being king over Israel."

27 And Samuel turned *his face* to go;
and [he] *Saul*[a] grasped the wing of his cloak,[b]
and [it was torn] *tore* it.[c]
28 And Samuel said to him:
"Yahweh has torn [the] *your* kingship [of] *from* Israel
[from being on you] *out of your hand* today;
and he has given it to your fellow,
who is better than you.
29 And [moreover, the Eternal One[a] of] Israel *will be divided into two*—
he will not *turn* [play false[b]],
and he will not repent;
for he is not *as* human—repenting."
30 And [he] *Saul* said:
"I have sinned.
[Now] *But* be sure to honor me in face of the elders of [my people] *Israel*
and in face of [Israel] *my people*;
and[a] turn back with me
that I may prostrate myself before Yahweh your God."
31 And Samuel turned back after Saul,
and [Saul] *he* prostrated[a] himself before Yahweh.

32 And Samuel said:
"Bring near to me Agag, king of Amalek."
And Agag came to him [in bonds[a]] *trembling*;
and Agag said to him,
"[Surely[b] the bitterness of death has turned aside.] *Is death so bitter?*"

33 And Samuel said,
"As your sword has left women bereft,
so shall your mother be more bereft than women."
And Samuel *slaughtered* [cut in pieces[a]] Agag before Yahweh at Gilgal.

34 And Samuel went to Ramah;
and Saul, he went up to his house at Gibeah [of Saul].
35 And Samuel did not see Saul further till the day of his death;
for Samuel mourned for Saul,
and Yahweh, he was sorry
that he had made Saul king over Israel.

12a. "Hand" (GT) is an overliteral rendering of *yd* (MT), which has the sense of "monument" here as in 2 Sam 18:18. The GT has "erected" in the past tense and may have read *wyṣb* as in 2 Sam 18:18; the ptc. *mṣyb* in MT, reinforced by *hnh* (MT and LT, but not B) is both more immediate and also more readily assonant with the problematic noun *mṣbt*.

b. The GT attests *ʾt-hrkb*, in place of MT's *wyʿbr*.

c. The LT does not share B's long plus.

13a. The GT attests not *ʾt-dbr yhwh* but *ʾt-ʾšr dbr yhwh*. Saul claims to Samuel that he has done exactly what Yahweh has complained to Samuel that he has not done (v. 11).

15a. "Destroy" (GT), as in v. 9 and again in v. 18.

17a. Here *skēptrou phylēs* may represent a double rendering of a single Hebrew word; yet it is the sg. *šbṭ* that each attests, and not pl. *šbṭy*, as in MT.

18a. This second rendering of the main instruction may be explained two ways: a frequent implication of Gk *anairein* is "do away with"; alternatively, "lift up" may be a literal rendering of *whrmt[h]*, which lacks just one consonant of MT's *whḥrmth*.

b. "Finish off" is found in 2 Chr 8:8—the sole context in BTH in which *hḥrym* (1 Kgs 9:21) may have been attested.

21a. The LT's "to sacrifice before Yahweh" may render an original *lzbḥ lpny yhwh*. If so, MT has lost *pny* from *lpny yhwh*, and B has lost *lzbḥ*.

23a. The MT and B divide this line differently: B after *qsm* and MT after *mry*. Here MT follows the usual derivation of *mry* from *mrh* ("rebel"), but B from *mrr* ("be bitter"). And B's *therapeian* is a mistaken correction of the transliterated *therapin* (from *teraphim*).

b. The GT has read *w-* in *wymʾsk* as a simple connective.

c. Here GT ends this verse as both GT and MT end v. 26. The phraseology is anticipated in 8:7.

27a. Like GT, here 4QSam[a] specifies Saul as subj.

b. Here DJD argues that 4QSam[a] requires another word after "his cloak," and it restores *wyʾṣr* ("and held on") on the basis of LT (*kai epeschen*) and Josephus.

c. The GT attests the same consonantal text at end as MT, but *qal* for *nipʿal*.

29a. In MT the word before Israel is *nṣḥ* ("splendor" or "duration"): though never elsewhere in HB a title of the Deity, *nṣḥ* does feature in a list of the attributes of the ideal king in 1 Chr 29:11. In GT *wnḥṣh* ("and will be divided") has been read before Israel. Just twice is *ḥṣh nipʿal* used in HB: in the corresponding prediction in Ezek 37:22 that the division into two kingdoms will not persist; and in Dan 11:4, of the division of Alexander's kingdom into four parts. Yet *nḥṣh* is rendered differently, and so independently, in B (*diairethēsetai*) and LT (*schisthēsetai*). The LT goes on to render MT's text by "the Holy One of Israel." What is completely absent from GT is any rendering of MT's opening and strengthening *gm*; and *gm* is elsewhere a component of pluses in MT. Yet *gm* is read in 4QSam[a]; and DJD 77 conjectures *yḥṣh* after it, which may be read either as *nipʿal* with Israel as subj., or as *qal* with Yahweh.

b. In HB *šqr piʿel* is used 5x, always negative, and once more with divine subj. (Ps 89:33 [34]). The commonly used *apostrephein* (B) mostly renders *šwb* or *sbb* (4QSam[a] reads *yšwb*); Israel is subj. of the two verbs in B, but the Deity in MT and LT. In MT this verse appears to contradict vv. 11 and 35; in GT Samuel is credited with the first prediction of the division of the kingdom.

30a. Against MT and GT, 4QSam[a] has no connective before *šwb*.

31a. With B and LT (but not Codex A), 4QSam[a] does not specify Saul as subj. of "prostrate."

32a. Only in Job 38:31 does *mʿdnt* ("bonds") occur elsewhere. Some have wanted here to derive the word from *ʿdn* ("delicacy"). The GT's *tremōn* seems to have derived the form from *mʿd* ("shake"), as, e.g., in 2 Sam 22:37. Did Agag think he was being set free, or know he was facing death?

b. Here *ʾkn* introduces the certainty of MT; but GT's question renders *hkn*, and lacks *sr* before *mr*.

33a. How precisely Samuel dispatches Agag is unclear: this is the unique instance of *šsp* (MT) in HB. The traditional "dismember" presupposes a link with the later biblical *šṣp*. The GT's choice of *esphaxen* may have been influenced by two sibilants followed by *p* in the unfamiliar Hebrew.

[10–16] Much is left unsaid about Samuel's reaction to the first divine response to the sparing of Agag and the best of the animals. Yahweh "regrets" having made Saul king, and Samuel is angry. "Regret" (always divine) is found in BTH (2 Sam 24:16, where what Yahweh regrets is an evil that he has started to do). Elsewhere in Samuel it occurs only three times, all in 1 Sam 15 (11, 29, 35). Yahweh regrets having made Saul king (vv. 11, 35), although this has not previously been attributed to him: making Saul king has been attributed to Samuel (8:22; 12:1) or the people (11:15). Samuel is angry; but is he angry with Yahweh, for an embarrassing change of mind, or with Saul? If Yahweh, then Samuel's anger anticipates David's when Yahweh kills Uzzah (2 Sam 6:7–8). Either way, his spending all night crying to Yahweh suggests intercession on Saul's behalf, guilty or not. Armed with a fresh divine word for Saul, he goes to meet him on his return from the south, is told that Saul has set up a monument at Carmel (a few miles south of Hebron), then turns (down to the Dead Sea valley) on his way to Gilgal. It is there that Samuel meets him. Saul greets him with a blessing (v. 13), as he has on an earlier occasion (13:10). That time he had been blamed for completing a sacrifice before Samuel came; this time, Samuel can hear the animals still lowing (15:14). Samuel's words in v. 17 repeat several key terms from ch. 9: "anoint as designate over Israel" (9:16); "small" and "staffs of Israel" (v. 21). Samuel's opening gambit about Saul's being "small in his own eyes" is rich in possible reference: it could recall his reluctance to become king; it could point humorously at the incongruity between his own self-estimate and his actual size; and it could represent an ironic reference to the monument that Saul has recently (15:12) erected in honor of his success. If Samuel has been angry when first learning of the divine regret (v. 11), the next-to-last detail in this story is his mourning over the king whom he will not see again (v. 35). Challenged by Samuel (v. 14) about their failure to destroy, Saul explains that the people have "spared" the prime sacrificial animals (from devotion to destruction on the battlefield)—but only in order to sacrifice them to Yahweh (at a duly constituted shrine). The term *myṭb* ("best") is found only in Gen 47:6, 11; Exod 22:5 (4; 2x); and 1 Sam 15:9, 15. Saul's interest in the "best" is resumed in the cognate *myṭyb lngn* in 16:17. (The *hipʿil* there recurs in Samuel only in 1 Sam 25:31.) The use of *herep* ("desist/stop") in v. 16 underscores the link with 2 Sam 24:16 (BTH //1 Chr 21:15), and also with 1 Sam 11:3.[51]

[17–23] Under further challenge (vv. 17–19), Saul holds his ground, confirms that he has brought Agag with him (for purpose unstated), and that the people have brought the prime animals precisely for sacrifice to Samuel's own God Yahweh at Gilgal—better, apparently, a great sacrifice at the sanctuary than a slaughter on the battlefield. Milgrom (2421) has offered a fresh reading of 1 Sam 13 and 15 within his discussion of Lev 27: "In chap. 13, the circumstances are transparent. The clash between Saul and Samuel is not ideological but personal: Saul had every right to officiate, especially in view of Samuel's tardiness, which endangered the welfare of his troops. In chap. 15, the tendentious nature of the composition is so blatant that Saul's claim that 'he had fulfilled the word of YHWH' (v 13b) must be upheld."

What are the dynamics of this debate? Is it only under questioning that the story of the whole affair emerges? Or is it under repeated challenge that the story is more acceptably fabricated? Samuel delivers the divine condemnation in formal poetry (22–23). When he puts the rhetorical question to Saul, we recall that we last read about Yahweh's "pleasure" in the report that Eli's sons did not listen to their father because Yahweh was pleased to put them to death (2:25). What gives Yahweh pleasure is attention to his will, not the receipt of (sacrificial) gifts. There are many smaller discrepancies between the two main textual traditions in this chapter. One of these shares a link to words of Balaam, with the principal issue of substance. Samuel's poetic oracle uses both divination (*qesem*) and "trouble" (*ʾāwen*) in 15:23a; and these nouns appear in the same context only once more in HB, in Num 23:23 and 21.

[24–26] Only now does Saul confess sin, admit his fear of the people, and beg a pardon that would be symbolized by Samuel's "returning" (*šûb* is very often used of repentance!) with him so that he might prostrate himself before Yahweh (24–25). Is he confessing something he has always known he has done wrong, or does he ultimately just accept Samuel and Yahweh as higher authority? Some readers will find it easy to suspect Samuel—and Yahweh too—of never having wanted Saul as king in the first place, and being eager to fault him at any opportunity: having blamed him on an earlier occasion (13:8–15) for not waiting long enough, Samuel now blames Saul for not slaughtering all the Amalekites in the immediacy of the battlefield. Still, while "sparing" on the

51. It is found also in Deut 9:14 and Ps 37:8. The longer form *hrph* is used in Judg 11:37; 2 Kgs 4:27; and the plural *hrpw* in Ps 46:11 (there traditionally "be still").

battlefield only to sacrifice later at Gilgal is a nice debating ploy, Saul never explains his intentions for Agag.

[27–31] What of the divine response? The term *nḥm nip ʿal* (11, 29, 35) is not paired elsewhere in the HB with one of the Hebrew verbs regularly employed for mourning and lamentation. But it seems sometimes to bear this sense, as at the end of Judges, when the rest of Israel are sorry about the fate of Benjamin (21:6, 15) and go on to do something about it. That God should regret things puzzles many a reader who expects God to have done things right in the first place. Such regret on Yahweh's part is commonly stated in HB in a stock formula (Gen 6:6; Exod 32:14; 2 Sam 24:16; Jer 26:13, 19; Jonah 3:10) "and Yahweh was sorry about the evil/disaster of which he had spoken." Yahweh's regret is not over a threat of future action, but over his past action in making Saul king. However, the most discussed aspect of this issue is not the statement of the matter at beginning and end (vv. 11, 35), but the intervening treatment of the issue (v. 29), which appears contrary, or even contradictory. Using an apparently freshly minted title for Yahweh, Samuel states (in MT at least) that he will neither play false nor be sorry.

Yahweh's regret (*nḥm*) is mentioned only once in BTH, where he is sorry (2 Sam 24:16) when he sees his destroying agent about to touch Jerusalem. Within the books of Samuel, it is only in that culminating chapter and here in 1 Sam 15 that this topic is addressed; and there are several other apparently significant links in vocabulary and theme between these chapters:

1. "count" (*pqd*)—2 Sam 24:9; 1 Sam 15:2, 4; plus, elsewhere in Samuel, 1 Sam 2:21; 11:8; 13:15; 14:17 (2x); 17:18; 20:6; 25:15; 2 Sam 3:8; 18:1
2. a separate total for Judah—2 Sam 24:9; 1 Sam 15:4; plus 1 Sam 11:8
3. "the word of Yahweh"—2 Sam 24:11;[52] 1 Sam 15:10, 13, 23, 26; plus 1 Sam 3:1, 7, 21; 2 Sam 7:4; 12:9[53]
4. "stop" (*hrp*)—2 Sam 24:16; 1 Sam 15:16; plus 1 Sam 11:3[54]
5. "sin"—2 Sam 24:10, 17; 1 Sam 15:23, 24, 25, 30; plus 1 Sam 2:17, 25; 7:6; 12:10, 19, 23; 14:33, 34, 38; 19:4, 5; 20:1; 24:12; 26:21; 2 Sam 12:13 (2x); 19:21
6. "lift/remove" (sin/guilt)—2 Sam 24:10; 1 Sam 15:25; plus 2 Sam 12:13

Two further shared elements are whether kings Agag and David will escape the fate of their people, and whether sacrifice is of any avail without obedience

52. Here as in 2 Sam 7:4 we cannot be sure that BTH had *dbr yhwh*: 1 Chr 21:9 has "and Yahweh spoke to Gad" (*wydbr yhwh ʾl-gd*), while 1 Chr 17:3 has "word of God" (*dbr ʾlhym*).

53. Further to the previous footnote, GT does not attest "the word of Yahweh" in 1 Sam 3:21; 15:13; 2 Sam 12:9.

54. Features 2 and 4 shared by 1 Sam 15 and 2 Sam 24 reappear only in 1 Sam 11, while feature 1 does occur in 1 Sam 11, but also more widely.

to the divine will. In the light of these comparisons, we have to ask whether it is enough to say simply that the composition of 1 Sam 15 has drawn on the language of 2 Sam 24.

There is textual ambiguity over just who grabs whose garment, which tears. But whether king has torn prophet's robe, or prophet king's robe, Samuel takes the opportunity to underscore what he has said by presenting the action as a parable of Yahweh's tearing from Saul the kingdom (vv. 27–28). Two anticipations are involved. The nearer one is of David's cutting off the edge of Saul's cloak in the cave, and Saul going on to admit that David is more in the right than he (see below on ch. 24); the further one, of Jeroboam and a later prophet and the division of Solomon's kingdom (1 Kgs 11:29–31).[55] Saul repeats his admission of sin but immediately—and hence we may suppose desperately—pleads for honor in face of his people, the leaders and the led (1 Sam 15:30). Once it is plain that Saul requires only to save face with humans, Samuel does accompany him to worship (vv. 30–31). Effective ruler again, Samuel, who has described himself as old when Saul takes power (12:2), must now complete the destruction of Amalek (15:32–33), famously hacking Agag to pieces. He never again sees Saul. We are reminded of words used to Saul about Samuel by the lad he took with him to search for his father's animals: "the man is honored; whatever he says will come for sure."

The most substantial textual discrepancy is over Samuel's response to Saul's catching hold of and tearing the edge of his robe (1 Sam 15:28–29). In v. 28 MT uses the relatively uncommon *mmlkwt* for kingship (8x in HB). Since this noun is never used with the possessive suffix, it is likely that "your kingship" in GT would attest *mmlktk* (as in 1 Sam 13:13–14) from *mmlkh*; however, the combination in GT of "from Israel" plus "out of your hand" is strange. Yet the testimony of GT in the following "verse" deserves respectful attention.

In v. 29 GT's first words belong with the previous verse and draw a second implication from the single image of the torn robe: the kingdom will not just be torn away from Saul, but Israel will also be torn into (two) parts. Only then does Samuel in GT say more about the Yahweh who tears: although the change in grammatical subject is not marked, the context makes it clear. In MT, by contrast, the opening words of v. 29 apply a fresh title to the divine subject of v. 28: the one who has torn is none other than "the *nēṣaḥ* of Israel." Two features lessen our confidence in the antiquity of MT's text here: the novelty of the title, and the presence of the strengthening *gam*—along with other markers of emphasis, *gam* ("also/even") is used more often in MT than is reflected in GT or attested in 4QSam[a].

There is a further textual difference at the beginning of the main statement in v. 29: in GT and 4QSam[a] we read *yāšûb* ("turn"), which is frequently paired with

55. The theme of "tearing the kingship" is found also in 1 Kgs 11:11–13, 29–36; 14:8; 2 Kgs 17:21.

the following "regret/repent," and not *yĕšaqqer* ("play false") as in MT. Both elements of MT's distinctive text seem to belong together: it is the "glory" or "durability" (whatever exactly *nēṣaḥ* means) of Yahweh that would be impugned by any expression of deceit or falsehood. The point that Samuel makes, according to 4QSam[a] and GT, is more local, which fits well into the argument of the whole dialogue: Yahweh may have regretted the original mistake over making Saul king but will neither turn from nor regret his decision to remove the kingship from this failed king. Verses 28–29 in MT are widely recognized as an adjustment to the main burden of the dialogue; and this will be true whether they are a later insert or an alteration to the earlier and better fitting text (at least in v. 29) of 4QSam[a] and GT. The closest parallel in HB to the thought, though not the wording, of MT is within the same statement of Balaam that includes "divination" and "trouble" (Num 23:19):

> El is not human, to tell a lie;
> nor an earthling's son, to display regret.
> Has he himself said, and will he not act?
> Or has he spoken, and will not set it up?

Samuel in MT appears to state this same general principle, apparently overriding the contrary claims in vv. 11 and 35. It would be possible to read "will not deceive and will not regret" as a hendiadys, "will not deceitfully regret"; and this would not conflict outright with the repeated statement that Yahweh has in fact regretted making Saul king. This could be squared with the next clause in GT: humans regret in their own way, but when Yahweh regrets, it is not as a human. Yet it is not easy to make this move in respect of the final clause, as MT has it: it is human to regret, but Yahweh is not human.[56]

The wider significance of the links between the words of Samuel and Balaam can only be weighed after discussing the connections of David's last (poetic) words (2 Sam 23:1–7) and several of Balaam's oracles. But we should simply note here that Amalek receives special mention in Balaam's final oracle (Num 24:20, immediately before the Kenites):

> The first of the nations was Amalek;
> but the last of him is toward destruction.

[32–33] Does Agag think he is being set free or know he is facing death? The rare *mʿdnt* has been read variously as "in bonds," "trembling," and "delicately"; and what he says is sufficiently cryptic, whether in MT and GT, as not to betray his inner feelings. However, if Agag's words are as hard to read as his

56. Kim makes no reference to the text-critical issues. His theological conclusion (26) is that, in face of God, the author becomes conscious of the limits of his knowledge, yet decides not to hide his deficiencies.

demeanor, Samuel's verdict is prophetically blunt: Agag will be done to as he has done, and yet another mother will be left bereft. The slaying of Agag has features of both execution and sacrifice. Samuel's judgment that the punishment will fit the crime suggests criminal process. And yet what happens is not simply "at Gilgal" but "before Yahweh" or "in Yahweh's presence" (in this respect, his death anticipates the death of seven of Saul's family in 2 Sam 21:9). There are regular elements of due order, or ritual, in judicial executions; but given the opaqueness of the unique verb *šsp*, it is unwise to say more. Amalek reappears only in Ps 83. But it is widely supposed that Haman the Agagite (Esth 3:1, 10; 8:3, 5; 9:24), with his visceral hatred of the Jews, is a descendant—and something of a "re-incarnation"—of Agag the Amalekite.

[34–35] In a sense, 1 Sam 15 underscores the end of the story of King Saul, an end that has already been signaled clearly almost as soon as it began (13:13–14), and may have been under threat ever since Samuel's dark words about "making the kingdom new" (11:14). Although Saul remains king till his death, reported in 1 Sam 31, it is equally true that Samuel anoints David as king in the very next chapter (16). Samuel's leave-taking is not simply preliminary; it is also "prophetic" in several senses. At the narrative level, we are told explicitly (even if also ambiguously) at the close (15:35) that Samuel never sees Saul again till the day of his death. The counterpart is also true, that Saul remains without access to divine counsel till his late summons to Samuel from the grave (28:3–19). And, third, the fourfold use of "the word of Yahweh" in this chapter (used only 6x more in both books of Samuel) together with Samuel's poetic oracle (vv. 22–23) combine to portray this Samuel as even more clearly "prophetic" than the orator who has earlier spoken in the language of Amos and Micah (12:3). Samuel's receipt of Yahweh's "word" (15:10) aligns him with Nathan "the prophet" (2 Sam 7:4) and Gad, "David's seer" (2 Sam 24:11), both from BTH.[57] Nonetheless, "the word of Yahweh" in 15:13, 23, 26 may mean Yahweh's command rather than his communication of information.

Insofar as 1 Sam 15 returns to the issue handled in 13:8–15a (both scenes have Samuel at Gilgal, declaring the end of Saul's kingship), its closing statement that Samuel does not see Saul again till the day of his death (15:35) invites reconsideration of some issues in ch. 14. This statement in the added ch. 15 simply makes explicit what is already implicit in an earlier version of the book, lacking ch. 15 and also David's escape to Samuel (19:18–24): the paths of Samuel and Saul never cross after 13:15 in this earlier version. Saul's failure to secure divine guidance through the resources of Ahijah is not due to Jonathan and the curse, but to his rejection by Samuel. In BTH, oracular consultation has been licit and successful for David until his encounter with Nathan the prophet;

57. It is likely that the authors of Samuel have adapted the wording of BTH in both passages, from "the word of God" (as in 1 Chr 17:3) and "and Yahweh spoke to Gad" (as in 1 Chr 21:9).

but he never again "asked of Yahweh." Saul has sought out Samuel as a diviner, but quickly finds that Samuel is a declarer of divine initiatives. Once Saul's own failure blocks off communication via Samuel, there is no other way.

This chapter plays several roles within the books of Samuel. The authors of Samuel have deliberately used materials copied from the final episode in BTH on David to build their anticipatory farewell to Saul. But it is also true that 1 Sam 15 reuses elements of 2 Sam 24 to offer a fresh reading of that culminating and troubling chapter. The purpose of this narrative is not principally to provide information about a historical Saul, but to provide us with fresh perspectives toward reading the story of David with greater insight. If Saul loses his kingship after disobedience to the divine will, and even after confession of his sin and an appeal to have its entailment cancelled, then why not David too? In what way is David different? If Agag swiftly joins the fate of his people after apparently surviving the *ḥērem*, then what about David who knows, as he watches the divine destruction, that the fault is his but still survives?

There are important respects in which the responses of Saul and David differ. Although David, even if belatedly, pleads that the guilt is his alone, Saul inculpates his people (15:21). And when, on his third mention of the people's role (v. 24), he lets slip that he has feared them, he tacitly recognizes his unfitness to rule. Though he now admits his sin (vv. 24–25), he asks for it to be removed. Samuel does not answer directly; but he refuses to accompany him to worship and confirms his rejection as king.

1 Samuel 16:1–12a

1 And Yahweh said to Samuel,
"How long are you mourning for Saul,
and I for my part have rejected him
from being king over Israel?
Fill your horn with oil,
and go.
I shall send you to Jesse [the Bethlehemite] *right to Bethlehem*,
for I have seen in his sons a king for myself."

2 And Samuel said,
"How shall I go?
And Saul will hear
and will slay me."

And Yahweh said,
"You will take in your hand a calf of the herd,
and you will say:
'To sacrifice to Yahweh am I come.'

3 And you shall summon Jesse to the sacrifice;
and [I,] I will let you know
what you will do;
and you shall anoint me
whomever I shall say to you."
4 And Samuel did *everything*
t[w]hat Yahweh said;
and he came to Bethlehem,
and the elders of the city trembled
meeting him,
and said,
"Is it peaceful, your coming, *o seer*?"
5 And he said,
"Peaceful: to sacrifice to Yahweh am I come.
Have yourselves consecrated,
and [come with me to the sacrifice] *rejoice with me* today."[a]
And he consecrated Jesse and his sons,
and summoned them to the sacrifice.
6 And it came about at their coming
and he saw Eliab;
and he said:
"Surely in front of Yahweh is his anointed."
7 And Yahweh said to Samuel:
"Do not look to his appearance or to the height of his stature,
for I have rejected him;
for not what man sees *does God see*;
for man looks to the eyes,
but Yahweh looks to the heart."
8 And Jesse called to A[b]*m*inadab,
and he [made him] pass*ed* before Samuel;
and he said:
"This one too Yahweh has not chosen."
9 And Jesse made Shammah pass;
and he said,
"This one too Yahweh has not chosen."
10 And Jesse made his seven sons pass before Samuel,
and Samuel said to Jesse:
"Yahweh has not chosen these."
11 And Samuel said to Jesse:
"Are the lads complete?"
And he said,
"There is still the smallest [left],

and look: he is shepherding among the sheep."
And Samuel said to Jesse,
"Send
and take him,
for we shall not [turn] *recline*[a]
till he comes here."
12a And he sent
and had him come—
and he was ruddy together with {being} attractive in eyes
and good in appearance *to Yahweh.*

5a. The LT appears both distinctive and conflate: "and recline with me today at the sacrifice."

11a. The Gk text here may have been the inspiration for LT in v. 5. It is much more specific than MT "turn": "turn aside"? "turn back"?

[1–2a] Yahweh's first words to Samuel not only resume the terms in which the narrator has closed the previous chapter, but reach farther back as well. His *ʿad-mātay* ("till when," "how long") nicely adapts some of the sounds of *ʿad-yôm môtô* ("till the day of his death") in 15:35; by subverting these, Yahweh may be mocking the fact that Samuel has gone into mourning before Saul ever dies. And the verb "mourn" (*ʾbl htpʿl*) also resumes 15:35.[58] Then the verbal structure of Samuel's chiding is an exact copy of Eli's scolding his mother (1:14): "Till when (will you make yourself drunk)?" Not since 1:14 has *ʿad-mātay* been used again;[59] and there too it introduces a verb in *hitpaʿel*. Yahweh insists that Samuel's mourning and Yahweh's own "regret" are not to be confused. Yahweh's regret is tantamount to rejection; Saul's replacement, already talked about in 13:14, is close to being identified. The LT repeats the opening words "And Yahweh said to Samuel" before "Fill your horn. . . ." And this exact repetition could indicate that the remainder of v. 1a had been a secondary addition intended to link the reports in chs. 15 and 16.[60]

Whether or not that is so, the use of "reject" (*mʾs*) in Samuel comes to its climax in this chapter (8:7; 10:19; 15:23, 26; 16:1, 7). It does not stem from the main source (it is never used in BTH), nor indeed from Deuteronomy; it appears in the Pentateuch only in Lev 26:15, 43, 44; and Num 11:20; 14:31.[61] The verb *mʾs* is most at home in Psalms and Job, and in the poetic rhetoric of

58. It is used 7x in Sam (never in BTH) and only 12x more in HB, always (?) in late texts: Gen 37:34; Exod 33:4; Num 14:39; Isa 66:10; Ezek 7:12, 27; Dan 10:2; Ezra 10:6; Neh 1:4; 8:9; 1 Chr 7:22; 2 Chr 35:24.

59. In Samuel–Kings it will be used only twice more: 2 Sam 2:26; and 1 Kgs 18:21.

60. Trebolle Barrera (71) points to a similar phenomenon in 17:34–37a.

61. The *hitpaʿel* of *ʾbl* ("mourned") is used also in Num 14:39 (as in 1 Sam 16:1).

Amos, Hosea, Isaiah, Jeremiah, and Ezekiel. As in the prophetic books, *m's* is used in 1 Sam 8–16 of both the people's or the king's rejecting Yahweh and his teachings (8:7; 10:19; 15:23, 26) and of Yahweh's rejecting them (15:23, 26; 16:1, 7). Eliab, good-looking like Saul, is similarly "rejected" by Yahweh. The verbs *m's* ("reject," 15:23, 26; 16:1, 7), *qr'* ("rend," 15:28), and *hmlyk* ("make king," 15:11, 35) occur together again in the reflection on the end of northern Israel (2 Kgs 17:20–21).

The end of Yahweh's instructions to Samuel do not just specify the town and family of his chosen king, but also for the first time use a key term of the whole story that follows: "I have seen (in his sons a king for myself)." The verb *r'h* ("see") not only recurs four times in vv. 6–7 (and its cognate *mr'h* in v. 7), but also is resumed in the search for a musician instigated by Saul (vv. 17–18). "I have seen for myself" resonates with Abraham's trust (Gen 22:8) that God had "provided" (this English verb means literally "seen in advance") for himself the means for an important project. To this rich mix, GT and 4QSam[b] report (end of 1 Sam 16:4) that Bethlehem's elders address Samuel as "seer" (*hr'h*). Yahweh here gives Samuel instructions about anointing a king "for myself"—Samuel's instructions relating to Saul have been to make him king "for them" (8:22). It is highly probable that this link was created by the author of ch. 8.

[2b–12a] Samuel's impatient response to Yahweh (16:2a) shows that he is all too aware that the Saul he mourns is far from dead and is still a potent source of danger. However, Yahweh supplies him with a cover story: the situation of David's anointing by Samuel will turn out not very dissimilar from Saul's—sacrifice by Samuel, (relative) privacy, process of selection superintended by the Deity. That he has come to Bethlehem to conduct a sacrifice might satisfy Saul. But his arrival in the town has its elders trembling (v. 4). We may compare Ahimelech's reaction to David's appearance at the sanctuary in Nob (21:1 [2]). The good folk of Bethlehem may remember the last time Samuel is known to have been involved in sacrifice to Yahweh: one king (Agag) was among the victims, and their own king (Saul) was pronounced a reject. It is hardly surprising that they seek reassurance that he has come in peace. Yet this is not full public sacrifice including the holocaust offering, but more intimate sacrifice within the family, such as Jonathan and David would use to excuse David from the king's table (20:6, 29). Similar sacrifices provided the context for the anointing of both Saul (9:12–13) and Absalom (2 Sam 15:12). In other reports the elders feature as representatives of the wider population at the acclamation of a king: David (2 Sam 5:1–3); Absalom (2 Sam 15:10–12); and Adonijah (1 Kgs 1:9–10). But their role here is reduced to this wary welcome.

The language of holiness and consecration (nouns and verbs related to *qdš*) is very rare in the books of Samuel. The only objects of the *pi'el* of *qdš* are Abinadab (1 Sam 7:1), to be in charge of the ark, and Jesse and family (16:5b). Whether it is ritually possible to "consecrate oneself," as the *hitpa'el* of *qdš* is often rendered, is less than clear; and so we have rendered Samuel's instruction (v. 5a) as "have yourselves consecrated." Joshua 7:13 is the only other passage in HB in which consecration (*piʿel*) is apparently achieved by issuing the instruction to become consecrated (*hitpaʿel*). Samuel prepares Jesse and family for the sacrifice, which is his excuse for being in Bethlehem, and invites them to it; but the text is not interested to tell us whether or not the sacrifice does take place: the real purpose of his visit takes over the report instead (vv. 6–13).

Samuel is immediately impressed by Jesse's firstborn. Some readers might suppose from his words ("Yahweh's anointed is in front of him") that they are standing by the altar. But the seer is rebuked for judging on the basis of externals:[62] this one is "rejected" (*mʾs*). The next—and indeed all the other six present—are "not chosen." The verb *mʾs* often bears the sense of "despise"; but here it is clearly the formal opposite of "choose." There is one more son. Though out of sight at the crucial moment, he is not like Saul (10:22) in hiding, but about his business among the sheep. He is fetched: Samuel will not allow the company to settle "around" the food till all are present. Like Saul in this respect (10:23), David's appearance is remarkable (16:12). Despite that—or not because of it (v. 7!)—he is the one. Only one other person in HB is described as *admônî* ("ruddy"): Esau at his birth (Gen 25:25). Esau is associated with Edom, east of the Arabah and southeast of the Dead Sea, with its characteristically red rock and soil; and *admônî* refers to red-brown color. Esau becomes known as a hunter, a man of the outdoors. Is that what is suggested here of David, or simply youth and the blush of health? It is impossible to judge, because different witnesses produce different assessments: Goliath will see the same David, describe him in almost identical terms, but scorn him (17:42).

1 Samuel 16:12b–16

12b And Yahweh said *to Samuel*,
"Up,
anoint [him] *David*,
for this one is [he] *good*."
13 And Samuel took the horn of oil
and anointed him in the midst of his brothers;
and the spirit of Yahweh came on David from that day and onward,
and Samuel rose
and went to Ramah.

14 And the spirit of Yahweh turned
from being with Saul,

62. See Schipper (2006: 79) on "a body fit for a king."

and an evil spirit from Yahweh terrorized him.
15 And Saul's servants said to him,
"Surely in fact an evil divine spirit is terrorizing you.

16 Let [your servants] be sure to speak before you—let them seek out [for our lord[a]]	16 Let *our lord* be sure to speak—*your servants are* before you—let them seek out

someone who knows,
who plays the harp;
and let it be,
when an evil divine spirit comes on you,
that he plays with his *hand* [harp],
and it is good for you."

16a. "Our lord" and "your servants" appear in each version but in different places—MT is more deferential.

[12b–13] Samuel appears to deal with the business in hand with very little speaking. It is here that the contrast with his anointing of Saul is most stark. No reported words to David either precede or follow the wordless action. After anointing David, Samuel is gone—back to Ramah (v. 13). We are not told whether Jesse's family and he ever do gather around the food. His initial exchange with Yahweh (vv. 1–2) provides two possible reasons. Every extra minute in Bethlehem adds to the danger of a hostile report back to Saul. And his mourning for Saul may be continuing through and beyond Yahweh's chiding. He has been instructed to take his oil horn to Jesse's household; and he does so—but minimally and with heavy heart. There is something final about his return to Ramah. He will never again take, nor be instructed to take, any further initiative. In no sense will he preside prophetically over David's reign as he has over Saul's. In fact, he will feature in only two further scenes, both of them probably written by a later author. In the first, David takes refuge from Saul with him in Ramah (19:18), but no word from Samuel is recorded. In the second, Saul has him brought up from the dead (28:11), and Samuel protests at the disturbance (v. 15).

It might be possible to plead, on the basis of the widely recognized and praised economy in biblical storytelling, that we should read into these few verses about David's anointing what we have learned from the more expansive report of the anointing of Saul. However, one particular feature encourages me to insist that contrasts between the two kings are uppermost: how the divine spirit relates to Saul and David. The spirit is reported as coming on Saul not directly at his anointing, but in two situations that follow. The first is an encounter with a band of prophets (10:10–13, with its counterpart in 19:20–24); and the second, his hearing the news of the impending outrage at Jabesh (11:5–6). In this latter case, Saul is described like Samson, on whom the spirit comes three times (Judg 14:6, 19; 15:14). But the situation with David is doubly different: it is reported here (16:13) that the divine spirit comes once and once only ("from that day and onward"); and this once-for-all characteristic is underscored by lack of any mention of divine spirit in connection with David throughout the much more extensive traditions relating to him. That is true at least of the prose material; there is one solitary exception: the opening of David's "last words" (2 Sam 23:2).

[14–16] The contrast could be described in a different but overlapping way. Saul has been described as anointed by Samuel, or by Yahweh, or by Samuel on behalf of Yahweh, whether as *nāgîd* or as *melek* over Israel, Yahweh's people. No such office is specified as Samuel anoints David—and there certainly is no vacancy (yet). However, immediately on being anointed (v. 13), he is identified as bearer of the divine spirit. Saul's experience of divine spirit continues to be episodic, but from this point always unfavorable. If there is a single point in the narrative where the shift between the two kings is concentrated, then this is v. 14. The first half of the verse spells out the implication of v. 13a: Yahweh's spirit is now with David and will remain on David; the spirit has therefore turned away from Saul. Verse 14b has been interpreted both as attempting theological precision and as proposing a fudge. Saul will continue to be affected (afflicted?) by a divine spirit; but that divine spirit will be not *the spirit of* Yahweh, but *a spirit from* Yahweh. The image of diplomatic—and not-so-diplomatic—relations is helpful here. Yahweh now recognizes David and not Saul as the legitimate king of Israel. Yahweh's agents still do business with Saul, but now they work to destabilize his position. All main versions transmit v. 14 the same way.

However, such unity is quickly lost; there is a preference in what follows to attribute Saul's condition to an evil spirit, or a divine spirit, or an evil divine spirit, rather than to "a spirit from Yahweh." The distinction between "the spirit of Yahweh" and other divine spirits somehow related to him appears to be a fresh coinage. If so, the narrator may have been influenced by the two relevant passages in his main source that distinguish between Yahweh himself and troublesome agents in his divine entourage: both the enticing "satan"[63] and the plague-dealing "messenger" in the report of David's census; and then the "spirits" attending Yahweh's court in the report of Micaiah's vision (1 Kgs 22:19–23), "a spirit of deceit" among them. The Book of Two Houses reports Nathan as telling David that Yahweh/God[64] is with him. Such a statement never reappears in 2 Samuel; the other occasions on which this is said are all concentrated at the beginning of the story of David

63. In this respect, I hold the opening of 1 Chr 21 to be more original than the opening of 2 Sam 24.

64. "Yahweh" in 2 Sam 7:3, but "God" in 1 Chr 17:2.

and will be noted when they appear.[65] Because the line that separates the black arts of the secret services from the methods of those they call the "terrorist" is so fine as often to disappear, I have succumbed to the temptation to translate *bʿt* by "terrorize" rather than the conventional "terrify." This verb is used in HB most often in Job[66]—but once more in Samuel, in David's song of deliverance (2 Sam 22:5–6 = Ps 18:4–5 [5–6]):

> For Death's breakers surrounded me, Belial's tides terrified me;
> Sheol's cords were round me, Death's snares faced me.

1 Samuel 16:17–23

17 And Saul said to his servants,
"Be sure to provide for me someone very good at playing,
and have him come to me."
18 And one from [the] *his* lads answered,
and said:
"Look: I have seen a son of Jesse the Bethlehemite:
knowing to play, and a *wise man* [hero in valor[a]], and a man of war,
and discerning in word, and someone of looks, and Yahweh is
with him."
19 And Saul sent messengers to Jesse,
and he said:
"Send to me David your son,
who is among [the] *your* sheep."
20 And Jesse took a heap of bread,[a] and a skin of wine, and one goat kid,
and he sent them by the hand of David his son to Saul.
21 And David came to Saul,
and stood before him;
and he loved him greatly,
and he became his armor-bearer.
22 And Saul sent to Jesse, saying,
"Let David surely stand before me,
for he has found favor in my eyes."
23 And it would come to be,
when a divine spirit came to Saul,
and David would take the lyre
and play by his hand,
and it would be refreshing for Saul,

65. See 1 Sam 16:18; 17:37; 18:14, 28; 20:13—18:12 is MT's plus, and Jonathan in 20:13 goes beyond what has been reported by the narrator.

66. Job 3:5; 7:14; 9:34; 13:11, 21; 15:24; 18:11; 33:7.

and it would be good for him,
and the spirit of evil would turn
from being upon him.

18a. Nowhere else in the OT does *anēr synetos* correspond to *gbwr ḥyl*.

20a. The opening of this verse teases the commentator with an interesting mix of textual and linguistic puzzles. The LT, though often conflate, may supply a large part of the answer: *kai elaben Iessai onon kai epethēken autō gomor artōn* ("and Jesse took an ass and placed on it an omer of loaves") retroverts to the unremarkable (and possibly original) *wyqḥ yšy ḥmwr wynḥ ʿlyw ʿmr lḥm*. This was already proposed in Budde (120), but with *wyśm*; however, Samuel never uses *śym ʿl* of physical placing, but *epethēkan* corresponds to *hnyḥw* in 6:18 (setting the ark on the oxen). It appears that the gutturals *ḥ* and *ʿ* could be confused—there is an unexpected case of *ḥ* in place of *ʿ* in 17:7 below—and haplography may have occurred as the copyist's eye jumped from (an original) *ḥmr* to *ʿmr*. However, confusion between the opening gutturals can lead to other explanations too. Thus *ḥmwr lḥm* is reminiscent of *ḥmr śʿrym* ("a homer of barley") in Hos 3:2. Then, though LXX *gomor* corresponds to *ḥmr* there and in Ezek 45:11, 13, 14; it corresponds instead to *ʿmr* in Exod 16 (6x). Play on two meanings of *ḥm(w)r* ("ass" and "heap") is nicely illustrated in Judg 15:16. It can be supposed that *ḥmr/ʿmr* was the amount of a "load," although *ʿmr* at one-tenth of an ephah suggests a much smaller amount. The term *gomor* is used once more, in 1 Kgdms 25:18, where it corresponds instead to the numeral "hundred" in MT.

[17–23] It is clear to Saul's staff that he is afflicted by a force beyond his control. One of them has seen "one of Jesse's sons" and reports so much good of David that he can hardly fail to complete his commendation with anything less than the claim that Yahweh is with him. In the form of the text transmitted by MT, this knowledgeable member of Saul's entourage, who is able to point the king in the right direction, is described exactly as is the servant who has directed him to Samuel (1 Sam 9). Among David's many attributes, it is by his skill with the lyre that he may serve Saul. Just as Saul's first encounter with divine spirit has been in the company of prophets who include musicians, so now a musician may help the terrifying spirit to pass from him. Saul's response is uncanny. His courtier has included several details in his commendation of David but has said nothing about his duties with sheep. And yet the disturbed king knows how to identify the correct one out of Jesse's sons (v. 19). Is it possible that he has information about Samuel's visit to Bethlehem?

Plucked from his sheep to be anointed king, David is now catapulted from the hillside to the heart of the court. In most of the many moves reported in this chapter, David is only acted upon: Yahweh looks him out; his father sends for him; Samuel anoints him; a courtier not only knows of him but has also seen him; Saul sends for him; his father dispatches him with a present to the king. When he arrives at court (comes to Saul), a relationship with the king begins. The two men interchange as grammatical subjects of the following verbs, although sometimes the logical subject is different from the grammatical one. On arrival, David "stands before" the king: a set phrase for being in his service. Saul loves him greatly—and trusts him to the point of making him his armor-bearer (Saul here the logical subject, although the narrator talks of "David's becoming" Saul's armor-bearer). Only after matters have proceeded so far does Saul seek confirmation from Jesse that these arrangements are in order: he tells David's father that he approves of his son, or that David has won his approval—David is the grammatical subject of "has found favor in my eyes," but a successful relationship is implied. And finally, when need be, David plays the lyre for Saul—and with success.

Saul's first response to David is of great love (v. 21). Apart from Hannah's being loved by her husband (1:5), David is the only character in 1 Samuel to whom "love" is directed. Saul is only the first of many to respond to David in this way: the king is followed by

- all Israel and Judah (18:16)
- his daughter, Michal (18:20)
- (a claim, at least, about) all Saul's servants (18:22)
- his son, Jonathan (20:17)[67]

It is only Jonathan's love for David that is explicitly recognized by David, and only once he is dead—at the end of David's elegy for Jonathan and his father (2 Sam 1:26).[68] What is the nature of this love? And do all of these individuals and groups "love" David in much the same way? Are they all simply responding to the hero, the champion, the good-looker, in whose direction all heads naturally turn? Or, especially in the case of the three named individuals, are the king and his daughter and his son all in some sense competing for David? At this point, we must leave the question for further reflection, but we can frame it along with another query.

The courtier who brings David to Saul's attention does so in a five- or six-part commendation that concludes, or is summed up, in the words "and Yahweh is with him" (16:18). Like so much other significant comment throughout 1 Samuel, this phrase anticipates an evaluation of David made early in the source text (2 Sam 5:10, BTH). More immediately, the courtier anticipates the narrator's judgment in 18:14. All the other uses of this and similar phrases are clustered in the same few chapters of 1 Samuel—the new beginning of the story of David—where the courtier and the narrator are echoed first by Saul himself (17:37; 18:28) and then by Jonathan (20:13). Loving David and recognizing

67. Anticipated in the MT plus of 18:1. There is another relevant instance of textual variation in 18:28: "Michal daughter of Saul" (MT) resumes 18:20; and "all Israel" (GT), 18:16.

68. The language of "love" will recur in 2 Samuel only in 12:24; 13:1, 4, 15; 19:6 (7).

that Yahweh is with him seem to be very closely related. It may simply be that, while humans "love" David, something less affective is reported of Yahweh—in the books of Samuel, he is said to "love" only the newborn Solomon (2 Sam 12:24).

The last words of this chapter pun nicely on the letters *rwḥ*, and also remind us (esp. in MT) of the immediate source of Saul's difficulties. When "a divine spirit" (*rûaḥ ʾĕlōhîm*) is on Saul, David plays, there is "space" (*rāwaḥ*) for Saul, and "the evil spirit" (*rûaḥ hārāʿā*) would turn away from him. The verb *rāwaḥ* is rare; yet it is used in a passive participle describing "spacious" rooms (Jer 22:14); and spacious rooms are also airy rooms into which a breeze (*rûaḥ*) may blow.

The statement made in v. 13, and only there, that "the spirit of Yahweh came on David" will correspond theologically to the statement made rather more commonly that "Yahweh was with him." It is the latter form of the theological claim that is rooted in BTH (2 Sam 5:10), and that we have seen anticipated in 1 Sam 16:18; 17:37; 18:14, 28; 20:13. If our hypothesis about the development of the materials in 1 Samuel is broadly accurate—that the first stories about David and Saul within 1 Sam 17–24, and about Saul before David in the older parts of 1 Sam 13–14, knew nothing of (the developed portrait of) Samuel—then this statement that "the spirit of Yahweh came on David" will not only correspond to but will also have been based on the rather more common claim that "Yahweh was with him." The "spirit" language will have been introduced to this book as part of the developing Samuel material. Taken with the note about Samuel's departure to his hometown (16:13), this observation suggests that we should read ch. 16 as the end of the story of Samuel as well as the beginning of the story of David. We have to ask whether David is already the joint leading character of most of 1 Sam 17–24 before he was anointed in 1 Sam 16.

Excursus 2: Afterword on 1 Samuel 9–16

The first chapters on Saul (before David comes on the scene) remain true to the principal source of the books of Samuel in at least one important respect. Saul has been introduced in BTH (1 Sam 31), only to fail and make way for another. Much of 1 Samuel is devoted to reporting what preceded this end. But the end is already in sight very soon after the beginning. Despite a series of positive indicators—anointing and signs and spirit-endowment and sacred lot and success in battle (1 Sam 9–11)—Samuel has told him openly as early as 1 Sam 13:14 that Yahweh has chosen his successor. For all that, Samuel is already now (15:35) in mourning for the Saul whom he would not see again till his death. His mourning for Saul faces in either one or both of two narrative directions: back to the people who are in mourning because Yahweh has caused so many deaths in Beth-shemesh (6:19); and forward to David, who begins mourning Absalom long before he dies (2 Sam 13:37).[69] It is also possible that Samuel's mourning has been simply

69. Notice proximity of *htʾbl* and *nḥm* at end of 2 Sam 13 (vv. 37, 39)!

symbolic of Yahweh's decision that King Saul is now effectively dead and finished; however, there is no clear indicator in the text that this is so. Yet the principal divisions of MT do not encourage pausing at Samuel's mourning, any more than Yahweh does (16:1). The chosen successor is now revealed, and his musical ministrations ameliorate the effects of the new spirit sent on Saul by Yahweh.

1 Samuel 17–24
Saul Rejected, David in Waiting

The third quarter of 1 Samuel charts the fraught relationship between two anointees (messiahs): Saul already divinely rejected before David is anointed; David still not king although very much the man of promise and recognized as the next king by both Saul and Jonathan, his expected heir. This portion also contains at least one (almost certainly secondary) return to an earlier theme: Saul among the prophets (19:18–24), resuming and reworking 1 Sam 10:10–16. The CL and Aleppo Codex share the major internal division at 18:16. The first and shorter section opens with the extended account of David's most famous exploit; it concludes by noting the people's glowingly positive reaction to David and the ambivalence of Saul. The longer section, more often divided in Aleppo than CL, demonstrates the varied reactions to David even within the house of Saul. Both Michal, who becomes David's wife, and Jonathan, who should be Saul's successor, protect David from their father. And Saul moves from fear and awe in face of David at the end of the first section (18:12, 15) to open admission at the end of the next (24:20) that he will be king.

1 Samuel 17:1–18:16 David, Goliath, and Saul

If Saul has fallen remarkably quickly from Yahweh's favor, so too does David from Saul's favor. And David's first and perhaps most spectacular triumph—and the popular reaction to it—are a large part of the cause. When we make such a comment, we need to remind ourselves that we mean "first" in the narrative before us. It may be that little if any of the story of David is historical. The source of the narrative is, unusually, still at hand. In the older Book of Two Houses, David's first reported external campaign after being anointed king was against the Philistines (2 Sam 5:17–25). And in a neighboring portion of that same BTH (now delayed to 2 Sam 21:18–22), Philistine giants slain by David's heroes included Goliath of Gath (his spear's shaft like a weaver's beam) and an unnamed man of great size who taunted Israel. The author of 1 Sam 17 has combined these several elements of his source and promoted Goliath to be young David's first victim, felled in solo combat. The quality of this memorable tale is rightly famous. Some of the complex development of the tale can also still be inspected, since it has come down to us in two quite different versions. Among students of textual criticism, the fame of this encounter and its immediate aftermath has another explanation: the texts of B and MT are more substantially different here than anywhere else in the Bible.

In the materials that MT and B share, they differ in detail, much as throughout the book. However, some whole scenes in MT are completely absent from B. The four largest of these take up a total of thirty-four verses: David is sent from home to visit his elder brothers in the ranks (17:12–31); the response of Saul and Jonathan to the success of their (unknown) champion (17:55–18:5); Saul's hurling his spear at David (18:10–11); and Saul's offer to David of his elder daughter's hand in marriage (18:17–19). Then there are also some shorter pluses, such as 17:41, 50; and 18:29b–30. Many attempts have been made to portray the shorter Hebrew text underlying B as a deliberate simplification of the more complex narrative in MT. However, the more economical theory appears preferable: that a shorter, simpler narrative (B) was substantially expanded to produce MT; rather than that the complex MT was first composed out of different sources, and the resultant text then simplified (B). The first and largest of the pluses in MT (17:12–31) is crucial to this argument; as we discuss it, we shall notice several indications that this was never (part of) an independently existing source text, but rather a deliberate supplement designed to indicate points of comparison and contrast between Saul and David as each first appeared on Israel's stage. Most frequently, throughout Samuel, 4QSam[a] supports the readings of B against MT, but not in this case. For three of the large pluses in MT, it has no evidence to offer; but it does have fragmentary testimony to 18:4–5, as well as to the short plus in 17:41.

1 Samuel 17:1–11

1 And *the* Philistines gathered their camp*s* for battle,
and they were gathered at [Socoh which belongs to Judah] *Succoth*[a] *of Edom*[b];
and they camped between [Socoh] *Succoth* and Azekah *Ephermem*, [at Ephes-dammim[c]].
2 Now Saul and the men of Israel gathered
and camped in the valley [of the terebinth];
and *these* arranged battle
to meet *the* Philistines.
3 And *the* Philistines were standing on the hill on this side,
and Israel were standing on the hill on that side,
[and the valley[a] was] *round about*[b] between them.
4 And [the in-between man[a]] *a powerful man* came out of the Philistine camp[s].

Goliath was his name, from Gath;
and his height was [six] *four* cubits and a span.[b]
5 And a [bronze[a]] helmet was on his head,
and with a plated cuirass he was clothed—
and the weight of the cuirass was five thousand shekels of bronze *and iron.*
6 And bronze greaves were on his legs,
and a bronze javelin between his shoulders.
7 And the "arrow"[a] of his spear was like a weaver's beam,
and [the] *its* "flame"[b] [of his spear] was six hundred shekels of iron;
and his [shield-] *weapons*-bearer walked in front of him.
8 And he stood
and called to Israel's line[s],
and said to them:
"Why do you come out
to draw up battle lines *against us*?
Am I not [the] *a* Philistine,
while you are [servants of] *Hebrews and* Saul?[a]
Select[b] for yourselves a man,
and let him come down to me.
9 If he is able
to fight with me
and strike me down,
then we shall be your servants.
But if I myself am able for him
and I strike him down,
then you will be as servants to us
and will serve us."
10 And the Philistine said:
"I myself despise Israel's lines [today in] this day.
Give[a] me a man,
and let us *both* fight *alone* [together]."
11 And Saul heard, and all Israel, those words of the Philistine,
and they were shattered
and very afraid.

1a. The GT's *Sokchōth* normally corresponds to MT's *sukkôt*, but here (2x) and in 2 Chr 11:7 to *śōkōh*.

b. The LT attests Judah here; it may be a mistake to suppose that B represents an original *Ĕdôm*: *Idoumaia* and *Ioudaia* are more similar in Greek than are their Hebrew counterparts; and Idumea later expanded northward into territory that had previously been Judean.

c. Either this name has been mauled in the Greek tradition or it represents a shorter name (without preposition) than MT. The MT is often compared with *bps-dmym whplštym* in the report in 1 Chr 11:13 of an encounter between David and the Philistines; MT in the synoptic 2 Sam 23:9 has *bhrpm bplštym*, the first element of which is not dissimilar to [*S*]*APHERMEIN* in LT here.

3a. In Codex A and LT, *aulōn* normally renders *ʿēmeq*, but here it corresponds uniquely to the MT *gayʾ*.

b. Normally B's *kyklō* represents some form of *sbb*.

4a. "The man of the space-between" (Fox).

b. That is, a palm-breadth.

5a. Not in B, but LT does read *chalkē*.

7a. The MT has *ḥēṣ*, but the more straightforward *ʿēṣ* is in 2 Sam 21:19 (the source verse in BTH). The LT has *xylon* here, as in 2 Kgdms 21:19, while B's *kontos* ("pole"), though more specific, can be taken as also attesting *ʿēṣ*. Is this a linguistic issue, to be compared with *ʿmr/ḥmr* (where LXX *gomor* also attests to *ʿmr*)?

b. Neither B nor LT renders *lahebet* lit., nor does either repeat *ḥănîtô* in this sentence. The GT *logchē* does mean "lancehead"; so we may be dealing with an idiomatic and economic rendering—yet the following *ep' autō* in LT may suggest a text different from MT.

8a. The LT reads "Hebrews of Saul."

b. The pl. imperative *brw*, as vocalized, is a unique instance of this *brh*: probably a by-form of the commoner *brr*, and to be distinguished from *brh* ("eat") used in 2 Samuel.

10a. Here the LT adds *oun* ("therefore").

[1–11] The story of Goliath begins with a Philistine military initiative. Their leaders are not named, nor is it said in so many words against whom they are preparing battle; but their action includes taking up positions between towns in the foothills of Judah (v. 1). "Saul and the men of Israel" draw up lines in response (v. 2). The two forces are on opposing hills, with the valley between (v. 3). The anonymous Philistine threat crystallizes into a massive individual challenge in the space between the armies: we are told the name of the "in-between man," his town, and his great height (v. 4); the armor protecting him is described in close detail (vv. 5–7a); and he has the services of a shield-bearer[1] (v. 7b). He not only looks huge; he also speaks big. There is no need, he says to Israel, for them to have drawn up battle lines (v. 8a); for he himself is "the Philistine." All they need to do is to search out a man to fight with him, to settle which people should serve the other (vv. 8b–9). He adds that he despises the lines Israel has drawn up: they should give him one man, and they would fight "together" (v. 10). Goliath's insult is directed against Israel (v. 10), although as David later repeats his words, he represents them as having been uttered against Israel's God (v. 36). Saul has led out his men in response to the Philistine initiative (v. 2) but is never specifically addressed by Goliath. His response to the champion's challenge is no different from that of "all Israel": all are "shattered"

1. Repeated in 17:41 (an MT plus), *nṣʾ hṣnh* is found elsewhere only in 1 Chr 12:25; 2 Chr 14:7.

(v. 11). Saul may stand head and shoulders above his people (10:23), but he has also once hidden himself among the baggage (10:22): this time, too, he is not to be the "man" for Goliath.

There is no other story quite like this in Samuel, or even in the Bible; and yet we can trace many of its origins. Conflict between Israel and Philistines is hardly novel; and "gather" (*'sp*), "battle," and "draw up [lines]" (*'rk*) are not unfamiliar. And yet all three are found in the same context—and also linked with *yaḥad* ("together")—only in 2 Sam 10 (BTH). Then battle with Philistines, involving a series of tussles with individual giants, of whom one is Goliath of Gath, the wood of whose spear is like a weaver's beam, while another giant "despises" Israel—these have also been reported in BTH (2 Sam 21:18–22). The Goliath of 1 Sam 17 is a composite of the separate Philistine giants in BTH. But there are also changes. Extra digits (six on each hand and foot; 2 Sam 21:20) have become great height (17:4): over four cubits (GT) and over six cubits (MT). Heavy armor is worn. The location has moved from Philistine Gath to a location in Judah. And a list of victories has become an account of a contest.

When Goliath calls for Israel to select a man so that they can fight "together," he gives that word a new sense that is never exactly repeated in HB: elsewhere men gather "together" to fight (as in 2 Sam 10:15), while here the challenge is for two men to fight "together." The closest comparison comes later in Samuel, when twelve men representing Benjamin and Saul's son counter twelve of David's servants, indulging in fatal "play" at the pool of Gibeon (2 Sam 2:12–17). This comparison is underscored when the two main forces are said to have met "together" (2:13) by the pool, and then sat separately with one party "on this side" and the other "on that side" (*mzh . . . wmzh*)—the latter phrase recurs in HB only in 1 Sam 14:4. However, the Bible has no parallel to an individual duel such as the Goliath of 1 Sam 17 proposes; and it is hardly surprising that GT interprets "together" (v. 10) by "alone."

The remarkable shaft of Goliath's spear may have come with his name and the name of his town from BTH. But the remainder of his armor (vv. 5–6) is another matter. The HB contains only one list of equipment at all similarly comprehensive; and that is the note in 2 Chr 26:14 detailing the provisions Uzziah makes for his army. But here everything detailed is being carried by one man, and everything is heavy bronze or iron. The mail (*širyôn*) is uniquely "scaly," and the leg "greaves" (*miṣḥâ*) are found nowhere else in HB. With so much other source material drawn from BTH, this report could have been crafted at any subsequent stage of the development of the book. But the nature of the armor, as well as the challenge to a duel between two champions, suggests the classical Greek world and a date no earlier than the Persian period. Although he is named once in this paragraph (v. 4), this longer story of Goliath is more concerned to stress his origins than his name. First Samuel is the book that deals more relentlessly with Philistines than any other in the Bible; and it is in this central chapter of 1 Samuel that "the Philistine" is used more often than anywhere else. When he throws down his challenge to the ranks of Israel (v. 8), he calls himself "the Philistine," and he calls them either "Hebrews" (GT) or "servants" (MT)—as we noted earlier, these Hebrew words are easily confused, both in looks (*ʿbrym* and *ʿbdym*) and in meaning.

1 Samuel 17:12–16

[12 Now David was son of an Ephrathite;
this {man was} from Bethlehem of Judah—
and his name was Jesse
and he had eight sons.
And the man—in the days of Saul, he was old
and advanced in "men."[a]
13 And the three big sons of Jesse went—
they went after Saul to war.
And the name of his three sons
who went to war
were Eliab the firstborn, and the second to him Ab/minadab, and the third Shammah.[a]
14 And David, he was the little one,
and the three big ones went after Saul.

15 And David was going and returning from Saul,
feeding his father's flock in Bethlehem.
16 And the Philistine approached, early and late,
and he presented himself for forty days.[a]]

12a. The LT attests the more likely *bʾ bšnym* ("advanced in years") rather than MT's *bʾ bʾnšym* ("advanced in men"). It is easy to see how the mistake had occurred.

13a. Here LT's *Samaa* may attest *šmʿh*.

16a. The LT adds "before Israel" at the end.

[12–14] Here David is introduced into the story of the battle, and in a rather leisurely way. We are told about his now elderly father with eight sons. The three biggest have followed Saul into the war, and these are named—the reference to "his second" (*mišnēhû*) uses the same terminology as 1 Sam 8:2 and 2 Sam 3:3. David is the smallest—and it is repeated that the three biggest have followed Saul. All this is clear, even if rather ponderous. These verses are the opening of a long plus in MT (vv. 12–31). This is surely additional material. However, it should not be understood as an import from a source external to the book (as often claimed). It is better seen as the result of continued organic development from the earlier shorter version of the story within its wider context. It needs both vv. 1–11 as introduction and what follows from v. 32 as its continuation (Barthélemy [54]). The information about Jesse and his eight sons is shared with the story of Samuel's anointing David: again only the three eldest and the youngest are named. The repeated mention of the intervening four sons may serve to emphasize David's junior status. On the other hand, father Jesse is said to be old (v. 12); we cannot assume that only three of his sons are old enough to bear arms. David is still responsible for his father's sheep.

[15–16] The final two verses bring the two major characters into narrative proximity for the first time. The second of these is unambiguous: the Philistine approaches early and late and presents himself for forty days. But what is said about David is more puzzling, however it is read. The verb *hlk* ("go") has been a very prominent feature of the opening statements. It is used three times in v. 13 and once in v. 14b, emphasizing that David's big brothers have gone "after Saul" (2x) and "into the war" (2x). What is now said about David opens with this same verb, and the use of the participle suggests continuity of action or state. Very widely, therefore, *hōlēk wāšāb* is read literally as meaning that David is [continually] going and turning back from proximity to Saul, for the purpose of feeding his father's flock in Bethlehem. David is moving between Bethlehem and the battle lines; and Goliath, for his part, is coming forward from the Philistine line twice a day for forty days. However, when *hlk* is closely paired with another verb as here, its idiomatic function is often to intensify the sense of the following twinned verb: David is "turning more and more away" from being by Saul, in order to feed father's sheep. Other examples of this use of the participle can be seen in 1 Sam 2:26; 17:41; 2 Sam 3:1 (2x); 15:12; and among these 1 Sam 17:41 is not only a further short plus in MT, but also describes the Philistine as coming nearer and nearer to David. Young David is certainly being contrasted with his older brothers. But is it that they are following "behind" Saul (vv. 13–14) while he is increasingly "away from" Saul, or is it that they are in the battle lines all the time while he is coming and going? The wider context may help clarify the question.

1 Samuel 17:17–18:5

[17 And Jesse said to David his son,
"Be sure to take your brothers this ephah[a] of parched grain[b] and these ten loaves
and run (them) to the camp to your brothers.
18 And these ten cuts of milk/cheese you will bring to the commander of the thousand;
and your brothers you will check for welfare,
and their tokens[a] you will take."[b]

19 Now Saul and they and every man of Israel were in the terebinth valley,
  fighting with the Philistines.
20 And David rose early in the morning,
and he let be the flock to a watcher,
and picked up
and went
  as Jesse had commanded him;
and he came to the wagon place[a]
  and the army[b] was going out to the lines
and they raised the war cry.
21 And Israel and Philistines drew up line facing line.
22 And David let be the baggage on him to the hand of the watcher of baggage,
and he ran to the line,[a]
and he came
and asked his brothers of their welfare.
23 And he was speaking with them,
and look the in-between man[a] was going up,
  Goliath the Philistine[b] his name,
  from Gath, from Philistine caves;[c]
and he spoke like these[d] words,
and David heard.
24 And every man of Israel,
  when they saw the man
they fled before him
and feared greatly.[a]
25 And the men of Israel[a] said:
  "Did you see this rising man?
  Surely to reproach Israel he was rising.
  The man
    who strikes him down
  the king will enrich with great riches;
  and his daughter he will give him,
  and his father's house he will render free in Israel."
26 And David said to the men standing with him:
  "What shall be done for the man
    who strikes down this Philistine
    and removes reproach from bearing on Israel?
  For who is this uncircumcised Philistine
    that he reproaches the lines of living God?"
27 And the people spoke to him in this way:
  "So shall it be done to the man

who strikes him down."
28 And Eliab his big brother heard
when he spoke to the men;
and Eliab's anger blazed at David,
and he said:
"Why ever did you come down?
And to whom did you let be those few sheep in the wilderness?
I, I know your pride and the evil of your heart,
for it was in order to see the battle that you came down."
29 And David said:
"What have I done now?
Was it not {but} a word?"
30 And he turned from his presence to face another,
and he spoke the same way;
and the people[a] returned him word as the first word.
31 And the words were heard,
that David spoke;
and they reported {them} in the presence of Saul,
and he took[a] him.]
32 And David said to Saul,
"Let not [a] the heart of [a human] *my lord* fall because of him.
Your servant will go
and fight with this Philistine."
33 And Saul said to David,
"You will not be able
to go to this Philistine
to fight with him,
for you are a youth
and he is a man of war since his youth."[a]

34 And David said to Saul,
"Your servant has been a shepherd for his father among[a] the sheep.
And the lion would come—and [with] the bear—
and would lift a sheep from the flock,
35 and I would go out after him
and would strike him down
and would deliver from his mouth.
And
if he rose against me,
I would grasp hold of his beard
and I would strike him down
and do him dead.

36 [Even the lion] and [even] the bear did your servant strike down
and the lion,[a]
and this uncircumcised Philistine shall be like one of them.
Shall I not go
and strike him,
and remove today reproach from Israel?
Who is this uncircumcised,
who [for he] has reproached the ranks of a living God."

37 [And David said,[a]]
"Yahweh
who has delivered me from the hand of the lion and from the hand of the bear,
he will deliver me from the hand of this Philistine."

And Saul said to David,
"Go,
and Yahweh will be with you."
38 And Saul dressed David in his *cloak*[a] [clothes],
and [put[b]] a bronze helmet on his head[,
and dressed him in a cuirass[c]].
39 And David bound his sword[a] over his *cloak*[b] [clothes],
and he [was too weary[c] to walk for he had not tested[d]] *toiled walking once and* twice.[e]
And David said to Saul,
"I am not able to walk in these,
for I have not tested (them)."
And *they*[f] [David] took them off him.
40 And he took his stick[a] in his hand,
and he chose himself five [smooth[b]] *complete* stones from the stream,
and he put them in the shepherd's vessel
which he had *for collecting* [and in the pouch[c]],
and his sling in his hand,
and he drew close to the Philistine.
41 [And the Philistine walked,
becoming nearer and nearer to David,
and the man carrying the shield in front of him.
42 And the Philistine looked[a]]
and *Goliath* saw David
and despised[b] him,
for he was a youth and ruddy together with [beautiful in appearance] *beauty of eyes*.

43 And the Philistine said to David,
"Am I a dog
that you are coming to me with stick *and stones?"*[a]
And David said,
"No—but worse than a dog."
And the Philistine cursed David by his gods.
44 And the Philistine said to David,
"Walk to me,
and I will give your flesh to the birds of the sky
and to the [beasts of the field] *cattle*[a] *of the* earth."[b]

45 And David said to the Philistine,
"You are coming to me with sword and with spear and with javelin;
but I am coming to you in the name of Yahweh *God* of Hosts, [God[a]] of Israel's ranks,
whom/which you have reviled *today.*
46 [This day] Yahweh will confine you *today* into my hand,
and I will strike you down,
and I will remove your head off you;
and I will give [as corpse] *your limbs and the limbs of* the Philistine camp this day to the birds of the sky and the beasts of the earth,
that all the earth may know
that there is a god *in*[a] [for] Israel,
47 and that all this assembly may know
that it is not by sword and by spear[a] that Yahweh will save;
for to Yahweh belongs the battle,
and he will give you into our hand."
48 And [it happened,
when[a]] the Philistine started and walked [and came near] to meet David[,
and David hurried
and ran to the line
to meet the Philistine].
49 And David put his hand into his vessel,
and took from there a stone,
and slung
and struck down the Philistine into his forehead;
and the stone sank *through his head-covering* into his forehead,
and he fell on his face on the ground.
[50 And David was stronger than the Philistine by sling and by stone;[a]
and he struck down the Philistine

and did him dead;
but no sword[b] was in David's hand.]
51 And David ran
and stood [by the Philistine] *over him*[a]
and took his sword
[and drew it from its sheath[b]]
and put him to death
and cut off [by it[c]] his head.
And the Philistines saw
  that their hero was dead,
and they fled.
52 And the men of Israel and of Judah started up
and they raised the war shout
and they pursued [the Philistines[a]] *them*
  till [you enter a valley[b]] *the entry of Gath* and up to the gates of [Ekron] *Ashkelon.*
And those pierced of Philistines fell on the road of the Twin Gates[c]
  and as far as Gath and as far as Ekron.
53 And the sons of Israel turned back from hot pursuit[a] of Philistines
and they plundered their camp.
54 And David took the head of the Philistine
and brought it to Jerusalem;
but his weapons he placed in his tent.

[55 And as Saul saw[a] David going out
  to meet the Philistine,
he said to Abner the army chief,
  "Whosever son is that lad, Abner?"
And Abner said,
  "By the life of your {good} self, O king,[b] I do not know."
56 And the king said,
  "You ask whosever son the youth is."

57 And as David came back[a]
  from striking down the Philistine,
Abner took him
and brought him before Saul;
  and the head of the Philistine was in his hand.
58 And Saul said to him:
  "Whose son are you, lad?"
And David said,
  "Son of your servant Jesse the Bethlehemite."

18:1 And it came to be,[a]
as he finished speaking to Saul,
Jonathan's self was bound to David's self
and Jonathan loved him as himself.
2 And Saul took him on that day
and did not allow him
to return to his father's house.
3 And Jonathan made—and David[a]—a covenant,
in his loving him like himself.
4 And Jonathan stripped himself of the cloak
that was on him,
and he gave it to David, and his clothes,
and as far as his sword and as far as his bow and as far as his belt.
5 And David went out:
in everything
on which Saul would dispatch him
he was successful;
and Saul placed him[a] over the men of war,[b]
and it was good in the eyes of all the people and also in the eyes of Saul's servants.]

17a. All 3 instances of *ʾêpâ* in FP (Judg 6:19; 1 Sam 1:24; 17:17) are transliterated *oiphi* in LXX, which corresponds also to *sĕʾâ* in 1 Sam 25:18.

b. The only case in HB where *qālîʾ* is spelled with the late-biblical and postbiblical final ʾ.

18a. The MSS of the Lucianic family transliterate *ʿărubbâ* variously as *erouba*, or *ersouba*, or *esouba*.

b. The LT adds the further clause "and you shall bring me their message," perhaps attesting *whbʾt-ly ʾt-šmʿtm*.

20a. The meaning of *maʿgālâ* is obscure, though it is often related in some way to *ʿăgālâ*, a "cart": it might (1) lit. mean a (cart) track or rut, extended to mean a military trench; or (2) a place where carts are drawn up (in a defensive laager [circle]). (3) The LT has *parembolēn*, which may instead attest *maḥăneh*, "army camp."

b. Here LT offers "and to the army which . . ."

22a. Again LT uses *parembolē*, this time corresponding to *maʿărākâ*.

23a. Here LT has *ho anēr ho amessaios*. Neither this adjective nor the variant *amassaios* or messaios is attested in LSJ, although the similar *mesaios* (retroverted from OL in LXX, ed. Rahlfs) is in LSJ and means "middle."

b. The expression *ho Phylistiaios* in Codex A and LT appears unique in LXX. The HB plus may have drawn "Goliath the Philistine" from the otherwise unique "the sword of Goliath the Philistine" in 21:9 (10) and 22:10 (2 Sam 21:19//1 Chr 20:5 calls him "Goliath the Gittite").

c. Almost certainly *mmʿrwt* is a slip for *mmʿrkwt*, attested in Q and LT.

d. Possibly "the former"?

24a. Here LT (more logically?) reverses the final two clauses.

25a. The LT has "a man from," which retroverts to *ʾyš m-*.

30a. Here LT does not attest "the people."

31a. The LT has read *wyqḥhw* as a pl. vb. ("and they took him"), to which it adds "and they brought him to Saul"; cf. "and Saul took him on that day" in the next major plus (1 Sam 18:2).

33a. The Gk. *paidarion . . . neotētos* does not catch the link between *nʿr* and *nʿryw* ("youth . . . his youth").

34a. Here *rʿh . . . bṣʾn* resumes the exact expression used earlier in the parent text (16:11 [,19]). Contrast MT's plus in 17:15 (*lrʿwt ʾt-ṣʾn*). In this case Gk. *poimainōn . . . en tō poimniō* creates a link not in the Heb. The LT has "for his father" after "in the flock."

36a. The word order in LT agrees with MT.

37a. Attested also by LT.

38a. A *mandya* (GT) is a [Persian?] woolen cloak. Deliberate assonance with *mdyw*?

b. Not in B, and LT sets the vb. "put" after the "bronze helmet," not before.

c. Also in LT.

39a. Here B (but not LT) takes David as a first obj. and "his sword" as second obj. of "girded," with Saul assumed to be subj., as he is in v. 38.

b. Here B repeats *mandya*, but LT uses *thōrakos* instead.

c. The MT's *wyʾl* is apparently a corruption from *wylʾ* ("was [too] weary to"). Only here does *kopian*, which corresponds most often to *ygʿ*, correspond to a form of *yʾl*.

d. The LT does attest these words after "once or twice" (see next textual note).

e. Just once does "once and twice" (B has *apax kai dis*) recur in LXX, in a plus in Deut 9:13. It may retrovert to *paʿam paʿămaim*, although that is not exactly attested anywhere in HB. The LT agrees with B over *apax kai dis* but is different and fuller in the previous words: B is briefer, "and he toiled walking"; and LT is fuller, "and David went lame in walking with them."

f. The LT has a sg. vb. and must intend David as subj. but does not specify him.

40a. Here B renders *mql* by the relatively rare *baktēria*, while LT has *rhabdos*, which both B and LT use in v. 43. They occur together in Ps 23 (22 LXX):4. Ordinarily a *rhabdos* would be lighter than a *baktēria*.

b. An adj. used as a noun: "smooth ones." The form is unique; B's *teleious* is a mistaken "correction" of the literal *leious* ("smooth").

c. Both *ylqwṭ* and *syllogē* are hapax in HB/OT; *lqṭ* means "gather" or "glean," and *syllogē* ("collection") can be used of what is "scraped together" for a living.

42a. The complete MT plus is represented in LT and attested also in 4QSam[a].

b. Here Codices B and A use *atimazein* for *bzh*, so comparing Goliath's disdaining David to the worthless fellows' disdaining Saul as a potential savior (1 Kgdms 10:27). The LT has *exoudenoun*, used in correspondence to *bzh* in 2 Kgdms 6:16 and also 12:10.

43a. The LT shares this small plus with B, but not the following response by David.

44a. The noun *ktēnesin* in B suggests domestic animals, but *thēriois* in LT means wild beasts.

b. The term *gēs* in GT corresponds better to *ʾrṣ* in v. 46 than to *śdh* here in MT.

45a. Here LT = MT.

46a. "In Israel" (GT) would normally correspond to *byśrʾl*, but MT has *lyśrʾl*.

47a. So also B, while unusually LT has the weapons in reverse order, and *machaira* for *rhomphaia.*

48a. Not attested in LT, which, however, does include the next two longer MT pluses. Here GT seems to have read simply *wyqm hplšty*. We see *whyh ky* followed by *yiqṭōl* in Gen 12:12; 46:33; Exod 1:10; 3:21; 12:25, 26; 13:5, 11, 14; 22:26; Lev 5:5; 6:4 (5:23); Deut 15:16; 26:1; 30:1; 31:21; Josh 8:5; 22:28; Judg 12:5; 21:22; 1 Sam 10:7; 25:30; Isa 8:21; 10:12; Jer 3:16; 15:2; 16:10; 25:28; Ezek 21:12; Zech. 13:3; but by *qāṭal* only in 1 Sam 1:12 (where the following *eplēthynen* [impf. or aor.?] corresponds to *hrbth*) and 17:48.

50a. Here LT adds "in that day" to the whole MT plus.

b. In LT is *rhomphaia*, as in v. 45, but not in v. 47.

51a. Here LT = B.

b. The LT = MT.

c. Here LT = MT.

52a. The LT = MT; but elsewhere in this verse, LT = B.

b. The letters of *gy'* and *gt* are readily confused.

c. Here B may be right to say "gates," as from *š'rym*.

53a. The regular term for pursue (*rdp*) in v. 52 is resumed by the rare *dlq* here. It lit. means "burn after," is used of pursuit only in Gen 31:36 and Lam 4:19, and conveys the sense of "hot pursuit." *ΕΚΚΛΙΝΟΝΤΕΣ* (B) is in error for *ΕΚΚΑΙΟΝΤΕΣ* (LT), induced by misreading *Α* as *Λ*.

55a. The clause-initial *wkr'wt* (lit., "and-as-seeing") is repeated in HB only in Esth 5:9. This linguistic feature, repeated in v. 57 below in *wkšwb*, may give an indication of the date of this expansion of MT.

b. Here LT adds "my lord" before "O king."

57a. This sentence opens like v. 55 (prep. + inf. + subj.); but while the main vb. in 55 (*'āmar*) has the same subj. and is *qāṭal*, here the subj. changes and the vb. (*way-yiqqaḥ*) is *wayyiqṭōl*.

1a. The verse opening in LT is fuller: "And it came to be, as David came to Saul and finished speaking to him, that Jonathan saw him. . . ."

3a. The LT adds "the king" after "David"!

5a. Here LT places the clause about David's appointment by Saul immediately after Jonathan's transfer (v. 4) of his (official) garments.

b. The phrase *tous andras tou polemou* appears to be a uniquely literal rendering of *'nšy hmlḥmh*; the sg. is rendered by *anēr polemistēs* in 17:33 and 16:18 (B), and by *anthrōpos polemistēs* in 16:18 (LT).

[17–33] If David has been coming and going all the time the Philistine has been calling for someone to take up his challenge (vv. 15–16), then we have to wonder whether the detailed instructions now given by his father (vv. 17–18) are part of this regular pattern, or whether they are special to this day. Does he always include a present for the officer? And does he always ask David to bring back some distinguishing token of evidence of his brothers' well-being—the rare *'rbh* here seems to be used in the same sense as the cognate (and quite as rare) *ʿrbwn* in Gen 38 (the distinctive items Judah leaves with his disguised daughter-in-law)? To ask these questions seems almost to answer them. It could be that none of David's previous visits has coincided with the twice-daily challenges by Goliath. It could be that the bounty for defeating the Philistine (v. 25b) has been set at a new level after forty days. And yet everything seems new to David, and his response to hearing Goliath's scorn appears to be instinctive and immediate.

In MT's expanded version of the story (vv. 12–31), the main action is triggered by the coincidence of a visit by David to his brothers and the Philistine's regular challenge. All the men of Israel flee from the giant in customary fear, saying (to each other, not to David), "Did you [pl.] see . . . ? Do you know the reward for killing him?" They repeat (v. 25) the keyword (*ḥrp*) reported by the narrator (v. 10) and drawn from the source (2 Sam 21:21): the Philistine is scorning and insulting Israel. It is not made clear whether and how far David has overheard his terrified countrymen—or how independent is his own response. In any case, he too repeats and develops the same key term. He first uses the related noun, saying that the killer of "this Philistine" will remove *ḥerpâ* from Israel (v. 26). As he then resumes the primary verb, he adds new detail: anticipating his words to Saul (v. 36), "this Philistine" is now "uncircumcised" and "[the ranks of] Israel" are now "the ranks of living God"—the latter point in much more distant anticipation of 2 Kgs 19 (Auld, 2004: 139). In Samuel, only Israel's leaders scorn Philistines as "uncircumcised": mortally wounded Saul already in BTH (1 Sam 31:4); Jonathan (14:6); and David both here and in his lament for Saul and Jonathan (2 Sam 1:20)—compare only Samson (Judg 15:18) and his parents (14:3). The formally plural *ʾĕlōhîm ḥayyim* ("living God") is found only in Deut 5:26 and Jer 23:36; and the related but stranger *ʾĕlōhîm ḥây* in 2 Kgs 19:4, 16 (= Isa 37:4, 17).

Responding to his people's fear in the face of the Philistine hero, David's taunt may be two-edged: on one level, it belongs with the sexual jibes men often use when together and in conflict; on another, it may mock his enemies' unripeness and unreadiness. As for his own side, they should recall how many oaths are sworn on Yahweh's life (*ḥy yhwh*)—by the life of that same Yahweh who is often called "Yahweh of hosts." Men of Israel should reckon themselves among the hosts of that living God.

David's big brother Eliab is enraged by his talk (v. 28). We readers know that he is one of the few who are privy to Samuel's having anointed the family's junior son. And we may suspect that he is jealous that the family's honor would be impugned by big talk in public on the part of the youngest member. He uses age-old tactics to return junior to his proper place: he has only a few sheep anyway; he is careless of their welfare; his concern for his brothers' welfare is no more than a pretense to let him view the action. However, upbraiding David now for entrusting his sheep to another seems strange if he has been visiting them regularly over the previous forty days. Eliab here uses the verb the narrator has used (*nṭš*) when reporting David's leaving sheep first of all (v. 20) and then luggage (v. 22) in safe deposit. Leaving his sheep in the care of a watcher has been implied in Jesse's commission to David to visit his brothers and attend to their needs. What his father would think about his not delivering his provisions directly to his brothers is not said. But another father (Saul's) has already shown (10:2) how a smaller concern should be "let be" (also *nṭš*) when a larger one emerges.

David says, "What have I done?" (1 Sam 17:29; 20:1; 26:18; 29:8) as often as all other biblical users of the question taken together (Num 22:28; Judg 8:2; 1 Kgs 19:20; Mic 6:3)—and the "now" added to the first such report neatly underscores how typical of him this protest is: this is far from the first time he has had to protest at injury to his innocence. David resumes talking to neighbors in the manner to which Eliab has taken offense, and he receives the same response as before (vv. 27, 30). When one word (v. 29) becomes quickly multiplied into many words (v. 30), the many words come to the ear of the king and result in a royal summons (v. 31). David now declares that he will fight with this Philistine, but Saul doubts whether a youth will prevail against a champion who has been a warrior since his youth (vv. 32–33).

The paragraphing in MT has coincided with the beginning of the long plus (v. 12), but the next break comes, not at its end, but after the first two verses of the continuation of the shorter shared text. In B, these two verses (32–33) follow immediately after the first report of Goliath's challenge (vv. 4–10) and the resultant terror of Saul and all Israel (v. 11). There David has needed no introduction to the battlefield or to Saul, because he is already part of Saul's staff (16:17–23). As we have seen already in vv. 12–16, much of the large plus in MT (vv. 12–31) could have been scripted from information already in the text. Jesse's present to his sons' commander reminds us of what he sent with David to Saul (16:20). And the terms in which David reports the Philistine's scorning of Israel's lines and their God (v. 26) anticipate his words in the shared text (v. 36). Fresh terminology is often a reliable mark of material of different origin. However, "free" (*ḥopšî*, v. 25) is the only term in all of twenty verses that is not also used in the wider context. The word itself is familiar from several other contexts in HB.[2] But elsewhere individuals "go out" or are "sent out" free; and only here do we read of a whole "house" being "made" free. Samuel has been uncomfortable about his mission to Bethlehem to anoint David (16:2) and has left for home as soon as he has done what he has come to do (16:13). Presumably David's family are no less uncomfortable after that occasion; and Jesse has been content to see David recruited into Saul's service. One function

2. Exodus 21:2, 5, 26, 27; Deut 15:12, 13, 18; Isa 58:6; Jer 34:9–16; Ps 88:5 (6); Job 3:19; 39:5.

of the large plus in MT may have been to underscore the loyalty of Jesse and his family to Saul, with three of his sons at the front and a handsome present to their commander.

Reading David's offer to Saul (v. 32) immediately after the report of the king's fearful response to Goliath's challenge (v. 11), as in the shorter text in B, is no more or less complicated than reading it after the long plus in MT. While in the new material in MT the volunteer has been brought to the king's notice by his talk, in the shorter B he has never left Saul's service since first being recruited to play before him (16:21–23). Saul and all Israel have been separately mentioned (v. 11) as being shattered in their fear of the Philistine. The MT and B differ over the precise terms of David's offer (v. 32). Each version of his offer resumes a different element of v. 11. "Let not the heart of a[ny] man [*'dm*] fall" (MT) corresponds to "all Israel," while "Let not the heart of my lord [*'dny*] fall" (B) answers to Saul; and the two Hebrew words are easily confused.

[34–36] When we first encounter David, we rather expect him to be nothing more than a "lad" (*na'ar*), but this is never explicitly stated in so many words. The first three sons of Jesse whom Samuel has inspected are named; the next four are not; after he has seen the seventh, the old man asks if he has seen all the "lads," and Jesse produces David (16:11). Saul asks for a "man" who can play well (16:17); and when one of his "lads" replies with a recommendation of David, two of his descriptors use "man": Saul claims David both as a "man of war" and a "man of looks." However, when David volunteers to fight with the Philistine, Saul calls him but a lad in contrast to a champion who has been a man of war since he was a lad (17:33). David makes a double response to the warning that he is too young to cope with a mature warrior. As shepherd to his father's flock, he has successfully dealt with lion and bear. If v. 35a (the rescue of the sheep from the lion's mouth) and v. 35b (the bearding and striking down of the predator when it reared up at him) report two aspects of the one rescue action, the claim is already impressive. But if David is reporting two stages in the exploit—that the sheep was first rescued before its captor was killed, and then the beast came for David—his credentials are all the more impressive. The uncircumcised Philistine will fare no better for scorning the battle lines of a living God (vv. 34–36).

[37a] In the shorter response, David now names that living God and credits him with saving him from lion and bear.

[37b–44] Persuaded now that he may be dealing with a credible fighter, Saul wishes David well; and his words (17:37b) to him echo the climax of his own lad's first recommendation of David (16:18): "and Yahweh will be with you." David's credibility comes from his experience of one-to-one combat with lion and bear. However, he is no regular "man of war": he has neither experience of nor immediate facility with regular arms and armor. We are now told, though without particular emphasis, that Saul dresses him in his own clothes, no less; and that he adds a bronze helmet and mail. David girds "his" sword over "his" clothes (presumably Saul's in both cases), but unable to walk, he takes them off. He finds at first trial what the Philistine champion discovers fatally late, that heavy armor constitutes an impediment, not a protection. The pieces of armed protection provided by Saul correspond strikingly to the elements of Goliath's armor (vv. 5–7). They are not said to be too heavy, but David is unable to walk, and what else could a bronze helmet be but heavy? Nor are David's own weapons of choice called "light." But the name of everything he does select (v. 40) plays on and hints at *qal*, the Hebrew adjective for "light" and "fast": most obviously his "stick" (*mql*) and "sling" (*qlʿ*), but also (with the key consonants reversed) the "smooth" [stones] (*ḥlqy*) and his "pouch" (*ylqwṭ*)—with this young champion in the making, words and reality are in perfect fit.

David now advances on the Philistine (v. 40b). The MT's longer version adds (v. 41) that the Philistine is also steadily approaching David, his shield-bearer in front of him. This late addition has interesting resonance later in David's story. "And he walked, coming nearer and nearer" (*wylk hlk wqrb*) is reported of only one other character in HB, of the first of the two messengers running to David with news of Absalom's death (2 Sam 18:25). David says there, "If he is alone, there is news in his mouth." When Goliath, preceded by his shield-bearer, does see David, he does not think much of him (v. 42). "Despise" or "scorn" (*bzh*) is a rare word in biblical narrative; in his low estimate of David, the Philistine is in "select" company: with the louts who brought no present to Saul (1 Sam 10:27), with Michal while watching David from her window as he accompanies the ark into Jerusalem (2 Sam 6:16, BTH), and with David himself in scorning Yahweh['s word] over Uriah and Bathsheba (2 Sam 12:9, 10).

Despising has to do with perception, or misperception. Goliath's first estimate of David—just like Saul's, when David has volunteered as champion—is of a "lad." The impression registered by the Philistine (v. 42) agrees with the narrator's description of the David summoned to meet Samuel (16:12). The first element is of a lad with the red flush of youth still on his cheeks. The GT ("eyes") and MT ("looks") go on to make different selections from the longer conclusion to that earlier picture; but what each offers is just a different aspect of the visual: GT emphasizes David's eyes, while MT returns our attention to Goliath's seeing. The longer text makes the link with the previous chapter even more explicit: "looked" (*wybṭ*) is used very sparingly in Samuel; but Yahweh has recently (16:7) warned Samuel not to "look" on the externals of Jesse's sons because Yahweh sees differently. In the longer text, Goliath repeats Samuel's mistake.

The scorn of the Philistine is all the greater because he has been insulted. His challenger is only a junior and is equipped only with "weapons" suitable for chasing away an unwanted dog. The Philistine resumes the wordplay already noted (v. 40) and develops it (v. 43). To David's approach with "sticks" (*mqlwt*), Goliath responds by cursing David; and the word selected here for "curse" (*qll*) literally means to "slight": to treat as light and insignificant. If all the tools collected by David are actually light, when compared with metal armor, and if all their names play on the word "light," the Philistine has now responded measure for measure: in his eyes, David is lightweight and contemptible. Having seen himself through David's eyes, not as a noble lion or bear, but as no more than a dog—and dogs are scavengers and pests in Near Eastern tradition—the Philistine threatens to turn David over to scavengers at large, whether birds of the air or "beasts of the field." Goliath's exact expression (*bhmt hśdh*) is unique (v. 44); and even "beasts of the earth" (*bhmt h'rṣ*) is rare (Deut 28:26; Isa 18:6 [2x]; Jer 7:33; 15:3; 16:4; 19:7; 34:20).

[45–54] But David is not to be outdone in the insulting foreplay customary before such a duel. In cursing by his god, Goliath has slighted the insignificance of the opposition. David's response ignores Goliath's god: he answers by claiming the name "Yahweh of hosts" as more effective than the heavy weapons brandished by the Philistine. David's boasts are bigger than the Philistine's: (1) The scavengers will have work in all the Philistine camp and not just with Goliath's corpse. (2) The whole land—or is it the whole earth?—will know that Israel has a God. And (3) everyone gathered will discover that Yahweh's deliverance is achieved without sword or spear. The development of the final point is left somewhat ambiguous: "The battle belongs to Yahweh, and [or but?] he will put you [all] in our hand." When the champion is laid low (without sword or spear), all Goliath's people will come into Israel's power. David uses a different term from Goliath for scavenging animal: his *ḥyt h'rṣ* (v. 46), while not unique, is found in only two contexts (Gen 1:25, 30; 9:2, 10; Ezek 32:4). The normal expression in HB is *ḥyt hśdh*. The culmination of David's speech, "The battle is Yahweh's," is said by no one else in HB. The closest comparator (text for comparison) is in 2 Chr 20:15: "Not yours is the battle but God's."

David has the last words, and they spur his opponent into action: it is only now (v. 48) that the shorter text talks of the Philistine's approaching David (contrast v. 41 in MT). He makes his move, and David responds with speed, runs to meet him, slings one stone, and fells his opponent. Like Dagon, the Philistine god before the ark in an earlier episode (5:3–4), Goliath falls on his face to the ground. The display for the public that Goliath is dead, though told in fewer words, has a more leisurely feel: David runs to a position by his fallen opponent, takes his (opponent's) sword, draws it from its scabbard, kills him, and with it cuts off his head. The desired impression is duly achieved: the enemy troops are left in no doubt but that their champion is dead, and they take to flight. No (Israelite) sword or spear has been used against their hero, and the Philistine ranks are in flight to their own cities, pursued by Israel.

That David should put his rival's armor in his tent (v. 54) is unremarkable. That he should bring his head to Jerusalem is a considerable puzzle, for that city is not even mentioned anywhere else in 1 Samuel; we will not read the report of its capture by David until 2 Sam 5; and it is not in Jerusalem, but in nearby

Nob, where we shall next meet Goliath's sword (21:9 [10]). Yet in considering this puzzle, we should perhaps keep in mind that in BTH, our author's major source, David's first battles with Philistines (including the older Goliath story) follow the capture of his new capital.

[55–56] While the shorter version of B moves immediately to the rejoicings across Israel as the army comes home (18:6), MT interposes brief scenes relating the impact of David on Saul and Jonathan. A tiny fragment of 4QSam[a] does contain parts of 18:4 and 18:5 (DJD 80). David has talked his way into becoming Israel's champion on the basis of his claimed prowess with lions and bears (vv. 32–37), and he has not let himself or his king down. It now appears (v. 55) that he has achieved this without Saul's being aware or taking the trouble to find out just who the shepherd is, who is so brimming with confidence.

There is no indication that Saul is feigning to Abner his ignorance over David's identity, or Abner to him. Another possibility is that Saul's nonrecognition of David is a sign of increasing unpredictability, even developing madness; and yet it is not until the next day (18:10) that a malevolent spirit impels him to try to kill David. However, it is sensible to explore other possibilities. Saul may have thought, when David rejects wearing his armor (v. 39), that he has also withdrawn from his challenge (Polzin 1989: 173). In that case, the king may have been no more aware that David was the youth going out to meet the Philistine than he has been of Jonathan's earlier solo exploit (1 Sam 14).

[57–58] When Saul asks Abner to make inquiries, the youngster is called not *naʿar* but *ʿelem*, which we shall find used of Jonathan's "pageboy" (20:22), and nowhere else in HB. Then the repetition of the same question—already put twice to Abner, then to David himself when he appears carrying Goliath's head—suggests that at least by this third time of asking the question, it is not to be understood simply or literally. After such a victory, David must have a higher origin, or at least a higher destiny, than simply to be son of Jesse the Bethlehemite. At one level, David's careful response ("I am the son of your servant . . .") is simply polite; but at another level, it may be designed to give Saul space to remember the promise, recorded in the earlier and even larger supplement to the shorter story, of freedom for the "father's house" of the man who kills the Philistine champion (v. 25).

[18:1–5] David's answer meets an immediately favorable response from both the king and his son. It is not easy to translate *nepeš*, which is so prominent in 18:1, 3. In each of its four appearances in BTH, it means "life" or "life force" (2 Sam 23:17; 1 Kgs 3:11; 8:48; 2 Kgs 23:3). It is very much commoner in Samuel as a whole.[3] The *nipʿal* of *qšr* ("bind, tie") is found in only one other

3. See 1 Sam 1:10, 15, 26; 2:16, 33, 35; 17:55; 18:1 (3x), 3; 19:5, 11; 20:1, 3, 4, 17; 22:2, 22, 23; 23:15, 20; 24:11 (12); 25:26, 29 (3x); 26:21, 24; 28:9, 21; 30:6; 2 Sam 1:9; 3:21; 4:8, 9; 5:8; 11:11; 14:7, 14, 19; 16:11; 17:8; 18:13; 19:6—and 23:17 (BTH).

biblical passage, where Neh 4:6 (3:38) records the completion, the completed linkage, of the rebuilt wall of Jerusalem. Though the verb need mean no more than "linked," the term often also throughout HB implies seditious ties (as in 1 Sam 22:8, 13; 2 Sam 15:31). And in a very short time, although in different words, Saul will in fact charge his son with disloyalty because of his attachment to David (20:30–31). Be that as it may, Saul's response for now, whether he is supportive of his son's affirmation of David or threatened by it, is to keep David within his own establishment. Jonathan makes the next move, making a covenant with David and passing to him the symbols of his status as first son of the king, including his weapons. And Saul in his turn follows this up by making David commander of his forces: so successful is David in this role that he pleases not only the generality of the people, but even Saul's own staff. In these few sentences, MT anticipates several themes developed more gradually in the following chapters of the shared text.

Quite apart from the question of whether Saul and Jonathan are acting in concert or in competition with each other, the language used to describe the moves of each toward David is in curious tension with the apparent reality. The *nipʿal* of a Hebrew verb (as in "was bound" of v. 1) frequently has overtones of mutuality, and not simply of passivity; and "love" is ideally mutual. And yet we are told nothing of David's response to Jonathan. Next, Saul does not make David an offer, but "took" him "and did not grant him [permission] to return. . . ." (v. 2). It would be natural to complete that sentence with the word "home"; but that would be to miss the significant echo with 17:25 (also an MT plus). The royal promise has been understood to include freedom for the victor's "father's house"; but victorious David is not free to return to his "father's house." Then there is the odd covenant: Jonathan neither makes a covenant "with" David (despite NRSV) nor imposes covenanted terms "upon" David. The verb is singular ("and Jonathan made a covenant, and David too"), corresponding to regular idiom when one party is clearly in the lead ("and Joshua rose early and the priests picked up the ark," Josh 6:12); and this covenant is made, without any content being stated, because he loves him—not because each loves the other. The statements of Jonathan's love for David (vv. 1b, 3b) anticipate what will be said in 20:17 (see below).

1 Samuel 18:6–13

6 And [it came to be
as they were coming,
as David was coming back
from striking down the Philistine,
and the women] *the dancers* came out
to meet David from all the cities of Israel [for the song and the dances:

to meet King Saul[a]] with timbrels and with rejoicing and with cymbals.[b]

7 And the women [at play[a]] spoke up
and said,
"Saul has struck down in his thousand(s), and David in his myriads."

8 And [Saul was very[a] vexed
and] this saying was bad in [his] *Saul's* eyes,
and he said:
"They have given myriads to David,
but to me they have given the thousands.
[Still for him—only the kingdom.]"

9 And Saul was eyeing[a] David from that day and onward.

[10 And it came to be on the morrow
and an evil divine spirit[a] fell on Saul,
and he played the prophet in the midst of the house;
and David played by his hand as day by day.
And the spear was in Saul's hand.

11 And Saul hurled the spear,
and said,
"I shall strike on David and on the wall."
And David turned from him twice.]

12 And Saul was afraid of David
[for Yahweh was with him
but from Saul he had turned].

13 And [Saul] *he* removed him from his presence,
and made him for himself commander of a thousand;
and he went out
and came in before the people.

6a. The LT is similar in extent to MT but has "the dancers and the singers [reverse order] came out to meet Saul the king."

b. If *šlšym* is derived from the very common word for "three," then it is the unique usage within MT of a form of this numeral to name a musical instrument ("triangle"? three-stringed instrument?). *kymbalois* (GT) appears to have read (this word as) *ṣlṣlym*, cognates of which are used here in Tg. and Syr. Then B is similar to MT in having three elements, each introduced by *en/b*, of which the first and last are instruments—and *charmosynē*, though corresponding to *twdh* in Lev 22:29, renders *śmḥh* twice in Jeremiah. The LT has five elements, of which the first and third are the same, and *en charmonē* is the fifth; but the second and fourth are further instruments, *en nablais* and *en kinyrais*; these quite often form a pair (as in 1 Kgdms 10:5 in the description of the prophets Saul would meet); but *nabla* and *kinyra* seem elsewhere always to correspond to *nbl* and *knwr* (from which they are derived).

7a. The LT's *hai choreuousai* resumes the term from v. 6 and so may attest *bmḥlwt*, as in 21:12; 29:5.

8a. The LT apparently attests *m'd* after rather than before *wyr'*.

9a. Apparently *'ôyēn* (Q) is a denominative vb. from *'yn* ("eye") rather than from *'wn*.

10a. The LT carefully renders *pneuma para theou ponēron*.

[6–9] At the end of the plus in MT, talk of David's pleasing the people (18:5) has neatly returned us to where the older story picks up from the Philistine defeat: the return home of the Israelite army and their leaders. And yet the longer and shorter texts are no sooner together again than they diverge. The shorter B (v. 6) has the singing and dancing women of Israel come out to greet David; and their "timbrels" and their "rejoicing" may well have been drawn from the celebrations described in BTH (2 Sam 6:5, 12) when David was bringing the ark to Jerusalem. But the longer MT has rebuilt the text. Although it still mentions David, it has the women meeting Saul, once David has killed the Philistine. Yet moving the focus to Saul simply underscores that Saul is now in second place. There is no disagreement between the texts over exactly what the exultant women are chanting: Saul has been hugely successful—but David many times more so. Hardly surprisingly, Saul takes this popular "welcome home" amiss. Saul notes, in another addition of MT (v. 8b), that the tide now swelling can carry David in only one direction: to the kingship. The critical observer might conclude from the same longer MT, which has earlier reported Jonathan and Saul as pressing advancement on David (vv. 1–5), that Saul and Jonathan have themselves contributed to such an outcome. The older shorter text had reported simply that Saul's displeasure at the chants had led him to "eye" David (v. 9). This unique instance of a verb made from one of the commonest of nouns could convey envy, or suspicion—or even suspicion leading to having David watched.

[10–13] "Eyeing" David also involves fearing him (v. 12); and fearing him leads to removing him from court by giving him a commission, as officer commanding a thousand troops (v. 13). This is a significant command: elsewhere 1 Samuel talks about "commanders of thousands and commanders of fifties" (8:12), and "commanders of thousands and commanders of hundreds" (22:7). However, the women's victory chant (v. 7) has just ascribed "thousands" (of Philistine dead) to Saul but tens of thousands to David. In giving David even a major command, is Saul also cutting him down to size?

Anticipating one of the first things the people say about David in BTH (2 Sam 5:2) when they approach him to be their king after Saul, his new command allows David to "go out and come in" before them (v. 13). The older shorter text underscores David's success, Yahweh being with him. Seeing David's success leads to more acute terror on Saul's side—but all his people, Israel and Judah, love David's leadership. The MT expands this report at two points: (1) The day after Saul begins to eye David, he is in the grip of a malign divine spirit and is beside himself. David is playing the lyre, and Saul is holding his spear. Twice[4] he tries but fails to pin David to the wall (vv. 10–11). (2) After the first mention of Saul's fear of David, MT repeats (v. 12b) two comments from ch. 16: that Yahweh is with David (v. 18) and (his spirit) has turned from Saul (v. 14).[5]

1 Samuel 18:14–16

14 And David had success in all his ways,
and Yahweh[a] was with him.
15 And Saul saw that he had much success,
and he was terrified[a] of him.
16 But all Israel—and Judah—loved David,
for he was going out
and coming in before the[m[a]] *people*.

14a. Here LT adds *pantokratōr*.

15a. The term *gwr* is relatively uncommon in HB[6]—it is not used again in FP; Gk. here renders it with *eulabeito* ("was cautious").

16a. At the end of the verse, GT (*lpny hʿm*) differs from MT (*lpnyhm*) by only one consonant.

[14–16] Here MT's additions to v. 12 simply anticipate and underscore the narrator's summary in this short main paragraph. David not only has success, but his success also is manifest to Saul. And he not only goes out and in before the people (v. 13b), but all Israel and Judah too love him for it. Saul has every reason to be terrified of David. The narrator's assessment of him at the end of his first test draws on language used about him soon after his introduction in BTH: "Yahweh . . . was with him" (2 Sam 5:10b); and "You it was who brought out and took in Israel" (5:2a). As we have noticed before, separate mention of Judah (though within Israel) does occur in Samuel, but that is unusual. David's family is from Judah; and the battle just concluded has been within the territory of Judah (17:1).

1 Samuel 18:17–24 David and Saul's Daughters

[17 And Saul said to David:
"Look, Merab is my elder daughter—
her will I give to you for wife.

4. This presumably counts the incident in 19:9–10, which MT and B share.

5. This expression is repeated in HB only in Judg 16:20 (Samson) and 1 Sam 28:15, 16 (Saul).

6. See Num 22:3; Deut 1:17; 18:22; 32:27; 1 Sam 18:15; Hos 10:5; Pss 22:23 (24); 33:8; Job 19:29; 41:25 (17).

However, become to me as a valiant son
and battle Yahweh's battles."
And Saul said,
"Let not my hand be on him,
but let there be on him the hand of the Philistines."

18 And David said to Saul,
"Who am I and who *my life,* my father's family in Israel,
that I should be in-law to the king?"
19 And it happened at the time of giving Merab Saul's daughter to David
and she herself[a] was given as wife to Adriel the Meholathite.]
20 And Michal, Saul's daughter, loved David,
and they informed Saul,
and the matter was right in his eyes.[a]
21 And Saul said:
"I shall give her to him
that she may be a trap for him,
and there was on Saul[a] [that there may be on him] the hand of the Philistines."
[And Saul said to David,
"By two[b] will you become in-law to me today."]
22 And Saul commanded his servants,
"Speak to David secretly, saying,
'See, the king has pleasure in you,
and all his servants love you.
Well then, become the king's in-law.'"
23 And the servants of Saul spoke in David's ear these words,
and David said:
"Is it a slight thing in your eyes
becoming the king's in-law,
when I am a poor and slighted man?"
24 And Saul's servants reported to him:
"According to these words did David speak."

19a. Before "was given" LT adds "she feared David and" (only in this chapter is Saul said to fear David: vv. 12, 29).

20a. The phrase *wyšr hdbr bʿyny* is found only in 1 Sam 18:20, 26; 2 Sam 17:4; 2 Chr 30:4—and with *yšr* (*qāṭal*) in 1 Chr 13:4. While B renders by *ēuthynthē* in 18:20, 26, LT has *ēresen* in 18:20, as also in 18:5 (MT and LT plus), where, however, MT has *wyyṭb* rather than *wyšr*.

21a. The LT accurately interprets MT, which here seems more original than B, which has wrongly identified "him" as Saul instead of David and has read the second *wthy* as introducing a comment instead of a wish coordinate with the preceding clause.

b. The LT's *en tais dynamesin* (pl.) is puzzling: *dynamis* is common in Kingdoms and corresponds mostly to *ḥayil* and *bĕḥayil. In virtute* (OL) may attest *bĕḥayi.*

[17–24] Both longer and shorter versions of the story now take up the theme of David and marriage to a daughter of Saul. In the shorter text (vv. 20–29a), Michal in one sense takes the initiative: her love for David is brought to the notice of her father, and he decides to use it against David. He sends some of his staff to act as marriage brokers and assure David that he would be an acceptable son-in-law to the king. We already noted (on 2:25) that Yahweh is subject of "be pleased" some half of the times it is used in HB. In many of the others, as here, a king is the subject. It is in fact the stock verb used in statements of the royal pleasure, or will. And Yahweh is of course the preeminent king. As proper in such negotiations, David says neither yes nor no but points out his humble status. His carefully crafted answer (v. 23b) challenges Saul's messengers to explore their own response to the proposal they have brought him: "Is it a slight thing in your view . . . ?" Cleverly, the last (*niqleh*) as well as the first (*nĕqallâ*) of the eight Hebrew words of his response plays on Goliath's slighting estimate of him (17:43). Given that he also calls himself "poor," his words can be taken as a polite way of saying he cannot come up with an adequate dowry. However, the term is also powerfully resonant with the keyword (*rʾš*) of Nathan's parable (2 Sam 12:1–4).

In addition to its small supplements and alterations to the story of Michal, Saul, and David, MT also prefaces to this report a shorter account of an earlier offer of royal marriage (vv. 17–19). Part of MT's largest supplement in 17:12–31 reports the bounty for killing the Philistine (v. 25). As almost typical of such stories, one of its terms is marriage to the king's daughter. Although Saul himself never confirms this popular claim in advance, and despite his fear of David and his recent attempt to spear him, he now offers David his elder daughter, Merab: the only conditions are that he should be "valor's son" to Saul himself and should fight Yahweh's battles. Saul here anticipates fair words spoken to David by Abigail (25:28, again MT but not B), but quite cynically: here, as in the matter of the hundred foreskins, it is Saul's expectation that the Philistines would dispose of David for him. Here too David demurs on first hearing the proposal. Here too there must have been an expectation of a marriage. But in this case, at the due time for her marriage to David, Merab is given to another husband.

The exploration of different perspectives on whether David is or is not a slight or slighted fellow, and whether becoming son-in-law to the king should be a slight matter for such a fellow, achieves greater resonance from Goliath's attitude to this rival. However, the first element in David's self-description has a more distant, but no less significant echo in the book. "Poor" (*rāš*) is only used within 1 Samuel at 18:23;[7] but it is anticipated by the related verb "impoverish" in the Song of Hannah (2:8). Though Yahweh brings people to poverty as to death, he also brings to riches as well as to life. The contrasting fates duly sketched (2:6–7) serve as preface to a more developed picture of upward movement from dust to royal anointing (2:8–10). What David knows—and what we the readers also know—is that David has already been anointed. But Saul's messengers will have been given no cause to doubt the response David sends back to their master, that he is a poor man and hardly fit for his daughter.

1 Samuel 18:25–24:22 David in Flight from His Father-in-Law

1 Samuel 18:25–19:10

25 And Saul said,
"Thus shall you say to David:
'The king has no pleasure in bride-price,[a]
but in a hundred Philistine foreskins—
to be avenged on the enemies of the king.'"
But Saul reckoned
to cast[b] [David[c]] *him* into the hand of the Philistines.
26 And his servants reported to David these words,
and the matter was right in David's eyes
to become the king's in-law.
And [the days were not full,
27 and] David rose
and went, he and his men,
and he struck down among the Philistines [two] *a*[a] hundred men,
and David brought their foreskins
[and they paid them in full[b]] to the king
[to] *and*[c] bec[o]ame the king's in-law;
and [Saul[d]] he gave him Michal his daughter as wife.

28 And Saul saw
[and he knew]
that Yahweh was with David;
and [Michal Saul's daughter] *all Israel*[a] loved him.
29 And Saul continued
to be very afraid of David,
[and Saul became enemy of[a] David all the time.

7. And it will reappear only once in 2 Samuel: in the case that Nathan brings to David, he repeatedly calls the wronged underling "the poor man" (12:1, 3, 4).

30 And the leaders of the Philistines went out,
and it came to be
whenever[a] they went out
David had more success than all the servants of Saul,
and his name was very precious[b]].

19:1 And Saul spoke to Jonathan his son and to all his servants
of putting David to death;
but Jonathan, Saul's son, took great pleasure[a] in David.
2 And Jonathan reported to David:
"Saul [my father] is seeking to put you to death.
Now then, be sure to take care [in the] *tomorrow* morning
and settle down in secret
and hide yourself.
3 And I myself will go out
and will stand by my father's side in the open
where you are;
and I myself will speak of you to my father,
and I shall see what,
and I shall report to you."

4 And Jonathan spoke good of David to Saul his father,
and he said to him,
"Let not the king sin over his servant, over David,
because he has not sinned toward you
and because his action is very good toward you.
5 And he took his life in his hand
and struck down the Philistine;
and Yahweh produced a great salvation [for all Israel].
[You] *And all Israel* saw
and were glad.
And why will you sin against innocent blood
putting David to death gratuitously?"
6 And Saul listened to the voice of Jonathan,
and Saul swore:
"As Yahweh lives, he shall not *die* [be put to death]."
7 And Jonathan called to David,
and Jonathan reported to him all these words;
and Jonathan brought David to Saul,
and he was before him as in former days.

8 And the war continued to be *against David*;
and David [went out] *grew strong*[a]

and fought against the Philistines,
and he struck on them a great blow
and they fled before him.
9 And [Yahweh's spirit, an evil one,] *an evil divine spirit* came upon Saul;
and he was sitting in his house, and his spear in his hand,
and David was playing by *his* hand*s*.
10 And Saul sought
to strike by spear on David [and on the wall];
and he removed {himself} from Saul,
and he made the spear strike on the wall.
And David fled,
and got away [on that night].

25a. The LT uses the appropriate technical term *edna* for the rare *mhr* while B has *doma*, a general term for gift.

b. Here B's *auton* precedes the inf., which suggests it is subj. rather than obj. of *embalein*.

c. In LT, *auton ton Dauid* follows *embalein*, leaving *auton* ambiguous.

27a. Here LT = B.

b. If this is the correct rendering, it represents a unique use of *ml'*, and the suf. should be f. Possibly a corrupt repetition of *wl' ml'w hymym* (itself an MT plus) at the end of v. 26. However, again LT = MT.

c. Here LT = B.

d. The LT = MT.

28a. Almost all the consonants in *kl-yśr'l* (B) reappear in *mykl bt-š'wl* (MT)—especially since *ś* and *š* were not distinguished. The LT has both "Melchol *his* daughter" and "all Israel," but before the sg. vb. *ēgapa*.

29a. Only here is *'yb* truly verbal with dir. obj., as in Exod 23:22. The assonance emphasizes the contrast with *'hb* (v. 16): only Saul in all of Israel and Judah is enemy to David.

30a. Only once does *wyhy mdy* + inf. occur in BTH; but the following verbal sequence differs in 1 Kgs 14:28 and in 2 Chr 12:11 (simple *qāṭal*, as here); cf. also 1 Sam 1:7; 7:16; 2 Kgs 4:8.

b. Here *śkl* as *qal* is unique in HB. And the vb. *yqr* is rare—26:21; 2 Kgs 1:13, 14; + 5x as qal.

19:1a. Generally *ḥpṣ* is used with *b-* as here and in 18:22, or with *l-* and an inf. as in 1 Sam 2:25 and Judg 13:23. Ironically, in both these passages the inf. in question is *hēmît* (put to death)!

8a. Most often *katischyein* corresponds to *ḥzq* in MT.

[25–27] Saul responds in kind to David's answer, naming a bride-price that would be no harder for a poor man than a rich man to afford (v. 25). Of course, Saul may recognize the boast implicit in David's reference to Goliath's misperception of him. Be that as it may, he now wagers impossible odds—impossible, at least in Saul's view, for David. Both Jonathan (14:6) and David (17:36) have scorned their enemies as "uncircumcised" (the Heb. more literally and positively means "foreskinned"). But in a sense they have learned their lines from the dying Saul in BTH, who fears being made (sexual) sport of by victorious Philistines. Here—seen at least from the vantage point of the older text—it is as if Saul is seeking preemptive vengeance on his enemies. One hundred Philistine foreskins would be a perfectly acceptable offering (David could hardly survive the attempt to collect them). But one hundred were duly produced (says B—but MT ups the feat to two hundred), and the marriage of David and Michal takes place.

[28–30] Saul's fear of his son-in-law is only increased by noting how both Yahweh and the people support him. In dispatching David against the Philistine giant, Saul has wished Yahweh to be with him (17:37). Faced now with abundant evidence that this is so, he becomes increasingly afraid of David.

As we reread the marriage of David and Michal as part of the expanded text in MT, we naturally understand it as ultimate fulfillment of the royal pledge to the eventual vanquisher of the Philistine champion. Despite Saul's growing hostility toward David, and despite her elder sister's being suddenly married off to someone else, Michal's love for David allows the bargain to be honored, even if only because her father can see advantage for himself in their betrothal. In the marriage agreement for Merab, Saul has required only David's valor in fighting the battles of Yahweh. In Michal's case, he tries to make this condition fatally specific.

[19:1–3] David's success and the popular acclaim that greet it are too much for Saul; and David falls out of Saul's favor as quickly as has Saul out of Yahweh's good graces. Killing David off has been a covert intention, when Saul sets the price for his daughter Michal; but it is now proposed by Saul in a broad circle (Jonathan and *all* his servants).

In the shorter B text, Jonathan has not been spoken of since he was ransomed by the people following his own great victory over the Philistine enemy (14:45). After two statements about Saul's pleasure or lack of it—that Saul is pleased with David (18:22) and that he has no pleasure in a dowry from him (18:25)—we are now told that Jonathan has "great pleasure" in David (19:1). His love for David will be reported later. But the key first word in this shorter (and probably older) text expresses royal approval on the part of the crown prince.

When Jonathan's own life was hanging in the balance, Saul was seeking to identify the "sin" (14:38) or "guilt" (14:41) that needed to be removed. Then too Saul had apparently been content to see a popular victor die. Jonathan is the first to use two expressions (19:2) whose significance is only gradually developed. The first is a phrase that will become a key expression in much of the rest of the book: Saul "is seeking" to kill David or strike him down. The statement is repeated some fifteen times in the following chapters,[8] till we read (27:4) that on David's (second) flight into Philistine territory, Saul ceases to "seek him." The other is his consequent advice to David to take himself off "in secret" (*sēter*) and hide.[9]

[4–7] Jonathan is not just "pleased" but "very pleased" (v. 1); and he makes it his business (vv. 4–5) to take up David's case with his father and save him from the king's "pleasure" (see the note above on the rendering of *ḥāpēṣ*). He moves to his father's side (*lĕyad* is used of officials in relationship to their superiors in Neh 11:24; 1 Chr 18:17 [where 2 Sam 8:17 has a different text]; 23:28; and may be a mark of later Heb.) and seeks to persuade his father not to involve himself in sin over David. Saul should not take the initiative in sinning, when not himself sinned against—especially since, far from sinning against Saul, David's behavior has been exemplary.[10] The people have earlier attributed a great deliverance to Jonathan (14:45)—he now, in vindicating David, attributes to Yahweh the recent deliverance from the Philistine: David's cause and Yahweh's cause are one and the same. Yahweh is credited with the great *tĕšûʿâ* associated with David's victory over the Philistines, as in 11:13 after Saul's victory in Ammon. The pattern has been set in BTH in 2 Sam 23:10, 12, where first one and then another of David's heroes has struck down (*wyk*) Philistines, and Yahweh has effected a great deliverance.

Shedding innocent blood is mentioned only here in the books of Samuel. It was not a topic of BTH or of the earlier classical prophets. But it became a topic of later prophetic tradition;[11] and in Kings, but not Chronicles (2 Kgs 21:16; 24:4 are Kings plus), it became an important element of the complaint against the archsinner Manasseh. Whether the preposition in *teḥĕṭāʾ bĕdām nāqî* is understood as "Would you sin *against* innocent blood?" or "Would you sin *by* [shedding] innocent blood?" this unique combination neatly threatens Saul with comparison with a principal villain of the books of Kings. Then in his final word "gratuitously" (*ḥinnām*), Jonathan anticipates Abigail's wise advice to David: even a fool's blood should not be shed without cause (1 Sam 25:31).[12] Saul not only pays attention to his son's powerful plea but confirms it in a repetition of the oath he used when Jonathan's life was in the balance (14:39)—an oath that is both brief and corresponds neatly to Jonathan's argument: just as Yahweh

8. See 1 Sam 19:2, 10; 20:1; 22:23; 23:10, 14, 15, 25; 24:2 (3); 25:26, 29; 26:2, 20; 27:1.

9. See below on 1 Sam 20:5, 19, 24; 23:19; 25:20; 26:1; 2 Sam 12:12.

10. The subjects of *ḥṭʾ* ("sin") in Samuel are (1) the people/Israel in 1 Sam 7:6; 12:10; 14:33, 34; (2) Samuel in 1 Sam 12:23; (3) Saul or Shimei in 1 Sam 15:24, 30; 19:4, 5; 26:21; 2 Sam 19:21; (4) David in 1 Sam 19:4; 24:11 (12); 2 Sam 12:13; 24:10, 17.

11. See Isa 59:7; Jer 7:6; 19:4; 22:3, 17; 26:15; Joel 3:19 (4:19); Jonah 1:14; cf. Deut 19:10, 13; 21:8, 9; 27:25; Pss 94:21; 106:38; Prov 6:17.

12. In terms of the development of the material, David himself has been the first to use the term *ḥinnām*, in 2 Sam 24:24 (BTH).

secured victory when David killed the Philistine, so just as Yahweh lives David shall not die. On that basis, Jonathan reintroduces David to the court (19:7).

[8–10] Neither David's success nor Saul's oath alters the wider situation: war with the Philistines continues, and (possibly because of David's prowess in it) Saul continues to want him dead. Now, for the first time in B,[13] he takes matters literally into his own hands—at least in a sense. For, though it is Saul's hand on the spear, he himself is in the grip of an evil "divine" force (so B—and MT identifies the spirit as Yahweh's). David's successful strike on the Philistines has turned them to flight; Saul's strike at David, though unsuccessful, has David in flight.

1 Samuel 19:11–14

11 And *on that night* Saul sent messengers to the house of David,
to guard him
and to put him to death in the morning.
And Michal his wife reported to David:
"If you do not rescue your life tonight,
tomorrow you will be put to death."
12 And Michal let David down through the window;
and he went
and he fled
and he got away.
13 And Michal took the teraphim[a]
and put them into the bed, and the goat [{hair} net] *liver*[b] at the head place;
and she covered them with a garment.
14 And Saul sent messengers
to take David,
and [she] *they* said,
"He is sick."

13a. Uniquely rendered by *kenotaphia* here and in v. 16.
b. Here *hēpar* is the stock rendering of *kbd*, whereas MT here reads the unusual *kbyr*.

[11–14] David's flight takes him at first no further than to the fragile security of his own house. Yet there, although still in range of Saul's men, David does have the benefit of Michal's counsel and assistance. There are some resemblances between this narrative and Gen 31: both concern a man, his wife/wives, and his father-in-law; both concern escape, concealment, and a search; and in both cases the concealment includes feigned indisposition plus household gods.

13. First Samuel 18:10–11 is an MT plus.

The presence in the tradition shared by MT and GT of this link between David/Saul and Jacob/Laban may have contributed to the MT plus earlier in the story (18:17–19) in which Merab is proposed as wife to David, prior to Michal.

1 Samuel 19:15–24

15 And Saul sent [the messengers]
to [see] David,
saying,
"Bring him up on the bed to me to put him to death."
16 And the messengers came;
but what they saw were the teraphim on the bed and the goat [net] *liver*
at the head place.
17 And Saul said to Michal,
"Why have you deceived me this way,
and sent off my enemy
and he got away?"
And Michal said to Saul,
"He himself said to me,
'Dispatch me.
Why should I put you to death?'"
18 And David, he fled
and got away
and came to Samuel at Ramah,
and reported to him all
that Saul had done to him;
and [he] *David* went, and Samuel,
and [they] *he* lived at Naioth.
19 And it was reported to Saul,
"David is in fact in Naioth in Ramah."
20 And Saul sent messengers
to take David;
and [he] *they* saw the company[a] of the prophets [acting the prophet],
and Samuel in position at his station over them;
and a divine spirit came upon the messengers of Saul,
and they acted the prophet [—they too[b]].
21 And they reported to Saul,
and he sent other messengers
and they too acted the prophet.
And Saul did further
and sent third messengers,
and they too acted the prophet.

22 And *Saul blazed with anger,*
and he too went to Ramah
and came to the [great] pit *of the threshing floor*[a]
that is [at Sekhu] *on the bare height*;
and he asked
and said,
"Where are Samuel and David?"
And someone said,
"In fact at Naioth in Ramah."
23 And he went there, to Naioth in Ramah;
and there came on [him,] him too, a divine spirit;
and he went [walking
and he acted] *acting* the prophet
till he came to Naioth in Ramah.
24 And he [too] stripped off his clothes,
and [he too] acted the prophet in front of [Samuel] *them*;[a]
and he fell naked all that day and all the night.
Therefore they say,
"Is Saul too among the prophets?"

20a. The noun *lahăqat* is unique to this verse. The most frequent rendering of forms related to *qāhāl* is *ekklēsia*. Within the narrative books of HB, *qāhāl* is most common in Chronicles–Ezra–Nehemiah, and its unique appearance in Samuel (unless attested here) is in 1 Sam 17:47.

b. In the last verses of this chapter, *gam-hûʾ/hēmmâ* ("he/they too") is used more than anywhere else in HB: 8x in MT, of which 5 are represented in B (cf. also ch. 28).[14]

22a. Both variants are much more similar in Hebrew: *bwr hgdwl* ("the great pit") and *bwr hgwrn* ("the threshing-floor pit"); and *śkw* ("Sekhu") and *špy* ("bare height").

24a. This textual variant may be related to the statement in 15:35 that Samuel did not see Saul again till the day of his death.

[15–17] The precise sequence of the following events is not made clear. Does Michal have inside information, or does a daughter simply intuit her father's next move? Does Saul intend that the prisoner be kept under guard in his own house overnight, or brought to the royal guardroom before being finished off the next day? Does Michal's prescience enable David's escape before

14. The term *gm* is used some 55x in 1 Samuel (MT), in some 50 pages of BHL; some 39x in 2 Samuel, in some 40 pages; some 54x in Jeremiah (MT) in 80 pages; but some 49x in Ecclesiastes in only 11 pages! The usage is very variable through 1–2 Samuel: 1 Sam 1–2 (4x); 4 (1x); 8 (2x); 10 (3x); 12 (4x); 13–14 (4x); 15 (1x); 16 (2x); 17–18 (2x); 19:20–24 (7x); 20–24 (8x); 25–26 (6x); 28 (9x); 31 (2x); 2 Sam 1–4 (9x); 5–8 (3x); 11–12 (7x); 13–20 (9x); 21 (1x). Of these only 1 Sam 31:5; 2 Sam 5:2 (2x); 8:11; 21:20 are attested in Chronicles, and hence securely derived from BTH.

Saul's men arrive? Or is she able to contrive his escape from a building they are already guarding? Are the men sent to take David (v. 14) the same as those sent to guard him (v. 11)? Much more important than the questions the text does not answer is what it does say. Michal first tells David that being rescued is not something that happens to you: it is something which you yourself have to do something about (v. 11). And then by her actions she adds a rider: or it is something that your wife has to do for you. Her excuse to her father, that David has threatened her life if she does not cooperate, is plausible. But her ruse with the sacred object[15] in David's bed, by which she wins him time to get clear away, surely demonstrates her complicity. The similarity to Gen 31:33–35 is striking.

The fivefold use of "rescue" (*mlṭ*) in 19:10, 11, 12, 17, 18 introduces a theme that pervades the following chapters: David's fleeing Saul and being rescued (20:29; 22:1; 23:13; 27:1). And it resurfaces twice in Samuel, very much later, after Absalom's death (2 Sam 19:5, 9 [6, 10]—there *pi'el* as in 1 Sam 19:11, not *nip'al*). Joab's reproof of David for shaming those who have rescued his life and the lives of his wives and household (19:5 [6]) is all the more poignant because of what happens to Michal after this incident. And one party in the civil war pleads to the other to restore the David who has rescued them from the Philistines but needs to flee before his son (2 Sam 19:9 [10]).

[18–20a] The next stage in David's first escape from Saul takes him to Samuel: he seeks out the man whose last recorded acts have been his own anointing and his removal to his hometown. The narrator does not say that David seeks refuge with him, but simply that he goes and tells him everything that Saul has done to him. No verbal response from Samuel is noted. However, when David goes, Samuel goes too; and they/he settle at Naioth. The report that comes to Saul is only that David is at Naioth in Ramah. That is sufficient to allow Saul to infer involvement by Samuel; and when he himself comes to Ramah (v. 22), he asks for Samuel and David (in that order). Saul dispatches messengers to "take" David (v. 20). There are many different sorts of "taking." David is taken by Yahweh into service (2 Sam 7:8, BTH), as by Saul (1 Sam 18:2, an MT plus); 1 Sam 17:31 and 57 (both MT plus) seem to imply a more neutral summons before the king. But here, as in 19:14, "taking" implies "arrest."

[20b–24] The remainder of this narrative has to be read in conjunction with the third of the signs promised by Samuel to Saul after anointing him (10:5–6, 10–13). There, when Saul came into proximity with a group of prophets, bystanders noted that something or other happened to him; he turned into another man; the spirit of Yahweh came on him; and he began to act as the prophets did ("prophesy"). Their presence was contagious, and Saul came under the same influence or power as controlled the prophets. Here (19:20–21) a similar contagious experience befalls three sets of messengers sent to arrest

15. Willi-Plein claims this as the oldest text in HB to use *trpym*.

David—similar, but different at least in some aspects of its description. Earlier Saul "encountered" the prophets: *pgʿ* (10:5) and *lqrʾt* (10:10); here, his messengers have only to "see" them to come under their influence. Earlier Samuel certainly knew all about it; now he is explicitly at the head of the prophets (19:20). Whatever is intended by the verb "prophesy" or "play the prophet" (*htnbʾ*), it is consonant both with walking the final part of the journey to Ramah (v. 23), and once there, with falling naked all day and all night (v. 24). Saul's behavior provokes the same question as before (10:13): "Is even Saul among the prophets?" With all his men and then Saul himself detained in such a trancelike or ecstatic state, it is possible for David again to take flight (20:1). Nakedness does appear occasionally elsewhere in the Bible's prophetic literature; but in Isa 20:1–3 and Mic 1:8 it seems to be more an acted sign than an involuntary reaction. We simply have too little information about prophetism in Israel or its neighbors.

At one level, this episode functions within the ongoing story to provide an escape for David. At another level, it seems sensible to understand this second account of Saul and the prophets as an exploration (*midrāš*) of the first. How does Samuel have knowledge of the prophets? Because he is at their head. What does prophetic behavior look like? It can be detected in someone when walking and also when lying naked for a day and a night. What is the force of "even" (*gam*) in the earlier saying about Saul? It means that not only his juniors and staff, but also Saul himself is susceptible to control by the spirit. More important than any of these lesser questions and answers is one large exegetical question. Did Saul's early encounter with the prophets after his anointing amount to divine affirmation? Not at all, according to this reading of the earlier passage. Confirmation may have come in Samuel's first two signs (10:2–4); but what was demonstrated in Saul's first coming under the power of the spirit is that divine limits are set to his exercise of royal discretion, and beyond these he cannot go.

1 Samuel 20:1–4

1 And David fled from Naioth[a] in Ramah,
and came
and said to Jonathan's face,[b]
"What have I done?
What is my wrong,
and what is my sin[c] in face of your father
that he is seeking my life?"
2 And [he] *Jonathan* said to him,
"It is unthinkable *of you*![a]
You shall not die.
Look, my father will not do[b] ['something'[c] big or] 'something' small,

and[d] not uncover my ear.
And why would my father conceal from me this 'something'?
It is not so."

3 And David [swore further[a]] *answered Jonathan,*
and said,
"Your father knows—he knows
that I have found favor in your eyes;
and he[b] said:
'Jonathan should not know this,
lest he be [pained[c]] unwilling.'[d]
However,[e]
as Yahweh lives and as your good self lives,[f]
as I said
there is not as (much as) a step[g] between me and death."[h]

4 And Jonathan said to David,
"What [says] *desires*[a] your very self
[that I should] *and what should I* do for you?"

1a. The GT's "from Auath" may have divided *mnwwt* differently—but "in Auath" (19:18, 19) cannot be explained so easily.

b. Here GT ("came before Jonathan and said") seems to reflect the same words, but in a different order.

c. Codex B ("have I sinned") reads the same consonants, but as the vb. (LT = MT).

2a. Presumably attesting *lk*, as in v. 9.

b. Here Q [= GT] is *l'y'šh*.

c. "Do 'something' [= you know what]" is normally threatening, as in Amos 3:7. Here LT = MT.

d. This *kai* (B) agrees with MT; but LT has *ho* ("which").

3a. No previous "swearing" by David is attested in 1 Samuel, where only Yahweh (3:14), Saul (19:6; 28:10), David (20:3 [MT], 42; 24:21, 22 [22, 23]), and Jonathan (20:17 [B]) are subj. of "swear." Jonathan's father is subj. of "make swear" (*hišbîă'*) in 14:27, 28, and Jonathan likewise in 20:17 (MT only).

b. The LT has "your father"; B = MT.

c. The term *n'ṣb* is used only in Gen 45:5; 1 Sam 20:3, 34; 2 Sam 19:3; Eccl 10:9. Each of the three instances in Samuel corresponds to a different vb. in B. This David who assumes that Saul will not want to cause grief to his son and heir will behave in like fashion to his own senior sons (1 Kgs 1:6 and 2 Sam 13:21 [LT and 4QSam[a]]).

d. Again LT is different: "report to David."

e. Adversative *wĕ'ûlām* is used 7x in Job and 9x elsewhere, including Judg 18:29; 1 Sam 20:3; 25:34; 1 Kgs 20:23.

f. The phrase *ḥy-yhwh wḥy npšk* is used only in 1 Sam 20:3; 25:26; 2 Sam 15:21; 2 Kgs 2:2, 4, 6; 4:30; and *ḥy npšk* alone in 1 Sam 1:26; 17:55; 2 Sam 14:19. The former expression belongs to life-and-death situations.

g. Here *pśʿ* is unique; the vb. is used once in Isa 27:4; cf. *mpśʿh* in 1 Chr 19:4, where the parallel 2 Sam 10:4 reads *štwtyhm*. Here B's *empeplēstai* (A has the related *peplērōtai*) may derive from the not dissimilar *śbʿ*.

h. Here B = MT; however, LT attests the longer *byny wbyn ʾbyk ʿd-hmwt* ("between me and your father till death").

4a. Only here in the OT does *epithymein* correspond to MT's *ʾmr*. It normally corresponds to *ʾwh* (*piʿel* or *hitpaʿel*), as in 1 Sam 2:16; 2 Sam 3:21; 1 Kgs 11:37 (all with *psychē* as subj.). The OG probably read *tʾwh*. In Lam 3:24 *ʾmrh npšy* may be the only other instance of *npš* as subj. of *ʾmr* (the commonest of Hebrew vbs.?).

[1–4] Jonathan has betrayed his father's intentions to David and then has secured a temporary reconciliation (19:1–7). After a further success against the Philistines, David was again in repeated danger from the king: the first time, he was able to evade Saul's spear; the next time, Michal actively assisted his escape; and then he was saved by the spirit of Yahweh and his prophets. After three escapes, he now puts a triple question to his brother-in-law: "What have I done?" is David's hallmark question, as already noted (on 17:29). The other two elements, "What is my guilt, and what is my sin in face of your father?" are here a protest of injured innocence and yet anticipate the wording of his own most comprehensive confession (2 Sam 24:10, BTH). Jonathan is fully aware of the fatal implications of such questions: he has already claimed to his father that David has not sinned against him (19:4). Confident that he enjoys the confidence of his father, he seeks to assure David that he is in no danger of his life. Jonathan's self-estimate is bolstered by the fact of his inclusion in an earlier "council of war" (19:1), but he has not reckoned sufficiently with the fact that he had spoken up for David on that occasion (19:4–6) and that the reconciliation he had brokered has most clearly broken down.

Despite having asked Jonathan for advice about his situation in the first place (v. 1), David now explains to him why he is unlikely to know; and David seeks to persuade him that death may be closer to him than Jonathan is to his father: in fact only a *peśaʿ* away (v. 3). There are two rhetorical masterstrokes in his short response. The first is to give this word for "step" its sole outing here in HB (the related verb is also used only once, in Isa 27:4); for it looks identical in Hebrew script and sounds quite similar to *pešaʿ*, which belongs to the same semantic family as "guilt" and "sin." Death is but a "step" (hardly distinguishable from "transgression") away. The other is to contrast his own situation with that of Yahweh and Jonathan. The double oath that opens his few words implies that Yahweh's life, and Jonathan's too, can be relied on—he, by contrast, is but a step away from death.

Repeated use of *nepeš* is a feature of the opening exchange between the two men. David's "life" has already been spoken of by Jonathan to his father ("He took his life in his hand," 19:5) and by Michal to David himself ("if you do not rescue your life," 19:11). Now David tells a Jonathan unwilling to believe him that Saul is seeking his life (20:1). In response to Jonathan's doubt (v. 2), he reaffirms the imminence of his death in an oath taken on the lives of Yahweh and of the king's son (v. 3). Jonathan's answer implicitly affirms equal concern for David's *nepeš* and its wishes (v. 4).

1 Samuel 20:5–8

5 And David said to Jonathan,
"Note it is new moon tomorrow.
And I, I [should] *shall* be sure *not*[a] to sit [with the king] to eat.
And[b] you will dispatch me,
and I will conceal myself in the field until the [third] evening.
6 If your father actually takes count of me,
you will say:
'David asked and asked[a] of me
to run to Bethlehem, his city,
for there is a sacrifice "of the days"[b] there for all the family.'[c]
7 If this[a] is what he says:
'Good,'
it is well for your servant;
but if he [is really flaming] *answers you* harshly,[b]
know that the ill has been completed/determined[c] by him;
8 and you will act loyally toward your servant,
for into Yahweh's covenant you have brought[a] your servant with you.
And if there does exist[b] wrong in me,
then put me to death yourself;
but as far as your father whyever would you bring me?"

5a. In v. 5a, LT = MT, stating David's obligation to eat with the king; B gives his decision not to do so.

b. No adversative is marked here, so making MT (and LT) the harder reading in v. 5a.

6a. The term *š'l nipʿal* is used only in 1 Sam 20:6, 28 and Neh 13:6.

b. The phrase *zbḥ hymym* appears to be a feature of 1 Samuel alone: 1:21; 2:19; 20:6; cf. *zbḥ hywm* in 9:12.

c. Does B's *phylē* attest a different Heb. (*šbṭ* or *mṭh*)?

7a. Codex B = MT; LT does not attest *kōh* ("thus") and also specifies "your father" as subj. of "says."

b. Here B = LT; both attest "answer you harshly," as found later (v. 10) also in MT, which has the sole attestation of inf. abs. of *ḥrh* in HB.

c. The vb. *klth* with *hrʿh* as subj. is found only in 1 Sam 20:7, 9; 25:17 (followed by *mʿm*) and Esth 7:7 (followed by *m't*).

8a. An interesting and unique biblical usage: elsewhere, when not following "ark," "covenant of Yahweh" is construed only with "abandon," "lest you forget," or "which is there." Here David acknowledges Jonathan's initiative; but presumably "Yahweh's covenant" is simply a striking abbreviation of "a covenant before Yahweh," such as the two men made according to 23:18.

b. Never is *yeš* used in BTH, but it is found in 1 Sam 9:11, 12; 14:39; 17:46; 20:8; 21:3, 4, 8 (4, 5, 9); 23:23; 2 Sam 9:1; 14:19, 32; 19:29; 1 Kgs 17:12; 18:10; 2 Kgs 2:16; 3:12; 4:2, 13; 5:8; 9:15; 10:15 (2x), 23. In this verse, the emphatic position of two phrases suggests a contrast between "as far as your father" and the earlier "into Yahweh's covenant."

[5–8] David takes up the invitation of the crown prince in a longer speech, with careful but rather curious emphases. At the new moon the next day, he has to be seated with the king at a meal: unusually, both elements of *ʾēšēb* ("I should sit") are stressed—both subject (using the independent pronoun *ʾānōkî*) and verbal idea (by means of the infinitive absolute). However, although he "must" be there, he asks Jonathan to dispatch him into "hiding" for a couple days. He is clearly now persuaded that Jonathan's advice to him back in 19:2 was thoroughly appropriate. Supposing he is actually remarked on by Jonathan's father, Jonathan should say that he had pressingly sought leave of him to dash to Bethlehem for a family sacrifice—David here echoing the excuse Yahweh had given Samuel should Saul challenge his visit to Bethlehem. The unusual term he uses for the "sacrifice" (*zebaḥ hayyāmîm*, precisely anticipated only in 1:21 and 2:19) is also close to what the young women of Ramah reported to Saul himself (*zebaḥ hayyôm* in 9:12 is formally ambiguous). Even if Saul has not yet received intelligence of David's actual anointing (1 Sam 16), this reminiscence of his own anointing might heighten his suspicion of David's reason for attending such a sacrifice at home.

A strong feature of the Hebrew in this chapter is the use of the strengthening infinitive absolute. The stakes are certainly high: David is in flight, and believes—even knows—that Saul is seeking his life. When he tells Jonathan, Jonathan strongly protests (20:2): "heaven forbid" (*ḥālîlâ*). David's responses (vv. 3, 5–8) are peppered with verbs emphasized in the same manner in Hebrew, although differently rendered above: "really knew" (v. 3), "be sure to sit" (5), "actually takes count" (6), "asked and asked" (6), and (in MT only) "is really flaming" (7). The use of this form of emphasis marks Samuel off from its main source in BTH: the only instance there of the emphatic infinitive absolute is in 2 Sam 24:24 (in the very last sentence it reports David as uttering).

Jonathan not only mediates between David and Saul, in the sense of achieving at least temporary reconciliation between them; he also in a real sense identifies with each (in turn). He is confident that there are no secrets between his father and himself (v. 2). It is precisely in the conversation between Yahweh and David (2 Sam 7) that loyalty (v. 15) and being "tipped off" (v. 27) are linked in BTH. As king's son, Jonathan gives David permission to be absent from the king's meal at the beginning of the month. When he himself becomes the target of his father's spear (1 Sam 20:33), he finally knows that David's life is really in danger. David plays to this changing role of Jonathan: even if guilt should be detected in him, there is no need to bring him to Saul—Jonathan himself has power of life and death (v. 8).

1 Samuel 20:9–42a (20:9–42)

9 And Jonathan said,
"How unthinkable of you!
For if I really know
that the ill has been determined from my father
to come against you,[a]
and if you do not go into your cities,
[will it not be what] I shall report to you?"

10 And David said to Jonathan,
"Who will report to me

if[a] your father answers you harshly?"	or what will your father answer you harshly?"

11 And Jonathan said to David,
"Come,
and [let us go out to] *remain in*[a] the field";
and the two of them went out to the field.

12 And Jonathan said to David,
"Yahweh, God of Israel, *knows* that,[a]
[if[b]] I shall examine my father about this time [tomorrow (or) the third day] *thrice*,
and it is in fact good for David,
shall I not then[c] send to you [and uncover your ear] *to the field*?
13 So[a] may Yahweh do to Jonathan,
and so may he continue—
supposing[b] [it shall be good[c] to my father] *I shall bring* the ill against you,
and I shall uncover your ear
and dispatch you,
and you shall go in peace,

and may Yahweh be[d] with you
as he has been with my father.
14 And will you not,
if I am still alive,
and will you not perform with me Yahweh's loyalty,
so that I do not die?
15 And will you not cut off your loyalty with my father's house forever;
even not when Yahweh cuts off the enemies of David, each off the face of the earth?"

16 The name of Jonathan being found,[a]
from the house of David
Yahweh will seek it out
from the hand of the enemies
of David.
17 And Jonathan went on
to swear to David[a]
that he loved
the life of the one who
loved him.[b]

16 And Jonathan decided
with the house of David:
and Yahweh will seek out
from the hand of the enemies
of David.
17 And Jonathan went on
to make David swear
by his love for him
that with his life's love he
loved him.

18 And Jonathan said [to him[a]],
"Tomorrow is new moon;
and you will be noted,
for your sitting place will be noted.[b]
19 And [on the third day] *three times*[a] you will [go far down] *be noted*,[b]
and you will come to [the] *your*[c] place
where you concealed yourself on the day of the deed,
and you will sit down beside that[d] [stone[e]] *ergab*.
20 And I, [the trio of] *three times* arrows [to the side] I shall shoot,
dispatching {them} to my target.[a]
21 And look, I shall send the lad, saying,[a]
'Go find *me* the [arrows] *dart*.'
If what I say to the lad is
'Look, the [arrows are] *dart*[b] *is* from you and this way,
take [them] *it*,'
then come,
for it is well for you
and there is no [matter] *word of Yahweh*, Yahweh lives.
22 But[a] if this is what I say to the youth,
'Look the [arrows are] *dart is* from you and beyond,'

go,
for Yahweh has dispatched you.
23 And as for the speaking
which we have spoken, I and you,
look: Yahweh is *witness* between me and you[a] forever."

24 And David concealed himself in the field,
and the new moon came,
and the king [sat over the food] *came to the table*,
to eat.
25 And the king sat at his sitting place as usual, at the wall seat,[a]
and [Jonathan rose[b]] *he was in front of Jonathan,*[c]
and Abner sat beside Saul,
and David's place was noted.
26 But Saul did not say anything on that day;
for he said *to himself*,
"It's an accident,
it appears[a] he is not pure;
he [must not be pure] *has not purified himself*."

27 And it came to be on the morrow of the new moon (the second),
and David's place was noted.

And Saul said to Jonathan, his son:
"Why did the son of Jesse not come, neither yesterday nor today,
to the [food] *table*?"
28 And Jonathan answered Saul
and said to him,[a]
"David [asked and] asked leave from me
to go/run to Bethlehem *his city*.[b]
29 And he said:
'Be sure to dispatch me,
for we have a family sacrifice in the city,
and my [brother himself has] *brothers have* commanded me.
Now then,
if I have found favor in your eyes,
let me surely get away[a]
and see my brothers.'
Accordingly he has not come to the king's table."

30 And Saul's anger waxed hot at Jonathan *greatly*,
and he said to him,

"Son of [the twisted one of rebellion] *girls who change sides*,[a]
have I not known
that you were [choosing for] *partner*[b] *of* the son of Jesse to your shame and to the shame of the uncovering of your mother?
31 For all the days that the son of Jesse is alive on the earth,
[yourself and[a]] your kingship shall not be established.
Well then, send
and take [him to me] *the young* man,[b]
for he is a son of death."

32 And Jonathan answered Saul [his father[a]],
and said to him,
"Why should he [be put to death] *die*?
What has he done?"
33 And Saul [hurled] *raised*[a] the spear toward [him] *Jonathan*,
to strike him down,
and Jonathan knew
that [that] *this evil* was determined from his father
to put David to death.

34 And Jonathan rose from the table in hot anger,
and did not eat food on the second day of the month,
[for he was troubled for David,]
for his father had [disgraced[a]] *concluded against*[b] him.

35 And it came to be in the morning
and Jonathan went out to the field, *as was arranged*[a] for David's appointment,[b]
and a small lad was with him.
36 And he[a] said to his lad,
"Run.[b]
Find for sure the [arrows] *darts*
which I am shooting."
And[c] the lad ran;
and he himself shot the [arrows[d]] dart,[e]
passing him by.
37 And the lad came to the place of the arrow
that Jonathan shot,
and Jonathan called after [the] *his* lad,[a]
"[Is not] *There*[b] *is* the arrow[c] by you and beyond?"
38 And Jonathan called after the lad,
"Quick!

Hurry!
Don't stand!"
And Jonathan's lad [gleaned] *collected* the arrow
[and came] to his master.
39 And the lad, he knew nothing.
However, Jonathan and David did know the matter.
40 And Jonathan gave his equipment to the lad
who was his;
and he said to him,
"Go,
[bring it] *enter*[a] to the city."
41 [The lad—he came[a]] *And as the lad came*;[b]
and David rose up from [by the Negeb] *the Argab*,
and he fell on his face on the ground,
and prostrated himself three times;
and they kissed each the other,
and they wept each with the other
till [David did most[c]] *a great completion*.
42a And Jonathan said to David,
"Go in peace,
which we two ourselves have sworn *in the name of Yahweh*, saying,
'Yahweh will be *witness* between me and you,
and between [my seed and] your seed forever.'"[a]

9a. Both B and LT are fuller than MT in v. 9b but differ from each other: LT has "and if not, I shall report to you into your cities"; B, "and if you do not go into your cities, I shall report to you." Has there been confusion between *tbwʾ ʿryk* and *lbwʾ ʿlyk*?

10a. "If" (GT) attests not the two words *ʾw mh* (MT), but simply their initial letters *ʾm*.

11a. Here LT = MT. And B's *menein* corresponds only here to *yṣʾ* but also 3x to *yšb*, which is part of the context in v. 19.

12a. The LT and B's *oiden* apparently attests *ydʿ*—accidentally omitted after *dwd*?

b. Here *hoti* (B) appears to support *kî* (MT); however, *hoti ean* (LT) could attest a conditional reading of the *kî* clause.

c. The expression *wlʾ ʾz* is unique to this passage. The phrase *kai ou mē aposteilō* (B) includes the third instance in this chapter of *ou mē* (formula of denial)—twice in v. 2 it corresponds simply to *lʾ*. But LT reads the positive *kai apostelō*.

13a. The LT precedes the oath formula with "And if it is bad."

b. The clause following this self-imprecation formula is introduced by *ʾim* in 1 Sam 3:17; 25:22; 2 Sam 19:14; 2 Kgs 6:31; by *kî* in 1 Sam 14:44; 20:13; 2 Sam 3:9; 1 Kgs 2:23; Ruth 1:17; and by *kî ʾim* in 2 Sam 3:35. In each other instance, *kî* clearly introduces a strong positive statement.

c. The construction here appears an odd mix of *yṭb* as *qal* and as *hipʿîl*.

d. The MT *wyhy* expresses a wish, while *kai estai* (GT) makes a positive statement.

16a. Here *eurethēnai* (B) may be an inner-Greek corruption from *exarthēnai* (cf. LT). The Hebrew underlying B and LT can be tentatively reconstructed with the help of MT as follows:

MT	*wykrt yhwntn ʿm-byt dwd wbqš yhwh myd ʾyby dwd*
B	*[wykrt] šm yhwntn mʿm-byt dwd wbqš yhwh ʾyby dwd*
LT	*ʾm ykrt lyhwntn ʿm-byt šʾwl wbqš yhwh myd ʾyby dwd*

17a. The LT agrees with B that Jonathan does the swearing, and with MT over the plus "in his loving him."

b. In the final clause (v. 17b), it is not clear how far GT represents a text different from MT or a free rendering of MT. Perhaps the earlier plus in MT and LT (at the end of v. 17a) was intended to clarify the meaning of this last clause. It is useful to include 18:1b, 3b in a table of comparisons:

18:1b MT +	*wyʾhbw yhwntn knpšw*	and Jonathan loved him as himself
18:3b MT +	*bʾhbtw ʾtw knpšw*	by his loving him as himself
20:17a MT +	*bʾhbtw ʾtw*	by his loving him
20:17b MT	*ky-ʾhbt npšw ʾhbw*	that (with) the love of himself he loved him
20:17b B	*ky-ʾhb npš ʾhbw*	that he loved the self of the one loving him

Does MT move to remove the idea of David's loving Jonathan?

18a. Here MT = LT.

b. Here MT = B; but LT attests the neater *whpqd ypqd mwšbk*, "and close note will be taken of your seating place."

19a. The *piʿel* of *šlš* occurs twice more (Deut 19:3; 1 Kgs 18:34), each in a different sense; here the sense is drawn from *šlšyt* (v. 12). The LXX uses *trisseuein* both here and at the beginning of the next verse (where MT attests the numeral "three").

b. Here B and LT's *episkepsē* may bear the same sense as *episkepēsē* in the previous verse.

c. The LT = MT; here B adds *sou* before (the relative) *hou*.

d. Reading not *hʾzl*, but *hlʾz* = *hlz* (see Garr 385, 389).

e. Again LT = MT; B's odd *ergab* may be a slip for A's *ergon*, which recalls *ergasimē* in the previous clause.

20a. Here B and LT both attest *lmṭrh* (MT), which refers to what is watched closely (normally prison, but here "target"). The initial *A* of *AMATTARAN* (LT) is a corruption of *L* (cf. Heb.).

21a. Here B = LT. The lack of "saying" in MT is very unusual.

b. The LT has the pl. *schizas* (chosen because it sounds similar to *ḥiṣîm*?). And B's unique nonword *gouzan* may be an inner-Greek corruption: *ΣΧΙΖΑΝ* > *ΓΟΥΖΑΝ*.

22a. Here LT = MT; but B has no *de* before *tade*.

23a. The LT adds "and between my seed and your seed."

25a. Here B = MT; but LT does not repeat "seat" (B has *kathedra* first with acc. after *epi*, then with gen.).

b. The term *prophthanein* (GT) is the stock rendering of *qdm piʿel* ("come before," "do [something] first"); MT's *wyqm* is a corruption of *wyqdm*, possibly influenced by the opening of v. 34, where *wyqm* is correct. Here *BA* 331 renders "placed himself in front of Jonathan."

c. The LT (*auton*) has Jonathan as subj. of the vb., as MT; but in B (*ton*) we assume that Saul is still subj.

26a. Here *symptōma* is a rendering of *mqrh*; and it seems that *phainetai* is a second translation.

28a. The GT plus provides the expected "say" before direct speech is reported (cf. note 21a above).

b. Both B and LT attest "his city" after Bethlehem; *poreuthēnai* (B) oddly follows the phrase; LT's *dramein* is in the more natural position.

29a. The vb. *diasōthēsomai* (B) is the more frequent rendering of *ʾmlṭh*: *apeleusomai* (LT) is used only here; yet I have taken it as a key indicator of the sense of *nmlṭ* throughout Samuel: Jonathan's advocacy would be particularly flat-footed if he had quoted David to his father as wanting to "escape" or "be saved." The term *nmlṭ* is a keyword of the narratives of David in flight from Saul (19:10, 12, 17, 18; 20:29; 22:1; 23:13; 27:1 [2x]); the other biblical chapters in which it is concentrated are Gen 19 (5x) and Judg 3 (3x). Also, *šlḥ piʿel* (1 Sam 19:17 [2x]; 20:5, 13, 22 [2x], 29; 24:19 [20]; 30:26; 31:9) often features alongside it (Gen 19:13, 29; Judg 3:18).

30a. The term *automolountōn* (B) is used of desertion in a military context; *BA* proposes that this has read the Heb. as being related to *mrwd* ("roaming," "homeless") rather than *mrd* ("rebel"). The LT plus *gynaikotraphē* ("woman-reared"), if an alternative rendering, is freer.

b. The GT's *metochos* ("partner") may attest a form of *ḥbr* (as 5x out of 9x in the Greek OT); only here does it correspond to *bḥr* in MT.

31a. Here LT = MT.

b. "The youth" (GT) may attest *ʾt-hʿlm* in place of *ʾtw ʾly* (MT).

32a. The LT attests only "his father," and not "Saul."

33a. Here GT reads *epēren* ("raised"), which normally renders *nśʾ* and nowhere else corresponds to *ṭwl*.

34a. The vb. *klm nipʿal* is used in BTH (2 Sam 10:5) and in 2 Sam 19:4; *hipʿil* in 1 Sam 20:34; 25:7; *hopʿal* in 1 Sam 25:15. The LT attests two *kî* clauses, as in MT; but B attests only the second. However, the second clause in LT is longer than in MT: "because his father had determined [*bouleuesthai* normally corresponds to some form of *yʿṣ*] to finish him."

b. Codex B's much shorter text is related to LT's: *synetelesen/syntelesai* appears to represent *klh* instead of MT's *klm*. In MT *klh* is also used in the same two chapters of 1 Samuel: 20:7, 9, 33; 25:17.

35a. The LT also has the apparently alternative rendering of *mwʿd*, but in reverse order to B.

b. In GT *mwʿd* is often rendered *martyrion*, though hardly appropriate to the context here.

36a. The LT specifies Jonathan as subj.

b. Here B = MT; but LT adds *sy*, as if it has read *ʾth* after the command "run." It may be responding to the following *egō*; however, the *ʾānōkî* so rendered is hardly emphatic, but simply marks the subj. of the participial vb.

c. The lack of connective in MT is surprising: perhaps "The lad—he ran."

d. Reading with a number of MSS and the VSS, *hḥṣym* ("the arrows"), and not as in CL, *hḥṣy* ("the half").

e. Here and in the next instance, LT offers forms of *belos* rather than *schiza*.

37a. The MT uses *naʿar* ("lad") throughout this episode for Jonathan's small servant, supported here by *paidarion* in LT. However, 4QSam^b has *ʿlmw* here, and B marks the shift with *tou neaniou*. The MT, supported by B and LT, has used *ʿlm* in 20:22 (and elsewhere only in 17:56 [MT +]). Oddly 4QSam^b and LT read the possessive, while MT and B do not.

b. The GT attests *šm* ("there"), not *hlwʾ* ("is it not"). The LT begins Jonathan's speech with an additional clause: "Quickly go and do not stand, for there . . ."

c. Again *hḥṣy* in MT. We find *ḥṣy* as a variant of *ḥṣ* only in 20:36, 37 (2x), 38 (K); and 2 Kgs 9:24 (DJD 234).

40a. Here B attests *bʾ* (*qal*) rather than *hbyʾ* (*hipʿil*), as in MT.

41a. Both the initial connective and the word order in GT, *kai* [*hōs*] *eisēlthen to paidarion*, suggest the more regular *wybʾ hnʿr*.

b. The LT adds "into the city."

c. Here *heōs* confirms MT's *ʿd*, and clearly *megalēs* (GT) corresponds to *gdwl* (cf. the MT *hgdyl*); *synteleia* most often renders a form of *klh*. The only (other) instances of *hgdyl* in FP are 1 Sam 12:24; 2 Sam 22:51 (both have Yahweh as subj.).[16]

42a (21:1). The LT has the longest text in this verse, sharing the two pluses of B and the one plus of MT.

[9–11] Jonathan's response (v. 9) opens with a further "heaven forbid" (as in v. 2), and combines this with David's emphatic "really know" (from v. 3). The wording of David's answering question about Saul's responding harshly to Jonathan (v. 10) may look in either or both of two directions. It may draw on BTH in 1 Kgs 12:13, with Rehoboam's harsh answer to his elders—the expression was available to any author of Samuel. But all the other instances of *qāšeh*, admittedly without "answer," are in later portions of the book (1 Sam 1:15; 25:3; 2 Sam 2:17; 3:39).

[12–17] The subparagraph in vv. 12–17 is particularly complex. Its grammatical and textual difficulties are especially acute in vv. 13 and 16. Before "to my father" (*ʾl-ʾby*, v. 13) we would expect *yyṭb* as *qal*; however, MT reads the verb as *hipʿil*, which better fits the following direct object: "the disaster." The GT reflects neither *yyṭb* nor the following *ʾl*; and after the oath formula, *kî ʾābî* is read as if *kî ʾābîʾ*: "Suppose I bring [bad (news) upon you]." Then, after mention of *ḥesed* (v. 15), it is not surprising that the opening *wykrt* (v. 16), pointed *qal* in MT, is given a positive sense, as in 11:2 and 22:8, where we also find *krt* without "covenant" (*bĕrît*) as its stated object. It is equally natural, after two occurrences of *krt hipʿil*, meaning "cut off" (v. 15), that both B and LT have read the correspondingly "negative" *nipʿal*/passive at the opening of v. 16.

16. Jobling (164) rightly notes that the textual evidence that David wept more than Jonathan is flimsy; and yet it is no more flimsy than the evidence he has not questioned (163) that Jonathan made David swear (20:17).

Yet, despite these formidable difficulties presented by the detail of the argument, its broad lines are clear, if surprising. Against Jonathan's further protestation that he will give David notice of an unfavorable verdict, David asks him (realistically, in light of vv. 30–34) to consider what would happen if his father gives him a rough response.[17] Jonathan insists that, even if his movement is restricted, he will send a message (vv. 12–13a). His wish that Yahweh will be with David as he has been with Saul (v. 13b) is neatly ambiguous. It takes off from the present uncertain times, but leads immediately (vv. 14–16) to an expected future in which Yahweh will be mopping up David's enemies—and among these Saul will be one of the has-beens: the house to which David should remain loyal is "mine," not "my father's" (v. 15).

The concluding sentence (v. 17) is shorter in GT and is formally ambiguous: we may more naturally read it as saying that Jonathan swears an oath to David because Jonathan loves David, who loves him; but it may be that Jonathan swears to David because David loves Jonathan, who loves him. However, given the reciprocal nature of true love, the ambiguity does not matter: Jonathan takes his oath to David because each of them loves the other. In itself, the longer sentence in MT is no less ambiguous: the principal shift is that Jonathan now has David attest formally to the situation between them. However, as we have noted above, the two Hebrew words added in MT to the end of v. 17a are repeated from 18:3b within a much larger plus, where they restate what has been stated more fully in 18:1b. In MT, in both chapters, it is always Jonathan who is said to love David, and he loves him no less than he loves himself. Here in 20:17, Jonathan makes David recognize formally that this is so; but David's own attitude to Jonathan remains unstated. Within 1 Samuel, it is Saul's love for David that is first noted (16:21). The theme of love for David is concentrated in ch. 18: vv. 1 (Jonathan [MT only]), 16 (all Israel and Judah), 20 (Michal), 22 (all [Saul's] servants), 28 (*mykl bt-š᾿wl* [MT, LT]; *kl-yśr᾿l* [B]); and then it reappears in 20:17 (Jonathan). In the shorter text of B, which lacks 18:1–5, Jonathan brings up the rear of a long list of others responding to David in love. In B it is 19:1–7 that supplies the first mention of Jonathan's first interest in David: "He took pleasure in David."

[18–23] Some of the language Jonathan uses is drawn ultimately from BTH in 2 Sam 7 and 10. This is most obvious in 1 Sam 20:15, where "loyalty," (royal) "house," "forever," and "David" all serve to anticipate 2 Sam 7:15–16. But it will be no less true of 1 Sam 20:23 and 42, where he insists that what has been spoken (v. 23) or sworn (42) between them should remain valid "forever." Yet it is David who has first appealed that Jonathan show loyalty (*ḥesed*) to him (v. 8). We might suppose that David and Jonathan envisage (vv. 10, 12) that Saul's

17. The phrase *ʿnh qšh* may have been adopted from 1 Kgs 12:13 (BTH), where Rehoboam's responses not only relate to hard labor but are also coarse.

hostility might restrict Jonathan's freedom, but that at least he could send David a message. From the code he now explains to David (vv. 18–23), it is now clear that he does not expect his movement to be restricted, although he may well be watched. He concludes his instructions (v. 23) with a further anticipation of language that we shall meet next in 2 Sam 7:7—there in Yahweh's mouth, but here referring to what they both have said: "the speaking which we have spoken, I and you." Jonathan's reference forward to the divine promise that would be so important to the house of David is underscored when he continues: "Look: *Yahweh* between me and you *forever*" (v. 23).

[24–26] The scene shifts to the seating arrangements at the court dinner (vv. 24–26). The places occupied by Saul, Jonathan, and Abner are presumably prescribed by protocol—David's too: hence his absence is all the more easily noted. Saul puts down to "chance" his absence on the first night of the new month. Outside Ecclesiastes (7x), *miqreh* is found only in Ruth 2:3; 1 Sam 6:9; and here (v. 26). In both Ruth and earlier in Samuel, it is not easy to distinguish between "chance" and Yahweh's secret causation. The fact that only Philistines and Saul speak of "chance" in 1 Samuel anticipates the significant use of the related verb three times in 2 Samuel.[18] Saul's first reaction is that David's absence is "just one of these things," and he goes on to suggest a reason: that he has become unclean in some way—and he repeats the reason to underline its plausibility. The category of "[un]cleanness" is quite as rare in FP as that of chance.[19] Either the same explanation cannot easily extend to a second absence, or at least a second absence makes it more necessary to check on what the real reason is.[20] Abner will play an important role in 2 Samuel 2–3 but has a much more restricted and possibly secondary role in 1 Samuel. He is mentioned as army commander (14:50) in the listing of Saul's staff; as such, he is appropriately at Saul's side here; he has a part to play in 1 Sam 26; and he appears in MT pluses in 17:55, 57. In this context, it may be significant that "pure" and "chance" are also rare within Samuel and probably late.

[27a] Here MT's paragraphing corresponds to the heightened tension caused by David's second nonappearance.

[27b–29] Saul's question to Jonathan appears very formally posed (v. 27b); and it elicits the full response suggested by David, but restated in Jonathan's own terms. One of the smaller changes in wording may be significant: "from me" (*mmny*) in v. 6 has become *mʿmdy* (v. 28), which is used only once more in HB; Saul himself has heard this more weighty option, on that one previous occasion, as he was receiving instructions from Samuel (10:2). Is the change

18. See below on 2 Sam 1:6; 18:9; 20:1.

19. According to Eccl 9:2, there is but one *miqreh* for the clean and the unclean.

20. On Deut 23:10 (11), where the related *qāreh* and *ṭāhôr* appear in the same context, Mandelkern calls the former a euphemism for *nocturna pollutio*.

in wording a small linguistic token of Jonathan's claiming authority to grant David's leave of absence? Jonathan's fuller explanation to his father (v. 29) about the clash of pressing obligations faced by David is neatly framed by a wordplay that encapsulates the whole: the first word is *šlḥny* ("dispatch me") and the final phrase is *šlḥn hmlk* ("the king's table").

If one neat play on words frames Jonathan's excuse for David's absence, another interesting allusion frames the whole of vv. 18–29. When the Queen of Sheba visits Solomon's court, she is amazed at "the eating at his table, and the seating of his servants" (1 Kgs 10:5, BTH). "Table" (*šlḥn*) and "seating" (*mwšb*) in one sense form an unremarkable pair; and yet they feature in only two chapters in Samuel: *šlḥn* in 1 Sam 20:29, 34; and 2 Sam 9 (4x)—and only once more (in 2 Sam 19:28 [29]); and *mwšb* only in 1 Sam 20:18, 25 and 2 Sam 9:12.[21] Both narratives deal with David's relations with the house of Saul, and in particular with Jonathan and his family.

[30–31] The rage Saul directs at Jonathan is crude and barely coherent. His opening verbal assault starts by insulting Jonathan's mother and finishes by claiming that Jonathan's behavior disgraces his mother. The king is fully aware that David constitutes a threat to Jonathan's succession to the throne: he should die. He finds something paradoxical—perhaps particularly unstable and dangerous—about a "son of death" who is also alive and flourishing.[22] Is he fit to die because he is in fact actively contagious and deals in death?

[32–33] Even if being called "son of death" by the king was not a formal sentence of death, Jonathan knows what "send and take him to me" implies. He asks on what grounds David should be put to death, apparently quite determinedly unaware that his father has just stated them. Without attributing it to David, he relays to his father David's characteristic (see above on 20:1) innocent question: "What has he done?" Saul's assault becomes physical. Now that he has himself become target of his father's spear, Jonathan appreciates that David's understanding of the situation is well founded.

[34] Jonathan leaves the table in a rage perfectly matched to his father's (vv. 30a, 34a). Codex B goes on to record the shortest version of the narrator's concluding and ambiguous comment (v. 34b): "[He did not eat that day] because his father had concluded against him"—against whom? The MT's different and longer ". . . for he was grieved for David because his father had disgraced him" leaves the identity of the final "him" no clearer, and hence neatly and ambiguously develops the identification of Jonathan and David.

[35–42a] This is further advanced in the closing subparagraph. The coded warning is acted out; the narrator assures his omniscient readers that Jonathan's arrow-retrieving boy knows nothing of what is passing between Jonathan and

21. There in a rather different sense, but what is significant is the use of the two words together.
22. Compare the proximity of life and "son of death" in 26:16.

David (v. 39). Jonathan dismisses the lad, and—whether confidently or recklessly—David proceeds to break cover. He falls before the king's son, prostrating himself three times. Each then kisses the other (we shall be reminded of this when we encounter another king's son, Absalom, greeting petitioners, in 2 Sam 15:5); and each then weeps with the other. The GT seems to maintain this mutuality to the end of v. 41, in an expression that may be rendered "until a great completion"; but MT, though no less obscure, suggests that David, who (in GT as well) has taken the initiative, is also the more affected.[23] David may have led in action, but Jonathan has the last words. As he wishes David a peaceful departure, he lays great stress on the mutuality of what they have sworn to eternity in Yahweh's name.

1 Samuel 20:42b–21:4 (21:1–5)

42b And [he] *David* rose
and went;
and Jonathan, he[a] came to the city.
21:1 And David came to Nob, to Ab/himelek the priest.
And [Ahimelek] *Abimelek*[a] trembled[b]
meeting David,
and said to him,
"Why are you alone,
and no man is with you?'
2 And David said to [Ahimelek[a]] the priest,
"The king, he commanded me something *today*;
and he said to me,
'Let not any man know anything about the matter
on which I am sending you
and about which I have commanded you.'
And the lads I have appointed to so-and-so's[b] place.
3 Now then,

have you under your hand	what[a] have you under your hand?[b]
five loaves? Put in my hand	Five loaves put in my hand,[b]
whatever is found."	or whatever is found."

4 And the priest answered David,
and said,

23. Alastair Moodie (contributing to the "Civil Partnerships Debate," in *Ministers' Forum*, ed. John Ferguson for the Church of Scotland, July 2006, 285), finds it "very possible that Jonathan was homosexual and that David was bisexual." Since we are told (2 Sam 4:4) that Jonathan had a son, this supposition seems very speculative. More important: since there is nothing erotic about Absalom's kiss when seeking to establish his claim to the throne, it may be overinterpretation to find (homo)eroticism in this narrative.

"There is no unhallowed[a] bread under my hand;
but there is holy bread,
if the lads have kept themselves [only[b]] from woman,
they may eat."

20:42a [21:1a MT]. Jonathan precedes the vb. in GT as in MT.

21:1[2]a. The LT = MT; but B reads *Abeimelech* throughout.

b. Of 12 instances of *existanai* in 1–4 Kingdoms, 8 (including this one) correspond to a form of *ḥrd*.

2[3]a. The LT does read "Ahimelech," but after "priest."

b. Here 4QSam[b] = MT. The plain Greek and the transcription in B appear to be a double rendering of a slightly different Heb. If they belong to different periods, they will attest all the more strongly to a text different from MT and 4QSam[b]: while *Phellanei* does correspond to *plny* in MT, *Maemōnei* may reflect *m'mny*, not *'lmny*; and *'mn* will underlie *Pistis*. Only *Theou pistis* is read in LT.

3[4]a. The GT attests *hyš* for MT *mh-yš*.

b. It is not easy to render idiomatically the repeated interchange between "under the hand" of the priest (in his control, available to him: vv. 3, 4, 8) and "in the hand" of David (vv. 3, 8).

4[5]a. Here GT uses *bebēloi* (lit., "able to be trodden") for "unhallowed"—possibly suggested by *derek/hodos* in v. 5 [6].

b. Different word order would be implied, but *'k* ("only") in MT may be a remnant of some form of *'kl* ("eat"), such as *w'klw* (G) or *w'kltm mmnw* (4QSam[b]). The LT differs in word order from B, but hardly materially.

[20:42b–21:4] Reading this short narrative is like trying to solve a puzzle with missing pieces, or a problem with too few clues. Jobling also confesses to puzzlement and looks ahead to chs. 27–29 for clues, whereas Polzin (1989) backtracks to chs. 10 and 13–14, where he finds parallels with Saul. The opening "and he upped and went" (20:42b [21:1]) is brief, and even abrupt. The two Hebrew words may simply convey that David wordlessly makes a move to break away from Jonathan's fulsome farewell (20:42a)—that David does simply do what the king's son has suggested and takes peaceful leave. And yet, since David has already been reported four times (19:10, 12, 18; 20:1) as being in flight from Saul, this departure appears to report the next stage in his flight, though the actual word "flee" will not be used again till v. 10 (11). What Jonathan calls "peace" his father would name rather differently.

David has fled first to his own house, then to Samuel, and then to Jonathan at an undisclosed location. His wife (Saul's daughter) and Samuel (who has anointed both Saul and himself) have both taken active steps to protect him; and now Saul's son, the "crown prince," has sworn solemnly to him. Since Jonathan apparently had the right to permit David to absent himself from his father's table, his "go in peace" here may be heard by David as more of a repeat exit permit than a simple farewell. He did not need to tell David that Saul's fury over the first permit has been demonstrated by spear as well as word.

Is the sanctuary at Nob the next objective in David's flight, or simply a staging point in his escape to Gath? We cannot know what David's intention toward the priest is. However, of those to whom David has turned since leaving Saul, the priest at Nob is the first who is said to tremble at his coming. The last time we met this term for fear (*ḥrd*) was at the trembling of Bethlehem's elders when Samuel arrives unannounced (16:4); and the next time will be Saul's own terror on observing the massing of the Philistine forces against him (28:5). The priest is suspicious that David has arrived without his usual retinue. We readers know that Saul himself knows nothing of the claimed secret royal mission. But blowing the cover of an official secret agent is always a serious offense, and we have to admire a skillful ruse that secures the silence—and compliance—of a subject loyal to Saul.

1 Samuel 21:5–24:15 (21:6–24:16)

5 And David answered the priest
and said to him,
"Surely woman is forbidden to us, *as* regularly, when I go out

on the way, all[a] the lads have been sanctified,	and the lads' equipment has been sanctified,
and is this path profane?	even if it was a profane path,
Therefore it will be sanctified[b] today through my equipment."	all the more today will it be holy by the equipment."

6 And the priest gave him [what was holy] *the loaves of the offering*,
for there was not bread there except the bread of the Presence,
which is removed from Yahweh's presence,
putting hot bread on the day of its being taken.
7 And there was there a man of Saul's servants on that day,
restrained[a] before Yahweh;
and his name was Doeg the Edomite,[b] chief[c] of the herders of Saul.
8 And David said to Ab/himelek,
"See[a] if there is here under your hand a spear or a sword.
For even my sword and even my equipment I did not take in my own hand,
because the king's matter was urgent."

9 And the priest said,
"The sword of Goliath the Philistine,
whom you struck down in the valley of the terebinth—
look, here it is wrapped in a garment [behind the ephod[a]].

If that is what you would take for yourself,
take it;
for there is not another here besides[b] it."
And David said,
"There is not its like;
give it to me."
And he gave it to him.[c]
10 And David rose
and fled on that day from before Saul,
and *David*[a] came to Achish king of Gath.
11 And the servants of Achish said to him,
"Is this not David, the king of the land?
Is it not of him that they spoke up in the dances, saying,
'Saul struck down in his thousands,
but David in his myriads'?"
12 And David took these words to his heart,
and he was very afraid of Achish king of Gath.

13 And he altered	13 And he altered it—
his face in his[a] eyes,	his "taste"—in their eyes,
and he made pretense on that day,	
and he drummed on the doors of the city,	
and he was distorted in his hands,	And he acted madly in their hands,
and he fell on the doors of the gate,	and he scratched on the doors of the gate,
and his spittle dropped on his beard.	And let his spittle drop on his beard.

14 And Achish said to his servants,
"Suppose you see someone acting crazily,
why would you bring him to me?
15 Am I lacking in crazy fellows
that you have brought this one
to act crazily over against me?
Shall this one come to my house?"

22:1 And David went from there
and [got away] *was saved and comes* to the cave of Adullam;
and his brothers hear[d] and [all[a]] his father's house,
and they [went] *go* down to him there.
2 And there gathered themselves to him every man in straits and every
man who had a creditor and every man bitter in spirit,

and he became leader over them,
and there were with him some four hundred men.
3 And David went from there to Mizpeh of Moab,
and he said to the king of Moab,
"Let my father and my mother surely come [down] *to be* with you
till I know
what God[a] will do for[b] me."
4 And he [comforted[a]] *encouraged* the face of the king of Moab,
and they stayed with him all the days
that David was in the fortress.

5 And Gad the prophet said to David,
"You shall not live in the fortress.
Come
and take yourself to the land of Judah."
And David went,
and came to the [forest of Hareth] *city of* Sareik.[a]

6 And Saul heard
that David was known of and the men
who were with him.
Now Saul was seated at Gibeah, under the tamarisk on the height,
and his spear was in his hand
and all his servants were stationed by him.
7 And Saul said to his servants stationed by him,
"Hear clearly, Benjamites/sons of my right hand,
to all of you [also] *really*[a] will the son of Jesse give fields and orchards;
or [of] all of you will he make captains of thousands and captains of hundreds?
8 For you have conspired all of you against me;
and there is no one uncovering my ear
at my son's deciding *a covenant* with the son of Jesse,
and there is none of you sick[a] for me and uncovering my ear,
that my son has raised up my servant against me [for an ambush]
as an enemy[b] as at this day."

9 And Doe*g*[q] the [Edomite] *Aramaean* answered—
now he was stationed [by the servants] *over the mules* of Saul—
and he said:
"I have seen the son of Jesse
coming to Nob to Ah/bimelekh son of Ahitub *the priest.*

10 And he asked for him of [Yahweh[a]] *God*;
and provision/catch he gave him
and the sword of Goliath the Philistine he gave him."
11 And the king sent
to call Ah/bimelech son of Ahitub and all [the sons of] his father*'s house*,
the priests who were at Nob;
and they came, all of them, to the king.

12 And Saul said:
"Hear well, son of Ahitub."
And he said:
"I am here; *speak,* my lord."
13 And Saul said to him:
"Why have you conspired against me, you and the son of Jesse,
in your giving him[a] food and sword
and asking for him of God,
[to rise toward me in ambush] *making him an enemy to me* as this day?"

14 And *he* [Ahimelech] answered the king
and said:
"And who among all your servants is trusty like David,
and the king's in-law,
and turning to your bidding,[a]
and honored in your house?
15 Today I began
asking for him of God.
How could it be thought of me!
Let not the king place anything on his servant, *or* on all my father's house;
for your servant knows no matter in all this, small or great."
16 And the king said:
"Die you surely shall, Ah/bimelech, you and all your father's house."
17 And the king said to the outrunners
who were stationed opposite him,
"[Turn] *Approach*[a]
and put to death the priests of Yahweh;
because their hand too is with David,
and because they knew
that he was fleeing,
and they did not uncover my ear."

But the servants of the king were not willing
to put out their hand
to [fall on] *sin against*[b] the priests of Yahweh.

18 And the king said to Doeg[q],
"You turn,
and fall on the priests."
And Doeg[q] the [Edomite[a]] *Aramaean* turned,
and he [himself[b]] fell on the priests *of Yahweh*,
and he put to death on that day [eighty-five] *three hundred and five* individuals,
each w/bearing a [linen[c]] ephod.
19 And Nob the city of the priests he struck with the sword,
man and woman, child and suckling, ox and ass and sheep, [with the sword[a]].
20 And one son of Ah/bimelekh son of Ahitub got away,
and his name was Abiathar,
and he fled after David.
21 And Abiathar reported to David
that Saul had slain *all* the priests of Yahweh.[a]
22 And David said to Abiathar:
"I knew *that*[a] on that day
that Doeg[q] the [Edomite] *Aramaean* [was there],
that report to Saul he surely would.
It is I who [turned on[b] every life] *am to blame for the lives* of your father's house.
23 Stay with me.
Do not be afraid;

for wherever I seek for my life a place,	for whoever seeks my life
I shall seek also for your life;	seeks your life;
for you have come under protection[a] with me."	for you are a duty of protection with me."

23:1 And [they[a]] *it was* reported to David,
saying,
"Look, *the* Philistines are making war at Keilah,
and they are plundering, *they are trampling down*[b] the threshing floors."
2 And David asked of Yahweh,
saying,
"Shall I go up
and (make a) strike on these Philistines?"

And Yahweh said to David,
"Go
and strike on the Philistines
and save Keilah."

3 And David's men said to him,
"Look, here in Judah we are afraid—
all the more so, supposing we go to Keilah,
[to the Philistine lines.[a]] *Into the booty of the Philistines shall we be moving?*"

4 And David continued further
asking of Yahweh.

And Yahweh answered him,
and said:
"Up!
Get down to Keilah,
for I am putting Philistines in your hand."

5 And David went, and his men, to Keilah,
and he made war on the Philistines,
and they fled before him
and he drove off their herds,
and struck on them a great blow;
and David saved the inhabitants of Keilah.

6 And it came to be
in the fleeing of Abiathar son of Ah/bimelekh to David to Keilah,
and he with David into Keilah went down, having an ephod [went down] in his hand.

7 And it was told to Saul
that David had come to Keilah;
and Saul said,
"God has [alienated[a]] *sold* him into my hand,
for he is shut in—
coming into a city with doors and gate bar*s*."

8 And Saul made the whole people hear[a] {the call} for war,
to go down to Keilah
to make an ambush for David and his men.

9 And David knew
that against him Saul was [devising] *not keeping silent*[a] the trouble;
and he said to Abiathar the priest,
"Bring near the ephod *of Yahweh*."

10 And David said:
"Yahweh, God of Israel, your servant has heard, surely heard,
that Saul is seeking to come to Keilah,
to bring ruin[a] to the city for sake of me.

11 Will he be excluded[a]?	11 Will the lords of Keilah deliver me into his hand?
And now, will Saul come down as your servant has heard?	Will Saul come down

Yahweh, God of Israel, be sure to report to your servant."

And Yahweh said,
"*He will be excluded.* [He will come down.]"
12 And David said,[a]
"Will the lords of Keilah deliver me and my men into Saul's hands?"
And Yahweh said,
"They will deliver."[bc]

13 And David rose, and his men, some [six] *four* hundred [men],
and they came out of Keilah,
and they went about
wherever they went about.
And to Saul it was reported
that David had got away from Keilah,
and he [ceased] *let go*[a] coming out.
14 And [David] *he* stayed in the desert, in the rock fortresses,[a]
and he stayed in the hill country in the desert of Ziph.
And Saul sought him all the days,
but [God[b]] *Yahweh* did not give him into his hand.
15 And David saw
that Saul was coming out[a] to seek [his life[b]] *David*,
and David was in the [desert of Ziph at Chorshah[c]] *dry mountain in the new Ziph.*

16 And Jonathan, Saul's son, rose
and went to David at Chorshah,
and he strengthened his hand by [God[a]] *Yahweh.*
17 And he said to him,
"Do not be afraid,
for the hand of Saul my father will not find you.
And you, you will be king over Israel;
and I, I shall be second[a] to you;

and even Saul my father knows so."
18 And the two of them made a covenant before Yahweh;
and David stayed in Chorshah,
but Jonathan, he went to his house.

19 And Ziphites went up *from the arid place* to Saul, to [Gibeah] *the hill*, saying,
"Is not David hiding himself with us in [the rock fortresses] *Nessara* [at Chorshah] *in the* new,[a] in the hill of Hachilah,
which is south of the Jeshimon?
20 And now, for all [the desire of[a]] your very life, O king, to come down, come down to us;
they have closed him off[b] [and it is for us to deliver him] into the hand*s* of the king."
21 And Saul said,
"Blessed are you of Yahweh,
for you have [had compassion on] *grieved for*[a] me.
22 Go surely,
make ready again,
and know
[and see[a]] his place,
where his foot is,
quickly there, who has seen him there;
where you have said[b], lest[c] for one has said to me that
he will be [very, very] cunning.
23 And see
and know [of all the hiding places where he might be hiding,
and come back to me for sure,[a]]
and [I] *we* will go[b] with you,
and may it come to be,
if he is in the land,
may I [grasp] *search out*[c] him among all the thousands of Judah."
24 And the[y] *Ziphites* rose
and went [to Ziph] before Saul;
and David and his men were in the desert of Maon[a] [in the Arabah] *at evening*[b]
south of the Jeshimon.
25 And Saul went, and his men
to seek him;[a]
and they reported to David,
and he went down to the rock
[and stayed] in the desert of Maon;

and Saul heard,
and he chased after David to the desert of Maon.
26 And Saul *and his men* went by the side of the hill here,
and David and his men by the side of the hill there;
and David became [hurried] *sheltered*[a]
going away from Saul;
and Saul and his men were [going round toward] *drawn up against*[b]
David and his men,
to grasp them.
27 And a messenger came to Saul, saying,
"Be quick
and go,
for Philistines have made a raid against the land."
28 And Saul turned back
from chasing after David,
and he went
to meet *the* Philistines.
Therefore they called that place the Rock of the Divisions.[a]
29 And David went up from there,
and settled at the [fortresses] *narrow spaces*[a] of En-gedi.[b]
24:1 And it came to be,
as Saul returned
from following Philistines,
and they reported to him, saying,
"Look, David is in the desert of En-gedi."

2 And *he* [Saul] took *with him* three thousand men, choice of
all Israel,
and he went
to seek David and his men, opposite the Wild-Goats' Rocks.[a]
3 And he came to the sheepfolds on the way,
and there was a cave there,
and Saul came to [screen his "legs"] *prepare* himself;[a]
and David and his men were settled in the depths of the cave.
4 And David's men said to him,
"Look! *this is* the day
on which Yahweh has spoken to you
['Look, I am] *of* giving your enemy/ies[a] into your hand,
and you shall do to him
as is good in your eyes.'"
And David got up
and he cut the border of the cloak belonging to Saul, secretly.

5 And it came to be after this,
and David's heart struck him
because[a] he had cut *the* [a] border [belonging to Saul] *of his* cloak.[b]

6 And he said to his men,
"Yahweh would hold it an abominable deed of mine[a]
if I were to do this thing [to my lord,[b]] to Yahweh's anointed,
to put my hand on him;
for he is Yahweh's anointed."
7 And David [ripped apart] *prevailed on*[a] his men by words,
and did not grant them
to rise [against[b]] *to slaughter*[c] Saul.
And Saul, he rose [from the cave[d]]
and went his way.

8 And David rose after [this
and went out] *him*[a] from the cave,
and *David*[b] called after Saul,
saying,
"My lord king."
And Saul looked behind him,
and David knelt, his face to the ground,
and did obeisance *to him.*

9 And David said to Saul,
"Why do you listen to the words of people,[a] saying,
'Look, David is seeking your ill.'
10 Look,[a] this day your eyes have seen
that Yahweh gave you today into my hand in the cave
and [said[b]] *I was not willing* to slay you,
and *I* had pity[c] on you
and I said,
'I shall not set my hand on my lord,
for he is Yahweh's anointed.'
11 [My father,[a] see,
just[b]] *And* see the border of your cloak in my hand.
[Truly when] I *myself*[c] cut the border of your cloak,
and I did not slay you.[d]
And Know
and see *today*
that there is not *ill* in my hand [ill] *or impiety* or rebellion,[e]
and I have not sinned against you

but you are [hunting] *binding*[f] my life,
to take it.

12 Yahweh judge between me and you;
and Yahweh champion me rather than you;
but my hand shall not be on you.

13 As the proverb of the ancient[a] says:
'From the evil comes out evil.'[b]
But my hand shall not be on you.

14 *And now*[a] after whom [has the king of Israel] *have you* come out, *king of Israel*?
After whom are you chasing?
After a dead dog?
After a single flea?

15 Yahweh be arbitrator and judge[a] between me and you.
And let [him] *Yahweh* see,
and let him settle my suit
and let him bring me justice away from your hand."

5[6]a. Like 4QSam[b], the GT has read *kl*, not *kly*, as in MT.

b. The GT's *hēgnismena* corresponds normally to *qdš hitpaʿel*; but MT has *qdš* as a noun.

7[8]a. In GT, *nʿṣr* is both transliterated and rendered appropriately by *synechomenos*.

b. Here B's *Dōēk ho Syros* might attest *dʾq hʾrmy*, rather than *dʾg hʾdmy* (LT = MT); however, B in Kingdoms has routinely altered Edomite to Syrian/Aramaean.

c. Only here is *ʾbyr* used in FP (MT), and it is not attested in GT, which presents him as herder (*rʿh*) to Saul's asses.

8[9]a. The translation follows LXX's *ide* ("see"); *wʾyn* in MT is a puzzle. For an instance of *ʾyn yš*, normally pointed, see Ps 135:17.

9[10]a. The plus in MT occurs also in 4QSam[b]; that immediately appears to support the judgment of Wellhausen that its omission in B is "tendentious," though he does not explain this. However, A and LT, uniquely in Kingdoms, use *epōmis* (lit., "on the shoulder") here, which is the standard rendering in the Pentateuch for *ʾēpôd*, and not as elsewhere the transliteration *ephoud*. That suggests that, if 21:10 MT and 4QSam[b] do have the original text, what A and LT attest is a "correction" of the shorter B.

b. As a rarely used preposition, *zwlt* is found elsewhere in Samuel only in 2 Sam 7:22//1 Chr 17:20—there too in otherwise unique relationship with *kmw*. Cf. also Deut 1:36; 4:12; Josh. 11:13; 1 Kgs 3:18; 12:20 (Kgs +); 2 Kgs 24:14; Isa 26:13; 45:5, 21; 64:4 (3); Hos 13:4; Ps 18:32 (but not 2 Sam 22:32, where *mblʿdy* is repeated); Ruth 4:4.

c. Here LT = B.

10[11]a. Again LT = B.

13[14]a. Here LT reads "their eyes" with MT, not "his eyes" with B. In all other details of the verse, LT = B, including reading 2 clauses more than the 4 in MT, or alternatively offering double renderings of clauses 2 and 3 in MT.

22:1a. Here LT also reads "all." In ch. 22 English versification matches MT and GT.

3a. The MT has anarthrous *ʾlhym*, while GT reads *ho theos*.

b. Hebrew *l-* can mean "to" or "for."

4a. This use of *nḥm* can be compared with *lnḥmw* (where Hanun, king of Ammon, is the obj.) in 2 Sam 10:2//1 Chr 19:2. An alternative approach is to treat *wynḥm* (used also in 1 Kgs 10:26) as equivalent to *wynyḥm* ("left them at rest") as in 2 Chr. 1:14; 9:25.

5a. The GT attests not *y'r* but *'yr*, and not *ḥrt* but *sryq* (B) or *sryk* (LT).

7a. Here *alēthōs* corresponds uniquely to *gam*. Is this deliberately ambiguous?

8a. Assonant *ḥōleh* ("sick") reinforces repetition of *gōleh* ("uncovering").

b. The GT attests *'yb* ("enemy") for *'rb* ("ambush").

10a. Here 4QSam[a] and Syr. agree with GT's "God" against "Yahweh" (MT).

13a. Here B renders *bttk lw* appropriately as *dounai se autō*; however, LT has the more puzzling *tou dounai seautō*, and it repeats *seautō* in the following phrase, where B has simply *autō*.

14a. Sometimes *sr 'l mšm'tk* (lit., "turning to your hearing") is (triply) emended to read *śr 'l mšmrtk* ("commander over your [body]guard"); *mšmrt* is much the commoner word and might even have been expected in this context—but that makes the rarer *mšm't* all the more effective.

17a. Here GT's *prosagagete* may attest *gšw* rather than MT's *sbw* (a unique correspondence). But cf. note 22b below.

b. The LT = MT; *pg' b-* is rendered lit. in v. 18 by *apanta eis*; the text underlying B in v. 17 may have been different from MT. Throughout Kingdoms, *hamartanein* is the stock correspondent to *ḥṭ'*; the only other exception is 1 Kgdms 26:18, where it corresponds to *'śh*.

18a. Again LT = MT.

b. The MT reads *hw'* before "the priests," while B attests the similar *yhwh* after it.

c. Here MT is followed by A, but not B or LT.

19a. The LT also repeats *epataxen* ("struck") before this phrase.

21a. Here LT has *kyriou*, which corresponds more readily to *yhwh*, but B has *tou kyriou*.

22a. In this sentence, LT has *hoti* once, MT has *ky* twice, and B has *hoti* three times.

b. The LT = B. As in v. 17, it could be that the LXX has read something quite different from MT's *sbty*: some have proposed *ḥbty* as the text underlying *aitios* ("guilty"); however, neither is *aitios* used anywhere else in OT books within HB, nor is *ḥwb* attested in *qal*.

23a. The vb. *phylassein* is the stock and very common correspondent to *šmr*; but only here and in 1 Chr 9:23 to *mšmrt*.

23:1a. Here LT = MT.

b. The LT has the same elements as B, but in a different order: "they are plundering the threshing floors and trampling."

3a. Here LT's *koiladas* may attest *m'mqy* for MT's *m'rkwt*.

7a. "Alienated" (in the legal sense of "transferred into other ownership") takes MT *nkr* as *pi'el* of a denominative vb. related to the common adj. "foreign." And B's *pepraken* (< *pernēmi* [LSJ 1395a]) attests the commoner *mkr*. To "sell into the power of" (*mkr byd*) with divine subj. is an idiom found only in Judg 2:14; 3:8; 4:2, 9; 10:7; 1 Sam 12:9 (but always in the narrative form *wymkr byd*, and not spoken as here [from B] *mkr byd*).

8a. Just once more *šm' pi'el* is used in HB, in 15:4 above, where Saul also is the subj. but with Amalek as the foe!

9a. Here B's *parasiōpa* also attests *mḥryš*—not the *mḥryš* intended in MT, but a homonym meaning "keep silence": misreading the Heb. in that fashion has required the insertion of the negative.

10a. Normally *šḥt* takes a direct obj.; but it is followed by *l-* also in Num 32:15; Deut 32:5.

11a. The GT attests the single word *hysgr*, repeating the *nip'al* (pass.) theme used in v. 7, while MT reads *hysgrny b'ly q'ylh bydw*, where the vb. is *hip'il* (active) with suf.

12a. Here GT or the underlying text may have lost text between the two instances of "And Yahweh said."

b. The MT also answers in a single word (contrast the opening of v. 11), and again offers the *hip'il* of *sgr* while B attests *nip'al*; LT = MT.

c. In vv. 11–12, DJD (245) summarizes the textual situation as follows: "4QSam[b] here presents the fuller, uncorrupted text. Thus in v. 11, where MT has suffered dittography and subsequent further corruption, 4QSam[b] stands with the Old Greek in preserving the more original reading; also here, where B has suffered haplography, 4QSam[b] with MT preserves the more original reading."

13a. Here *anienai* for *ḥdl* is unique to 1 Kingdoms—9:5; 12:23 B; 23:13.

14a. Codex B's *en Maserem en tois stenois* first transliterates then translates what was before it; but that seems not to have been *bmṣdwt*, as in MT: normally in LXX *stenos* renders *ṣr*, and so both transliteration and translation attest *-ṣr-* rather than *-ṣd-*. The evidence is repeated in v. 19 below: there the transliteration is different (*Nessara*), but again attests *-ṣr-*. In both verses, LT reads *Messeram*, so attesting the same text as B. There is evidence in Isa 29:7 of similar confusion between *mṣdth* (M) and *mṣrth* (1QIsa). Codex B attests not *bhrbmdbr* but the very similar *bmdbrbhr*. LT = MT. Here B and LT have different but related additional text: B has *en tē gē tē auchmōdei*; LT has *en tē Kainē eis to oros to auchmōdes*; B's additional "in the arid land" may be a further interpretation of *bmdbr*, already rendered by the normal *erēmō*. Apart from Mic 4:8 (where we find *pyrgos poimniou auchmōdēs* in puzzling correspondence to *mgdl 'dr 'pl*), *auchmōdēs* is found only in 1 Kgdms 23:14, 15, 19; 26:1 (and Ziph occurs in all four verses). The LT's *Kainē* here is also found in B in vv. 15, 16, 18 below, where MT has *ḥršh*, but OG may have read *ḥdšh* ("new").

b. Here LT = B. Their agreement here and regarding the plus after "ephod" in v. 9 above may lend support to MT's *'lhym* here.

15a. The MT has *qāṭal*; but B's *exerchetai* suggests a ptc.

b. The LT has simply "him."

c. B reads not *ḥršh* but *ḥdšh*, and understands it as "Novel."

16a. Is "God" always more original than "Yahweh" in FP? Here LT = MT.

17a. In 2 Sam 3:2–3 (and in 1 Sam 17:13 [MT +]) *mšnh* follows *bkwr* in a listing of a father's sons. The only other instance in Samuel is in the textually questionable 1 Sam 15:9 (in pl.).

19a. Apparently GT has again read *ḥdšh*, as in v. 14.

20a. "Desire" is found only once (Hos 10:10) as an independent noun: elsewhere only in the combination *'wt npš*, as in Deut 12:15, 20, 21; 18:6; 1 Sam 23:20; Jer 2:24.

b. In place of *kekleikasin auton* (B), LT has *apokekleismenoi gar eisin* ("for they have been closed off").

21a. Codex B's *eponesate* ("toiled") may attest not *ḥml* but *ḥlh* ("be sick"), as in 22:8.

22a. Here LT = MT. The MT plus is *wr'w*: the preceding *wd'w* shares consonants with *'wd*.

b. Codex B retroverts to a consonantal text (*mhrh šm 'šr 'mrtm*) not dissimilar to MT (*my r'hw šm ky 'mr*). After these words, LT attests a longer and easier transition than either MT or B: *ky ʾmr šʾwl pn ʿrwm yʿrm hwʾ*. In v. 27 below, *mhrh* is part of the shared text (pointed as a noun, but in the context of a command, it was used also in 20:38).

c. Here B's *mēpote (panourgeusētai)* might suggest *ʾl* for MT's *ʾly* and that MT's *yʿrm* has been repeated. However, in 2 Sam 1:20; 17:16; 20:6, *mēpote* corresponds to *pn*, and in 17:16 follows soon after *mhrh*.

23a. Again LT = MT.

b. Each of the four verbs at the beginning of v. 22 is resumed in v. 23 (MT), provided that we accept that *ʾl-nkwn* alludes back to the earlier *hkynw*.

c. Here B's *exereunan* ("search out") corresponds in the Book of the Twelve and Lamentations (4x) to *tpś*, which differs in just one letter from *ḥpś* (MT).

24a. As in B; but LT translates as "witness, overhearer."

b. The GT attests *bʿrb* rather than *bʿrbh*.

25a. In LT the obj. is "David."

26a. *skepazesthai* corresponds to forms of *str* in 1 Sam 26:1; Isa 28:15; Zeph. 2:3. On the other hand, it is assonant with MT's *nḥpz*.

b. Codex B has *parenebalon*, but LT has *pareplagiazon* ("were going obliquely").

28a. This understanding of *ḥlq* also underlies *meristheisa* in GT; but BDB (325) proposes the homonym "smoothness" as more original.

29a (24:1). This third instance of *en tois stenois* (24:1 LXX) does not follow a transliteration, in accord with 23:14, 19; but the fourth and last does transliterate (24:22 [23 LXX]).

b. *Engaddei* in 24:1 B agrees with MT; however, LT reads only *Gaddi*.

24:2[3]a. Here 24:1 LT's "the hunt[ing ground] of the deer" could retrovert to *ṣydt hʾylym*: a multiple inner-Hebrew confusion with MT's *ṣwry hyʿlym*. At first B's *Eddaiem* appears to attest a very different text; however, *ΕΔΔΑΙΕΜ* and *ΕΛΛΑΕΙΜ* look similar, and so we may be dealing with the remnant of a transcription of a text similar to MT or the text behind LT.

3[4]a. In v. 4 GT, *paraskeuasasthai* means "to prepare oneself." This vb. corresponds to different Heb. at each of its several occurrences and has been a useful workhorse. Both Hebrew and Greek expressions are presumably euphemisms for Saul emptying his bowels.

4[5]a. Verse 5 K is pl., but Q along with GT are sg.

5[6]a. Simple *hoti* corresponds in v. 6 GT to *ʿl ʾšr*.

b. Some Heb. MSS of v. 6, as well as OG, repeat *knp hmʿyl* as in the previous verse. Anarthrous *knp* after *ʾt* is not normal.

6[7]a. Almost always *ḥlylh* is followed by *l-* identifying the one who should not do the action in question. The remainder of the clause (in v. 7 MT) follows in several patterns: the action forsworn is specified most often by *m-* with the inf. (Gen 18:25; 44:7, 17; Josh. 24:16; 1 Sam 12:23; 26:11; 2 Sam 23:17; 1 Kgs 21:3; 1 Chr 11:19) and sometimes by *ʾm + yiqṭōl* (1 Sam 24:6 [7]; 2 Sam 20:20; Job 27:5). There are two differences in the transmission of the single instance in BTH: 2 Sam 23:17 has *yhwh mʿśty* (the other instance of a suf. on the inf. is 1 Kgs 21:3) while 1 Chr 11:19 has *mʾlhy mʿśwt*. Here B is absolutely literal: *Mēdamōs moi para kyriou*. See above on 12:23.

b. Here LT = MT.

7[8]a. This correspondence of *peithein* (v. 8 GT) with *šsʿ* is unique.

b. In fact not *ʿl* but *ʾl*.

c. Here B has *thysai*, but *thanatōsai* appears in LT.

d. This phrase is attested in LT, but at the end of the clause, which suggests secondary revision.

8[9]a. The LT attests a mix of MT and B: *wyṣ' dwd 'ḥry š'wl*.

b. Here LT = B.

9[10]a. Are "the words of people" human words, or everyone's words?

10[11]a. Here B = MT; however, v. 11 LT reads not a second *idou* (after its use in the previous verse), but *kai ge*—either an inner-Greek alteration or attesting *wgm*.

b. Here LT = B. However, *et cogitavi* ("and I thought," Vulg.) may have read the first *w'mr* as the second is pointed in MT.

c. The MT *wtḥs* appears to require *'ynk* as subj., while *kai epheisamēn* (GT) may attest *w'ḥs*.

11[12]a. Unlike B, the LT does attest *w'by*, but apparently as an extension to the predicate (*mšyḥ yhwh*) of the final clause in the previous verse.

b. Here LT = B, apart from the (transitional) *kai patēr mou*.

c. Again LT = B. Both may attest *'nky krty* rather than *ky bkrty*.

d. Codex B appears to attest the more straightforward *krty 't-hknp wl' hrgtyk*.

e. In place of MT's *wpš'*, B has *oude asebeia kai athetēsis*, but LT *oude athetēsis oude asebeia*. Each noun and the related vb. is used elsewhere in Kingdoms for *pš'*.

f. Here B's *desmeueis* (*syndesmeueis* in LT) may attest *ṣrr* rather than *ṣdh* (HRCS, Suppl. 332).

13[14]a. Neither B (*hē parabolē hē archaia*) nor LT (*en parabolē archaia*) is exactly as MT: both read *qdmny* as a true adjective, but in B the phrase is definite while in LT it is indefinite.

b. The GT does not share the symmetry of MT; however, *plēmmeleia* corresponds to *rš'* nowhere else, but only to (the assonant) *m'l* in Joshua, or some form of *'šm* elsewhere.

14[15]a. Here in v. 15 LT = B.

15[16]a. MT points *špṭ* as a vb., while B renders it as a second noun after *dyn*. Also, LT = B.

[5–8] The divergence between the texts at 21:5 (6 GT, MT) may relate to the strangeness of the term *ḥōl*. Only here is it used in the narrative books—in fact, only here in HB, apart from Lev 10:10 and four times in Ezekiel,[24] always as here in contexts where a distinction is made between "sacred" and "profane." When Saul explained to himself David's absence from his own table at new moon, he thought in terms of a different priestly contrast: between "pure" and "impure" (20:26). We cannot know how the practice at Nob concerning the sacred loaves corresponded to the regulation in Lev 24:5–9, where twelve fresh loaves were to be arranged in rows each Sabbath, and normally only priests could eat the old ones removed that day. Indeed, outside this narrative we have no other information about Nob as priestly settlement or town with a holy

24. Ezekiel 22:26; 42:20; 44:23; 48:15.

place.[25] David has requested five, or whatever (v. 3)—one presumes out of those properly available to the priests (v. 6).

Much is opaque about the exchanges between David and the priest. The priest has questioned David's arriving alone (v. 1). Does he thereby articulate the reason for his fear at David's coming, or seek to mask it? David's response in terms of instructions from "the king" may have been deceptively ambiguous: the priest would suppose that David means Saul, while David himself could have King Yahweh in mind.[26] Is David really interested in both food (v. 3) and a significant weapon (v. 8), or does he talk of loaves simply as a device to open the conversation? Or, supposing his interest is really in food, does David only require to raise the question of weapons once he has become aware of the presence at Nob of a nonpriest who is also a leading member of Saul's staff (v. 7)?

Just how Doeg is "restrained" (*neʿĕṣār*) before Yahweh (v. 7 [8]) has led to much speculation, some of it quite extravagant. What could or should an Edomite be doing at a sanctuary of Yahweh? Is his presence there legitimate or illegitimate? Is it a matter of voluntary restraint in pursuit of a vow, or of candidacy for full incorporation into the community of Israel? Or is it involuntary detention? The text appears to give no clues at all to answer any of these questions; in any case it is more sensible to appeal first to the resources that the text does offer. In almost every instance of the *nipʿal* of *ʿṣr* in HB, the subject of "was restrained" is "plague" (*maggēpâ*): 2 Sam 24:21, 25 (//1 Chr 21:22); Num 16:48, 50 (17:13, 15); 25:8; and Ps 106:30. Such plague is always at Yahweh's direction; I suspect that the core text of this group is the story of the plague following David's census in BTH (2 Sam 24//1 Chr 21). Within Samuel–Kings, the restraint of Doeg is the only instance of *ʿṣr nipʿal* apart from the census story and the one other exception: 1 Kgs 8:35 (//2 Chr 6:26) speaks of the heavens as being restrained (from giving rain). There too, Yahweh is responsible for the restraint of the rain. Given how Doeg will act against the priests, it is entirely suitable that he is described in terms appropriate for a pestilential blow: not simply "restrained," but "restrained before Yahweh." It may also be textually significant that another form of the same Hebrew word has just been used (v. 5 [6]) of women being "under restraint" (*ʿăṣurâ*) as far as David's men are concerned? Personal restraint (*mʿṣr*) is commended in a verse from Proverbs (25:28) already cited in our discussion of

25. Elsewhere in HB, Nob is mentioned only in Isa 10:32, at the end of a list of places on the approach to Jerusalem from the north; and in Neh 11:32, in a list of towns inhabited by Benjamin.

26. Polzin 1989: 195, links David's explanation to Jonathan's statement (20:22) that if David needs to go, it is because Yahweh is sending him off. However, sending someone off (*šlḥ piʿel*) is not the same as sending them on a mission with instructions.

1 Sam 3:1: "A city broken into, without a wall, is a man for whose spirit there is no restraint."

[9–15] Two factors give added resonance to the terms in which David restates what the priest says when indicating the whereabouts of Goliath's sword (v. 9): "There is none like it." One fact is that only Samuel says exactly the same, when presenting Saul to the people as their king: "There is no one like him" (10:24). And the other is the close connection between sword and spear and Saul's kingship from beginning (13:22) till the two reports of his death (31:4–5; 2 Sam 1:6). However, there is a further interesting echo. David used Goliath's sword to cut off his head after felling him with his sling and five stones. Now he leads up to his request for the (return of the) sword (v. 8) by asking for precisely five loaves or whatever (v. 3).

With Goliath's sword in hand, David does now explicitly "flee" (v. 10 [11]). Although the priest refers to his former foe as Goliath "the Philistine" rather than Goliath (more precisely) "of Gath," it remains extraordinary that it is precisely to Gath among all of the Philistine cities that David flees. Especially when equipped with such a weapon as Goliath's own sword, he can hardly have hoped to escape detection. Achish's courtiers recognize him as David and describe him (uniquely in HB) as "the king of the land" (v. 11). The only near parallel, the plural "the kings of the land" in Josh 12:1, 7, introduces lists of kings of city-states. The courtiers may think of David as only a local kinglet; however, the expression they use appears prescient of his future greatness. Indeed they recall to their king the chants about David's greater success than Saul's, measured in myriads of Philistine slain (v. 11), and David feels immediately vulnerable and afraid (12). The idiom here of putting someone's words in one's heart (taking someone's words to heart [v. 12]) recurs in HB only in Job 22:22. This is the only point in the whole story of David in which fear is reported of him, although once Jonathan will urge him not to be afraid (23:17).[27]

The wording of the following verse is textually uncertain, and MT stands in curious relationship to Ps 34. In some respects, the version preserved in B appears preferable. Despite its apparent consistency, the regularity of "his eyes . . . his hands . . . his beard" is deceptive. Codex B's possessives are ambiguous (the beard is David's, but the eyes will probably belong to Achish, while the hands could belong to either). The MT seeks to clarify this distinction with its change to "their eyes . . . their hands." "Face" is object of "alter" only in Job 14:20 and in B here. Equally, it is only in MT and the superscription to Ps 34 that "taste" is attested as object of "alter." There are two grounds for giving priority to the Psalm: the syntax of the suffix on "alter" is more straightforward in the

27. On this basis, but without support in ancient texts, RSV rereads *wyr' ky* (23:15) not as "saw that" but as "was afraid because."

superscription;[28] and "taste" is integral to this acrostic poem (each line beginning with the next letter of the Heb. alphabet): "taste (*ṭʿmw*) and see that Yahweh is good" opens the appropriate line in alphabetic sequence (34:8 [9]). On the other hand, *ṭaʿam* does occur once more in 1 Samuel, where David blesses Abigail's "discretion," or possibly "decision" (25:33). Of course the superscription of Ps 34 has David feigning madness before Abimelech, who drives him away, while in 1 Sam 21 it is before Achish. In other respects, the longer text in B may be secondary: "made pretense" may seek to explain "altered his face/taste"; and "drummed on the doors of the city" may be a variant of "fell/scratched on the doors of the gate." The MT stresses the effect of David's actions on his audience ("their eyes . . . their hands"); B tells of his use of his own body ("his eyes . . . his hands . . . his beard").

It could be purely coincidental that, *hthll* in Hebrew has two quite separate meanings: "act madly," as in 1 Sam 21:14, and "give praise," as in Ps 34:3. And yet, given all the other links just noted, this is far from likely to be a coincidence: "lack" (*ḥsr*) is found in the long books of Samuel just once more (1 Sam 21:15 [16]; 2 Sam 3:29), and of Psalms just once more (23:1; 34:10 [11]). David's "craziness" as recognized by Achish is described in a different term (*šgʿ*), used relatively seldom in HB. In 2 Kings 9, one and the same word is used (slightingly) by Jehu's staff (v. 11) of the "crazy fellow" from among the prophets whom Elisha has sent to anoint their master, and also by the watchman in Jezreel (v. 20) of the "craziness" of Jehu's driving. If Jehu could be recognized by his driving, we may ask whether that was (impressively) manic or simply worryingly erratic? Both Deut 28:28 and Zech 12:4 threaten Yahweh's "striking" someone with "craziness"; and in each passage this is associated with both astonishment and blindness. Then Hos 9:7 speaks of the prophet as a fool and "the man of the spirit" as crazy, while Jer 29:26 speaks of every crazy fellow who prophesies being put in the stocks. Is it in fact "straightforward craziness" that Achish detects in David's simulation (1 Sam 21:14–15 [15–16]), or the craziness of a prophet?[29] Or would Achish—would anyone else—have been able to distinguish between different causes of "possession"? Be that as it may, the David who seeks refuge with Saul's enemy from Saul's spear-hurling madness is now seeking, via simulated madness, to protect himself from (well-founded) Philistine accusations. The response of Achish is hardly complimentary to his own staff: far from thanking them for reminding him that David has an anti-Philistine record, he simply queries the need to add another madman to those already around him. The next time David

28. The suffix appears to anticipate the object expressed next. The phraseology in MT is almost identical to that in Ps 34:1 (E: superscription), but there the suffix on the infinitive is subjective, not objective.

29. On David as "prophet," see further below on 1 Sam 25:34; 2 Sam 23:1–7.

takes himself out of Saul's territory to Achish of Gath (1 Sam 27), there is no word of this earlier episode.

[22:1–4] In flight first—and still—from Saul, and now also from Achish, David escapes to a cave in the borderlands between their territories. Typical of such a desperate situation, he is joined there only by his family and by similarly desperate men (vv. 1–2). This cave of Adullam has featured in the older, shorter David story in BTH (near the end in Samuel, but near the beginning in Chronicles and probably also in BTH—2 Sam 23:13//1 Chr 11:15): while there, David is joined by some of his "thirty" chiefs and is overheard longing for water from his home spring at Bethlehem, then under Philistine control. This extended introduction to the older story builds on both the location and the family interest, but reduces the reputation of his "heroes" by calling his associates discontents and debtors, while increasing their number from thirty to four hundred.

David's next move was eastward, near the Dead Sea, to the far side of Judah. The otherwise unknown *miṣpēh mô'āb* could refer to a lookout within Moab (east of the Dead Sea) or a lookout (within Judah) eastward over Moab. If the *mĕṣûdâ* (vv. 4–5) is, or is like, the Masada just west of the Dead Sea of later and continuing fame, it certainly commands a good view into Moab. The king of Moab now grants David's father and mother asylum; and that tradition of good relations between Moab and a Bethlehem family will be related to the story of Ruth (see above, on the opening chapter of Samuel).

[5] Anointed, although in secret, and now leader of his own forces, though outlaws, David is a king in the making. Anointed by a prophet (Samuel), he also has advice volunteered him by a prophet (Gad). David's receipt of prophetic advice, like his ability to inquire successfully of Yahweh (23:1–5), are both themes drawn from BTH—and in both respects Saul is correspondingly deficient (see further on ch. 28). Gad (v. 5) is also known from the older David story. The account of the census in BTH has known him as "Gad, David's seer"; but it is as "Gad the prophet" that he appears here (2 Sam 24:11 MT and 24:19 LT add "the prophet" to the title "seer"). Gad counsels David to move from a prominent position (however apparently secure)—but just where to is unclear: neither a forest called Hareth nor a town called Sareik is otherwise known.

[6–8] David's flight from Saul has taken place in several stages; but only now is Saul reported to have any knowledge of his whereabouts. He himself is holding court at Gibeah, his spear formally in hand, and under a tamarisk tree. The *'ešel* is little known in HB: Abraham planted one in Beer-sheba, where he "called on the name of Yahweh" (Gen 21:33); and according to 1 Sam 31:13, the bodies of Saul and his sons will be buried under one in Jabesh, although 1 Chr 10:12 identifies that tree as an oak (*'ēlâ*). The Greek *aroura* corresponds to *'šl* at each of its three occurrences in HB (see Gen 21:33; 1 Sam 31:13). The main entry (LSJ 245b) records *aroura* simply as "tilled land"; however, the LSJ Suppl. (51b) attests it as also equivalent to the goddess *Gē* (earth); *BA* 347 notes the range of renderings in Tg. and VSS and suggests that the reason for coyness is that in Egypt the tamarisk is sacred to Osiris.

Saul addresses those around him as *bĕnê yĕmînî*. The only other example of this precise pairing (Judg 19:16) forms part of a note that the inhabitants of Gibeah were Benjamites. We noted above (on 9:21) that Saul described himself as a Benjamite. Here, where he is addressing his entourage, the expression is capable of double entendre: "you Benjamites" or "you sons of my right hand." Even his own tribe—even his right-hand men—have failed to keep him up to date. Jonathan used the expression "tip off" (lit., "uncover the ear") three times in ch. 20: he would have expected his father to keep him privily informed (20:2), and he promised to keep David similarly informed (vv. 12–13). Saul now complains to his entourage that none of them is supplying him with intelligence about his son. Keeping open the channels for relevant information is the essence of a good relationship. In BTH, David has used it of his relationship with Yahweh (2 Sam 7:27).

Saul has earlier insulted Jonathan grossly about his parentage (20:30); and now he insults both his staff and his son. Now Jonathan is accused of having "set up" (*hēqîm*) Saul's "servant" against him (v. 8). The other (supposedly "right-hand") "sons" are no better than the "son of Jesse"—Saul has not called him "David" since he fled from court. If they are not already in the pay of the son of Jesse, they must be banking on his future largesse. Fields (*śādôt*) and vineyards (*kĕrāmîm*) have an unpleasant resonance in Samuel and Kings. Samuel has warned his people (8:14) that a king will take the best of them to give his servants. Naboth loses his vineyard (1 Kgs 21) to royal skulduggery. And even closer to home, one of Saul's family, Mephibosheth, will lose his field to a mischievous servant's currying favor with David (2 Sam 16:1–4). "Conspiracy" or "revolt" (*qešer*) is known in many courts and governments. David will suffer from the revolt of one of his sons (2 Sam 15:31); and three of his successors in Jerusalem would be killed in "conspiracies" (2 Kgs 12:21; 14:19; 21:23, 24—all BTH). But within the books of Kings, it is a principal feature of the ever-changing dynasties of northern Israel.[30]

[9–11] The second time Doeg is mentioned, his position is described in a *nipʿal* participle as it was the first time; and *nṣb* here is assonant with *nʿṣr* there. It is natural to suppose from *nṣb ʿl* that Doeg stands in the same relationship to the servants of Saul as these servants to Saul himself (v. 7). However, GT renders the phrase, not by *parestēkōs autō* (as in v. 7) but by *kathestēkōs epi tas hēmionous*—Saul's *hēmionoi* ("asses") make their only other appearance in 1 Kingdoms in 21:7 [8 LXX], where Doeg is introduced as their *nemōn* ("herder"). Elsewhere in Kingdoms, the term renders *prd* or *prdh*, normally of a royal mount (*onos* is the normal rendering for *ʾtwn* or *ḥmwr*, as in 1 Sam 9).

30. See 1 Kings 15:27; 16:9, 16, 20; 2 Kgs 10:9; 15:10, 15, 25, 30.

Doeg responds to Saul's angry challenge by denouncing the priest of Nob for his assistance to "Jesse's son" (vv. 9–10). He goes on to claim eyewitness status ("I saw")—21:7 (8) had reported only his presence at Nob and had offered no information as to whether he was fully aware of what was going on. He gives the priest whom the son of Jesse met at Nob his full name: Ahimelech son of Ahitub, and reports three actions without expressing any evaluation. It appears that the order of his report (v. 10) is climactic: consulted the Deity for him, gave him food, and gave him Goliath's sword. The second and third elements are stated emphatically, with object before verb. It is his first statement, however, that surprises the reader. Indeed, it is Doeg's first claim that may rankle most with Saul. We have not been told that David has sought an oracle; so that element of Doeg's testimony may represent either pure mischief, or merely his own assumption, however natural, and not something he witnessed. We may suppose from Saul's summoning the whole priestly clan to come from Nob (v. 11) that he has already decided Ahimelech's fate before speaking to him.

[12–13] Saul charges the priest with being joint conspirator with Jesse's son (v. 12), just as shortly before (v. 8) he has charged all his entourage with conspiracy (*qšr*). He rehearses the same three details as Doeg; however, he mentions provision of food and sword first, and only then the divine consultation. It appears that Saul's summary of the evidence against the priest is also climactic. Saul is never reported as having successful access to the Deity. When the priest invited him to submit his tactics to divine scrutiny, and he did so (14:37), no answer came. What has now rankled even more with Saul is the idea of the priest's exercising his divinatory role on behalf of a rebellious subject. Saul changes the order of the three elements from Doeg's report and ignores the earlier disjunctive word order. The origins of the sword are passed over, and food and sword are lumped together in one giving. Indeed, in his representation of Doeg's evidence, Saul rewords *ṣydh* as simply "food." And yet Doeg's own term has interesting associations. Sometimes it refers, apparently quite neutrally, to provision for a journey, as in Josh 1:11 and 9:11. However, in Gen 27:3, where Isaac instructs Esau about his blessing, it is something hunted (cognate with the verb *ṣwd*). We may wonder just how far it is intended to play on *mṣwdh* just mentioned (22:4, 5) or on *mṣdwt* (23:14, 19) or *mṣwdh* (24:23) to come. The whole context in these chapters is of hunter and hunted—and Saul and David each play both roles. In game-shooting terms, Saul has the apparent advantage of the larger band of beaters; but it is David who twice symbolically captures Saul (1 Sam 24 and 26). When Doeg saw David at Nob, he recognized him as a lone "stalker." It appears that, when the king reduces *ṣydh* to mere "food," he may have missed some of Doeg's point.

[14] Ahimelech's robust response seeks to defend David's reputation (v. 14) before his own (v. 15). The priest's defense of David (he calls him by his given name, and not "son of Jesse" with Saul and Doeg) makes four brief, balancing, and interrelated points. The first and fourth use the assonant and mutually reinforcing participles *ne'ĕmān* and *nikbād*. The qualities of trust, truth, and reliability stated in the one are recognized and valued in the other: the David who is trusted and reliable among Saul's servants is also honored in his whole household. Then the first and third ground David's reputation for reliability in his attention to Saul's wishes. And finally, the relatedness of second and fourth underscore the more domestic sense of "house[hold]": David as Saul's son-in-law has an intimate relationship to the royal house. The trust, truth, and reliability claimed by the priest are the very antithesis of Saul's charge of revolt and conspiracy.

The outer balancing participles have interesting resonances within Samuel and its main source. In 2 Sam 23:19, 23 (BTH), *nikbād* notes the honored role of Abishai and Benaiah among David's select heroes; and we read in 23:23 that Benaiah is set by David to his *mišma'at*. Whatever exactly this very rare word means (we have rendered it for 1 Sam 22:14 as "bidding"), it is used in Samuel only of Benaiah in relation to David, and of David in relation to Saul.[31] It is very likely that *ne'ĕmān* has also been drawn from BTH: the word plays an important role in 2 Sam 7:16 and 1 Chr 17:23, 24—but at a different point in each version of that chapter (cf. the comment below on 1 Sam 27:12). Yet the priest's use of this term has a terrible resonance for readers of this book. It has been used twice in 1 Sam 2:35 of the trusted, reliable priest, for whom Yahweh will build a secure, reliable house in replacement of Eli's; and Ahimelech is himself a descendant of that same rejected Eli. Samuel has been described as "reliably secured" (*ne'ĕmān*) as prophet (3:20), as something of a down payment on the rejection of Eli's house, and also to Saul himself as *nikbād* (9:6). And Abigail will shortly promise David such a secure, reliable house built by Yahweh (25:28). The priest's words have their own echoes; but these sound all the more striking when uttered all together by a scion of one house that is already operating in borrowed time to another such. It is only in 1 Sam 2:27–36 that we find "father's house" clustered (4x in GT, and 5x in MT) as also in 22:11, 15, 16, 22.

[15] When the priest turns to his own defense, he says nothing about food or sword. As for the charge of consulting the Deity on David's behalf, his response is quite as brilliantly crafted as his defense of David—and at several levels. First of all, it is ambiguous. "Perish the thought" is an implicit negative; but is the priest denying that he has begun divining for David at all, or only denying that he began that day? He could be suggesting that a false claim has been made about his actions that day. He could be suggesting that he has been acting this way for some time—and in complete innocence, because he held David to be a trusted member of Saul's house. What is said is very clever: however the facts of the matter turn out, he cannot be shown to be a liar. And his word choice is equally effective: "I began" (*hḥlty*) and "Perish the thought" (*ḥlylh*) share

31. And the only other reference in HB is Isa 11:14.

most of the same letters and may be even more closely related; and at least the second of these, *ḥālîlâ* ("it would be a profanity," or "perish the thought"), is cognate with the very term *ḥōl* ("common" or "profane"), which has been part of his discussion with David in 21:5–6. It is the business of a priest to be able to distinguish between sacred and profane (Lev 10:10; Ezek 22:26; 44:23); and hence, when a priest says *ḥālîlâ*, he should be recognized as knowing what he is talking about. Moreover, when he protests to the king that "he does not know a matter/thing [*dābār*]," he confirms that David has kept faith with what he has claimed (21:2 [3]) to be Saul's own instruction: "Let no man know anything of the matter." Aware too of all his fellow priests summoned with him, he seeks to exculpate his whole "father's house" (v. 15).

[16–17] Saul does not engage in any discussion of what the priest has said. He is already convinced of his guilt: Saul had not asked whether Ahimelech has conspired against him, but simply why. Sentence of death on the priest and his whole clan is expressed in all brevity. And it is not even to the condemned that Saul explains his verdict, but rather to his own guard who should carry out the sentence: the priests have not only given aid to someone they knew to have been in flight from the king, but have also brought no news of the matter to the king. In the first (1 Sam 9:15) and last (2 Sam 7:27, BTH) instances of "uncovering the ear," Yahweh himself is the provider of privy information to Samuel and David. Where the provider is human, the context is always the relationship between Saul and David: either Jonathan's passing on to David privileged information from his father (1 Sam 20:2, 12–13), or Saul's complaining about others not passing information to him about David (22:8, 17). Saul complains about the priests (v. 17) that "their hand" is with David; however, he now finds that his own guard will not extend "their hand" against the priests—what price they pay for this disobedience is not recorded.

[18–19] Doeg is a foreign trusty. Without family links or a shared tradition to bind him to Saul's people, his loyalty is only to his master. In part of the biblical tradition, the people of Edom, to which he belongs, is a particularly reviled neighbor. Doeg has just heard the priest's definition of reliability in the royal household—which includes attention to the king's wishes—and he does carry out the bloody sentence, apparently in two stages: first those eighty-five males of an age to function as priests, who have appeared before Saul with their chief, and then the whole remaining population (human and animal) of Nob. The description of totality (v. 19) is similar to Samuel's grim instructions about the annihilation of the Amalekites in 15:3.[32] It adds to the scandal: Doeg

32. In BTH (2 Sam 6:19 = 1 Chr 16:3), "from man to woman" (English idiom would prefer "both man and woman") expresses the totality of those who received food from David. Here as elsewhere in the Bible the context is much less benign; and, as here, the list of those under threat is much longer.

is more punctilious over the destruction of priests in Israel than Saul has been with Agag and the Amalekites.

[20–23] But one does get away. The names of Abiathar and Ahimelech are anchored in the list of King David's officials in BTH (2 Sam 8:17//1 Chron 18:16). Since *yeter* means "remnant," *ʾb-ytr* ("father of a remnant") is a particularly suitable name for a sole survivor. When he reaches David, he makes no mention of Doeg but puts on Saul the whole blame for the slaughter of Yahweh's priests. David, however, immediately admits that he was aware not only that the Edomite was present that day but also that he was sure to make a report to Saul. Although there is textual uncertainty over the verb in v. 22b, MT does appear rhetorically effective: Saul has commanded first his guard and then Doeg to "turn and fall on" the priests; however, David concedes that the fatal "turning" has been his own. There is even greater uncertainty over the precise terms in which David undertakes responsibility for Abiathar (v. 23), but none over the fact itself.

This bloody episode resonates with elements from end to end of the books of Samuel. The priests of Nob were of the family of Eli, which had come under terrible threat at the beginning (1 Sam 2). The annihilation of a priestly town just outside Jerusalem by Doeg, who has been restrained "before Yahweh," anticipates the divine envoy of destruction, who stops his terrible work just short of Jerusalem (2 Sam 24). David has coerced the priest at Nob over the showbread just as he will coerce Joab over taking a count of Israel—and then in both cases he accepts responsibility. And yet, despite his own admission and the hint of divine initiative in the matter, it will be convenient to David's progress that Abiathar points his finger at Saul alone.

[23:1–3] Now David is acting independently of both Saul and Achish; he has an armed force loyal to him and is, so to say, an embryonic ruler. The source of David's information about Philistine depredations at Keilah (v. 1) is not provided. Especially if it has come from the townspeople themselves, they do not appear to be particularly grateful to him (vv. 7–13). The drafting of the narrative is fresh. "Plundering the threshing floors" (v. 1) is not at all formulaic. Appropriately, this story of the future king's consulting Yahweh about tackling the Philistines at Keilah draws on and anticipates two narratives at the beginning of BTH. "And Philistines were making war on" are the very first words of the synoptic material in Samuel (1 Sam 31:1); and David's first campaign after fully becoming king of Israel also involves double consultation of the Deity (2 Sam 5:19, 23). The third and only other instance of the phrase *pělištîm nilḥāmîm* (1 Sam 28:15) is part of the report on Saul's desperate attempt at En-dor to secure divine guidance. That confirms two points: both that this linkage is significant, and that Doeg's report of the priest at Nob's seeking divine guidance for David has particularly incensed Saul.

[4–5] Double consultation of the Deity may anticipate 2 Sam 5 (BTH); but the statement following his second asking (v. 4),[33] that Yahweh does answer him, serves to align David explicitly with Samuel (1 Sam 7:9) over against Saul (14:37; 28:6, 15). In the older David story (2 Sam 8:6, 14),[34] it is Yahweh who saves David. The story of Saul maintains this tradition; positively, he gives credit to Yahweh; when his early detractors asked (1 Sam 10:27), "In what way will this fellow save us?" they spoke with greater prescience than was first apparent. What is said here about David himself as the savior (vv. 2, 5) is quite unusual.

[6–9] While the report to Saul (v. 7) about David's presence in Keilah is obviously after David's campaign there (vv. 1–5), it is less clear how the arrival of Abiathar with the ephod (v. 6) relates chronologically with what precedes. But it is easier to see how it relates to what follows. The reported arrival in David's camp of the surviving priest with the ephod implies that Saul must be drawing on his own judgment when he deduces that God has turned David over to him. Whether that transaction is stated in commercial (GT) or legal (MT) terms, Saul describes David as in some sense God's property. While describing a town or wall as being furnished with gates and bar or bar and gates (v. 7) is common enough in HB, it occurs nowhere else in Samuel.[35]

The ephod is used in David's next inquiry of Yahweh (vv. 9–12), as it will be again in 30:7; and the note about the arrival of this sacred object (v. 6), even if secondary to the drafting of vv. 1–5, may be intended to suggest that the ephod was also used in the first inquiry.[36]

[10–12] Be that as it may, the second two-stage dialogue between David and Yahweh has a quite different flavor from what goes before. In the first case, Yahweh's answer is marginally longer than David's opening question (v. 2), and Yahweh responds at still greater length (v. 4) to a follow-up question, which is not cited. However, in this next case, David—at least in MT[37]—poses two much more detailed questions; and to each of these Yahweh responds in a single Hebrew word: "He'll-come-down" (v. 11) and "They'll-hand-over" (v. 12). Such a one-word response is unique in Judges and Samuel.

[13–15] The opening statements of the next subparagraph (vv. 13–15) sit rather oddly together. When Saul learns that David has escaped from Keilah, and that he and his men are roaming where they will, he ceases going out

33. The phrase used for "repeating" the action (*wysp ʿwd*: [lit.] "and added again") also borrows from 2 Sam 5:22.

34. As also in 1 Sam 11:13; 14:23, 39; 17:47; 19:5; 2 Sam 22:3, 28.

35. Both 2 Chr 8:5 and 14:6 are Chronicles plus in BTH context.

36. There are similar issues in 2 Sam 5–6 about the relatedness of ark and consultation of Yahweh.

37. In B, there is only one lengthy question and one one-word answer.

in pursuit (v. 13), but only for a time: not only shall we find that much the same will have to be reported again (27:4), but more important, Saul is already searching for him in the very next verse (23:14)! We cannot have confidence in our reading of David's residences (v. 14). The principal Greek versions differ from each other and differ from MT. The nomenclature in MT is both similar to and different from the listing of Judah's towns in Josh 15:20–62. These are grouped in four areas: the third area is the hill country between Hebron and Jerusalem (vv. 48–60), and the fourth is the desert alongside the Dead Sea (vv. 61–62). There is no surprise at all that David lives in *mĕṣādôt* ("fortresses") in the desert (1 Sam 23:14), for the En-gedi (*ʿên-gedî*) area boasts many Masada-like rock outcrops. That he should next live "in the hill country in the desert of Ziph" may imply a classification different from Joshua 15: there the location of Ziph is set not in the hill country but in the area to the south (*negeb*, in the Negeb) of it—presumably "the desert of Ziph" is the parched area toward the east and the Dead Sea. That he lived first in one and then in another corresponds to "they moved about where they moved about" (v. 13).

Saul is in competition with the Deity as well as with David. The last words of v. 14 and the first of v. 15 are opposite sides of the same coin: no gift is made of David by the divine giver; and David is quite aware of what Saul is doing. Since he sees and knows the threat, David may well be finding his situation precarious; however, there is neither ancient textual witness nor logical requirement to read *wyrʾ* ("and he saw," v. 15) as if it were *wyyrʾ* ("and he was afraid") with RSV and McCarter.[38]

[16–18] Though father Saul cannot find David, son Jonathan can and does (v. 16). Strengthening someone's hand is a regular Hebrew idiom for encouraging them; but nowhere else in HB does such encouragement come "in" or "by" God. At their previous encounter (20:42), Jonathan's farewell words to David were that both had sworn by Yahweh that Yahweh would be between them and between their descendants forever. He now concedes for the first time that David will enjoy what is normally the right of a monarch's firstborn son: David and not Jonathan will be king over Israel. At his next meeting with David (24:20), Saul will confirm that this is also his understanding. Jonathan sees his own new role as *mišneh* (v. 17), the term used in 2 Sam 3:3 and 1 Sam 17:13 (MT plus) for a second son. It is the precariousness of such a role[39] that has him both encouraging David and seeking to bind David in a formal covenant before Yahweh. If there is a distinction between (simply) swearing and making a covenant, then the latter is the more formal. As the balance between the two men

38. The verb *wyrʾ* has David as subj. again in the very similar 26:3, 5. Just how he "sees" is another matter.

39. In many monarchic societies, the succession of one brother was followed quite quickly by the elimination of the others.

shifts, greater effort is required on the part of the weaker to maintain stability. By noting that their covenant is enacted "before Yahweh," the narrator may be suggesting that even before Saul's death, Jonathan is anticipating the initiative of the elders of Israel afterward (2 Sam 5:3). With Jonathan's departure to his house (v. 18), he also departs from the action of the book. He will be mentioned next (31:2) only as dying at Philistine hands, next to his father.[40] Not that his death will mark the end of interest in him. Quite apart from David's memorable elegy, Jonathan's household and his (re)burial will continue to occupy the new king in 2 Samuel.

[23:19–24:1] Jonathan's last words before leaving the action of the narrative include the promise that his father will not find David (v. 17). He himself has accepted that David will be next king of Israel. However, even if part of his father has anticipated that outcome, another part is unwilling to give up and submit to his fate without a struggle. That part of Saul also enjoys the continuing support of at least some of his subjects. What the people of Keilah would do, even though they have been delivered from the Philistines by David, the people of Ziph now do: offer to hand David over to Saul (vv. 19–28). Jonathan has withdrawn to his house; but the people of Ziph resume the key word *str* ("hiding"), which he first introduced (19:2): they report that David is still practicing Jonathan's advice to keep his whereabouts "secret."

There are two preliminary—and possibly related—critical issues. One is that many of the details of this story are textually uncertain. And the other is that much of the wording reappears in 26:1–5, although there is it David who checks Saul's position for sure rather than Saul checking David's. Mention of the Maon desert no less than three times in 23:24b–25 appears to be an insistent demand that the reader remain aware of the location of the action. Although Jeshimon reappears in Numbers, Isaiah, and Psalms,[41] Hachilah is unique to 1 Sam 23:19 and 26:1. Saul thanks the Ziphites (23:21); but the texts divide over the precise terms in which he expresses his gratitude, and each resonates with other parts of the narrative. According to MT, he blesses the Ziphites for having compassion on him (*ḥmltm*); and Saul is casting himself rather pitifully as a comparator with Agag, on whom he himself took pity (15:9), or with Mephibosheth, whom David would spare (2 Sam 21:7) from a similarly grisly fate. However, GT attests *ḥlytm* (lit., "were sick"), and has Saul compare the people of Ziph in the south of Judah favorably and in contrast with his right-hand men from Benjamin (22:8).[42] Ironically, it is a renewed report of a Philistine attack that

40. Reminiscent of Samuel, who departs for his home in 15:34, has one brief nonspeaking role in ch. 19, dies in 25:1, and is summoned back from the grave in ch. 28.

41. See Num 21:20; 23:28; Isa 43:19, 20; Pss 68:7 (8); 78:40; 106:14; 107:4—cf. *yěšîmôt* in Ps 55:15 (16)?

42. McCarter also links 23:21 with 22:8; but proposes emending *ḥlh* to *ḥml* there.

saves David from further harassment by Saul. The expression "against the land" (v. 27) recalls how the staff of Achish described David as "the king of the land" (21:11), and also Abner's question (2 Sam 3:12), "Whose is the land?" At the beginning of this chapter, David has offered protection against the Philistines; now Saul attends to this proper duty of a king.

[24:2–7] The books of Samuel, and especially 1 Samuel, report many situations from two or more perspectives. The downfall of the house of Eli is predicted twice. There are several apparently culminating stages in Saul's becoming king. Saul comes twice under the influence of a band of prophets. David is freshly introduced twice to Saul. Saul's death is twice narrated. But the reports in 1 Samuel 24 and 26 of David's sparing Saul's life when he has the opportunity to take it are in a class of their own. Despite offering the longest examples of such multiple narratives, they are also the most similar to each other. Of all the possible comparators, the briefer stories in 1 Samuel 10 and 19 of Saul and a band of prophets come closest. However, these are located at some distance from each other, and each has a distinct role to play in the larger narrative. At the same time it is relatively straightforward to argue that the second depends on the first, and also that it plays something of a midrashic role: it explores and seeks to answer some of the puzzles in the earlier, shorter story. What are the physical manifestations of "acting the prophet"? And what exactly does the popular saying "Is Saul also among the prophets?" mean? Such comparison with 1 Sam 10 and 19, however, simply invites contrast.

First Samuel 24 and 26 occupy (compete for?) almost the same space in the larger narrative and are separated by only one (though itself quite extended) episode. And that episode, concerning David, Nabal, and Abigail, both separates them and is also intimately related to them both. When they are considered in isolation, it is much harder to decide which version of the sparing of Saul depends on which: readers of Samuel have debated that question for generations. And yet the simple critical conclusion that one is almost certainly primary in the narrative and the other secondary is underscored by two further and neighboring pairings. One of these is much briefer: the double notification of the death of Samuel (in 25:1, immediately after ch. 24; and in 28:3, one short episode after ch. 26). It seems reasonable to suppose that what has prompted the resumption (in 28:3) or secondary anticipation (in 25:1) of this notice of death and burial is the insertion of a block of new material, including a fresh version of the sparing of Saul and the innocence of David. The other is the double report of David's seeking sanctuary from Saul with the Philistine Achish of Gath: first and briefly in 21:10–15, then at greater length in chs. 27–29. The resultant matching panels are reinforced by contrasts, such as David's successful pair of double inquiries of Yahweh (23:1–5, 6–14) and Saul's total failure to achieve communication with Yahweh by any method (28:3–25).

A lot of detail is provided in the opening verses of ch. 24 to locate this incident quite precisely (24:1 = 24:2 BHS, etc.). On the basis of good intelligence, David is tracked down by Saul at the head of a large choice force. The description of the force cannot fail to remind us of the campaign at the beginning of his reign (13:2). There Saul "chose" three thousand out of Israel to deal with a Philistine threat. Here, in a striking reversal, he gives up pursuit of Philistines to lead a force, again of three thousand, "choice" out of all Israel, to hunt David. And the David he is hunting has recently liberated Keilah from the common Philistine foe (23:1–5)!

But the roles of hunter and hunted become immediately reversed when each chooses the same large cave for a different purpose. In this defined space inside the cave, it is David effectively now who has not only the larger force, but also the benefits of intelligence and surprise. David's men interpret Saul's off-guard position as a heaven-sent opportunity. Their words have often been translated as the realization of an earlier divine promise: Yahweh told you once that he would put your enemy into your hand—and now he has done so. It has quite as often been noted that such a divine promise has never been brought to our attention by the narrator. And so readers have rightly wondered whether David's men in the cave are seeking to persuade him, as Nathan and Bathsheba would do later when he is on his deathbed (1 Kgs 1), of something that had never been said. It could be so; and yet *ʾāmar* (*qāṭal*) need not refer to past time—and very often does not so refer, especially within the stock introduction *kōh ʾāmar yhwh* ("Thus says the Lord"), where the "perfect" is called "prophetic," or even "performative." From such a perspective, the men may have been urging David to recognize the facts in front of his face: seeing Saul delivered defenseless before them should be tantamount to hearing a divine utterance.

Urged by his men to do to Saul whatever seems good to him, David does approach the king . . . and cuts off the edge of his robe, but immediately regrets his action. Cutting the royal robe has sometimes been interpreted as a symbolic killing, or at least a symbolic castration of the king. The terms in which his action and also his regret are stated have, each of them, a unique link with one other passage in Samuel (and indeed the whole HB). David's heart would strike him again when the results of his ill-considered census are brought to him (2 Sam 24:10)—and only in these two passages in HB is *lēb* ("heart") the subj. of *hikkâ* ("strike"). Just as the later counting of his people (though incited by Yahweh) is a foolish sin, so taking advantage of Saul in the cave (though offered the chance by Yahweh) is something to regret. The kingdom is a gift long promised to David, but it should not be taken by him. And his deliberate cutting of the edge of Saul's robe recalls its apparently more accidental tear when grasped by Samuel (1 Sam 15:27). In only these two passages is a robe (*mĕʿîl*) said to have an edge (*kānāp*). Samuel has interpreted that earlier rending of the robe as signifying that Saul would shortly lose the kingdom to someone better than himself: David will shortly (24:10) reject the claim of those who say he is seeking what is bad for Saul; and Saul will concede (v. 18) that David has repaid good for his own bad. It is far from clear what is meant by David "ripping apart" his men (v. 7): is it that he "tore into" them in anger? Or divided them into rival parties?

[8–15] David's presentation of his case to Saul occupies the whole middle third of the narrative; it represents the only part of the story in which this account in ch. 24 is significantly longer, and more fully developed, than that in ch. 26. He bows low before Saul, as never reported before—though he did prostrate himself before Jonathan (20:41). David then tells Saul what has passed between his men and himself in the cave; he produces the piece cut from Saul's robe as evidence, not of an assault begun on the (trappings of) kingship, but of his innocence and good faith (v. 11). At this point we can detect an interesting shift in David's account of his actions.[43] At the time when he cut the garment (v. 5), his heart struck him. From the parallel at the end of the books of Samuel (2 Sam 24:10), we might deduce that he regretted having done—or having been about to do—something that was wrong. However, when he comes to explain cutting the garment to Saul, he anticipates the second part of the selfsame verse in the census story to make a quite different point. After numbering his people, he expresses the wrong done in three terms: sin, guilt, and folly. Now the garment fragment "in his hand" is produced as evidence of "an absence of wrong or of rebellion in his hand": he has not sinned against Saul. Here the triple description (wrong, rebellion, sin) is applied to disclaim any mischief. Indeed, if there is any "malice aforethought," it pertains to Saul, who has been lying in wait for him.

And this leads to another relevant intertext, suggested in turn by a further significant pairing, this time of the verb "lie in wait for" (*ṣdh*), which is unique to 1 Sam 24:11 and Exod 21:13. The law in the so-called Covenant Code determines death as the penalty for striking someone fatally (Exod 21:12), and then continues with a limiting clause (v. 13): "If he did not 'lie in wait,' but the Deity let him fall into his hand, I shall appoint for you a place to which he should flee." David's men have as good as urged him that Yahweh has let Saul fall into his hand: although already in the cave, they have not been lying in wait for Saul. David now points out to Saul that in fact matters are quite the other way round: that they are in flight from him, and he has happened on their hideaway. On the other hand, David may have been concerned lest their hiding in the cave could

43. Campbell (1:252) explains the tension between David's actions and words inside the cave and his explanation to Saul outside the cave in terms of different earlier versions combined by the storyteller. However, he does not note the wider links within Samuel, just as he later overlooks (255) that David has already been anointed by Yahweh.

be misrepresented as insidious. In any case, he has no interest in adding to his requirement of safe refuge. More important still: Saul is not just any chance victim—and not even just any enemy put in David's way. Saul is Yahweh's anointed (v. 6); and David, already himself anointed of Yahweh, has every interest in promoting the sanctity of that status.

David's self-defense before the king includes a further variant (v. 11) of the pairing "know and see," which we have found characteristic of 1 Samuel. In this case, the "seeing" is much anticipated. The complaint against David (as quoted by David) has been introduced by "Look!" (v. 9), and David's own answer begins the same way (v. 10). Saul is invited to realize that his eyes have already "seen" the evidence that exonerates David. If this is a straightforward past tense, as it is regularly rendered, then David is calling on Saul to recognize that he can only be where he now is if he has first been in the cave when Saul was there. The call to the human king to "see" is reinforced at the beginning of v. 11, in advance of the familiar "know and see"; and David concludes his appeal by calling on the divine judge to "see and settle" the case in his favor (vv. 12, 15).

After defending his own innocence before his king, David now appeals to Yahweh against Saul. The case should be taken up by Yahweh (v. 12a), but no action taken by David (v. 12b). Saul is not directly accused, but the saying quoted (v. 13a) is a cap that fits; yet David will not take action (v. 13b). The king's expedition against David is absurdly out of proportion: dead dogs and single fleas do not warrant even a search party, let alone a full-blown hunt (v. 14). And the appeal concludes (v. 15) with an extended restatement of the opening statement (v. 12a). Although it is masked in the translation above, this peroration opens and closes with the first word of v. 12: David's call to Yahweh to *špṭ*. Judging in the fullest sense is not simply discriminating neutrally "between" the merits of one claimant and another. Once the truth has been "seen," the complaint has to be upheld; and especially when the injured party has less means than the wrongdoer, "bringing justice" has to involve protection "out of [his] hand" (v. 15).

1 Samuel 24:16–22 (17–23)

16 And it came to be,
  as David was finishing
    [speaking] these words *speaking* to Saul,
and Saul said,
  "Is this your voice, [my] son[a] David?"[b]
And Saul lifted up his voice
and wept.
17 And [he] *Saul* said to David,
  "You are [more] right [than I] *beyond me*;

for you, you have dealt me what is good,
but I, I have dealt you what is ill.
18 And you, you have related [to me] today
what good you have done with me,
how Yahweh delivered me into your hand,
but you did not slay me.
19 And supposing someone find his enemy *in distress*,
and send him off in a good way,

Yahweh too will requite him good,	Yahweh, he will repay you good against this day
As you have acted today.	as you have acted to me.

20 Now then, look, I *myself*[a] know
that king you surely will be,
and the kingdom of Israel will come up into your hand.
21 Now then, swear to me by Yahweh
that you will not cut off[a] my seed after me
and that you will not destroy[a] my name from my father's house."
22 And David swore to Saul,
and Saul went to his [house[a]] *place*;
and David and his men,[b] they went up to the fortress.[c]

16[17]a. The v. 17 GT *teknon* does not represent the suf. "my" in MT's *bny*.

b. Here B = MT. The LT completes the exchange, suggesting *wyʾmr dwd ʿbdk hmlk* ("and David said, 'Your servant, O king.'")

20[21]a.Here GT *egō* attests *ʾnky*.

21[22]a. Codex B may attest the verbs in reverse order.

22[23]a. Here LT = MT.

b. The closing formula resembles 23:18, with an implied disjunctive ("but") before the second party: person's name before *qāṭal* vb.

c. Before the translation *stenēn*, *Messara* is yet a third transliteration—after *Maserem* (23:14) and *Nessara* (23:19). Only here do B and LT share the same transliteration; however, LT's *eis Messara tēn stenēn* appears more authentic than *eis tēn Messara stenēn* in B.

[16–19] The narrator's opening words ("as David was finishing") appear to underscore that David has made rather a long speech. Codex Aleppo has a blank line here, and not at 25:1. It seems banal to suggest that Saul is really checking David's identity, unless he is simply playing for time. We may say "Is it really you?" when we have not seen someone for a long time; but that too is inappropriate here. I suggest two bases for an interpretation of the king's words. The first is that listening to someone's voice is a common idiom for paying attention to what they have to say. The second is that Saul's response to what David has had to say is to raise his voice—and weep. Only one character in all of BTH weeps: Huldah interprets the weeping of Josiah as repentance

(2 Kgs 22:19). And that fits the situation here too. Saul like Josiah is coming to terms with an awful reality.

No one else in the pages of the Hebrew Bible utters Saul's first words of response, "Is this your voice?"[44] The terms in which Saul completes his question, "my son David," are no less interesting. Two obvious remarks can be offered: he is replying in kind to David, who has addressed him as "my father" (v. 11); and David after all is his son-in law. But it is also true—and it may be more significant—that up to this point Saul has always used "my son" to refer to Jonathan, the crown prince (1 Sam 14:39, 40, 42; 22:8), and that he will never do so again. This same Jonathan has recently described himself as the second son (23:17). Saul and Jonathan may not be in contact with each other; but their words to David complement each other. Saul's speech begins by calling David "my son" for the first time; it ends by talking quite explicitly about David's becoming king over Israel.

Saul concedes David's whole case. David has been suitably oblique about charging the king with being *rāšāʿ* (v. 13); although the term is used nontechnically of the "wicked" person, it is also used forensically of the "guilty" person. And the king is responsible for justice. However, the king, as judge, is quite direct in pronouncing his verdict: it is David who is "in the right" or "innocent" rather than himself. The term *ṣādîq* is the juridical opposite to *rāšāʿ*. This "judgment" by Saul has its closest biblical parallel in Judah's words about his daughter-in-law Tamar (Gen 38:26). The similarity does not lie just in the words of the verdict, but also in the nature of the evidence that leads to the verdict. It is when items of their personal property are produced that Saul, like Judah, is persuaded of the innocence of the one they have been considering as guilty. In recognizing the articles, they have to admit (at least to themselves) the full circumstances in which these have come into the hands of the accused.

In explanation of his verdict, Saul first summarizes his grounds (v. 17b). Once more *gāmal* is used in the narrative of 1–2 Samuel, of the recompense that David offers but Barzillai seeks to turn down (2 Sam 19:37). The verb is found mostly in poetic contexts, which makes "render" or "deal" appropriate in English. Saul's words here echo the psalmist's hope in Ps 18:20–21 (21–22) = 2 Sam 22:21–22). The word is also used in Gen 50 of the three-way transaction between Joseph, his brothers, and the Deity. Then Saul rephrases the evidence that David has provided him (vv. 18–19): Yahweh has put Saul in David's hands, but he did not take advantage; anyone finding their enemy would finish him off, but David did not. Next, Saul addresses the issue David has raised, first with his own men (v. 6) and then with Saul (v. 10): in response to David's not

44. Saul repeats his own exact words in 26:17; but otherwise the nearest comparison is in Gen 27:22, 24.

acting against the anointed of Yahweh, Saul declares that he is fully aware that David will become established as king of Israel.

[20–22] Saul finally comes to his plea. Jonathan has earlier sought from David his sworn protection when Yahweh would remove all of David's enemies (20:15). And more recently the king's son has achieved a covenanted declaration that he would be second to David (23:17–18). Saul now requests an oath from David that he will not institute a purge of Saul's whole house: it is a man's descendants who preserve his name. The fact that he begs David to swear not to "cut off" his "seed" or descendants gives greater credence to the suggestion that the earlier "cutting" of the hem of his cloak was actually perceived by Saul as a symbolic castration. The final words of his plea concern the elimination of his name from his "father's house," echoing Samuel's early declaration to him (9:20). David does so swear (24:22a). The irony in this desperate appeal by Saul is that he himself has earlier listened to Jonathan's "voice" and sworn solemnly to him that David would not be put to death (19:4–6). He must have hoped that also in this matter David would continue to render him good for evil. As for David, despite Saul's declarations, he takes himself and his men to the protection of the stronghold (24:22b).

1 Samuel 25–2 Samuel 3
End of Saul, Response of David

With the departure of Jonathan to his house and the death of Samuel, in 1 Sam 25–30 the cast of Israel's leaders is reduced to only David and Saul, and Saul has just declared unambiguously that he knows (what we readers also know) that David will become king. We should remind ourselves that the authors of 1 Samuel are bound by the facts of the tradition they have inherited: Saul with Jonathan and others of his sons were killed in a battle with Philistines at the north end of the central highlands (1 Sam 31, BTH). David had previously led Saul's forces, but was not part of the defeat on Mount Gilboa; thus he was available to be approached by Israel's representatives and to become their new king (2 Sam 5, BTH). Neither could Saul be killed by David; nor could he be succeeded by his son and expected heir.

After anointing David, Samuel has barely impinged on David's story. He has had no role within the older story of David as king; and with his death, this great figure who has dominated the first half of 1 Samuel is now fully removed from the national scene. Following his burial, David (whether he has been present there or not) heads south. Already in ch. 24, David has chosen not to take even an apparently heaven-sent opportunity to acquire the kingship there and then. And already in their notice of Samuel's death (25:1b), the authors of 1 Samuel are distancing the king-to-be from the northern locus of Saul's demise, placing him closer to Hebron, in the southern highlands, where Israel's elders will find him in their quest for a new king. The preparations for David's innocent succession to Saul are now in place, including a clear suggestion of why he did not fight alongside Saul and his sons against the common enemy on Gilboa. In short, the narrative could have proceeded directly from 1 Sam 25:1 to the beginning of the older and still normative tale in 1 Sam 31. And it may once have done so. What we read in 1 Sam 25–30 further demonstrates David's innocence in the matter of Saul's death. It is made plain that this is his own deliberate choice (ch. 26); but the external circumstances are also laid out that drove him still deeper into the south (chs. 27, 29–30). This section also further demonstrates Saul's total unsuitability to be king of Israel (ch. 28).

However, David and Saul are far from the only principal characters in the final chapters of 1 Samuel. The first (added) quarter of 1 Samuel opens with the story of Hannah; the last similarly opens with the story of Abigail (ch. 25). Several features or scenes in the chapters that follow are doublets of material we have already read. David will have Saul in his power once again. David escapes once again from Saul to Achish in Gath. The contrast is further explored between David, who can successfully consult his God, and Saul, who cannot. In the return to these topics, the opportunity has been taken to rework some themes, but also to heighten our anticipation of Saul's end and David's emergence as king over Israel. The role of Jonathan is not further developed in this context. There is also teasing ambiguity over whether David does or does not participate in the national celebration of the funeral for Samuel. "All Israel" assembles for it; and David moves southward from the fortress after it. But we are left to assume that Saul leads the mourning and to wonder whether David is there at all.

Each of the first two sections marked in CL opens with a report of Samuel's death and burial, which effectively also forms a bracket round chs. 25–27. And the second division, placed just before the end of ch. 30, draws attention to the new theme, made fully explicit in a short paragraph (30:26–31): David's cultivation of the elders of Judah. The presents that David sends to the leaders around Hebron set the scene for a new development in this early story of Israel's kings: the distinct identity of Judah. The Book of Two Houses had located the split between Judah and Israel later, following the death of Solomon (1 Kgs 12//2 Chr 10). The books of Samuel locate the antecedents of this split at, and even just before, the beginnings of David's royal power. (No separation between 1 and 2 Samuel is marked in CL: the next blank line follows 2 Sam 3:5.)

The main divisions in CL map less well in 2 Samuel than in 1 Samuel on the structural and developmental divisions we have detected. Second Samuel 1–4 not only lies between 1 Sam 31 (BTH) and 2 Sam 5–8 (BTH) but is also in itself a clearly unified block of text. It begins and ends with death meted out to messengers who think they are bringing good news to David, whether about the death of Saul or about the murder of one of his surviving sons. It also includes David's elaborate elegy over Saul and Jonathan, and his shorter notice of the murdered Abner. The link that David makes with Nabal as he mourns Abner provides just one of many unmissable connections between 2 Sam 1–4 and 1 Sam 25–30. The fact that the messenger who brings Saul's regalia to David is an Amalekite (2 Sam 1), when David has just been avenging himself on the Amalekite people (1 Sam 30), is another. And these thematic connections are underscored by numerous significant links in terminology.

The heightening of tension and expectation throughout 1 Sam 25–2 Sam 4 is very effective. We have noticed in 1 Sam 25–30 how several already-familiar topics are revisited, and the movement toward Saul's death is accordingly slowed. Given the many links between 1 Sam 25–30 and 2 Sam 1–4, it is likely that David's two-stage progress toward kingship over Israel after Saul's death is also part of a later reshaping of the material, and not integral to the first draft of 1–2 Samuel. Because CL makes a break at the end of 2 Sam 3 but not after ch. 4, we shall comment on 2 Sam 4 with what follows.

1 Samuel 25:1–28:2 David Separates from Saul

1 Samuel 25:1–26:9

1 And Samuel died,
and all Israel were[a] gathered,
and they mourned for him
and they buried him at his house at Ramah.
And David rose
and went down to the desert of [Paran] *Maan*.[b]

2 And there was a man in Maon,[a]
and his [activity] *flock*[b] was in Carmel;
and the man was very great,
and he had a flock of three thousand and a thousand goats;
and it came to be in shearing[c] his flock in Carmel.
3 And the name of the man[a] was Nabal,
and his wife's name was Abigail.[b]
And [the] *his* wife was good of sense and *very good*[c] [fair] of appearance;
but the man was hard and evil in deeds,[d]
and [he] *the man* was [as his heart] currish.[e]
4 And David heard in the desert
that Nabal was shearing his flock.
5 And David sent ten lads,
and [David] said to the lads,
"Go up to Carmel
and come to Nabal
and bid him well in my name;
6 and say thus:[a]
'For [life] {*all*} *time*.[b]
And you, peace; and your house, peace; and all that you have,[c] peace.
7 Now then, *look* I have heard

that your shepherds	that you have shearers.[a]
are now shearing for you who	Now the shepherds that are yours

have been with us in the desert.
We have not shamed them;
and nothing has been counted[b] to them all the days of their being in Carmel.

8 Ask your lads
and let them tell you,
and may [the[a]] *your* lads find favor in your eyes,
for upon a good day have we come.
Be sure to give
what your hand finds [to your servants and[b]] to your son David.'"
9 And [David's] *the*[a] lads came,
and they spoke to Nabal according to all these words in David's name[;
and they rested].
10 And Nabal *upped*[a]
and answered David's servants
and said,
"Who is David?
And who is Jesse's son?
Today servants have multiplied
who are breaking away each from his master[s[b]].
11 And shall I take my food and my [water] *wine*[a] and my slaughtering*s*
which I have slaughtered[b] for [my shearers] *those shearing my*
sheep,[c]
and shall I give them to men
of whom I do not know
where they are from?"
12 And David's lads turned about[a] on their way
and returned
and came
and reported to [him] *David*[b]
according to [all[c]] these words.
13 And David said to his men,
"Each of you, gird on his sword."
[And they girded on each of them his sword;
and David too girded on his sword;[a]]
and there went up after David some[b] four hundred men;
and two hundred, they settled by the equipment.
14 And to Abigail wife of Nabal one [lad[a]] from the lads reported, saying,
"Look, David sent messengers from the desert
to bless our lord
and he [screamed at/preyed on] *turned away from*[b] them.
15 And the men have been very good to us
and [we] *they* have not [been] shamed us,[a]
and we have not counted anything (as missing)
all the days we [have moved about] *were*[b] with them
And as we were in the field[.

16 T]*they* have been a wall close by us both night and also day,
all the days we were with them, feeding the flock.
17 Now then, know
and see
what you should do,
for the ill toward our lord and upon all his house is complete,
while he is too much a son of no use[a]
to speak[b] to him."
18 And Abigail made speed
and took two hundred loaves and two skins of wine and five sheep prepared
and five measures[a] of parched grain and a hundred bunches[b] of raisins
and two hundred lumps of pressed figs,
and she put them on the donkeys.
19 And she said to her lads,
"Pass on before me;
look, I am coming behind you."
But to her husband Nabal she did not report.
20 Now she was riding on her donkey
and going down under cover[a] of the mountain;
and look, David and his men were going down to meet her,
and she came on[b] them.
21 And David, he said,
"[Surely it was falsely] *In fairness*[a] *it was unjustly* that I looked after everything
belonging to this fellow in the desert;
and there was not anything counted {missing} of all that was his,
and he has returned me ill instead of good.
22 So may God do to [the enemies of[a]] David,
and so may he go on doing,
if I leave remaining of all
that is [his[b]] *Nabal's,*
till the morning, a pisser on the wall."
23 And Abigail saw David,
and she made speed
and came down from her donkey,
and she fell in face of[a] David on her face,
and she did obeisance *to him*[b] on the ground[.
24 And she fell] on his feet,
and she said,
"Mine [my very own[a]] my lord is [the] *my* guilt.
Be sure to let your servant speak in your ears,
and hear the words of your servant.

25 Let my lord be sure not to put his heart to this man of no good, [upon Nabal,[a]]
for as his name so is he:
Fool is his name
and Folly attends him.
And I, your servant, I did not see [my lord's[b]] *your* lads
whom you sent.
26 Now then, my lord,
as Yahweh lives and by the life of your own self,
as Yahweh has held you back
from entering on [blood(guilt)] *innocent blood*[a]
and saving your hand for you,[b]
now then let your enemies and those who are seeking[c] ill for my lord
become as a fool/Nabal.[d]
27 And now *take the* [this] blessing
which your servant has brought to my lord,
[let it be given] *and give it*[a] to the lads [moving about at my lord's feet] *standing near*[b] *my lord.*
28 Lift away for sure the rebellion of your servant;
for Yahweh will certainly make for my lord an established house,
for [it is Yahweh's wars which my lord] *my lord's war Yahweh*[a] is fighting,
and ill shall not be found in you [from your days] *ever.*[b]
29 And someone arose[a]
to pursue you
and to seek your very life,
but the life of my lord was bundled up in the bundle of [the living with] *life beside* Yahweh [your] *the* God;
and as for the life of your enemies, [he] *you* would sling it away in midst [of the hollow] of the sling.
30 And it will be the case,
for/supposing Yahweh will do for my lord according to all
that he has declared the good upon you,
and he will order you as designate over Israel,
31 And this will not be for you a staggering and a collapse [of heart] for my lord,
[and] shedding blood gratuitously, and *saving* my lord*'s hand* [saving] *for* himself;
and Yahweh will do good for my lord,
and [you will] remember your servant *doing good to her.*"

32 And David said to Abigail,
"Blessed is Yahweh, God of Israel,
who sent you [this day]
to meet me;
33 and blessed is your [discretion[a]] *manner*
and blessed are you
who have restrained[b] me this day
from entering into blood(guilt),
and saving me my (own) hand.
34 But in fact,[a] as Yahweh, God of Israel, lives,
who has restrained me
from doing you ill,
had you not hurried
and come to meet me,
then I had said,

'There shall not be left	there would not have been left
for Nabal till light of morning	for Nabal till light of morning
a pisser on the wall.'"	a pisser on the wall."

35 And David took from her hand
what she had brought him;
and to her he said:
"Go up in peace to your house.
See, I have listened to your voice,
and I have [raised[a]] *chosen* your face."
36 And Abigail came to Nabal;
and look: he had a feast [in his house like the feast] of a king;[a]
and Nabal's heart was good on him,
and he was exceedingly drunk;
and she did not report to him a word small or great till light of morning.
37 And it came to be in the morning,
[as the wine left Nabal] *when Nabal slept off the* wine,[a]
and his wife reported to him these words;
and his heart died within him,
and he became *as* stone.
38 And it came to be about ten days,
and Yahweh smote Nabal
and he died.
39 And David heard
that Nabal was dead,
and he said:
"Blessed[a] is Yahweh

who has disputed the dispute about the reproach to me from the hand of Nabal:
his servant he has restrained from ill,
and Nabal's ill Yahweh has brought back on his head."
And David sent
and spoke for Abigail
to take her for wife.
40 And David's servants came to Abigail to Carmel,
and spoke to her
saying,
"David, he has sent us to you
to take you for wife for him."
41 And she arose
and did obeisance, face to the ground,
and she said:
"Look, your handmaid is your maidservant,
for washing the feet of [the] *your* servants [of my lord]."
42 And [she made speed
and] Abigail arose
and rode on her donkey,
and five lasses were those walking at her feet,
and she followed after the messengers of David,
and she became his wife.
43 And Ahinoam, David had taken[a] from [Jezreel] *Israel*,
and both of them became his wives.

44 And Saul, he gave Michal his daughter, David's wife, to Palti son of Laish[a]
who was from Gallim.[b]
26:1 And the Ziphites came *from the arid land*[a] to Saul to Gibeah,
saying,
"[Is David not] *Look, David is*[b] hiding himself *with us* in Gibeah of Hachilah[c] in face of the Jeshimon[?]"
2 And Saul arose
and went down to the desert of Ziph,[a] and with him three thousand men, choice/youth of Israel,
to seek David in the desert of Ziph.
3 And Saul camped in Gibeah of Hachilah,[a]
which is in face of the Jeshimon on the way,[b]
and David was settled in the desert;
and [he] *David* saw
that Saul had come after him to the desert.

4 And David sent scouts,
and he knew
that Saul had come [for sure[a]] *ready from* Keilah.[b]
5 And David arose *in secret*
and came to the place
where Saul [had camped] *was* lying;[a]
[and David saw the place where Saul had lain down[b]],
and Abner son of Ner the leader of his host *was there*;
and Saul was lying in the covered wagon,[c]
and the people were camping round about him.
6 And David spoke up
and said to A[h]*b*imelekh the Hittite and to Abishai son of Zeruiah, brother of Joab, saying,
"Who will [descend] *enter*[a] with me to Saul to the camp?"
And Abishai said,
"I will [descend] *enter* with you."
7 And David came, and Abishai, to the people by night;
and Saul was in fact lying asleep in the covered wagon,
and his spear pressed into the ground by his head,
and Abner and [the] *his* people were lying round about him.

8 And Abishai said to David,
"[God] *Yahweh*[a] has today delivered your enemy into your hand*s*.
And now I shall [surely[b]] strike him with the spear [right[c]] into the ground one time,
and I shall not do it to him a second time."
9 And David said to Abishai,
"Do not [destroy[a]] *disparage* him.
For who puts out his hand against the anointed of Yahweh
and is cleared?"

1a. Codex B = MT; but LT has this first vb. in sg.

b. The LT has *Epēkoon* ("Listener" or "Witness").

2a. Here B = MT, but LT has "in the desert."

b. In Kingdoms *poimnia* (pl.) corresponds always elsewhere (19x), except for 3 Kgdms 21:27, to *ṣ'n* (sg). In LT, *ergasia* renders MT.

c. Codex B = MT; however, LT adds *autous* as a subj. to the infin. *keirein*: "in their shearing."

3a. Here B's *onoma tō anthrōpō* might suggest it read *šēm lā'îš*.

b. The name *Abeigaia* reflects an easy corruption from *-GAIL* to *-GAIA* (Λ to A).

c. Here CL = B.

d. The commonest rendering of *m'll* is *epitēdeuma*.

e. Codex B's *kynikos* ("currish, churlish") has apparently read an adjectival derivate of *klb* ("dog").

6a. Overwhelmingly *kōh* precedes forms of *'āmar*; however, on the analogy of *sb htyṣb kh* in 2 Sam 18:30, it may be held to have similar force here, where it follows *'āmar*.

b. What then follows *kōh* is quite puzzling. (1) The combination *lĕ* + *ḥāy* (sg.), if that is what MT intends, is unique. (2) The Vulg. "to my brothers" (*fratribus meis*) makes good sense, and may have read *leḥāy* as the equivalent of *lĕ'eḥāy*—there is a further example in v. 33 below of the suppression of *'ālep*. (3) It is not clear to what Heb. *eis hōras* (GT) might be retroverted—the rendering above is indebted to LSJ 2036a.

c. Here B = MT, but LT has "everything yours" before "your house."

7a. The pause (*'atnāḥ*) in MT disrupts the sentence as read in GT.

b. Here and in v. 21, as well as in v. 15 (where MT has *pqdnw*), B has apparently read *npqd* as first person pl. *qal yiqṭōl*. Overwhelmingly the common *entellesthai* renders the equally common *ṣwh*; but, in 1 Kgdms 25 (3x) and in Isa 13:11, exceptionally *pqd*.

8a. Here LT = MT.

b. Also here, LT = MT.

9a. Again LT = MT; however, against MT and B, the LT has both vbs. in sg.: *erchetai* and *lalei*.

10a. Also in 20:34 *kai anepēdēsen* is used of Jonathan's jumping up angrily from table: there MT has *wyqm*, which OG may have read here—and yet, would it not be odd to have two coordinate verbs before the (change of) subj. is stated?

b. The pl. *'dnyw* (MT) is odd in this distributive sentence.

11a. Here LT = B.

b. Noun and vb. are cognate with the m. noun rendered "butcher" in 9:23, 24; and with the unique f. form in 8:13.

c. Again LT = B.

12a. Although the neuter pl. *paidaria* refers to persons, LT has the sg. *apestraphē*, but B the pl. *apestraphēsan*, more expected in LXX usage. The very common *apostrephein* most often corresponds to *šûb*, but to *hpk* in Judg 20:41; 2 Chr 9:12 (but the par. 1 Kgs 10:13 [12] has *wtpn*); Prov 10:32; Dan 10:16. *DCH* reports intrans. meaning "turn round/back" in Judg 20:39, 41; 1 Sam 25:12; 2 Kgs 5:26; 2 Chr 9:12; Ps 78:9; plus 2x in Sirach and 2x at Qumran.

b. Here LT = B.

c. The LT = MT.

13a. Again LT = MT.

b. Here B = MT; but LT lacks *hōs*.

14a. The LT = MT; both, however, appear to have conflated "one lad" with "one from the lads." Here, in contrast to 16:18, it is B that repeats the formulation found first in 9:3 when introducing a junior who has important information to pass on.

b. The GT may have read *wyṭ mhm* for MT's *wy'ṭ bhm*.

15a. The OG has apparently read the same consonants as 3d pl. *hip'il* + first pl. suf., rather than first pl. *hop'al*, as in MT.

b. The GT appears to attest simply *hyynw* for MT's *hthlknw*.

17a. Here B paraphrases, using *loimos* adjectivally ("pestilent") for *bly'l*.

b. The MT appears to require *mdbr* to be read as a comparison. The expected retroversion of GT would be *wl' ldbr*.

18a. The Gk. *oiphi* will be a transliteration of *'ēpâ*, as 8x in six OT books; uniquely here, MT specifies a different "measure," which is rendered elsewhere by forms of *metron* (4 Kgdms 7:1, 16, 18; 2 Chr 4:5). The terms *'ph* and *s'h* do share two consonants.

b. Likewise, *m'h ṣmqym* are part of Ziba's provisions for David in 2 Sam 16:1. However, OG specifies instead *gomor en staphidos*. The term *staphis* corresponds to *ṣmwq* in two or three other instances in Kingdoms and Chronicles, while *gomor* corresponds to *'ōmer* in Exod 16 (6x), to *ḥōmer* in Ezek 45 and Hos 3:2, and (strangely) to *ḥāmôr* with *leḥem* in 1 Kgdms 16:20. The Gk. will have read what it transliterates; perhaps the tradition behind MT substituted a numerical equivalent for the older measure—unless *m'h* is a confusion for *s'h* (see note 18a above).

20a. Here *skepē* corresponds to *str*, as only elsewhere in Isa 16:4; Ps 61:4.

b. The root *pgš* is used in a neutral sense in Gen 32:18; 33:8; Exod 4:27 (in each case *lqr't* is found close by; and a *brkh* [v. 27] is part of the meeting between Esau and Jacob [Gen 33:11]).

21a. The term *isōs* seems much weaker than *'ak* but does correspond to it once more (Jer 5:4).

22a. Elsewhere "the enemies of David" feature only in 20:15, 16.

b. Here LT = B.

23a. The phrase *l'py dwd* is the unique instance of pl./dual const. of *'p*. The OG *enōpion* corresponds normally to *lpny*, and we would expect *'l-'pyh* to produce *epi prosōpon autēs*. The GT may have rendered "before David on her face and did obeisance on the ground." The repetition of *wtpl* has suggested to many commentators a secondary addition. Trebolle Barrera (81–82) holds only "fell at his feet" to be original.

b. The LT = B.

24a. Alter notes the ambiguity of initial *bî*: (1) the particle of entreaty or (2) "on me." It is also the first word of what Hannah says to Eli in 1:26.

25a. Here LT = MT.

b. Again LT = MT.

26a. Here, as in v. 31 (MT sg. *dam*), GT attests *dam nāqî*, but supports MT in v. 33 with *haimata*. It is important to clear David from acting as Saul might have (19:5) or Joab or Manasseh will (see comment on 1 Sam 25:29 below and footnote 16).

b. The Hebrew inf. abs. could be understood as logically coordinate with "held back" (Gibson [127, *rem.* 4] takes "hand" as subj. of the inf.; and *DCH* takes *l-* as mark of the obj.), but the rendering above follows GT, which takes it as coordinate with the immediately preceding inf. "entering."

c. Here B = MT, but LT offers the sg. part. *ho zētōn*, presumably implying Saul.

d. The GT takes *nbl* as the proper name.

27a. Here LT = B.

b. Again LT = B. Nowhere else does *paristanai* corresponds to *hthlk brgly*, but rather to *nṣb* or *'md lpny*. On the other hand, *hthlk* in 25:15 above is also not lit. rendered in OG.

28a. Here LT = B.

b. Again LT = B.

29a. Codex B (*kai anastēsetai*) offers a positive statement, while LT (*kai ean anastē*) introduces a hypothesis. Both may attest *wqm* for MT *wyqm*, and this is read by many scholars. Caquot and de Robert attempt a faithful reading of MT similar to the rendering above.

33a. The NRSV offers "good sense." And RSV renders Prov 11:22 as "Like a gold ring in a swine's snout is a beautiful woman without discretion." But would "taste" not suffice? The correspondence of *ṭʿm* and *tropos* here is unique, unless one includes 1 Kgdms 21:13 A, where B reads *prosōpon*.

b. The vb. is not *klh*, but *klʾ* (the noun *keleʾ* means "prison"). As in 6:10 (only other use of vb. *klʾ* in FP), the *ʾālep* is not written.

34a. Here *wĕʾûlām* is a strong adversative, used already in 1 Sam 20:3—but most often in Job (10x).

35a. "To raise someone's face" (Hebrew idiom for holding in regard) has caused problems for the translators: in 2 Kgs 3:14 (the only other instance in Sam-Kgs) the rendering is woodenly literal. Here B offers "chosen" (*hēretisa*), but LT appropriately "had regard for" (*enetrapēn*).

36a. The LT = MT, except "of the kings."

37a. Here LT = B.

39a. Codex B renders appropriately with *Eulogētos*, but LT transliterates as *Barouch*.

43a. The past perfect is chosen here, simply because Ahinoam is mentioned before Abigail where this information is recapitulated in 27:3.

44a. Here B offers *Ameis*, and LT *Iōas*.

b. Codex B offers *Romma*, and LT *Goliath*.

26:1a. The GT uses the rare *ek tēs auchmōdous*, as in 23:14, 15, 19 above.

b. The GT *idou* attests *hinnēh* rather than *hălôʾ*.

c. Codex B has *tō Chelmath*. It also renders *gbʿh* (Gibeah?) both times by *bounos* ("hill").

2a. Here B = MT; but LT both here and at the end of the verse reads not *Zeiph* but *tēn auchmōdē*.

3a. B now offers *tou Echela*.

b. The word order in LT (*Iessemoun tou epi tēs hodou*) makes more explicit than MT and B that this Jeshimon is the one on his route.

4a. The term *ʾel-nākôn* is used also in 1 Sam 23:23 (MT + and A +). Here B uses *hetoimos* ("ready"), as does A in 23:23; but that would be more natural for *nākôn* alone. "For sure" more naturally emphasizes the level of David's knowledge, while "ready" describes Saul's state of preparedness—and establishing that is the more natural business of the scouts.

b. The LT does not attest (*ʾel-*)*nākôn* at all, but reads "behind him to Ziklag."

5a. Here GT attests *škb*, not *ḥnh*.

b. The LT shares this plus with MT, yet uses not *katheudein* but *koiman*—both stock equivalences for *škb*.

c. Here and in 26:7, *lampēnē* is used to render *mʿgl*, which reappears in the same sense in 1 Sam 17:20 (MT plus).

6a. The GT uses *eiseleusetai* ("will go *in*") here and in Abishai's response.

8a. The LT = B.

b. Here LT = MT.

c. Again LT = MT.

9a. The term *diaphtheirēs* (A and LT) corresponds better to MT's *tšḥyt* than B's *tapeinōsēs* (which corresponds most often to *ʿnh*, though never in 1 Kingdoms).

[1] The note about Samuel's death and burial (v. 1a) is remarkably terse. The event is recalled again in similar terms in 28:3; presumably only one of these verses preserves the original report. The passing of Samuel is clearly relevant to what follows in 1 Sam 28; however, that may simply explain the repetition of the notice there. The proposal advanced in this commentary is that this is the primary location of the notice. It is here that a simple narrative past tense (*wayyiqṭōl*) is used to describe the great man's passing: *wymt šmwʾl*, "And Samuel died." By contrast, 1 Sam 28:3 resumes a previous report: *wšmwʾl mt*, "Now Samuel, he had died." There has been a long silence about Samuel before his death notice. After the confrontation at Gilgal (15:34), he withdrew from Saul and went home to Ramah. Yahweh interrupted this withdrawal with the command to anoint David, after which Samuel again returned to Ramah (16:13). David next went to Ramah and appealed for his help (19:18). The situation of a long-delayed death-and-burial notice is somewhat reminiscent of the notices in 2 Kings of the deaths of Jezebel and of Elisha, both at quite some distance from the last reported major action. And yet their deaths are much more fully reported than Samuel's (2 Kgs 9:30–37; 13:14–21). It almost seems as if Samuel is hanging on to life till Saul has articulated directly to David his awareness that David will follow him. Saul has finally accepted what Samuel has told him long before (13:14), that his kingdom will not last and that Yahweh has sought out a successor of whom he approves more.

The extreme brevity makes it hard to interpret what is said about David in the following half verse (1b). In the previous verse (24:23), the simple *qāṭal* verb placed after the subject "David and his men" expresses a contrast: when Saul has heard David take an oath to him, he went home; *but* David and his men—they took themselves to a place of safety. However, after "all Israel" has buried Samuel, David simply upped (*wayyiqṭōl*) and left for the desert. This gives at least some reason for us to conclude that David was part of "all Israel" in paying respect to the old leader before going off to the desert. Exactly which desert is a problem. The GT identifies the desert area near Maon. This takes David back to the area repeatedly specified in 23:24b–25, and which we are just about to learn is also the territory of Nabal; this is clearly the more straightforward reading. The MT's "desert of Paran" belongs further south and is mentioned only in texts from the Pentateuch. Ishmael and his mother had settled there (Gen 21:21), and it was Israel's first stopping place after leaving Mount Sinai (Num 10:12). Could MT intend to suggest that David sets out for

Paran, but pauses in the neighborhood of Maon on the way there or the way back? If so, the point could have been stated more clearly; and yet the syntax in this part of the text is unusual.

[2–3] The opening of the next subparagraph (v. 2) is unique within HB: no other independent clause is composed simply of *ʾîš* ("man") plus a prepositional phrase.[1] Introductions to fresh characters within HB narrative normally move more quickly to provide the individual's name. Here instead, topography is indicated, location of activity is more precisely specified, importance of the character is underscored by the size of his flocks, even what he is currently doing with his flocks is defined (all in v. 2): the increase in information and lengthening delay serve to emphasize our surprise at his name, when finally we are told that a man who meets sufficient criteria for "greatness"[2] is named or at least nicknamed "Fool."[3] Since "flock" (*ṣōʾn*) can include goats as well as sheep, the separate mention of the thousand goats is ambiguous: they could be a subset of the flock of three thousand, or an addition to it. This arithmetic ambiguity is like the occasional separate mention of Judah within or in addition to Israel. And this numerical link provides the first of several hints that "Fool" is in some sense a character double for Saul.

The prominence and oddity of his striking name are further increased by what follows. His wife has a much more positive-sounding name ("Happy Father"?); after learning her name, we are told that she has good sense as well as a beautiful appearance. Such high praise of her is followed in turn by comment on his character. Nabal is described first as *qāšeh*. This adjective is used of "hard" labor, "hard" fighting, "blunt" answers. However, it is used twice more in Samuel of people. David says of Joab and Abishai that they are more *qāšîm* than he (2 Sam 3:39); and Hannah describes herself to Eli as *qĕšat rûaḥ* (1 Sam 1:15), "hard of spirit." Perhaps Hannah, no less than Nabal and the sons of Zeruiah, should be thought of as "obstinate" or "determined." No one else in HB is described exactly like Nabal, as "evil in deeds" (*raʿ maʿălālîm*); however, the prophets frequently complain elsewhere about their people and "the evil of their deeds"; and in one case (Judg 2:19), "deeds" and "obstinate" are closely linked.[4]

The culmination of the introduction to Nabal is also its most controversial element. The official "reading" in MT (Q) of the last word of the Hebrew text is *kālibbî*, or "Calebite." The GT has read the same four consonants (*klby*) as an

1. Yet B may attest it in 9:1—*kai anēr ex uiōn Beniamein.* Here in 25:2, GT reads *kai ēn anthrōpos. . . .*

2. Barzillai (2 Sam 19:32–33) and Job (1:3) are similarly described, and both were rich.

3. Other meanings have been proposed for his name; yet I doubt that the name would have been so long delayed had it not been so appropriate.

4. Judges 2:19: *lōʾ hippîlû mimmaʿălĕlêhem ûmiddarkām haqqāšâ* ("they did not let fall any of their deeds or of their stubborn way").

adjective from *keleb* ("dog"). However, neither "Calebite" nor "doglike" occurs elsewhere in HB. The consonants actually written (K) in MT are *klbw*; and that does make perfectly good sense: "as his heart." After all that has been said about Nabal and his wife, the final element may be "and he was a Calebite" or "and he was doglike" or "and he was according to his heart." In favor of the K, the final option, there is a close parallel in BTH (2 Sam 7:21): *kĕlibbĕkā*, "[because of your word and] according to your heart [you have done all this greatness]."[5] The orientation of Caleb's heart is manifest in behavior that is in fact the very opposite of [Yahweh's] greatness. In favor of the gentilic, we could plead the locality called "the Negeb of Caleb" at the other end of this section of the book (1 Sam 30:14). And, given the low estimate of dogs in Samuel and HB generally, the interpretation in GT should in no way be discounted. We should recall that David has just likened himself ironically to "a dead dog" (24:14 [15]). In the absence of pejorative associations of Caleb, "doglike" and "according to his heart" appear to offer a better negative climax to the introduction.

[4–8] When David hears about the shearing, he makes contact with Nabal, but not directly (vv. 4–8). He schools his ten lads very precisely about what they should say. After the full pleasantries, they should point out to Nabal that they know they have come "on a good day," and ask for "whatever his hand finds"; this more normal expression reassembles the separated "[under your] hand" and "[what is] found" of David's own approach to the priest at Nob (21:3 [4]). Something about that earlier request went terribly wrong: whether that David represented himself at Nob or was unaccompanied, or that the form of words he used had been unusual. If "good day" (25:8) means a festal day, David may have higher expectations of hospitality, including security.

[9–12] In whatever way he has come to reflect on that tragic situation, each element of this new approach is different—be it a simple request for food, or a challenge to another supposed Saul loyalist. Nabal rejects the lads' approach out of hand. His questions about David (v. 10) are in no sense a request for information: he knows precisely who David is and who his father is. What he is questioning is David's significance; he seems to be drawing together two elements in the earlier narrative. After David killed Goliath, Saul asked after David although they had already met (17:55–56). And each time David has been called "Jesse's son" (and not by his own name), it has been in the mouth of an angry and contemptuous Saul (20:27, 30, 31; 22:7, 8, 13) or by Doeg when answering Saul (22:9). In fact "son of Jesse" on its own is used exclusively by critics: Sheba ben Bichri (2 Sam 20:1), and "all Israel" (1 Kgs 12:16, BTH), in addition to Saul, Doeg, and Nabal. When "son of Jesse" follows David, it is a neutral surname.

5. We may also compare the alternate forms *klbbw* in 1 Sam 13:14; Deut 20:8; and *klbbk* in 1 Sam 14:7; Ps 20:4 (5).

David's messengers have been asked to make repeated use of *šālôm* (4x in vv. 5–6: "well," "peace"). But Nabal is not persuaded: he does not trust David; and there is no question of his sharing his food only to be cheated later. His answer could have Ps 41:9 (10) in mind: *gam-ʾîš šĕlômî ʾăšer-bāṭaḥtî bô ʾôkēl laḥmî higdîl ʿālay ʿāqēb* ("Even the man of my peace, whom I trusted, who was eating my bread, has 'enlarged'[6] against me his heel"). The use in the psalm of an expression using *ʿāqēb* is suggestive of another fraught biblical relationship: Laban's cheating and being cheated by his (heel-catching) relative *yaʿăqōb* (Jacob; Gen 29–31). As many commentators have noted, both "LaBaN" and "NaBaL" are the other name read backward.

[13] Nabal's lack of hospitality is met by the same response as David will make to the Amalekite sack of Ziklag: four hundred men advance in company with David, while two hundred stay with the baggage (v. 13), anticipating 30:9–10. After the opening verses, where there are fewer links (unless already "the Negeb of Caleb"), this lengthy narrative shares many expressions with the latter part of 1 Samuel, and most particularly with the two neighboring chapters. The story of David, Nabal, and Abigail is framed by the two reports of David's sparing Saul's life. And with each of them and both of them, it also shares several themes and terms, some unique to these narratives within 1 Samuel, while others are at least uncommon in the rest of that book. It plays something of a parabolic role in relation to these immediate neighbors.

David is operating on the margins of Nabal's space, as he is of Saul's. He has aided Nabal's herdsmen and made no demands on them thus far, just as he has protected Saul's border areas (most recently at Keilah). However, he is no more welcome at Nabal's feast than he would be at Saul's. Nabal, like Saul, has returned him evil for good. And yet, while David's own followers urge their reluctant master to kill Saul (24:4), it is now David who leads them in a raid to punish Nabal; though he explains to his men that they should wait for Yahweh or fate to put an end to the king (26:10), it requires Abigail to urge him to wait for Yahweh to act for him (25:29).

Nabal is often presented as an "alter ego" of Saul, and several similarities have already been noted. But there is an all-important difference: he does not enjoy the protection (from David at least) of being Yahweh's anointed. Important as the connections are between this narrative and those immediately framing it, there are also interesting links elsewhere in the books of Samuel. Several of these are in 2 Sam 3: Michal's new husband (1 Sam 25:44) is mentioned again (2 Sam 3:13–16). When David mourns Abner's death (3:33), he asks, "Should Abner die as a *nābāl* dies?" The sons of Zeruiah, responsible for Abner's death (3:27–30), are called *qāšîm* (3:39; cf. 1 Sam 25:3). David claims

6. Obad 12 uses *higdîl* with "mouth" to create a phrase implying boasting.

innocence of any bloodguilt (*dĕmê*) relating to Abner (2 Sam 3:28; cf. 1 Sam 25:26, 33).[7]

[14–17] The narrator has already (25:3) led us to expect well of Nabal's wife; and this predisposition is reinforced by the terms in which Nabal's staff seek her help. Their spokesman is "one from the lads," but on this occasion not one chosen out of the available staff pool (9:3), nor even responding to a direct question (16:18). In tune with his master's wife, this "lad" knows when to take the initiative. His sketch of the problem is crisply delivered (25:14–16) and underscored (most of v. 17). David has sent his men to "bless" his master (v. 14). This "greeting" sent to Nabal has consisted of polite words, or polite words that mask seeking an invitation to the shearers' feast. When Abigail offers David a *bĕrākâ* in v. 27, it consists of much more than words.

[18–20] The appeal itself—quite as economical—is a fresh variant of "know and see" (v. 17), which is used somewhat differently at each appearance. Here the knowing may focus on Abigail's grasp of the report she has just been given, while the seeing relates more to what she should do about it. Her immediate response comes in action relating to "provisions." We should recall that the classic illustration of "vision" referring in the HB to what we normally call "provision" is Abraham's dark response to Isaac's question about the lamb for their sacrifice: "God will see for himself the lamb" (Gen 22:8).

Speed seems characteristic of Abigail (4x out of 13x in 1–2 Samuel). It is not a general characteristic of biblical women; but Abigail's bustling is matched by Rebecca (Gen 27) and by Samson's mother (Judg 13:10). Since she is already hurrying, her order to her staff to pass on before her (v. 19) adds to the impression of speed. The rations that Abigail prepares (v. 18) have elements in common with those sent by Jesse to King Saul (16:20): bread, wine, and a kid; and those used to revive the Egyptian slave (30:11–12): bread, water, figs, and raisins (the last two, *dblh* and two *ṣmqym*, are emergency rations used to restore the exhausted Egyptian in 30:12). But quite the closest parallel is Ziba's provision for the fleeing David in 2 Sam 16:1. The accounts share two asses, two hundred loaves, and one hundred bunches of raisins. In addition Abigail brings two skins of wine, not one; five prepared sheep; five measures of parched grain; and two hundred cakes of figs. Ziba adds a hundred of summer fruit. Abigail's asses are more heavily laden—but Ziba's are intended as royal mounts. Immediately afterward (16:7–8), Shimei hounds David as "the man of bloods" and "the man of Belial/'No-good.'"[8]

[21–22] The staff on both sides are well able to read the situation. David's men need no more than his crisp order to gird on their swords. Nabal's men

7. Also on bloodguilt, cf. 1 Sam 25:31 as located between 1 Sam 19:5 and 1 Kgs 2:31.

8. "The man of Belial" (1 Sam 25:25) is found again only in 2 Sam 16:7 ("the men of Belial" only in 1 Kgs 21:13).

know from their master's treatment of David's men what David's response will be. Abigail's swift attempt to intercept David is delayed briefly by the narrator (vv. 21–22) as he clarifies David's intentions. Whether he ever voices them to his men or only to himself is immaterial. His threat to eliminate Nabal and all his men has a double resonance. It is expressed in terms similar to Saul's wish to move against Philistines (14:36): only in these two passages in all of HB is the *hipʿil* of *šʾr* ("leave remaining") used with a first-person subject ("we" or "I"); both passages envisage a night raid lasting till morning light. And Saul's proposal did not receive any response of divine approval (14:37). Then all the other threats (other than 1 Sam 25) against "every pisser on the wall" are uttered by the Deity: in the words that came to him in his fit of temper, David may have been overstepping the mark (v. 22).

[23–31] Abigail's speech (vv. 24–31) must be one of the longest in Samuel. She is not only a beautiful woman, but a wise one as well. As we shall see, her approach to David anticipates in several respects the approach of the wise woman from Tekoa engaged by Joab (2 Sam 14). If Nabal's response to David's messengers reminds us of a psalm, this whole narrative could be read as an illustration of the second half of Prov 11. The relationship with Prov 11:22 is particularly interesting:[9] "A gold ring in a pig's snout is a beautiful woman who departs *ṭāʿam*."

Abigail is beautiful (v. 3), and David's praises her *ṭāʿam* (v. 33): see below on the meaning of this term; one of the issues for interpreters of this story is just how far this human "gold ring" is seeking to disengage herself from her "pig's snout." There is an urgency and breathlessness about her: she says "and now" (*wʿth*) three times in vv. 26–27; and this way of speaking is yet a further illustration of the speed with which she habitually acts.[10] However, the most striking element in her whole address to David (vv. 24–31) is the fact that she calls him "my lord" as many as fourteen times.[11] Nabal's staff twice (vv. 14, 17) speak of him to Abigail as "our lord"—presumably they include her in this description: they no doubt think of Nabal as Abigail's "lord" too. The narrator calls him more neutrally "her husband" or "her man" (v. 19), while to David she herself calls Nabal "this man of Belial" (lit., v. 25 MT).

Abigail's repeated use of "my lord" when speaking to David seems to work at three different levels. It reinforces the intensity of her supplication. It helps to bring about a relationship between them. And within the whole narrative, it functions to redirect our attention away from Saul and toward David as the natural recipient of the address "lord." This is particularly true of the immediate context

9. Also cf. Prov 11:26 and Abigail.

10. Expressed by *mhr* (25:18, 23, 34, 42).

11. In 25:24, 25 (2x), 26 (2x), 27 (2x), 28 (2x), 29, 30, 31 (3x). The term *ʾādôn* is used 13x more in the remainder of 1 Sam 24–26; and 11x more in all the rest of 1 Samuel.

in chs. 24–26; for David himself twice reinforces with the words "the anointed of Yahweh" his own use of "lord" in relation to Saul (24:6 [7]; 26:16), and in each speech addresses Saul as "my lord the king" (24:8 [9]; 26:17). The wise woman from Tekoa will almost always address David as "my lord the king"; and while Abigail cannot do that, she does explicitly look forward to David being *nāgîd* over Israel (25:30) and associates his battles with Yahweh's (25:28).

Like the wise woman of Tekoa (2 Sam 14:9), Abigail opens her address (1 Sam 25:24) by taking the guilt (*ʿāwôn*) on herself. David will do the same (2 Sam 24:10), although he will ask that the guilt be removed. On an earlier occasion (1 Sam 20:8), David had—more characteristically even if only implicitly—disclaimed guilt in words that Absalom would later use (2 Sam 14:32): "If there is guilt in me, then put me to death." David, Abigail continues, should waste no more attention[12] on Nabal (1 Sam 25:25) than Saul on the donkeys that had already been found (9:20): neither was of any further consequence. "As his name, so is he" (*kšmw kn-hwʾ*) offers an echo of "and he was as his heart" (*whwʾ klbw*)—the consonantal form of the text at the end of v. 3. Her husband's heart and name are well matched.

Having admitted her own responsibility for what she has not done, she moves to save David from the consequences of what he is set on doing. But the language that she uses is almost without parallel in HB and may be deliberately imprecise, creating space for reflection. Here *bôʾ bĕdāmîm* (vv. 26, 33) is a unique expression;[13] but the plural of *dām* ("blood") does refer elsewhere to the entail of multiple or successive bloodshed associated with bloodguilt or blood feud. The expression *hôšēaʿ yādĕkā lāk* ("your hand do your own saving," vv. 26, 33) does have one parallel, in Judg 7:2.[14] Taking matters into his own hands might accord with custom; but it would not be wise. Having offered him her gift/blessing for the men who have "gone about" with him (*hthlk* happens to be used next at the end of the report of a similar "blessing," in 30:26–31), she asks him (v. 28) to take away her "transgression" (*pešaʿ*). This term is used only once more in the books of Samuel (and never at all in Chronicles): David himself has just asserted to Saul (24:11 [12]) that there is neither transgression nor evil in his hand and that he has not sinned against him. Since, as used by David, these terms seem broadly synonymous, we may suppose that Abigail is now hoping not to be held to her opening gambit—not to have to bear the guilt of her household. Her exact words are used once more in HB: to Joseph by his brothers on the instruction of their father (Gen 50:17). Joseph and David

12. The term *śîm* is construed with *lēb* again in Samuel only in 2 Sam 18:3, where his lieutenants tell David that even as many as half of his men are of no significance beside himself.

13. First Kings 2:33 contrasts *dmym* and *šlwm*.

14. The parallel in Judges seems a meager basis for Vermeylen (151) to call "se sauver par sa propre main" Deuteronomic.

should behave with the generosity of God. She builds on what the priest of Nob has said to Saul, that David is *neʾĕmān* in Saul's house (22:14), and anticipates Nathan (2 Sam 7:16) in assuring David that Yahweh will build him an "established house" (*bayit neʾĕmān*). This actual phrase recurs only in 1 Sam 2:35 and 1 Kgs 11:38, although 1 Sam 22:14 is also relevant. In each case the language is drawn from 2 Sam 7:16 (BTH). Abigail finds little distinction between David's wars and Yahweh's wars (25:28). In fact, MT talks of David as fighting Yahweh's wars, while GT has Yahweh as fighting David's.[15]

Abigail's words in v. 29b stress both *ṣrr* and *qlʿ*: in balancing phrases, each appearing first as a verb and then as a noun. When she talks of "slinging" and the "sling," she is surely recalling the means by which David put an end to Goliath's challenge, as he entered onto the national stage. In context, there can be little doubt that the previous *ṣrwrh bṣrwr* ("bundled in the bundle") is intended as a positive image, in contrast to being slung away. But it is typical of the author's love of ambiguity and wordplay that there is a second noun *ṣĕrôr*, which means "pebble" (2 Sam 17:13; Amos 9:9), though it is not actually used in the Goliath story. The theme of David's leaving vengeance to others and (still) getting his own way points forward to 1 Kgs 2. An immediate connection between "blood" (*dām*) shed gratis (*ḥinnām*) is made only once more in HB (1 Kgs 2:31).[16]

Toward the end of her speech (v. 30), Abigail returns to the language of 2 Sam 7 (BTH): the only other instance in HB of "good" (*ṭwbh*) following "speak/declare" (*dbr*) is in 7:28; and "leader" (*ngyd*) also appears in 7:8—however, that term is used with "command" (*ṣwh*) only in non-BTH portions of Samuel–Kings (1 Sam 13:14; 25:30; 2 Sam 6:21; 1 Kgs 1:35). In the immediate context of 1 Kgs 14:7; 16:2, where *ngyd* follows *ntn*, we also find two further instances of "piss on the wall" (14:10; 16:11)—the only other instances, apart from 1 Sam 25:22, 34, are in 1 Kgs 21:21; 2 Kgs 9:8. Her closing request to "remember your handmaid" (v. 31) immediately after "taking vengeance himself" (if that is what it means) corresponds to her becoming David's wife immediately after Yahweh takes Nabal's life (vv. 38–39): a nice illustration of how closely Yahweh's and David's actions are aligned.

[32–35] David repays Abigail in kind: her words and actions and Yahweh's words and actions are also convergent. He blesses Yahweh for sending her to

15. Given the use of "Yahweh-War" as an alternative to "Holy War" in some historical discussion (under the influence of Rudolf Smend's *Jahwekrieg*), it is important to recognize that the term has an uncertain biblical pedigree. "Yahweh's wars" (pl.) occur 3x in HB (the sg. is never found in MT). However, in 1 Sam 18:17 the expression is part of a large plus in MT; here in 25:28 there is disagreement over who is fighting whose wars; and in Num 21:14 *mlḥmt* is read not as pl. but (more naturally) as sg. in LXX, which also divides the clauses differently from MT.

16. The phrase *špk dm* ("shed blood") is used in Samuel–Kings only here and in 1 Kgs 2:31 (Joab); 18:28 (prophets of Baal); and 2 Kgs 21:16; 24:4 (both have Manasseh as subj, with *dam nāqî*).

him, in words (*brwk yhwh . . . ʾšr*) that anticipate Hiram (1 Kgs 5:7 [21]), Solomon (1 Kgs 8:15), and the Queen of Sheba (1 Kgs 10:9) in BTH.[17] And David blesses Abigail for restraining him, declaring on Yahweh's life that, if she had not held him back and met him . . . Hold back (*mnʿ*, vv. 26, 34) and restrain (*klʾ*, v. 33) are practically synonymous; if there is a distinction, it is that in most parts of HB, Yahweh is quite the commonest subject of *mnʿ*.[18] Similarly, it is always Yahweh in the books of Kings who through a prophet threatens every "pisser on the wall"; however, here (vv. 22, 34) David utters the threat on his own initiative. See below on 2 Sam 23:1–7 for David as prophet. With David and Abigail each sharing divine characteristics, the emerging relationship could be said to be "made in heaven."

The semantic range of *ṭāʿam* (v. 33) is quite broad: from "taste," through "discretion and judgment," to "decision and decree." Is it the freshness of her speech that has impressed David with its "taste"? Or is it her quick "decision" to come running to head him off? Proverbs 11 was cited above. Job 12:20 provides another relevant intertext:

> He removes the speech of the trusted [*neʾĕmānîm*],[19]
> and takes away the *ṭāʿam* [discernment] of the elders.

[36–38] "A word small and/or large" (v. 36) resumes "a *dābār* small or large" (22:15, said by the priest to Saul; neither has an exact parallel in HB) and compresses "a large *dābār* or a small *dābār*" (20:2, said by Jonathan to David): the resumptive "these words" (*haddĕbārîm hāʾēlleh*, v. 37) includes large and small. Mention of the wine going out of Nabal (v. 37) plays nicely on another *nbl* (*nēbel*, "wineskin"). The unique expression "his heart died within him" (v. 37), following so soon after the merriness of his heart (v. 36), usefully reminds us that Nabal does have a heart (cf. *klbw*, v. 3).

[39–40] The expression *ryb ʾt-ryb* (v. 39) was also used in the parallel narrative (24:16), of Yahweh's taking up David's case. The phrase with which David resumes here is otherwise unique in Samuel–Kings. He uses *miyyad* ("from the hand of") in 24:16 too when invoking Yahweh as his vindicator against Saul. Israel (and the living God) have suffered *ḥerpâ* at Philistine hands, and so will Tamar at Amnon's hands; it appears that "disgrace" is best removed by another.

17. The other ten instances in HB (not counting the BTH refs in Chronicles) are in Gen 24:27; Exod 18:10; 1 Sam 25:32, 39; 2 Sam 18:28; 1 Kgs 1:48; 5:7 (21); Ps 66:20 (*ʾĕlōhîm* not *yhwh*); Ruth 4:14; Ezra 7:27.

18. Yahweh is subject of *mnʿ* in Gen 30:2; Num 24:11; 1 Sam 25:26, 34; Ezek 31:15; Amos 4:7; Pss 21:2 (3); 84:11 (12); Prov 30:7; and Neh 9:20; and the passive in Num 22:16 implies the deity. David and Ahab are the only other subjects in rest of FP. "His servant he has restrained from ill" (1 Sam 25:39) is reminiscent of Ps 19:13 (14: "Even from the insolent, restrain your servant") and Gen 20:6 ("I restrained you from sinning against me").

19. See above on v. 28.

Although quite a stock phrase,[20] it is remarkable again just how relevant an intertext is provided for both expressions by a single verse from a psalm (74:22):

> Arise, O God, take up your case [*rybh rybk*];
> remember your shame [*ḥrptk*] from the fool [*mny-nbl*].

"[Returning his evil] on his head" is unique; the closest parallels in FP are 1 Kgs 8:32 BTH and Josh 2:19.

[41–43] Abigail's response (v. 41) to David's messengers is interesting. First of all, she treats his representatives, his ambassadors, as she has David himself—doing full obeisance before them on the ground. And then she says that she is ready to serve them below her status. It is not always easy to detect the difference between *ʾāmâ* ("handmaid") and *šipḥâ* ("maidservant"). However, where they are clearly distinguished, as here, the *šipḥâ* has the lower status. Writing of Ruth, Sasson (81) notes that on her first encounter with Boaz (Ruth 2:13), she describes herself as *šipḥâ*. He comments on her new self-description in 3:9: "By now using the term *ʾāmāh*, Ruth imagines herself as ranking among those females who might be taken by a freeman either as a concubine or as a wife." For the widow of Nabal, about to be wife to David, the term *ʾāmâ* might already suggest self-abasement; but describing herself as a *šipḥâ* and ready to wash the feet of David's staff is to go a stage still further.

[44] Possibly under the influence of the subparagraph break (which happens to be shared by B), the verb in v. 44 is often rendered as a past perfect: "[Saul] had given." However, such a reading runs counter to the situation at the end of neighboring episodes, where one of the rivals does one thing, but the other does something different. There is no need for us to suppose that Saul's action over Michal has happened earlier: it would represent a natural response by the king to the death of Nabal and David's two new marriages. The names of Michal's new husband are given here as Palti son of Laish (*lyš*), but in 2 Sam 3:15 as Paltiel son of Lush (*lwš*). Gallim occurs elsewhere in HB only in Isa 10:30, beside *lyšh*, in a text that goes on to mention Nob, which has already featured in 21:1; 22:9, 11, 19.

[26:1–5] When we read the opening of ch. 26, it is as if nothing has happened since the middle of ch. 23; it is not just that 26:1 offers a briefer and lightly modified version of 23:19, but that 26:1–5 as a whole shares many unique features with 23:19–26. "Choice of Israel" (v. 2) is plural, agreeing with "thousands," while "choice out of all Israel" in 24:2 was singular, agreeing with the collective noun *ʾîš*. The form of the expression here may anticipate a selection that Joab makes when in a tight corner in BTH (2 Sam 10:9); but the parallel text in 1 Chr 19:8 is slightly different. Those critics who prefer to understand

20. Pss 43:1; 74:22; 119:154; Prov 22:23; 23:11; 25:9; cf. also Mic 7:9; Jer 50:34; 51:36.

longer versions of texts as expansions of earlier shorter ones give the priority here to 1 Sam 26. Beyond that, David's challenge to his men ("Who will go down with me to Saul, to the camp?") resumes his earlier question to the Deity in 23:11 ("Will Saul go down [against me]?"). At Keilah (ch. 23) and in the cave at En-gedi (ch. 24), it was a matter of Saul's entering space held by David; in the cases of Nabal at Carmel and Saul's camp, it is David who does the entering.

[6–9] And yet there is novel content in this final subparagraph. The note about Michal and Palti[el] functions as something of a transition toward 2 Sam 3; and mention of Joab's brother Abishai as David's comrade (26:6–9) offers a more surprising anticipation of the David story in 2 Samuel following Saul's death. Neither Joab nor this brother will appear (again) until after Saul's death, after David's transfer to Hebron, and after his anointing there. Not only does the mention of Abishai come as a surprise, but also the fact that he is introduced as brother of a Joab of whom, as readers of Samuel, we have heard nothing. This is one of the several portions of Samuel that have to be read in the light of what we encounter later in the book rather than what comes before: the first readers of Samuel knew Joab and Abishai from the older BTH. Abner too (26:5) is better known in 2 Samuel but has already been encountered in 1 Sam 14:50; 20:25 (and 17:55, 57 [MT plus]). Though listed as head of the army (14:50) and appropriately mentioned as seated beside Saul at a special dinner (20:25), it is only here and in a late addition to the Goliath story that he is reported as doing anything until after Saul's death. There is no mention of any role for him in the battle in which Saul and his sons die, and he was unknown in BTH. Both David and Abishai see the vulnerability of Saul asleep among his men (v. 7); but it is Abishai who interprets this as God's putting David's enemy into his hands: he volunteers to strike the king fatally with a single stroke of Saul's own spear. David responds that no one can make a hostile move on the anointed of Yahweh and remain in the clear (v. 9).

1 Samuel 26:10–14

10 And David said,
"As Yahweh lives, Yahweh will surely [smite[a]] *train* him,
or his day will come
and he will die,
or he will come down into battle
and be [swept away] added.[b]
11 It would be a profanity for me from Yahweh{'s view}
to put out my hand against the anointed of Yahweh.
Now then, take to be sure the spear
that is at his head
and the jug of water,
and let us go on our way."

12 And David took the spear and the jug of water from by Saul's head,
and they went their own way.[a]
And no one was seeing
and no one was knowing
and no one was waking,
but all of them were sleeping
because Yahweh's deep sleep had fallen on them.
13 And David crossed over to the other side
and stood on top of the hill afar;
the [space] *way* between them was large.
14 And David called to the people
and to Abner son of Ner *he* spoke,[a] saying
"Are you not answering, Abner?"
And [Abner answered[b]
and] *he* said,
"Who are you that [have called to the king] *are* calling?"[c]

10a. Here *paisē* (A, LT) corresponds better to MT's *ygpnw* than B's unique *paideusē*. Can *-deu-* be a secondary expansion?

b. That is "[added] to the account."

12a. This at least appears to be the sense of Gk. *kath' heautous*.

14a. The LT = B.

b. Here LT = MT.

c. The LT is longer than B: ". . . that are calling me? Who are you?" The participial form *qwr'*, attested by OG, is nicely resumed and played on by *qōrē'* = "partridge" (v. 20).

[10–14] David is confident that, one way or another, Saul will be removed from the scene; but he cannot himself contemplate such a hostile move (vv. 10–11). By using the oath formula in his first statement (v. 10), then solemnly forswearing action on his own part (v. 11), what David says comes closer than any other speaker in the book to the words of the people when they insisted to Saul that Jonathan should not be put to death (14:45). His opening words envisage three options for Saul's removal, in uncanny anticipation of the three options he himself will later be offered after counting the people (2 Sam 24:13). And the way in which two of the options are phrased underscores the relevance of this link: being "smitten" by Yahweh suggests plague; being "swept away" in battle (MT) uses the verb (*sph*), which may have originally stood in 2 Sam 24:13 (we find it still in the parallel version in 1 Chr 21:12). The GT's "added" misreads the verb as a form of *ysp*, or of *'sp* ("gather").[21]

Yes, Abishai should take hold of the spear—but only to remove it along with Saul's water jug. They make off through a camp experiencing a preternaturally deep sleep, like Jonah during the storm on the ship (1:5), or Adam when his rib

21. There is no *nip'al* theme of *ysp*, but there is of *'sp*.

was removed (Gen 2:21), or Sisera exhausted after battle (Judg 4:21). Taking up a safe position at a considerable distance, David taunts Abner for failing to look after a master who is none other than Yahweh's anointed, and shows him the spear and jug as evidence (1 Sam 26:15–16). (Abner will survive Saul's death, only to meet his own end at the hands of Joab, the brother of Abishai, David's companion here [2 Sam 3:27].)

1 Samuel 26:15–24

15 And David said to Abner,
"Are you not a man?
And who is like you in Israel?
And why [have] *are* you not watch[ed]*ing*[a] [for] your lord the king?
For one of the people has come
to destroy the king, your lord.
16 Not good is this thing you have done.
As Yahweh lives, surely you are sons of death,
who [have not watched[a]] *are watching* over your lord,
over the anointed of Yahweh.
Now then see [where[b]] the king's spear [is],
and the jug of water [which was] *where are the things* at his head*?*"
17 And Saul recognized the voice of David,
and he said
"Is this your voice, my son David?"[a]
And David said,
"[My voice it is] *Your servant*, my lord the king."[b]
18 And [he] *David* said,
"Whyever is my lord[a] pursuing after his servant,
for what have I [done] *sinned*[b]
and what in my hand is *found*[c] evil?
19 Now then, let my lord king be sure to hear the words of his servant.
If it is [Yahweh] *God*[a] has incited you against me,
let him smell an offering.
And if it is human beings,
they are cursed before Yahweh,
for they have driven me out today
from being joined in Yahweh's holding
saying,
'Go serve other gods.'
20 Now then, let not my blood fall to the ground over against
Yahweh's face;
for the king of Israel has come out
to seek [a single flea] *my life*

as [one chases the partridge[a]] *long-eared owl chases* in the hills."

21 And Saul said,
"I have sinned.
Return, [my[a]] son David,
for I shall not do you ill [again[b]],
against the fact that my life has been precious in your eyes [this day.[c] Look].
And today,
I have been foolish
and I have been very greatly in error."

22 And David answered
and said,
"Look: the king's spear,[a]
and let one from the lads cross over
and take it.

23 And Yahweh, he will return to each man his righteousness[a] and his faithfulness
as Yahweh has given you today into (my) hand,
but I was not willing
to put out my hand against the anointed of Yahweh.

24 And look: as your life has been great [this day] *today in this* in my eyes,
so let my life be great in Yahweh's eyes,
and let him hide/protect[a] *me,*
and he will deliver me from all ill."

15a. Here LT = B.

16a. The LT uses the present tense with B, as in vv. 14–15; but here like MT includes "not."

b. The interrogative adv. *ʾy* precedes spear, but *ʾt* (obj. marker) precedes jug. Similarly LT and B place *pou esti* ("where is?") differently: LT near the beginning, after "see," but B only after the flask of water. Both B and LT read the ungrammatical *kai ho phakos tou hudatos* (nom., not accus.), which suggests they did not read *ʾt* before *ṣpḥt*.

17a. Perhaps a conversational gambit?

b. Here LT attests a combination of MT and B: "My voice, my lord; your servant, lord king."

18a. Codex B = MT; but LT, as before and after, has "my lord king."

b. In Kingdoms the correspondence between *hamartanein* and *ḥṭʾ* is total (some 35x), apart from this one instance; the only other biblical exception is Ezek 35:6, where MT and GT differ from each other more, but MT does also use a form of *ʿśh*.

c. Here LT = B, both repeating the otherwise unique expression used in 25:28 (we wonder how to distinguish that rendering of MT from "What is evil in my hand?").

19a. Both B and LT use the article for *ho theos*.

20a. Here *hqr'* may be subj. or obj. of *yrdp*: if "partridge," then obj.; if "owl," then subj. Is the assonance of Heb. *qōrē'* and Gk. *-korax* deliberate?

21a. The LT = B.

b. Here LT = MT.

c. Like MT, the LT sets the time reference before the sentence break; however, MT alone reads *hnh*.

22a. The official "reading" (Q) of MT ignores the apparent art. at the beginning of "spear," and GT agrees. The MT's consonants could be read as "Look, the spear, O king."

23a. Here GT reads *ṣdqtw* as pl. We find the opposite variation between MT and B in 1 Sam 12:7.

24a. Codex B's *skepazein* corresponds to *str* in 26:1 and in a few other places in the OT; and *ekspasai* (LT) can correspond to both *nṣl* and *mlṭ*. The most economical explanation is that the reading in LT started as an alternative to the shared *exeloito*, and what we find in B is an inner-Gk. corruption.

[15–18] David taunts Abner and his men (v. 16) in terms that Saul has earlier used of him (20:31).[22] Here, as there, "son[s] of death" may mean pestilential[23] fellow[s], and hence deserving to be put to death. And here, as there, "son[s] of death" is used in immediate proximity to "life": "sons of death" belong in a different sphere from Yahweh, who lives. Saul recognizes David's voice as he taunts Abner (v. 17), although Abner himself may not have done so (v. 14b).[24] David confirms his identity and immediately complains about Saul's pursuit of him. He puts to Saul the question that is more characteristic of him than of any other biblical figure (v. 19): "What have I done?" David has asked it of Jonathan (20:1); he will ask it of Achish (29:8); and—in a substantial masoretic plus (17:29)—he has asked it of his elder brothers; and here he asks it of Saul.

[19–20] His next words (v. 19) resonate with both end and beginning of the books of Samuel: if it is Yahweh who has "incited" Saul against him, let him smell an "offering." David here utters the only explicit anticipation of "incite" in 2 Sam 24:1 (and GT preserves this link), where Yahweh will "incite" David to count his people (BTH). At the end of that census episode (2 Sam 24:25), David would offer up whole burnt offerings and *šĕlāmîm* sacrifices. And he appears to take a very cavalier attitude to the issue ventilated in the narrative about Eli's house, about whether sacrificial offering is acceptable to Yahweh as expiation for certain sorts of guilt.[25] It is not clear whether the word *mnḥh* (an essentially more flexible term) has a more precise reference here and in 2:17, 29 and 3:14.

22. The phrase is used again twice in 2 Samuel—12:5; 19:28 (29).

23. "Sons of *Môt* [Death]."

24. I am supposing that Abner is asking a real question. But his words can be a protest or a warning about the impropriety of anyone noisily hailing a camp where the king is asleep.

25. See further Auld 2002: 77–78.

The rare verb *spḥ* (v. 19) is found in the related 1 Sam 2:36 (there in the *qal*). David is fugitive, and Eli's sons will be; and in both contexts the alternate possibilities are voiced: is the problem between humans or with Yahweh?[26] If it is only men who have persuaded Saul, then being cursed "in face of" Yahweh would be a punishment fit for their crime of driving David out, "away from" Yahweh: away from Yahweh means, emotively, into the territory of other gods (v. 19). "Yahweh's holding" (*nḥlt yhwh*) recurs in HB only in 2 Sam 20:19; 21:3; and Ps 127:3. "Other gods" (again with "serve") reappear in Samuel only in 1 Sam 8:8. "Before Yahweh" is where both Agag (1 Sam 15:33) and Saul's seven descendants (2 Sam 21:9) meet their fate. Appropriately, only Saul has uttered a curse (using *ʾrr*) in all of 1–2 Samuel. In using the plural of "cursed," we may presume that David is discreetly cursing Saul: if he uses the regular singular, he could be construed as cursing the king to his face.

However carelessly or carefully David expresses himself here, one element in his implied theology deserves comment. The Philistine priests and diviners (6:2) operated with a choice between Yahweh's ark and chance. Saul will shortly swear to the medium at En-dor by Yahweh that no guilt would chance on her (28:10). But "chance," which would also be cited by an Amalekite and by the narrator, does not come into David's reckoning. He operates with only two options: Saul has been enticed against him either by Yahweh or by humans. And whichever is the case, divine or human, the action has been deliberate and deserves the appropriate response. His opponents have sought to remove him from God's (GT) or Yahweh's (MT) heritage with the words "Go serve other gods." "Chance" is something David never speaks of; and "other gods" is terminology he ascribes to others. Yahweh is the only divine force recognized by David. So soon after "other gods" (*ʾlhym ʾḥrym*), the phrase "over against Yahweh's face" (v. 20) is reminiscent of *ʿl-pny* (traditionally "before me") at the beginning of the Decalogue.

[21] David has anticipated the opening of the census story in BTH (2 Sam 24:1); Saul responds with a set of variations on David's confession within that same story. David will admit that he has sinned greatly, ask that his guilt be removed, and underscore his admission of guilt by noting he has also been very foolish (24:10). Here Saul admits to having sinned, but not greatly (1 Sam 26:21). He will do nothing bad (here anticipating the older text of 2 Sam 24:17) to David. He has played the fool, but not greatly. What has been very great indeed has been merely his unwitting mistake (v. 21). Saul's variation of the final words David will later use is triply interesting: uniquely in HB it uses the *hipʿil* rather than *nipʿal* of *skl*; it tries to defuse the implications of "folly" by attaching a term for unintentional mistake; and it is to that second verb that

26. Only here does *spḥ* correspond with *stērizesthai* ("be firmly set/fixed").

he attaches not just "very" (David's multiplier) but "a very great deal." He claims implicitly that his folly is not culpable, but very, very venial: it was unintentional.

David may have suggested that, if he were forced by others into the service of "other gods," it would not be his fault. Saul replies with a similar abdication of responsibility. It is fascinating to observe how each man picks up and develops hints from the other's language. David has suggested that an offering should suffice if it should turn out that it was Yahweh who has incited Saul against him: if the instigation came from Yahweh, then neither man is to blame; if neither man is to blame and it was all a mistake, then the appropriate offering should meet the case. Saul's response (v. 21) culminates in the verb *šgh*: precisely the sort of unwitting behavior (*šggh*) for which priestly teaching prescribes a sacrificial offering.

[22–24] David's answer is symbolic: to invite one of Saul's staff to retrieve his spear. Here, as in 9:3; 16:18 (MT); 25:14 (B), we have to ask whether "one from the lads" suggests just any one—or whether only a select junior will be ready to retrieve the royal emblem from a David who has been able to remove it from the heart of the camp.

The spear (v. 22) is prominent in this narrative (see also 7, 8, 11, 12, 16), and throughout 1 Samuel it is particularly associated with Saul. At the beginning of his reign, swords and spears are so rare in Israel that only he and Jonathan have them (13:22). Saul is seen with his spear in his hand (18:10 plus; 19:9; 22:6); and—as he dies—he is leaning on it (2 Sam 1:6). And Saul throws his spear (18:11 plus; 19:10; 20:33) precisely at those potential rivals (David his commander and Jonathan his son) who might be king in his place. By returning the royal spear, David is demonstrating that, although he has temporarily removed it, he has no current designs on either Saul's life or his kingdom. Barbara Green (2003a: 388; 2003b: 96–98) discusses why only the spear and not also the water is offered for return. Though Saul has promised to do David no further harm (v. 21), David seeks no further assurance from him, but instead appeals to Yahweh (v. 23) to reward his faithful and righteous behavior (*ṣdqh*) and save his life as he has saved Saul's. The noun *ṣdqh* is not common in Samuel–Kings; however, it is practiced by David in 2 Sam 8:15 and by Solomon, according to 1 Kgs 10:9 (both BTH); and the formulation here is close to 1 Kgs 8:32 (also BTH). Paired with it here is *ʾmwnh*, which is even rarer in Samuel–Kings—used only of reliable temple restorers in 2 Kgs 12:15 (16); 22:7 (BTH). Abishai has earlier spoken about "God's" giving David's enemy into his hand (v. 8). David now attributes this to Yahweh (v. 23).[27]

27. The phrase *ntn byd* has Yahweh as subj. in 1 Sam 14:10, 12; 17:47; 23:4; 24:4, 10 (5, 11); 26:23; 28:19; 30:23; and "God" as subj. in 1 Sam 14:37; 23:14; 26:8.

1 Samuel 26:25

25 And Saul said to David,
"Blessed are you, [my] son [David[a]].
You will both go on and on doing,
and also go on and on being able."
And David went [on his way] *to his place*,
and Saul, he returned to his [place] *way*.

25a. The LT does attest "David," but not "my."

[25] These words elicit an unusual blessing on David by Saul (26:25).[28] The verb "do" is normally followed by an object naming what is done; and the verb "be able" is normally followed by a verb naming a specific sort of action. Here both of these verbs are not only left open and unspecific, but also emphasized by duplication. Any translation must be tentative: "You will do what you like (or go on and on doing), and be wholly able so to do." At one level, Saul is congratulating David for achieving what should have been impossible, extrapolating from his successful penetration of the royal camp. However, the oddity of the expression is lessened if we recognize its origins. If the Book of Two Houses was the controlling narrative and set the agenda for the books of Samuel–Kings, and if 1 Samuel is a substantial anticipatory commentary on that earlier narrative, then Saul's blessing will have Micaiah's vision of Yahweh in mind. Micaiah's report to Ahab concludes with Yahweh's words to the lying spirit: "You will entice and you will also[29] be able (succeed); go out and do so" (1 Kgs 22:22). As in Saul's blessing, "can" and "do" are the key words: they offer assurance of successful deception—and at Yahweh's command. In receipt of such a blessing, David does go out and does successfully dupe Achish, by means that include total ruthlessness. Is this also in accordance with the divine will?

David has made no direct accusation against his king: Saul has been misled either by Yahweh or by humans—and if the latter, then they should be cursed.

The words of Saul do not just close this scene. They are also the last words Saul ever addressed to David. It may be for this reason that this scene's ending is transcribed as a full paragraph. Saul's words represent a double reversal. He addresses David as if an independent actor, and he recognizes David as "blessed." Samuel's major statement about the future has ended (12:25) by speaking of the consequences of doing real evil (*r" hip'il* doubled by use of inf. abs.) for people and king alike. Saul, who has admitted doing David unmerited evil (26:21), ends his statement with a double evocation of Samuel's

28. It is also somewhat ironic, since he has earlier blessed the Ziphites for locating David (23:21).

29. Even the *gam* of the source text becomes a (repeated) feature of Saul's blessing.

conclusion: emphatic *gam* ("also") used twice, each time introducing a verb doubled by use of an infinitive absolute. (Or does Samuel negatively anticipate Saul's blessing of David?) Appropriately, each goes a different way. The contrasting destinations appears to suggest settled and unsettled existence; but B and MT (= LT) are not agreed over which is appropriate for whom. In 23:22 and 27:5, a "place" is associated with David, and in 26:5 with Saul. However, in 24:22 (23), OG has Saul "departing to his place [MT: 'house']."

Excursus 3: Retrospect on 1 Samuel 24–26 Recurrent Narratives in Samuel

Up to this point, we have read 1 Sam 24–26 largely as three separate narratives. However, they share too many features for such separate reading to be wholly satisfactory. This is most obviously true of chs. 24 and 26; but it is also true of the intervening chapter, which has many significant links with each. Before we say more, we should satisfy ourselves as to quite how much the two outer stories share:

1. Saul pursues David with a force of 3,000 men in the desert country to the southeast of Judah (24:2; 26:2).
2. Where Saul stops, he is vulnerable (24:4; 26:4–7).
3. David's companion[s] tell him that God has given his enemy into his hand (24:4a; 26:8).
4. David secretly takes something royally significant and recognizable from Saul (24:5b; 26:11b–12).
5. David refuses to "put out his hand against" (*šlḥ yd b-*) the anointed of Yahweh (24:6–7, 10 [MT: 7–8, 11]; 26:9–11a).
6. David presents Saul with the proof of his goodwill (24:11–12; 26:16).
7. David addresses Saul as "my lord the king" (24:8; 26:17) and as "the anointed of Yahweh" (24:6, 10; 26:16).
8. David complains about being pursued (*rdp*) (24:14 [15]; 26:18–20).
9. Saul recognizes David's voice and calls him "my son" (24:16; 26:17).
10. Saul declares himself in the wrong (24:17; 26:21).
11. David is recognized as *ṣdyq,* or at least implicitly claimed as *ṣdqh* (24:17 [18]; 26:23).
12. The pair of verbs "see and know"[30] is used in both—but differently (24:11; 26:12).
13. The rare *piʿel* of *sgr* is in both, with Yahweh as subject and Saul as object (24:18 [19]; 26:8).
14. "Bless" is used in both (23:21; 26:25).
15. Both draw on David's confession in 2 Sam 24:10, 17 (1 Sam 24:11; 26:21).
16. The phrase *tḥt . . . hywm hzh* occurs in both (24:19 [20]; 26:21)

30. With 14:38, the usage of this phrase is concentrated in chs. 23–26. Note the discussion of seeing and knowing in Pamuk 92–97 (there in terms of the art of blind miniaturists).

The comparisons can be stated in different ways. The two stories clearly share the same structure: in each, David has Saul in his power in the dark, is urged to kill him but instead removes a distinctive and symbolic item from the king, proves the rightness of his cause, and wins Saul's approval. Moreover, they also share a significant amount of distinctive wording; and the distribution of that wording maps only partially on the common elements of structure and story line. And this point is quite as true if we identify 1 Sam 23:19 as the opening of the first narrative instead of 24:1—Saul's blessing of David (26:25), for example, to which nothing in ch. 24 corresponds, echoes his blessing of the Ziphites (23:21). Both of the outer panels of this apparent triptych draw on David's confession in the census story. In the first, David is denying that he has sinned; and in the second, it is Saul who is admitting his folly. And both share significant wording with the story of David, Nabal, and Abigail.

Some language of 1 Sam 25 is shared with the surrounding chapters (D = David):

Term	**1 Sam 25**	**1 Sam 23:19–24:23**	**1 Sam 26**	**Elsewhere in 1 Samuel**
3,000	v. 2 sheep	24:2 (3) *bḥwr*	v. 2 *bḥwr*	13:2 *wybḥr*
hdbrym h'lh	vv. 9, 12, 37	24:16 (17)		5x; & 2 Sam 7:17; 13:21; 14:3, 19
mhr	vv. 18, 23, 34, 42, all for Abigail	23:27, request to Saul		4:14; 9:12; 17:48; 28:20, 24
bstr/msttr	v. 20, Abigail	23:19 D	v. 1, D	19:2; 20:5, 19, 24, all D; & 2 Sam 12:12
'śh + inf. abs.	v. 28		v. 25	2 Sam 9:7
blessed, *brwk*	vv. 32, 33, 39 D	23:21, Saul to Ziph	v. 25, Saul to D	15:13, Saul to Samuel; & 2 Sam 18:28
bless, *brk pi'el*	v. 14, D to Nabal			2:20; 9:13; 13:10; & 2 Sam 6:12, 18, 20; 7:29; 8:10; 13:25; 14:22; 19:39 (40); 21:3
do obeisance to a human	vv. 23, 41, Abigail to D & servant	24:8, D to Saul		20:41; 28:14 (Saul to Samuel); & 2 Samuel (12x)

pursue, *rdp*	v. 29	23:25, 28; 24:14 (15)	vv. 18, 20	7:11; 17:52; ch. 30 (3x); & 2 Sam 2 (3x); chs. 17–20 (4x[31]); 22:38; 24:13
smite, *ngp*	v. 38		v. 10	4:3; & 2 Sam 12:15
see and know	v. 17 (reversed)	23:22, 23; 24:11	v. 12	14:38
enemy	vv. 22, 26, 29	24:4, 19	v. 8	13x
ryb 't-ryb	v. 39, Yahweh	24:15, Yahweh		
pšʿ	v. 28	24:11 (12)		
hšyb, divine subj.	vv. 21, 39		v. 23	2 Sam 15:8, 25; 16:8, 12; 22:21, 25
rʿh	vv. 17, 21, 26, 28, 39 (2x)	24:9, 11, 17 (MT: 10, 12, 18)	v. 18	6:9; 10:19; 12:17, 19, 20; 20:7, 9, 13; 23:9; 29:6
ṭwbh	vv. 21, 30	24:17, 18, 19 (MT: 18, 19, 20)		1 Sam 2:24; & 2 Sam 16:12; 17:7, 14; 18:27

The priority of 1 Sam 24 over 1 Sam 26, or the other way round, has been debated over the generations, and at length, without clear conclusion. The model proposed in this commentary for understanding the development of the books of Samuel allows the question as generally posed to be (usefully) sidestepped. At least a version of 1 Sam 24 had concluded the first main draft of the story of Saul and David (1 Sam 9–24). Then 1 Sam 25–26 was first drafted as a supplement to this story. But that does not exclude the possibility of backward influence from them on ch. 24. First Samuel 26 appears to have more connections than ch. 24 to wider themes in Samuel. And yet 1 Sam 24 seems more closely linked than ch. 26 to ch. 25: the story of David and Nabal offers parabolic comment on 1 Sam 24, from which the David of 1 Sam 26 has learned: ch. 26 reads like a midrash on ch 24, from *trdmt yhwh* (26:12) to final blessing by Saul (v. 25). Psalm 37—with its unconcern over the current success of the wicked, its mention of "his day" coming (v. 13), its waiting for vindication—makes an interesting intertext with 1 Sam 24–26: the wealthy wicked of the psalm have aspects of both Saul and Nabal.

31. First Samuel 17:1 in MT only; GT has read *w'rdh*, without *p*.

1 Samuel 27:1–6

1 And David said [to] *in*[a] his heart,
"Now I shall be [swept away] *added*[b] *in* one day [by] *to* the hand of Saul;
there is no good for me but to get away [completely] to Philistine land,
and *if* Saul [will despair of] *is* seeking me further in all the territory of Israel,
and I shall get away from his hand."
2 And David arose
[and crossed over, he] and [six] *the four* hundred men who were with him,
to Achish[a] son of [Maoch] *Ammach*[b] king of Gath.
3 And David settled with Achish [in Gath[a]], he and his men, each man and his house,
and David and his two wives, Ahinoam the Jezreelite and Abigail wife of Nabal the Carmelite.
4 And it was reported to Saul
that David had fled to Gath,
and he did not continue further seeking him.

5 And David said to Achish,
"If [I have] *your servant*[a] *has* in fact found favor in your eyes,
let there be given me a place in one of the towns of the countryside,
and let me settle there.
And why should your servant settle in [the royal] *a* city *ruled by a king*[b] with you?"
6 And [Achish] *he* gave him on that day Ziklag.
Therefore Ziklag has belonged to the king[s][a] of Judah till this day.

1a. The GT appears to attest *blbw*.

b. Here GT appears to render a form not of *sph* but of *ysp*; see on 26:10 above. In v. 4 below, GT does have the expected *prosetheto* for *ysp* (Q).

2a. The GT offers *Agchous* throughout this chapter: does Gk. *-gch-* represent a Heb. double *k*?

b. In this sentence, LT agrees with MT is saying "crossed over" and 600, but with B over *Agchous*; however, it gives that king's father's name as *Achimaan*. *Ammach* (B) may represent *ʿmk*, rather than *mʿwk*, as in MT.

3a. The LT is still fuller: "king in Gath."

5a. Here LT = B.

b. The vb. *basileuein* is very common in the Gk. OT; but this may be the unique instance of the pass. Only in Dan 9:1 is *mlk* (*hopʿal*) attested, but in the sense "was made king." Again LT = B.

6a. Here LT = MT.

[1–4] Despite Saul's blessing David (26:25), David's private estimate of his situation is less secure (27:1). David has spoken to Abishai (26:10) about the coming of Saul's day for dying or about his being swept away in battle (precisely what Samuel threatened for the people and their future king in 12:25). But now David broods over his own fate in very similar terms. "One day," although ostensibly used in the sense of our "someday,"[32] will also deliberately resume "his day will come" (26:10). And the thought that David too might be "swept away" (MT) is stated in the third of only three occurrences of *sph nipʿal* in FP (MT).[33] Each of these is in 1 Samuel; and the second, like the use of "day," was also a significant element of 26:10. David has "escaped" before; but the triple use of *nmlṭ* ("get away")[34] in this opening verse is most reminiscent of his first escape from Saul (the term was used four times in 19:10–18). On that occasion, David escaped to Samuel and was pursued by Saul. On this occasion he escapes to the Philistines. Again Saul will seek out Samuel (ch. 28).

David speaks of the "land" (*ʾereṣ*) of the Philistines but of the "borders" or "territory" (*gĕbûl*) of Israel (v. 1). It is not easy to decide whether he intends a deliberate contrast in geographical terminology. The "land of the Philistines" is mentioned again in 1 Sam 29:11 and 30:16, apart from the immediate source of the phrase (31:9, BTH)—and again (within FP) only in 1 Kgs 4:21 (5:1) and 2 Kgs 8:2–3. The term "borders" is never connected with Philistines. The "borders of Israel" are mentioned in 1 Sam 7:13; 11:3, 7; and 2 Sam 21:5; but the "land of Israel" only in 1 Sam 13:19. The "land of Judah" is used in 1 Sam 22:5; 30:16—but "borders of Judah" never in Samuel (and in all of HB, only in Ezek 48).

Mention of David's wives (v. 3) ties this narrative to the end of ch. 25, and indeed to the chapters that follow. They reappear in 30:5; 2 Sam 2:2; 3:3; and in the broad context of each a form of the verb *ḥzq* ("be strong") is used (2 Sam 2:7, *qal*; 1 Sam 30:6 and 2 Sam 3:6, *hitpaʿel*). Although well represented in BTH, forms of this verb are relatively infrequent in nonsynoptic portions of 1–2 Samuel.[35] The evidence is accumulating that 1 Sam 25–30 and 2 Sam 1–4 represent a connected and developed stratum of the book. But we should also note one piece of possible counterevidence: the name of Achish's father is given here (v. 2) as if we are meeting him for the first time: that may suggest that this chapter was drafted prior to the previously reported episode about David and this king of Gath (21:10–15). Saul's response to the news of David's flight

32. The combination *yôm ʾeḥād* is very rare in HB; it has quite different force in Gen 33:13 (a single day) and Zech 14:7 (continuous day).

33. But see below on 2 Sam 24:13.

34. Genesis 19 is the other HB context which links *nsph* and *nmlṭ*.

35. Also *ḥzq hitpaʿel* is only in 1 Sam 4:9 and 2 Sam 10:12 (BTH); *qal* only in 1 Sam 17:50 (MT plus); 2 Sam 10:11 (2x), 12 (all BTH); 13:14, 28; 16:21; 24:4 (BTH).

to Gath (v. 4) is similar to when he heard that David had escaped from Keilah (23:13)—he broke off his pursuit.

[5–6] Now apparently safe from Saul's attentions, David asks his Philistine host for "a place," or "space," for himself. In a phrase unique within HB, he requests space in one of the "towns of the open country." Elsewhere *śādeh* is what lies outside a town, as in the description of Hebron, which was assigned to Caleb, while its fields or open country were given to a priestly family (Josh 21:11–12//1 Chr 6:55–56 [40–41]). In this exceptional case, *śādeh* appears to refer to the territory of Gath lying outside Achish's royal city of Gath. By seeking to move outside Achish's capital, David may be testing how far he is under surveillance as a refugee. Ziklag is granted him without further ado and apparently thereby becomes a personal holding of the kings of Judah (v. 6, "till this day").

If we recognize the cluster of significant terms at the end of this short narrative as deliberate anticipations of the great dynastic chapter (see below on the links between v. 12 and 2 Sam 7), we are better able to recognize the preparatory hints scattered through this first portion: the promise of a safe "place" (1 Sam 27:5), where violent men will no longer be able to oppress (2 Sam 7:10); "kingdom" (1 Sam 27:5; 2 Sam 7:12); "to this day" (1 Sam 27:6; 2 Sam 7:6). Still earlier (1 Sam 27:3) it is noted that David's "house[hold]" (2 Sam 7:18, 19, 26, 29) is also in the care of Achish.

1 Samuel 27:7–12

7 And the number of the days
that David settled in Philistine countryside
were [days and[a]] four months.

8 And David went up and his men,
and they made a raid[a] on *all* the Geshurite [and the Gir(ga)zite] and the Amalekite,
for they were settling[b] the land that is from "Ever"[c] as you come to Shur
and toward [the land of[d]] Egypt.[e]

9 And *he*[a] [David] would strike the land,
and he[b] would not keep man or woman alive,
and he[b] would take flock and herd and donkeys and camels and clothing;
and he returned and came to Achish.

10 And Achish said *to David*,
"[{To . . .}] *On whom* have you raided today?"
And David said *to Achish*,
"Against the south[a] of Judah and against the south of the Jerahmeelite[b]

and against the south of the Qen*iz*ite."

11 Neither man nor woman would David keep alive to bring to Gath,
saying,
"Lest they report *to Gath* against us, saying,
'Thus David acted.
And this was his justice all the days
that he settled in Philistine countryside.'"

12 And Achish was confident[a] in David, saying,
"He has become utterly obnoxious in his people, in Israel;
and he [has/will become] *will be*[b] my servant forever."

7a. Here LT = B.

8a. The LT has a much fuller text: "on everyone approaching and made a raid on." Also, LT's second of three names is *Iexraion*.

b. The f. ptc. in MT is surprising—B does not read *hnh* as a pl. pronoun but renders by *idou*; then its *katōkeito* may attest a pass. form of *yšb*.

c. Both *Gelampsour* (B) and *Gelamsour* (A) appear to have read *šûrâ* immediately after *mēʿôlām*. Perhaps *anēkontōn* represents something like *bwʾk*, as in Josh 23:14 (B).

d. Quite often *ʾrṣ* is a secondary addition; however, here *ths* before *Aigyptou* could be a corruption of *ghs*.

e. In the second half of this sentence, LT is unusually much shorter than MT or B: "[the land] from Geshur and up to the land of Egypt."

9a. The LT has pl., "they."

b. The GT has both final vbs. pl.

10a. Here GT treats the three instances of *negeb* as directional, replacing it by the wind direction *notos* ("south").

b. Codex B's *Iesmega* could represent the otherwise unknown *yšmʿh*. The LT reads *Aermōn*.

12a. Here B oddly makes David to be subj. of the rare pass. *episteuthē*; in 3:21 it corresponds to *nipʿal ʾmn*.

b. The LT = B here.

[7–12] The period of David's being settled in "Philistine countryside" is defined (v. 7), then referred to later in the chapter (v. 11b), using a topographical expression found only where the length of the sojourn of the ark is defined as seven months in 1 Sam 6:1. The length of this sojourn is given as simply "four months" in GT, but as "*yāmîm* plus four months" in MT. The refugee from Saul is far from being confined in Ziklag. He busies himself with many raids and achieves a complete deception of Achish. The details of the peoples he raids are textually uncertain. However, despite the quantities of booty he brings back to Achish, these do not include human slaves, who could betray their origins; and he passes off the victims of his plundering as peoples in and near the south of Judah. Achish has no reason not to trust David (v. 12). David can take double confidence in Achish's operating by the rule that his enemy's enemy is his friend: David is not only in flight from King Saul but must also (as a result of these claimed depredations) have become in Achish's eyes thoroughly obnoxious among his people.

The closing verse includes some striking adaptations of language drawn from Nathan's dynastic oracle and David's response in 2 Sam 7:3–29 (BTH). Although nowhere else combined as here (*ʿebed ʿôlām* = "perpetual servant"), *ʿebed* and *ʿôlām* occur more densely separately in David's prayer than elsewhere in HB; and "in Israel" in apposition to "in his people" anticipates "my/your people Israel" in 2 Sam 7:7, 8, 10, 11, 23, 24. Its opening verb *wyʾmn* is read as *hipʿil* in MT (*heʾĕmîn* is detected only here in 1–2 Samuel), but as *nipʿal* in GT, which can be compared with 1 Sam 2:35; 22:14; 25:28, and which will have been drawn from the same key chapter of BTH, though differently placed now in 2 Sam 7:16 and 1 Chr 17:23–24. The confidence of Achish is further reflected in his emphatic use of the infinitive absolute in both 27:12 and 28:1.

We could add that the term for being found wholly objectionable (stinking) has also been derived from a neighboring portion of BTH: 2 Sam 10:6. And there is more! Our author finds space within even a short episode to give double emphasis to David's wholesale slaughter of the humans he captures on these raids. His practice of killing "man and woman" is stated (v. 9); and when it is restated (v. 11), "man and woman" is promoted to the head of the clause. What David does to these peoples is the very opposite of what is reported about Joab in a related synoptic context, though not now in Samuel, but only in 1 Chr 11:8. The last sentence of the Chronicler's report of the taking of Jerusalem notes that Joab "preserved alive the remainder of the city." We shall discuss (below on 2 Sam 5:6–10) the evidence that the authors of Samuel have airbrushed Joab—and his magnanimity—out of their version of Jerusalem's capture.

With Saul's blessing of David still ringing in our ears (26:25), and noticing the several words Achish anticipates from the end of 2 Sam 7, we might well suppose that Achish shares the whole conclusion of the dynastic chapter: "and with your blessing shall the house of your servant be blessed forever." When blessing David, Saul has predicted quite unspecifically that David will be remarkable in his ability to achieve things. Rendering Achish wholly pliable to his wishes is David's first such success. But if it is by duplicity that David achieves Achish's trust, how does this reflect on the confidence that David expresses in the establishment of his house by Yahweh? Do the links with 2 Sam 7 serve only to ridicule Achish? Or do they also tend to subvert the image of David and the later confidence of the Davidic house? Not all the Philistines are so readily duped: the more critical role played by the staff of Achish in 1 Sam 21:11 is resumed later in the book (1 Sam 29:3–5) by his fellow kings.

The morality of David's actions would need to be probed and discussed even if this narrative and what immediately precedes it contained no allusions to other parts of Samuel–Kings. But, as we noted in our first comment on Saul's blessing (26:25), other links do sharpen the issues. There are three certain instances of the verb *yākōl* in BTH (1 Kgs 8:11; 9:21; 22:22 [2 Kgs 18:29 is uncertain]). If the Book of Two Houses is the controlling narrative that has set the agenda for the books of Samuel–Kings, and if 1 Samuel is a substantial anticipatory commentary on that earlier narrative, then Saul's statement within his blessing that David "will be able" (from *yākōl*) may have a second relevant passage in mind. The account of Solomon's reign in BTH talks about people who are not of the sons of Israel and whom the sons of Israel "had not been able" to destroy (1 Kgs 9:20–21). David's expeditions from his Philistine stronghold are as successfully devious as the lying spirit (1 Kgs 22:22); and the totality of destruction that others in Israel cannot achieve within Israel, David is able to achieve on its southern margins: "He let live neither man nor woman" (1 Sam 27:9, 11).

To add to the list of controlling parallels, both David and Solomon are credited in BTH with practicing (doing) justice (*mišpāṭ*) and righteousness (*ṣĕdāqâ*): "David was practicing justice and righteousness for all his people" (2 Sam 8:15); and the Queen of Sheba blesses Yahweh for making Solomon king in order "to practice justice and righteousness" (1 Kgs 10:9). David's "righteousness" has apparently been exemplary in chs. 24–26. And yet, with these twin "texts" of BTH in our ears, it is hard not to find the comment "Thus did David practice and thus was his justice all the time that he lived in Philistine open country" (v. 11b) somewhat ironic. Unlike many translators, I have ascribed all these words to the hypothetical captives; but of course the narrator is speaking through them (Bar-Efrat 1:350). They certainly underscore Samuel's early warning about the *mišpāṭ* of a future king (8:11).

One corollary to this discussion is the total inadequacy of translating *mišpāṭ* by "practice" or "custom." We may have to debate whether or not the narrator was well disposed to David. But there can be no doubt that 1 Samuel wants to warn us that kingship implies the use of means that many will find dubious. Campbell (1:274) may be strictly correct to say that there is no word in this chapter of Yahweh's intervention; and yet, for those who remember the "texts" (BTH) as they read the "commentary" (1–2 Samuel), Yahweh's encouragement cannot be far from their minds.

1 Samuel 28:1–2

1 And it came to be in those days,
and Philistines assembled[a] *in* their camp [in force]
to go out[b] to make war on Israel;
and Achish said to David,
"Know for sure
that with me you will go out [in the camp] *to* war,[c] you and your men."

2 And David said to Achish,
"Therefore *now*[a] you [yourself] will know
what your servant will do."
And Achish said to David,
"Therefore guard of my head[b] I will set you for all time."

1a. Here LT's act. vb. agrees with the *qal* in MT. The middle voice in B corresponds better to a *nip'al*, as in 28:4. Apart from 1 Sam 7:5–6, *qābaṣ* is used in Samuel only in this central, and later, portion (1 Sam 25:1; 28:1, 4 [2x]; 29:1; 2 Sam 2:30; 3:21).

b. The GT apparently read not *lṣb'* (which MT attests in only four late biblical contexts: Num 4; 31; Josh 22; 1 Chr 12), but the similar *lṣ't*.

c. Here 4QSam[a] supports *lmlḥmh*, as attested by GT here, not *bmḥnh* (MT); but 4QSam[a] does not support the following "you and your men," over which MT and GT agree.

2a. The GT *nyn* attests *'th*, not *'th*.

b. Here GT renders as "chief bodyguard."

[1–2] "In those days" (*bayyāmîm hāhēm*) are normally the opening words of an independent statement. It is rare to find the phrase prefaced as here by the connecting *wayĕhî* (elsewhere only in Exod 2:11, 23; Judg 19:1), although that is common in the case of the singular "in that day." The Philistine decision to make war on Israel forces Achish to clarify the situation of the refugee. What he says to David (*yādōa' tēda'*) has the same emphatic structure (using the inf. abs. alongside the finite vb.) as what he has just said to himself in 27:12 (*hab'ēš hib'îš*): the complete certainty that David will be included among the forces of Achish corresponds to his total unacceptability within his own people, Israel. David answers that Achish also has something to "know"—just what David (taking up again the words of Saul's blessing in 26:25) will "do." And that unspecific commitment is enough for the gullible Achish to make Saul's one-time bodyguard his own bodyguard—and for an unrestricted period (v. 2).

1 Samuel 28:3–30:25 Saul Prostrate; David Legislating

1 Samuel 28:3–25

3 Now Samuel had died,
and all Israel mourned him;
and they buried him in Ramah [even] in his town.
And Saul had removed the bottles[a] and the experts[b] from the land.
4 And the Philistines were gathered[a]
and they came
and camped in Shunem,[b]
and Saul gathered [all] *every man of* Israel,
and they camped in Gilboa.

5 And Saul saw the Philistine camp;
and he was afraid
and his heart[a] trembled greatly.
6 And Saul asked of Yahweh;
but Yahweh did not answer him:
  [even] by dreams, [even[a]] by the Urim,[b] [even[a]] by the prophets.
7 And Saul said to his servants,
  "Seek for me a woman, a bottle-mistress,
  and let me go to her,
  and let me inquire by her."
And his servants said to him,
  "There is in fact a woman, a bottle-mistress, in En-dor."
8 And Saul disguised himself
and dressed in other clothes,
and he went and two men with him,
and they came to the woman by night;
and he said *to* her,[a]
  "Divine for me, I insist, by the skin-bottle,
  and raise for me
    whomever I say to you."
9 And the woman said to him,
  "Look, you yourself[a] know
    what Saul did:
    how he cut off the 'bottles' and the 'expert[s]'[b] from the land.
  And why are you striking[c] at my life,
    putting me to death?"
10 And Saul swore to her [by Yahweh[a]], saying,
  "As Yahweh lives, guilt will not happen on you in this matter."
11 And the woman said,
  "Whom shall I raise for you?"
And he said,
  "Samuel you should raise for me."
12 And the woman saw Samuel,
and she[a] cried out with a great voice,
and the woman said to Saul:
  "Why have you deceived me?
  You are Saul."
13 And the king said to her,
  "Do not be afraid;
  [for what] *say whom*[a] have you seen?"
And the woman said to Saul,
  "Gods did I see,

rising from the earth."
14 And he said to her,
"What was his form?"[a]
And the woman said,
"An [old] *erect*[b] man rising,
and he is wrapped in a robe."
And Saul knew
that it was Samuel;
and he knelt face on the ground
and did obeisance *to him.*

15 And Samuel said [to Saul],
"Why have you caused me disturbance,[a]
raising me up?"
And Saul said,
"It is very tight[b] for me;
and Philistines are making war on me;
and God has turned from me
and has not answered me still—even by hand of the prophets, even by dreams;[c]
and I called to you
to let me know
what I should do."

16 And Samuel said:
"And why do you ask me,
and Yahweh has turned from you
and come to be [your adversary] *with your* neighbor?[a]
17 And Yahweh has done to you
as [he[a]] *Yahweh* spoke by my hand,
and Yahweh [has torn] *will tear*[b] the kingdom from your hand
and give[n] it to your neighbor, to David.
18 Just as you did not listen to Yahweh's voice
and did not 'do' the heat of his anger on Amalek,
accordingly this deed has Yahweh done to you this day.
19 And Yahweh will give[a] Israel [too] with you into Philistine hands,
and tomorrow you and your sons [{will be}] with [me] *you will* fall,[b]
the camp of Israel [too][c] Yahweh will give into Philistine hands."
20 And Saul made speed
and fell his full height[a] on the ground,
and was greatly afraid at the words of Samuel.

Power [too[b]] there was not in him [any more],
for he had not eaten food the whole day and [the] *that* whole night.
21 And the woman came to Saul,
and she saw
that he [was very disturbed] *made very great* haste;[a]
and she said to him,
"Look, your servant listened to your voice,
and I put my life in my hand,[b]
and I heard the words
you spoke to me.
22 Now then, you too be sure to listen to the words of your servant,
and let me put before you a piece of food,
and eat;
and let there be power in you
that you may go on your way."
23 And he refused;[a]
and he said,
"I shall not eat."
And his servants broke through to him,
and the woman too,
and he listened to their voice
and rose from the ground
and sat on the couch.
24 And the woman had a stall{-fat} calf[a] at home,
and she made speed
and sacrificed it;
and she took flour
and kneaded it
and baked of it[b] unleavened loaves.
25 And she brought them before Saul and before his servants,
and they ate;
and they rose
and went [in[a]] that night.

3a. The GT has "ventriloquists" (*engastrimythous*), as throughout this chapter.

b. A pair in 2 Kgs 21:6 again, where Gk. also renders by *gnōstas*.

4a. Here, unlike 28:1, MT and OG agree over *nipʿal*/middle.

b. Here B and LT both read *Sōman*.

5a. It is also possible that Saul is the grammatical subj. and "his heart" locates the trembling.

6a. The GT connects only with *kai* in LT, before each element, like *gam* in MT; in B, only before elements two and three. It appears there was a predilection for *gam* in Samuel (MT)—cf. 19:20–24.

b. Here GT renders, as in Num 27:21, by *en tois dēlois*—however, that corresponds in Deut 33:8; 1 Sam 14:41 to *ʾûrîm*. One may wonder how GT envisaged "prophetic" at the end of a series, following "dreamlike" and "clear."

8a. Here LT = B.

9a. Notice the emphasis: it is unlikely that she already knows she is speaking to Saul (see v. 12); more likely, she is suggesting that everyone knows Saul's earlier purging action.

b. Here LT differs from B and offers *apophthengomenous* ("speak plainly/pointedly")—used once each for five different Heb. terms in HB.

c. Is there a deliberate suggestion of *nwqš* ("be trapped") in *nqš* ("strike")? Or are *nqš* and *yqš* variants? The Gk. *pagideueis* apparently attests *yqš* (*qal*).

10a. The LT has Saul swearing "by God."

12a. Here LT specifies "the woman" too, perhaps because the Gk. vb. does not mark the f. subj.

13a. Codex B may attest *ʾmry my*. The LT has elements of both MT and B: the question is "what" rather than "whom"; and its "say" follows the question.

14a. The GT with *ti egnōs* has apparently not read *mh tʾrw*; has it read *mh ydʿt*? This question (in MT) is posed twice in Job, in 15:9 ("What do you know that we do not?"); 34:33 ("What do you know? Declare.").

b. Neither *orthion* (B, LT, unique in OT) nor *orthrion* (A, rare in OT) appears to attest MT's *zqn*.

15a. The Gk. *parenochlein* ("cause great annoyance") is used to render at least six different Hebrew vbs., once each.

b. The GT does not maintain the link with David's words in 2 Sam 24:14.

c. Here B = MT; but LT adds the third element, *oute en dēlois*.

16a. The OG's *meta tou plēsion sou* may attest something like *ʿm rʿk*, of which *ʿrk* (MT) may be an unintended contraction.

17a. Apart from the second *kyrios*, B = MT in the first part of this sentence. However, LT does not specify the [divine] subj. of either vb.; and more interesting, it reads "to him" rather than "to you."

b. The LT = B.

19a. Here GT and MT agree over the future reference.

b. Again LT is different: "You and Jonathan your son < will be > with me."

c. The LT adds "with you."

20a. Presumably both *hestēkōs* (B) and *apo tēs staseōs autou* (LT) are suggesting that Saul did not crumple to the floor, but fell rigid.

b. This verse, like 19, has an instance of *gam* not attested in GT. But LT does add "and you."

21a. The GT repeats *speudein*; the correspondence with *mhr* at the beginning of v. 20 is quite the most common, but it corresponds to *bhl* 6x, including Exod 15:15 (just following mention of *rgz* [1 Sam 28:15] and Philistines) and Judg 20:41 (the culmination of the battle at Gibeah).

b. Apparently a stock idiom: Judg 12:3; 1 Sam 28:21; Ps 119:109; Job 13:14.

23a. May *wymʾn* ("refused") in the case of Saul be intended to echo *wyʾmn* ("was confident") in the recent case (27:12) of Achish?

24a. Codex B has *damalis nomas* ("grazing heifer"); and LT, *moscharion galathēnon* ("little sucking calf").

b. Here *wtphw* is written defectively (from *ʾph*).

25a. The MT uses the preposition, but not 4QSam[a] or GT.

[3] It is the next stage in the Philistine muster, their encampment at Shunem, that provokes Saul's response in mustering Israel and their encampment at Gilboa. (Gilboa as the scene of Saul's demise is determined by the start of BTH in 1 Sam 31.) But before this is reported (v. 4), the narrative pauses to provide two pieces of background information. About the death and burial of Samuel (v. 3a) we have already read in almost identical terms in 25:1a. But Saul's purge of *ʾōbôt* and *yiddĕʿōnîm* from the land (v. 3b) has not previously been reported to us. (We shall encounter a similar situation in 2 Sam 21:1–14.) There seems to be no suggestion that Saul's "reform" was consequent on Samuel's death. Like the reminder of Samuel's death, the notice of the removal of the illicit intermediaries is stated in an independent *qāṭal* verbal form. Both separate pieces of information are simply necessary for understanding what follows.

Leviticus forbids turning to either *ʾōbôt* or *yiddĕʿōnîm* on pain of death (19:31; 20:6, 27); and Deut 18:11 declares, "There shall not be found in you a bottle-asker [*šōʾēl ʾôb*]." Probably the warnings against such in Torah depend on the account of King Manasseh in BTH (2 Kgs 21:6), who is criticized for these and several more illicit religious practices. The book of Isaiah offers three rather more informative intertexts. The woman consulted by Saul says she sees "gods going up from the earth" (*ʾlhym ʿlym mn-hʾrṣ*); and Samuel complains of Saul's disturbance "bringing me up" (*lhʿlwt ʾty*). Isaiah speaks (8:19), in the context of *ʾōbôt* and *yiddĕʿōnîm*, of a people consulting "its god[s]" (*ʾlhyw*), and then of the Egyptians consulting such (19:3), and also of a voice speaking from low out of the earth (29:4). Just as the end of 2 Kgs 21:1–18, elaborating suggestions already made in BTH, blames Manasseh for the collapse of Jerusalem and the end of the Davidic line of which he was a part, so too Saul's desperate flirtation with divination and necromancy brings his royal house to an even more immediate end.

The term *yiddĕʿōnîm*, derived from *yādaʿ* ("know"), is transparent. In a nice anticipation of the gnostics, GT calls them the *gnōsteis*: they are the "knowledgeable," the "experts." The term *ʾōbôt* is the plural form of *ʾôb*, which is a bladder or a (skin) bottle, and has presumably been the medium's familiar prop, such as a crystal ball would become in much later times. We never meet *yiddĕʿōnîm* in HB without *ʾōbôt*;[36] but whether they refer together to one sort of

36. See Lev 19:31; 20:6, 27; Deut 18:11; 2 Kgs 21:6 (//2 Chr 33:6); 2 Kgs 23:24; Isa 8:19; 19:3. However, we do find *ʾôb* on its own in Isa 29:4 and 1 Chr 10:13.

intermediary, or separately to two, is beyond our power to settle. It may be that such "experts" gained (or at least presented the results of) their knowledge by use of these "bottles."

[4–5] Fear is reported often enough in 1 Samuel, but probably nowhere else in such heightened terms as in this chapter. When Saul sees the Philistine forces encamped (v. 5), he not only "fears," but also "his heart trembles," exceedingly so. So desperate is he in his terror to make contact with Samuel, that—somewhat ironically—he commands the "bottle-mistress" not to fear but to tell him what she has seen (v. 13). When Samuel confirms (v. 19) what Saul has already deduced (v. 5), Saul falls prostrate. And when the woman approaches the prostrate king (v. 21), she sees that he is not just "terrified," but also terrified to an exceeding degree. This strong word *bhl* is found again in Samuel only in 2 Sam 4:1, of the terror of Israel on learning of Abner's death (a further indication of the relative homogeneity of 1 Sam 25–30; 2 Sam 1–4).

[6–7] "Dreams" are mentioned only here in Samuel (vv. 6, 15). We may suppose from their sole mention in Kings that they are viewed as an acceptable means of divine communication within this section of biblical tradition (Samuel–Kings): 1 Kgs 3:5, 15 specify as a "dream" what the older BTH had simply called a "night vision." Finding each of the licit routes blocked (v. 6), Saul asks his staff to seek out (*biqqēš*) for him a woman who has an *ʾôb*, for him to make inquiry (*dārаš*) by her. This word *biqqēš* has been the key term in the extended narrative of Saul's search for David, which he has only just given up (27:4). Saul is now embarked on another desperate search. Only once before did we meet *dāraš*, in the story of Saul's first—and equally unsuccessful—search: for his father's donkeys, when he first met Samuel at the encouragement of his servant (9:9). Here Saul's staff is able to tell him that there is a "bottle-mistress" at En-dor (v. 7). This place name makes only two other appearances in HB. Psalm 83:10 (11) locates the destruction of Jabin and Sisera at En-dor, by the Kishon torrent,[37] though the Song of Deborah mentions neighboring Taanach and Megiddo by the Kishon instead (Judg 5:19–21). And Josh 17:11 (though not the related Judg 1:27) includes it among the Canaanite towns that Manasseh (the tribe, not the king) could not hold. Both passages may suggest a locality where Israelite traditions are not strong.

[8] What Saul does next has two sets of significant links. The only other passage in HB where "disguise" and "dress oneself" and other "clothes" appear together (1 Kgs 22:30) also follows making an "inquiry" of Yahweh (22:5, 7). There in the source text (BTH), the disguise also proves ineffectual: Ahab, king of Israel, is killed by an "innocent" arrow. It is noteworthy that Ahab,

37. In Ps 83:10 (11), En-dor is sometimes emended to En-harod, to make it agree with Judg 7:1. However, Ps 83:7 (8) also contains a rare reference to Amalek, mentioned similarly in 1 Sam 28:18.

who will be compared in 2 Kgs 21:3 with the wicked Manasseh (see above), is another of the literary models for Saul. It is also striking that this alignment of Saul with Ahab follows so quickly on the heels of the association between David and the divinely prompted lying spirit of 1 Kgs 22. Then "other" (1 Sam 28:8), especially so soon after "seek out" and "inquire," also takes us back to Saul's early encounters with Samuel and prophets. On the one hand, the king who has to don "other clothes" in an attempt to gain access to Samuel is a poor reflection of the young man newly anointed by the same Samuel. The prophet then promised that Saul would be made an "other" man and given an "other" heart when he came in contact with the prophetic musicians (10:6, 9). He is more like the later Saul, who tried to capture David from Samuel's protection: he first sent messengers, and still "other" messengers; when finally he had to go himself, he had to strip off his "clothes" (19:20–24). To complete the set of correspondences with that second report of Saul and the prophets: the end of 1 Sam 19 is the passage with the densest concentration of the emphatic *gam*, which is prominent here too (28:6, 15).

Now disguised, Saul asks the "bottle-mistress" to *qāsam* ("divine"?) for him by means of her *ʾôb*, and to "raise up" for him whomsoever he tells her. His earlier suppression of the mediums demonstrates that he has considered them important. The terms *qāsam* and *ʾôb* are found again together only in Deut 18:10–11, where the list of illicit divinatory procedures is even fuller than in the BTH source (2 Kgs 21:6). Balaam was a *qōsēm* (Num 22:7; 23:23; Josh 13:22). Samuel's formal oracle (1 Sam 15:23) links *qesem* with sin and rebellion; and the Latter Prophets (Mic 3:7; Jer 14:14; Ezek 13:6; Zech 10:2) associate the term with falsity. Whatever *qāsam* means precisely, the word is used in only one other place in Samuel: Saul's anxious inquiry of the woman here aligns him with the desperate Philistines, consulting their priests and diviners (1 Sam 6:2). And *hôdiʿunû* ("let us know") there may play on the paired term *yiddĕʿōnîm* here (28:3).[38] Three licit means of learning Yahweh's will have all failed Saul (v. 6); these licit means are balanced in this account by three terms associated with false divination and sorcery (vv. 7–8).

[9–11] The woman does not deny what she can do, but instead protests (v. 9) that her would-be client must "know" what Saul has done to the "knowers": why then is this client set on an entrapment that would be fatal for her? And, just as the Philistines have operated with a distinction between Yahweh and "chance," so Saul swears to her by Yahweh (whom we readers know he cannot reach) that no guilt will "chance on" her. Without further prevarication, the woman now asks whom she should raise for him. Is she simply making conversation to sound out a customer? Or has she become persuaded, now that he has taken an oath, that he is serious?

38. Compare the play on *ydʿ* in v. 9.

[12–14] Enlightenment appears to come to the woman in a single flash: in recognizing Samuel as he rises, she also recognizes Saul—and she complains loudly (v. 12) about his deception[39] of her. Her protest ends with the nicely ambiguous *wĕʾattâ šāʾûl*: either "and you are Saul," or "and it is you who are asked for"! Ever since the beginning of the book, there has been play on Samuel, the "asked-for" son, and Saul, the "asked-for" king. However, although the woman has recognized both Samuel and Saul, she has only told or scolded Saul about the second element in her illumination. He reassures her and presses her for what she has seen. She replies with a general and plural expression: "Gods [or spirits?] rising from the ground [or underworld?]." Is she reporting, or wasting time, enjoying her power, increasing the drama? In any case, he is impatient for information about only one single figure: "What is his form [or shape, or appearance]?" Told that there is an old man rising, wrapped in a cloak, Saul knows that it is Samuel and prostrates himself, face to the ground. The king of Israel, as never before reported, "does obeisance" to a higher authority. It is only here that the term for doing formal homage is found with Saul as subject. However, Saul has also been reported on the ground before Samuel in 1 Sam 19:24. There it was asked for the second time whether he too was among the prophets. Here it is quite clear that he has no independent access to the Deity.

[15] "Disturb" seems too tame a rendering for Samuel's accusation. *rgz hipʿil* is used of shaking great objects like heavens (Isa 13:13), earth (Isa 14:16; Job 9:6), kingdoms (Isa 23:11)—and, in Job 12:6, even God. However, Saul is not at all put off: he has called for Samuel (in whose presence he has just done obeisance) because God has turned from him (v. 15). This expression provides the material for the MT plus in 18:12.[40] We may recall another link with their first meeting: just after Samuel anointed Saul, he promised to come to him after seven days' wait and (using the very same terms) let him know what he should do (10:8).

[16–19] Samuel refuses to be an alternative to Yahweh, who has already made his position clear (v. 16). There is no space between Yahweh and himself that can be exploited. Although the final battle has not yet taken place, Samuel gives striking grounds for insisting on their identity of view: Yahweh has already confirmed in action (v. 17) what Samuel has said. By the next day, Saul and his sons will be with Samuel, and his army will be in Philistine hands; but the kingdom is already given to David. When David is called Saul's *rēaʿ* (v. 17) this clearly does not at all imply friendship: often translated "neighbor," the group-jousting scene in 2 Sam 2:16 suggests rather "opposite number."

39. The verb *rimmâ* is used where Laban tricks Jacob over Rachel (Gen 29:25); the Gibeonites trick Joshua and Israel (Josh 9:22); and Michal tricks her father with a dummy David (1 Sam 19:17).

40. Other parallels are Judg 16:20; and 1 Sam 16:14 (and 23) where the subj. is *rûaḥ*. Does that amount to a suggestion that 1 Sam 16:14–23 is relatively late? And 16:1–13 too?

Samuel utters from beyond the grave a three-part threat (vv. 17–19): (1) The kingdom is to be torn from Saul's hand and given to his "neighbor" David (repeating what he has said in 15:28). (2) Saul and his sons are to join Samuel tomorrow. (3) The army of Israel is to be given into the hands of Philistines. This may remind us of the three signs he promised to encourage Saul when he first anointed him (10:1–8). It is only at beginning and end of his reign that Saul receives such declarations from Samuel. And it adds to this suggested patterning that a meal provided by another precedes the promises in 10:1–8 and follows the promises in 28:17–19.

[20–25] A king or commander seeking a divine oracle before a battle would hope for positive encouragement: the classic "Do not be afraid." Saul receives the very opposite: his great fear (v. 5) returns, and he speedily falls (v. 20)—no longer in the formal posture of obeisance, but full length on the ground, almost like the statue of Dagon in presence of the ark (1 Sam 5:3–4). "The full of his stature" recalls the only other use of *qômâ* in Samuel (16:7, where Yahweh warns Samuel when reviewing Jesse's sons not to "regard the height of his stature"), which itself reminds readers that the young Saul's tallness is one of his defining features (9:2; 10:23). Falling prostrate is the most obvious physical manifestation of Saul's fear at Samuel's words. Absence of strength, because he has not recently eaten, may explain why he cannot move. The medium now became solicitous hostess. She puts to him (v. 22) the same diagnosis as the narrator has already offered (v. 20): the problem is absence of strength (*kōaḥ*).[41] By listening to him, she has taken her life in her hands; she now wants to take responsibility for his welfare. Under pressure from both his aides and the woman,[42] he agrees to her offer of food.

Despite warnings about her sort elsewhere in HB, this unnamed medium from En-dor is presented very sympathetically. She is an engaging character, offering hospitality to the king about to die, readily killing an animal of her own to feed an unexpected visitor (quite the opposite of the rich man in Nathan's parable). As for the portrayal of her professional competence, the Samuel she summons up speaks exactly like the narrator's Samuel. Except for the prediction at the end of his speech that Saul and his sons will join him tomorrow and that the camp of Israel will by then be in Philistine hands, everything else is repeated from earlier utterances before his death. In "making speed" to provide food for him, the woman resembles Abigail (4x) in her attention to David. Indeed,

41. Though far from uncommon in HB, "strength" appears only twice more in Samuel (1 Sam 2:9; 30:4).

42. There is a proliferation of *gam* ("also," "both/and") in this chapter (10x): 6 (3x), 15 (2x), 19 (2x), 20, 22, 23—cf. 6x in the prophetic context of 19:20–24. This may be a further indication of the relative lateness of the material. It is used some 100x in Samuel (MT), but only 4x in all of BTH—significantly, perhaps, only in the Saul and David material (1 Sam 31:5; 2 Sam 5:2; 8:11; 21:20), and never in synoptic portions of Kings/2 Chronicles.

along with Abigail and Hannah, this so-called witch is one of the main female characters in Samuel. The deft speed of her provisioning is conveyed, not just by the use of the verb "hurry" (v. 24), but also by the following cascade of eight verbs within only twice as many words (vv. 24–25). The slaughter of her fatted calf (v. 24) is a clear instance of *zbḥ* meaning slaughter for food, as possibly also in 2 Sam 6:13. The only other instance in HB of *zbḥ qal* with a female subject is the prejudicial Ezek 16:20, where the offerer is the whore Israel.

It is not just the mere mention of Amalek in 28:18 that refers back to 1 Sam 15. There in 15:28 is the only other passage in Samuel to speak of "rending the kingdom" from Saul (28:17). Hosea 11:9 is the only other passage in HB where anger is the object of the common verb "do" (*ʿśh*). However, "doing [or not doing] Yahweh's hot anger" is another way of referring to carrying out the ban and has another interesting resonance. The end of the related narrative in Josh 7 about Achan/r who compromised the totality of the ban on Jericho reports that, after the malefactor was stoned, "Yahweh turned from his hot anger."

There is a move among commentators to link 1 Sam 28 + 31 as the account of Saul's final night and day of life, into which we find woven the case for David's innocence in respect of Saul's death in 1 Sam 27 + 29–30 + 2 Sam 1. If, however, much of the Amalek theme in Samuel is late, then Saul's death (1 Sam 31) may originally have been preceded immediately by the note of Samuel's death in 25:1. Adam (2009: 27–43) presents 1 Sam 28 as a comment on Saul's destiny from a "late prophetic" point of view, influenced by the treatment of *nekuia* in Homer's *Odyssey* 11 and the *Persians* of Aeschylus.[43]

1 Samuel 29:1–3

1 And Philistines gathered all their camp*s*[a] to Apheq,
and Israel were camping at [the spring] *Aeddon*,[b]
which is at Jezreel.
2 And the Philistine lords were passing over by hundreds and thousands,
while David and his men were passing over at the rear with Achish.
3 And the Philistine leaders said,
"[What are these Hebrews?] *Who are these passing across*?"[a]
And Achish said to the Philistine leaders,
"Is this not David, servant of Saul, king of Israel,
he has been with us who has been with me
days, this second year,[b] these days or these years,
and I have not found in him anything
from the time of his fall*ing in with me* till this day."

43. Couffignal offers an Oedipal reading of 1 Sam 28.

1a. Here LT = B.

b. The LT = MT. Codex B may attest *bʿyn dʾr ʾšr* ("at En-Dor which," cf. 28:7), with *dʾr* being lost from MT because of its similarity to *ʾšr*.

3a. Again LT = B.

b. The LT has the more straightforward "who has been with me already a second year of days."

[1–3] Jezreel is named as the focus of the struggle; and that is where Israel is encamped (v. 1). After a preliminary encampment at Aphek, as once previously (4:1), the Philistines also moved up there (29:11). Later Jezreel will be the place from which the bad news would come to the family of Saul (2 Sam 4:4). The original report of the battle in BTH has spoken simply of Mount Gilboa (31:1, 8). We would need to know whether Jezreel refers to the whole valley, or simply to the city of the same name, which will feature again in the story of Jezebel and Naboth (1 Kgs 21), before we could locate MT's unspecified "spring" (v. 1). If, however, we read En-dor with GT, then Jezreel may more likely refer to the whole valley. The narrator lingers over his view of the whole Philistine camp's assembling (v. 1), as their leaders pass our gaze at the head of hundreds and thousands, and David and his men bring up the rear with Achish (v. 2). As in the earlier part of ch. 14, there is play (vv. 2, 3) on two different pronunciations of *ʿbrym*—"Hebrews" (*ʿibrîm*) and "crossers-over" or "passersby" (*ʿōbrîm*)—with MT and GT making different decisions in v. 3 on which is appropriate.

This is the final piece in the "Hebrew" puzzle of the books of Samuel. The MT and GT agree in only three (or four) cases in reading "Hebrews": 1 Sam 4:6, (9); 13:19; 14:11. In two further passages (1 Sam 13:7; 29:3), MT and GT have read the same letters, but MT has read these as "Hebrews" while GT has rendered by "crossers-over" or "passersby." In two cases (1 Sam 13:3; 14:21), MT has read "Hebrews" (*ʿbrym*), but GT "servants" or "slaves" (*ʿbdym*), while in 1 Sam 17:8 we meet the opposite situation. The context is always Philistine. Where "Hebrews" is attested in GT, it is always in Philistine speech (4:6, 9; 13:19; 14:11; 17:8); and Philistines are speaking also in 29:3 (MT). However, in MT we also find the narrator (13:7; 14:21) and Saul (13:3) speaking of "Hebrews."

When challenged by his colleagues, clumsy Achish does his case no favors by describing David ambiguously (v. 3) as "the servant of Saul, king of Israel." He goes on to give David the same accolade as Samuel was able to extract from his own people (12:4, 5), or David from Nabal's staff much more recently (25:7, 15, 21): "I have found in him nothing" (29:3) means that, to my knowledge, he has taken nothing from me: nothing has been counted as missing.

1 Samuel 29:4–30:25

4 And the Philistine leaders were angry with him,
and the Philistine leaders said to him,

"Turn the man back
[and let him return] to his place,
where you have [reckoned him] *set him down.*
But let him not come out with us to battle,
and [he shall not become for us as adversary in the battle[a]] *let him not be a plotter in the camp.*
And with what will this fellow [become pleasing to] *be reconciled with* his lord?
Surely with the heads of these men.
5 Is this not David
of whom they sang in their dances, saying,
'Saul has struck in thousands, and David in myriads'?"

6 And Achish called to David,
and said to him,
"As Yahweh lives, you have been straight and good in my eyes
and your going out and coming in with me in the camp.
Indeed, I have not found ill in you
from the day of your coming to me to this day.
But in the eyes of the lords you are [not[a]] good.
7 Now then, return
and go in peace;
and you shall not do ill in the eyes of the lords of the Philistines."

8 And David said to Achish:
"What have I done,
and what have you found in your servant
from the time that I have been before you till this day,
that I should not come[a]
and fight with the enemies of my lord king?"
9 And Achish answered
and said to David,
"I know
that you are good in my eyes[, like a messenger of god[a]].
However, the Philistine lords have said,
'He shall not go with us into battle.'
10 Now then, rise early in the morning, and the servants of your master
who have come with you,
and *go to the place*
where I set you down;
and do not put a pestilent word[a] in your heart,

for you are good before me;[b]
and be early in the way [{all} rise early in the morning],
and have light[c] and go."
11 And David rose early, he and his men,
to go [in the morning[a]],
to [return to] *guard*[b] Philistine land.
But the Philistines went up
to *make war against*[c] Jezreel.

30:1 And it came to be
on the arrival of David and his men at [Ziklag] *Keilah*[a] on the third day
—now Amalek had raided toward south and toward Ziklag,[b]
and had struck Ziklag
and burned it by fire.
2 And [they took captive] the women [who were] *and all that were*
in it from small to great;[a]
they put no man *or woman*[b] to death
but took them prisoner,[b] and they [drove them
and] went on their way—
3 and David came, and his men, to the city.[a]
And look: it was burned by fire,
and their women and their sons and their daughters, they were taken
captive.
4 And David raised, and the people who were with him, their voices,
and they wept
till there was not in them power
to weep *further*.[a]
5 And David's two wives, they were taken captive:
Ahinoam the Jezreelite and Abigail wife of Nabal the Carmelite.
6 And it was very tight[a] for David,
for the people spoke
of stoning him;
for the soul of the whole people was bitter, each over his sons and over
his daughters;
and David strengthened himself[b] in Yahweh his God.

7 And David said to Abiathar the priest, son of Ahimelech,
"Bring near [surely to me] the ephod."
[And Abiathar brought the ephod near to David.[a]]
8 And David asked of Yahweh,
saying,
"Shall I pursue after this band?[a]

Shall I overtake it?"
And he said to him,
"Pursue.
For you will overtake for sure,
and you will deliver for sure."
9 And David went, he and [six[a]] *four* hundred men who were with him,
and they[b] came to the wadi of the Besor,
and the remainder stopped.[c]
10 And [David] *the remainder* pursued, [he and] *some* four hundred men,
and two hundred men stopped
who [were too dead[a] to cross] *settled across* the wadi of the Besor.[b]
11 And they found an Egyptian man in the countryside
and took him to David *in the field/open*;
and they gave him food
and he ate
and they gave him water
to drink.
12 And they gave him a slice of dried figs [and two bunches of raisins[a]],
and he ate;
and his spirit returned to him.
For he had not eaten food
and he had not drunk water three days and three nights.

13 And David said to him,
"Whose are you?
And from wherever are you?"
And the Egyptian lad said,
"I'm servant of an Amalekite man;
and my lord abandoned me,
for I have been sick, today a third.
14 We for our part had raided the south of the Kerethites[a]
and against what belongs to Judah
and against [the south of Caleb] *Gilboa*;[b]
and Ziklag we burned by fire."
15 And David said to him,
"Will you bring me down to this band?"
And he said,
"Swear to me *surely* by god,
you will not put me to death,
and you will not deliver me into the hand of my lord,
and I will bring you down to this band."[a]

16 And he brought him down *there*;
and they were seen abandoned over the face of the whole earth,
eating
and drinking
and celebrating with all the great booty
they had taken from the land of Philistines and from the land of Judah.
17 And David *came upon them*
and struck them down from the [twilight] *morning star*
and till the [evening] *afternoon* [of their[a]] *and on the* morrow;
and[b] not a man of them got away, apart from four hundred young men
who rode on the camels
and fled.
18 And David delivered all that Amalek had taken.
And his two wives did David deliver.
19 And there was none missing of them,
from small to great, and *from booty*[a] to sons and daughters, and [from booty[a]] to all
that they had taken of theirs.
Everything David brought back.
20 And [David[a]] *he* took the whole flock and herd.
[They drove before those cattle, and they] *and led it away in front of the booty*,[b]
and of that booty it was said
"This is David's booty."
21 And David came to the two hundred men,
who had been [too dead to] *set free from*[a] follow*ing* after David,
and he had made them settle at the wadi of the Besor,[b]
and they came out
to meet David
and to meet the people
who were with him;
and David drew near to the people
and asked of their well-being.

22 And every bad and worthless man of the men *of war*[a]
who had gone with David
spoke up;
and they said,
"Because they did not [go with me] *pursue with us*,[b]
we shall not give them of the booty
that we delivered,

except each man his wife and his [sons] *children*.
Let them lead them and go."

23 And David said,
"You shall not so do, my brothers,
in that Yahweh has given to us[a]
and guarded us
and given the band
that came against us into our hand.
24 And who of[a] you will listen to[a] this word?
'*Because they are not less than you*.[b]
As the division of the one
who goes down into battle
so is the division of the one
who sits by the baggage:
together they divide.'"

25 And it was from that day and onward,
and he established it for a statute and precedent for Israel to this day.

4a. Here *mlḥmh* (MT) corresponds to *mḥnh* (GT); contrast end of 28:1.

6a. The LT = MT.

8a. How significant is the break in normal idiom (*bw'*, v. 8): one normally "goes out" (*yṣ'*) to fight (1 Sam 8:20; Zech 14:3; Dan 11:11) or (challenges) enemies (to) "come" (*bw'*) to fight against one (Josh 11:5; Judg 5:19). Notice the normal (out-in) pairing in 1 Sam 29:6; cf. 2 Sam 5:2 (BTH).

9a. Again LT = MT.

10a. In 1 Kgdms 1:16; 2:12; 10:27; 25:17, 25; and probably also in 30:22 (where B's word order differs from MT), *loimos* corresponds to *bly'l*; but *logon loimon* appears unique in the Gk. OT.

b. Here B offers *enōpion mou*, though *en ophthalmois mou* in v. 9. The LT reads *en ophthalmois mou* both times and follows it both times with *[kath]ōs angelos theou*.

c. The LT is again fuller, repeating "in the way" before "let it be light for you."

11a. Here LT = MT.

b. But here LT = B.

c. The inf. *polemein* appears before *epi Israēl* in B but after the phrase in LT. Is the shorter MT original?

30:1a. Here LT = B.

b. The LT only adds here: "David and his men departing from Ziklag on the third day."

2a. Again LT = B except that "all" is neuter in B (*panta*) but m. in LT (*pantas*). This phrase is linked by the punctuation to what precedes.

b. Throughout this sentence, LT = B.

3a. Here B = MT; but LT, in place of "the city," has the fuller "Ziklag on the third day."

4a. Here LT = B.

6a. This phrase is replicated only once (of Israel), in Judg 10:9. The m. form (*wyṣr l-*) is found in Gen 32:7; Judg 2:15; 2 Sam 13:2.

b. The vb. *ḥzq* (*hitpaʿel*) is commonest in Chronicles (15x)—cf. also Daniel and Ezra (3x). The other nine instances are Gen 48:2; Num 13:20; Judg 20:22; 1 Sam 4:9; 30:6; 2 Sam 3:6; 10:12; 1 Kgs 20:22; Ezek 7:13; 2 Sam 10:12//1 Chr 19:13 is the sole instance in BTH.

7a. The LT = MT.

8a. In its four instances in this chapter (and in 1 Chr 12:21), the Hebrew corresponding to *gdwd* in MT is transliterated in B (*geddour*), but never elsewhere—presumably it has already been corrupted in the underlying text to *gdwr*. The witnesses to LT vary between *systremma* ("crowd, band"), which corresponds to *gdwd* in 2 Sam 4:2; 1 Kgs 11:24; and *systrateuma* ("common campaign"), which corresponds to *qšr* ("conspiracy") in 2 Kgs 14:19. Presumably the otherwise unknown *systreuma* is corrupt.

9a. Again LT = MT.

b. Here B = MT; but LT has sg.

c. Again B = MT; but LT has "and he left there two hundred men."

10a. The verbal form is used only here and in v. 21 below—a denominative from *pgr* ("corpse")?

b. Again LT is different in this verse: "And he pursued with four hundred men. And the two hundred men lay concealed to guard, who remained beyond the wadi of the Bosor."

12a. Here LT = MT.

14a. The *l* in B's *Cholthei* is supported in several other texts.

b. This appears as *Cheloub* in LT.

15a. Here B = MT; but at the end LT adds "And he swore to him."

17a. This apparent suf. form on *mḥrt* is unique.

b. The LT prefixes "and he put [them] to death."

19a. The LT represents *mšll* in both positions.

20a. Here LT = MT.

b. The LT = B.

21a. Presumably a contextual guess. Interpreting *pgrw* (MT) is not easy: this verb form, repeated from v. 10, is otherwise unique. The proposed translation "were too dead to ..." supposes that it is a denominative from the common *peger* ("corpse": "were too 'corpsed' to . . ."); Instead of *eklythentas*, LT has *apoleiphthentas*.

b. Here B offers *Beana* (?< *bʿnh*).

22a. Again LT = B.

b. Yet again LT = B; *katadiōkein* is the stock rendering of *rdp*, as already 11x in 1 Kingdoms, but here MT uses the colorless *hlk*.

23a. Codex B = MT; but LT specifies the obj. as "the enemies."

24a. Translators agree that the preposition *l-* must be rendered differently in *lkm* and in *ldbr hzh*. The GT has taken the first as possessive (B shares the word order of MT; but LT reads *tōn logōn hymōn toutōn*,"these words of yours"). Others choose "Who will listen to you in this matter?"

b. The LT shares the same plus as B, but finishes with "us" not "you."

[4–5] To Achish's defense of David, his colleagues make a doubly knowing response (v. 4) in insisting that David go back to "his place" (27:5). And they play on the exact terms of the good-conduct formula used in the Nabal story, whether *l' npqd . . . m'wmh* (*pqd nip'al*, 25:7, 21: "not anything was counted") or *l' pqdnw . . . m'wmh* (*pqd* in *qal*, 25:15: "not anything did we count"). The place to which David should return is the one "which you accounted" (*hpqdtw*, *hip'il*) to him. Thereby they skillfully suggest to Achish that he has lost to David something important: he has knowingly made over a significant piece of real estate, the town of Ziklag. The Philistine lords do not want David in their ranks lest he deceive them in the battle. They see only one way in which this "servant of Saul" could "ingratiate himself" again with his old "lord": that would be by making a collection of their heads for Saul (v. 4). Here *rṣh* (*hitpa'el*) is unique; this verb occurs only once more in Samuel (there in *qal*). In 2 Sam 24:23 (see p. 618) it is part of a small plus, not in the Chronicler's version. One of the interesting crosscurrents between the two versions of the census story is nicely exemplified in the immediately preceding words: the Philistine leaders warn Achish that David will prove to be an adversary (*śāṭān*); and it is a *śāṭān* that is blamed for David's trouble in 1 Chr 21:1. The leaders warn here of a collection of their heads, to please David's master. David has certainly been informed earlier in his relationship with Saul that it delights the king to receive other Philistine body parts as a bride-price (18:25). And the lords remind Achish of the song[44] to which people have danced once in Israel: David used to be ten times more dangerous to Philistines than Saul.

Prompted by the song, it is possible for us to view this chapter as an extended variation on a theme within ch. 21. When the lords of the Philistines here (29:3) start their questioning of Achish about the aliens among them, he answers them just as his own servants there (21:11 [12]) answered him: "Is this not David. . . ?" And then, in their displeasure at his response, they in 29:5 make their own selection from 21:11. They know about the David who is the hero of the song. Comparing the two stories adds depth to the ambiguous description of David in 29:3.

21:11	David, . . . king of the land
29:3	David, servant of Saul, king of Israel

Who is being said to be king of Israel? How ironically is David being called "servant of Saul"? Achish extends the description when he sends David on his way, (gullibly?) describing David's men as "the servants of your lord who came with you" (v. 10).

44. The contexts in which *'nh* means "sing" may all be quite late: Exod 15:21; 32:18; Num 21:17; 1 Sam 18:7; 21:11 (12); 29:5; Isa 13:22; 27:2; Jer 25:30; 51:14; Pss 88:1 (E: superscription); 119:172; 147:7.

As for their knowing talk about "place"—we should note that (within the books of Samuel) it is only in this longer variant of the David and Achish story (vv. 2, 6, 7) that the Philistine lords are called *serānîm*, as they were in 1 Sam 5–6. These *serānîm* reckon that David is as dangerous in their midst now as the ark was formerly: each should "turn back to its/his place" (5:11; 29:4).[45]

[6–7] Having spoken up for David once in the company of his fellow lords, Achish does not do so again. Faced with their anger and their counterarguments (vv. 4–5), he backs down and asks David to go quietly (vv. 6–7). Although Achish himself is the model of straightforwardness in this narrative, this gullible king of Gath assures David of his own confidence in him. David responds with his characteristic (innocent or mock innocent?) "What have I done?" Is David unconscious of his own deviousness, or is this repeated question a deliberate element in his strategy? Ambiguity, if not deviousness, is nicely illustrated in David's talk of fighting "against the enemies of my lord the king": though all who hear him would suppose that loyalty to Achish is meant, a good advocate might have him acquitted of such treachery before a future tribunal in Israel.

[8–11] To David's challenge Achish now responds with what looks like the extravagant flattery one expects from subject to king. Two further characters in Samuel will compare David to a divine messenger: the woman of Tekoa (2 Sam 14:17, 20) and Mephibosheth (19:27 [28]). And yet, since Achish gets so many things wrong, and since this narrative has possible anticipations of beginning and end of the census story,[46] it is fair at least to ask whether there is also irony in his comparing David to a divine messenger: the only *mal'ak yhwh* in BTH is the divine destroyer that David's conduct lets loose.

David, like Achish before him (v. 3b), makes only one protest (v. 8) over the ruling by the Philistine lords; once it is answered (vv. 9–10), he too acts as requested (v. 11). He makes an early departure for Philistine territory, while the Philistines themselves advance further toward Jezreel. And this action of both parties conveniently distances him from what will happen to Saul. Whether Achish has been aware of the ambiguity in David's answer (v. 8) is another matter: "the enemies of my lord the king" could mean the armies on either side of the coming conflict.[47]

[30:1–6] Two narratives featuring David and Amalekites (1 Sam 30 and 2 Sam 1:1–16) frame the account of Saul's death (1 Sam 31). Saul's removal by death from the kingship over Israel does not occur till long after Samuel's words of rejection, uttered in the wake of an earlier campaign against Amalek

45. And we have already noted that Philistines assembled at Aphek in both 4:1 and 29:1.

46. The deceptive *śāṭān* at the beginning of the census account (though no longer in the Samuel version of the census [2 Sam 24:1]) and the vb. *rāṣâ* at its end (2 Sam 24:23), which may have inspired the unique *hitpa'el yitraṣeh* in 1 Sam 29:4.

47. David's answer is much more careful, and much less clear than McKenzie (101–2) appears to allow.

(15:26). These words of Samuel might suggest to a modern reader that Saul will soon be deposed. As it is, the long delay over replacing Saul together with renewed prominence of Amalek as a significant force invite review of the earlier presentation of the theme of Amalek as Saul's nemesis. Saul's end may have been long delayed, but the narrative has recently prepared us well for a reappearance of the Amalekites in force. They were among the southern neighbors against whom David was carrying out raids from Ziklag (27:8); and Samuel recalled from the underworld told Saul again exactly why Yahweh has become his enemy (28:16–18).

Amalek features only once in BTH, in a list of neighboring peoples that David has subdued and booty from whom he dedicates to Yahweh (2 Sam 8:11–12).[48] The extended narrative response (1 Sam 30) to the mention of Amalek among the peoples raided by David from Ziklag (27:8) fleshes out both brief reports. In these David stories, as in Ps 83,[49] Amalek has no status among Israel's ancestral enemies as specially abhorred. To the contrary, the narrator's insistence that the Amalekites have killed no one on their Ziklag raid (1 Sam 30:2) must be intended to reflect on the fact that in his raids David by contrast left no one alive (27:9)—and would deal quite as ruthlessly with these Amalekite raiders (30:16–17).

David has just been identified to Saul by Samuel (28:17) as the "opposite number better than him" (15:28) to whom the kingship over Israel would be passed. However, the narrator's remark that David and his men weep so much that they no longer have strength (*kōaḥ*) for weeping (v. 4) precisely invites comparison with Saul (28:20, 22). The setback at his base in Ziklag in fact almost leads to David being stoned by his own men (v. 6). Talk in this description of his people's *nepeš* being "bitter" invites us to see David's situation looking Janus-like in two directions. It looks back to the formation of his band at Adullam (22:2), where some of those who joined him were "bitter in soul"; if this attitude has lifted during the period of their successes, it is hardly surprising that it should recur when they experience serious setback. But it also looks forward to the advice given by Hushai to Absalom when he has David on the run: "You know that your father and his men are mighty men and bitter in soul, like a bear bereft" (2 Sam 17:8). The prospective glance reminds us of the continuity of experience from David before he became king, onward to David as king: more than once David is in deadly peril from within.

The following words (v. 6) also look backward and forward. Insofar as they recall Jonathan's strengthening David's hand in God, when he was in flight from Saul and fearing for his life (23:16), they remind us that David is now

48. Outside the Pentateuch (but not Leviticus), Judges, Samuel, and Chronicles, Amalek appears only in Ps 83:7 (8).

49. Psalm 83 was mentioned above (on 28:7) because of its rare mention of En-dor.

doubly alone: Jonathan is no longer available to give support,[50] and here it is his own men and not Saul who provide the immediate threat. They also anticipate the openings of 2 Sam 2 and 3. We shall learn that, while David is becoming stronger and stronger and Saul's "house" correspondingly weaker (3:1), Abner is "strengthening himself" or "seeking to become strong" in Saul's house (3:6). The suggestion may be that David's power grows precisely because he seeks strength in Yahweh.

[7–12] In response to the danger from his own men, David reacts exactly as he has when he learned of danger from Saul (23:9–12): he calls for Abiathar to arrange an oracular consultation of Yahweh by means of the ephod. The success of the consultation and the success of the following action are both in marked contrast to the final stages in the story of Saul, who fails in both (chs. 28 and 31). It is hard to read of David's consulting Yahweh by means of the ephod (v. 7) as anything other than supplying the specific content of how David consolidates his position in or by Yahweh (v. 6). Yet, in MT at least, a subparagraph break separates vv. 6 and 7. In ancient biblical manuscripts, one principal function of a larger-than-usual space between sentences is to underline decisive action or speech by one of the principal characters (often God, king, or prophet), as reported in the new sentence.

Again in contrast to Saul's failure to elicit a response from Yahweh by any means (28:6, 15), David's inquiry of Yahweh is answered, and his hopes are affirmed in the strongest terms (v. 8). To heighten this contrast, the linguistic structure of the oracle (two verbs without object or further specification, each emphasized by the infinitive absolute) resembles the structure of Saul's unusual blessing (26:25). Gentle handling of an Egyptian slave produces the intelligence David requires (vv. 11–12). One further element of the contrast between Saul in ch. 28 and David here serves to confirm the prescience of Hannah. The remedy for Saul's lack of strength was food; the remedy for David's weakness is consultation of Yahweh. Apart from the medium at En-dor and the narrator, Hannah is the only user of *kōaḥ* in all of Samuel (2:9; cf. 28:20, 22; 30:4): what she says might be paraphrased as "It is not strength that makes a male a real man."

[13–21] Presumably David does swear the oath the Egyptian demands (v. 15) before leading those who have saved his life to his old masters. The Amalekite raiders, as their pursuers catch up with them, present themselves in two ways (v. 16): as "*nĕṭušîm* over the whole face of the earth"; and as "eating and drinking and *ḥōgĕgîm*." The first participial phrase suggests inadequately tended sheep, "spread out" (cf. 1 Sam 17:28), or even "maiden Israel" abandoned on her land,

50. The controlling text of BTH has Jonathan reunited with his father in death on Gilboa (1 Sam 31).

with no one to pick her up (Amos 5:2).[51] The only other instance of the second of these puzzling participles is in Ps 42:4 (5), which describes a festal procession. Our translation above proposes "celebrating" (Alter [186] has "reveling"). The closest parallel to the complete phrase is "eating and drinking and happy [*śĕmēḥîm*]" in 1 Kgs 4:20.[52] They are easy targets for David's slaughter, except for a group of young men equal in number to David's force who are able to make their escape on camels (v. 17). David's takings included everyone and everything looted from Ziklag, not least his own wives.

For reasons that (because of the textual uncertainty already discussed) are not wholly clear, David gave leave to two hundred of his total force of six hundred from the final leg of the pursuit (vv. 9–10). Yet, after a long forced hike, it is hardly surprising that a good portion of the party was already "corpse-like."

[22] When the main force returns, the rascals among them want those who have stayed behind left out of the distribution of spoils: they should retrieve only their wives and children, and take themselves off, leading their families (v. 22)—apparently contemptuously, they use the same verb (*nāhag*) of the families as is used of animals, not just in vv. 2 and 20 but elsewhere in HB as well.

[23–24] David responds by quoting or propounding a ruling that a whole army should share and share alike: both those who fight and those who stay with the baggage. The terms of David's ruling appear to restate generously the situation of the two hundred who have not persisted with the pursuit till the end. At the time of their staying behind, they are reported (vv. 9–10) as having simply come to a stop or standstill (*ʿmd*); but David gives them credit for the same division of responsibility as operated when he set out to punish Nabal (25:13). There are other links with the Nabal story. No sooner is the rule propounded than its significance is extended. David's whole band may share equally, but they do not share the whole booty. Some is sent to elders in Judah. This, like the food offered by Abigail to David for his men (25:27) and like Jacob's present to Esau (Gen 33:10–11), is called a "blessing." This is divine generosity, not the churlish meanness of a fool.

[25] What follows in its own subparagraph (v. 25) invites us to recognize greater significance in what at first sight seems to be simply an off-the-cuff response to a delicate situation. The rare and apparently formulaic pairing of *ḥōq* and *mišpāṭ*, both in the singular (in the plural, these two nouns, separately or together, constitute a Deuteronomic cliché for the instructions that Moses sets before his people) and joint objects of the verb *śîm*, is reproduced only in Exod 15:25 and Josh 24:25, where Moses or Joshua "established for him [Israel] a 'statute' and 'precedent.'" In each case this formal resolution follows conflict

51. The related *nipʿal* is used of the Philistines in the valley of the Rephaim (2 Sam 5:18, 22); however, since 1 Chr 14:9, 13 uses a different verb, we cannot be confident what BTH reported.

52. The Jewish festal greeting *ḥāg śāmēaḥ* appears to be postbiblical.

or dispute.[53] Although David's whole "people" at this point are his six hundred men and their families, and although he is not yet king of Israel, his judgment in this matter is treated as a ruling still valid for all Israel at the time of writing.[54] And yet, however important it may or may not have been in the aftermath of other later battles, David's ruling is even more crucial to immediate concerns. After all, only one other character in the books of Samuel was located "beside the baggage"; that was the young Saul (10:22)—not positioned there on guard duty but lurking there in hiding. If David's ruling is to serve as a continuing precedent, then its first test will come in the battle looming between Saul and the Philistine lords. The same David who supplies a noble reason for the nonparticipation of a third of his force in the pursuit of Amalek has a powerful motive for presenting his own dispatch back to Philistine territory in a similarly positive way. By this ruling, he seeks valid title to some of the spoils from a coming battle in which he will take no active part. Like Saul before him, he hopes to progress from staying by the baggage to kingship over Israel!

Excursus 4: Patterns near the End of 1 Samuel

Fokkelman has nicely observed the contemporaneity of what is happening in the north at Saul's end (1 Sam 28 and 31), and in the south in David's noninvolvement in that end—at least until Saul is actually dead (1 Sam 27//29 and 1 Sam 30//2 Sam 1).[55] David's victory in the south and Saul's defeat in the north are simultaneous. And Calum M. Carmichael (private communication) has observed how each account of Saul's death corresponds fitly with what precedes it in each of these contemporaneous strands. Saul's hastening of his actual dying (1 Sam 31) mixes life and death as his summoning of Samuel from the realm of the dead has done (1 Sam 28). And the Amalekite's claimed role before David in dispatching Saul (2 Sam 1) corresponds immediately to David's campaign against the Amalekites (1 Sam 30), who have sacked the town given him by Achish (1 Sam 27), and more distantly to Saul's failure to dispatch the Amalekite king (1 Sam 15).

These several observations are open to the hypothesis that an earlier version of 1 Samuel had moved directly from Samuel's death (25:1) via Saul's postmortem interrogation of him (ch. 28), to Saul's own death (ch. 31). When the later "Amalekite" stratum was added to the book, the narrator knew of Saul's visit to the medium on the night before the battle and noted (15:35) that Samuel did not see Saul "till the day of his death." In at least negative support of this approach, the list of vocabulary common to David and Saul and David and Absalom prepared by Rezetko (46–49) has no items in 1 Sam 24; 28; 31. It is also true that 1 Sam 28 draws on 2 Kgs 21 (BTH) and could therefore belong to an early stratum of Samuel. But need it be distinguished from the stratum immediately contiguous to it? If 1 Sam 31 was once a beginning (of BTH), need

53. The only other instance of "statute and precedent" is "taught" by Ezra (7:10).

54. A similar ruling is attributed to Yahweh through Moses in Num 31:25–31.

55. Fokkelman 2010: 43–45. See also Bar-Efrat 1:353.

any material have separated the deaths of Samuel and Saul in the first draft of the new "book" of 1 Samuel? Even at a more advanced stage, the presentation of their origins is intermingled ("asked for"). And with Samuel dead and Saul's recognizing that David will be king, Saul can die after Samuel.

1 Samuel 30:26–2 Samuel 3:5 David at Hebron and the Death of Saul

1 Samuel 30:26–31

26 And David came to Ziklag,
and dispatched [of the booty] to the elders *of the booty*[a] of Judah, *and* to his neighbor*s*,
saying,
"Look a blessing to you from the booty of Yahweh's enemies."

27 {It was} to those in Beth[el[a]]*syr*
and to those in Ram[oth]*a*[b]-negeb
to those in Yattir
28 and to those in Aroer[a]
and to the Ammadei[b]
to those in [Siphmoth] *Saphei*
and to those in [Eshtemoa] *Estheie*[c]
and to those in Gath
and to those in Keimath
and to those in Saphek
and to those in Theimath[d]

29 and to those in [Rakhal] *Carmel*[a]
and to those in the towns of [the Jerahmeelite] *Jezreel*[b]
and to those in the towns of the Qen*iz*ite[c]
30 and to those in [Hormah[a]] *Iereimouth*
and those in [Bor[b]-ashan] *Beer-sheba*
and to those in [Athakh] *Noo*[c]
31 and to those in Hebron
and to all the places
where David moved about, he and his men.

26a. Even later in LT, after the "neighbors."
27a. Here LT = MT.
b. The LT = B.
28a. Here LT has *Arouēl*.
b. The LT has *Arikain*.
c. Here LT has *Nothōm*.
d. Neither 4QSam[a] nor LT shares the four-name plus in B.

29a. Here LT = B. The MT has lost the *-m-* of the familiar name and transposed *krl* as *rkl*.

b. The LT, like B, has *Israēl*.

c. Here 4QSam[a] reads *hqnzy* with GT. The same variation between "Qenite" and "Qenizite" occurs also in 27:10 above.

30a. The LT's *Erma* may attest "Hormah" (MT).

b. Here LT = B. *Bor-* and *Beer-* may simply be alternate vocalizations of the same word.

c. Again LT is different: *Nageb*.

[26–31] There is a high degree of instability in the text of these verses. (1) Although marked as a new paragraph in MT, space does not allow recognition of such a break in 4QSam[a]. (2) "From the booty" appears immediately after "and dispatched" in MT, between "elders" and "Judah" in B, immediately before "saying" in LT, while the reconstruction of 4QSam[a] deduces that the word had been repeated in that text: first where we find it in MT, then as attested in LT. (3) Codex B and LT do attest some form of *rʿ* ("neighbor") as in MT, although both attest plural, not singular. However, DJD (98–99) accepts the long-standing emendation to a form of *ʿr* ("city"). A list of cities certainly follows; however, they can also be reasonably presented as neighbors of Ziklag. Those in receipt of David's "blessing" are described as "the elders of Judah." These reappear in Samuel only in 2 Sam 19:11 (12), to be reproved for their tardiness in welcoming David back as their king following Absalom's revolt. David has been recently reminded by Abigail (25:27) of the usefulness of a tangible "blessing" in securing favor. She too has used the verb "move about" (*hthlk*), in MT at least. A more significant echo may be of David's abandoning Keilah and "moving about" with his men wherever they "moved about" (23:13). We now learn some of the locations covered by that earlier cautious form of words.

The list is reminiscent of the topographical chapters in Joshua in two respects. It is only in Josh 17:16 that we find another instance of *lʾšr . . . wlʾšr* ("to those in . . . and to those in"). And several of the names appear in the list of Judah's cities in Josh 15 and Simeon's in Josh 19, and the Levitical cities from both in Josh 21 and 1 Chr 6. Hormah precedes Ziklag in Josh 15:30–31 and 19:4–5; and *ʿtr* (though not the unique *ʿtk*) appears immediately before *ʿšn* in Josh 15:42 and 19:7. Kenites and Jerahmeelites feature here among David's beneficiaries (30:29 MT). When asked by Achish about his raiding activities, David has claimed (27:10) them among his victims. The Kenites were good neighbors of Judah to the south and are well spoken of wherever they are mentioned in the books from Exodus to 1 Samuel.

1 Samuel 31

1 And [the] Philistines were fighting [with[a]] *against* Israel;
and the[b] men[c] of Israel fled before [the] Philistines,

and they fell pierced on the hill of the Gilboa.
2 And Philistines pressed on Saul and his sons;
and Philistines struck down Jonathan and [Abi]*Yo*nadab[a] and Malchish[u]a, Saul's sons.
3 And the fighting became heavy toward Saul,
and the archers[a] found[b] him—men with the bow[c]—
and he [writhed greatly from the archers] *was wounded*[d] *under the* breastbone.[e]
4 And Saul said to his armor-bearer:
"Draw your sword
and run me through with it,
lest these uncircumcised come
and they run me through[a]
and do their will[b] with me."
But his armor-bearer was not willing,
for he was very afraid;
and Saul took the sword
and fell on it.
5 And the armor-bearer saw
that Saul was dead,
and he too fell on his sword
and died with him.
6 And Saul died, and his three sons and his armor-bearer,
[even all his men,[a]] on that day together.
7 And the men[a] of Israel
who were on the other side of the valley and on the other side of the Jordan
saw
that the men[a] of Israel had fled
and that Saul and his sons had died;
and they abandoned the*ir* cities
and fled,
and [the] Philistines came and settled in them.

8 And it came to be on the morrow
and [the] Philistines came
to strip the pierced,[a]
and they found Saul and his three sons,
fallen on the hill of the Gilboa.
9 And they [cut off[a] his head] *turned him over*
and stripped his weapons;
and they dispatched *them*[b] in Philistine land round about

to inform [the house of[c]] their idols and the people of the good news.

10 And they placed his[a] weapons in the house of Ashtaroth;
and his body they thrust on the wall of Beth-Shan.

11 And the inhabitants of Jabesh-gilead heard [about it,[a]]
what [the] Philistines had done to Saul.

12 And they arose, every man of worth,
and walked all the night,
and took the body of Saul and the bodi[es] of *Jonathan*[a] his son[s] from the wall of Beth-Shan;
and [came] *brought them* to Jabesh
and burned them there.

13 And they took their bones
and buried them under the [tamarisk] "{*goddess*} *Earth*" at Jabesh;
and they fasted seven days.
And it came to be after the death of Saul
(and David, he had returned from striking down the Amalekite)
and David settled in Ziklag two days.[a]

1a. The LT's *en* renders MT in a literal way.

b. Here LT has no article, but it does before the following Philistines.

c. "Men" is pl. here in Samuel, as in v. 7; but 1 Chr 10:1 uses the less familiar collective "man of Israel."

2a. This is "Aminadab" in LT.

3a. Here *akontistēs* is unique here in the Gk. OT, though *akontizein* is used (4x) for *yrh* in 1 Kgdms 20.

b. Only in the parallel 1 Chr 10:3 is "archer" the subj. of "find."

c. The combination *ʾnšym bqšt* is unique in HB.

d. Normally *traumatizein* corresponds to a form of *ḥll*, but here uniquely of *ḥwl*.

e. Only here is *hypochondrion* found in the Gk. OT.

4a. The vb. *apokteinōsi* ("kill") in LT (4 MSS) appears to be an inner-Gk. alteration of *apokentēsōsi* (B and MS 82).

b. The vb. *empaizein* corresponds to *ʿll* (*hitpaʿel*) more often (6x) than any other single rendering.

6a. Here LT = MT.

7a. Twice pl., "men of Israel"; but 1 Chr 10:7 uses the sg. collective *ʾîš yiśrāʾēl* (as in v. 1) at the beginning of the sentence and leaves the subj. of "fled" unstated. In both cases Chronicles will represent the text of BTH—cf. 1 Kgs 8:2//2 Chr 5:3 (and probably 2 Sam 23:9, where the parallel verse has been lost from 1 Chr 11).

8a. Here *nekrous*, but *traumatiai* in v. 1 for *ḥllym*.

9a. The vb. *krt* ("cut"), as in 1 Sam 17:51; 1 Chr 10:9 uses *nśʾ* ("lift"), which could underlie *apheilen* in 1 Kgdms 17:51—yet *aphairein* does correspond to *krt* in 1 Kgdms 5:4 and 24:5, 6; 1 Chr 19:4; and Isa 9:14 (13; where the obj. is again "head"). The LT follows MT and renders by *apokephalizousi*; in 17:51 it agrees with B. Here B could retrovert to *wyšybw ʾtw* or *wysbw ʾtw* (*hipʿil* of *šwb* or of *sbb*).

b. Here LT = MT.

c. The LT = B.

10a. Codex B = MT; but LT has "Saul's."

11a. The LT = MT.

12a. Here LT = B.

13a. Codex B treats each of the four "books" of *Basileiai* (Kingdoms) as an independent book, with its text starting at the top of a fresh page. Not only so; but at this point it reports the same words twice: at the end of 1 Kingdoms, as 31:13b, and at the beginning of 2 Kingdoms, as 1:1. The LT reports them only once.

With this chapter, a new dimension enters our reading of Samuel. After the lengthy fresh introduction by the authors of Samuel (and Kings), we have now reached the beginning of the older narrative (BTH) that they have inherited, then radically expanded and made their own. Here and in the synoptic portions of 2 Samuel, part of our task will be to consider (and where possible to decide) how far these authors have modified what they took over—and where they may have betrayed their own interests by so doing. At several points, especially from v. 6 onward, the version in Samuel of this opening chapter is different from and fuller than the parallel in 1 Chr 10. It has been argued,[56] I think successfully, that where briefer, the version in Chronicles is prior; and that some of the pluses in Samuel belong together as part of a deliberate rewriting of the report.

[1–7] At first sight, the narrative does not linger over any details of the battle: the initiative or pressure came from Philistines, Israel was unable to resist, and there were casualties on Gilboa (v. 1). And yet the opposite is the case. The opening verses only gradually zoom in on the most important details. Israel is worsted in the battle (v. 1); even the king and his sons do not escape (v. 2); Saul is writhing (?) because of the enemy archers, but not killed outright (v. 3). Saul takes responsibility for his own death (vv. 4–6). Only after all this had been observed does a wider flight take place from surrounding towns, with Israelites being replaced by Philistines (v. 7). The same main points are made by the Chronicler, with differences in detail only toward the end. The main lexical problem is the identity of the final verb in v. 3. The more straightforward option is offered by GT: a form of *ḥll* ("pierce"). But MT both here and in 1 Chr 10 appears to read a form of *ḥwl* ("twist, writhe"). This verb is used both positively of dancing and negatively of quaking in fear; it also describes the pains of childbirth. Following MT leaves open the question of whether Saul has already been wounded, or whether he simply knows that he is staring death in the face—and likely mistreatment beforehand or afterward. Samuel adds mention of the armor-bearer alongside Saul and his sons, (consequentially) alters "all his house" to "all his men," and adds "on that day"

56. Ho, supported by Knoppers (525).

(v. 6). In the following verse, Samuel increases and repositions the witnesses from "those *in* the valley" to "those *across* the valley *and those across the Jordan*," and alters what they see from "that *they* had fled and that Saul and his sons were dead" to "that *the men of Israel* had fled and that Saul and his sons were dead."

The wounded Saul expects abuse or mischief at the hands of his victorious enemies. The range of *ʿll* (*hitpaʿel*) ranges from petty to gross abuse: what Balaam suffered from his ass (Num 22:29), what the Levite's concubine suffered at the hands of the scoundrels in Gibeah (Judg 19:25), what Yahweh inflicted on Egypt (Exod 10:2; 1 Sam 6:6), and whatever King Zedekiah feared that the Jews who had deserted to the Chaldeans might do to him (Jer 38:19). Saul's expectations prove not unreasonable in light of what is done to his dead body; so he asks his armor-bearer to finish him off. In an age where the ethics of assisted suicide are much discussed, close attention to this biblical scene is understandable. The relevance of an ancient battlefield to modern medical issues is not immediately obvious. And yet, like every medic, the normal duty of the armor-bearer is to help his charge stay alive—but this one is asked by his king to do the opposite.

Even although it conjures up an image of what is seen from some distance in once-Israelite territory, this report of Saul's end is told in the narrator's own words, and that means also with his own authority. His version of the matter is only slightly altered from the source text. In our next section we shall have to consider how far his view is subverted by the very different account brought to David by an Amalekite.

[8–13] The second subparagraph (vv. 8–13) describes in rather greater detail what happens to the bodies of Saul and his sons after their deaths. The Chronicler's version is again shorter and closer to the BTH original. According to this, the Philistines take the good news of their victory to their people and their idols by removing Saul's head[57] and armor and parading these till their final display in a temple or temples (one of them dedicated to Dagon), in a location not specified by the text. On hearing of this, the valiant men of Jabesh in Gilead remove the bodies of Saul and his sons (Saul's body being headless?), presumably from the battlefield, and take them for burial under an oak in their own city.

The more important differences in Samuel are these: (1) The MT has Saul's head "cut off" before his armor is stripped, while in Chronicles his armor is stripped before his head is "lifted." (2) The Deities in whose temple Saul's armor is put are specified as Ashtaroth (1 Sam 31:10); Chronicles has simply "their god[s]." (3) His body (not only his head) is displayed on the wall of Beth-shan (*bêt-šān*, 1 Sam 31:10), not *bêt-dāgôn* (1 Chr 10:10). (4) The men

57. Here 1 Chr 10:10b reads quite differently: "and his skull they thrust into the house of Dagon" (cf. 2 Sam 18:14 of lances thrust into the heart of Absalom?).

of Jabesh make a night trip to retrieve the bodies from Beth-shan.[58] (5) Before burial, they burn the corpses. (6) The bones are buried under a tamarisk (1 Sam 31:13), not an oak (1 Chr 10:12).[59]

Several other comments are appropriate: (1) Nowhere else in HB are Philistines said to worship Ashtaroth (1 Sam 31:10). (2) No theft is involved in 1 Chr 10 of what has already been removed by the victors, and hence no night journey from Jabesh is necessary. It is surely the version in 1 Sam 31 that is reflected in the account in 2 Sam 21 of the ultimate reburial of Saul and his family; in that later chapter the word "steal" is used to describe the action of the "lords" (*baʿălê*) of Jabesh (21:12). (3) In 1 Sam 31, burning the recovered corpses may have been intended to forestall any further Philistine attempt to reacquire recognizable trophies. (4) The different texts of v. 9 in MT and B encourage combining the issues of clause order and of word choice. Here B makes no mention of Saul's head and reports only that "they turned him over [or brought him back?] and stripped his armor." Noting that the Chronicler is not explicit about the Philistines' "cutting off" Saul's head, Lestienne (*BA* 415) suggests that B has further attenuated the report of this outrage. I prefer McCarter's suggestion (1:441) that the different location of Saul's beheading in the majority tradition in Samuel and in Chronicles is evidence that it has been secondarily introduced into each, presumably on the basis of what was reported of Goliath's head (1 Sam 17:51).

Ho makes a series of apt observations but may have deduced from them more than they can bear. He nicely demonstrates (1) the several links between Samuel pluses in 1 Sam 31 and 2 Sam 21 (esp. 21:12); (2) the similarity of the battle scenes in 1 Sam 17 and 1 Chr 10 in a valley and how the heads of Goliath and Saul are dealt with; (3) that the number of Saul's sons (just three) given in 1 Sam 14:49 and 28:19 agrees better with 1 Chr 10:6 (where they are specified as "his whole house") than with 1 Sam 31:6; and (4) that 1 Chr 10 is more consistent with the favorable attitude to Jabesh in 1 Sam 11 than the use in 2 Sam 21 of the pejorative verb "stole." However, Ho's conclusion that the "common source" included "a story of the Rise and Fall of Saul" does not follow. It may be instead that several elements elsewhere in 1 Samuel were drafted on the basis of the earlier version of the death of Saul; and that 1 Sam 31 was then subsequently redrafted in light of 2 Sam 21. There is similar evidence that portions of both 1 and 2 Samuel were drafted on the basis of a version of 2 Sam 24 that has since been revised in important details.

58. For the "body," 1 Chr 10:12 uses *gwpt*, not *gwyt* and the verb *wyqḥw*, not *wyśʾw*, and again has no mention of the wall of Beth-shan.

59. The parallel passage in 1 Chr 10:12 has *ʾlh/drys* ("oak"). On the "tamarisk," see above on 22:6. In Gen 21:33, *ʾešel/aroura* is also used in a Philistine context.

2 Samuel 1:1–27

1 And it came to be after the death of Saul
(and David, he had returned from striking down the Amalek*ite*),
and David settled in Ziklag two days.
2 And it came to be on the third day
(look: a man was coming from the camp from *the people*[a] *of* Saul,
and his clothes were torn
and there was earth on his head),
and it came to be on his coming to David,
and he fell to the ground
and did obeisance *to him*.
3 And David said to him,
"From wherever do you come?"
And he said to him,
"From the camp of Israel I have got away."
4 And David said to him,
"What was *this* [the[a]] word?
[Be sure to] tell me."
And he said
that the people fled from the battle;[b]
and a large number [too] fell of the people,
and they died;
and Saul too *died* and Jonathan his son died.[c]
5 And David said to the lad, the one informing him,
"How do you know
that Saul died and Jonathan his son?"
6 And the lad said, the one informing him,
"By pure chance I was on the hill of the[a] Gilboa
(and look: Saul was leaning on[b] his spear,
and look: the chariotry and the lords of the horsemen caught up with him).
7 And he turned behind him,
and he saw [me[a]],
and he called to me,
and I said,
'I'm here.'
8 And he said to me,
'Who are you?'
And I said to him,
'I am an Amalekite.'

9 And he said to me,
'Take sure stand over me,
and do me to death;[a]
for dizziness[b] *dread darkness* has seized me,
for all[c] [the continuation of] my life is in me.'
10 And I stood over him,
and I did him to death;
for I knew
that he would not live after his collapse.
And I took the diadem
that was on his head
and the bracelet[a]
that was on his right arm,
and I brought them to my lord—here."
11 And David took hold of his clothes
and tore them,
and all his men who were with him[a] [too] *tore their clothes.*
12 And they mourned
and they wept[a]
and they fasted till the evening over Saul and over Jonathan his son[b]
and over the people of [Yahweh] *Judah*[c] and over the house
of Israel,
because they had [fallen] *been struck down*[d] by the sword.

13 And David said to the lad, the one informing him,
"Wherever are you from?"
And he said,
"I am son of an Amalekite resident."
14 And David said to him,
"How were you not afraid
to put out your hand
to destroy the anointed of Yahweh?"
15 And David called to one from the lads,
"Come near.[a]
Fall on him."
And he struck him down
and he died.
16 And David said to him,
"Your blood be on your head;
for your mouth—it spoke up against you, saying,
'I, I did to death the anointed of Yahweh.'"

17 And David keened this keening over Saul and over Jonathan his son;
18 and he said,
"To teach the sons of Judah[a] [bow]."
Behold it is inscribed on the Book of the Just.[b]
19 He said:
1.1 "[Your beauty] *Erect*[a], O Israel, *for your dead* pierced on your heights![b]
How have heroes fallen!
20 1.2 Tell it not in Gath, bear no good report in Ashkelon's open places,
Lest the daughters of Philistines rejoice,
lest the daughters of the uncircumcised exult.
21 1.3 Mountains in the Gilboa, no dew and no rain on you[a] nor fields of offerings.[b]
For there the shield of heroes was abhorred,[c] the shield of Saul unanointed with oil.

22 2.4 From blood of pierced, from fat of heroes,
Jonathan's bow was not turned *empty* back
and Saul's sword did not return empty.
23 2.5 Saul and Jonathan—loving each other and delightful,
not separated; comely[a] in their life;
in their death too they were not parted—
swifter than eagles, more heroic than lions.

24 3.6 Daughters of Israel, weep for Saul;
weep for the one[a] who clothed you in crimson with luxuries,[b]
who hung gold ornament[b] on your clothing.
25 How have heroes fallen amid the battle!
3.7 Jonathan, pierced on your heights.[a]
26 I am vexed over you, my brother Jonathan—
you delighted me exceedingly.
Your love for me was more marvelous[a] than[b] the love of women.
27 How have heroes fallen—and the tools of battle[a] perished."

2a. The MT reads the second element in *mʿm* as "with," but B as "people." The LT appears to conflate both readings: "from the camp of the people (that was) with Saul." The expressions "the people of Saul/David" are never attested in MT.

4a. Here DJD (103) reconstructs 4QSam[a] as having included "this" like GT. The noun *dābār* means "situation," as in 2 Sam 14:20.

b. Codex B = MT; however, LT adds "from the camp."

c. The LT = MT, in reading "died" once only.

6a. Here B = MT, but LT has no article.

b. The GT uses here the pass. "supported on"—elsewhere only in Judg 16:26 for *nišʿān*, where again the context is struggle with Philistines, and again a whole house is to be brought down with the protagonist.

7a. Here LT = MT.

9a. The *polel* form *mōtēt* (vv. 9, 10, 16) is relatively uncommon. In 1 Sam 14:13 and 17:51, it is used of finishing off the fallen.[60]

b. There is a possible connection with a (rare) vb. *šbṣ* that appears to mean "decorate" or "plait." The Gk. term *deinos* is relatively uncommon outside Wisdom, and is nowhere else paired with *skotos*. Here LT = B.

c. The LT attests "still" but not "all": "and still my life is in me." In MT, *ʿwd* must be read as a noun suggesting continuance, restoration, or repetition.

10a. The Gk. term *chlidōn* can mean an ornament for arm or ankle.

11a. The sentence in LT is shorter than MT or B and ends with "him."

12a. Codex B has "fasted" before "wept."

b. Here B = MT; but DJD (104) finds that "the line would be long even with the omission of *bnw* ("his son").

c. The LT = B. Neither expression is frequently attested, and in Hebrew they differ only by the presence or absence of a *d*: *ʿam yĕhûdâ (yhwdh)* is used in 2 Sam 19:41; 2 Kgs 14:21//2 Chr 26:1 (LXX reads "people of the land"); Jer 25:1, 2; 26:18; Ezra 4:4; and *ʿam yhwh* in Num 11:29; 16:41 (17:6); Judg 5:11; 1 Sam 2:24; 2 Sam 1:12; 6:21 (not in BTH, and B attests simply *ʿmw*, "his people"); 2 Kgs 9:6; Ezek 36:20; Zeph 2:10 (LXX attests *yhwh ṣĕbāʾôt*).

d. Normally, including 7x in Kingdoms, *plēssō* corresponds to *nkh*, as also here in 4QSam[a], which has *nkw*[61] (DJD 103)—but in MT here, as only in 2 Chr 29:9, the passive corresponds to *npl*.

13a. Paragraphing in 4QSam[a] corresponds to MT.

15a. Here B = MT; however, LT rather strangely has both commands and reports in the pl.

18a. Again B = MT; but LT adds "Israel and [Judah]."

b. The analysis in seven strophes and three stanzas is adapted from Fokkelman (2001: 5–13).

19a. Here B's *stēlōson* and also LT's *akribasai* appear to attest the imperative of the vb. *yṣb* or *nṣb* (with which *maṣṣēbâ* is cognate): "Make monument."

b. The LT's "about your dead" corresponds to *ʿl-bmwtyk* ("on your heights," MT). Here LT may have read the shorter *ʿl-mtyk*. Codex B (rendered above) attests both phrases and may be conflate.

21a. The MT has no vb.; but B reads *mē katabē*; and LT, *mē pesoi*.

b. Here B = MT; but LT ends the line "upon your heights, mountains of death" < *ʿal-bamôtêka hārê māwet*?

c. The vb. *prosochthizein* ("to be wroth with," *LSJ* 1522a) corresponds to a form of *gʿl* elsewhere only in Lev 26 (4x).

60. It is used also in Judg 9:54; Jer 20:17; Pss 34:21 (22); 109:16.

61. It is *puʿal*, as in Exod 9:32.

23a. The LT does not attest the B plus *euprepeis*.

24a. Here LT = MT.

b. Codex B and LT agree in rendering both by *kosmos* in v. 24.

25a. The final phrase quite different in LT, which attests *lammāwet tĕḥallēl lî*.

26a. Here LT appears to have read *nplh* instead of *npl'th* (MT).

b. Apparently LT read *k*- rather than *m*-.

27a. The LT's *skeuē epithymēta* may attest *kĕlê ḥemdâ* (as in 2 Chr 32:27) or *kĕlê maḥămadêhā* (as in 36:19).

[1] Second Samuel opens with a formula used in just three other biblical contexts, Gen 25:11; Josh 1:1; and Judg 1:1: "Now it came to be after the death of *X*." The deaths in question are those of Abraham, Moses, Joshua, and Saul; and those of Abraham and Saul have been reported in the middle of a book. We are reminded immediately after these opening words (v. 1) just where David has (not) been when Saul died. He has been far from the national catastrophe on Gilboa; and yet he has been doing exactly what a leader of Israel should be doing: slaughtering Amalekites. This first insert (2 Sam 1–4) into the original BTH is framed by two very similar accounts of men who believe David will benefit them for killing or claiming to kill Saul or one of his sons: in his response to the second of these messengers (4:10), David will recall the first.

The apparently earlier and shorter narrative within 1 Samuel of the transition from Saul to David has already placed David in the south of the country (25:1), before the final struggle of Saul against the Philistines began well north on Gilboa. Part of the function of the longer version, created by the addition of 1 Sam 25–30, is to strengthen David's alibi: he accepts Abigail's good counsel that he should not himself move against a fool (ch. 25); he turns down a second chance of finishing off Saul himself (ch. 26); he proves to the satisfaction of his patron in Gath his willingness to join the Philistine muster (ch. 27), but is sent back to the south at the insistence of Achish's colleagues (ch. 29); then, to save his own and his men's families and possessions, he has to go still further south and further out of range of the coming northern battle (ch. 30). For readers unfamiliar with the terrain, the relevant timing is spelled out at the very beginning: David has been at Ziklag all the time it took someone to travel there from Gilboa (1 Sam 30:1).

[2–5] This bearer of bad news presents himself like the unnamed messenger whose news from the battlefront brought on Eli's death (1 Sam 4:12) and like Hushai, who will tell David of the death of another great foe (2 Sam 15:32). On each occasion the messenger's clothing is rent (though the term for garment differs in each case), and (this feature in identical terms) there is always earth on his head. David's question about where the new arrival comes from is as ambiguous in Hebrew as in English (1:3; the only other character in HB to frame the question in exactly these terms is Yahweh in addressing the satan in

Job 2:2). The man chooses to answer, not in terms of his origins, but in terms of his most recent journey: he has got away from Israel's camp. His use of *nimlāṭ* (v. 3) is interesting: in 1 Samuel it has been used eight times of David (19:10, 12, 17, 18; 20:29; 22:1; 23:13; 27:1), overwhelmingly in connection with David's escapes from Saul or his camp; and once of Abiathar, son of Ahimelech, in escaping the purge by Saul and Doeg (22:20). Ironically (for we have not yet been told the origins of the messenger), it has been used for the tenth and most recent occasion in 1 Samuel (30:17) of the escape from David by the young Amalekite camel riders.[62] Once more *nimlāṭ* will be used in 2 Samuel (4:6) in the balancing story of Ish-bosheth's assassination.

David's opening question is less precise than Saul's to Abner about David himself (1 Sam 17:55), or Saul's even more direct question to the messenger: the dying king came more quickly to the point (2 Sam 1:8). But the exact words of David's next question (*meh-hāyâ haddābār*, v. 4a) have not been heard since Eli's interrogation of the messenger in 1 Sam 4:16, and they will not be heard again in the books of Samuel. Appropriately, these reports, requested in identical terms by Eli and David, are presented according to the same structure: the fate of the main force is related first, and the named casualties last. In 2 Sam 1:4, Saul and Jonathan are the climactic figures, while in 1 Sam 4:17 the loss of the ark was reported as even more significant than the death of Eli's sons. It is difficult to know whether we should pass on quickly, supposing we have simply read a second instance of a stock, stylized report of defeat and casualties—how many different ways can such information be packaged in a minimum of words?—or whether we should linger and draw out the comparisons and contrasts.

No contrast is offered between the two messengers in the way they make their report or their report is received. The first messenger is simply described as a Benjamite (1 Sam 4:12), and we might suppose the same of the second (2 Sam 1:2) when we are told that he comes from the camp, from the people of (or from proximity to) Saul. Readers are as surprised as hearers when he later lets slip that he is an Amalekite. Should we compare David and Eli as receivers of the bad news, and suppose that at least a slow-burning fuse has been lit under David and his house? Or should we simply contrast the young man of action and of the future with the old man (and his daughter-in-law), whose house is already under divine threat?

[6–10] There is no mention of Saul's spear in the first report of his death (1 Sam 31); there his own sword was the means of his death. The spear on which the Amalekite now reports Saul leaning (v. 6) has on occasion been thrown at David (1 Sam 18:10–11; 19:9–10) and at Jonathan (20:33); and it

62. Should *nimlāṭ* and *bāraḥ* be compared or contrasted as "elude," "give the slip"? They are frequently used together; perhaps *nimlāṭ* marks the success of the flight.

also features prominently in the second account of David preserving Saul's life (1 Sam 26:7, 11, 12, 16, 22). The term *nēzer* (2 Sam 1:10) is most common in Leviticus and Numbers. In these books it is associated with consecration; the sense (by extension) of "crown" is proposed. But a homonym (?) means "flower"; stylized flowers (as well as feathers) were used in or as the headdress of kings—certainly from the Achaemenid period. It is found in two royal psalms (89:39 [40]; 132:18). However, perhaps the most important parallel is the royal context in 2 Kgs 11:12 (BTH), where the priest puts the *nēzer* on young king Joash in the renewal of kingship after Athaliah's seizure of power. Nonetheless, the term *ʾeṣʿādâ* present here is quite rare (Num 31:50; Isa 3:20). Campbell (2:21) rejects the idea that the royal insignia brought by the Amalekite are intended to depict David as Saul's legitimate heir: he understands David, by going into immediate mourning, as rejecting the insinuation that he is eager for the crown. But that may be a false opposition: it is quite as likely that David is content to receive the tokens of legitimacy at the same time as (apparently) deploring the means.

The messenger may claim "pure chance" in his encounter with the dying Saul (v. 6). However, the patterning of "chance" encounters in Samuel is far from accidental. It is only in this first one in 2 Samuel[63] that the main verb (*qrʾ*) is strengthened by the infinitive absolute. That is a feature of reported speech in the books of Samuel: it functions to draw particular attention to the claim. His emphatic choice of language might even alert an attentive reader to the surprising admission he is about to make. He is talking to David of "happening" on Saul, in a book in which happenstance has been spoken of only by the Philistine enemy (1 Sam 6:9) and by Saul himself (20:26). Israel is viscerally opposed to Philistines . . . and to Amalekites. "Happen" is certainly not a word that David uses, nor is it ever used about him. He might have agreed with the Philistine diviners' choice: either by chance or by Yahweh.

[11–12] David at first ignores the explosive admission. Just as David has been at sufficient distance not to know what was happening on Gilboa, so the messenger who has been on Gilboa knows nothing of David's recent dealings with his own people. David and his men tear their clothes like the messenger (vv. 2, 11). David's court will mourn similarly for Abner (3:31) and for Amnon (13:31). The repetitive rhetoric of v. 12 (the three verbs, "lamented . . . wept . . . fasted," followed by the four objects of the mourning, "Saul and . . . Jonathan, . . . the people of Yahweh/Judah, . . . the house of Israel") already suggests mourning that is more than cursory, even before we come to David's immortal elegy. But we are not told at what hour during the third day the messenger has arrived in Ziklag; it may be that a ceremony (including a fast) that lasts only "till evening" (v. 12), and hence less than one full day, deserves to

63. The others are noted by the narrator in 2 Sam 18:9; 20:1.

be contrasted with the seven-day fast being observed at much the same time in Jabesh (1 Sam 31:13).

[13–16] We have seen that the narrator of 1 Sam 31 has largely repeated, and hence endorsed, the narrative in his source relating Saul's death, provided in the chapter that begins BTH. We are not told there whether Saul's armor-bearer is motivated by the duty of his own office (to look after his master) or by respect for Saul's kingly office; but something restrained him from respecting Saul's stated wishes. In that report by the narrator himself, the mortally wounded king has then himself to contrive the speeding of his own dying. The Amalekite, by contrast, claims to David to have done just what the king requested. He agrees wholly with the narrator that immediate death was what Saul wanted. If we can trust the Amalekite, we might wonder why Saul needed to know his identity—possibly to satisfy himself that it was not a Philistine who found him alive. We might even wonder whether Saul would have recognized it as grimly fitting that it be an Amalekite who should finish off the very king who had been blamed for not finishing off on the battlefield an earlier king of his own people.

It is just possible to combine into one interlocking story the different accounts of Saul's death provided by the narrator and the Amalekite, but it probably is not wise to do so. I suspect that we readers should understand what David cannot know: that the messenger is offering him a self-serving fiction, or at best an embroidered version of the truth. David may not have been minded to trust this foreigner; but the Amalekite is able to prove that he had access to the royal body in advance of the Philistines, for he is carrying Saul's royal insignia. Polzin (1993: 2–10) proposes that the narration uses the Amalekite as a double, not only for David, but also for the Deuteronomistic Historian. His "story about the death of Saul is, after all, fundamentally accurate. It is the History's task to kill Saul off." The messenger transfers the regalia to the new king.

The three portions of this chapter can be read as sequential: we can suppose that David's questioning of the messenger resumes after the first impromptu mourning, and is followed by a more formal ceremony. But it may be preferable to read the interrogation and dispatch of the Amalekite and the following memorable lament as supplementary detail to the summary account we have already read. Several elements of vv. 1–12 are resumed in vv. 13–16. In particular, David's questions to the messenger take a similar form: "Wherever are you coming from?" (v. 3) is only slightly simplified to "Wherever are you from?" (v. 13); on each occasion the follow-up question is introduced by the same "how?" (*ʾêk*, vv. 5, 14), as will be so memorably repeated in his elegy (vv. 19, 25, 27). Now David's attention is focused on the man himself (v. 13), and his words can no longer be (mis)understood as an interest in the starting place of the messenger's most recent journey (v. 3). The man has already identified himself as an Amalekite in his report of the words he has exchanged with the dying Saul (v. 8). Now, under further questioning by David, he immediately moves to ameliorate that admission by claiming that his father is a resident alien (*gēr*). Whether, given the news and gifts he has brought David, he thinks he needs the protection expected from his father's status is not stated. If David does recognize his words as an implicit claim for protection, he implicitly brushes this aside: even he, an Israelite strongman, has twice (1 Sam 24 and 26) refrained from laying hands on Yahweh's anointed when Saul came into his power. In the report of the second occasion (26:9, 11), he used the exact expression with which he now (v. 14) charges the Amalekite (*šlḥ yd b-*). One person's mercy killing is another person's murder. What the Amalekite has sought to portray as a coup de grâce, David proclaims to be regicide.

Outside the books of Samuel, we encounter the phrase "Yahweh's anointed" only once more in HB; and there (Lam 4:20) some of the rich significance of the expression is explored:

> Our nostrils' breath, Yahweh's anointed, has been caught in their pits,
> of whom we had said: "In his shadow shall we live among the nations."

The anointed king was the very air Israelites breathed: protected by his shadow, they lived as a nation among the nations. On hearing the Amalekite's news, David and his men mourn not only the king and his son but also the whole people and house of Israel (v. 12): on the death of the king, the very life of the nation is under threat.

The messenger claims to have done for Saul what the dying king wanted; he may have brought the royal diadem and bracelet to David, not because David is known to crave them, but simply for safekeeping because he was known as the commander of Israel when Saul was still alive (5:2). If so, he is cruelly rewarded: killed off to the sound of David tendentiously accusing him of words he has never uttered: "It is I who have done to death the anointed of Yahweh." David's command to one of his men to "fall on" the Amalekite is echoed in just two contexts in all of Samuel and Kings. The first is Saul's command first to his own men to "fall on" the priests of Nob, and then to Doeg when his own men would not "lay hands on" the priests (1 Sam 22:17–18). The other is the series of executions ordered by Solomon (1 Kgs 2:25, 29, 31, 34) on the advice of his dying father, which secured the new king's royal power (2:46). These parallels and the hyped misquotation will provide reliable clues as to how the narrator proposes we should view this scene: they make us suspect again (compare, most recently, 1 Sam 26:22) that "one from the lads" does not mean the same as just "any one of the lads."

[17–18] Following the frequent example of the ancient Greek translators, the use of "keened/keening" in the rendering above deliberately plays on the sound of the Hebrew *qîn*/*qînâ*. David's move into formal poetry is not simply for the occasion, but for the record: this dirge should be both taught to others and written down. It should be taught to the "sons" of Judah. In recent times, he has been sending presents from his booty to the "elders" of Judah in several cities around Hebron (1 Sam 30:26); and the "men" of Judah will shortly (2 Sam 2:4) anoint him as their king. Insofar as this David is speaking to a future people of Judah, he may be insisting that Israel is the same people, and that Israel's leaders deserve honor in death. As for the written record, GT supports MT in stating that this is to be added to "The Book of the Just" (*spr hyšr*). The same document is mentioned in Josh 10:13. However, a Greek plus in 1 Kgs 8:53 mentions a "Book of the Song," and *spr hšyr* would be a straightforward title for a collection of poems.

[19–27] Grief, like surprise, regularly expresses itself in questions. The refrain "How have heroes fallen?" (2 Sam 1:19, 25, 27) has double resonance. Most immediately, the David who utters this triple "how?" (*ʾêk*) to everyone present has already interrogated the Amalekite in identical terms (vv. 5, 14). The longer alternate form of the same interrogative (*ʾêkâ*) heads three of the five acrostic poems that constitute the book of Lamentations (1:1; 2:1; 4:1) and provides the book with its Hebrew name. It may be more than accidental that, as noted just above, the sole mention of the exact phrase "Yahweh's anointed" outside Samuel occurs toward the end of the third of these acrostics (Lam 4:20).

Despite the several textual uncertainties, some of the recurring and some of the opposing themes of the poem are clear:

- The wish that news not reach the Philistine cities lest their womenfolk begin to celebrate (v. 20) corresponds to the command to Israel's daughters to weep for Saul (v. 24).
- Love and delight characterized the relationship between Saul and Jonathan in life, and this is underscored by their togetherness in death (v. 23). But the delight of David in Jonathan and the love of Jonathan for David are true to an even higher degree (v. 26).
- The previous observation is underscored by the way in which *nplʾth* ("was wonderful," v. 26) plays on the recurrent *nplw* ("have fallen") of the refrain (vv. 19, 25, 27): the wonder of their love is anything but fallen/failing.
- The mutuality and togetherness of Saul and Jonathan in life and death (v. 23) is both affirmed and subverted by giving them parallel but separate recognition in death: Saul should be specially mourned by Israel's women (v. 24); Jonathan is claimed by David himself on the basis of a love greater than women's (vv. 25b–26).
- The repeated *bmwtyk* ("your heights," vv. 19, 25), the hilltops on which they died, looks very similar to *bmwtm* ("in their death," v. 23); and there are many smaller clusters of shared consonants in much closer proximity.

- The verb *ḥll* ("pierced," sg.) is used in close proximity to *gb*[*w*]*rym* ("heroes") at beginning (v. 19) and near the end (v. 25). But in v. 22 we find it in the plural, even closer to *gbwrym*—separated only by *mḥlb* ("from fat of"), which shares consonants with both.
- The hilltops of Gilboa (*glb'*) are cursed (v. 21) because a shield was "abhorred" (*ng'l*)—a not very common verb, chosen probably because it uses three of Gilboa's four letters: Gilboa has abhorrence built into its very name.[64]
- The fact that "Jonathan, pierced on your heights" (v. 25b) resumes the poem's opening words "Your beauty, O Israel, pierced on your heights" (v. 19) may suggest, but does not require, that only Jonathan is intended as the referent of Israel's beauty.
- The parallelism of the separate recognition is confirmed by the repetition after each (vv. 25a, 27) of the lengthened refrain, which in each case ends in the word "battle."
- This repetition of "battle" gives all the greater prominence to the poem's very last words, "tools of battle." "Tools of battle" is normally understood as a term for weapons.[65] However, "heroes" are the subject of the previous verb, and *'bd* ("perish/wander," v. 27) normally has a personal or an abstract subject. Together these observations powerfully suggest that Saul and Jonathan, who have themselves been very effective with sword and bow (v. 22), were finally discarded by a personified Battle as rejected implements.[66] Alternatively, we may compare Ezek 32:27 (footnoted above): the tyrants just reviewed "will lie with heroes fallen, . . . who went down to Sheol with their tools of war."[67]
- The repeated question, if not also the triple echo of the book called "How," contributes powerfully to the dirge. The third "how" (v. 27) follows close on the heels of the second (v. 25), and leads almost immediately to silence.

It is no surprise that Gath is the first representative of the Philistine homeland. It is well known to David as the city of Goliath his opponent and of Achish

64. Amos similarly plays on several place names: Gilgal and Beth-awen (5:5); Lo-debar and Karnaim (6:13).

65. See 1 Sam 8:12; Jer 21:4; 51:20; Ezek 32:27; 1 Chr 12:33.

66. The term *'bd* occurs in the book of Judges only in the final line of the Song of Deborah ("So perish all your enemies, O Yahweh," 5:31); and otherwise in the books of Samuel only in 1 Sam 9:3, 20, of the "wandering" or "loss" of the asses belonging to Saul's father.

67. Later tradition almost certainly links these two passages: the word after "fallen" had originally been *m'wlm* ("forever") as in LXX, but in Ezek 32:27 MT we read the similar *m'rlym* ("because of the uncircumcised").

his protector. And the David of 1 Sam 27 is expert in not having the truth told in that city. With Ekron, Gath has marked the Philistine border toward the hill country (1 Sam 7:14; 17:52). Coastal Ashkelon is much deeper into their territory; it appears elsewhere in Samuel only in the story of the return of the ark, and as one member in a list of five cities (1 Sam 6:17).

Israel's women have chanted David's and Saul's victories over Goliath and his people (18:7); but now the tables will be turned. Jonathan has scorned the Philistines as "uncircumcised" (14:6); and David speaks of Goliath in similar terms (17:36); David earned marriage to Saul's daughter with a heap of foreskins; and the dying Saul has feared (sexual?) mishandling by the uncircumcised victors. Apart from one backward reference to that bride-price (2 Sam 3:14), David's words here bring this catalog of barrack-room insults in the books of Samuel to a close. They are reminiscent of the scatological humor in the plagues on the Philistines (1 Sam 5–6).

Polzin (1993: 12–15) writes of elegy as eulogy and suggests that, just as David refused to do Saul harm when he could so, here he refuses to say ill of him: a nation needs to salute its dead leader. The use of "heights" (*bmwt*) in the inclusio (vv. 19 and 25) emphasizes a term that elsewhere throughout the larger narrative we know as pejorative. Then the elegy resumes in vv. 19, 25, and 27 two key terms from the report in 1 Sam 31 (BTH), each repeated in vv. 1 and 8 there: "pierced" or "slain" (*ḥllym*) and "fall" (*npl*). Connected in this lament with *bmwt*, the other sense of *ḥll* becomes more prominent: "pollute," "profane," "defile." Another nice ambiguity in connection with "heights" is whether *ṣby* means "glory" or "gazelle." Again "blood" and "fat" (v. 22) belong equally to ritual and to martial sacrifice. The daughters of Israel should weep (v. 24), just as the daughters of the Philistines should not rejoice (v. 20).

Fokkelman (2010: 21–23, 27) draws attention to the links between the poems near the beginning, middle, and end of Samuel; he finds it particularly significant that v. 23 (the pivotal verse of the whole Samuel composition) is precisely where life and death appear in inverted quotation ("in their life; in their death too") of Hannah's Song, which told (1 Sam 2:6) of Yahweh's "bringing to death and bringing to life"—inverted quotation being a sign of inverted genre.

Clearly, by the end of the poem, David has detached Jonathan from his father—Jonathan who proved his loyalty to David over against his father—and that may be a ground for understanding the opening *ṣĕbî* (v. 19) as referring only to Jonathan (so Fokkelman, 2001: 7, 12 on the basis of the pattern of names in the whole poem). Polzin stresses the parallel with *gibbôrîm* and assumes that *ṣĕbî* (MT)[68] refers to Saul and Jonathan together. However, such lines of

68. Given the several links between the messengers' reports, it is important when translating MT not to use "glory" for *ṣĕbî*, because that has already been used in the ark and Eli story for Hebrew *kābôd*.

interpretation work only for MT: in GT the opening word of the poem is read as imperative, and the dead being celebrated are plural. "Love" can have a political or diplomatic sense in HB, denoting the loyalty properly shown by a vassal to a superior. But David sings of something more personal: Jonathan's love was more marvelous than the love shown by women.

2 Samuel 2:1–7

1 And it came to be after that
and David asked of Yahweh, saying,
"Shall I go up into one of the cities of Judah?"
And Yahweh said to him,
"Go up."
And David said,
"Where shall I go up?"
And he said,
"To Hebron."
2 And David went up there, and also his two wives, Ahinoam the Jezreelite and Abigail wife of Nabal the Carmelite.
3 And his men
who were with him
David brought up, each man and his household,
and they lived in the cities of Hebron.
4 And the men of Judah came
and anointed David there as king over the house of Judah.
And they reported to David, saying,
"The men of Jabesh-gilead—they have buried Saul."

5 And David sent messengers to the men of Jabesh-gilead,
and said to them,
"Blessed are you of Yahweh,
who have performed [this] *the* loyalty *of God*[a] with your lord,
with Saul,
and have buried him.
6 And now may Yahweh perform with you loyalty and trust;
and I too will do with you this good thing
because you have done this good thing.
7 And now let your hands be strong
and come to be men of valor;
for your lord Saul is dead;
and moreover me have the house of Judah anointed as king over them."

5a. Here 4QSam[a] has a combination of MT and B: "this loyalty of God."

[1–4] David's question to his God "Shall I go up . . . ?" is the first of two anticipations of 2 Sam 5 (BTH)—here anticipating the question in 5:19 in face of a Philistine attack. However, the following preposition is not *'l/'l* as there but *b-*. There is no mention of any hostilities between David and his men and the people of Hebron and the surrounding towns. This appears to be a peaceful "ascent" into one of the highest areas of the hill country of Judah. His move—accompanied by his two wives and his men and their households—is described (vv. 2–3) in terms quite similar to their earlier move out of Saul's way to Gath (1 Sam 27:3). Not only is no conflict mentioned, but also "the men of Judah"[69] come and anoint him king there over "the house of Judah" (v. 4). With Saul now out of everyone's way, David and his people with their families move their base up into the hill country, where he and his men used to roam (1 Sam 30:31), and out of the old Philistine protectorate of Ziklag, where they have learned of Saul's death and have mourned him (2 Sam 1:1).

The source-document (BTH) had already placed David's anointing by Israel in Hebron (5:1–3). And the new story of David in the developed book of Samuel anticipates this by reporting him anointed king of Judah seven years before the approach from (northern) Israel. Second Samuel retrojects into the story of David a Judah-Israel polarity that the older source had known only from the division of Solomon's kingdom on his death, and that barely surfaces in 1 Samuel. Insofar as the story of the punishment that follows David's census (2 Sam 24, BTH) anticipates this later polarity, it also counts Judah separately from Israel; we have seen this anticipated in turn in 1 Sam 11:8 and 15:4.

[5–7] Anointed by Judah in Hebron well to the south, David learns immediately that "the men of Jabesh"[70] in Gilead (to the distant northeast) have buried Saul. First Samuel 31 has reported less specifically that "men of worth" have buried Saul in Jabesh. The traditional paragraphing, and even verse division, report both the anointing and the burial news within a single sentence. David responds to the news about Jabesh with an embassy to this city that delivers a very complimentary overture. We readers recognize that his message to these Transjordanian northerners, who have taken care of Saul's remains, opens with the very words used by Saul to the people of Ziph in Judah who have betrayed David's whereabouts to him: "Blessed are you of Yahweh."[71] Both Saul and David are ready to flatter communities distant from their own power base.

69. Not "the elders of Judah" (who appear in Samuel only in 1 Sam 30:26; 2 Sam 19:11 [12]), although it is "the elders of Israel" who officiate in 5:3 (BTH).

70. Exactly as they are styled in 1 Sam 11:1, 5, 9, 10.

71. Outside 1 Sam 23:21; 2 Sam 2:5, this greeting is found in pl. only in Ps 115:15 (the first line of the psalm speaks of "loyalty"). It is even rarer in sg.: m. in 1 Sam 15:13 (where Saul claims to have established the divine word); f. in Ruth 3:10 (where Boaz praises Ruth for her "loyalty").

There is a deal of ambiguity in both subparagraphs. It is unclear (v. 4) whether the men of Judah have told David about Saul's burial in Jabesh, or otherwise unidentified messengers have done so. Then the ancient witnesses divide over whether the men of Jabesh-gilead are expressing their own loyalty or divine loyalty to Saul, just as they have divided over what Jonathan was expressing to David. Even in the shorter text (MT), the word order in v. 5 may have David deliberately suggesting that in burying Saul, Jabesh is acting loyally toward their (divine) lord. And David goes on (v. 6) to lead them to expect that Yahweh himself will repay them for what they have done for their lord in burying Saul. The noun *ḥesed* ("loyalty") is used only within speech in the books of Samuel, and never in the words of the narrator, as follows:

In 1–2 Samuel	**Speaker**	**From**	**To**
1.15:6	Saul	Kenites	Israel
1.20:8	David	Jonathan	David
1.20:14	Jonathan	David/Yahweh[72]	Jonathan
1.20:15	Jonathan	David	Jonathan's house
2.2:5	David	Jabesh-gilead/ *God*[73]	Saul
2.2:6	David	Yahweh	Jabesh-gilead
2.3:8	Abner	Abner	house of Saul
2.7:15	Yahweh	Yahweh	David
2.9:1, 3	David	David	house of Saul
2.9:7	David	David	Mephibosheth
2.10:2	David	David	Hanun
2.10:2	David	Nahash	David
2.15:20	David	Yahweh	Ittai
2.16:17	Absalom	Hushai	his friend David
2.22:51	David	Yahweh	his king, David

Yahweh speaks only once (2 Sam 7:15) about his *ḥesed* toward David; and David echoes these words of Yahweh at the end of his song (22:51). The only other *ḥesed* in the Davidic part of BTH concerns the expected mutual loyalty between David and the Ammonite kings (2 Sam 10). Apart from David, who speaks of *ḥesed* in four narrative contexts in addition to 2 Sam 10 (1 Sam 20; 2 Sam 2; 9; 15), Saul, Abner, and Absalom are the only humans to use the term.

David uses the term "lord" (*ʾădôn*, in the plural of dignity) to express the position of Saul in relationship to Jabesh—twice (vv. 5, 7), and hence with

72. Codex B does not attest *yhwh*.

73. Codex B does attest *h'lhym*.

emphasis. David appears to have an almost complete monopoly over the use of this term, as with *ḥesed*. Joab and Orna both address David as "my lord, the king" in BTH (2 Sam 24:3, 22);[74] and throughout 2 Samuel many anticipate their example, from the Amalekite messenger and Abner onward.[75] And David talks to Ziba (9:9, 10; 16:3) as well as the men of Jabesh about Saul as his lord (in the past).[76] Within First Samuel, Abigail has addressed David as "my lord" no less than fourteen times in 1 Sam 25:24–31. But with just one exception,[77] it is only David who addresses Saul in this manner—and he does so with some irony, precisely in the two contiguous situations where Saul's "mastery" over himself is most obviously in question (1 Sam 24:6, 8, 10 [7, 9, 11]; 26:17). It is between these two scenes describing Saul in David's power, and as if to emphasize where lordship truly resides even while Saul remains alive and king, that Abigail's almost obsessive repetition of the term is located.

The associations of David's final words to Jabesh are no less interesting. He has wished for them a divine response to what they have done for their late king, and has promised them a good response from himself (v. 6). However, this partly hoped for and partly promised future does not just answer to Jabesh's actions in the past (v. 5b): further readiness on Jabesh's part is commended (v. 7a), and they in their Transjordanian north should be aware that David has been anointed as their king by the house of Judah (v. 7b).[78] We have already noted that David has greeted Jabesh in the words used by Saul to the people of Ziph. Absalom's briefing to his men who will assassinate his elder brother Amnon (13:28) provide the closest parallel in Samuel to David's words (v. 7a) encouraging Jabesh.

2 Samuel 2:8–9

8 And Abner son of Ner, leader of the army of Saul—
he took Ish-bosheth son of Saul
and brought him over to Mahanaim.
9 And they made him king to Gilead and to [the Ashury[a]] *Tashiry* and to Jezreel,
and over Ephraim and over Benjamin and over Israel as a whole.

74. Only two more synoptic texts (2 Sam 10:3; 1 Kgs 22:17) use "lord"; then 1 Chr 12:19 (20) draws on 1 Sam 29:4 for its use of the term. And 2 Chr 2:14, 15 (13, 14); 13:6 demonstrate that Chronicles is not opposed to using the term.

75. See 2 Sam 1:10; 3:21; 4:8; 11:9, 11, 13; 14:9, 12, 15, 17 (2x), 19 (2x), 22; 15:21 (2x); 16:4; 18:28, 32; etc.

76. As also Nathan addresses David himself in 2 Sam 12:8 (2x); etc.

77. The priest Ahimelech, son of Ahitub (1 Sam 22:12).

78. Within BTH, "the house of Judah" is unique to 1 Kgs 12:21.

9a. Here DJD (104) reconstructs *gšr*, but without comment. McCarter (2:83) notes that it is the reading of Syr and Codex v. Also, B would retrovert to an otherwise unknown *tšyry*, while LT reads *Ezri*. Alter (203) notes that it is "simplest" to read MT as a mistake for "Asherite."

[8–9] Abner's initiative is reported after the men of Judah anoint David, and after David's dealings with the men of Jabesh in Gilead. In this context it is striking that Gilead heads the list of the territories named by Abner. But the Hebrew narrator has not provided any close temporal coordination with these relevant actions. The translation above follows B, in which the order of the report mirrors the order of events. However, MT could equally plausibly be read as offering background to what has just been reported: "Now Abner . . . had {already} taken Ish-bosheth." David's actions and words in Ziklag (2 Sam 1) have preceded his move to Hebron and his recognition as king. Only gradually do we come to learn that Saul's death results in two king-makings. The verb "make someone king" (*himlîk*) is used in the books of Kings of the appointment of many of David's successors, from Solomon to Josiah. But in Samuel we find it in connection with Saul (1 Sam 11:15; 12:1; 15:11, 35) and now his son (2 Sam 2:9), but never with David. David is never said to be "made king"; instead, he is "anointed as king" (2 Sam 2:4; 5:3).

The genealogies of Benjamin in 1 Chronicles give Eshbaal as the name of Saul's fourth son (8:33; 9:39). A few Greek MSS attest Ishbaal here too, and these are almost certainly closer to the original form of his name. In 2 Samuel, however, not only MT but also the dominant Greek tradition has altered this name compounded with Baal into the explicitly discreditable Ish-bosheth, or "Man-of-shame." We found the comparable Jerub-besheth in 1 Sam 12:11 for the Jerub-baal known in Judg 6–9. If DJD is right in detecting double haplography in 2 Sam 2:15 (see below), this is important for the question of the name of this son of Saul: elsewhere in 4QSam[a], as in four of the five Lucianic Greek MSS, he is always Mephibosheth. If the Chronicler did accurately record his name as *ʾšbʿl*, we may wonder whether a narrator has deliberately and prejudicially named Saul's son by the Hebrew cognate of Phoenician *ʾtbʿl*—Jezebel's father (1 Kgs 16:31).

Each of the new kings already has or is keen to develop relations to Gilead. Collision between them is inevitable. The very name Mahanaim ("Twin Camps," v. 8), east of the river Jordan, makes it a useful setting for stories of conflict. It makes one appearance in Genesis (32:2 [3]), and that mention is strategically placed between two of Jacob's difficult relationships: just after his finally peaceful parting from Laban, and before his reconciliation with Esau. In Joshua it helps to mark the border between Gad and the half-tribe of Manasseh (13:26, 30). And it appears in the buildup to both of the intra-Israel conflicts that 2 Samuel reports. In this first one, Abner makes Saul's son king there

(2:8); moves from there to Gibeon (v. 12), prominent in the early kingship of Solomon (1 Kgs 3); and returns there after heavy losses (v. 29). Then, as soon as it is reported that the fleeing David has arrived in Mahanaim, we are told that Absalom (whose rebellion, like David's kingship, has begun in Hebron) "crossed the Jordan with all the men of Israel" (2 Sam 17:24). These cities, which serve as the rival bases, provide only the first of many links between the reports of the two civil wars in this book.

2 Samuel 2:10–3:5

10 Forty years old was Ish-bosheth son of Saul
    at his becoming king over Israel,
and for two years he was king.[a]
However, the house of Judah, they followed David.
11 And the number of the days
    that David was king in Hebron over the house of Judah
came to be seven years and six months.

12 And[a] Abner son of Ner went out, and the servants of Ish-bosheth son of Saul,
    from Mahanaim to Gibeon.
13 And Joab son of Zeruiah and the servants of David, they went out *from Hebron*
and met them by the pool of Gibeon altogether;
and these settled by the pool on one side,
and those by the pool on the other.
14 And Abner said to Joab,
    "Let the lads surely rise up
    and make sport before us."
And Joab said,
    "Let them rise up."
15 And they rose up
and passed by on a count *of the servants of* [twelve of] Benjamin,[a]
    [and] *twelve* of Ish-bosheth son of Saul, and twelve of the servants of David.
16 And they grasped each on the head of his fellow, and his sword in the side of his fellow,
and they fell together.
And that place became called the field of the rocks that is at Gibeon.
17 And the fighting was extremely hard on that day;
and Abner was smitten, and the men of Israel, before the servants of David.

18 And there were there the three sons of Zeruiah, Joab and Abishai and Asahel;
and Asahel was light on his feet, like one of the gazelles that are in the open.
19 And Asahel pursued after Abner;
and he did not turn aside,
going to right or to left, from following Abner.
20 And Abner turned behind him
and he said,
"Is that you, Asahel?"
And he said,
"It is I."
21 And Abner said to him,
"Take yourself off to your right or to your left
and catch yourself hold of one from the lads;
and take for yourself what is stripped from him."
But Asahel was not willing
to turn
from following him.
22 And Abner continued further
saying to Asahel,
"You turn
from following me.
Why should I strike you to the ground?
And how should I raise my face to Joab your brother?"
23 And he refused
to turn;
and Abner struck him with the back of the spear on the belly
and the spear came out behind him,
and he fell there;
and he died where he was.
And everyone
who came to the place
where Asahel had fallen
and died
stood still.
24 And Joab and Abishai pursued after Abner;
and the sun came {home};
and they, they came to Givat Ammah,
which is opposite Giah on the way to the desert of Gibeon.
25 And the sons of Benjamin gathered themselves behind Abner
and became one band;[a]

and they took their stand at the head of one hill.
26 And Abner called to Joab
and said,
"Forever shall a sword consume?
Do you not know
that it will be bitter at the last?
And how long will you not say to the people
to turn back
from following [their] *our* brothers?"
27 And Joab said,
"As [God] *Yahweh*[a] lives,
surely,
had you not spoken,
then from morning the people would have been raised up,[b] each after his brother."
28 And Joab sounded on the horn,
and all the people stood still,
and they no longer pursued after Israel,
and they did not continue further
to fight.
29 Abner and his men, they walked in the Arabah all that night;
and they crossed the Jordan,
walked all the cleft,
and came to Mahanaim.
30 And Joab, he turned from following Abner,
and gathered all the people,
and there were counted {missing} from the servants of David nineteen men and Asahel.
31 And the servants of David,
they had struck down from *the sons of*[a] Benjamin and [among] *from* the men of Abner;
three hundred and sixty men died.
32 And they picked up Asahel,
and they buried him in the grave of his father,
which was in Bethlehem;
and they walked all the night, Joab and his men,
and it grew light for them in Hebron.
3:1 And the war was long between the house of Saul and the house of David.
And *the house of* David was becoming stronger and stronger,
and the house of Saul *was* [were] becoming weaker and weaker.

2 And sons were born to David in Hebron:
and his eldest was Amnon, to Ahinoam the Jezreelitess;
3 and his second was [Chilab[a]] *Dalouia*, to Abigail [wife of Nabal] the Carmelite*ss*;
and the third was Absalom, son of Maacah daughter of Talmai king of Geshur;
4 and the fourth was Adonijah, son of Haggith;
and the fifth was Shephatiah, son of Abital;
5 and the sixth was Jithream, to Eglah, wife of David.
These were born to David in Hebron.

10a. Although translated in GT, v. 10a is absent from 4QSam[a].

12a. There is no space in 4QSam[a] corresponding to the *sĕtûmâ* ("closed") layout before this verse in MT.

15a. Here 4QSam[a] reads *lbny bnymyn ʾyš . . .* : DJD (105) explains MT as resulting from double haplography: "twelve belonging to the sons of Benjamin, each belonging to Ish-bosheth."

25a. Each use of *ʾăguddâ* is distinctive: Exod 12:22; 2 Sam 2:25; Isa 58:6; Amos 9:6.

27a. Here DJD (107) reconstructs *yhwh* with B, noting (1) that it is preferred in the oath formula (Driver) and (2) that it is preferred in 4QSam[a].

b. The vb. *ʿlh nipʿal* is found predominantly in late contexts (Exod 40; Num 9; 10; 16; Jer 37). The context in Jer 37:11 is also military.

31a. The MT has suffered the same haplography of *bny* before *bnymn* as in v. 15 above.

3:3a. The MT's *klʾb* is otherwise unknown. Instead of relating this to *klb*, Dhorme (220) attractively sees in the letters *lʾb* a dittograph of the first letters of the following *lʾbygl* ("of Abigail"). Because 4QSam[a] supports GT's shorter reading after Abigail (MT's "explicating gloss" being held to reflect 1 Sam 27:3; 30:5; 2 Sam 2:2), DJD (109) reconstructs the reading of 4QSam[a] as either *dlyhw* or *dlyh*, corresponding fairly closely to *Dalouia* (GT).

[10–11] The lack of the stock information about Ishbaal's age when he becomes king and how long he reigns (10a) in 4QSam[a] corresponds to its absence from 2 Sam 5:4–5, which provides similar information about David. The GT reads both with MT, but B lacks the similar information about Saul in 1 Sam 13:1 (where 4QSam[a] is not extant). However, all our texts do include the length of David's reign in Hebron (v. 11). The note about the house of Judah continuing to follow David (v. 10b) reads better within the shorter text in 4QSam[a], where it immediately qualifies or clarifies the meaning of the territory sketched in v. 9. "Israel as a whole" should not be [mis]understood as including Judah. After these divergences, quite a lengthy paragraph follows with remarkably little textual variation.

[12–13] There is no question of his new king's ordering Abner back across the Jordan. Abner himself remains the dominant force within Israel. He takes

(v. 12) "the servants of Ish-bosheth son of Saul" to Gibeon, immediately to the northwest of Jerusalem and just within the traditional territory of Benjamin. There is an important sanctuary there, where Solomon will be granted a vision at the beginning of his reign (1 Kgs 3:1–15, BTH).[79] But another prominent feature is its great water pool. A force of David's men, led by Joab, take up a counter position on the other side of the pool (v. 13).

As the story of the contest by the pool of Gibeon begins, Joab is already the leading figure among David's "servants." However, the narrator never explains how or when Joab has come into David's service. We meet him first by proxy, when Abishai is oddly introduced as "Joab's brother" in an earlier standoff with Abner (1 Sam 26:6). In the text shared by Samuel and Chronicles, Joab is first met within the summary listing of David's leaders (2 Sam 8:15–18) where he is the army commander. But in the Chronicler's account of the taking of Jerusalem, Joab has already become commander by successfully meeting David's challenge (1 Chr 11:6, 8). Gibeonites will complain to David (21:5) that Saul tried to destroy them completely from within Israel. Though the books of Samuel make no other mention of this, Gibeon seems here to be already just a town within Israel: there is no mention of Gibeonites there, as a separate people.

[14–17] Abner proposes to Joab that some of the lads should "play" before them. "Play" seems heavily ironic, in view of the outcome, unless something like sportive martial arts or jousting has been intended. Twelve represent Benjamin or the house of Saul, and twelve "the servants of David." No preliminary moves are described, only the scene of interlocking mutual destruction (v. 16)—and that could seem nothing other than the product of deft choreography if it were not for its ending and its entail. Abner's men (now styled "the men of Israel") are routed in the very severe fighting that ensues (v. 17).[80]

[18–22] Yet Abner himself does have two successes, against the flow of the battle as summarized here. The story of young gazelle-swift Asahel pursuing the older and stronger Abner is well told (vv. 19–23): how can Abner face Asahel's brother if he kills him? Abner even offers Asahel the spoil from "one from the lads." This phrase, unique to Samuel, which has its first outing at the very beginning of the story of Saul (1 Sam 9:3), has its last (v. 21) from his general's mouth soon after his death. In each of the other cases, the junior introduced (in 1 Sam 9:3; 16:18; 25:14; 26:22; 2 Sam 1:15) as "one from the lads" has gone on to demonstrate particular insight or perform a distinctive task. And that may suggest here that Abner, while warning Asahel not to continue pursuing himself, challenges him to take his spoil from the choicest of the juniors.

79. A later scene in this book will feature "the great stone" there (20:8).

80. "Extremely" (v. 17, *'d-m'd*) is rarely used in HB. Twice more it appears in Samuel: 1 Sam 11:15 (in the earlier story of Saul and Jabesh); 25:36; and elsewhere in Gen 27:33, 34; 1 Kgs 1:4; Isa 64:9, 12 (8, 11); Pss 38:6, 8 (7, 9); 119:8, 43, 51, 107; Lam 5:22; Dan 8:8; 11:25.

[23–29] Asahel's own death briefly stops everyone in their tracks (compare the description [20:12] of Joab's later killing of Amasa). It is no longer a matter of (even fatal) play between the lads: the leaders are now fully involved (v. 24). Asahel's brothers chase Abner till he falls in with a group of Benjamites who close ranks round him. Abner, who issued the original challenge to "play," but had then himself been chased first by Asahel and then by Joab and Abishai, now asks whether the sword should go on devouring forever (v. 26). In response, Joab does call off the general pursuit, but what he says to Abner is far from clear (v. 27). Does he mean: "Had you not spoken now, we would have pursued you through the night till morning"? Or: "Had you not spoken the way you did this morning, none of this would have happened?"

[2:30–3:1] David may have lost twelve of his lads, and Asahel, and a few more; but the losses to Saul's house are almost twenty times greater (vv. 30–31). Hardly surprisingly, the narrator remarks (3:1) that the house of David is getting stronger and stronger, and the house of Saul more and more weak. The lack of unity in the house of Saul is economically suggested in MT by the move from singular after "house of David" to plural. However, 4QSam[a] agrees with GT over keeping to the singular, and it also reads *byt* ("house) before the second "David."

Several features of this whole narrative resonate, but puzzlingly, with elements of the national story in, but also beyond, 2 Samuel. It is only within 2 Samuel that individuals are finished off by being struck on the *ḥōmeš* (2:23; 3:27; 4:6; 20:10). This term, presumably for the belly or abdomen, is unknown elsewhere in HB.[81] Division within the original kingdom diminishes both sides. The older narrative in BTH had told of a threat of armed strife after the death of Solomon (1 Kgs 12:21–24); and we have noted that the phrase "house of Judah" (2:7) may deliberately anticipate that passage.

[2–5] The information in the final subparagraph about David's family is also provided in 1 Chr 3:1–3. In its present position, it seems to be a secondary addition (v. 6a resumes 1a, or v. 1a anticipates 6a). In 1 Chr 3:1 (MT) Abigail's son is named not Chileab but Daniel, but *Dalouia* appears again in some of the Greek tradition.[82] The sixth mother (2 Sam 3:5 and 1 Chr 3:3) is described simply as David's "wife." The others are given their place of origin, or are said to be so-and-so's daughter or (former) wife. Has nothing else been known of Eglah ("Cow")? The claims made (by David?) in several of the names have interesting resonance: Amnon is related to *'mn*, the word used of a "sure" or "established"

81. The suggestion should probably be resisted to explain the term as the "fifth rib," on the basis of the common word for "five" (*ḥmš*).

82. Because (1) the divine element in some names changes, (2) Gk Λ and Δ are easily confused, and (3) Heb. *d* could corrupt into *n*, Dhorme (289–90, n. 3) proposes *ddyh* or *ddy'l* as the original underlying the many variants.

house; Ab-salom ironically links "father" and "peace"; and Adoni-jah and Shephat-iah acknowledge Yahweh as lord and judge.[83] It is these Hebron-born sons that supply characters for the narratives in 2 Sam 13–20.

2 Samuel 3:6–30 David, Abner, and Joab

6 And it came to be in the coming-to-be[a] war between the house of Saul and the house of David,
and Abner had been strengthening himself in the house of Saul.
7 And Saul had a concubine,
and her name was Rizpah daughter of Aiah;
and *Mephibosheth son of Saul* said to Abner,
"Why have you come to my father's concubine?"
8 And Abner became very heated because of the words of [Ish-] *Mephi*-bosheth,
and he said,
"Am I a dog's head [belonging to Judah[a]]?
Today I was acting loyally with the house of Saul your father and toward his brothers and toward his friend,
and I have not [let you be found in the hand] *defected to the house* of David;
and you have counted against me guilt over [this] *a* woman[b] today.
9 So may God do to Abner
and so may he go on doing to him
if,
as Yahweh has sworn to David,
so I do not do for him:
10 making the kingdom pass from the house of Saul
and setting up the seat of David over Israel and over[a] Judah
from Dan and as far as Beer-sheba."
11 And [he] *Mephibosheth* was no more able
to return Abner a word, from his fear of him.

12 And Abner sent messengers to David
to Tailam[a] where he was suddenly | In place of him,[a] saying, "Whose land?"
saying,
"Make your covenant with me;
and look—my hand is with you,

83. Jithream (*ytr'm*) is ambiguous: *'m* is "people," but *ytr* can signify either "remainder" or "excess/wealth."

to turn toward you all *the house of* Israel."
13 And he said,
"Good. I on my side will make a covenant with you.
But one word I ask of you, saying,
'You shall not see my face
except [before[a]] your bringing me Michal daughter of Saul
at your coming to see my face.'"

14 And David sent messengers to [Ish-]*Mephi*-bosheth son of Saul, saying,
"Give *me* my wife, Michal,
whom I betrothed [for myself] for a hundred Philistine foreskins."
15 And [Ish-]*Mephi*-bosheth sent
and took her from *her* husband, from Paltiel son of Laish.
16 And with her came her husband,
weeping more and more,
following her as far as [Bahurim] *Barakim*;[a]
and Abner said to him,
"Off, turn back,"
and he turned back.
17 And Abner's word came to be[a] with the elders of Israel:
"Even yesterday, even the day before, you have been seeking David as king over you.
18 And now act!
For it is Yahweh has said to David,
'By the hand of David, *I shall* save my people Israel
from the hand of the Philistines and from the hand of all their enemies.'"
19 And Abner too spoke in Benjamin's ears;
and Abner too went to speak in David's ears in Hebron
all that was good in Israel's eyes and in the eyes of all the house of Benjamin.
20 And Abner came to David at Hebron, and with him twenty men;
and David made for Abner and for the men who were with him a feast.
21 And Abner said to David,
"Let me rise
and go
and gather to my lord the king all Israel;
and let them make with you a covenant
and you will be king in all
that your spirit desires."
And David dispatched Abner,
and he went in peace.

22 And note David's servants and Joab came from the raid,
and much booty they brought with them;
but Abner was not with David at Hebron,
for he had dispatched him
and he had gone in peace.
23 But Joab and all the army who were with him, they came;
and people reported to Joab, saying,
"Abner son of Ner came to *David* [the king[a]],
and he dispatched him
and he went in peace."
24 And Joab came to the king
and he said,
"What have you done?
Look! Abner has come to you.
Whyever have you dispatched him,
and has he gone [on his way[a]] *in peace*?
25 *Did not*[a] You know Abner son of Ner,
that to deceive you he came,
and to know your going out and your coming in,
and to know all that you are doing."

26 And Joab went out from David
and sent messengers after Abner,
and they brought him back from the well of Sirah;
but David, he did not know.
27 And [Abner returned] *he returned Abner*[a] to Hebron;
and Joab took him aside to the middle of the gate
to speak to him quietly;
and he struck him down there on the belly,
and he died for the blood of Asahel his brother.
28 And David heard afterward;
and he said,
"I am clear—and my kingdom—with Yahweh forever of the bloodguilt of Abner son of Ner.
29 Let it devolve on the head of Joab and *on* [to] the house of his father.
And let there not be cut off from the house of Joab one who has a flux or a skin complaint or who grasps a spindle or falls by the sword or lacks food."
30 And Joab and Abishai his brother—they [slew] *laid in wait for*[a] Abner on account of the fact that he put to death Asahel their brother at Gibeon in the fight.

6a. "In the developing war" would be a more idiomatic rendering of "in the war coming to be" (*bhywt hmlḥmh*).

8a. The GT does not include the words "belonging to Judah." Does this "addition" in MT imply that MT has read *klb* as "Caleb" rather than simply "dog"? Here DJD (107–10) includes the words in its lengthy reconstruction of vv. 8–9, but without comment.

b. Here *ʿwn hʾšh* carries the article in MT, but not in B. The rendering above supposes this to have demonstrative force. In cst. *ʿwn* usually refers to guilt incurred by (not inflicted on) the following "ruling" noun.

10a. The scroll 4QSam[a] does not repeat "over" before "Judah" (as in MT[84] and GT).

12a. Here LT reads the shorter and simpler "to Hebron"; and this is followed by Josephus and adopted by DJD (111) as the likely reading of 4QSam[a]. It is not easy to see how the variants in MT and B are related, or indeed how each could separately have arisen.

13a. The MT's additional "before" (*lpny* lit. means "in front/face of") is probably a mistaken repetition of the earlier *pny* ("my face").

16a. Here GT attests a different (form of the) name.

17a. Both 4QSam[a] and B have the simpler *wyʾmr* for MT's *wdbr . . . hyh*.

23a. Here 4QSam[a] agrees with GT against MT's use of the title, not the name.

24–25a. The MT's *hlwk* and the GT's *hlwʾ* differ in only one letter; the larger textual issue is whether GT's "in peace" is original in this verse, or added from the end of v. 23. Here DJD (114) prefers to read the negative question with GT; but it finds no room in its reconstructed line for GT's "in peace."[85]

27a. While Greek *kai epestrepsen* could be transitive or intransitive, and LT is ambiguous, B is probably wrong to make Abner the obj. of the vb.

30a. Various proposals have been made of a Heb. vb. that GT might have rendered by the rare and precise *diaparetērounto* ("laid in wait"), but none has matched the clear reading (*...ʿw*) in 4QSam[a], very plausibly restored as *ngʿw*. The discussion in DJD (115) proposes "smite" as the sense of *ngʿ ʿl*; however, LXX[A] and LXX[B] in Judg 20:34, 41 use three different renderings of this Heb. expression: "touched," "met," and "reached." It seems not impossible that "laid in wait for" also renders *ngʿ ʿl*.

[6] The effect of what is said about Abner in v. 6b is all the more powerful if read, as probably originally intended, immediately after v. 1: the house of David is going from strength to strength. Of the house of Saul, the opposite is true; yet within that weakening house, the figure of Abner represents an exception—the word used about him ("strengthening himself") is another form of the expression used about David's house ("becoming stronger"). Ahead of this explicit statement, we had already noted how Abner is not caught in the downward current of the destiny of Saul's house.

[7–8] The precise sense of Abner's opening words in v. 8 must remain unclear. In self-deprecation, David once described himself to Saul as a "dead

84. Here DJD (110) wrongly cites MT as reading "upon Judah and upon Israel" instead of "over Israel and over Judah."

85. One is surprised at that judgment: the long previous line as reconstructed in DJD has 47 letters and 12 spaces; with *bšlwm*, the line in question would have 46 letters and 12 spaces.

dog" (1 Sam 24:14 [15]), just as Mephibosheth will later do to David (2 Sam 9:8). When Shimei (a further member of Saul's household) curses David, Joab's brother calls him a dead dog and volunteers to remove his head (16:9). However, there is no close parallel in Samuel or elsewhere in HB to a person's calling oneself a dog's head. We may well suppose that a dead dog's head is liable to be removed and played with as a makeshift ball. If so, then clearly Abner does not see himself as similarly expendable. He is far from dead: the repeated "today" at beginning and end of the main statement in v. 8 plays an important role, conveying his lively impatience.

Abner puts his loyalty to the house of Saul up to this point on record, but strangely; we are left wondering how far his anger has affected what he does and does not say. His claim of positive loyalty is stated in more general terms: Saul's house, his brothers, and his friends. His loyalty to the new incumbent from that house, whom he has put on the throne, is stated only negatively: that he has not handed him over to David. And (contemptuously?) Abner would have his king believe that his own choice of bed partner (v. 7) is no proper royal concern. In a later scene (16:20–22), Absalom (whose name we have just met for the first time in v. 3) openly takes David's concubines as an act of deliberate public policy put to him by an adviser. In this ironic prelude, Abner neither accepts nor rejects the truth of the sexual complaint against him, but vows now to transfer the kingdom to David from the house of Saul. Rizpah herself will reappear in Gibeon briefly (21:10–11), albeit in a memorable role.

[9–11] Many of the elements of 2 Sam 3 anticipate elements throughout BTH: much of 5:1–3 (Hebron, all Israel, even yesterday, even the day before, make a covenant); seat, kingdom, and "raise up" from ch. 7; showing loyalty, from ch. 10; guilt, Israel and Judah, and from Dan to Beer-sheba, and returning someone a word, from ch. 24; deceive, from 1 Kgs 22:20–22. However, the statement (2 Sam 3:9) about an oath of Yahweh in favor of David is quite striking. First, no such oath from Yahweh in favor of David is reported elsewhere in Samuel–Kings. Then Yahweh is only reported as swearing an oath once more in Samuel–Kings, and that is his oath to the house of Eli (1 Sam 3:14). But Abner's words to Saul's son do echo what David's men have said to him when he had Saul in his power in the cave (1 Sam 24:4 [5]).[86] In each case it is unclear whether the speakers are inventing a divine word to suit their purposes, or whether they are deducing the divine will from their reading of the situation. Abner may well have reckoned that it requires a (claimed) divine oracle to trump the obligations of his *ḥesed* to the house of Saul.[87]

86. First Samuel 24 does use the language of swearing: Saul asks David to swear to him by Yahweh (v. 21 [22]), and he does so (v. 22 [23]). Then "from Dan to Beer-sheba" is used in both 1 Sam 3:20 and 2 Sam 3:10. And 2 out of 5 mentions of "dog" in Samuel are 1 Sam 24:14 (15); 2 Sam 3:8.

87. See further on 5:2 below.

[12–13] Abner's ambassadors to David's court in Hebron open (only in MT) with a puzzling question: "Whose land?" or "To whom does land belong?"—just "land," not "the land," as it is often translated. However, the main business of his messengers is to deliver the quite straightforward offer that, in return for terms sworn by David, Abner will deliver all Israel to him. What comes back from David is a double reply. Covenanted terms will certainly be offered. However, only by meeting a further condition will Abner be admitted into David's nearer presence—"see my face" is emphasized by being repeated within a single sentence (v. 13)—only if he brings David's first wife along with him to Hebron. We can be sure that Abner, who has just been accused by his own king of unfaithful relations with a woman in Saul's harem, fully understands the meaning of restoring Saul's daughter to David: reestablishing David's legitimacy in and with Saul's family. We are given no reason to suppose that Abner knows that the most senior member of Saul's house after the old king himself has already pledged himself to David in covenant (1 Sam 23:18). That was enacted "before" or "in face of" Yahweh. Abner will not even see David's face if he does not meet his terms.

[14–16] After speaking about her to Abner, David then actually demands his (former) wife Michal directly from Saul's son, Michal's (half-)brother. And he reminds him just how many mutilated Philistines this dynastic marriage has cost him. Our two main textual traditions continue to differ over this Saulide's name. The MT calls him Ish-bosheth; GT attests Mephibosheth, attributing to him the same name as his nephew, son of Jonathan (2 Sam 4; 9). When David sends his demand for Michal's return straight to the head of the house of Saul, has he supposed that Abner is actually representing Saul's son (as was his duty) rather than betraying him? Or, building on his awareness of Abner's machinations, is David trying to find out directly for himself just how weak Saul's son really is? As it turns out, it is Saul's son who issues the command to Michal's current husband: all Abner has to do is send the grieving Paltiel home (vv. 15–16).

[17–21] Abner's preparatory negotiations are carried out in two stages: first with the elders of Israel (vv. 17–18), and then with Benjamin (v. 19). On our standing assumption that BTH is the principal source text, the narrator typically is here drawing on two portions of that earlier narrative. Reminding "the elders of Israel" of what they have long ("even yesterday, even the day before") wanted, anticipates 5:2–3. And the notion that the whole people is constituted of Judah, Benjamin, and Israel is drawn from the situation that will face Rehoboam after Jeroboam's defection (1 Kgs 12:21–24). Having checked with both parties to the further then nearer north of Judah, he makes his report to David. David makes him a feast; this presumably implies that he has been allowed to see David's face. He now speaks to David of covenanted terms, not offered to himself by David, but to be offered by Israel to David. Whereas Samuel told

Saul (1 Sam 9:20) that all Israel "coveted" his father's house, Abner now offers David kingship over all he "desires" (v. 21). David dismisses him peaceably.

[22–25] Joab has been out of town on a successful raid. It is too much for him to learn on his return that his brother's killer has been his king's guest—and has left in peace. The unpalatable facts of "dispatch" from Hebron and "in peace" are repeated (v. 22) and repeated (v. 23)—and then taken up by Joab in reproach to his king (v. 24). This last time, the textual tradition divides: GT repeats "in peace"; the implication of MT's closing infinitive may be that Abner is able to go from Hebron and keep on going. It is significant that Joab's words to David, like Abner's to the northerners, combine elements of two portions of BTH. Anticipating the role of the later Ammonite leaders wary of David in 2 Sam 10, he warns that such foreign interest in David's "goings and comings" (5:2 again) is suspicious. No response from his king is reported. Has David a shrewd idea of what will transpire?

[26–30] Joab tricks Abner into returning to Hebron. City gates have several chambers within them, for elders' meetings and judicial deliberations—but also where guards can be stationed when attack is expected. Joab takes his rival aside, without proceeding further into the city, and avenges his younger brother's death with a blow matching Abner's when he struck Asahel down (2:23; 3:27, 30). The narrator assures us that David knows nothing of this beforehand: we cannot be sure whether this is true in actual fact, or only by turning a diplomatic blind eye. When he is told, the king makes elaborate protestation of his innocence, not only for the present but also for posterity. Not only he but also his kingdom too is innocent—they are not simply innocent, but also innocent in divine perspective—and not only now but also forever (v. 28). He may be protesting too much! The image that follows (v. 29a) may be adapted from Jer 23:19 (repeated in 30:23), where it is a tempest that spins and revolves over the head of the wicked. In similar fashion, the bloodguilt from Abner's death should swirl[88] over the head of (wicked) Joab—and over his extended family (corresponding here to David's "kingdom").

The following words betray the source of the strange "forever" in David's seemingly extravagant protestation of innocence: as so often, the author of Samuel has drawn on a passage from BTH. The second divine vision granted to Solomon (1 Kgs 9:3–5) offers a combination unique within BTH of four elements, each of them relevant to this passage: three words and an issue. The three linguistic links are the negative "not be cut off," the positive "forever," and the term "kingdom"; the shared and all-important issue is the integrity of David. The opening words of the threat in 2 Sam 3:29b have been compared to Josh 9:23; but it may be more helpful to compare these words (and Josh 9:23) with 1 Kgs 8:25 and 9:5 (both BTH), where they introduce the divine promise that

88. Rabbinic Hebrew is cited in support of a quieter "hover over" (McCarter 2:118).

David's house will never lack someone sitting on Israel's throne, provided only that his sons continue walking before Yahweh as he has. The author of Samuel links "kingdom" and "forever" from his source text to his claim of innocence. "Innocent" (*nqy*) links this passage backward to his account of the David/Saul conflict (1 Sam 26:9) and forward to the Absalom story (2 Sam 14:9). But our author detaches "not be cut off" from its original promissory context, and uses it (as also in Joshua) to introduce a threat: here a comprehensive fivefold threat. The first pair and last pair among the five specific details are clear. Leviticus 15 legislates at length for gonorrheal discharge, while Num 5:2 simply declares that the leper and the person with such a discharge must be put out of the camp. Then falling by the sword and lacking food speak for themselves. Controversy surrounds only what implement (*plk*) is grasped in the middle element. The basic sense of GT's *skytalē* is club or cudgel; but the word is also used of any handle of that length or shape. *plk* has been interpreted as "spindle" and supposed to have effeminate associations; however, *plkm* is interpreted as "crutches" in a Phoenician inscription (McCarter 2:118). With disabilities like those that David is calling down on Joab, this slayer of a kingmaker will never himself be able to be king, nor any member of his extended family (see further on 2 Sam 9 below). It is hardly accidental that David curses Joab for avenging the death of his brother at Gibeon in the same terms that Joshua cursed the deceiving Gibeonites.

2 Samuel 3:31–39 David Laments Abner

2 Samuel 3:31–32

31 And David said to Joab and to all the people
    who were with him,
        "Rend your clothes
        and gird on sacking
        and bewail before Abner";
    and King David was walking behind the bier.
32 And they buried Abner at Hebron;
and the king raised up his voice
and wept [toward] *over* Abner's grave;
and all the people wept *over Abner*.

[31–32] David now fears guilt by association and presides over Abner's funeral in Hebron. Joab and "all the people who were with him" join in the lamentation for their leader's rival. The "him" is ambiguous and could refer to Joab or to David. "The people" (*hāʿām*) is a very flexible term in the books of Samuel. The precise group in question in any particular passage often needs to be deduced from the context and is most readily identified by its leader. "The people" with Joab were earlier identified as "the servants of David" (v. 22) and "all the army that was with him" (v. 23). They were David's rather than Joab's "people."

Two links in wording set this passage in context. "Gird" (*ḥgr*) is used quite frequently in Samuel;[89] and the command to gird on sacking is given in Isa 22:12; Jer 4:8; 6:26; 49:3—then, using a different verb, in Jonah 3:8. In Jer 4:8 too it is followed by *spdw*, "bewail"; there too the king and all of his establishment are appalled. Then "raised up his voice and wept" (2 Sam 3:32) also describes Saul's response in 1 Sam 24:16 (17) when he learns that David had him in his power but spared his life. Saul's next words speak volumes, not just on what David has refrained from doing to himself, but also on what Joab has just done: "Who has ever found an enemy, and sent the enemy safely away?" (1 Sam 24:19 [20]).

2 Samuel 3:33–37

33 And the king keened [toward] *over* Abner,
and said:
"As [a fool dying] *Nabal's death* should Abner die?

34 Your hands were not bound,	**34** Your hands not bound,
nor were your feet	and your legs—
in fetters.	to brass fetters[a]
You/he did not advance	they had not been brought.
like Nabal;	Like falling[b]
before sons of wrongdoing you	before the sons of depravity
fell."	you fell."

And all the people went on weeping over him.
35 And all the people came
to have David eat while it was still day;
and David swore, saying
"So may God do to me
and so may he continue,
supposing
before the sun comes home
I taste food or anything at all."
36 And all the people—they took note;
and it was good in their eyes,
as all
that the king did
was good in the eyes of all the people.

89. With ephod in 1 Sam 2:18; 2 Sam 6:14; with sword in 1 Sam 17:39; 25:13 (3x); and probably to be understood with "new" in 2 Sam 21:16.

37 And all the people—and all Israel—knew on that day
that it had not been from the king
to put Abner son of Ner to death.

34a. For DJD (117), "The preferred reconstruction of the original [couplet], not found exactly in any extant text, is as follows:

ʾsrwt ydyk lʾ bzqym
rglyk lʾ bnḥštym hgš
Your hands bound by no manacles
Your feet not locked in bronze fetters."

b. While DJD prefers *knpl* in 4QSam[a] with MT, it recognizes that *knbl* with GT is a possible reading.

[33–37] The introductory "keened" immediately recalls to us the introduction to David's elegy over Abner's royal masters (1:17): here both introduction and lament are very much briefer. The rare word used for "feed" (*brh hipʿil*) looks in the opposite direction. Used in various forms, it is one of the keywords of the Absalom and Tamar story (13:5, 6, 7, 10); but it is also part of the account of David's determined fast while his first son by Bathsheba is dying (12:17). There he is the guilty party; but here he has vigorously protested his innocence in respect to Abner's death. We find the cognate noun *brwt* only twice in HB; and it may be significant that both are again occasions of distress and elegy: Ps 69:21 (22) and Lam 4:10.

David again delivers the elegy but does not praise Abner as he has praised his royal kinsmen (1:19–27): Abner has fallen as a fool who has not looked out for himself against the wicked. The ambiguous Hebrew can be translated as GT has, specifying Nabal as the archetypal fool. The king's words of lament draw again on the resources of BTH: he links "and bound him in brass fetters" from the end of BTH with "the sons of depravity" near its beginning. Zedekiah will be put on the throne in Jerusalem by the king of Babylon, but then he rebels. He sees his sons slaughtered and has his own eyes put out, before he is taken to Babylon (2 Kgs 25:7). By contrast, Abner's return to Hebron has been quite unforced. Then Nathan has promised a secure planting of Israel under the monarchy, immune from the depredations of those like earlier "sons of depravity" (2 Sam 7:10). And the author of 2 Samuel anticipates Nathan's words by providing, in his account of assassinations in chs. 3–4, two samples of such nation-threatening depravity.

"All the people," though recently returned from a successful raid led by Joab (3:22), have been paying close attention to David's action—close and approving attention. They dominate these sentences, five times in as many verses; and they are clearly persuaded of David's innocence—not only they, but "all Israel" as well. "All the people" must again have been all *David's* people. This short paragraph sees the first outing of a rare verb (*bārâ*) meaning "eat," which is found only in three contexts within 2 Samuel. In each case the person being fed is somewhat fragile, whether David after a fast (3:35; 12:17) or Amnon during (pretended) illness (13:5, 6, 10).

2 Samuel 3:38–39

38 And the king said to his servants,
"Don't you know
that a prince and a great man, has fallen this day in Israel?
39 And I for my part today am tender and anointed king—
but these men, the sons of Zeruiah, are harder than me.
Let Yahweh repay the doer of the evil according to his evil."[a]

39a. Though found in both MT and GT, there is no room in 4QSam[a] for the closing pious comment. Yahweh is also invoked as subj. of *šlm piʿel* in 1 Sam 24:19 (20)—there by Saul in favor of David.

[38–39] David has emerged unscathed from close scrutiny by "all the people." It seems all the more appropriate that they are now described again as "his servants," as in v. 22. David's claim to be "tender" (*rak*) is his third anticipation in short order of a series of actions for which Josiah will be praised by Huldah (2 Kgs 22:19): tearing his clothes (2 Sam 3:31), weeping (v. 32), and now being tenderhearted (v. 39).[90] It adds to the already-considerable evidence that the author is drawing many of the king's words from BTH. However, given what happens to Josiah, there may be some irony in the alignment of David with his unfortunate successor. Huldah goes on to tell Josiah that he will die and be peaceably buried with his fathers, and will not (himself) look on the ill that Yahweh is bringing against "this place." The royal claim to be tender is also reminiscent of the vision (Zech 9:9) of a future righteous king who will be "meek" (*ʿny*). David's protests against Joab and Abishai, which culminate in his dying advice to Solomon to have the elder brother assassinated (1 Kgs 2:5–6), begin here.

Excursus 5: Retrospect on 2 Samuel 3

The previous few sections of translation and comment have followed ancient (and premasoretic) paragraphing. However, several linguistic and thematic links between 2 Sam 3 and 1 Sam 25–26 deserve closer attention:

90. The recognition of this link may be sufficient evidence against the rendering "weak" in RSV.

- David dismisses Abigail in "peace" (25:35) and Abner too—this is emphasized by repetition (3:21, 22, 23).
- The term *mšth* ("feast") occurs in Samuel only in 1 Sam 25:36 and 2 Sam 3:20; David is more generous than Nabal, but his guest falls like Nabal.
- Abigail and Ahinoam (25:43) reappear as mothers in 3:2–3—in Hebron!
- Michal's new husband (25:44) is mentioned again (3:13–16).
- When David mourns Abner's death, he asks, "Should Abner die as a fool [*nābāl*] dies?" (3:33).
- The conflict between the sons of Zeruiah and Abner is prefigured in 1 Sam 26 (but not 1 Sam 24–25).
- The sons of Zeruiah, responsible for Abner's death, are called *qāšîm* (3:39), and Nabal is *qāšeh* (25:3).
- David claims innocence of any bloodguilt (*dĕmê*) relating to Abner and Nabal (3:28 and 25:26, 33).[91]
- Also notice two links between 1 Sam 24 and 2 Sam 3: *šlm* ("repay") in 24:19 (20) and 3:39; "Lifted up . . . voice and wept" in 24:16 (17) and 3:32 (elsewhere in Samuel only in 1 Sam 11:4 and 2 Sam 13:36).

91. Also cf. 1 Sam 25:31 between 1 Sam 19:5 and 1 Kgs 2:31.

2 Samuel 4–9
David Secures His Throne

As we argued in the introduction to this volume, almost all of the material in the central four chapters (5–8) was reproduced from BTH. But the authors of Samuel made at least one large-scale change: moving to their new coda (2 Sam 21–24) the listing of some of David's heroes (now 23:8–39) and a few select exploits. The earlier BTH, like 1 Chr 11:10–47, still featured these heroes immediately after the report of David's taking Jerusalem. The order in Chronicles underlines how important a group of loyal personal followers (11:10–47) is in David's success in becoming king over Israel (11:1–9); and this link is reinforced in the following substantial plus in 1 Chronicles (12:1–40). Some of these heroes are involved in conflict with Philistines (11:12–19). As we shall see in our discussion of 2 Sam 6, it is more difficult to decide whether Samuel or Chronicles maintains the order in the Book of Two Houses of David's Philistine campaigns and the start of his movement of the divine ark toward Jerusalem.[1]

Assuming for the sake of argument that the Chronicler has preserved, but also extended, the main lines of the older account in BTH, we can detect a number of ways in which this older pattern is also reflected within Samuel. The Philistines are David's principal enemy, from beginning to end. Whether the story of David as king is bracketed by 2 Sam 5:17–25 and 23:9–17, or by 1 Chr 11:12–19 and 20:4–8, the Philistine menace is there from first to last; that is anticipated close to the beginning of the David story, in 1 Sam 17. Equally, thirty of David's heroes come to him at the cave of Adullam (1 Chr 11:15); this early approach is anticipated in 1 Sam 22:1–2. Seen from this perspective, the moves made by the author of Samuel have given sole prominence to David, both at the beginning of his story (Goliath in 1 Sam 17) and at the outset of his reign over Israel (2 Sam 5). As for his "heroes," they are introduced as a band of discontents (1 Sam 22:1–2), and their full listing has to await the very end of the story (2 Sam 23).

As already with the first account of Saul's death (1 Sam 31), it is worth reading the synoptic chapters of 2 Samuel from two perspectives: first, as joint witness with their parallels in 1 Chronicles to a possibly older account of David;

1. For greater detail, see also Auld 2010b.

and next, as part of the whole story of David in Samuel that has developed from their roots. The largest connected block of synoptic material is represented by 2 Sam 5–8, starting with Israel's leaders' approaching David and finishing with a short list of his principal staff. Almost all of the material in these chapters is repeated within the more extended 1 Chr 11–18—but not all; and it is arguable that the several (mostly brief) pluses represent special interests added by the author of Samuel, rather than unwelcome or irrelevant details deleted by the author of Chronicles. Our commentary on these chapters will try to distinguish between the text and its meaning in BTH, and how this was developed and reshaped by the authors of Samuel.

The CL makes no major break at the end of either 2 Sam 4 or 2 Sam 8, and hence we shall discuss chs. 5–8 within this larger portion of 2 Sam 4–9. Beginning (2 Sam 4) and end (2 Sam 9) of this portion of the book make clear that the David who now becomes king of Israel is innocent of the ending of Saul's house.

2 Samuel 4:1–5:16 Ishbosheth Killed; David King of Israel in Jerusalem

2 Samuel 4:1–12

1 And *Mephibosheth*[a] Saul's son heard
  that Abner had died in Hebron;
and his hands were weak,[b]
and all *the men of*[c] Israel were terrified.
(2 And two men *were* gang chiefs[a] *of* [belonged to[b]] *Mephibosheth* son of Saul;
the name of the one was Baanah
and the name of the second was Rekab,
sons of Rimmon the Beerothite of the sons of Benjamin;
for Beeroth [too] was reckoned to *the sons of* Benjamin.
3 And the Beerothites escaped to Gittaim
and became resident aliens there till this day.
4 Now Jonathan son of Saul had a son crippled in his legs.
He was five years old at the arrival of the report about Saul and Jonathan from Jezreel,
and his nurse picked him up
and fled.
And it came to be in her hurrying
  to flee
and he fell
and was lamed.
And his name was Mephibosheth.)

5 And the sons of Rimmon the Beerothite, Rekab and Baanah, journeyed
and came as the day was hot to the house of [Ish-]*Mephi*-bosheth;
and he was having his noonday liedown.

6 And see the doorkeeper
of the house
had been cleaning wheat
and she nodded and fell asleep;
and Rekab and Baanah the brothers escaped notice.[a]

6 And they—they came into the middle
of the house
taking {wheat},
and they struck him on the belly,
and Rekab and Baanah his brother got away.

7 And they came to the house,
and [he] *Mephibosheth* was lying on his couch in his bedchamber;
and they struck him
and they put him to death
and they removed his head
and they took his head
and they went by way of the *west* [Arabah] all the night.

8 And they brought the head of [Ish-]*Mephi*-bosheth to David in Hebron;
and they said to the king,
"Look at the head of [Ish-]*Mephi*-bosheth son of Saul your enemy,
who sought your life.
And Yahweh has given my lord the king *the* vengeance *over his enemies as* this day from Saul *your enemy* and from his seed."

9 And David answered Rekab and Baanah his brother, sons of Rimmon the Beerothite,
and said to them,
"As Yahweh lives
who has ransomed my life from all distress,

10 surely the one who reported to me, saying,
'Look, Saul is dead'
(and in [his] *my*[a] eyes he was as one bringing good news),
I caught hold of him
and I slew him at Ziklag,
to whom I had to give good news.

11 And now[a] wicked men have slain an innocent man in his house on his bed.
And now shall I not seek his blood from your blood
and remove you from the land?"

12 And David commanded [the] *his* lads
and they slew them;
and they cut off their hands and their feet

and hung them by the pool at Hebron.
And the head of [Ish-]*Mephi*-bosheth they took,
and they buried it in the tomb of Abner *son of Ner* in Hebron.

1a. Here 4QSam[a] reads Mephibosheth with B, but not "men of."

b. The GT renders *rph* ("become weak") by *eklyesthai*, used of bows being unstrung or implements becoming unserviceable.

c. Israel is treated as pl. in MT and 4QSam[a], like the house of Saul in 3:1 (MT).

2a. "Gang chief" (*śr-gdwd* in sg.) reappears in HB only in 1 Kgs 11:24.

b. Here MT (*hyw*) and 4QSam[a] (*wyhy*) offer a vb., but B attests the pron *whw'*.

6a. Codex B's "escaped notice" (*dielathon*) is hapax in LXX, while *nmlṭw* (MT) is common.

10a. Here DJD (122) adopts the reading of GT and Syr, in which David admits that Saul's death is good news for him.

11a. Dhorme (304) compares *'p ky* here with *w'p ky* in 1 Sam 23:3.

[1] Saul's son may have been impotently silent in face of Abner's threat to turn Israel over to David (3:11); but his reaction to Abner's death (v. 1a) is no less akin to paralysis. And we are told that the response of "all Israel" (v. 1b) is terror, debilitating emotion like that of Saul when he heard Samuel's message through the medium at En-dor (1 Sam 28:21): *nbhl* is used in only these two contexts in all of Samuel–Kings. This is rather more surprising in that we readers have already been told that "all Israel" is aware that David is not implicated in the death of their commander-in-chief (2 Sam 3:37).

[2–3] The report that starts in 4:1 continues in 4:5. The interruption consists of two pieces of background information. The first (vv. 2–3) introduces the two assassins, naming them in reverse order to the main narrative (vv. 5, 6, 9). The late Abner may have held the same position in Saul's establishment as Joab in David's. But Baanah and Rekab are about business similar to Joab's (3:22). In the ancient history of the England-Scotland border, they would have been termed "reivers": officially sanctioned adventurers and freebooters. One of David's heroes is a "Beerothite" (2 Sam 23:37, BTH). Is it pure coincidence? Or would readers familiar with the information that this hero from Beeroth is also armor-bearer to Joab already be "smelling a rat"? Beeroth itself is always one of the same group of three or four towns (Josh 9:17; 18:25; Ezra 2:25; Neh 7:29). In Ezra and Nehemiah, Beeroth is one of the long list of towns that lost exiles to Babylon. Gittaim (2 Sam 4:3) reappears in HB only in Neh 11:33, as one of the towns in Benjamin to which exiles returned. The repetition of Benjamin (v. 2) may insist that it is precisely at home there, and not in wider "all Israel," that the house of Saul is in trouble. And the role of Beeroth and Gittaim in Ezra and Nehemiah may suggest that the immediate backdrop to this story may be tensions within the portion of postexilic Yehud north of Jerusalem.

[4–8] The second piece of background (v. 4) reports the accident that led to the laming of Jonathan's son Mephibosheth, whose story is taken up again in 2 Sam 9. Rightly or wrongly, MT has not named Saul's successor in v. 1, while GT and 4QSam[a] agree that he is called Mephibosheth. The MT calls him Ishbosheth in vv. 5, 8, and 12; ungrammatical wording makes it likely that that name has dropped out of v. 2. Many experts are persuaded that MT is correct in naming Saul's son and grandson differently. However, the very fact that the author has chosen to introduce Jonathan's lame son precisely here can and perhaps should be taken as indicating that he recognizes the need to distinguish between two identically named descendants of the late king. In v. 6 B and MT offer such different texts that it appears impossible to explain one version of the story on the basis of the other. The MT is certainly redundant but is far from offering the only example of redundancy in Samuel. At this point 4QSam[a] offers no help. Whether the sons of Rimmon take the western route (GT), or travel by the Arabah (Jordan and Dead Sea) valley, and hence by the eastern route (MT), their way south to Hebron is not direct.

As they present David with the head of his presumed rival (vv. 7–8), the assassins give voice for the last time to one of the most often repeated themes of the books of Samuel, that Saul has "sought" to destroy David['s life].[2] God's "granting vengeance" reappears in 2 Sam 22:48, there quickly followed by deliverance from "enemies" (v. 49). Saul uses the cognate verb in 1 Sam 14:24 and 18:25, where he expects vengeance over his own enemies. When David wishes in Saul's hearing (1 Sam 24:12 [13]) that Yahweh will avenge him over Saul, he does not use the word "enemy"—and yet the absence of the word speaks volumes. Here in MT the assassins avoid the term "enemy," as David had, while in B they make David's private reaction (see below on v. 10) explicit.

[9–12] "As Yahweh lives who has ransomed my life from all distress" reappears exactly only in 1 Kgs 1:29, where David is again the speaker—this time to Bathsheba; but divine deliverance "from all distress" echoes his words to Saul in 1 Sam 26:24. As he develops his reply, David takes up the keyword "seek" in delivering his verdict on their action. Saul's son has been innocent—it is his killers who are guilty. Since a person's life is intimately associated with their blood (Gen 9:4–6), David will now "seek" that innocent man's blood from the guilty assassins' hands (2 Sam 4:11). Here again it is instructive to read the phraseology of the developed books of Samuel from the perspective of the major source. The proximity of this final instance of the Saul-seeking-David theme to the original (BTH) theme of Philistines-seeking-David (5:17) neatly

2. The term *bqš* with Saul or his agents as subject and David or his life as object is used no less than 13 times in 1 Samuel (19:2, 10; 20:1; 22:23; 23:10, 14, 15, 25; 24:2 [3]; 26:2, 20; 27:1, 4). In a neat reversal, David asks Saul why he listens to those saying David is "seeking" his ill (1 Sam 24:9 [10].

underscores the enormity of what Saul has long been determinedly about: trying to do for the Philistine enemy their work of destroying the anointed David.

David himself draws attention to the parallel with the story of the Amalekite and Saul, with which the author of Samuel has opened his new introduction (2 Sam 1–4) to the narrative of David as king. The Amalekite foreigner proved his account of Saul's death by delivering the royal regalia to David. The Benjamite fellow tribesmen authenticate their action by producing their king's own head. Since Saul's son has only been "made king" by Abner (2:8–10), he cannot be called "the anointed of Yahweh" like his father, on whom David has twice refused to lay hands (1 Sam 24:6 [7]; 26:9). But David insists on the innocence of their victim no less than on their guilt (2 Sam 4:11). Presumably only the culpable hands and feet of the murderers are put on view at a public space in Hebron (v. 12a). David has taken entirely literally his threat to have their hands pay for the blood of their victim. As the story ends, the narrator shifts our attention from their severed limbs to proper burial for their victim's head.

2 Samuel 5:1–3

1 And all the staffs of Israel came to David, to Hebron;
and they said *to him* [saying[a]],
"Look at us:
we are your bone and your flesh.[b]
2 Yesterday too and the day before as well,
when Saul was king over us,
you have been the one leading Israel out and in;
and Yahweh said to you,
'You, you will feed my people Israel;
and you, you will be as prince over Israel.'"
3 And all the elders of Israel came to the king, to Hebron,
and King David made for them a covenant at Hebron before Yahweh;
and they anointed David as king over *all* Israel.

1a. The LT reads *kai legousin* ("and they say"). Here 4QSam[a] and 1 Chr 11:1 read simply *l'mr*.

b. The GT renders as "bones" and "flesh[s]"—both pl.

[1–3] On Saul's death, Israel approaches David in Hebron on the triple basis of relatedness, of past record, and of claimed support from Yahweh. And the "Israel" that makes the approach is "all Israel": the "Israel" over which Saul has been king, and the "Israel" that has been worsted by Philistines when he was killed. The relationship between vv. 1–2 and v. 3 can be read in two ways: as two stages in the one process, or as two aspects of it. Either a first approach is made to David by unspecified representatives of Israel (vv. 1–2), and then this is later confirmed between David and the elders (v. 3); or else it is only gradually made clear that the approach to David in Hebron was made on Israel's behalf by its "elders." More important is the silence within this report: it is only indirectly that Yahweh is credited with the initiative over making David king over Israel. Israel claims divine support, as well as relatedness to David and shared experience with him; and David responds by making a covenant in their favor "before Yahweh." Yahweh is there for both sides; but Israel and David are the partners. It is rather like the official view of Christian marriage: it is undertaken "before God" and commonly witnessed among others by a member of the ordained clergy; but the only partners in the covenant are the human couple.

The role here of the "elders" is particularly significant. In BTH, Israel's elders appear only twice: where David becomes king, and when Solomon brings the ark into his new temple (1 Kgs 8:1). And it is precisely these two roles that were anticipated by the elders in 1 Samuel: removing the ark from Shiloh after defeat by the Philistines (4:3), and requesting Samuel to appoint a king (8:4). In BTH, elders make two further appearances: as Rehoboam consults over what response to make to the people of Israel (1 Kgs 12:6, 8, 13); and as Josiah prepares to have the book of the law read (2 Kgs 23:1). The clear separation of the roles played in 1 Kgs 12 by "all Israel" and the elders should encourage readers to ponder carefully before conflating them in the much briefer 2 Sam 5:1–3.

Both beginning and end of the story of David in BTH recall the story of Job. Later, at the end of Samuel, we shall discuss the more obvious divine incitement of the hero (David) to sin (24:1). But more relevant here is the Satan's challenge to Yahweh (Job 2:3–6) that if Job's bone and flesh are touched, he will curse Yahweh. Yahweh tells the satan that he may have his will but must spare Job's life. Seen from Job's perspective, when Israel says, "We are your bone and your flesh" (2 Sam 5:1), they may be implying, "and you, David, are our life." And if he has not only led them out in battle, but also brought them home (v. 2a), this is no exaggeration: he has proved that he is their life.[3] Job certainly assists our reading of the words of Israel's leaders; but there is a closer significant link. In BTH, this sole use of "bone" (*ʿṣm*, m. sg.) has immediately followed the report of the burial of Saul and his sons (1 Sam 31:13), where the plural of the feminine form *ʿṣmh* is used of their bones. Their bones have been burned and have therefore been buried without flesh. The David whom they address is altogether more substantial. Though never so used in BTH, *ʿṣm* can also bear the sense of "selfsame."

The claimed divine word to David (2 Sam 5:2b) is reported in the speech of Israel's leaders. But is it court flattery, or do they deduce it from observation, or do they have knowledge of an oracle having been delivered to David? First

3. Compare the discussion of life, breath, and the anointed of Yahweh on 1:16 above.

Samuel 16 and 17 both present David as shepherd of his father's sheep, but they do not suggest that his future role will be as shepherd of God's people. Israel's leaders anticipate Nathan—in BTH it is they who first mention Yahweh; and David also recognizes that Yahweh is the source of his kingship (2 Sam 5:12) before ever Nathan speaks (ch. 7). Earlier interpretations offered to David of the divine will (such as 1 Sam 24:4 [5]; 26:8) anticipate this passage.

Just as it is Israel who interprets the divine will, so it is Israel who does the anointing of David. It is difficult to read this short account fresh, as the original readers of BTH had read it; for there have been so many narratives within Samuel already of anointing[4] and "kinging."[5] Throughout 1 Samuel, it is Samuel or Yahweh who is said to anoint Saul or David. Only 2 Sam 2:1–7 prepares the readers of the books of Samuel as we know them for corporate anointing. The only other case of anointing in the older BTH occupies something of a mediating position. After the removal of his mother Athaliah, Joash is kinged and anointed by an anonymous grouping, among whom the priest Jehoiada plays a leading role (2 Kgs 11:9–12). We should note that the narrator uses the terms "king," "anoint," and "covenant," while the people speak of "feeding" and "my people," and the controversial *nāgîd*. The verb that is rather prominent by its absence is "choose": election may be implied in the narrative, but it is not stated.

While 1 Chr 11:1—and so presumably BTH before it—reports simply an approach to David by "all Israel," Samuel specifies that "all *the tribes of* Israel" are involved. Are these intended to be distinct from "the elders of Israel" (v. 3), or are the "elders" one and the same as the "staff[holder]s" of Israel?[6] Despite the fact that Israel and its elders have taken an initiative in approaching David and he has accepted their approach, it is important not to translate v. 3 as "King David made with them a covenant in Hebron": *lāhem* normally means "to them" or "for them," and that is appropriate here too—David grants their request and becomes king over them; he does not enter a mutual pact with them.

2 Samuel 5:4–10

4 David[a] was thirty years old at his becoming king;
and forty years he was king.
5 In Hebron he was king over Judah seven years and six months;
and in Jerusalem he was king thirty-three years over all Israel and Judah.[a]

4. See 1 Sam 9:16; 10:1; 15:1, 17; 16:3, 12, 13; 2 Sam 2:4, 7; 3:39.

5. See 1 Sam 8:22; 11:15; 12:1; 15:11, 35; 2 Sam 2:9.

6. Although *šbṭy yśr'l* is known in synoptic contexts (1 Kgs 8:16; 14:21; 2 Kgs 21:7), it is likely that its appearance within synoptic contexts in 2 Samuel is secondary—see below on 7:7; 24:2.

6 And [the king] *David*[a] and his men went to Jerusalem, to the Jebusite
who settled the land,
and [he] *it was* said to David, saying,
"You shall not come here,

for the blind and the lame	except for the blind and the lame
opposed,	turning you away,[b]

saying,
'David shall not come here.'"[c]

7 And David captured the citadel of Zion (that is, the city of David).

8 And David said on that day,
"Any one striking down Jebusite,

let him attack by dagger[a]—	let him reach by the pipe—
even the lame and the blind[b]	even the lame and the blind,[b]
and those hating[c] *David's very self.*"	hated of[c] David's very self."

Therefore people will say,
"Blind or lame—he shall not come to the House *of Yahweh.*"

9 And David settled in the citadel,
and he called it the city of David;
and David built round about from the Fill and [to] the House.

10 And David went on and on
becoming greater;
and Yahweh [God[a]] of hosts was with him.

4a. Here 4QSam[a], like 1 Chr 11, lacks vv. 4–5.

5a. Codex B has a different order from MT: "Seven years and six months he was king in Hebron over Judah; and thirty-three years he was king over all Israel and Judah in Jerusalem." The LT is almost identical to MT in word order, but "corrects" the arithmetic to "thirty-two years and six months."

6a. First Chronicles 11:4 reads "David" with GT, not "the king"; followed by "and all Israel," not "and his men" (MT and GT). See further on 7:1–3.

b. After the first *hnh*, 4QSam[a] clearly reads *ky hsyt* . . . (and not *ky ʾm hsyrk*, as in MT). This is variously restored as *ky hsytwk* or *ky hsytwhw* ("for they have enticed you/him").[7]

c. "Saying . . . here" may either be resumptive repetition if the shorter text in 1 Chr 11 is primary, or the cause of an accidental loss of text if 2 Sam 5 is primary.

8a. The GT's *paraxiphis* may refer to a small "dirk" (short dagger) worn beside the larger sword, although OL renders this simply as *gladium*. The GT may have read *ṣnwt* (as in Amos 4:2), not *ṣnwr*.

b. Here 4QSam[a] has the second "blind and lame" in the same order as first and third.

c. Also, 4QSam[a] reads none of *śōnʾê* ("hating," GT), *śĕnuʾê* ("hated of," Q), nor *śānʾû* ("they hated," K)—but instead *śnʾh* ("it hated"): David's soul is the subj., not the obj. of

7. But Herbert (1994) argues for *ky ʾm hsyrwhw* ("surely [the blind and the lame] have turned you aside") as the formulation underlying all the attested readings.

the hate. In two of these readings, it is the lame and the blind who do the hating, and in two it is David's *nepeš* (4QSam[a] is largely convergent with MT).

10a. Only MT adds "God": the GT and 4QSam[a] and 1 Chr 11:9 all read simply *yhwh ṣb'wt.*

[4–5] The joint negative testimony of 4QSam[a] and 1 Chr 11 makes it virtually certain that at this point the older book of Samuel (like BTH) did not include the summary chronology of David's reign in Hebron and Jerusalem (vv. 4–5). In any case, such information is normally part of a king's death notice; and what we are told here simply anticipates 1 Kgs 2:11. It reinforces a distinction between "Judah" and an "Israel" that does not include Judah and that is in tension with the "all Israel" mood and language of vv. 1–3.

[6–10] The city, or at least a part of it, becomes called "the city of David" (vv. 7, 9) by virtue of David's acquisition of it; it is to "the city of David" that the ark will be brought (6:10, 12, 16). No further mention of "the city of David" is made within the story of David, whether in the older BTH or in 2 Samuel. However, this locus remains prominent through most of BTH where, apart from the next two references (relating to Solomon[8]), all the others are to be found in records of royal burials;[9] and there are a few pluses in Kings.[10] The prominence of this site in the older record of so many kings in Jerusalem makes it certain that the first readers of its initial mention, here in connection with David, would have at the front of their minds that they are being told something about Jerusalem's royal necropolis. It is harder to be confident about the expectations of later readers, for 2 Chr 32:5, 30; 33:14; Neh 3:15; 12:37; and Isa 22:9 all concern repairs to an established architectural feature of Jerusalem and make no reference to its purpose before the time of Hezekiah.

Other terms relating to Jerusalem in this pericope are remarkably rare, whether in BTH or more widely in Samuel–Kings. Jebus[ite] reoccurs only in the account of census and plague (2 Sam 24:16, 18) and within what becomes the stereotyped list of original inhabitants of the land (1 Kgs 9:20)—all BTH. Similarly, Zion reappears in BTH only in 1 Kgs 8:1;[11] and "the stronghold of Zion" is unique to David's acquisition of the city. Elsewhere in BTH, David's

8. As in 1 Kgs 8:1; 9:24.

9. See 1 Kgs 11:43; 14:31; 15:8, 24; 22:50 (51); 2 Kgs 8:24; 12:21 (22); 14:20; 15:7, 38; 16:20 (although 2 Chr 28:27 denies that Ahaz was buried with his predecessors).

10. See 1 Kgs 2:10; 3:1; 11:27; 2 Kgs 9:28. Of these pluses, 1 Kgs 2:10 and 2 Kgs 9:28 report the burials of David himself and of Ahaziah; 1 Kgs 3:1 anticipates 9:24; and 11:27 concerns a detail of Solomon's building works.

11. "Daughter Zion" (2 Kgs 19:21) and "Mount Zion" (19:31) are much more at home in Isaiah (37:22, 32).

stronghold (*mṣdh*) is outside Jerusalem, to the (south)west.[12] The title Yahweh of Hosts (v. 10) is used only in the Davidic portion of BTH (3x),[13] and then very sparingly in Samuel–Kings,[14] by comparison at least with the books of the Latter Prophets.

Two main features distinguish the version of this short narrative in Samuel from that in Chronicles, making it much harder than usual to reconstruct the text of BTH: the role of the blind and lame in Samuel, and of Joab in Chronicles. The following basic report is shared:

6 And [David and his men][15] went to Jerusalem, to the Jebusite who settled the land, and he said to David, "You shall not come here. . . ." 7 And David captured the citadel of Zion (that is, the city of David). 8 And David said . . . , "Whoever strikes the Jebusite . . ." 9 And David settled in the citadel, and he called it the city of David; and David built round about from the Fill and [to] the House. 10 And David went on and on becoming greater; and Yahweh God of hosts was with him.

The first issue over which they differ totally relates to the role of Joab—he figures twice in the Chronicler's report but not at all in the Samuel version. The first variance follows what David begins to say about striking down the Jebusite. Chronicles continues with a straightforward sentence that includes a simple and repeated wordplay: "[Whoever strikes the Jebusite] first [*br'šwnh*] shall become head [*r'š*] and commander; and Joab son of Zeruiah went up first and became head." Not only so—if Chronicles here reproduces BTH, it also offers a straightforward introduction of David's closest lieutenant, who will be with him till the final scene (2 Sam 24//1 Chr 21), where he tries to save his king from persisting in his own folly. Without such a report, the subsequent introduction of Abishai as Joab's brother comes as rather strange. The second is at the end of the note on David's building work (1 Chr 11:8), which is understood very differently. What it literally says is this: "as for Joab, he was letting/making live the remainder of the city." Understood literally, it suggests that, while David takes responsibility for building work at a key central fortification, Joab is responsible for not putting the remainder of Jerusalem's population to the sword, but "letting them live." Understood figuratively, David builds in

12. See 2 Sam 23:14; compare also Yahweh as David's rock and stronghold in 22:3. The plus in 2 Sam 5:17b may have been necessitated by the author of Samuel reorganizing substantially the material inherited from BTH. In 1 Chronicles, and perhaps originally, 11:16 (= 2 Sam 23:14) precedes 1 Chr 14:8 (= 2 Sam 5:17a).

13. See 2 Sam 5:10; 7:8, 26 (6:2, 18; 7:27 are Samuel pluses).

14. As in 1 Sam 1:3, 11; 4:4 (MT); 15:2; 17:45; 2 Sam 6:2 (not 4QSam[a]), 18; 7:27; 1 Kgs 18:15; 19:10, 14; 2 Kgs 3:14; 19:31.

15. Samuel has "the king and his men," while Chronicles has "David and all Israel."

one area and Joab in another: "reviving" the rest of Jerusalem. The two issues are not necessarily linked; however, if the author of the present text of Samuel deleted both mentions in his source of Joab's role, we judge it more likely that he also adjusted the previous clause describing the locus of David's building work. Let us compare 2 Sam 5:9b (MT) and 1 Chr 11:8a (MT):

2 Sam 5:9	*wybn dwd sbyb*	And David built round about
1 Chr 11:8	*wybn hʿyr msbyb*	And he built the city round about
2 Sam 5:9	*mn-hmlwʾ wbyth*	from the Fill and houseward.
1 Chr 11:8	*mn-hmlwʾ wʿd-hsbyb*	from the Fill and as far as the surrounds.

The alternative account in Samuel starts (in MT at least) with mention of an enigmatic *ṣinnôr*. Normally understood here to mean something like "water shaft," this word occurs only once more in HB, in a context speaking of the watery deeps (Ps 42:7). Commentators and archaeologists have mostly supposed that David's men gained entry to Zion by ascending one of the partly natural clefts through the karst rock, which normally gave Jerusalem's inhabitants safe access to the spring below. However, given (1) that Chronicles preserves a wholly different text, and (2) that we can see good reason why the author of Samuel changed it, and (3) that GT attests not *ṣnwr* but *ṣnwt*, it is unwise to build too much historical reconstruction on a possibly unreliable text.[16]

Samuel does not just mention the enigmatic blind and lame, about whom Chronicles is silent, but features them three times—and that in a relatively short report that has several other important pieces of information to convey. From a formal, text-critical point of view, we also observe how remarkable it is that precisely where Samuel substantially differs from Chronicles, the versions of the Samuel text differ most among themselves. Such a feature is sometimes to be interpreted as evidence of a more recently altered text, where the alterations have not yet become standardized.

If we had no information beyond this short report, we might fairly suppose that the blind and the lame here are simply the Jebusite native inhabitants: a (boastful) claim is being made that the city is sufficiently impregnable that even disadvantaged citizens can defend it. But seen from a wider perspective, such a reading becomes less convincing. The phrase "blind and lame" reappears only twice in HB. Deuteronomy prescribes that domestic animals with such a blemish may be eaten locally on a par with wild animals, but may not be offered in sacrifice (15:21). And that rule squares with people here saying that blind

16. Commenting on the many differences between their related short accounts, Holm-Nielsen (39) wisely finds it "unlikely that the author of Chronicles knew the Books of Samuel in their present form."

and lame should not come to the "house" [of the Lord] (2 Sam 5:8b). More positively, Jeremiah includes blind and lame, along with pregnant women and mothers with infants, in the company of exiles whom Yahweh will gently lead home (31:2–9).

No one else in Samuel is described as "blind" (*ʿiwwēr*). However, when we later find one of Saul's sons described (2 Sam 9:13) and describing himself (19:26 [27]) as "lame" (*pissēaḥ*), we may fairly ask ourselves if we have been given a clue to what is being suggested here.[17] The larger class of Hebrew *qiṭṭēl* adjectives, to which both these belong, describes disabilities, including those of character. When we first learn of the damage to Mephibosheth's legs, it is differently described (4:4). Only one character in the books of Samuel is marked out with damaged legs: Jonathan's surviving son. And similarly, only one character is identified as having impaired sight: Eli (1 Sam 3:2; 4:15). In each case their physical impairment is taken as a symbol of unfitness for office of a house (royal or priestly) that deserves to be supplanted. Neither merits a role in David's city, or in Yahweh's "house" there.

Writing Joab out of David's beginnings in Jerusalem was easy for the author of Samuel. He has already introduced David's commander and right-hand man in 2 Sam 2–3. Joab is now well known from that new material and needs no introduction here. A further motivation for the author of Samuel may be deduced from later in the book, from one of the additions to the older report of the campaign against Rabbah, the Ammonite capital. Once Joab has neutralized the opposition in that city, he asks David to complete the campaign lest the victory be ascribed not to David but to himself (12:27–29). Our Samuel author leaves no possibility for such misunderstanding in the case of the city that has come to be known as "city of David." The BTH had already commented (5:10) that David goes on and on becoming greater. Writing Joab out of this story—for the sake of David's greater glory—is further reinforced by moving the list of David's heroes to the book's end; originally in BTH, as still in Chronicles, the list immediately followed, and it mentions Joab three times (2 Sam 23:18, 24, 37). Both changes to the source material further increase David's reputation by removing any immediate mention of his colleagues at the time.

Yet was this out of respect for David? Or was our author raising David up even higher before an even more spectacular fall? We need to recall (see above on 1 Sam 27:9, 11) how the Chronicler reports, right after the taking of Jerusalem, that Joab "kept alive the remnant of the city" (1 Chr 11:8), just before stating (with Samuel) that David goes "on and on becoming greater." Many scholars read this statement metaphorically and understand it as a further comment on the physical rebuilding of Jerusalem: David is responsible for the area near the Fill and the House, while Joab "revives" or "restores" the remainder

17. Schipper (2006: 64–69).

of the city. But if the Chronicler intends it literally, Joab's magnanimity toward those in Jerusalem who survive the takeover of their city will be seen as contributing to and not diminishing David's growing reputation. And this may have been what BTH also intended. There should always be a good reason for supposing that an author of Samuel makes a deletion from his source. Here it is not so much a deletion as a removal: by displacing talk of keeping alive from 2 Sam 5 to 1 Sam 27, turning a humane note in the original (as in 1 Chr 11:8) into its opposite there, and introducing hatred into his retelling of BTH on the taking of Jerusalem (2 Sam 5:8), the author of Samuel leaves us to imagine the fate of the city's people at David's hands.

2 Samuel 5:11–16

11 And Hiram king of Tyre sent messengers to David and cedar wood
and craftsmen in wood and craftsmen in stone [of Kir[a]],
and they built a house for David.
12 And David knew
that Yahweh had established him as king over Israel
and that his kingdom had been raised up[a] for the sake of his people Israel.
13 And David took further [concubines[a] and wives] *wives and concubines* from Jerusalem
after his coming [from] *to* Hebron,
and there were born [further] to David *further*[b] sons and daughters.
14 And these are the names of those born to him in Jerusalem:
Shammua and Shobab and Nathan and Solomon;
15 and Yibhar and Elishua and Nepheg and Yaphia;
16 and Elishama and Eliada and Eliphelet.

11a. Both 4QSam[a] and LT read *ḥršy qyr* while B attests *ḥršy 'bn* and MT is conflate. The noun *qîr* means "wall," but it is also a place name (whether in Babylon or, when normally followed by *Hareśet*, in Moab). Since no distinction is made in an unpointed Hebrew text between *ś* and *š*, deliberate wordplay may well be involved. Construed with *'bn* (MT), *qyr* may more likely be the place name; LT renders it as "wall." First Chronicles 14:1 has the same two phrases as 4QSam[a] in 2 Sam 5:11, but details "wall" before "wood."

12a. Here MT's *niśśā'* can be *pi'el* or *nip'al*; the pass. in GT opts for the latter and need not assume *niśśē't* of 1 Chr 14:2—a m. vb. is acceptable, provided that the f. subj. has not yet been stated. Unvocalized *nś'* (4QSam[a]) could also be *qal.*

13a. The scroll 4QSam[a] also has "concubines" first. The LT has "wives and concubines" with B, but "from Hebron" with MT.

b. With GT and 1 Chr 14:3, the scroll 4QSam[a] reads "further" after "David." The order in MT is unique.

[11–12] We have already noted that David's becoming king and the completion of Solomon's temple are linked by the role played in both by Israel's elders (5:3; 1 Kgs 8:1, 3). This is quickly reinforced by Hiram king of Tyre's cooperation with both (2 Sam 5:11; 1 Kgs 5; 7; 9). Saul may have fallen in battle with Philistines who have dominated (at least) the southern Palestinian coastal territory. But a friendly approach to David and his successor is made from further north along the Levantine littoral. Hiram provides encouragement both in word (messengers) and deed (wood and craftsmen). David understands this support, when added to his previous successes, as divine endorsement.

[13–16] David may have recognized that his success in Jerusalem and his reputation abroad are due to Yahweh. But it is noteworthy that the names he gives to his sons born in Jerusalem do not feature his patron Deity: none begin with Jeho- (or Jo-) nor end with -iah (< -yahu); but 4 of the 11 begin with El-. Equally, his successes may have been "for the sake of his people Israel"; but his wives are taken, not from Israel, but "from Jerusalem." For his sons born in Jerusalem, 4QSam[a] reflects the same list of 11 names as MT. The LT lists 13 names, prefaced with their total. And B follows the 11 shared with MT and 4QSam[a] with a further 13 names (24 in all in vv. 14–16), many of which appear to be alternate forms or transcriptions of the 11 also in MT and 4QSam[a]. Of the 11 sons in the apparently primary list, only Solomon's name appears in the subsequent narrative.

Only in this passage within Samuel–Kings (v. 13) do we find "concubine" (*plgš*) in a BTH context. The word itself (possibly originally vocalized *palagš*) is almost certainly the same word as we know in Greek as *pallax* or *pallakē*; and it was not very widely used in HB.[18] It is possible that the word is neither Greek nor Semitic in origin. Esther and Song of Songs are late biblical books, and the story of the Levite concubine in Judg 19–20 is widely reckoned as one of the latest elements in that book. First Chronicles 14 mentions only "wives" (or more strictly, "women"), and is generally credited with improving David's image. It is more likely that "concubine" was added in 5:13 as part of the wider "concubine" theme in 2 Samuel (8x). Samuel–Kings and Chronicles are at one in mentioning *pallakes* only in connection with early kings (Saul, David, and Solomon in Samuel–Kings; and Rehoboam in Chronicles), while the genealogical portions of Genesis and 1 Chr 1–9 are dealing with still more ancient figures.[19] The apparent antiquity of these characters is probably

18. See Gen 22:24; 25:6; 35:22; 36:12; Judg 8:31; 19–20 (11x); 2 Sam 3:7 (2x); 5:13; 15:16; 16:21, 22; 19:5 (6); 20:3; 21:11; 1 Kgs 11:3; Ezek 23:20; Song 6:8, 9; Esth 2:14; 1 Chr 1:32; 2:46, 48; 3:9; 7:14; 2 Chr 11:21 (2x).

19. Abraham's brother, Abraham himself, Israel, and Esau's son in Genesis; and Abraham, Caleb, David, and Manasseh in Chronicles.

in inverse relationship to the recent introduction of the term into Hebrew. The Chronicler's introduction of "concubines" into the older BTH narrative about Rehoboam has the same disparaging function as their association in Samuel and Kings with David and Solomon.

2 Samuel 5:17–25 King David and the Philistines

2 Samuel 5:17–21

17 And Philistines heard
that they had anointed David as king over Israel,
and all Philistines went up
to seek David;
and David heard,
and he went down to the fortress.
18 And Philistines came,
and they [spread out in] *fell on*[a] Rephaim Valley.
19 And David asked of Yahweh, saying,
"Shall I go up [against] *to the* Philistines?
Will you give them into my hand?"
And Yahweh said to David,[a]
"Go up;
for I shall wholly give the Philistines[b] into your hand."
20 And David came into Baal-Perazim,[a]
and David struck them down there,
and he said,[b]
"Yahweh has broken through my[c] enemies before me,
like water breaking through."
And therefore that place was called Baal-Perazim.
21 And they abandoned there their *gods* [images];
and David and his men picked them up.

18a. Here GT's *synepesan* is used both in 2 Sam 5:18, 22 and in the parallel 1 Chr 14:9, 13. It is a better rendering for *wypšṭw* there than *wynṭšw* here.

19a. Here DJD deduces from vertical alignment that there was no place for "to David."

b. The scroll 4QSam[a] supports MT in reading the final "Philistines" unusually with the article. This is part of a larger Samuel plus: the divine response in 1 Chr 14:10 is simply *'lh wnttym bydk*—with no strengthening inf. abs. and no "Philistines."

20a. The GT has read *mm'l* for *bb'l* at the beginning of the verse ("from Upper Breaches"—compare NETS), and similarly at the end.

b. Codex B has read David after, not before, "and he said'; LT has "David" twice.

c. Here B offers "the Philistine enemy" for "my enemies" (MT and LT).

[17–19] What Philistines hear (v. 17) is exactly what has earlier been reported (v. 3): that "they" (the people of Israel and their elders, not a prophet or divine representative) have anointed David king—in 1 Chr 14:8, the verb is passive: "that David had been anointed king."

We have already seen that Saul's "seeking" David's destruction is a major theme of the books of Samuel, from 1 Sam 19:2 to 2 Sam 4:8. In the older BTH, the verb is used much more sparingly, yet no less significantly. There, in addition to 2 Sam 5:17, it is used only once more, so setting up a contrast between the beginning of David's rule and the end of Solomon's (1 Kgs 10:24). News of the anointing of David brings an immediately hostile response from Philistia; however, the significance of David's house after the lapse of only one generation is clearly claimed in the report of "all the [kings of the] earth seeking Solomon's face, to hear his wisdom." When Philistines go to "seek" David, he first takes shelter in a fortress, then asks "of Yahweh."

The synoptic parallel in 1 Chr 14:10 has David asking of "God," and we cannot be sure whether BTH would have read "God" or "Yahweh." Though DJD (123) reconstructs *yhwh*, in the absence of contrary evidence this edition of the scroll defaults toward agreement with Samuel (MT + GT) rather than Chronicles. This is the final mention in Samuel of Yahweh's putting someone in their enemies' hands. Three times in 1 Samuel, "God" is used in this expression, and not "Yahweh": 14:37 (of Saul); 23:14 (of Saul); 26:8 (of David, in words spoken by Abishai). Is the link between David and Yahweh stronger?

Neither the location nor the means he uses to make his inquiry is specified. In the source as we understand it, the ark has already begun its journey toward Jerusalem. It is already in the house of Obed-Edom (as in 1 Chr 13:13–14), and David's descent toward Philistia (as in 1 Chr 14:8) will take him closer to it. However, even if such a hint may just be heard in Chronicles and BTH, it is absent here. Yet we can speculate, from the importance of the verb "ask" (*š'l*) early in 1 Samuel, that our author was conscious of the assonance between this term for inquiry of God and the name of the deceased King Saul.

As noted above, the Chronicler attests a shorter version of the divine answer (v. 19b): one closer to the form in which the question has been asked: "Will you give them into my hand?" It is possible that the strengthening infinitive absolute, very much a feature of the book of Samuel, was never used in BTH. We shall see at the end of this volume that the most debatable instance may be in 2 Sam 24:17 // 1 Chr 21:17 (inf. abs. is rare in Chronicles); but LT and 4QSam[a] in 2 Sam 24:17 read differently and may be more original. The MT uses a term for idols (2 Sam 5:21) found more in Hosea (4:17; 8:4; 13:2; 14:8 [9]) than any other biblical text.[20] Its only other use in Samuel is also in a

20. Compare also Isa 10:11; 46:1; Jer 50:2; Mic 1:7; Zech 13:2; Pss 106:36, 38; 115:4; 135:15; 1 Chr 10:9; 2 Chr 24:18.

Philistine context based on BTH (1 Sam 31:9). In both cases GT reads "gods," as does 1 Chr 14:12 (but not 10:9).[21] The pejorative *ʿṣbym* (MT) is assonant with *ʿzb* ("abandon").

[20–21] If we had not already been thinking about the ark as possible locus for David's inquiry, the term used to describe the divine involvement against the Philistines should make us alert to the possibility. "Burst through" or "breach" (*pāraṣ*) is a key element in the story of Uzzah immediately below (6:8). This further evidence is enough to justify Yahweh's being termed "Lord of Breaches" (5:20 MT).

2 Samuel 5:22–25

22 And Philistines continued further
going up,
and they [spread out in] *fell on* Rephaim Valley.
23 And David asked of Yahweh,
and [he] *Yahweh* said,
"You shall not go up[a] *to meet them*.

Turn from them, and come to them near Weeping.[b]	Turn to behind them, and come to them from opposite Balsams.
24 And it shall be as you hear the sound of the confinement from the groves[a] of Weeping, then you will come down[b] to them, for then Yahweh will[c] come out before you to smite in the battle[d] of the Philistines."	24 And let it be as you hear the sound of a step on the tops of the balsam trees, then you should be {alert}; for then Yahweh has[c] come out before you to strike down in the Philistine camp."[d]

25 And David did so,
as Yahweh had commanded him;
and he struck down Philistines from [Geba] *Gibeon*
till you come to Gezer.

23a. The divine response is a strong prohibition, using *lʾ* + impf., as in the Ten Commandments.

b. The GT reads *bkʾym* as if related to *bkh* ("weep").

21. Yet in 1 Chr 10:10 we do find "house of their gods" where 1 Sam 31:10 has "house of the Ashtaroth."

24a. Here GT may represent not *br'šy* ("on the heads," MT) but either *b'šry* or *m'šry* ("in/from the groves"). But a cst. pl. of *'ăšērâ* is nowhere attested in HB.

b. The GT apparently reads *trd*, not *tḥrṣ*.

c. In an unvocalized text, *qāṭal* (MT) and *yiqṭōl* (GT) of *yṣ'* ("come out") are indistinguishable.

d. Here GT appears to render *bmlḥmh* for *bmḥnh* (MT). And 1 Chr 14:15 reads *'t-mḥnh* (as also in v. 16).

[22–23a] The Philistines have suffered a reverse but are able to resume their attack. "Go up" (vv. 17–19, 22–23) appears to have the sense of "make a frontal attack on." Facing a second hostile Philistine move, David again consults the Deity. For economy, the narrator does not repeat the question; however, it is implied in the terms of the divine prohibition "You shall not go up" (v. 23). This does not imply that Yahweh will not be with David or that he is facing defeat this time—simply that a stratagem other than attack is appropriate on this occasion.

This is the last time that anyone will "ask of Yahweh" in the pages of Samuel. Such oracular inquiry has been a regular feature of 1 Samuel, as indeed of Judges as well. In the older BTH, David's double inquiry (vv. 19, 23) represents the first and last occasions of such seeking of the divine will. The next time he seeks divine counsel, it is via Nathan the prophet, and by then the ark is in Jerusalem (7:1–3). Although the David story in BTH was much expanded as the book of Samuel was produced, this divinatory transition was respected.

[23b–25] Unusually, it is MT and not GT in vv. 23b–24 that is very close to 1 Chr 14:14–15; and that may make it more likely that GT has been working from a corrupted text. In the final verse, however, GT and Chronicles agree over "Gibeon to Gezer." There is considerable confusion in modern times—and probably because there was also confusion in ancient times—over the place names Geba (*gb'*), Gibeah (*gb'h*), and Gibeon (*gb'wn*), just north of Jerusalem: should they be understood as three separate places, or just two—or even one? All three name forms are attested in BTH. King Asa of Judah stops Baasha of Israel in rebuilding Ramah, and uses his materials to build Geba (of Benjamin) and Mizpah (1 Kgs 15:22//2 Chr 16:6). Ittai son of Ribai, one of David's heroes, comes from "Gibeah of the sons of Benjamin" (2 Sam 23:29//1 Chr 11:31). And Gibeon is the location of Solomon's first vision (1 Kgs 3:5//2 Chr 1:3). The addition "of Benjamin" in 1 Kgs 15:22 (2 Chr 16:6 reads only "Geba") may suggest that what is called Geba there is one and the same as the Gibeah that has been home to Ittai. The common testimony of GT and Chronicles to "Gibeon" (5:25) is to be taken seriously. Whether Geba (MT) represents deliberate or accidental change is another matter.

2 Samuel 6:1–9:13 Consolidation in Jerusalem

2 Samuel 6:1–23

1 And David again collected every youth[a] [in] *from* Israel, [thirty] *some seventy* thousand.

2 And David upped
and went
—and all the people who were with him[a]—
from the lords of Judah *in ascent*,
to bring up from there the ark of God,
over which is proclaimed [the name] the name of Yahweh of Hosts,[b]
who is throned *upon* the cherubim.

3 And he had the ark of Yahweh ride on a new cart; and he bore it into[a] the house of Aminadab, which was on the hill; and Uzzah and his brothers, the sons of Aminadab, were driving the cart	3 And they had the ark of God ride on a new cart; and they bore it from the house of Abinadab, which was on the hill;[b] and Uzzah and Ahio,[c] the sons of Abinadab, were driving the new cart.
	4 And they bore it from the house of Abinadab, which is on the hill,
with the ark, and his brothers were walking in front of the ark.	with the ark of God, and Ahio was walking in front of the ark.
5 And David and the sons[a] of Israel were playing before Yahweh with harmonious instruments,[b] with strength and with songs, and with lyres and with harps and with tambourines and with cymbals and with pipes.	5 And David and all the house of Israel were playing before Yahweh with all cypress wood, and with lyres and with harps and with tambourines and with castanets and with cymbals.
6 And they came to the threshing floor of Nodab, and Uzzah stretched out his hand upon the ark of God	6 And they came to the threshing floor of Nachon,[a] and Uzzah stretched out to the ark of God;

to catch hold of it; and he seized it because the ox let it drop— to catch hold of it.[b]	and he caught hold of it because the oxen let it drop.
7 And the anger of Yahweh blazed on Uzzah, and God struck him down there and he died there beside the ark of Yahweh before God.[c]	7 And the anger of Yahweh blazed[a] on Uzzah, and God struck him down there {upon the};[b] and he died there beside the ark of God.

8 And David was blazing,
because Yahweh burst through with a burst-through on Uzzah;
and that place was called Perez-Uzzah till this day.
9 And David feared Yahweh on that day,
and he said:
"How shall the ark of Yahweh come to me?"[a]
10 And David was not willing[a]
to turn the ark *of the covenant* of Yahweh toward himself, up to the city of David;
and David deflected it to the house of Obed-edom the Gittite.
11 And the ark of Yahweh settled at the house of Obed-edom the Gittite three months;
and Yahweh blessed *the whole*[a] *house of* Obed-edom and all *that was* his [house].
12 And it was reported[a] to King David, saying,
"Yahweh has blessed the house of Obed-edom and all that is his on account of[b] the ark of God."[c]
And David went
and brought up the ark of God from the house of Obed-edom to the city of David with joy.

13 And there were with them bearing the ark seven choirs[b] and sacrifice: a bull[22] and a fatling.	13 And it was the case[a] that, when those bearing the ark of Yahweh had stepped six steps,[c] he sacrificed a bull and a fatling.[d]
14 And David was rotating with harmonious instruments before Yahweh;	14 And David was rotating with all strength[a] before Yahweh;

and David was girt with a linen ephod.[22]

22. The LT has "sacrifice of a bull."

15 And David and all the house of Israel were bringing up the ark of Yahweh with a shout and with a horn blast.

16 And *it happened with* the ark of Yahweh [had been[a]] coming into the city of David;
and Michal the daughter of Saul looked out through the window
and saw King David
dancing
and rotating before Yahweh;
and she scorned him in her heart.

17 And they brought[a] the ark of Yahweh,
and they set it firm in its place within the tent
that David had stretched out for it;
and [David] *he* offered up holocausts before Yahweh and *šělāmîm*.

18 And David completed
offering up the holocaust*s* and the *šělāmîm*;[a]
and he blessed the people in the name of Yahweh of Hosts.

19 And he distributed for all the people,
for all the [throng] *power* of Israel,[a] *from Dan to Beer-sheba*,
for both man and woman, for each, one round of bread, one roll,[b]
and one [raisin] cake *from the frying pan*;
and the whole people went each to their house.

20 And David turned
to bless his house;
and Michal daughter of Saul came out
to meet David;
and she *blessed him*
and said,
"How honored today is the king of Israel,
who today is revealed to the eyes of the maidservants of his staff,
like the total revealing of one of the [empty fellows] dancers."[a]

21 And David said to Michal,

"Before Yahweh I shall dance. Blessed is Yahweh[a] who has chosen me	"Before Yahweh who has chosen me
rather than your father, and rather than all his house, ordering me designate over the people of Yahweh, over Israel—	rather than your father, and rather than all his house, ordering me designate over the people of Yahweh, over Israel—
and I shall disport and I shall dance before Yahweh,	and I shall disport before Yahweh,

22 and I shall be further so revealed,[a] and I shall become lowly in your eyes; but with the maids of whom you have spoken, shall I be honored."	22 and I shall become still slighter[a] than this, and I shall become lowly in my eyes; but with the maids of whom you have spoken, with them shall I be honored."

23 And Michal, daughter of Saul, she had no child till the day of her death.

1a. "Youth" (GT) is one proper rendering of *bāḥûr*; the other is "choice one."

2a. Here 4QSam[a] is fuller: ". . . with him to Baalah, that is Kiria[th jearim, which belongs] to Judah."

b. Here DJD finds no place for *ṣbʾwt*.

3a. The LT agrees with MT in reading "from the house" in v. 3 as well as v. 4.

b. Here DJD assumes *bgbʿt qryt yʿrym* for *bgbʿh* of MT and GT.

c. In unvocalized Heb. *ʾḥyw* is ambiguous. GT renders it as pl. "his brothers"; MT points it as sg., which some render "his brother" and others read as a proper name.

5a. Like GT here, 4QSam[a] reads "sons of Israel."

b. The list is even longer in B and appears to contain double renderings. Both 4QSam[a] and GT, like 1 Chr 13:8, read *[b]kwl ʿz [w]bšyrym* in place of *bkl ʿṣy brwšym* (MT); but GT prefaces this with what appears to be a rendering of a doublet starting with *bkly . . .* All versions continue with a list of five instruments, of which the first three appear constant—except for the judgment in DJD that vertical alignment is better served by reversing items 2 and 5 in GT:

4QSam[a]	*wbknwrwt w[bḥllym] wbtpym wbm[nʿn] ʿym [wbnbly]m*
GT	*wbknrwt wbnblym wbtpym wbmṣltym wbḥlylym*
MT	*wbknrwt wbnblym wbtpym wbmnʿnʿym wbṣlṣlym*
1 Chr 13:8	*wbknrwt wbnblym wbtpym wbmṣltym wbḥṣṣrwt*

Here *mṣltym* and *ṣlṣlym* are alternative forms from the same vb. *ṣll* ("tingle/quiver") > "cymbals"; and *mnʿnʿym* are "shakers."

6a. The term *nwdn* (4QSam[a]) lies between the readings of MT (*nkwn*) and B (*nwdb*). But LT has them arrive at the threshing floor of Orna the Jebusite. Here 1 Chr 13:9 reads *kydn*.

b. Only B, but not LT or MT, repeats at the end Uzzah's attempt to grasp hold of the ark. The phrase repeated in B renders surely *lʾḥz bw*, an early variant of *wyʾḥz bw*. Likewise 1 Chr 13:9 uses the inf. *lʾḥz* yet also uses *ʾtw* after it. See further below.

7a. The vb. *ḥrh* is used only in 6:7, 8 in all of BTH (if we take the wording of 2 Sam 24:1 to be secondary to 1 Chr 21:1).

b. The expression *ʿl-hšl* is a notorious puzzle, long explained as a corrupt shortening of *ʿl ʾšr-šlḥ ydw ʿl-hʾrwn* ("on account of the fact that he had put his hand on the ark") in 1 Chr 13:10, a reading largely confirmed by 4QSam[a]. The information about his touching the ark has been supplied in the previous sentence and is not repeated in B (which at this point is even shorter than MT).

c. In 4QSam[a] (as in 1 Chr 13:10), the sentence concludes simply "and he died before God." Codex B conflates this reading with MT.

9a. Here 4QSam[a] concludes with the proto-Lucianic plus: *wybwʾ ʾrwn yhwh.*

10a. First Chronicles 13:13 notes simply that David did not: it does not use *ʾbh* ("was willing").

11a. The LT is shorter than B, without "whole" before "house."

12a. Here v. 12b corresponds to 1 Chr 15:25; but v. 12a is Samuel plus. It also uses the vb. *ngd* ("was reported"): this does occur 3x in portions of Samuel repeated in Chronicles (2 Sam 7:11; 10:5, 17), but is very much commoner in nonsynoptic portions—and is used more often in Samuel than in any other book of the HB.

b. The term *baʿăbûr* ("on account of") is used 3x in the David story of BTH (5:12; 7:21; 10:3), but also in 1 Sam 1:6; 12:22; 23:10; 2 Sam 6:12a; 9:1, 7; 12:21, 25; 13:2; 14:20; 17:14; 18:18–6:12a, though within a BTH context, is Samuel plus.

c. In vv. 11–12a we see that 4QSam[a] agrees with MT; but DJD (124) reconstructs it as continuing the plus also in LT: *wyʾmr dwyd ʾšyb ʾt hbrkh ʾl byty.*

13a. The MT opens with *wyhy*, while GT attests *wyhyw*; but 4QSam[a] reads *whyh.*

b. The noun *choros* ("dance" or "band") renders *ḥebel* in 1 Sam 10:5, 10; and the reconstruction in DJD uses *ḥblym* here. In the more normal sense of "lines" or "cords," *ḥblym* occurs within a Samuel plus in 2 Sam 8:2, and also in 2 Sam 17:13; 22:6. It was presumably a measure like the (now archaic) chain.

c. The GT is much briefer; 4QSam[a] is similar in length to MT, but differs as reconstructed: where MT has the pauses coming after "six steps," the reconstruction in DJD (124) is most easily read with "seven choruses" in apposition to the subject.

d. In v. 13b, the scroll 4QSam[a] agrees with 1 Chr 15:26b: "seven bulls and seven rams"; MT corresponds more loosely.

14a. Here, unlike in v. 5, the phrase *bkly-ʿz* attested by GT is an alternative to *bkl-ʿz*, not an addition to it. McCarter (2:166) follows the Heb. attested by GT but takes *kly* as sg., "a sonorous instrument."

16a. Here MT opens *whyh*, but 4QSam[a] (and 1 Chr 15:29) have *wyhy.*

17a. Both B and LT open with the historic present.

18a. Here DJD insists that there is no space in 4QSam[a] for *whšlmym.*

19a. The parallel 1 Chr 16:3 opens simply (and probably more originally), "And he distributed for every man of Israel." The correlation of *hāmôn* with *dynamis* is rare but not unique (1 Kgs 20:28 [21:28 LXX]; Jer 3:23; Ezek 32:24). Elsewhere in 1–2 Samuel, *dynamis* renders only the positive military terms *ḥayil* or *ṣābāʾ*; but only the latter is ever (2x!) construed with "Israel" (1 Kgs 2:32; 2 Chr 25:7).[23] The term *hāmôn* with "Israel" is quite as rare: 2x in 2 Kgs 7:13. The fact that the corresponding phrase is differently placed in B and LT also indicates secondary expansion.

b. The noun *ʾešpār* is otherwise unknown; the assonant *escharitēs* is bread baked over a brazier.

20a. The GT may have read *hrqdym* for *hrqym.* Has a more original *hrqym* been expanded into the "dancers" expected from the wider context? Or has an original *hrqdym* been moralized into "empty" or "vain"?

23. But notice 2 Sam 20:23, where "Israel" is in apposition to "all the army" (*ṣābāʾ*).

21a. Within the Greek plus, B attests *brwk yhwh* but LT *ḥy yhwh*, which may indicate that the added material is secondary.

22a. Here GT appears to have read not *wnqlty*, but *wnglyty*.

[1–8] Several surprises face readers of the books of Samuel as we know them. Meeting the ark of God again after a silence lasting thirty chapters is surprising enough. Conflict with Philistines is again part of the context; and the attentive reader may have recognized Eli in David's recent words about the blind (5:6, 8). But it seems strange for the author to leave such connections implicit and to have no helpfully explicit reminder of Shiloh, of Dagon and his temple, or of golden representations of tumors. Of course, if this account of David and the ark is older than the narrative in 1 Sam 4–6—and I am far from the first to have argued that—then the matter is less strange.

In MT this whole chapter is an undivided paragraph; however, 4QSam[a] has clearly marked paragraph breaks after vv. 8 and 18. The relationships between the different main versions available to us of this paragraph in Samuel (MT, B, LT, 4QSam[a], and the parallel paragraph in Chronicles)[24] are unusually complex and betray considerable interest in rethinking the detail of what is described. Dietrich (236) proposes recognizing three sections: vv. 1–12, 13–19, 20–23, with blessing in each (vv. 11, 12, 18, 20). As noted above, the partial recapitulation of v. 11 in 12a is a Samuel plus; however, the other three instances stem from BTH. The chapter division at the end of 1 Chr 13:14 corresponds also to a break after 6:11. (The question should at least be asked whether the procession to Jerusalem was composed prior to the collection from the house of Obed-edom.) Verses 3–4 exhibit greater textual variety than even the norm within Samuel. The shifting terms in which the ark is described, and in particular the association with it of "God" or "the Deity" (*h'lhym*) and of Yahweh, are unusual and therefore interesting.

- All versions refer at the outset to "the ark of God," but immediately designate this as the appropriate locus for naming Yahweh (v. 2).
- There is variation in the next sentence (v. 3) between "the ark of God" (MT, LT, Chr) and "the ark of Yahweh" (B, 4QSam[a]).
- What follows (v. 4, in Samuel only) is mostly repetition of the larger part of v. 3; it may have started as an alternative version of it (stating that Ahio walked in front of the ark, rather than that Uzzah and Ahio/his brothers were driving the ark).
- All versions of Samuel (4QSam[a] is reconstructed here) have the festivities played out before Yahweh (v. 5), but Chronicles has them before God.

24. Where, significantly, MT and GT agree—quite often the Hebrew tradition in Chronicles is close to GT + 4QSam[a] in Samuel, and the Greek to MT in Samuel.

- All versions of Samuel have Uzzah touch "the ark of God" (v. 6), but Chronicles simply says "the ark."
- There is unanimity, for the first time since v. 2, that it is Yahweh's anger that blazes on Uzzah (v. 7); however, though all versions of Samuel go on to specify that God strikes him down, Chronicles leaves the subject Yahweh to be assumed from the previous clause.
- Both B and LT state that Uzzah died "near the ark of Yahweh"
- All versions except Samuel MT state that Uzzah died "in front of God."
- Samuel MT appears to combine these statements into the compressed "near the ark of God."
- There is unanimity that it is Yahweh who has burst out on Uzzah (v. 8).[25]

The Chronicler's text is the shortest of these variants; and in almost every respect I take it to be the most original. Even the longer Samuel (MT) never uses the wording "the ark of Yahweh" in the opening 8 verses. It is where other hands in the complex Samuel tradition have made additions and changes that they have tended to alter "God" to "Yahweh."

Granted that all this is so, what was the point of maintaining carefully the presumably original expression "the ark of God" at the same time as making clear how closely this ark is associated with Yahweh? It is Yahweh's fatal anger that blazes out when it is touched (vv. 7–8). And yet there seems to be little point in supposing that it is only in the course of this scene, only after Uzzah's death, that it becomes clear that the God of the ark is none other than Yahweh: Samuel (MT), though not Chronicles, states that it is before Yahweh that the associated musical celebrations are taking place. And all versions state at the

25. The occurrences of ark and names of God can be tabulated as follows, after Rezetko (303–18; S = verse in 2 Sam 6; C = verse in 1 Chr 13):

S/C	**Sam MT**	**Sam B**	**Sam LT**	**4QSam[a]**	**Chr MT &GT**
2/6	Ark/God	Ark/God	Ark/God	Ark/God	Ark/God
2/6	Name/YHWH	Name/YHWH	Name/YHWH	Name/YHWH	Name/YHWH
3/7	Ark/God	Ark/YHWH	Ark/God	Ark/YHWH	Ark/God
4/	Ark/God	Ark	Ark/God	Ark/YHWH	
4/	Ark	Ark	Ark	Ark/YHWH	
5/8	YHWH	YHWH	YHWH	YHWH	God
6/9	Ark/God	Ark/God	Ark/God	Ark/God	Ark
7/10	YHWH	YHWH	YHWH	YHWH	YHWH
7/10	God	God	God	God	
7/10				Ark	Ark
7/10	Ark/God	Ark/YHWH	Ark/YHWH		
7/10		Before God	Before God	Before God	Before God
8/11	YHWH	YHWH	YHWH	YHWH	YHWH

outset that "the ark of God" either bears his name or is the place where Yahweh is to be named (v. 2). I take it that the most natural English rendering is "the divine ark." Here and there, scribes responsible for this or that manuscript of Samuel may have slipped into writing "Yahweh" to replace "God"; however, unlike the next paragraph, this one remains free from contamination by the later phrase "the ark of the covenant [of Yahweh]."

The phrase including "the cherubim" (v. 2) has more puzzles associated with it than its familiarity might suggest. The phrase *yōšēb hakĕrubîm* is rendered "seated *upon* the cherubim" in GT; but the Hebrew expression (which is found with Yahweh [of Hosts] in 1 Sam 4:4; 2 Kgs 19:15//Isa 37:16, and independent of Yahweh in Pss 80:1 [2]; 99:1) includes no preposition (corresponding to "upon") and hence leaves the reader to deduce the relationship between the seated one and the cherubim. The cherubim will be depicted on temple panels close to the innermost sanctuary and, in sculpted form, within the inner sanctum; we may deduce that these beings have been among the closest members of Yahweh's entourage. They are almost certainly depicted with bodies of winged lions, and with heads like either eagles or humans. Since their wings may function to conceal Yahweh, it may be preferable to understand the phrase to mean seated or enthroned *between* or *among* the cherubim.

The infinitival phrase "to catch hold of it" (v. 6), shared with 1 Chr 13:9 and repeated in B, doubtless attests to an early variant of the finite verb "caught hold of it" in MT. But B's longer text in addition uses a stronger finite verb. It appears that the translators were striving for the correct nuance. How powerful or how violent was Uzzah's "grasp"? Was it simply by touching the ark and seeking to aid its passage that he was found at fault, or did he pay the price for a hold that sought to control it? It is only here that the verb *ʾḥz* is used in BTH; but each of its other occurrences in the books of Samuel report a seizing preparatory to death.[26]

The report of Yahweh's hot anger (v. 7) and of the resultant and corresponding hot anger of David (v. 8) are both unique within BTH. David's anger is reported again later in 2 Samuel (12:5; 13:21); and he is anticipated by Saul (1 Sam 11:6; 18:8; 20:30), Samuel (15:11), David's brother Eliab (17:28 MT), and Abner (2 Sam 3:8). In each case, as here, David's anger is sparked by the report of injury to a person for whom he is responsible. A continuation of Yahweh's anger is noted toward the end of Samuel, and within a BTH context—in the Samuel variant at the very beginning of the census story (24:1).

The two neighboring accounts of Yahweh's "breaking through" destructively, on the Philistines and on Uzzah (in whichever order), need to be examined together. The breakthrough on the Philistines is compared to a flood; and the name Uzzah is related to the Hebrew word *ʿōz* ("power, might"). This term

26. As in 2 Sam 1:9; 2:21; 4:10; 20:9.

for power is often associated with Yahweh, not least in Ps 132, which celebrates David's efforts to find a dwelling place for the Almighty:

> Arise, O Yahweh, and go to your resting place,
> you and the ark of your might. (v. 8)

In light of the psalm, the name Perez-Uzzah can be understood as "Breakthrough of Might"; but in our story it clearly means "Breakthrough on Uzzah." The verb *prṣ* is construed with *b-* once more in BTH, in the report of King Jehoash of Israel breaking through on a section of the wall of Jerusalem (2 Kgs 14:13). Psalms 60:1 (3); 80:12 (13); and 89:40 (41) lament or complain about Yahweh's bursting through the people's defenses. However, the close of Exod 19 offers a rather closer parallel, with Yahweh's delivering a series of warnings to Moses at the beginning of the Sinai report. They can be read as a commentary on what Uzzah did and should not have done. The people should not tear through toward Yahweh to see, lest many of them fall (v. 21). Even the priests who approach Yahweh should be consecrated lest Yahweh break out on them (v. 22). When Moses responds (v. 23) that the people will not be able to go up because Yahweh has already given instructions that the mountain be put out of bounds and consecrated, Yahweh simply reiterates (v. 24) that neither priests nor people should tear through to ascend toward Yahweh, lest he break out on them.

Yahweh's outbursts are clearly not partisan: they can be directed against an attendant of the ark no less than against the Philistines. In 1 Sam 4–6, the divine affliction of the Philistines occurs before the similar fate of the men of Beth-shemesh (6:19–20); the order may correspond to a pattern already established in BTH, as found still in 2 Sam 5–6. In 1 Sam 4–6, however, there is this difference, that the suffering of the Philistines is intimately associated with the ark.

[9–15] The note about David's fear (v. 9), as also about his anger (v. 8), is a unique statement about a king or ruler of Israel in BTH. The explicit statement of his unwillingness (v. 10) may be a Samuel plus; but it is in the spirit of the characterization of this king already in BTH and much more fully developed in Samuel.

It is likely that both the texts rendered in our translation above (MT and B) reflect the same accidental yet significant loss from v. 12. LT and OL and Josephus all report words David spoke after learning of the blessing enjoyed by Obed-edom: "I shall turn the blessing to my house." And there is space for these words in 4QSam[a].

[16–20a] Having completed the public aspects of bringing the ark to Jerusalem, including blessing the people (v. 18), David then feeds and dispatches the populace "each to his house" and finally returns to his own house to bless it. In our discussion of ch. 7, we shall notice how each of the four Hebrew words of 6:20a becomes a key element of the following chapter. Verses 19b–20a, which serve now to introduce the end of 2 Sam 6, were originally (in BTH) the end of the ark story. In one respect the older wording may have been augmented—and rather strangely. We noted above that the Chronicler describes the beneficiaries of the royal bounty simply as "every man of Israel."[27] The longer text in Samuel probably results from secondary expansion (see above); but the (apparently positive) use of *hāmôn* with "Israel" is surprising (v. 19): elsewhere in Samuel (1 Sam 4:14; 14:16, 19; 2 Sam 18:29) it refers only to the thronging tumult of an army in defeat. The larger part (6:20b–23), added by the author of Samuel, shows Michal acting out her earlier and interior response (seeing and despising in her heart, v. 16) to the arrival of David and the ark. The exchange between David and Michal that results from her upbraiding is significant at several levels.

[20b–23] We readers who know the story of Michal as told in 1 Sam 18–19; 25:44; and 2 Sam 3:13–16, remember that Michal has been David's wife first, then wife to another man, and has then [been] returned to David. To the reader of BTH—as still to readers of Chronicles unfamiliar with the books of Samuel—2 Sam 6:16 has been the first introduction to Michal; here she is called "daughter of Saul," not "wife of David." Although she "comes out" to meet David as he returns to bless his house, it is not stated—though it may be suggested—that it is out of *his* house that she comes. We can only be sure that it is out of the house through whose window she has seen his arrival that she comes. The reader of BTH has been told only two things about Saul and his family up to this point: that the former king of Israel and his three sons are dead, and that David has been his general. No ancient reader would be surprised to learn that a successful commander has been bound into the household of the king by marriage to his daughter. But that has not been reported in BTH. Still, it may be the very suggestiveness of this source text that encouraged the inventiveness of the author of Samuel. We readers of the whole story of Michal as told in Samuel are also aware that the Michal who now sees David through a window and scorns him once let David down through a window because she loved him (1 Sam 19:12).

When Ahimelech is vouching for David to Saul (1 Sam 22:14), two of the four attributes listed are that he is married to the king's daughter and honored in all his household. Glory or honor (*kābôd*) ought to be manifest in a king; but Michal does not find this—or no longer finds this—manifested in David's behavior. Her use of Ahimelech's words is bitterly ironic. It is an unstated something else about David that has been made shamelessly manifest in David's dancing: self-exposure in the presence of women (*ʾāmâ* is never

27. If it represents the older BTH text here, it may do so also in 1 Chr 10:1, 7//1 Sam 31:1, 7, where (*kl-*) *ʾyš-yśrʾl* is also read. However, Rezetko (224) prefers to argue that *ḥayil* or *ṣābāʾ* was original in 2 Sam 6:19 and was "generalized in MT Chronicles to *ʾyš* on the basis of 1 Chron 10:1, 7?."

used in BTH or Chronicles).[28] Michal might well have known what we can read in Prov 25:2, that the *kābôd* of kings is finding things out: finding things out, yes—but not showing them off. The longer text attested in Greek adds that Michal "blessed" David. That reads so oddly in English—a scolding is a strange form of blessing—that a few remarks are appropriate. The oddity could be lessened by rendering the Hebrew word *brk*, which underlies the Greek, as "greet" rather than "bless"; this is one of many occasions on which "greet" would be the most idiomatic translation: scolding may be an unwelcome form of greeting, but it is far from unknown. However, if we opt for more normal English, we lose an important strand in the thread of "blessing," which runs right through chs. 6–7.

David responds to issues raised both by the narrator and by Michal. The narrator has called Michal "Saul's daughter": David observes that Yahweh has now chosen himself rather than her father or any member of his house. He uses the verb "order" or "command" with the noun *nāgîd* ("leader"), just as Samuel has in 1 Sam 13:14 when telling Saul that Yahweh has ordered a replacement for him. Then the keyword of her complaint has been *nglh* ("being revealed," 3x in v. 20). In v. 22 according to B, he takes up exactly her word and promises what she is bound to see as further base exposure. However, in MT, he takes it up by punning on it (*nql*) and states that he is prepared to become still more slight and abased even in his own eyes. In B, David returns Michal's own word to her; in MT, he recalls the self-deprecatory language he has used when Saul has sent messengers offering him marriage to Michal (1 Sam 18:23), and which reappears nowhere in the books of Samuel (but cf. 1 Kgs 16:31; 2 Kgs 3:18). Michal has objected to what David has done in face of the servant women. David responds that, whether exposed in her eyes or slighted in his own, he will receive honor and glory from precisely these women. The only other time the books of Samuel report musical rejoicing and playing is just earlier in 1 Sam 18,[29] on David's return from striking down Goliath, when it is precisely the women from all the towns who greet Saul with the wounding words that David is ten times more successful than himself (vv. 6–7).

Michal's own shame (the unstated opposite of David's honor) will consist in her perpetual childlessness. Her fate anticipates that of David's ten concubines (2 Sam 20:3). Infertility was regarded as a form of disability. If Michal has no child by either husband, this represents another slight on the family of Saul.[30] A paragraph that has begun with largesse for all, and a blessing for David's house, ends with a manifest curse on the daughter of Saul, irrespective

28. It is found in 1 Sam 1:11 (3x), 16; 25:24, 25, 28, 31, 41; 2 Sam 6:20, 22; 14:15, 16; 20:17.

29. In fact "rejoicing" (*śimḥâ*) is used in Samuel only in 1 Sam 18:6 and 2 Sam 6:12, and "drums" (*tuppîm*) only in 1 Sam 10:5; 18:6 and 2 Sam 6:5.

30. Schipper (2006: 93).

of whosoever's house has served as her vantage point for seeing and despising David's celebrations.

2 Samuel 7:1–29

1 And it came to be,
when the king had sat in his house,
and Yahweh, he had [given rest for him] *left him an inheritance*
round about from all his enemies,[a]
2 and the king said to Nathan the prophet,
"See well;
I am sitting in a house of cedar,
but the ark of God is sitting[a] amid the screen."
3 And Nathan said to the king,
"All that is in your heart, go[a]
do;
for Yahweh is with you."

4 And it came to be in that night
and the word of Yahweh came to Nathan, saying,
5 "Go
and say to my servant, [to[a]] David,
'Thus has Yahweh spoken:
"[Is it] *It is not*[b] you who will build for me a house for my dwelling.[?]
6 For I have not dwelt in a house
from the day of my bringing up the sons of Israel from Egypt to this day,
and I have been moving about in a tented dwelling,
7 in all that I have moved about in all the sons of Israel.[a]
Have I *actually* spoken [a word[b]] with one [of the] staff[s][c] of Israel
whom I commanded
to feed my people Israel,[d]
saying,
'Why have you not built for me a house of cedar?'"'
8 Now then, thus shall you say to my servant, [to] David,
'Thus has Yahweh of Hosts spoken:
"I, I have taken you from the pasture, from behind the sheep,
to be leader over my people, [over] Israel.
9 And I have been with you

in all that you have walked,
and I have cut off all your enemies before you,
and I [shall make] *have made* for you a great[a] name,
like the name of the great ones who are in the earth.
10 And I shall set a place for my people, for Israel,
and I shall plant him,
and he will dwell in his position,[a]
and he will not tremble any more,
and the son[s] of depravity will not continue to humiliate[b] him as at first,
11 [and] since the day*s* that I commanded judges over my people Israel.
And I shall give you rest from all your enemies;[a]
and Yahweh will declare to you
that a house [for you will Yahweh make] *you will build for* him.[b]
12 When your days are full
and you lie with your fathers,
I shall establish your seed after you,
which will come out of your loins,[a]
and I shall set firm his kingdom.
13 He, he will build a house for my name,
and I shall set firm [the] *his* seat [of his kingdom[a]] forever.
14 I shall be to him as father,
and he shall be to me as son,
in whose doing wrong I shall punish him by a staff of men
and by strokes of humans.
15 But my loyalty [I[a]] will not turn from him
as I turned it from [Saul[b]] *those*
whom I turned from before [you[c]] *me*.
16 And [your] *his* house and [your] *his* kingdom shall be established forever before you:
[your] *his*[a] seat shall be firm forever.'"'"
17 According to all these words and according to all this vision,[a]
so did Nathan speak to David.

18 And King David came
and sat before Yahweh;
and he said:
"Who am I, Lord Yahweh,
and what is my house,
that you have [brought] *loved* me to this point?

19 And [this too] I was *extremely* little in your eyes,[a] Lord Yahweh,
and you spoke even [to] *about* the house of your servant afar;
and this is the instruction of the human,[b] Lord Yahweh.
20 And what shall David continue further
to speak to you?
And you yourself know your servant, Lord Yahweh.
21 [For the sake of your word] *Through your servant*[a] *you have acted*
and in accordance with your heart you have done all this greatness,
letting your servant know.
22 Accordingly you are great, Lord Yahweh;
for there is none like you,
and no god apart from you,
in all that we have heard by our ears.
23 And who is like your people, like Israel,

another nation in the earth,	one nation in the earth,
which God	which God
has led to redeem for himself	has gone to redeem for himself
as a people,	as a people,
and to set you a name,	and to set for himself a name,
and to do greatness	and to do for you the greatness
and show, for you to drive out[a]	and fearful things for your land
before your people, which	before your people, which
you redeemed for yourself from Egypt,	you redeemed for yourself from Egypt,
nations and tents.[b]	nations and its gods.[b]

24 And you have set firm for yourself your people Israel,
for yourself as a people forever;
and you yourself, Yahweh, have become for them as God.

25 And now, [Yahweh God] *my Lord*, the word
that you have spoken about your servant and [about] his house,
[set it up] *confirm*[a] *it* forever, *Yahweh of Hosts, God of Israel,*
and [do[b]] *now*
as you have spoken.
26 [And] let your name be great forever [,saying,
'Yahweh of Hosts[a] is God over Israel';
and the house of your servant David shall become set firm before you.]
27 [For you,[a]] Yahweh of Hosts, God of Israel,
you have uncovered the ear of your servant, saying,
'A house shall I build for you.'
Accordingly your servant has found his heart[b]
to pray to you this prayer.

28 And now, Lord Yahweh, it is you who are God,
and your words shall be true;
and you have spoken to your servant this good thing.
29 And now [be favorable[a]] *begin*
and bless the house of your servant,
to be forever before you;
for it is you, Lord Yahweh, who have spoken;
and from your blessing the house of your servant will be blessed forever."

1a. "And . . . enemies" is a Samuel plus, within which B (but not LT) has read *hnḥylw*, not *hnyḥ-lw* (see further on 7:11). Deuteronomy 12:10 uses both verbs (*yšb* and *nwḥ*) in close proximity.

2a. Here 1 Chr 17:1 does not repeat the part. *yōšēb*.

3a. "Go" is a Samuel plus.

5a. There are many instances of apposition in this chapter; repetition of the preposition is very common in Samuel MT, but not in Samuel GT or Chronicles.

b. Samuel GT agrees with 1 Chr 17:4 over the negative.

7a. The sentence division in the translation above is suggested by the discussion in DJD (129) of the small fragment of vv. 6–7 that appears to require a space after "Israel."

b. This is one of at least three occasions in the books of Samuel where GT has read a form of *dbr* as verb, but MT as a noun. The others are in 1 Sam 15:13 and 2 Sam 13:20.

c. Here 1 Chr 17:6 reads neither *šbṭ* (Samuel GT) nor *šbṭy* (Samuel MT), but *špṭy* ("judges").

d. "Israel" after "people" is a Samuel plus.

9a. "Great" before "name" is a Samuel plus.

10a. Often *taḥat* refers to (proper) position, which is not necessarily "beneath."

b. Here 1 Chr 17:9 reads not *lʿnwtw* but *lbltw* ("wear him out").

11a. Also, 1 Chr 17:10 reads, "and I shall make all your enemies kneel"; this may reflect the original reading of BTH, where this vb. is used in *hipʿil* in 2 Sam 8:1, and in *nipʿal* in 2 Kgs 22:19.

b. Here B retroverts to *byt tbnh-lw*, and LT to *byt ybnh-lw*; however, the difference between them probably reflects inner-Greek confusion of Codices E and S. Chronicles agrees with MT.

12a. 1 Chr 17:11 has "which will be of your sons" for "which will come from your loins." The phrase *ʾšr yṣʾ mmʿyk* is found only in Gen 15:4 (Abraham and David), while *ʾšr-yṣʾ mmʿy* is used in 2 Sam 16:11 (David and Absalom).

13a. Here 1 Chr 17:12, like Samuel GT, has simply "his seat."

15a. 1 Chr 17:13, like GT, reads not *yswr* but *ʾsyr*.

b. Saul is mentioned here only in Samuel MT, not in Samuel GT or in Chronicles.

MT	*wḥsdy lʾ-yswr mmnw kʾšr hsrty mʿm šʾwl ʾšr hsrty mlpnyk*
GT	*wḥsdy lʾ-ʾsyr mʿmw kʾšr hsrty mʾšr hsrty mlpny*
Chr	*wḥsdy lʾ-ʾsyr mʿmw kʾšr hsyrwty mʾšr hyh mlpnyk*

c. 1 Chr 17:13 ends the verse in sg.: *mʾšr hyh lpnyk*. And GT supports MT over the repetition of *hsrwty*, but concludes the sentence with first-person suf.

16a. In v. 16b, GT ("his seat") has the support of Chronicles; however, 1 Chr 17:14a offers, "And I shall have him stand in my house and in my kingdom forever."

17a. The LT takes v. 17a as the conclusion of v. 16, and 17b as a short independent sentence.

19a. Here LT has aspects of both MT and B: "And these small things have become smaller before you."

b. In place of *wz't twrt h'dm* (MT), we should possibly read *wtr'ny twr h'dm* [*hm'lh*]—"and have shown me the 'generation' [to come]." The synoptic parallel (1 Chr 17:17) has *twr* and may mean "turn," or (if defectively written for *tw'r*), "appearance." Admittedly, *r'h* is not prominent in this chapter, even though its topic is a vision; in fact, it is used only once (v. 2, *qal*).

21a. The LT conflates: "Through your words and through your servant."

23a. Here 1 Chr 17:21 reads *lgrš*, which DJD includes in its restoration here and assumes GT has read.

b. Both MT and B have a difficult ending: MT has *w'lhyw*, and B attests the very similar *w'hlym*. The term *w'lhym* ("and gods") is very close to each and makes excellent sense. But we should note that Chronicles has neither: either BTH finished its sentence with "nations," or the Chronicler chose to delete mention of other gods.

25a. The form *pistoun* pass. is the stock rendering (9x) of *'mn nip'al*; and *pistoun* act. (B) corresponds to *qwm hip'il* here; *'mr* (1 Kgs 1:36); and *'md hip'il* (1 Chr 17:14). However, *pistōthētō* (LT) may attest *y'mn* (*nip'al* jussive), which is the reading in 1 Chr 17:23 and is reconstructed in DJD.

b. Only one Hebrew letter separates "and do" (*w'śh*) from "and now" (*w'th*).[31]

26a. "Lord of Hosts, God of Israel" is addressed within v. 25 (B) and is part of a statement in v. 26 (MT). The shorter B is clearly in error here: a copyist's eye has jumped from the first "Lord of Hosts" to the next. The MT has the support of both LT and Chronicles; DJD, noting that "saying" (*l'mr*) is required to fill the line, argues that B has suffered a haplography restored in LT.

27a. The LT shares the emphatic opening *ky-'th* of MT and 1 Chr 17:25.

b. "Found his heart" appears unique to this passage in HB, presumably meaning "found courage." The LT adds the explanatory "[found his heart] in God," and 1 Chr 17:25 has simply "found" without obj. (quite as unique in this sense).

29a. The MT's *hw'l* is clearly read in 4QSam[a], rather than *hḥl*, retroverted from GT.

[1–3] In BTH this short paragraph opened by resuming the terms in which the previous one left off. We left the synoptic material in 6:20a, talking of David, his house, and blessing. And this whole scene that follows opens with David in his house (7:1), and is brought to a conclusion with talk of "blessing" (7:29). The connection at the beginning is even closer, because *yšb* ("sat" or "dwelt," 7:1) uses the same letters as *wyšb* ("and he turned back," 6:20). The wording of 7:1–3 masks this link somewhat because in each of its sentences David is no longer referred to by his own name but by his title, "the king." By

31. Wrongly *w'nh* in DJD 131.

contrast, and more originally, the shorter parallel passage in 1 Chr 17:1–2 uses "David" three times. This is part of a much wider phenomenon: Samuel–Kings uses the title "the king" rather than a king's own name much more often than Chronicles in synoptic passages.[32] And it is significant that this is only one of several differences in this paragraph (see the textual notes on each verse): it is beyond doubt that the paragraph has been rebuilt in Samuel or in Chronicles or in both.

The major Samuel plus (v. 1b) can be read as aligning the kingship of David with the larger story of early Israel, whether we follow the reading in MT or in GT. It is a feature of the pluses in Samuel–Kings, identified by comparison with shorter variants in Chronicles, that there is a higher level of textual variation between MT and GT than in synoptic passages (but see below for exceptions to any such rule). Yahweh gives Israel "rest" (MT) in Deuteronomy (3x) and Joshua (5x), and gives Israel "inherited possession" (GT) in Deuteronomy (2x).[33] Since David's active campaigning is far from over, as will be reported in the next chapter, it seems a little strange for the author of Samuel to have added either of these notes. However, GT's version of this note need not refer to Israel's more distant history. Samuel has declared to Saul (1 Sam 10:1) that Yahweh has anointed him over his "heritage": GT may be noting that Yahweh has now given David this heritage in preference to his enemies—and for the author of Samuel these "enemies" would certainly include Saul and his family. Explicit reference to the much earlier history of Joshua's times is more readily found in MT's text.

The divine ark has been moved to Jerusalem and settled in a tent that David had prepared for it. But while its move to Jerusalem had meant blessing for the house of Obed-edom, it had also meant death for Uzzah. Moving the ark had apparently taken place on David's own initiative (unlike the Philistine campaign, where he had taken divine advice); now David is being scrupulous over seeking proper advice before any further action. It is a feature of the few prophetic narratives shared by Samuel–Kings and Chronicles that the king takes the initiative over consulting the prophet: Jehoshaphat and Ahab summon Micaiah son of Imlah (1 Kgs 22), and then Josiah sends a delegation to the prophetess Huldah (2 Kgs 22). In each case these prophets give their own opinion first. Only afterward do they receive a divine response, and that "word of Yahweh" countermands or supplements what they have said.

David's first word to Nathan is a striking opening gambit to a prophet: "See clearly" (v. 2) is the only use of the common verb for "see" (*rʾh*) in this whole

32. On the issue of "David" or "the king," see textual note on 5:6 above and comments on ch. 24 below.

33. It is Joshua, rather than Yahweh, who is said to give Israel possession—although of course on Yahweh's instructions (Deut 1:38; 3:28; 31:7; Josh 1:6).

chapter, unless it should be restored in v. 19 (see textual note). The twin facts of residence that David reports to Nathan—the mismatch of accommodation for God and king—are obvious for all to "see"; but Nathan is invited to "discern" the appropriate implication. He immediately gives David carte blanche—and does so in language that again picks up the end of the previous scene. Michal has "seen" David; believing she understood the significance of what she was seeing, she despised him "in her heart" (6:16). David now asks Nathan to "see." Presumably believing that Nathan understands what he sees, Nathan tells David to do "all that is in his heart." Michal saw and distrusted David; Nathan saw and trusted him.

According to Avioz (16), the problem about David's proposal from the perspective of ancient Near Eastern practices is that there has been no prior divine injunction to build a temple. In strict terms, however, David has made no proposal: much more diplomatically, he has simply remarked on an imbalance of housing provision. It is Nathan's response that first commends action. While David has contrasted the living arrangements of the ark and himself, Yahweh's response through Nathan brings Israel into the frame in each of vv. 6, 7, and 8.

[4–5] Whether we read the opening of Yahweh's response (v. 5b) as a negative statement (GT) or as a question implying a negative (MT), our interest must focus on the emphatic independent pronoun "you": David has no proper role as house builder for Yahweh. He is a newcomer to a long-existent relationship: Yahweh has a history of roaming within his people, and he has had previous shepherds to feed his people; but to none of these has he complained over lack of a cedar house. David is his new shepherd, and Yahweh has won for David a great reputation. But if there is any question of "setting" a "place" (and both verb and noun have an important role in temple talk), it is Yahweh's business to set a "place" for Israel (v. 10), and to plant (*nṭ'*) his people where they will dwell (*škn*). Here Yahweh is surely recalling his ark's being set up in its "place" amid a "tent" that David has "stretched out" (*nṭh*—note the assonance with *nṭ'*)[34] for it (6:17), as well as the nearer sentence (7:6) at the end of which we find "dwelling place" (*mškn*) in apposition to "tent."[35] Yahweh quietly makes the point that, in his actions with the ark, David has already anticipated what is Yahweh's proper business in respect of his people.

[6] The use of the verb "bring up" (*h'lh*) for the divine action of freeing Israel from Egypt (v. 6) is hardly remarkable: throughout HB it frequently alternates with "bring out" (*hwṣy'*). But the choice of this alternative here means that the

34. I am inclined to suggest that, in 7:10, *nṭ'* ("plant") neatly combines the sound of *nṭh* ("stretch out") with the fixity of "erect/setup," both from 6:17.

35. Within Samuel–Kings, *mškn* is unique to 2 Sam 7:6, while the verb *škn* occurs only in 2 Sam 7:10; 1 Kgs 6:13; 8:12; "tent" (*'hl*) is used in connection with the ark only in 2 Sam 6:17; 7:6; and 1 Kgs 8:4; and *śym mqwm* occurs only in 2 Sam 7:10 and 1 Kgs 8:21 (Kings +).

report of Yahweh's earlier action for his people corresponds to David's action in respect of Yahweh in "bringing up" the ark (6:15) and "offering up" sacrifice (6:16–17).[36] Such symmetry provides a helpful background to the discussion as to whether there should be similar reciprocity over the provision of houses for each other. This is only one of several examples of significant wordplay as key relationships are explored.

[7–11] We have found the common verb "commanded" (*ṣwh*) used in the sense "appointed" (v. 7) in three earlier portions: 1 Sam 13:14; 25:30; 2 Sam 6:21. In each of these, the object is *nāgîd* ("designate"). These three anticipations of the language of 2 Sam 7 have combined elements from "to become designate over my people" (v. 8) and "commanded judges over my people" (v. 11). However, Yahweh's speech includes a more local resonance with *ngyd*: David may have been appointed to such a role (v. 8), but it is Yahweh himself (note the emphatic move within v. 11 from Yahweh's speaking in first person to using his own name in third person) who will declare (*hgyd*) whether and when any house should be built for himself. The conflict between vv. 5 and 11 in B is only apparent (Schenker 178–79): permission for David to build Yahweh a house will apply only when David has conquered all his enemies.

It is in the two sections of the Book of Two Houses, in which David and Solomon are speaking to Yahweh,[37] that we find clustered most often the repeated insistence that Israel is Yahweh's people: "Israel, my/your/his people." Within BTH, this usage is anticipated in 2 Sam 5:2 (the first words spoken to David) and 12. Whenever this language is used elsewhere in Samuel, it is derivative and anticipatory.[38]

[12–17] The statement about punishment (v. 14b) is a plus in Samuel. The wording is a mixture of Ps 89:32 (33; *šbṭ* and *ngʿym*) and possibly 2 Sam 7:19 (*ʾdm*). Punishment of (only?) human proportions is perhaps to be contrasted with punishment on a divine scale; and yet David chooses divine afflictions for his people to suffer after he counts them (2 Sam 24:13–14). And the mention of Saul in MT (but not in GT; v. 15) must also be secondary. As with the previous chapters whose content has been drawn substantially from BTH, it is from the material peculiar to Samuel that we may deduce the special interests of its authors. Where Samuel (GT) = Chronicles, we may be reasonably confident that we are dealing with the text inherited from BTH. Within the consensus view of the relationship of Samuel and Chronicles, it is arguable that the Chronicler might have deleted mention of a king in whom he was much less interested. But no such reason can explain the nonmention of David's predecessor in the Greek

36. All *hipʿil* of *ʿlh*.

37. See 2 Sam 7:7 (MT), 8, 10, 11, 23, 24; 1 Kgs 8:16, 30, 33, 34, 36, 38, 41, 43, 66—with their parallels in Chronicles.

38. See 1 Sam 15:1; 27:12; 2 Sam 3:18.

versions of Samuel. These versions are probably also more original in making the divine declaration end "from before me" (v. 15). The GT is right to assume a plurality of those whom Yahweh has previously needed to remove from his presence. Yahweh has originally stated a much more general rule than it has become. The MT in both Samuel and Chronicles has narrowed the focus to the one who was moved out of David's way, whether named (Samuel) or unnamed (Chronicles). The counterpart within the books of Samuel to this divine promise to the house of David, as reported by Nathan, is the divine curse reported in 2 Sam 12, following David's adultery with Bathsheba. There (12:7–8) the same Nathan talks of Yahweh's having delivered David from Saul and having given him everything of Saul's. It seems that MT here has further improved this correspondence by specifying Saul's name.

In this same verse (15), Yahweh himself promises his "loyalty" (*ḥsdy*) to David's son. In corresponding fashion, the Solomon of BTH will twice speak of it to Yahweh (1 Kgs 3:6; 8:23). In the conclusion of his Song (2 Sam 22:51), David expects that Yahweh will deal loyally with his anointed; and that Song (v. 26) like Hannah's (1 Sam 2:9) also speaks of Yahweh's loyal devotee (*ḥāsîd*). David in BTH will claim that his embassy to king Hanun of Ammon is motivated by mutual *ḥesed* (2 Sam 10:2). There is considerable overlap between 2 Sam 7//1 Chr 17 and Ps 89. The psalm speaks of the "vision" (v. 19 [20]) received by David; and many other key terms are shared: *ḥesed* is one recurring theme in the psalm (vv. 1, 2, 14, 24, 28, 33, 49 [2, 3, 15, 25, 29, 34, 50]), and *ʿôlām* another (vv. 1, 2, 4, 28, 36, 37, 52 [2, 3, 5, 29, 37, 38, 53]). What is vital for the exegesis of 2 Sam 7 is to decide in which important respects it is distinctive—for example, that the vision is imparted to David via Nathan. The "seeing" role of Nathan is emphasized both by David's opening words (v. 2), though he may not have intended them so, and the narrator's conclusion (v. 17).

[18–24] Following such a positive response from the prophetic intermediary, David now addresses Yahweh directly. Each party is formally titled: it is King David who enters and addresses him as "Lord Yahweh."[39] Given the way ch. 7 has opened, with David "seated" in his own house, it is striking that he now enters and "takes his seat before Yahweh." Following 2 Sam 6:5, 14, 16, we might suppose that sitting "before Yahweh" means taking a seat in front of the ark; yet we should recall that David has made a covenant for Israel "before Yahweh" (5:3) before there is any mention of the ark in BTH.

David's first move in response to the divine words is to suggest in rather stuttering confusion that Yahweh has gone too far in his generosity (vv. 18b–21). The term *hălōm* ("here," v. 18) is found in only ten other passages in HB[40]

39. Or "God Yahweh" in 1 Chr 17:16.

40. Genesis 16:13; Exod 3:5; Judg 18:3; 20:7; 1 Sam 10:22; 14:36, 38; Ps 73:10; Ruth 2:14; 1 Chr 17:16.

and never combined with *ʿad* except in the parallel, 1 Chr 17:16. The unique combination *ʿad-hălōm* ("to this point") may well have been chosen precisely because of its assonance with the dominant phrase, which it politely seeks to limit. The phrase *ʿad-ʿôlām* ("forever") clusters three times toward the end of the divine speech in vv. 13–16, and it is taken up as a prominent feature of the king's response.[41] David's modest "to this point at least" (v. 18) is perhaps better developed in B's version[42] of the immediately following words: "and I was extremely small in your eyes." Rendering *lmrḥwq* (end of v. 19a) as simply "afar" recognizes that, in itself, the expression can point either backward or forward. The following half verse is too uncertain textually as a basis for interpretation.

David's second move is to recognize and restate (vv. 22–24) what Yahweh has said (vv. 6–7, 10) about the priority of his relationship with his people, which he intends David to serve. The incomparability of Yahweh is stated (v. 22) in terms found elsewhere in HB only in the Latter Prophets (Isa 26:13; 45:5, 21; 64:4 [3]; Hos 13:4), with Ps 18:31 [32] (but not the parallel in 2 Sam 22:32!) as the sole exception.

[25–29] In the second part of his prayer before Yahweh (vv. 25–29), David develops the theme that most concerns himself: the divine promise to him of a (royal) house. Not a word is spoken about a house that might be built for Yahweh; there is no further mention of the imbalance in the matter of housing between God and king, over which David has consulted Nathan at the outset.[43] Yahweh has dealt with the issue briefly (v. 13) and made it the responsibility of David's successor; David makes not even a polite show of dissent. The divine titles are different and fuller in Samuel than in Chronicles. Here DJD (on 7:27) suspects that MT in 25–27 has arisen either by [accidental] dittography or [deliberate] expansion of one or more of the [divine] epithets to conform with the others. "Confusion has entered the versions as well." The conclusion of the prayer in 1 Chr 17:27 ("For it is you, Yahweh, who have blessed and are blessed forever") is certainly briefer than in 2 Sam 7:29. The Chronicler's shorter version in turn is more similar to the last words of the long Ps 89: "Blessed is Yahweh forever. Amen and amen."[44] This is the first return to the theme of blessing since 6:18, 20, while other key terms from the end of ch. 6 have reappeared several times: the occasion is now ripe for the theme of blessing to be stressed.

Certainly this report of the exchange between the father of Jerusalem's royal line and his God is far from being a simple historical report. Those who read it in

41. Three times in vv. 24–26, followed by *lʿwlm* twice in v. 29.

42. Apart from the points noted above on vv. 19, 21, LT agrees with B against MT throughout.

43. Schenker (177–181) argues that, in the shorter GT at least, the "house" about which Yahweh prays to Yahweh is the temple.

44. Unless that verse should be better understood as a doxology at the end of book 3 of Psalms.

the Book of Two Houses, after the collapse of Jerusalem with its temple and its monarchy, and still later in Samuel and Chronicles, would have been poignantly conscious of the irony of familiar words such as "set firm" and "established" and "blessed"—and perhaps especially the repeated "forever."

2 Samuel 8:1–18

1 And it came to be after this,
and David struck down Philistines
and [made them kneel] *turned*[a] *them*;
and David took the ["Bridle of the Mother-City"] "*separated off*"[b] from the hand of Philistines.
2 And he struck down Moab,
and he measured them by line,
making them lie down on the ground;
and he measured *the* two lines for putting to death,
and the [full of the line[a]] *two lines* for keeping alive;
and Moab came to belong to David as servants bearing tribute.
3 And David struck down Hadadezer, son of Rehob, king of Zobah,
when he went to [turn back] *set up*[a] his "hand" in the river *Euphrates*.[b]
4 And David captured from him one thousand *chariots and* seven [hundred] thousand horsemen and twenty thousand men of foot;
and David [hamstrung] *paralyzed* all the chariotry
and left remaining of it one hundred chariots.
5 And Aram of Damascus came
to help Hadadezer king of Zobah;
and David struck down in Aram twenty-two thousand men.
6 And David placed *a* post[s] in Aram of Damascus,
and Aram came to belong to David as servants bearing tribute;
and Yahweh saved David everywhere he went.
7 And David took the shields[a] of gold
which *he* had *made* [belonged to] *against* the servants of Hadadezer,
and he brought them to Jerusalem.
And Susakim king of Egypt took them
on his coming up to Jerusalem in the days of Jeroboam son of Solomon.
8 And from [Betah and from Berotay,[a]] *Masbak,*
King David took from the *choice* cities of Hadadezer,
[King David took] very much bronze.

9 And To*u*[i] king of Hamath heard
that David had struck down all the army of Hadadezer.

10 And To*u*[i] sent [Joram] *Ieddouran* his son to King David
to ask of his welfare
and to bless him
because he had made war on Hadadezer
and struck him down,
because *he had fallen to*[a] Hadadezer [had been the man of
To*u*[i]'s wars];
and in his hand were vessels of silver and vessels of gold and vessels
of bronze.
11 These too King David consecrated to Yahweh with the silver and the gold
that he had consecrated from all the [nations] *cities*
that he subdued:[a]
12 from [Aram] *Edom* and from Moab and from the sons of Ammon
and from Philistines and from Amalek,
and from the booty of Hadadezer son of Rehob king of Zobah.[a]
13 And David made a name;
on his returning [from striking]
he struck down [Aram] *Edom* in *Gebelem* [the Valley of Salt], eighteen
thousand.
14 And he set in Edom *a* post[s],
in all Edom [he set posts],[a]
and all Edom became slaves to [David] *the king*;
and Yahweh saved David
everywhere he went.
15 And David was king over [all] Israel;
and [David] *he* was performing justice and right for all his people.
16 And Joab son of Zeruiah was over the force;
and Jehoshaphat son of [Ahilud] *Aheia* was recorder;
17 and Zadok son of Ahitub and Ahimelech son of Abiathar were priests;
and [Seraiah] *Asa* was scribe;
18 and Benaiah son of [Jehoiada] *Janak* was *counselor*
and the Creti and the Peleti;[a]
and the sons of David: [priests] *leaders at court* they became.

1a. The Gk. *tropoun* corresponds to *knʿ hipʿil* in the synoptic 1 Chr 18:1, and elsewhere only in Judg 4:23.

b. The GT's *tēn aphōrismenēn* may retrovert to *ʾt-hmgrš*, which shares some consonants with *ʾt-mtg hʾmh*; the term *hʾmh* is unique in HB.

2a. "The full of the third line" (LT) is accepted into the reconstruction of 4QSam[a] (DJD 133).

3a. The infin. *epistēsai* is used also in the synoptic 1 Chr 18:3; where MT has *lhṣyb*, not *lhšyb* as here.

b. The GT attests *pĕrāt*, as also reconstructed in DJD, read in 1 Chr 18:3, and required by Q.

7a. *šeleṭ* is parallel to *māgēn* ("shield") in Song 4:4.

8a. Here DJD (134) suggests that the original text may have read *wmbʾrt*, and that the *ʾālep* later quiesced. First Chronicles 18:8 reports the names as *ṭbḥt* and *kwn*.

10a. The Gk. *keimai* is used in wrestling terminology of taking a fall.

11a. "Which he subdued" is a Samuel plus: the *piʿel* of *kbš* is unique to this verse.

12a. First Chronicles 18:11 ends with "and from Amalek" and lacks all mention of Hadadezer.

14a. The second clause is redundant and absent from 1 Chr 18:13. The MT restates the whole first clause, and B gives only a part of it.

18a. Codex B strictly attests one different consonant in each name: *whklty whplṭy*. Apart from the parallel 1 Chr 18:17 and the recapitulation in 2 Sam 20:23, these reappear in 2 Sam 15:18; 20:7; 1 Kgs 1:38, 44. In both 2 Sam 20:23 and 1 Chr 18:17, Benaiah is described as "over" (*ʿl*) these forces: presumably a second *ʿ* was lost after *yhwydʿ*, and then the *l* corrupted to *w*.

[1–3] David's armored foreign policy is sketched in a series of brief notes. There seems to be no strong temporal force in the opening "And it came to be after this": it simply links this collection of notes to the previous narrative; and the clause has a similar (and simple) connective function in 10:1; 13:1; 21:18. The first note (v. 1) returns to the Philistine theme of ch. 5. Apart from here (MT) and Job 40:12, "made kneel" always (8x) has Yahweh as subject. The remainder of this opening note is obscure, whether in MT or GT. The twin senses of "house," played on in ch. 7, are further developed in ch. 8. David's successes abroad both add to the reputation of his own royal house (v. 13) and also contribute booty for his God's treasury within the divine house (vv. 8, 11). After all, Yahweh is the one who is credited with David's victories (vv. 6, 14).

An attack on Moab (v. 2) results in its becoming subject to David. The detail in the center of this verse about brutal treatment of Moabite captives (two-thirds of them slaughtered) is not part of the Chronicler's shorter text. By adding it to this report, the author of Samuel reinforces what has just been noted about "making kneel" being something Yahweh normally does. Giving David the decision over life and death creates an ironic echo of the "credo" at the core of the Song of Hannah (1 Sam 2:6), where Yahweh is said to be the one who causes death and life.

In the third note, it has been debated whether it is David or the king of Zobah who is going to do something at the river. The text is formally ambiguous on the point; but McCarter (2:247) has cogently argued for David as the implied agent. Zobah was the Aramean region east of the Anti-Lebanon mountain range in the area of Damascus, and hence between David and the Euphrates. Associated with the verb "turn back" (*lĕhāšîb*), as in MT, and possibly in the sense of "restore," "hand" refers to the king's power. With the probably more original "erect" (*lĕhāṣîb*), attested in GT and read in Chronicles, "hand" refers to a standing monument. The common word "hand" (*yad*) is also the regular Hebrew term for the (erect) male member—and by extension, for other erections such as standing stones, symbolizing dominant authority. The consonantal text in MT is distinctive in not specifying the Euphrates as the river. If *pĕrāt* has been deliberately deleted in that tradition, it could have been in order to favor David as claiming authority near some unspecified river closer to Jerusalem; yet McCarter notes that even more-distant Egyptian kings aspired to march to the Euphrates and leave a memorial there to their achievement. Be that as it may, the only other erectors of memorials in the books of Samuel are David's rivals Saul (1 Sam 15:12) and Absalom (2 Sam 18:18). However, we cannot know how the author of these passages read the ambiguous 2 Sam 8:3 of his source.

[4–8] In the case of the Zobah forces, it is not the humans, but the great majority of the horses that David renders useless (v. 4). Many a Hebrew reader would note with a wry smile that a king whose name implies "help" (*ʿēzer*) from (the god) Hadad also needs help from Damascus (v. 5). Unlike Moab, which is closer and may have been intimidated by the atrocity to its captives (v. 2), the more distant Damascus requires the establishment of one or more fortified positions to guarantee its client status (v. 6a). The note that Yahweh has "saved" David in all these ventures (v. 6b) is followed by notes about tribute in metals (vv. 7–8). Though MT and GT differ over word order and city names (v. 8), they agree over using the title "king" with David. The Chronicler, as frequently, uses only the name here but adds the title in v. 10 (see further on 7:1–3 and 24:2).

[9–18] The first note in this fresh paragraph describes how some of the tribute that comes to David is brought voluntarily, perhaps on the basis that "my enemy's enemy is my friend." Joram (v. 10 MT), apparently a Yahweh name, is surprising in this context. If original, the name is possibly a token of submission to David. However, the parallel in 1 Chr 18:10 reads *hdwrm*, which is partly supported by B. The first expression used for greeting David (*lšʾl-lw lšlwm*) is found only here in BTH. However, it is taken up (but with the word order varied) in 1 Sam 10:4; 17:22; 25:5; 30:21[45]—and compare 2 Sam 11:7. The identical expression is found only in Jer 15:5, while the word order found in 1 Samuel is replicated in Gen 43:27; Exod 18:7; and Judg 18:15. Compare also the playful *šʾlw šlwm yrwšlm* in Ps 122:6 (traditionally "Pray for the peace of Jerusalem").

The opportunity is then taken (v. 11) to make clear that all the precious metals gained as tribute by David were dedicated to Yahweh. There are two surprises among the nations listed as subdued (v. 12) in this material shared

45. How many more expressions in 1–2 Samuel are used for the last time within 2 Sam 5–8? Cf. *nśʾ klyw* 4x in 1 Sam 31 (BTH) and also in 1 Sam 14 (9x) and 16:21 (and in Judg 9:54, but never in Kings); and *nśʾ kly ywʾb* in 2 Sam 23:37 (BTH) and also in 2 Sam 18:15.

with 1 Chr 18: no campaign against Ammon has yet been reported (that will follow in 2 Sam 10//1 Chr 19); and no mention of Amalek appears elsewhere in the synoptic account of David (or indeed of any other king). David's dealings with Amalek have been handled in 1 Sam 30 (not part of BTH); but even in a wider Samuel context, the mention here of Ammon is noteworthy.

Because of the similarity of Hebrew *r* and *d*, confusion between Israel's neighbors *ʾrm* (Aram) to the northeast and *ʾdwm* (Edom) to the southeast is widespread throughout HB, as between MT and other witnesses to the text (vv. 12–13). The variation between "from striking" (v. 13 MT) and "he struck" (GT) corresponds to this basic confusion. In MT, on his return from striking down Aram, David establishes posts in Edom; but in GT, it is on his return from somewhere unspecified that he strikes down Edom and then set posts there. Three interlinked considerations lead us to prefer the Greek reading in v. 13: a later incident in the time of king Amaziah, geography, and the parallel passage in Chronicles. Amaziah is reported to have defeated "Edom" (2 Kgs 14:7) or "the men of Seir" (2 Chr 25:11) by the Valley of Salt, ten thousand in number. Apart from 2 Sam 8//1 Chr 18, this is the only mention of "the Valley of Salt," except for the superscription of Ps 60—thus confirming that we are dealing with the valley where the "sea of salt" (the Dead Sea) is located, which forms part of the border of Edom, but not for Aram, well to the north. Appropriately, 1 Chr 18:12 reports defeat for Edom, not Aram. However, 1 Chr 18 and Ps 60 have more to contribute to the understanding of 2 Sam 8 than simple confirmation that GT was correct to preserve "Edom." Each attributes Edom's defeat to a different victor: Chronicles to Abishai, son of Zeruiah, and Ps 60 to Joab (his brother). It is hardly likely that these other books would have removed one of his own victories from David's credit. We should conclude instead that the author of Samuel reattributed to David a victory over Edom by one of Zeruiah's sons—perhaps to ensure that David's reputation is not outdone by Amaziah, one of his minor successors.

Many take *šēm* ("name," v. 13) to mean a physical memorial or monument, of the sort for which *yad* was earlier used (v. 3). It is true that these two nouns are combined in the gracious promise of *Yad wā-Šēm* (Isa 56:5) to those whose mutilation will deny them the progeny to continue their name—memorably reapplied to victims of the Shoah in modern Jerusalem's Holocaust memorial. But the whole phrase has been added by the author of Samuel; and it has to be said that "make" is not the expected verb for such a sense of "name."

The two halves of v. 15 state an ideal situation: David is king over the whole of Israel, and in favor of his whole people he practices law and right. The individual nouns *mišpāṭ* and *ṣĕdāqâ* form a frequent word pair within a poetic line, each reinforcing the other in prophetic poetry. However, this phrase *ʿśh mšpṭ wṣdqh* is relatively rare: it is found once more in BTH, where the Queen of Sheba congratulates Solomon on doing what is lawful and right (1 Kgs 10:9); but otherwise it nowhere reappears in all of Samuel–Kings or Chronicles. On the other hand, the behavior it describes is claimed for Yahweh in Jer 9:24 (23) and Ps 99:4; and it is used as the standard by which to judge kings in Jer 22:3, 15; 23:5; 33:15; the matter is stated more generally in Ezek 18:5, 19, 27; 33:14, 15, 16, 19, but may have kings in mind, while princes are explicitly mentioned in 45:9. Several of the passages in Jeremiah and Ezekiel are apparently playing on the name of King Zedekiah (*ṣdq-yhw*).

The narrator in one case and the Queen of Sheba in the other attribute to David and Solomon the practice of godlike justice. This shared statement in BTH of the gold standard becomes a benchmark for royal behavior in Jeremiah, and perhaps Ezekiel too. But, while the successor narratives of Samuel–Kings or Chronicles preserve it, they never mention it again. One further detail of this verse is unique, certainly within BTH and apparently also within Samuel as a whole: when Israel is referred to as "my/your/his people,"[46] the possessive always refers to Yahweh except here. It is precisely here, where David's practice of justice is implicitly compared to Yahweh's, that Israel is said to be "his people."

This paragraph concludes with the summary record of David's "cabinet," based on BTH. Joab, commander of the army, is mentioned first. We noted (above on 5:6–10) that BTH, like Chronicles, probably ascribed his prominence to his role in the taking of "the city of David." Just as the author of Samuel removed Joab from that scene, so in 8:13 his brother Abishai lost credit to David for the victory in Edom. Benaiah is reported as commander of the (somewhat mysterious) Cherethites and Pelethites.[47] Readers of BTH have already been familiar with him from the account of David's three and thirty heroes, now in 2 Sam 23:20–23. At the culmination of that short account of his exploits, he is said to be over David's *mšmʿt*, a term that appears only in a similarly enigmatic statement of David's role in Saul's household (1 Sam 22:14) and in Isa 11:14 (see on 2 Sam 23:23).

The other principal puzzle in this listing comes at the end. "Priests" (v. 18 MT) is particularly surprising following the naming of the two priests in v. 17. Many scholars have supposed that *khnym* is a mistaken replacement for whatever word was interpreted by the several ancient versions as implying some sort of prominence; and McCarter (2:255) notes that a mechanical mistake could have resulted from the presence of *khnym* (v. 17) in the same position on the line above. Especially if "priests" was read by MT by mistake, it appears surprising that it was allowed to remain in the text. Kings in the ancient Near East did have a cultic function, and it is far from impossible that king's sons were priests. The one Hebrew verb in vv. 15–18 comes in this final element

46. As in 2 Sam 5:2, 12; 7:7, 8, 10, 11, 23, 24.

47. John Van Seters (at SBL Vienna 2007) interpreted these as Greek mercenaries: "Cretan" archers and lightly armed "peltasts" (troops armed with a light shield or *peltē*).

and, possibly emphatically, at its very end. Its implication may be that David's sons were not originally priests—there were already duly constituted priestly families (v. 17)—but in the course of time, the king's sons *became* priests. Such a claim in a later period would have been hostile to the royal family, and implicitly critical of the non-Levite father who allowed it to happen. Similar mischief is reported of Micah (Judg 17:5–6), at a time when "there was no king in Israel; all the people did what was right in their own eyes."

Four features toward the end of this chapter combine to give the reader the clear impression that an end is being approached: the roundup of tributary neighbors (v. 12), the note that David is victorious wherever he goes (v. 14), the corresponding assertion about his practice of justice at home (v. 15), and the list of his chief officials (vv. 16–18). Yet the story of David continues: more briefly already in BTH, but much more extensively in Samuel.

2 Samuel 9:1–13

1 And David said,
"Does there[a] still exist someone who is left over of the house of Saul,
that I may show loyalty with him for the sake of Jonathan?"
2 And the house[a] of Saul had a servant,
and his name was Ziba;
and they called him to David,
and the king said to him,
"Are you Ziba?"
and he said,
"*I am*[b] Your servant."
3 And the king said,
"Isn't there[a] still a man of the house of Saul
for me to practice divine loyalty with him?"
And Ziba said,
"There is still a son of Jonathan—smitten in the feet."[b]
4 And the king said [to him],
"Where is he?"
and Ziba said to the king,
"In fact [he is] in the house of Machir, son of Ammiel, [in] *from* Lo-debar."[a]
5 And King David sent
and took him from the house of Machir, son of Ammiel, from Lo-debar.
6 And Mephibosheth,[a] son of Jonathan, son of Saul, came to *King* David
and fell on his face
and prostrated himself *to him*;

and David said *to him*,
"Mephibosheth,"
and he said
"Your servant, in fact."
7 And David said to him,
"Do not be afraid,
for I shall really practice loyalty with you for the sake of Jonathan your father:
I shall return to you all the land[a] of Saul your father;
and you shall eat food at my table perpetually."
8 And he *Mephibosheth* prostrated himself
and said,
"What is your servant,
that you have [turned to] *looked on* a dead dog like me?"[a]
9 And the king called to Ziba, Saul's "lad,"
and said to him,
"Everything
that belonged to Saul and to all his house
I give to the son of your lord.
10 And you shall work the land for him, you and your sons and your servants;
and you shall bring [and it shall be[a] food] *loaves*[b] for the son of your lord,
and he shall eat [it] *loaves*,
but Mephibosheth, son of your lord, shall eat perpetually food at my table."
And Ziba had fifteen sons and twenty servants.
11 And Ziba said to the king,
"According to everything
that my lord the king may command[a] his servant,
so shall your servant do."

And Mephibosheth was eating at David's table[b] like one of the king's sons.	"And Mephibosheth is eating at my table[b] like one of the king's sons."

12 And Mephibosheth had a small son,
and his name was Micha.
And all who were settled[a] in Ziba's house were servants to Mephibosheth.
13 And Mephibosheth was settled in Jerusalem,
for at the table of the king—perpetually—he was eating.
And he was lame in both feet.

1a. Only four more times does *hky* appear: Gen 27:36; 29:15; 2 Sam 23:19;[48] Job 6:22.

2a. Codex B suggests *wmbyt*, but LT supports MT.

b. Not all GT MSS read *Egō*.

3a. Interrogative *h'ps* is unique.

b. Jonathan's son was introduced in the same, otherwise unique, terms in 2 Sam 4:4—we can compare *nkh-rwḥ* in Isa 66:2, and also the Aramaic-like adj. forms in Isa 16:7 and Prov 15:13; 17:22; 18:14.

4a. The GT offers several variants: B and LT have *Ladabar*, but all attest a single word, not two as MT.

6a. Here B transliterates MT as *Memphibosthe*, but LT and OL read *Memphibaal* (also in vv. 10, 11, 12, 13). The genealogy of Saul is given twice by the Chronicler, in the almost identical 1 Chr 8:33–34 and 9:39–40. There, Jonathan's son is given three times as *mryb bʿl* and once as *mry-bʿl*.[49] It is hotly debated whether *mry-* or *mpy-* is more original.

7a. The usage of *śdh* requires close review, to detect whether deliberate ambiguity is in play here or whether it is sufficiently clear that only Saul's family property is intended. Codex B renders "every field"; LT, "all the fields."

8a. The GT like MT uses the definite art., "the dead dog." It renders *kmwny* by *ton omoion emoi*; however, it is more likely here that *k* identifies, rather than compares: "the dead dog that I am."

10a. Codex B has the present *estin* for MT's *hyh*; but LT offers the closer *hypērchen* (impf.).

b. Here B uses sg. *arton* to render only its third attestation of *lḥm*.

11a. For MT's *yṣwh*, Codex B offers perfect *entetaltai*.

b. Other VSS offer "his/your/the king's table." "My table" (MT) must imply that Ziba is still speaking.

12a. Here B's *autou* is not anticipated in MT. Its *katoikēsis* means "settlement, habitation."

[1–6] This gem among stories has important relations with at least five others. It anticipates the immediately following chapter, which was part of BTH, on showing loyalty where loyalty is due. It takes up several issues from the long chapter on David, Jonathan, and Saul in 1 Sam 20. It is jarringly reminiscent of David's acquisition of Jerusalem. It looks forward to the very last words of the books of Kings. And the clue to some of its language is to be found in the breathless praise of Solomon's court by his most famous royal visitor.

There was a royal house even closer than Ammon (ch. 10), to which David was also indebted. David came to prominence as leader of Saul's forces. He inherited the throne when Saul died on the field of battle with his three warrior

48. But 1 Chr 11:21 is different; and the reading in Samuel is textually uncertain.

49. And Saul's fourth son is given as *'šbʿl*.

sons. And concerning Jonathan's family, David has made the most solemn undertakings to Jonathan, who died with his father and whom David has eulogized most memorably.

It is very hard to decide how ironically *ḥesed* is used here. The first occasion on which David spoke of *ḥesed*, it was to Mephibosheth's father (1 Sam 20:8); and in turn it was precisely "Yahweh's *ḥesed*" that Jonathan called on David to exhibit (20:15). David later praised the loyalty shown to (the dead) Saul by the people of Jabesh in Gilead (2 Sam 2:5–6). Then Abner claimed *ḥesed* to the house of Saul (2 Sam 3:8), as he angrily rebuffed Saul's son who had complained about his relationship with Rizpah. Thus *ḥesed* has an honorable pedigree in the books of Samuel. For its roots in BTH, see below on 10:2.

[7–13] David's speeches to Jonathan in 1 Sam 20:3, 5–8 were replete with emphatic infinitives absolute, and he uses another now to his son: "I shall really practice" (2 Sam 9:7). His last words in 1 Sam 20:8 included the distinctive—and possibly late—*yeš* ("there is/exists"); and his first words here (2 Sam 9:1) use it again. (See further below on the usage of *yeš*, found altogether 13 times in Samuel.) At the conclusion of the long scene between them, David prostrated himself before Jonathan (1 Sam 20:41), as he was later to do before Saul (24:8 [9]); and now Jonathan's son prostrates himself before David (2 Sam 9:6, 8). As if Mephibosheth has been schooled in all these pregnant scenes, he takes upon himself David's words to Saul (1 Sam 24:14 [15]) when he describes himself before David as a "dead dog" (2 Sam 9:8). Then again Mephibosheth is to eat at David's table (vv. 7, 10, 13), just as David was due to eat at Saul's (1 Sam 20).

There are so many obviously significant pairings that we have to ponder the meaning of two other interesting links that relate particularly to the steward Ziba. David tells him (2 Sam 9:9–10) that he is restoring to Mephibosheth all Saul's property, and that he (Ziba) and his family will have the duty of working the land for him. The land is called *śādeh* ("field[s]"); and that in itself is unremarkable—except that it is also the term used throughout 1 Sam 20 for where all the private discussions and coded archery took place between Jonathan and David (20:5, 11, 24, 35). More striking is the fact that the noun *môšāb* is used in the books of Samuel only in these two chapters. It is related to *yšb* ("sit/dwell") and thus means either a sitting place or a dwelling place. It is used in the first of these senses in 1 Sam 20:25, of the habitual place where the king sat at table, and (20:18) of the place where David was expected to sit, from which any absence was easily noted. But what does "the whole *môšāb* of the house of Ziba" mean (2 Sam 9:12)—surely not "the whole table place"? "The whole household of Ziba were servants of Mephibosheth" would have been a straightforward sentence; but what of "the whole *môšāb* of the house . . ."? That is more easily rendered as above: "All who were settled in Ziba's house."

Similar play on the meanings of the common verb *yšb* continues in the next statement (v. 13). Here again the most obvious sense is "Mephibosheth lived/was settled in Jerusalem." And even that is a surprising enough thing to read here about someone with damaged feet, in the light of what we have read about the blind and lame in 2 Sam 5:6, 8—they will turn David back; David hates them; they shall not enter the house. Lest there be any mistaking the significance, the last words of this chapter take pains to underscore the fact that Saul's grandson "with the damaged feet" (v. 3) is wholly "lame"—"lame in both feet." Are we to suppose that David is prepared to break his more recent rules about Jerusalem in favor of an even more ancient bond with Jonathan? When he finds out that Jonathan's son is disabled, does he realize the inadequacy of what he let his people know when they were taking over Jerusalem?

The words could bear that inference. And yet David's words, no less than his actions, are always very difficult to "read." All Saul's private farm is to be restored to his grandson, but certainly not his wider state lands. A king's grandson, with his property restored, is to eat at the king's table—but at his own expense. The farm income is to be used to finance his upkeep at the king's table (where we might expect the eating to be at royal expense). Mephibosheth is being "treated loyally"! But the following remarks suggest that he is really also being mocked. Back to the meanings of *yšb*: when a king is said to "sit," the implication is often that he is sitting enthroned, that he is ruling. Mephibosheth "sat" in Jerusalem, eating always at the king's table.

That next-to-final sentence looks backward and forward. David insists that Saul's grandson should never be absent from David's table, in the manner that David absented himself from Saul's table. Mephibosheth should not be allowed to stray from the normal discipline of the king's family; he should not be allowed to compromise David's security, as David's own son Absalom would later do when he is granted leave of absence to go to Hebron (2 Sam 15–18). But the word "continually" in that sentence (*tāmîd*) looks much further forward than any relationship between David and Mephibosheth. Within Samuel it is only used in this paragraph, and it is stressed there (vv. 7, 10, 13). But it is to reappear twice at the very end of 2 Kings, where we learn that a new king of Babylon sets one of his captives, Judah's last king, in a seat higher than the other kings in Babylon: he changes out of his prison clothes and eats food "continually" in the presence of the king; he has a portion given him by the king "continually," day by day, as long as he lives (2 Kgs 25:27–30). In that situation too, just as Mephibosheth has been disqualified for kingship by being lamed (2 Sam 4:4), Zedekiah is disqualified by being blinded (2 Kgs 25:7). To keep one's prisoner under house arrest rather than in prison is a form of preferential treatment and may be represented as an instance of the practice of loyalty. Already in our discussion of 1 Sam 20, we suggested that some of the court language there may have been drawn from what the Queen of Sheba sees at

Solomon's court.[50] We are now in a position to strengthen that proposal. That queen is amazed not just at "the eating at his table, the seating of his servants" (1 Kgs 10:5), but also at the good fortune of "your servants, those standing in front of you *always*" (10:8).[51]

The treatment of Saul's descendant at the hands of David and of David's remote descendant at the hands of the king of Babylon are comparable. We are left to ponder the significance of such a comparison for the fate of either house. Second Samuel 9 could have been read during the exile as a quiet jibe against the imperial power: the entertainment of the exiled king was being financed by revenues from his land. Equally, if it was written sufficiently long after the fall of Jerusalem, in a time of tension between old Judah and old Benjamin within new Yehud, it could have conveyed that there was absolutely no hope for a descendant of Saul.

There is just one point in this narrative (v. 11b) where Mephibosheth's eating arrangements are not associated with the word "always"; and it is all the more striking that this part verse has come down to us in different wordings. The Greek version is widely accepted as more original. There, "Mephibosheth was eating at David's table like one of the king's sons" is a comment by the narrator. It is natural to read MT as continuing what Ziba says to the king: "Mephibosheth is eating at my table like . . ." And such a statement by Ziba would be open to at least two quite different interpretations. In the one, Ziba is claiming that his present treatment of his master is up to royal standards. In the other, Ziba, while accepting David's instructions, is daring to modify them: he is content with David's orders to manage Saul's estate for his master's benefit, but he intends that his master will continue to enjoy royal treatment at his (Ziba's) own table.

The movement of the narrative in this remarkable chapter appears to end with v. 11. Verses 12a and 12b read almost like footnotes. However, the narrator's commentary in v. 13 comes like a wake-up call: "Do you realize the significance of the story I have just told you?" Perhaps it is deliberate that the reader is left wondering throughout this chapter till its very end just whether Mephibosheth is or is not among those hated by David? The emphatic final words, "both feet," as soon as they are spoken, leave little doubt. Such further specification of *psḥ* is unique to this verse. Allusion is clearly being made here to 2 Sam 5:5–8, where *psḥ* is used three times, as well as to v. 3 above—the dual form earlier in the story is not simply recapitulated, but is reinforced here in *šty rglyw* ("both feet"). There is only one other case where such a dual, referring to paired parts of the body, is similarly strengthened; and that is "both ears" (*šty*

50. It may not be without significance that both Zedekiah and the Queen of Sheba were mentioned in our discussion of 2 Sam 8:15.

51. See further Schipper (524).

ʾ*znyw*) in 1 Sam 3:11; 2 Kgs 21:12 (and Jer 19:3, where the normally shorter LXX does attest *šty*).

An indication of the relative dating of this narrative may be available in the use of *yeš* ("there is/exists"). Of some 132 instances (Mand.), 15 are from Ecclesiastes, 8 from Chronicles–Ezra–Nehemiah (none from synoptic passages), 5 from Ruth–Lamentations–Esther, 1 each from Jonah and Malachi, 13 from Proverbs, 12 from Job, 2 from Isaiah 43–44. The 12 from Kings are all found in 1 Kgs 17–2 Kgs 10; similarly the 13 from Samuel are all from nonsynoptic passages (1 Sam 9:11, 12; 14:39; 17:46; 20:8; 21:3, 4, 8 [4, 5, 9]; 23:23; 2 Sam 9:1; 14:19, 32; 19:28 [29]), and all within direct speech. An interesting subset of these passages exhibits further links to 2 Sam 9:1. (1) Second Samuel 19:28 (29) also relates to Mephibosheth. (2) The term *yšnw* (*yš* with the third m. suf.) is used only by Saul, and when seeking information (1 Sam 14:39; 23:23), just as David is doing here. (3) In 1 Sam 14:39, it is also used in proximity to an infinitive absolute. (4) It is used in proximity to practicing loyalty in 1 Sam 20:8. (5) In 1 Sam 14:39 and 20:8, Saul and David are speaking about sin or guilt, as also Absalom in 2 Sam 14:32. Finally, the 20 from Genesis[52] are largely in passages otherwise related to Samuel (11 are in the Joseph story).[53]

52. See Gen 18:24; 23:8; 24:23, 42, 49; 28:16; 31:29; 33:9, 11; 39:4, 5, 8; 42:1, 2; 43:4, 7; 44:19, 20, 26; 47:6.

53. Auld 2011a sets the context.

2 Samuel 10:1–13:33
Disloyalty and Disaster

It is only in the case of these four chapters that we have chosen to define as a separate section of the commentary the material between one blank line in CL and the following blank line. The fact that this body of text narrates the transition from David's success to its unraveling offers thematic justification. At its heart (chs. 11–12) is the story of David and Bathsheba and Uriah and Joab and Nathan. From the beginning of this section we reckon LT the better witness to OG than B, although some scholars set the transition at 11:2. The translation below reflects the differences between MT and LT.

2 Samuel 10:1–19 Joab Defeats Ammon and Aram

1 And it came to be after this,[a]
and the king of the sons of Ammon died,
and Hanun[b] his son reigned in his place.
2 And David said,
"I shall practice loyalty with Hanun son of Nahash
just as his father practiced loyalty with me."
And David sent to console[a] him, by hand of his servants, about his father;
and David's servants came to the land of the sons of Ammon.
3 And the princes of the sons of Ammon said to Hanun their lord,
"Is David honoring your father in your eyes,
in that he has sent you comforters?
Is it not[a] in order to investigate the city
and spying [it] out *the city* and overthrowing it
that David has sent his servants to you?"
4 And Hanun took David's servants
and shaved [half of] their beards
and cut their "clothes"[a] in half to *the ascent to* their bottoms[a]
and dispatched them.
5 And they informed David *about the men,*[a]
and he sent to meet them;

for the men were very ashamed.[b]
And the king said,
"Stay in Jericho[c]
till your beards grow
and come back."
6 And the sons of Ammon saw
that [they stank[a] to David] *the servants of David were ashamed.*[a]
And the sons of Ammon sent
and hired Aram [of] *and* Beth-Rehob and Aram of Zoba (twenty thousand foot), and the king of Maacah (a thousand men), and Ish-Tob[b] (twelve thousand men).
7 And David heard,
and sent Joab and all the army,[a] the warriors.[b]
8 And the sons of Ammon went out
and drew up[a] battle at the opening of the [gate[b]] *city*,
and Aram of Zoba and *Beth*-Rehob and Ish-Tob and Maacah were on their own in the field.
9 And Joab saw
that the battlefront had come to be toward him before and behind,
and he chose from [all the choicest in] *every youth*[a] *of the sons of* Israel,
and *they* drew [them] up[b] to meet Aram.
10 And the rest of the people he put in the hand of Abishai his brother,
and [he] *they* drew [them] up to meet the sons of Ammon.
11 And [he] *Joab* said *to Abishai*,
"If Aram is too strong for me,
then I will have you as deliverance;[a]
and if the sons of Ammon are too strong for you,
then I will go to deliver you.
12 Be strong
and let us strengthen ourselves,
and *let us fight* for our people and for the cities of our God.
And as for Yahweh, he will do what is good in his eyes *for us*."
13 And Joab drew near and the people who were with him for battle on Aram,
and they fled before him.
14 And the sons of Ammon—they saw
that Aram fled,
and they fled before Abishai
and came to the city.

And Joab turned back from the sons of Ammon
and came to Jerusalem.
15 And [Aram] *the sons of Ammon* saw
that [it was smitten[a]] *Aram stumbled* before Israel,
and they gathered together.
16 And Hadad-ezer[a] sent
and brought out Aram

which is across the river Chalaama,	which is across the river,
and they came to Helam[b] and Soba;	and they came to Helam;
and Sabee leader of the army of Hadad-ezer was before them.	and Shobach[c] leader of the army of Hadad-ezer was before them.

17 And it was told to David.

And he gathered all Israel
and crossed the Jordan
and came to Helam;
and [Aram drew up to meet David[a]] *David was drawn up against Syria*,
and they did battle with him.
18 And Aram fled before Israel,
and David slaughtered of Aram seven hundred charioteers and forty thousand horsemen;
and Shobach leader of its army he struck down
and he died there.
19 And all the kings,[a] the servants of Hadad-ezer, saw
that they [were smitten] *stumbled* before Israel;
and they made [peace] *terms* with Israel[b]
and became their servants;
and Aram [were] *was* afraid[c] to deliver the sons of Ammon any longer.

1a. The point in the books of Samuel from which LT is reckoned the better witness to OG than B is normally given as either 2 Sam 10:1 or 11:2

1b. The LT vocalizes the name as *Annan*, and B as *Annōn*.

2a. Here GT's *parakalesai* means "call on, encourage, console."

3a. Codex B's introductory *Mē* anticipates a negative response: "You don't mean . . . ?" A positive answer is signaled by LT's *ouchi*. In the following, B has *all' hopōs ouchi*, but LT only *all' hopōs*—there a more literal rendering of MT would have transposed *hopōs* and *ouchi*. The GT does not render *wlhpkh*; instead, its inf. *kataskepsasthai* here appears to repeat the sense already present in the immediately preceding subjunctive *kataskopēsōsin*—each could render *wlrglh*. The LT repeats *tēn polin* in place of B's *autēn* after the second vb. By contrast, 1 Chr 19:3 reads "the land" after the third vb. ("to investigate and to overthrow and to spy out the land"). "The land" is supported by Tg. to Samuel.

4a. Both *mdwyhm* and *štwtyhm* are unusual forms: the root of the former appears to be not *dwh* but *mdd* or possibly a by-form *mdh*—the noun *md* is used of a "measure" of clothing or carpeting; KBL derives the latter from *št* but Mandelkern from *šyt* (the word is found elsewhere only in Isa 20:4), not *šth*—1 Chr 19:4 uses the equally rare *mpśʿh*. The added *anabolēs* in LT may be explanatory. "Bottom" is deliberately ambiguous and may refer either to the garment or to the men's buttocks.

5a. Here 4QSam[a] reads with GT and 1 Chr 19:5; B offers *hyper*, but LT *peri*.

b. Codex B's *ētimasmenoi* (small variants within GT) means "dishonored" rather than "ashamed." Elsewhere in Samuel, *klm* ("ashamed") reappears in 1 Sam 20:34; 25:7, 15; 2 Sam 19:3 (4).

c. Here 4QSam[a] uniquely reads simply *yrḥw*, without the preposition *b*.

6a. The Heb. *bʾš* ("stink") and *bwš* ("be ashamed") are frequently confused, and often their similarity is played on. In MT, Ammon was stinking "in David" (*bdwd*). Codex B had the same text before it as 1 Chr 19:6 (*ʿm-dwd*) but did not read this as "with David"; instead it understood "the people of David" as subj. of "be ashamed." The LT achieves a similar sense but has apparently read *ʿbdy dwd* ("the servants of David").

b. With Ish-Tob, cf. *ṭbʾl* in Isa 7:6.

7a. The MT has the force of "all the army, the elite." The LT's *stratian tōn dynatōn* has read *ṣbʾ* (like 1 Chr 19:8), not *hṣbʾ*. Codex B's *pasan tēn dynamin tous dynatous* renders each element in *kl-hṣbʾ hgbrym* appropriately but does not catch the difference in the Heb. words.

b. The *gbrym* feature again in 1 Sam 2:4; 2 Sam 1:19, 21, 22, 25, 27; 16:6; 17:8; 20:7; 23:8, 9, 16, 17, 22; and we meet the sg. *gbwr* in 1 Sam 9:1; 14:52; 16:18; 17:51; 2 Sam 17:10; 22:26 (originally *geber*?).

8a. The vb. *ʿrk* is unique to this chapter in BTH: complemented in this verse by *mlḥmh* (as in 1 Sam 17:8), and in 9, 10, 17 by *lqrʾt . . .* (as in 1 Sam 4:2); 1 Sam 17:2 combines both.

b. Codex B's "door of the gate" is more precise than MT; however, LT's *ton pylōna tēs poleōs* renders *šʿr hʿyr* or *ptḥ hʿyr*.

9a. The GT's youth[s] is an appropriate rendering but fails to catch the Heb. wordplay.

b. The GT renders *qal wyʿrk* with the middle voice *paretaxanto* (and in v. 10), although the active vb. is perfectly common in Greek.

11a. The parallel in 1 Chr 19:12 uses the expected *tšwʿh* rather than *yšwʿh* as here. Since both are routinely rendered by *sōtēria*, GT cannot help to fix the original reading in Samuel.

15a. The vb. *ngp* (*nipʿal*) is well anchored in BTH—cf. also 2 Sam 10:19; 1 Kgs 8:33; 2 Kgs 14:12; and parallels in 1 Chr 19:16, 19; 2 Chr 6:24; 25:22. Where the *qal* is used (though never in BTH), Yahweh is normally subj.—cf. the neighboring 2 Sam 12:15; and this may also be implied in the (impersonal) *nipʿal*, as here. The GT uses the active *eptaisen* (pl. in v. 19), meaning "stumbled" or "blundered." The expression *ngp lpny* was drawn from vv. 15, 19 for use in 1 Sam 4:2; 7:10 and 2 Sam 2:17, just as *nbʾš* (v. 6) for use in 1 Sam 13:4 and 2 Sam 16:21.

16a. The GT transliterates (and in v. 18) as *Adraazar*.

b. Here GT's *Ailam* renders *ḥylm* as a place name; it is possible that the earlier *Chalamak* (B) or *Chalaama* (LT) is a variant rendering of the same or a similar Hebrew term.

c. For *šwbk*, here and in v. 18, we have *šwpk* in 1 Chr 19:16, 18. The LT's *kai Sōba* is clearly intended as a second place name after *Ailam*, while the immediately following *Sabee* is the military chief. While this may reflect a conflation of two interpretations, it is striking that neither transliteration reflects the final *-k* of MT and B.

17a. The MT of 1 Chr 19:17 agrees with Samuel GT, and GT agrees with Samuel MT.

19a. "All the kings" is a Samuel plus. McCarter (2:270) suggests that *hmlkym* first entered the text as a correction of *hml'kym* in 11:1.

b. In 1 Chr 19:19, the servants of Hadadezer make peace *ʿm-dwyd* rather than *ʾt-yśrʾl*. The GT in Samuel agrees with MT that Israel is the agent, not David; but LT has the Aramaeans make a covenant with Israel, while in B they desert to Israel.

c. Chronicles has Aram "unwilling" (*wlʾ-ʾbh*) rather than "afraid" (*wyrʾw*) to continue saving Ammon.

[1–5] Second Samuel 10 is related to 2 Sam 5–8 in interesting ways and reads as something of an afterthought to ch. 8. Although, like that earlier chapter, it is introduced by "And it came to be after this," the content may be intended as a supplementary flashback: we have already seen Hadadezer defeated there (8:3–8), and Ammon as one of the several neighbors bringing David tribute (8:12). Grace is a characteristic of Yahweh; and one of the texts that describes him as "gracious" (Exod 34:6) also states that he practices "loyalty" (2 Sam 10:2). As for David, we have noted above (on 8:15) that both his own practice of justice and the description of Israel as *his* people serve to align him with Yahweh, while one of the promises conveyed by Nathan implies that Yahweh's *ḥesed* will remain with David (7:15). If *ḥesed* characterizes Yahweh's behavior, it should also mark David's. His "practice of loyalty" (10:2) toward a royal line that has just lost its head is the immediate source of the expression that is even more prominent in 2 Sam 9.[1]

We have observed that David's opening position is consonant with everything that we have learned so far. And this is no less true of the Ammonites. Most of their neighbors to the east of the Rift Valley (the Arabah), both south and north, have already been attacked by David, forced to pay tribute, and some of them occupied; and now David is sending them an "embassy" when their

1. The phrase *ʿśh ḥsd* is construed with *ʿm* in Gen 24:12; 40:14; 47:29; Josh 2:12 (2x), 14; Judg 1:24; 1 Sam 15:6; 20:14; 2 Sam 2:6; 3:8; 9:1, 3, 7; 10:2/1 Chr 19:2 (2x); 1 Kgs 3:6//2 Chr 1:8; Ruth 1:8. "Yahweh" or "God" is subject of *ʿśh* in Gen 24:12; 2 Sam 2:6; 1 Kgs 3:6—and with the verbs "turn" (*swr*) in 2 Sam 7:15 and "keep" (*šmr*) in 1 Kgs 8:23 (both BTH). First Kings 3:6 is the only instance of *ʿśh ḥsd* that comes after the synoptic 2 Sam 10. This is another expression whose use apparently culminates in reports relating to the earliest kings—or better, really starts there and then is projected backward.

king is new and potentially vulnerable. The advice given to the new king is quite reasonable. And yet the situation is more complex. Although the Ammonites may well be aware that David has gone on the offensive against Philistines (5:17–25; 8:1), Moabites (8:2), Aramaeans (8:3–6), and Edomites (8:13–14), he has also received help volunteered from Tyre (5:11) and tribute from Hamath (8:9–10). Against such a varied background, it should cause little surprise that there have been orderly relations[2] between David and Hanun's father: of the six closest neighbors of Israel listed in Amos 1:3–2:3, Ammon is the only one whose relationship with David is so far unreported in BTH. Unreported but not unmentioned: Ammon is listed in the earlier summary note (8:12) as subdued by David and contributing gold and silver. This may be yet another case of the narrator offering a report of something whose details are only later provided; but if so, the connecting phrase "And it came to be after this" (2 Sam 10:1) has been only loosely used.

When we learn that the new king of Ammon is called "Gracious Son of Snake" (vv. 1–2), we may expect some surprises. We are given no opportunity to find out the real purpose behind David's embassy, for Snake's son is persuaded by his advisers that David's solicitous concern for his Ammonite neighbor is far from genuine. The reader is offered no access to David's motives. There is a good deal more interesting and very effective wordplay in the Hebrew. The key verb *šlḥ* ("send") has already (vv. 2–3) been used three times before the narrator introduces the assonant *glḥ* ("shave") to describe Hanun's treatment of the ambassadors whom David has sent to him; *glḥ* is always used in the *pi'el* and here is resumed by *šlḥ* (this time in the *pi'el*) at the finish of v. 4b.[3] On the return of those he has sent, David's message (v. 5b) starts and finishes with forms of *yšb* ("sit/dwell") and *šwb* ("return"); and following *nklmym* ("ashamed," v. 5) we find attested in GT the semantically similar *bwš* (also assonant with *yšb* and *šwb*) in place of the easily confused *b'š* ("stink") in MT. In a story including all these correspondences in sound, it seems all the more appropriate for McCarter to note the correspondence in folktale between eyes and testicles, which underscores the appropriateness of the punishment (v. 4) meted out by Hanun to suspected spies. The shame they experience is probably caused quite as much by the failure of their mission (cf. Jer 14:3) as by their physical appearance: the one is powerfully symbolic of the other. Things go wrong for David but end up turning out in his favor. Those to whom he will show *ḥesed* soon stink to him. "Stink to" (v. 6 MT) has the support of Chronicles and provides a more immediate and explicit recognition

2. "Orderly" may characterize better than "friendly" the relations implied by *ḥesed*.

3. The frequency of *šlḥ* (*qal* 7x, *pi'el* 1x, within 16 verses) is matched in the following chapter (*qal* 11x, *pi'el* 1x, in 27 verses). For comparison, *šlḥ qal* is used 10x in 2 Sam 1–9, and 21x in 2 Sam 13–24; and *šlḥ pi'el* 4x in 2 Sam 3 and 3x in 2 Sam 13–24.

of the trouble ahead; but the note (v. 5) that David's ambassadors have been "shamed" (*klm*) already implicitly recognizes the danger.[4]

[6–8] First Chronicles 19 gives us access to an earlier draft of this chapter in two quite different ways: both its context and its actual text. Readers of this episode in 1 Chr 19, as within the earlier and shorter BTH, meet it immediately after 1 Chr 18 (which corresponds to 2 Sam 8); and in several respects the Chronicler's wording appears more reliable. Verses 6–7 are the only portion of the chapter extant in 4QSam[a]. This is one of the portions of Samuel in which 4QSam[a] and Chronicles attest a longer and apparently better text of Samuel; and this should predispose us to greater sympathy for distinctive readings elsewhere in 1 Chr 19 over against the majority witnesses in 2 Sam 10.[5] The longer text reads as follows:

> And the sons of Ammon saw
>   that they had become stinking to David,
> and Hanun and the sons of Ammon sent a thousand talents of silver
>   to hire for themselves from Aram-Rehob/Naharaim
>   and from Aram-Maacah
>   and from Aram-Zobah
>   chariotry and horsemen.
> And they hired for themselves thirty-two thousand chariots
>   and the king of Maacah and Ishtob;[6]
> and they came
> and they camped before Medaba;
> and the sons of Ammon gathered from their cities
> and came for war.

It can hardly have come as a surprise to the Ammonites that their humiliation of David's ambassadors would be taken as "stinking" behavior by the king who had sent them. Be that as it may, when they saw that it was so, they recruited mercenary allies in large number. David's own response on hearing this was to send Joab with the whole army. We were reminded as recently as 8:16 that he was its leader; but here, in an unusual collocation of terms, the narrator adds that this force (*ṣbʾ*) consists of, or is accompanied by, the heroes (*gbrym*) or mighty men (some of whose exploits are reported in ch. 23). The Ammonites themselves draw up their lines by their city gate, while their Aramean allies occupy more open ground.

4. It appears that GT, under the influence of *klm* (v. 5), has (mis)read *bwš* (another word for "shame") for *bʾš* ("stink")—*klm* and *bwš* are frequently paired, especially in Jeremiah and Ezekiel.

5. Compare the textual notes on vv. 3 and 19 above.

6. Here 4QSam[a], like LT, reads Ishtob as a proper name; Chronicles offers the colorless "and his people."

[9–14] Seeing that he is dealing with an enemy in two locations, Joab selects some elite troops to face the Arameans with him, and puts the remainder under the command of his brother to face the Ammonites.

The narrator does not make clear whether Joab's words reported in vv. 11–12 were private encouragement to Abishai or were intended for wider hearing. Though seemingly unremarkable at first, they are in fact unusual in several respects. The plan itself that they describe is straightforward: only after engaging the enemy will Joab know whether the division of troops between the brothers was the right one—if not, and one comes under enemy pressure, the other can help. "Deliver" or "save" (*hwšy*) is not a common verb in BTH; and, when we meet it first (2 Sam 8:6, 14) and last (2 Kgs 19:34) in these synoptic texts, Yahweh is delivering David (2 Sam 8), or else Jerusalem (2 Kgs 19) "for the sake of David." Heard in this larger context, it may be significant that there is no place in Joab's pre-battle words of encouragement for "our king."

Here one military chief will save the other, if the opponent is too strong for him. The repeated "strong" (*ḥzq*) of the two enemy forces in v. 11 is matched in v. 12 by a doubled call for the brother generals to "be strong" and "exhibit strength" (*qal* followed by *hitpaʿel* of the same verb). They should have, and should manifest, this strength "for the sake of our people and for the cities of our God." "Cities of our god" is unique in HB—and the sg. "city of our god" can be found only in Ps 48:2, 8, and referring to Jerusalem. Defining the people of Israel by its cities is unusual in HB. We shall find below (15:2–3) that Absalom uses "city" in a trick question-and-answer with those who ask him for help: they should identify themselves with the tribes of Israel and not its cities. Then, in the only other context in which BTH uses "what is good in his eyes" (*hṭwb bʿynyw*, 2 Sam 10:12), it is again part of a hope for divine favor, this time in the words of the Jebusite to David (2 Sam 24:22). Eli has used it similarly in 1 Sam 3:18, as will David in 2 Sam 15:26; 19:18 (19).[7] We are given no detail about the victory achieved, simply that Joab and his men return to Jerusalem with their task accomplished.

[15–16] Their enemies are in confusion and our ancient texts even differ over which enemy saw that the other was in trouble. Yet, even as Joab and his forces are returning to Jerusalem, their enemies are regrouping; and David is told.

[17–19] This time, David himself takes to the field—at the head, not of the army and elite troops, but of "all Israel." He does not just put the enemy to flight again, but inflicts large casualties. And the "servants of Hadadezer" (so the synoptic version in 1 Chr 19) draw the appropriate conclusion. Our account

7. Compare 1 Sam 18:8, 20; 2 Sam 12:9.

in Samuel goes one step further (v. 19) and identifies his subordinate allies as "kings," like the picture in Isa. 10:8 of the boastful Assyrian: "Are not my commanders all kings?"

2 Samuel 11:1–27 David, Bathsheba, and Uriah

1 And it came to be at the turn of the year,[a]
at the time when [messengers] *kings* "go out,"
and David sent Joab, and his servants with him, and all Israel,
and they destroyed the sons of Ammon
and beseiged Rabbah.
But David was sitting in Jerusalem.

2 And it came to be at eventime,
and David rose from his couch
and went to and fro on the roof of the king's house
and saw a woman washing [on] *from* the roof,[a]
and the woman was of very good appearance.
3 And David sent
and asked about[a] the woman;
and [he] *they*[b] said,
"Isn't this Bathsheba, daughter of Eliam, wife of Uriah the Hittite?"[c]
4 And David sent messengers
and took her;
and [she[a] came to him] *he came to her*
and he lay with her;
now she was [purifying herself] *washed* from her uncleanness;[b]
and she returned to her house.
5 And the woman became pregnant,
and she sent
and informed David,
and said,
"I am pregnant."[a]
6 And David sent to Joab, saying,[a]
"Send to me Uriah the Hittite."
And Joab sent Uriah to David.
7 And Uriah came to [him] *David*;
and David asked after Joab's welfare and after the people's welfare
and after the welfare of the battle.
And he said,
"*It is well.*"[a]

8 And David said to Uriah,
"Go down to your house
and wash your feet."[a]
And Uriah went out of the king's house;
and there went out after him [the "portion"[b]] {*one*} *of the attendants* of the king.
9 And Uriah lay down at the door of the king's house with all the servants of his lord;
and he did not go down to his house.
10 And they informed[a] *King* David, saying,
"Uriah did not go down to his house."
And David said to Uriah,
"Are you not coming 'from a way'?
Why have you not gone down to your house?"
11 And Uriah said to David,
"The ark of God[a] and Israel and Judah are living in huts,[b]
and my lord Joab and the servants of my lord are camping on the face of the field.
And I—shall I come to my house
to eat
and drink
and lie with my wife?
By your life[c]—by your very life—I shall not do this thing."
12 And David said to Uriah,
"Stay right here today as well;[a]
and tomorrow I shall dispatch you."
And Uriah stayed in Jerusalem on that day,
and [from] *on* the morrow[b] **13** David called for him,
and he ate before him
and drank;[a]
and he made him drunk;
and he went out in the evening
to lie on his bed with the servants of his lord;
but to his house he did not go down.
14 And it came to be in the morning
and David wrote[a] a letter to Joab,
and sent[a] it by hand of Uriah.
15 And he wrote in the letter, saying,
"Put[a] Uriah opposite[b] the strenuous battlefront,
and turn back from him
that he be struck down
and die."

16 And it came to be as Joab was [watching] *besieging*[a] the city,
and he put Uriah to the place
where he knew
there were valiant men.
17 And the men of the city went out
and did battle with Joab,
and there fell some of the people, [of the servants] *according to the word*[a] of David,
and[b] Uriah the Hittite [also] died.
18 And Joab sent
and informed David of all the details of the battle.[a]
19 And [he] *Joab* commanded the messenger, saying,
"As you finish all the details of the battle,
speaking to the king,
20 if the king's anger rises
and he says to you,
'Why did you approach the city to fight?
Did you not know
that they would shoot from the wall?
21 Who struck down Abimelech son of [Jerub-besheth] *Jerobaal*?[a]
Did not a woman throw down on him a piece of a millstone[b] from the wall,
and he died in Thebez.[c]
Why did you approach the wall?'
say,
'*The men were too strong against us,*
and they came out against us into the field,
and we were on top of them right up to the gate of the city,
and the missiles were overloaded on your servants from the wall,
and there died from the servants of the king some eighteen men;
and your servant Uriah the Hittite has [also[d]] died.'"
22 And the messenger *of Joab* [went.[a]
And he] came *to the king in Jerusalem*
and announced to David [everything with which Joab had sent[b] him.]
all the news of the war;
and David raged with anger against Joab
and said to the messenger,
"Why did you approach the city to fight?
Did you not know
that you would be hit from the wall?
Who struck Abimelech son of Jerobaal?
Didn't a woman throw on him a piece of a millstone from the wall

and he died in Thamessei?
Why did you approach the wall?"
And the messenger said to David,
23 "The men were too strong against us,
and they came out to us in the field,
and we came to be on top of them right up to the [entrance of the gate] *gates of the city*.
24 And [the archers shot toward] *the missiles were overloaded on* your servants[a] off the wall,
and some of the servants of the king died;
and your servant Uriah the Hittite died [too]."

25 And David said to the messenger,
"You shall say this to Joab,
'Do not let it be bad in your eyes—this matter;
for the sword may devour this way and that.
Strengthen your warring on the city,
and tear it down'
[and encourage him[a]]."
26 And the wife of Uriah heard
that Uriah her husband had died;
and she lamented for her lord.
27 And the mourning passed;
and David sent
and [added[a] her] *took Bathsheba* to his house,
and she became his wife
and she bore him a son,
and the thing
that David had done
was bad[b] in Yahweh's eyes.

1a. Beyond the synoptic 1 Chr 20:1, *tšwbt hšnh* is found just 3x—in 1 Kgs 20:22, 26, where the king of Aram moves against Israel, and in 2 Chr 36:10, where the king of Babylon sends for Jehoiachin.

2a. Here DJD reconstructs the longest variant attested in Greek as best filling the space in 4QSam[a]: "and he saw from upon the roof of the king's house a woman bathing"; but it favors the short Syr reading as the most original: "and he saw a woman bathing."

3a. In GT, *tēn gynaika* is the direct obj. of *(ex)ezētēsen*.

b. In MT and B it is not clear whether it is David or another who suggests the woman's identity; LT's pl. *eipon* clarifies that it is not David.

c. Here 4QSam[a] ends by noting, like Josephus, that Uriah is Joab's armor-bearer.

4a. "She came to him" (MT) may suggest joint culpability. The later mention of the death of Abimelech at the hands of a woman may also be intended to suggest that Uriah's death is not caused by David alone.

b. The scroll 4QSam[a] does not read "from her uncleanness": though attested in both MT and GT, this is an addition to explain *mtqdšt*, which 4QSam[a] does read.

5a. Codex B's very literal *Egō eimi en gastri echō* probably attests *ʾnky hrh*, as in 4QSam[a], which is the actual order found in Gen 38:25 (the only other biblical occurrence of this phrase), but the opposite of MT word order here. However, LT supports MT, with *Syneilēpha egō*. Actually, 4QSam[a] reads the fuller *hnh ʾnky hrh*, with *hnh* reinforcing the independent pronoun as in 1 Sam 8:5; 10:22 (DJD 139).

6a. The MT is unusual in lacking "saying" before direct speech not otherwise introduced by a speaking word.

7a. At the end LT adds: "and he said, 'It is well [*šālôm*].'" This verse in Hebrew is still dominated by the sounds *š-l-ḥ* plus *m*.

8a. At the end of v. 8a, DJD reconstructs with Josephus, "and lie with your woman," as filling the space requirements in 4QSam[a].

b. On *mśʾt hmlk*, the textual tradition is very confused. Codex B offers a literal rendering of MT: *arsis tou basileōs*; but LT has *tōn parestēkotōn tō basilei* (this might retrovert to *mšrty hmlk*: in 13:17 *proestēkota* corresponds to *mšrt*). Given the several connections between the books of Samuel and Genesis, and especially the Joseph stories there, it is interesting that MT here appears to use *mśʾh* in a sense shared with Gen 43:34—food provided from the ruler's house or table (rather like the contemporary "take away" or "carry out"). Note the further link in v. 13 of eating, drinking, and becoming drunk in the presence of the great man.

10a. Here 4QSam[a] opens with *wygd* (presumably *hopʿal*), not *wygdw*.

11a. Codex B, like MT, has "the ark."

b. The GT renders *skwt* alliteratively by *skēnais*. McCarter argues that the place name Succoth is meant, and that Joab's base camp is there; but the parallelism of Joab and other leaders camping in open ground appears compelling. First Kings 20:12 depicts kings in the field resident in *skwt*.

c. For MT's *ḥyk*, DJD argues 4QSam[a] has space for the more common *ḥy yhwh*.

12a. Codex B's *kai ge* may attest *wgm*—LT has *kai*. Is B a conflation of MT and LT?

b. The term *wmmḥrt* is found elsewhere only twice in Leviticus—in 19:6 it ends a clause, as here in MT and B; in 7:16 it starts a clause, as here in LT. The LT can retrovert either to *wmmḥrt qrʾ* or to *wyhy mmḥrt wyqrʾ*.

13a. Here B follows MT closely; however, LT's pass. *emethysthē* for *wyškrhw* suggests that Uriah, not David, is the subj. of "he ate before him and drank."

14a. The LT uses the historic present for both verbs.

15a. In place of MT's pl. *hbw*, GT offers sg., whether *Eisagage* (B) or *Parados* (LT).

b. The MT's *ʾl mwl pny* appears pleonastic; B offers the simpler *ex enantias*, and LT only *eis*.

16a. Here LT uses a variant of the vb. it uses for *ṣwr* in v. 1.

17a. The LT appears to have read not *mʿbdy* but *mdbr*.

b. The LT and the majority Gk. tradition supports MT; however, B's "and they died, and also" retroverts to *wymtw wgm*: this requires two instances of *wāw* more than MT.

18a. Codex B's plus at the end of the verse, *lalēsai pros ton basilea*, is unique, likely inspired by the identical "all the news of the war" in both vv. 18 and 19.

21a. Here B makes Jerub-baal/Jeroboam to be "son of Ner"; elsewhere in MT and GT, Ner is father of Abner and/or of Kish, and so belongs in Saul's wider family.

b. This report of the woman's action uses exactly the same terms as Judg 9:53. On its own, *pelaḥ* can refer to a "millstone," presumably strictly meaning a "slice" of stone (in 1 Sam 30:12 it is a slice of cake). And *rekeb* on its own can also refer to an upper millstone (Deut 24:6). The GT's *klasma mylou*, here and in Judg 9:53, means "a fragment of a millstone."

c. In place of *b* in MT's "Thebez," GT attests *m* or *mn*.

d. Again B offers *Kai ge* for MT's *gam*.

22a. After the first two words in MT, Codex B offers *Iōab pros ton basilea eis Ierousalēm*. And after the final Joab of MT, both B and LT offer a substantial recapitulation of vv. 19b–21. The messenger's explanation in v. 23 reads more easily if David is actually reported as complaining as Joab predicts he will. One effect of the repetition of these words is to delay David's receipt of the news of Uriah's death. Is this the interest of an armchair commander in tactics, or a ploy to conceal his interest in the other news? The MT is shorter, but it is not easy to decide whether also more original.

b. The vb. *šālaḥ* (*qal*) + suf. occurs some 40x, almost always with divine subj. In 3 (or 5) cases in 2 Kgs 18–19//Isa 36–37, Sennacherib is the subj.; however, he is portrayed as an equivalent if not greater deity. The usage here with Joab as subj. is unique.

24a. The GT reads *ʿbdk* as pl., with Q.

25a. Codex B supports MT in attaching the f. suf. to "pull down" and m. suf. to the final *piʿel ḥzq*—the obj. is presumably "Joab." However, LT "omits" *wḥzqhw*.

27a. Here B's *synēgagen autēn* is the literal rendering of *wyʾsph*; and it also renders *ʾsp* in the similar 1 Sam 14:52 and 2 Sam 6:1. However, LT's *elabe* may have rendered a different underlying text, resuming 11:4 and anticipating 12:9, 10.

b. Here the Gk. *kai ponēron ephanē* corresponds to *wyrʿ* (MT), while in v. 25 *ʾl-yrʿ* was rendered *Mē ponēron estō*.

[1] The story of David, Bathsheba, Uriah, and Nathan is one of the best-known in the Bible. The main lines of the narrative are only too clear. David's army is on campaign, but he is not in the field with them. He sees the wife of one of his officers washing, sends for her, and lies with her. She finds she is pregnant and tells David. To disguise his paternity of her child, David has her husband summoned back to Jerusalem, but he refuses to visit his home. David gives instructions that, on his return to the campaign, Uriah be left exposed to the heat of the battle, and he is killed. Nathan the prophet confronts David with what he has done and radicalizes the divine promise he has already delivered.

The story was already linked in ancient times with the great penitential Ps 51. It anticipates the sin of David in 2 Sam 24 and leads to a restating of the divine promise issued as recently as 2 Sam 7: both of these chapters are integral elements of BTH and both involve a prophet or seer. And it is the sole narrative involving a prophet that is contributed by the author of Samuel to the account of David as king (Gad is briefly mentioned in 1 Sam 22:5 while David is still in flight from Saul). The telling of the story can be called both restrained and detailed: some of the detail is so lightly sketched as to be easily misunderstood. There are several powerful resonances with the census story—specifically with the beginning of that story, where Joab tries to prevent the count of the people but is overruled by David and, despite his opposition, needs to direct it (2 Sam 24:3–4). The ancient scribes have left several traces of their varying attempts to cope with the detail.

If the larger divine-human setting of this story is provided by 2 Sam 7 and 24, the more local human setting is also drawn from BTH, from the older account of David's relations with Ammon. The earlier contours of the story of David and the Ammonites can still be read in 1 Chr 19:1–20:3. This new episode, located at the end of the campaigns against Ammon, occupies the same position relative to them as had the census story in BTH, which it powerfully and suggestively anticipates. The much extended and powerful fresh composition within 2 Sam 11–12 has not simply used the end of the older Ammonite story as a backdrop: it also explores some of its gaps. Sending Joab to lead his army and do battle is no novelty for David. Even when Ammon has the help of some Aramaean allies, Joab has successfully completed a campaign against them and returned to Jerusalem (10:6–14). David himself has become involved only when the worsted Aramaeans enlist many more reinforcements (10:15–19). At the beginning of the new campaigning season, Joab returns to do battle in Ammon. And this time it is actually stated that David stays on in Jerusalem. However, even this detail (11:1 = 1 Chr 20:1) is only rendered problematic or suggestive in the context of the new story spun from it. We may assume that David stayed in Jerusalem the first time he sent Joab to Ammon (10:7). It was only because David subsequently become involved in the second stage of that campaign that the narrator found it useful to note the next time David dispatches Joab that the king himself is again uninvolved. And this time Joab is leading out not just the army but "all Israel" (like David in 10:17).

[2–5] Other details of the new story have also been drawn from the old context. The not-very-common temporal marker *lĕʿēṭ* ("at the time of") is reused in the phrase "at the time of the evening" (v. 2). And the verb that dominates the new story is also drawn from the old v. 1. This story about the misuse of authority reports eleven sendings: no other chapter of HB, however long, uses "send" more than seven times. In the context of the new story, the inherited verb describing his continued presence in Jerusalem becomes nicely ambiguous: *ywšb* can mean not only "dwelling" or "staying," but also "sitting." Within 11:1 read on its own, the verb suggests "staying." But read as the introduction to David enjoying an afternoon siesta (v. 2), the more leisurely "sitting" becomes no less attractive a reading. The MT has added to the wordplay in this opening sentence by replacing the original "kings" (*hmlkym*, as still read in both GT and

1 Chr 20:1) with "messengers" (*hml'kym*). This deliberate "mistake," in writing "when messengers go out to battle, David sent Joab," heightens the expectation of readers that trouble must be coming. It is a clever comment on David himself, and on Joab, who will act as his message boy in sending Uriah back to Jerusalem and on to his death in the field.

David's viewing a woman as he walks on his roof terrace (v. 2) is a scene that has fascinated—and been exploited by—storytellers, painters, filmmakers, as well as commentators. The story of the following encounter is very briefly told and leaves many gaps to be filled in by (voyeuristic) imagination. But the attentive reader is also guided by the wider text. David's "going about" (*hthlk*) on his roof should take us back to 1 Sam 23–30. When Jonathan left him, David and his men started going about where they went about (23:13); Abigail brought a present for those who were going about at his heels (25:27); and David sent presents to the elders of Judah in several locations where he went about (30:31). David when roaming had "form": predatory and unscrupulous. And during this earlier roaming, he gained two wives, at least one of whom had already been married and was very beautiful.

Huge attention has been directed to the nature of the washing or bathing being done by the woman whom David observes from his roof: ritual or nonritual, proactive or reactive. I have translated *rḥṣt* (v. 2) by "washing" rather than "bathing," mostly because the same verb reappears in the MT in David's instruction to Uriah to go home "and wash [his] feet" (v. 8). But the distinction in NRSV (and how many more?) between "bathe" (v. 2) and "wash" (v. 8) has an ancient pedigree: it follows the different verbs in GT, which distinguish between what might often be done in a bathhouse (v. 2) and more limited rinsing off (v. 8).

Only three women are described in HB as "washing": none of them belongs to Israel, but each bears responsibility for one of Israel's leaders. The daughter of Pharaoh finds Moses as she washes in the river (Exod 2:5) and goes on to adopt him. Ruth from Moab is instructed to wash before her nighttime encounter with Boaz (3:3), with whom she will become an ancestress of David. And this woman, who we learn is wife of a Hittite, is to become Solomon's mother. Although three instances are insufficient to prove the existence of a stock theme, such a literary context should serve to set limits to social-historical speculation about ritual washing in ancient Israel.

Unlike Ruth and Pharaoh's daughter, this woman is observed as she washes—indeed, it may have been precisely to protect the latter from being watched that the servants of the Egyptian were walking on the riverbank at the time. This woman is observed, and is observed as being very good looking. The description of Bathsheba is used of only two other women in HB: Rebekah (Gen 24:16; 26:7) and Vashti and other young women (Esth 1:11; 2:3). The books of Samuel are remarkable for their attention to the looks of principal characters: the attractiveness of David, Tamar, and Absalom is also noted. And Abigail is even more fully described (1 Sam 25:3): *ṭwbt-śkl wypt tʾr*. David arranges for inquiries to be made about her, although apparently simply to confirm his own supposition[8] that she is the wife of one of his own officers, and possibly daughter of another.[9] His next sending is not for intelligence but for action; the action is described very quickly: in the Hebrew of vv. 4–5, half of the words are verbs. All but one of the ten verbs simply advance the story line in a manner that occasions no surprise and requires little comment: "sent . . . took . . . came . . . lay . . . returned . . . conceived . . . sent . . . reported . . . said . . ." The man's role is described more briefly in [at least three of[10]] the first four verbs, and the woman's in the remaining five or six. David has frequently been "taking" (v. 4) throughout the books of Samuel. However, since this story develops the "sending" theme from the parent 2 Sam 10, we should notice that the last "taking" of which we have read was of David's servants by the king of Ammon (10:4), and they too were taken to be mistreated by Hanun.

The tenth and only controversial verb appears in a participial comment: it is not one of the nine contributors to the main story line just listed. And unless there is a clear indication to the contrary, the action described in the participle *mtqdšt* should be understood as contemporaneous with the action in the previous main clause "and he lay with her while she was . . ." The *hitpaʿel* of a Hebrew verb can describe what one does to or for oneself: *mtqdšt* can mean "was consecrating herself." But a verb in the *hitpaʿel* can also describe showing oneself (rightly or wrongly) as being in a certain state. She might be either demonstrating that she is *qdš*, or making herself out to be *qdš*. Only once else in HB can we find a singular subject of the *hitpaʿel* of *qdš*[11]—and there (Ezek 38:23) it is no less than the Deity who is "making himself out to be holy" or "demonstrating his holiness."

The MT and 4QSam[a] agree in reading this participle (*mtqdšt*); and it is reasonable to suppose that it represents the original text. If so, then LT has doubly obscured the situation: first by using a Greek perfect participle to render the Hebrew participle; and second by using the verb *louō* ("wash/bathe") to render *mtqdšt*. The GT (LT and B) use *louomenēn* (correctly in the present participle) in v. 2 to render *rḥṣt* ("washing"). For LT, the woman *is bathing* herself when David sees her (v. 2) and she *has bathed* herself when he lies with her (v. 4). Put

8. It has been suggested that the subject of "said" is impersonal: "and someone said"; but the plural is more often used impersonally, as at the beginning of v. 10 ("and they reported").

9. Bathsheba's father may be the same Eliam as is enumerated in 2 Sam 23:34 as son of Ahithophel the Gilonite, just a few names before her husband, Uriah the Hittite (23:39). However, we read quite different names in LT.

10. The fact that a subject comes to her king when he sends for her (MT) does not imply her complicity in adultery—and GT's reading "and he came to her" lacks any such suggestion.

11. Normally it is priests (and Levites) in the plural who "consecrate themselves" or "demonstrate their consecrated state."

another way, LT understands the washing (v. 2) and purifying (v. 4) to be the same process in time and essence. However, this is almost certainly mistaken.

The MT has the support of 4QSam[a] in reading *mtqdšt*, but not in adding *mṭmʾth* to the two-word circumstantial clause. This term has proved to be no less controversial than the participle that it supplements and interprets. The LT and B are clearly familiar with the text of MT, and both offer a rendering: B has the more regular and general *akatharsia* ("impurity"); LT offers the more precise *aphedros* ("menstruation"). These two Greek terms are very closely associated with each other throughout the legislation on menstruation and other impurities (Lev 15:16–33); but no form of *qdš* is found throughout these detailed paragraphs. It is also true that the normal opposite of "impure" (*ṭmʾ*) is "pure" (*ṭhr*), not "sacred/holy" (*qdš*). Saul suspected that David must not be "pure" when he absented himself from eating with him (1 Sam 20:26). The mismatch in categories ("consecrating herself from her impurity/uncleanness") tends in the same direction as the text-critical evidence: that the shorter text of 4QSam[a] is more original, and that "from her impurity" is a secondary attempt to explain just what Bathsheba is doing or demonstrating at the time when David lies with her.[12] These sacral terms are very rare in the narrative books; but we find Naaman instructed to wash (*rḥṣ*) in order to become pure/clean (*ṭhr*) in 2 Kgs 5:10–14.

The long-standing interpretation of this "circumstantial" phrase is that at the time of intercourse (or at least when observed by the king immediately beforehand), the woman is still attending to ritual washing following her monthly period. However, three critical points have to be conceded: *ṭmʾh* is not the normal Hebrew term for menstruation; *qdš* is never used in connection with menstruation; and the postbiblical Jewish institution of ritual bathing following a woman's period is unknown in HB (unless here!). Since there is only one other instance of the *hitpaʿel* of *qdš* with a singular subject, it seems more sensible to start an interpretation from Ezek 38:23: Bathsheba is demonstrating something about herself. Neither prophet nor narrator ever blames her as being complicit in an adulterous affair. In the immediately following and consequential tale of Ammon's rape of Tamar, Tamar desperately asks her half brother to seek permission from the king. But there is no one to whom Bathsheba can appeal beyond the king, when David himself is making advances on her—no one except God and her own conscience: "while she was declaring herself holy" (v. 4, 4QSam[a]).

[6–8] Pregnant with the king's child, Bathsheba does the next sending (v. 5), and her message causes a further flurry of sending (v. 6). David greets Uriah, sent back from the front, with a series of questions: about the welfare of Joab

12. The detailed discussion of this verse by Chankin-Gould and others makes no reference to the absence of "from her uncleanness" from 4QSam[a].

and the army and the campaign. Whatever responses Uriah makes do not detain the narrative. David's purpose in having Uriah sent is not to receive a bulletin from the front, but to reunite husband and wife; and so he sends him on his way in two two-word commands: "go-down to-your-house, and-wash your-'legs'" (v. 8a). Since *regel* can refer to the whole limb from hip to toe, or any part of it, the king's second instruction might simply wish his officer the refreshment of a foot wash. However, since "the legs" are regularly used as a euphemism for the genitals, not least in the portion of Ruth (3:4, 7) just mentioned, he is more likely giving him permission to sleep with his wife. Uriah does not leave the king's house alone. The GT has him accompanied by (at least) one of the king's staff; and MT is more specific: a portion of rations leaves with him.

[9–11] When David learns that he has gone no further than the palace gate, he asks why after a journey he has not gone to his own house. His response is eloquent and damning, especially from the mouth of an army officer. Why should he go to his house when the ark and Israel and Judah are in temporary quarters—and when even the commander is camping on the face of the field?[13] And why, by implication, should even the king be in his house in Jerusalem when the ark and all his people are in temporary quarters? David himself has noted the mismatch between the ark's situation and his own (7:2, BTH); Uriah now links "the ark" from 2 Sam 7 with "Israel and Judah" from another text in BTH (2 Sam 24:9). Once his king protested to the priest at Nob that he and his men were sexually abstinent on a mission. How can he, Uriah, go home and lie with his wife? These culminating words suggest that Uriah has understood the sexual import of David's instruction to wash his "legs." His refusal to carry out the king's command is prefaced by an oath on David's life. For Rashban, the medieval Jewish commentator, Uriah is justly killed for his triple disobedience to David's orders to go to his house. (He also notes that all officers leave a bill of divorce behind before going into battle.) However, Rashi suggests that it is Uriah's talking about "my lord Joab and the servants of my lord" (v. 11) that costs him his life: saying these words to David amounts to disloyalty. They might also have led to the tradition shared by 4QSam[a] (v. 3) and Josephus that Uriah is Joab's armor-bearer.

In his eloquent refusal to take rest in his own home (v. 11), Uriah mentions the temporary situation of the ark first; and that has suggested to many readers that he is pointedly reminding David of the sentiment ascribed to him in Ps 132: that he will not go to his home or get on his bed or allow sleep to his eyes till he has found a resting place for Yahweh and his ark (132:3–5). That seems very likely; however, it does not of itself solve the conundrum of how to read together the first two principal elements of his disclaimer (in v. 11):

13. Normally what is "on the face of the field" has been discarded, or is even dung (2 Kgs 9:37; Jer 9:21). But in 1 Sam 14:25, the wild honey eaten by Jonathan was found there.

The ark and Israel and Judah are living in huts,
and my lord Joab and the servants of my lord are camping on the face of the field.
And what of me . . . ?

Does the first line state the general national situation, and does he only in the second line turn to the campaign against Ammon? Or does the first line also refer to the current hostilities? More particularly, does the mention of the ark tell us no more than we have learned in 2 Sam 6 and the beginning of 2 Sam 7—that the ark is now in Jerusalem, but not yet in its final home? Or does Uriah tell us that the ark is in the field with the people, as we found it back in the time of Eli? The answer is relevant to our understanding of 15:24–25 below.

[12–15] David changes tack. Uriah should remain in Jerusalem for the remainder of the present day and return to the campaign the next day. He calls for the man and feasts him and makes him drunk . . . and the narrator's next few words about Uriah ("and he went out in the evening to lie on his bed . . .") leads the reader to wonder whether David's new tactics have worked. However, even when drunk, the loyal officer's bed is "with the servants of his lord"; his refusal to comply with David's repeated instruction is underlined in the final words of v. 13: "and to his [own] house he did not go down." The keyword "send" has played no part in the report of David's dealings face-to-face with Uriah, neither in his repeated instructions to go home nor in his call to a meal. But "send" reappears in David's Plan B. Uriah is sent back to Joab, bearing his own death certificate. David's letter to his commander only sketches a plan, but it is quite explicit about the expected outcome: Uriah should die.

[16–24] The king and his principal henchman understand each other well. Joaḇ's dispatch of Uriah to his death takes up no more narrative space (vv. 16–17) than David's sending him back to the field (vv. 14–15)—or indeed than the adulterous rape that starts the spiral of events (vv. 4–5). Much more narrative space is required for the preparation of deception, whether earlier the stratagem to cover David's fathering of the child (vv. 6–13), or now the terms in which David should learn of Uriah's death (vv. 18–24). Even if Joab understands David, it appears that the new messenger who will carry the news to Jerusalem is to be as ignorant of what it is all about as David believes Uriah to be—or at least public opinion (we cannot know whether Uriah's refusal to visit his home represents only his soldier's code or also the refusal of even a loyal soldier to act as willing pawn for a king who has taken his wife).

But what is the extent of Joab's understanding? In the story of the census, which this story anticipates at several levels, David forces Joab to carry out a mission of which he deeply disapproves (24:3–4). It is an attractive suggestion that Joab instructs his messenger to cite the case of Abimelech, not just killed outside a city wall but killed by a woman, because he knows or thinks he knows what it is all about—because he intuits that a woman is involved in this fatal story too.

The death of Uriah is viewed from four perspectives: what David instructs; what Joab actually does; how Joab briefs his messenger; and what the messenger actually says when the time comes. What Joab does takes twice as many words to tell (vv. 16–17) as the orders David has given (v. 15b). And even in MT's shorter version, the message Joab gives the messenger is twice as long again (vv. 19b–21). The lengths of vv. 19b–21 and 22b–24 are more similar to each other whether we are reading the shorter version in MT without the longer repetitions or the longer GT, which includes them (4QSam[a] is not extant after v. 20). How we read together Joab's coaching of his messenger and the envoy's actual performance before his king depends to an extent on which version we are reading. In the longer Greek text, the audience with the king proceeds just as Joab has expected, and just as he has briefed his messenger; and the messenger is almost word perfect in what he says to David. The shorter text of MT does allow us to imagine a similar scenario—but simply one that is narrated as briefly as possible, but with two assumptions: that Joab does know how David will react, and that the messenger will respond exactly as he has been told. But MT is also open to a quite different reading. The messenger, like all good and trusted emissaries, is entrusted to improvise at his own discretion; and he chooses to put the death of Uriah in the context of further losses than Joab has specified.

[25–27] Separating vv. 25–27 as a subparagraph in MT underscores the contrast between what Yahweh takes amiss (v. 27b) and David's advice to Joab through his envoy about what *not* to take amiss (v. 25). But it also emphasizes the innocence of the woman at the center of the story. When she hears of her husband's death, she observes the appropriate mourning for Uriah, who in the space of a very few words is called both her "man" and her "lord" (v. 26). It is David, and not she herself, who is waiting for the end of that period of lamentation: as soon as it is over, he sends and takes/adds her to his household, and she becomes his wife (v. 27a). As suggested in the note above, the context of "took" (GT) is more local, and that of "added" (MT) more distant—but also more damning. It is more acceptable for a king to take into his service every able or choice warrior who comes to his attention than every beautiful woman whom he eyes. Though a common verb, it is only here in MT that *ʾsp* ("add") has a female object.

Only at the end of this series of verbs comes one where the feminine subject corresponds to real activity on the woman's part: and—appropriately for someone added/taken to his house—even her "giving birth" is "for him." David alone is to blame for what has been done. There has been no consent on the part of Uriah's wife. This short paragraph is bracketed by the rival perspectives of David (and, he hopes, Joab) and of Yahweh. And the theme of eyes and perspectives is resumed in another subparagraph (12:11–12). The message that follows Yahweh's displeasure begins the following paragraph. David has advised Joab to reckon Uriah's death as an accident of war and to strengthen his assault on Rabbah, which should be "torn down" (the verb *hrs*, uncommon in prose narrative, has been drawn from BTH—it survives in 1 Chr 20:1).

2 Samuel 12:1–25 Nathan Rebukes David

1 And Yahweh sent Nathan *the prophet* to David,
and he came to him
and said to him:
"*Explain to me this case.*
Two men there were in one city, one rich and one poor.
2 The rich had very many flocks and herds.
3 And the poor had nothing but one small ewe lamb,
which he had bought
and saved for himself[a]
and kept alive
and raised with him and his children together:
from his [portion] *food* she ate,
from his cup she drank,
and in his bosom she lay;
and she came to be to him like a daughter.
4 And a traveller came to the rich man,
and he was sparing
of taking from his own flock or herd
to prepare for the wayfarer
who came to him;
and he took the poor man's lamb
and prepared it for the man
who came to him."
5 And David's anger was very hot against the man;
and he said to Nathan,
"By Yahweh's life, the man who [does[a]] *did* this is death's son.
6 And the lamb he shall repay fourfold,[a]
because he did this thing
and did not spare."
7 And Nathan said to David,
"You are the man *who does this*.
This is what Yahweh, God of Israel, says:
'I, I anointed you as king over Israel;
and I, I delivered you[a] from the hand of Saul;

8 and I gave you [the house] *everything* of your lord
and *his* [the] wives [of your lord] in your bosom,
and I gave you the house of Israel and Judah;
and if too little *for you*, I will add for you like these and more so.[a]
9 Why[a] have you scorned [the word[b] of] Yahweh,
doing what is evil in *his* [my] eyes?
Uriah the Hittite you have struck down with the sword,
and his wife you have taken as your wife;
and him you have slain by the sword of the sons of Ammon.
10 Well then, a sword shall not turn from your house forever,
on account that you have scorned me
and taken the wife of Uriah the Hittite to be your wife.'

11 Thus has Yahweh said:
'I am in fact raising[a] evil against you from your house,
and I shall take your wives before your eyes
and give them to your neighbor[s],
and he shall lie with your wives before the eyes of this sun.
12 For you, you acted in secret, but I, I shall do this thing in face of
all Israel and in face of [the] *this* sun.'"

13 And David said to Nathan,
"I have sinned against Yahweh."

And Nathan said to David,
"Yahweh too has transferred your sin;
you shall not die.
14 On account of the fact that you have [despised] *provoked*,
yes, [despised[a]] *provoked among* the enemies[b] [of] Yahweh in
this matter,
even[c] the son born to you shall die, yes, die."[d]
15 And Nathan went to his house;
and [Yahweh] *God*[a] smote the child
that Uriah's wife had borne to David,
and it became sick.[b]
16 And David sought God[a] on behalf of the child,
and he kept a fast,
and he came
and spent the night
[and lay] *in sacking*[b] on the ground.
17 And the elders of his[a] house rose up against[b] him,
raising him from the ground;

but he was not willing
and did not eat[b] food with[b] them.
18 And it came to be on the seventh day,
and the child died.
And David's servants were afraid
to inform him
that the child had died;
for they said,
"Look.
While the child was alive,
we spoke to him *of raising him from the ground*,
but he did not listen to our voice;
and how shall we say to him
'The child has died'?
He will do a mischief."
19 And David saw
that his servants were whispering among themselves;
and David understood
that the child was dead;
and David said to his servants,
"Has the child died?"
and they said,
"He has died."
20 And David rose from the ground
and washed
and anointed himself
and changed his clothes
and came to the house of [Yahweh] *God*
and prostrated himself *to him*;
and he came to his house
and asked *to eat food*,
and they placed food for him
and he ate.
21 And his servants said to him,
"What is this thing you have done?
For the sake[a] of the child alive you fasted[b]
and wept
and stayed awake;
and
as the child died
you rose[b]
and ate food *and drank*?"

22 And [he] David said,
"While the child was alive,
I fasted
and wept,
for I said,
'Who knows?
Yahweh may show me favor
and the child may live.'
23 But now he has died.
Whyever should I fast?
Shall I be able
to bring him back again?
I am going to him,
but he shall not come back to me."
24 And David comforted Bathsheba his wife;
and he [came] *spoke*[a] to her
and lay with her.
And she conceived
and bore a son,
and he called his name Solomon.
And Yahweh, he loved him.
25 And he sent by hand of Nathan the prophet,
and he called his name Jedidiah/"Yahweh's beloved,"
[for the sake] *by the word*[a] of Yahweh.

3a. The OL does not attest the plus in GT.

5a. MT uses the [perpetual] ptc. "who is [always] doing," which is more effective than the aorist participle in GT "who has done [a single act]."

6a. Codex B says "sevenfold."

7a. Some Gk. MSS have the more grammatical *ho rysamenos* instead of the more literal *errysamēn* of B. The LT has *egō* on its own twice, not *egō eimi*, and *exeilamēn* for *errysamēn* ("protect, rescue").

8a. Here B offers *kata tauta* for MT's *khnh wkhnh*, and LT has *kathōs tauta*. Each may have read *khnh* alone. The duplication is unique; the single form is found also in Gen 41:19 and Job 23:14.

9a. Codex B has causal *hoti* in place of interrogative *mdwʿ*, and LT has *kai ti hoti*.

b. The LT does not attest *dbr* (cf. 1 Sam 15:13 above).

11a. The participial *hnny mbyʾ* suggests continuity appropriate to "forever."

14a. The majority tradition in GT, including LT, has *parorgizōn parōrgisas* ("make angry"); B has *paroxynōn parōxynas* ("provoke, irritate"). The very different renderings, word after word, in B and LT, raise acutely the question whether one is revised from the other or each is an independent translation. Just once more is *nʾṣ* used in Samuel: in 1 Kgdms 2:17 GT renders it with *ēthetoun* ("disregard").

b. Here 4QSam[a] clearly reads *dbr* ("word") for MT's *ʾyby* before *yhwh*. Also, LT's *en tois hypenantiois*, whether before or after *ton kyrion*, may attest *bʾybym*.

c. For MT's *gam*, B typically has *kai ge*, LT *kai* alone, and Codex A nothing. How far does this *gam* resonate with that in v. 13?

d. Here 4QSam[a] has the pass. *ywmt* (attested in GT): "shall be put to death."

15a. The MT's *yhwh* is supported by B; however, 4QSam[a] supported by LT reads *ʾlwhym*.

b. The final *wyʾnš* is not present in 4QSam[a] but is attestedby GT. This is a unique occurrence of the finite vb.: it is known otherwise only as *qal* pass. ptc. *wyʾnš* probably dropped out of because of its similarity to the following *wybqš*.

16a. For MT's *ʾt-hʾlhym*, 4QSam[a] offers *mn-yhwh*.

b. Here 4QSam[a] with [*wb*]*ʾ wyškb bśq ʾrṣʾ* supports (*ekoimēthē*) *en sakkō* of LT and much of GT.

17a. The LT agrees with MT. Codex B's *tou oikou* without *autou* may attest *hbyt* rather than *bytw*; or "his" may have been accidentally omitted.

b. Here 4QSam[a] has three readings that differ from MT: *ʾlyw* for *ʿlyw*, *brh* for *brʾ*, and *ʾwtm* for *ʾtm*.

21a. Several witnesses prefer *bʿwd* (as in v. 22) for *bʿbwr* here (as also in v. 25); the lack of article with *ḥy* may go more easily with *bʿwd*.

b. Notice attractive wordplay on *ṣamtā* ("fasted") and *qamtā* ("rose").

24a. The Gk. *lalein* renders *dbr* in both 11:19 and 12:18; and hence LT has probably read *wydbr* here—however, B supports MT's *wybʾ*.

25a. The LT attests *bdbr* for *bʿbwr* in MT and B.

[1–6] Yahweh's sending Nathan to David (v. 1) is inseparably linked with his bad opinion of David's action (11:27b). But it is typical of the ancient manuscript tradition that the decisive action of a principal character is placed at the head of a new paragraph or chapter. This is the second of three encounters reported between David and Nathan. In 2 Sam 7, Nathan is first consulted by David and goes on to offer his own opinion about the building of a house, before receiving the authentic divine word in a subsequent vision. This was typical of the older narrative in BTH: Josiah's dealings with the prophetess Huldah follow a similar pattern (2 Kgs 22:11–20). But here, in a style more familiar in the developed books of Samuel and Kings, Yahweh and his prophet take the initiative and confront the king. In the third (1 Kgs 1:11–40), Nathan encourages Bathsheba to be the first to inform the ailing David about the coronation of Adonijah and "remind" him of his "commitment" to have Solomon succeed him, and then the prophet reinforces her message.

It is often claimed that 12:1–25 as a whole is secondary because we expect a name-giving to follow immediately after the report of the birth (11:27a). However, it is precisely the absence of what we normally expect—an absence underscored by its presence in the case of the second child born to the same parents (12:24)—that adds to the poignancy of this tale. The child's imminent death is announced as soon as it is born: it seems there is no need to name a child that will not be.

Nathan's parable is brilliantly crafted. The situation of the two (human) characters is sketched very briefly in single-word strokes (vv. 1–3) till we reach the one little lamb, whose depiction is lingered over in loving detail. And when the prophet describes the ewe lamb[14] ("ate . . . drank . . . in his bosom she lay" [12:3]), he cannily—even uncannily—repeats to David almost word for word what Uriah has said to him ("Shall I eat, drink, and lie with my wife?" [11:11]). The climax of the description ("and she came to be to him like a daughter" [*bat*]) plays on the first element of Bath-Sheba's name. Similarly, when Nathan later expands on the divine judgment and reports Yahweh's declaring that he has given David "Israel and Judah" (v. 8), he again repeats a formulation unusual in Samuel ("Israel and Judah"), which David has already heard from Uriah's lips (11:11).

But the clever links go far wider than the immediate context. The offending action, as Nathan describes it (whether it is simply a story told to the king or an apparent case brought to him for judgment, as explicitly in LT), has been against a "poor" man; and this is repeatedly stressed (12:1, 3, 4). The particular word used here for "poor" is relatively uncommon in most of HB: outside Samuel, it is used only in Ps 82:3; Eccl 4:14; 5:8 (7); and fourteen times in Prov 13–29. Psalm 82 is a powerful evocation of impartial judgment, by which the rights of the needy and poor are to be maintained. Only one other person is so described (or better, so describes himself) in all of 1–2 Samuel. David (now called on to judge) has called himself *rāš* (the same word as here) when querying the offer made to him of marriage to Saul's daughter (1 Sam 18:23). He should have a particular fellow feeling for someone else so described. But the connection is even more telling: when David protests that he is too "poor" to afford the bride-price for the king's daughter, Saul grandly tells him that the evidence (counted in their foreskins) of one hundred dead Philistines will suffice. Saul has assumed that such an attempt will cost David his life. David survives and marries Michal; but now by engineering Uriah's death at enemy hands, he shows that he has learned well from Saul.

It is not easy in English to catch the double use of *ḥāmal* in vv. 4 and 6. I have used "spare" because it works in both contexts; but the Hebrew verb has the richer connotation of "have compassion." No difficulty over securing a suitable rendering in English should obscure the fact that this verb—so important in the story of Saul, Agag, and Samuel (1 Sam 15:3, 9, 15), which finalized the rejection of Saul—reappears precisely in the story in which another prophet pronounces divine judgment on David. It is otherwise used only twice in these books, where Saul praises the people of Ziph for their compassion to him in betraying David's whereabouts (1 Sam 23:21) and where David has

14. The f. *kbśh* is much rarer than the m.: it is prescribed as a sacrifice alongside two (m.) *kbśym* in Lev 14:10 and Num 6:14; and is used also in Gen 21:28–30.

compassion on Jonathan's son (2 Sam 21:7). Two further links underscore the connection with Samuel's conveying the divine rejection of Saul: "despise" (*bzh*), also from 1 Sam 15:9, reappears in 2 Sam 12:9, 10; and "word of Yahweh" (15:10, 13, 23, 26) is used in 2 Sam 12:9 (MT).

In 1 Sam 20:31, as in David's angry outburst here (v. 5), it is in passion that Saul identifies David as "son of death" (*bn-mwt*). There (1 Sam 20:32) Jonathan immediately voices the more judicial question: Should the "son of death" also "be put to death"? But does "son of death" mean "dead man" (as in "You're a dead man") or "Death's agent"? Hebrew has no upper case letters with which to distinguish personal names. But we should remember that Death (*Môt*) was a god throughout Israel's neighbors. Is it already a verdict, or simply an accusation? When Mephibosheth uses the similar expression "men of death" in 2 Sam 19:28 (29), he is apparently accusing his own (Saul's) family: they "have never been other than deadly to you." Then in 1 Kgs 2:26, as in 1 Sam 20:31, we again find the issue of not putting to death this "man of death." When David calls the rich man of Nathan's parable a "son of death" (12:5), he uses a much more flexible expression than the verdict Nathan will shortly utter (12:14): "he shall surely die." There Nathan reintroduces "son," as independently significant, into the discourse from 11:27; and he also suggests the opposition of Death to the living Yahweh (by whom he swears), just as Saul has done (1 Sam 20:31).

[7–10] The killing of Uriah is mentioned twice in Nathan's accusation (v. 9), and the taking of his wife just once:

> Uriah the Hittite you have struck down with the sword,
> and his wife you have taken as your wife;
> and him you have slain by the sword of the sons of Ammon.

Nathan does not charge David with the original act of adultery but concentrates on David's responsibility for Uriah's death. He has not himself wielded the sword. However, by taking Bathsheba and adding her to his wives, he has demonstrated his interest in Uriah's death even though the killing was achieved by Ammonite agency. Nathan's statement of the divine complaint is very like Elijah's against King Ahab (1 Kgs 21:19). In order to acquire Naboth's vineyard, Jezebel arranges for scoundrels to lay false capital charges against Naboth. On his execution, the king goes to take what has now become royal property, only to be faced by "Thus says Yahweh, 'Have you murdered, and also taken?'" Elijah's direct denunciation is more typical of prophets in the narrative books of the HB; Nathan's more oblique parabolic approach entraps the powerful and scheming David.

"You have scorned me" (v. 10) is a more precise resumption of LT's shorter "You have scorned Yahweh" (v. 9) than of MT's longer "You have scorned the word of Yahweh." Given the context of murder and adultery, we should recall the singular *dbr yhwh* in Deut 5:5 (unique there within Deuteronomy), which introduces precisely the Decalogue. The conjunction of "your house" and "forever" in words spoken by Nathan (middle of v. 10) reminds us powerfully of what Yahweh has promised in 2 Sam 7:11–13. That David's house will forever now be under the sword turns the earlier promise into a threat.[15] David's attitude to Yahweh and his standards has been like that of the worthless fellows to Saul's accession as king (1 Sam 10:27), or Goliath's to a stripling opponent unworthy of him (17:42), or most recently Michal's to seeing David's dancing before the ark: simple contempt (2 Sam 6:16).

[11–12] Links have already been noted between Nathan's words to David in this chapter and in 2 Sam 7: "house" and "forever" (v. 10). There is a further link in the next short subparagraph (vv. 11–12). In 2 Sam 7:12, Yahweh is to "raise up" (*hqym*) David's "seed" after him; now here he is raising ill over him out of his own house. The ill will relate to David's women, though it is not specified just how it may relate to his "seed." David has learned subterfuge in his dealings with Saul. Both noun and verb forms of *str* ("secret") are used of him in 1 Sam 19:2; 20:5, 19, 24; 23:19; 26:1. And now, even as king, the ways of secrecy are still typical of him. However, some of the language in this short unit is unique within the books of Samuel. Samuel invited criticism of himself in face of Yahweh and his anointed (1 Sam 12:3); Saul begged Samuel to honor him in face of the elders of his people and of Israel (15:30). But Yahweh's own declaration, as cited by Nathan, promises action that will be taken in face of the sun and all Israel.

[13a] David's response to the terrible and sufficiently specific threat is given in all brevity and accorded its own subparagraph in MT. David has once denied sinning against Saul (1 Sam 24:11 [12]). But here—as in 2 Sam 24:10, 17 (BTH), which this story anticipates—the admission of sin is made without any excuse or prevarication. Nathan has reported Yahweh's claim that Yahweh himself has been scorned by David's behavior; and David simply admits that his sin has been against Yahweh. Pss 10 (vv. 3, 13–14) and 74 (vv. 10, 18) are useful intertexts. In Ps 10, the wicked not only scorn Yahweh but boast he will not call them to account; and Ps 74 complains of the enemy, an impious people, scorning Yahweh's name. Through Nathan, Yahweh does call wicked David to account.

[13b–25] It is often asked why the child still must die if David is forgiven after his admission of sin. But full forgiveness with release from punishment is not in question (Stoebe 2:309). The term *hʿbyr* is well known in the books of Samuel and always implies movement from one place or side to another. It

15. In an oral preface to the paper published as Fokkelman (2010) the author likened Nathan's three roles in Samuel–Kings to the Hegelian scheme: promise of an eternal house (2 Sam 7: thesis); sword eternally against that house (2 Sam 12: antithesis); Solomon securely on the throne (1 Kgs 1: synthesis).

is used of Jesse's parading his sons in front of Samuel (1 Sam 16:8–10), or of Jonathan's shooting an arrow past his servant (20:36). It is used of bringing David and his household back across the Jordan (2 Sam 19) and of transferring the monarchy from the house of Saul to the house of David (3:10).[16] Thus *hʿbyr* does not mean "forgive," or at least does not mean "forgive" in the sense of wish away, or remove the sin into nothingness. David has already been warned by Nathan (v. 11) that trouble will be raised up from within his house. His confession leads to the response that he will not (immediately) die for his crime, but that the first piece of trouble in his house will be the death of the child just born.

This story offers an anticipatory commentary on the older census story (2 Sam 24). At this point it is both briefer and more explicit than the master tale. There David asks for his guilt to be transferred (24:10), and it is only after Israel has been substantially damaged that he asks that his own house and he himself should take responsibility (24:17). Here he is told immediately of the cost to his house and to his new son of what he has done. It is only in 2 Sam 12:13 and 24:10, within HB as a whole, that *hʿbyr* takes *ḥṭʾt* ("sin") or *ʿwn* ("wrong, guilt") as its object.[17]

The position of Dhorme (363) is not that the whole of ch. 12 is secondary, but only the first half. Dhorme argues (360) that the return of Nathan to his house (v. 15a) concludes the story in 12:1–15a, and he notes that Yahweh's stroke on the child (v. 15b) follows naturally after the note on his displeasure (11:27). He quotes the departure of Hannah after her song (1 Sam 2:11) as similar; and Stoebe adds the departures of Samuel (1 Sam 15:34), Jonathan (21:1), and Bathsheba (2 Sam 11:4). I find the three examples from 1 Samuel convincing. However, the nearest of Stoebe's proposed parallels points me in the opposite direction. If the others do rightly suggest a pattern of return home as signal of section end, then the departures of Bathsheba and Nathan disrupt this pattern. The results of what has passed between David and Bathsheba and between David and Nathan are not yet obvious when Bathsheba and (later) Nathan leave the king's house for their own place: the actions are not yet complete, and both have to do with the child. Several scholars (such as Rudnig 2010) believe they can lay bare much more complex literary stratification in this story.

Many commentators share the surprise of David's staff at his apparently abnormal behavior both before and after the death of his child. Calum M. Carmichael (private communication) urges that David's emotions are very mixed

16. Given the extent to which v. 13 resonates also with 1 Sam 2:22–25, it is interesting that MT reads *maʿăbirîm* in 2:24.

17. The term *ḥṭʾt* is also obj. of these vbs.: *ksh* ("cover"), Ps 85:2 (3); *nśʾ* ("bear, lift"), Gen 50:17; Exod 10:17; 32:32 (the alternative Moses poses is that Yahweh "wipe away" him from his book); 1 Sam 15:25; *lqḥ* ("take"), Deut 9:21; *hsyr* ("turn away"), Isa 27:9; *mḥh* ("wipe away"), Isa 44:22; and, though doubtfully, *sph* ("sweep away"), Isa 30:1; cf. also Isa 6:7; Ps 109:14; Neh 4:5 (3:37). Psalm 51 uses the images of washing and purifying.

up: on seeing a woman, he sends for her; on hearing Nathan's story, he overreacts; he mourns before, not after, his child's death. But David has been told—and we have no evidence that his staff knows this—that his sick child will die. And we readers know what the characters in the books of Samuel cannot know: that this story is shaped in part by themes from 2 Sam 24. There, though David's guilt is transferred to his people, he opts for the punishments in which Yahweh might demonstrate his mercy, and his people are not totally destroyed. Here, though he sees his son struck down, he desperately intercedes. David's actions, at this point at least, are far from unreasonable.

David will seek (*bqš*) the Deity (v. 16) once more, in connection with the three-year famine (21:1)—another narrative with close links to 2 Sam 24. In the sense of "on behalf of," *bĕʿad* is relatively uncommon; it is used already in 2 Kgs 22:13 (BTH) in connection with an inquiry of the Deity in difficult times, and also in entreaties by Samuel (1 Sam 7:5, 9; 12:19, 23). The people of Jabesh fast when burying Saul (1 Sam 31:13), and then David and his people when they hear that Saul and Jonathan are dead (2 Sam 1:12). Yet fasting is part of entreaty at Mizpah (1 Sam 7:5–6); and there are complaints in prophetic books that we have fasted but no one has heard. If we are to give sense to MT at the end of v. 16, it may be that David is lying prostrate, rather than kneeling with forehead on the ground (the more regular position of submission). The alternative text shared by 4QSam[a] and GT is closely linked with 1 Kgs 21:27 (the only instance in HB [MT] where "lie" (*škb*) is combined with sacking), where the acted penitence of Ahab leads to postponement of judgment. Either this tradition may have adjusted the text to highlight a comparison between David and Ahab, or MT may have avoided the comparison. Here (v. 17), as in 3:35 above, *brʾ* (a by-form of *brh*) is used for "eat" rather than the common *ʾkl*.

There are several stories in HB about death or danger to children. These often include their mother, and appropriately use the Hebrew *yeled* rather than *bēn* ("son"). Like the Scots "bairn" ("child"), *yeled* is cognate with the verb "bear/born." And yet no other story in HB is so replete with forms of *yld* as this one. The "bearing" is done by "the wife of Uriah" (11:26–27; 12:15); but it is insisted that he is "born to" David (11:27; 12:14). David seeks the Deity on behalf of "the lad" (12:16); but *yeled* ("bairn") or "the son born" (*habbēn hayyillûd*) is the preferred term (12x) in connection with his unnatural death (12:14–23).[18]

The verb *ḥnn* ("favor, be gracious") is used as often in the Psalms as in the rest of HB together, and almost always in a request to Yahweh to be gracious to the worshiper. When David uses it here (v. 22) within his explanation of

18. The precise sequence in v. 20 of *rḥṣ* ("wash"), *swk* ("anoint"), and *śmlh* ("garment") is found also in Ruth 3:3. The same terms for washing and anointing are found in Ezek 16:9, followed by a different term for fresh clothes. Notice also 2 Sam 14:2; 2 Chr 28:15.

behavior that his staff has found strange, he prefaces it with "Who knows?" This recalls the cautious hopefulness or hopeful caution of Yahweh's statement to Moses: "I will favor whomever I will favor" (Exod 33:19). It is particularly reminiscent—but ironically so—of key elements in the couple of verses at the very heart of the book of Amos (5:14–15):

> Seek good and not evil, in order that you may live;
> And so let Yahweh . . . be with you, as you have said.
> Hate evil and love good, and set right judgment firm at the gate.
> Perhaps Yahweh will be gracious . . .

Both Exodus and Amos safeguard divine freedom: neither text promises Yahweh's favor. David's recent behavior has played fast and loose with Amos's preconditions for even hoping for divine grace. However, he has acknowledged his sin; he has been told that his sin has been moved away from him—and so, "who knows?"

This "grace" word introduces an echo of the beginning of the trouble with Ammon (2 Sam 10:2–4) just before we turn to its final resolution here. "Grace" is what King Hanun did not exhibit when David sent messengers to "console" him. And here the mention of grace (12:22) is quickly followed (v. 24) by the only other instance of "console" (*nḥm* [*piʿel*]) in the books of Samuel.

In 2 Sam 7, action was taken (by Nathan, 7:3) without first consulting Yahweh himself; here, Nathan is sent to rename the second child "Yahweh's beloved" (v. 25) in place of his given name "Solomon" (v. 24). The textual difference in its final phrase may reflect different views on how to solve the ambiguity over the subject of the last sentence (v. 25): "for the sake of Yahweh" (MT) suggests that David sends Nathan with news of the name change; but "by the word of Yahweh" (LT) reinforces the view that Yahweh himself has sent his prophet. The new name itself, *yĕdîd-yāh*, means "Beloved-of-Yahweh." The root *ydd* is either actually related to or at least plays on *dwd*: vocalized as *dôd*, the term *dwd* denotes several close family relationships; but it is best known in Samuel vocalized as *dāwīd*, or David. The name of this second son born by Bathsheba to David hints at a claimed relationship between David and Yahweh—all the more interesting to know which of them instructed the name change.

2 Samuel 12:26–31 Ammon Despoiled, Enslaved

26 And Joab fought at Rabbah of the sons of Ammon;
and he captured the royal city.
27 And Joab sent messengers to David,
and said,
"I have fought in Rabbah;

and I have also captured the city of water.[a]
28 Now then, gather the rest of the people
and camp over against the city
and capture it,
lest I myself capture the city
and my name be proclaimed over it."
29 And David gathered all the people
and went to Rabbah
and fought in it
and captured it.
30 And he took the crown of their king[a] off his head;
and its weight was a talent of gold and of precious stone
and it came to be on David's head;
and the plunder of the city he brought out in very great quantity.
31 And the people
who were in it
he brought out
and [set[a]] *sawed* with saws and iron cutters[b] and iron[c] axes;
and he made them pass by in [brickworks[d]] *Maddeba*;
and so he did to all the cities of the sons of Ammon.
And David returned to Jerusalem, and all the people.

27a. Some MSS and versions read not *mym* but *mlwkh*, expected from the end of v. 26; Dhorme (362), however, and Stoebe (2:313) follow Wellhausen (185–86) in reading *hmym* in v. 26.

30–31. These verses correspond to 1 Chr 20:2–3.

30a. Codex B offers a double reading of *mlkm*, "their king," with LT and MT; and (the god) "Milcom."

31. LT renders a text very similar to MT in shape.

a. Codex B's opening *kai ethēken* renders MT's *wyśm*; however, LT's *kai dieprisen* appears to render *wyśr* ("and he sawed") of 1 Chr 20:3. Here DJD prefers to restore *wyśrm*, from which both MT and LT + Chronicles had corrupted, each by the loss of a different consonant. Dhorme (363) argues that "sawed" does not fit the tools mentioned and hence that "placed" or "imposed" (*wyśm*) is a better reading.

b. Here B does not represent *wbmgzrt hbrzl*, which LT renders as *kai skeparnois sidērois*—"and {with} iron {carpenters'} axes."

c. The shorter text in Chronicles "omits" the second *hbrzl* and the following three words in Samuel, which are quite differently handled in GT: Codex B has them drawn through the brickworks, and LT led round in Madeba.

d. For K's *bmlkn*, Q reads *bmlbn*, presumably understanding this much like B (*lĕbēnâ* means "tile" or "brick")—cf. either Nah 3:14 or Jer 43:9.

[26–30] The prevailing assumption in this commentary is that where the Chronicles version of a report is briefer, it is also normally more original. The

Chronicler simply and briefly informs us that Joab assaulted Rabbah and "tore it down"[19] (1 Chr 20:1b); and this may remind us that the same author earlier ascribed to the same Joab the key activity in the capture of Jerusalem (11:6, 8). The Chronicler goes on to report (v. 2) that David removes the crown of Milcom/their king from his head, weighs it, and it comes to be on David's head. But it is quite unclear in this shorter Rabbah story just from whose head David takes the crown: the original wearer's or Joab's. The wording of 2 Sam 12:26, 30 is almost identical; but the ambiguity has been all but removed by the choreography of vv. 27–29 drafted by the author of Samuel. Here a politically sensitive general fights against Rabbah (that tones down the original, which reports that he struck it and tore it down), but takes (only?) the royal city, and sends a report back to his king that he has taken the "city of water," and that David should come lest his general get the credit for taking Rabbah. The narrator's account of Joab's victorious action, and his own report of it, and David's victorious action—these are all told in the same pair of verbs ("fight" and "capture"), neither of which figures in the Chronicler's shorter report, although he uses both in neighboring reports. (The "remainder of the people" [v. 28] is drawn from 2 Sam 10:10 [BTH].) In the context of such apparent deference on Joab's part, it is unlikely that he would have dared to wear the Ammonite crown.

The Joab of our longer Samuel version has recently been given an object lesson in David's readiness to contrive the elimination of insubordinate officers; but this does not mean that he is now without influence, provided it is carefully used. When he dispatches envoys to Jerusalem, in the last of the many "sendings" of 2 Sam 11–12, there may be something of an echo of Bathsheba's "sending," once pregnant (11:5b). He is implying, "You may have initiated something when you sent me to Ammonite territory; but now I have something in my power to which you are going to have to react."

Some readers have suggested that the final capture of Rabbah needs to await David's being forgiven; they have wondered how far the chronology of the Rabbah campaign has become stretched by the report of the birth of a second child to David and Bathsheba. David's dealings with Bathsheba started during that campaign; and the report of them took over center stage and became extended far beyond that of the campaign, coming to include the birth of not just one but two children. But there is absolutely no need to read the end of the campaign as chronologically later than the birth of Solomon. What is delayed is not the end of the campaign, but only the report of its end.

[31] There are several uncertainties over the wording of the final verse. Mention of some tools has encouraged many scholars to support the emendation

19. In his substantial rebuilding of this story here in 2 Sam 12, the author of Samuel removes the verb *hāras* ("tear down") and uses it instead in David's instructions to Joab in 11:25 (see above on 11:25).

of *h'byr* ("made pass") to *h'byd* ("made work"). However, tools could be used for different purposes; and it is far from clear whether this note is reporting forced labor or (remembering 2 Sam 8:2) gratuitous cruelty. Dhorme (363) suggests that the forced labor David imposes on the Ammonites comes close to the oppression of the Hebrews by the Pharaoh. When so much is uncertain about this verse, it may be useful to recall that *h'byr* is used (for example, in 2 Kgs 16:3; 17:17; 21:6; 23:10; Jer 32:35; Ezek 20:31; 23:37) of offering [by fire] one's sons [and daughters] *lmlk* {to Moloch}.

2 Samuel 13:1–22 Absalom, Tamar, and Amnon

1 And it came to be after this—
and of Absalom, David's son, there was a [beautiful] sister *very beautiful in form,*[a]
and her name was Tamar;
and Amnon, David's son, loved her.
2 And there was distress for Amnon,
making himself ill on account of Tamar his sister,
for she was of marriageable age;
and it was marvelous[a] in Amnon's eyes
doing anything to her.
3 And of Amnon there was a companion,
and his name was Jonadab,[a] son of Shimeah, David's brother,
and Jonadab was a very wise man.[b]
4 And he said to him,
"Why are you so reduced, son of the king, morning by morning?
Will you not inform me?"
And Amnon said to him,
"Tamar, my brother Absalom's sister—I love her."
5 And Jehonadab[a] said to him,
"Lie on your bed
and make yourself ill;[b]
and your father will come
to [see] *visit*[c] you,
and you will say to him,
'Please let Tamar my sister come *and attend on me*[d]
and feed me food;
and let her prepare the meal in my sight,
in order that I may see
and eat from her hand[s[e]].'"
6 And Amnon lay down
and made himself ill,

and the king came
to see him,
and Amnon said to the king,
"Please let Tamar my sister come [to me]
and let her heart-shape before my eyes two heart-cakes,
and let me eat from her hand."
7 And David sent to Tamar in the house, saying,
"Please go to the house of Amnon your brother
and prepare food for him."
8 And Tamar went to the house of Amnon her brother,
and he was lying down;
and she took the dough
and kneaded
and heart-shaped it before his eyes
and boiled the heart-cakes.
9 And she took [the pan[a]] *into which they pour*
and poured it before him;
and he refused to eat.
And Amnon said,
"Remove everyone away from me";
and they [went out] *removed* everyone, away from him.
10 And Amnon said to Tamar,
"Bring the food to the chamber[a]
and let me eat from your hand."
And Tamar took the heart-cakes
that she had made
and brought them to Amnon her brother, into the chamber.[a]
11 And she offered some to him
to eat,
and he grasped her
and said to her,
"Come lie with me [my sister[a]]."
12 And she said to him,
"No, my brother, do not humiliate me;
for it is not done[a] so in Israel.
Do not do this *foulness*[b] [churlishness].
13 And I, where would I take my shame?
And you, you would become [like] one of the fools[a] in Israel.
Now then, please speak to the king,
for he will *surely* not hold you back from me."
14 But he was not willing
to listen to her voice,

and he was too strong for her
and he humiliated her
and he lay with her.
15 And Amnon hated her with a very great hatred.
In fact the hatred
with which he hated her
was greater than the love
with which he had loved her;
and Amnon said to her,
"Up; out!"
16 And she said to him,
"No, brother,
for great is the final wrong
beyond the first

"On account of
this greater wrong
than the other

that you did with me,
sending me off."
But he was not willing
to listen to her.
17 And he called his lad, his [page] *house-guard,*[a]
and said,
"Please send this one off—away from me—outside;
and lock the door after her."
18 And she was wearing a lengthy robe,[a]
for this is how the king's daughters of marriageable age used to dress in tunics.[b]
And his page[c] removed her outside,
and locked the door after her.
19 And Tamar took ash *and put it* on her head;
and the lengthy robe
that was on her
she rent;
and she put her hand on her head[a]
and went on her way,
crying out more and more.
20 And Absalom her brother said to her,
"Was it Aminon your brother who was with you?
Well then, my sister, keep silent.[a]
He is your brother;
do not put your heart to [this matter[b]] *saying anything*."
And Tamar settled—a desolate[c] woman—in the house of Absalom her brother.
21 Now King David, he heard all these things,

and became very heated.
And he did not grieve the spirit of Amnon his son
because he loved him,
because he was his firstborn.[a]

22 But Absalom did not speak with his brother, neither bad nor good,
for Absalom hated Amnon
because[a] he had humiliated Tamar his sister.

1a. Here GT's *kalē tō eidei sphodra* attests not MT's *yph*, but the fuller *ypt mr'h m'd*—a combination never precisely attested in MT, although Adonijah is *ṭwb-t'r m'd* (1 Kgs 1:6).

2a. Here *wypl'* is differently rendered: B has *hyperogkon* ("immoderate[ly big]"), and LT *ēdynatei* ("was unable").

3a. Both 4QSam[a] and LT attest "Jonathan" throughout, not "Jonadab."

b. Codex B's "wise man" seems to render MT more lit.; however, LT's "was sensible" (*phronimos*) is used more commonly in LT than *sophos*.

5a. MT uses the longer form of the name here, but reverts in vv. 32, 35.

b. The term *hthl* is often rendered "play sick," but it is the same form as we met in v. 2. Codex B has "show weakness," but LT has "pretend/profess to be troubled." The LT reflects real sickness in v. 2, but pretense in vv. 5, 6.

c. The LT (uniquely) appears to attest *lpqdk*, not *lr'wtk*.

d. There is space in 4QSam[a] to accommodate LT's plus.

e. The LT follows MT (sg.), but B offers "from her hand*s*."

9a. Codex B offers *to tēganon* ("frying/sauce pan") for MT's *hmśrt*, while LT has *eis ho apocheousin*.

10a. The MT uses *ḥdr* twice, and LT offers *koitōna* ("bedchamber") twice; but B varies between *tameion* ("closet"), used also in Gen 43:30, and *koitōna*.

11a. The MT's "my sister" is supported by B.

12a. Again MT's "it is not done" is supported by B.

b. For *nblh*, B has *aphrosynēn* ("folly") and LT *akatharsian* ("foulness").

13a. For *nblym*, both LT and B have *aphronōn*. That may suggest that LT read *ṭm'h* in v. 12.

16a. Here LT makes better sense. Its opening *'l 'ḥy* appears to have corrupted into MT's *'l-'wdt*, and then the elements of a main clause have been rearranged as a subordinate clause. Codex B offers a translation close to MT in this verse but has included "greater the last evil than the first" as an odd plus within v. 15; apparently it has included both variants, one in place and the other out of place.

17a. In place of "attendant" (MT), GT has the fuller reading, lit., the "one standing in front of his house."

18a. The *ktnt* (MT) worn by Tamar has become the assonant *chitōn* in GT (they may be the same word). It is specified in MT as *ktnt psym* (elsewhere only Joseph's garment in Gen 37). In later Hebrew and Aramaic, *pas* means the palm of the hand or sole of the feet—hence *astragalōtos* ("covering the ankles," LT) and *karpōtos* ("to the wrist," B).

b. Tamar's *m'ylym* have become undergarments in LT and overgarments in B. The term is used also in 1 Sam 2:19; 15:27; 18:4; 24:4, 11 (5, 12).

c. In this verse, *mšrtw* is rendered, as more commonly, *ho leitourgos autou*; this can refer to a public or a private servant.

19a. Trebolle Barrera (104) notes that LT, with the rest of the Greek tradition apart from B, attests the shorter "and Tamar took dust and put it on her head"; the disorder in MT (and B) was first caused by the addition of the clause about Tamar's rending her tunic.

20a. The term *hḥryš* ("be silent") reappears in 2 Samuel only at the very end of the Absalom story (19:11), with the people reprimanded for staying dumb about bringing back David.

b. The LT reads *ldbr* as vb., not noun (as in MT); cf. 1 Sam 15:13; 2 Sam 7:7. Codex B combines both readings.

c. For the unusual *wšmmh*, B has *chēreuousa* ("in widowhood") without the connective, while LT has *chēreuousa kai ekpsychousa* ("expiring").

21a. Here LT's substantial "plus" at the end of this verse has the support of 4QSam[a]: the text had become shortened in MT when the eye of the scribe jumped from one *wlw'* to the next.

22a. Perhaps LT's *anth' hōn* is a "correction" to better Greek, or B's *epi logou hou* is "corrected" toward the Heb. *'l-dbr 'šr*, an idiom found apparently only in three contexts close to each other in Deuteronomy, in 22:24 (2x); 23:5.

[1a] The Hebrew wording at the opening of the chapter is contorted. "And it came to be after that" immediately follows the report in the source text of David's return to Jerusalem from Rabbah. The BTH, as 1 Chr 20:4–8 still does, moves straight on to fighting with Philistines in the Rephaim Valley. The author of Samuel has delayed that report (still introduced by the same phrase) until 2 Sam 21:18–22. But he has also retained the old transitional formula here in its original position, although immediately left high and dry.

[1b–2] It is not made clear just how the description of Tamar as *'almâ* (often rendered "virgin") relates to what Amnon experiences as "wonderful." The term *pele'* is often associated with the "marvelous" (miraculous) actions of Yahweh. Nothing is too wonderful or impossible for Yahweh (Gen 18:14; Jer 32:17, 27; Zech 8:6). As far as humans are concerned, there is nothing wonderful about keeping the laws (Deut 30:11); yet even judges may find a particular case impossible to decide (Deut 17:8). Is doing something to Tamar part of a delicious fantasy, or something that in his eyes would require a miracle? Is it because, though of marriageable age, Tamar is not married? If she has been married, like Bathsheba, might she be more rather than less available? Or does Amnon, like some men, have fantasies about deflowering virgins?

[3–7] Amnon's companion belongs to David's wider family. Ancient tradition, Hebrew as well as Greek, has divided over whether he is known as Jonathan or as Jonadab. Whichever name was original was presumably simply misheard at some stage in the tradition. In case the reader is intended to see the meaning of his name bearing on how his role is perceived, we should note that Jonathan means "Yahweh has gifted," and Jonadab "Yahweh stirs/impels." Whatever his name, he has a reputation for "wisdom" (*ḥokmâ*)—and in Hebrew that very much includes (practical) skill. Though an important element in the Solomon story, the words "wise" and "wisdom" are extraordinarily rare throughout the books of Samuel—in fact only 2 Sam 13:3; 14:2, 20; 20:16, 22. Especially if Amnon thinks that getting his way with Tamar would take a miracle, a companion described as "very wise" is just what he needs. Jonadab diagnoses Amnon as being *dal* (v. 4). David's eldest son is already being described in the same terms as the fading house of Saul: "becoming more and more reduced" (3:1). We have met Amnon only once before: in the immediately following note of his birth (3:2a). Ironically, the only other occurrence of *dal* in the books of Samuel is in Hannah's song, which describes Yahweh as raising such people from the dust (1 Sam 2:8).[20]

[8–13] The relatively extended dialogue between Amnon and Tamar makes us notice, if we have not already, that not a single word of direct speech was reported between David and Bathsheba. Is Bathsheba just the wife of one of David's officers, while Amnon and Tamar as half brother and half sister share the same royal blood and have equivalent status?

Another feature of this chapter is the rare verb *brh* (eat): 5, 6, 10—with the cognate noun also in 5, 7, 10. The only other occurrences in Samuel (2 Sam 3:35; 12:17) are in the context of lamentation—and in fact the only other instance in the Bible[21] is the awful image in Lam 4:10 of Jerusalem's compassionate women boiling their own children for food. The KBL notes cognates implying either strength or freedom; it argues that *brh* implies invalid diet. Both features are combined in 12:17.

It is not easy to render the play on words related to "heart" (*lbb*) in vv. 6 and 8. At one level, *lbbwt* may have simply been heart-shaped cakes or dumplings that were supposed to give one heart—just as "cordial" is so called because of its presumed benefit to the *cor* (Latin for "heart"). And the *piʿel tlbb* may, quite as innocently, be the cognate verb for making such beneficial heart shapes. It is only here in all of HB that verb and cognate noun are so used. But it is not just the outcome of this baking-and-eating scene that should make us wonder whether something altogether more suggestive is going on.

The noun is otherwise unknown; but the verb "hearten" in *piʿel* is used once more, and again with a feminine singular subject within some lines of the Song of Songs (4:9–10) that have several other word links with this portion of Samuel:

20. Hannah's words might better describe Gideon: he, in the only other use of *dal* in FP, calls his own clan "the most reduced in Manasseh" (Judg 6:15); yet his end too may be read as a warning to future leaders.

21. *brh* in 1 Sam 17:8 is a unique homonym.

You have heartened me, my sister, bride;
you have heartened me with one [glance] from your eyes,
with one jewel from your necklace.
How beautiful are your endearments, my sister, bride;
how much better are your endearments than wine.

"Heartened," "sister," "eyes," "beautiful"—these are all part of the immediate context in 2 Sam 13. And "your endearments" (*dōdayik*) picks up on *dwd/ydyd* and Yahweh's beloved (Jedidiah), discussed just above (12:25). The emphases on Tamar as Amnon's (and not just Absalom's) sister (vv. 5, 6) and on Amnon's seeing her with his eyes as she prepared what would hearten him constitute a remarkable echo of the words of the lover in the Song.

It is not easy to suppose that writer and readers of the story of Amnon and Tamar were ignorant of these lines of the Song, or possibly of the traditional love poetry on which the classic Song drew. Who knew this Song? If the prince's friend and counselor knows it, then his advice is all the more erotically fraught. If King David knows the Song (despite the fact that Solomon and even his own tower feature in it!), then his response to Amnon's request is at best reckless, at worst complicit. And if our author knows the Song, then at least this part of Samuel may be from quite late in the biblical period. And what about Tamar? Is it only men who make up the audience when love-poetry is recited? Does she know the Song? How close to a dangerous wind does she know she is sailing when she visits her half brother to "bring him heart"? When she tells Amnon to wait and to ask David for her properly, is she desperately playing for time in order to get away? Or does she know full well that the king who has sent her on such a loaded mission will not withhold her from her half brother (v. 13)? And, if so, where does it all go wrong?

There is another set of instructive links, this time within the books of Samuel. First Samuel 25 and 2 Sam 13 are the only narratives in Samuel to use "withhold" (*mnʿ*), and the only narratives to feature "fool" and "folly" (*nbl/nblh*) except for David's short elegy over Abner (2 Sam 3:33). A gift of food helped Abigail win her way into David's affections (25:26–31). The quickest way to a man's heart . . . ! Amnon is son of Ahinoam, whom David married around the same time as Abigail (25:43). And "heart" also plays a prominent role in 1 Sam 25:25, 31, 36, 37. Tamar may have erred in using the *nābāl* word to describe what she realizes Amnon is about to do to her. Only the almost-proverbial Nabal (1 Sam 25) and then Abner in the manner of his death (2 Sam 3:33) are so described in all of Samuel and Kings; and it may be too much for David's first son to be compared with such associates of Saul. Shameless folly (*nblh*) and the culpable fool (*nbl*) appear twice as often in the poetry[22] as in the prose

22. See Deut 32:6, 21; Isa 9:16; 32:5, 6; Jer 17:11; 29:23; Ezek 13:3; Pss 14:1; 39:8 (9); 53:1 (2); 74:18, 22; Prov 17:7, 21; 30:22; Job 2:10; 30:8; 42:8.

texts[23] of the Hebrew Bible; and this language may have been more originally at home in the broad wisdom tradition represented in these poetic/prophetic materials.

[14–18] Amnon would not listen to Tamar (v. 14). "Was not willing" (*l' 'bh*) is a feature of this chapter (vv. 14, 16, 25) and also of its immediate neighbors (12:17; 14:29).[24] On Amnon's side, the hatred that follows the snatched liaison is greater than the love that led to it (v. 15). For Tamar too, being sent away by Amnon is worse than what Amnon has done "with" her (v. 16). When she says "with her" and not "to her," she may be pleading that a future together should be the result of what they have done together. Amnon appears instead to confirm his knowledge of the Song only by subverting it: when his love becomes hate, so the "locked garden," there an image of the sister-and-bride (Song 4:12), becomes his quite literal door—locked against the sister he has forced. Apart from 2 Sam 13:17–18 and Song 4:12, *n'l* is used meaning "lock" only once more in HB (Judg 3:23–24). And if any further confirmation of the literary link is required, the very next verse of the Song begins with *šlḥyk* ("your shoots, or channels"), cognate with *šlḥ* ("send"), a key verb of 2 Sam 13 (vv. 7, 16, 17, 27).

[19–20] With ashes on her head and her long robe torn, Tamar moves to make her wronged status public. Ordered instead by her brother to keep silent, she stays in his house "devastated." This strong word is used just twice more in all of Samuel–Kings: in 1 Sam 5:6, it describes the literal devastation of Ashdod by Yahweh; and in 1 Kgs 9:8 (BTH), in Solomon's second vision, it anticipates the appalled reaction of those who witness how Yahweh will have ruined the Jerusalem temple if Solomon's successors depart from Yahweh's standards. Given all the suggestive talk of baked hearts, it seems a very unfeeling choice of words when Absalom urges his sister not to "put her heart" to the situation (v. 20).

[21–22] David is said to be angry when he hears what has happened; but he does nothing. Perhaps he is mute in face of Nathan's threat. The plus in GT and 4QSam[a] may be original, but its language is unusual: the books of Samuel speak only of the divine spirit, except for "bitter-spirited" Hannah (1 Sam 1:10); and if DJD is correct in retroverting *elypēse* ("grieved") to *'ṣb*, the only "spirit" ever "grieved" elsewhere in HB is also the divine one, on account of human disobedience (Isa 63:10). The verb *'ṣb* (*qal*) is used in a similar sense in 1 Kgs 1:6, where David also refrains from intervening in the activities of Adonijah,

23. See Gen 34:7; Deut 22:21; Josh 7:15; Judg 19:23, 24; 20:6, 10; 1 Sam 25:25; 2 Sam 3:33; 13:12, 13.

24. In BTH, "was not willing" is used only in 3rd m. sg. (1 Sam 31:4; 2 Sam 23:16, 17; 2 Kgs 8:19—and possibly also in 2 Sam 6:10; cf. 1 Chr 13:13; and 1 Chr 19:19; cf. 2 Sam 10:19). In 3rd m. sg., it is found in (other) Samuel–Kings pluses also in 2 Sam 2:21; 12:17; 13:14, 16, 25; 14:29; 1 Kgs 22:49 (50); 2 Kgs 13:23; 24:4—and with other subjects in 1 Sam 15:9; 22:17; 26:23.

next in line to Absalom.[25] The exact expression used (v. 22) of his own total silence toward Amnon ("neither bad nor good") is unique; but the nearest parallel comes in God's advice to Laban to speak neither good nor ill to Jacob when he felt wronged by him (Gen 31:24, 29). Saul's great love for David (1 Sam 16:21) may quickly have turned to something else; and Michal who had once loved David (1 Sam 18:20) came to despise him (2 Sam 6:16). But Amnon's love for Tamar is the first in Samuel said to turn to hatred. These familiar polar opposites will reappear only in Joab's biting criticism of a confused David (2 Sam 19:5–7).

2 Samuel 13:23–33 Absalom's Revenge on Amnon

23 And it came to be at two years' time,
and here was sheep-shearing for Absalom at Baal Hazor near [E]*Go*phraim,[a]
and Absalom called all the king's sons.
24 And Absalom came to the king
and said,
"May it please you, there is shearing for your servant;
may the king and his servants go with[a] your servant?"
25 And the king said to Absalom,
"Please, my son, let us not all go,
and it will not be too heavy for you."
And he[a] pressed[b] on him,
but [he] *the king* was not willing
to go,
and he[c] blessed him.
26 And Absalom said,
"If not,[a] then please let Amnon my brother go with us."
And the king said,
"Why should he go with you?"
27 And Absalom pressed on him,
and he sent with him Amnon and all the sons of the king.
And Absalom prepared a banquet like the banquet of the king.[a]

28 And Absalom commanded his lads, saying,
"Look[a] [out], please:
as Amnon's heart becomes merry[b] with the wine,

25. And *'ṣb nip'al* is used in a similar context in 1 Sam 20:3, of Saul's not disappointing Jonathan, and in 1 Sam 20:34, of Jonathan's being disappointed on behalf of David. But in none of these cases is "spirit" part of the phrase.

I shall say to you,
'Strike Amnon
and put him to death.'[c]
Do not be afraid.
Is it not[d] I who command you?
Be strong
and be valor's sons."

29 And Absalom's lads did to Amnon
as Absalom commanded.
And all the sons of the king got up
and rode each on his mule
and fled.

30 And it came to be—they on the way—
and the report came[a] to David, saying,
"Absalom has struck down all the sons of the king,
and not one of them is left."

31 And the king got up
and rent his clothes
and [lay] *sat*[a] on the ground;
and all his servants were stationed by him with rent[b] clothes.

32 And [Jonadab] *Jonathan* son of Shimeah brother of David spoke up
and said,
"Let not my lord *the king* say,
'All the lads, the sons of the king, *have died* [they have put to death].'
For Amnon alone is dead.
For[a] at Absalom's word it was something set,[b]
from the time of his forcing Tamar his sister.

33 Now then,[a] let not my lord the king take[b] any matter to his heart,
saying,
'All the sons of the king are dead,'
for instead[c] Amnon alone is dead."

23a. Here B follows MT's *Ephraim*, but LT offers *Gophraim* (from *ʿprym*, with *ʿayin*, not *ʾprym*).

24a. Codex B's *meta* agrees with MT's *ʿm*, and LT's *pros* with *ʾl* in 4QSam[a].

25a. The LT specifies Absalom as subj. of "pressed" and "the king" as subj. of "was unwilling."

b. Here 4QSam[a], as in v. 27 and also 1 Sam 28:23, reads a form of *pṣr* rather than of *prṣ*. The vb. *pṣr* is rarer, used in MT only in Gen 19:3, 9; 33:11; Judg 19:7; 1 Sam 15:23; 2 Kgs 2:17; 5:16, and bears only one of the senses attested for *prṣ*—"urge."

c. David is the subj. of "bless" in 2 Sam 6:18, 20//1 Chr 16:2, 43 (BTH) and in 2 Sam 19:39 (40).

26a. Here *wl'*; cf., with the same force, also 2 Kgs 5:17.

27a. The unique instance in MT of *mšth hmlk* is 1 Sam 25:36. There is space in 4QSam[a] for the longer reading. Again haplography has caused the loss in MT: from one instance of "of the king" to the next.

28a. Absalom's first words to his father had been *hnh-n'* (v. 24). To his subordinates he says instead *r'w-n'* (like Jonathan and Saul in 1 Sam 14:29; 16:17).[26]

b. The closest parallel is in Esth 1:10: *kṭwb lb-hmlk byyn*; however, notice also a further connection with Nabal in 1 Sam 25:36: *wlb nbl ṭwb ʿlyw*.

c. For "put to death," 4QSam[a] uses not *hipʿil* but *poʿlel* of *mwt* (as MT in 1 Sam 14:13; 17:51; 2 Sam 1:9–10, 16).

d. The LT (and OL) apparently do not represent *hlw'* (notice the plene spelling).

30a. Here the identical *whšmʿh b'h* appears only in 1 Kgs 2:28; but cf. also 2 Sam 4:4; Jer 10:22; Ezek 21:12 with *bw'* (inf).

31a. The LT's *kai ekathisen* retroverts to *wyšb* for *wyškb* of MT and B.

b. The MT's *qrʿy* is supported by LT, while *dierrēxan* in B appears to read *qrʿw*.

32a. Here B supports the simple *ky* of MT, while LT has read *ky-'m* with MT and GT in v. 33.

b. The LT (and OL) explain that Absalom "was in anger to him," probably having read *ky ʿl 'p hyh lw 'bšlwm*; MT, supported by B, reads a very similar group of consonants: *ky-ʿl-py 'bšlwm hyth śwmh*. Codex B reads the difficult *śwmh* as *śymh* (f. pass. ptc.), "placed/lying."

33a. Trebolle Barrera (104–9) holds that "well then" is the classic mark of resumption after the insertion of v. 32b.

b. With *'l-yśm*, cf. 1 Sam 22:15; 25:25—and also *'l-tšyty* in 2 Sam 13:20, in similar sense and also with "heart" as object.

c. Trebolle Barrera (109–11) has a useful excursus on the rendering of *ky 'm*.

[23–27] Earlier in his career, David wanted to attend Nabal's shearing party but had been refused. Now he refuses to attend such a party when invited. Though surprised at the specific invitation for Amnon (v. 26), David consents to Amnon's joining all his brothers. As earlier with Tamar, he seems ready to let Amnon walk into quite foreseeable trouble.

[28–30] Absalom's encouragement to his lads to be strong and become valor's sons (v. 28) has links in two directions: it will later be echoed in Hushai's warning to the same Absalom that David and his men are similarly valorous (17:10). But it also recalls David's encouragement to the men of Jabesh-gilead (2:7): he thanked them for loyally burying Saul, their lord; and then—with no apparent logical connection—he added that it was himself that Judah had

26. In 2 Sam 7:2, David introduces his remarks to Nathan with *r'h n'*, but with *hnh* in the parallel 1 Chr 17:1.

anointed. In bidding his men strike down David's eldest son, Absalom is also implicitly asking them to recognize a new political reality.

Even without the longer text including the "king's feast" (v. 27), Amnon continues to emulate the eponymous Nabal at his end. The heart of each is "good" with wine when death comes. Yet despite the many comparisons, there is an important difference between the stories of the two fools. Yahweh has an explicit role in the one, but not the other. Abigail credits Yahweh with holding David back from bloodguilt (1 Sam 25:26); Tamar tells Amnon that David will not hold her back from him (2 Sam 13:13). It is Yahweh who puts an end to the life of Nabal, diminished by the stroke brought on by Abigail's news on the morning after his royal drinking bout. But it is Absalom's men who do so for Amnon when he is inebriated. Yahweh has taken a key role in confronting David and in bringing a measure of restoration. But his name and influence are nowhere visible in this immediately following narrative. Solomon's new name may claim that David remains Yahweh's beloved; but what takes place between Amnon and Tamar is the beginning of the sword out of David's own house. Bathsheba may have been blameless; but Tamar appears to have been quite as foolish as she blames Amnon for being.[27]

Many readers have attributed this change in religious atmosphere to different religious attitudes in the source material available to the author[s] of Samuel. Second Samuel 9–20, from which Yahweh is almost completely absent, has been very widely held to represent the larger part of a once independent account of David's court—or, with 1 Kgs 1–2, of Solomon's succession—close in spirit to the independent and not-very-"Yahwistic" material at the heart of the book of Proverbs. The story as told is the product of a remarkable period of "enlightenment," of a "world come of age." The several human characters, guided by their own wisdom or the lack of it, take responsibility for their own actions. However, a series of comparisons between 1 Sam 25 and 2 Sam 13, which their shared language invites readers to draw, point in a very different direction. There Yahweh was credited with holding David back from the bloodguilt that would have resulted from killing off a fool who offended him. Here Tamar appears as foolish as the fool who rapes her. She invokes no divine sanction against the action her half brother proposes, and speaks only of "daddy" not holding them back from their action—a father who raped the wife of one of his officers, and then had him killed. Humans are now acting independently; and Yahweh has apparently withdrawn from the scene (to reappear only in 17:14). For the author of Samuel, it was a given of the history that he knew (BTH) that Solomon was David's successor. In his much enlarged account of the begin-

27. The story of the rape of Jacob's daughter Dinah by Shechem supplies an instructive intertext (Gen 34), not least because they share the expressions "folly" and "it is not done so" and "in Israel."

nings of David's line, he introduces Solomon, marks him as special recipient of divine pleasure, then passes over his development in total silence. At the same time, he shows David, once the sure-footed recipient of divine favor, committing the most heinous crimes himself; then, despite the divine warning, he makes careless mistakes over (not) guiding his family.

No valor needs to be shown by Absalom's brothers. All the king's sons ride away, each on a mule (v. 29). And it is in a forest, on a mule, that Absalom meets his end (18:9). His brother Solomon will be placed on the king's (female) mule in 1 Kgs 1:33, 38, 44.

[31] When David's new baby fell sick, following Nathan's threat that he would die and that the sword would never leave David's house, David pleaded with God and lay on the ground fasting (12:16). Now, on the report that Absalom has killed all his other sons, he again lies on the ground, having first risen to tear his clothes (v. 31). The action of rending of clothes is normally ascribed to the king or leader. The BTH reports first Athaliah and then Josiah as tearing their clothes;[28] and we find the same action reported of Ahab,[29] an unnamed king of Israel,[30] and Hezekiah,[31] all within pluses in Kings. We can compare Reuben (Gen 37:29); and Jephthah (Judg 11:35). Nevertheless, the arrival on the scene of someone whose clothes are already "rent" involves someone lesser in status, and often a messenger.[32] Here, although his subordinates also have torn clothes, they do not join him on the ground; but equally they do not try to raise him from the ground as they had in the previous instance (12:17), perhaps finding his reaction to this news more appropriate.

[32–33] Before the arrival of his other sons, Jonadab has briefed his king (vv. 32–33) on what has happened and why. And then, when they do all arrive safely, he notes ambiguously, and with a grim satisfaction that only he and we readers can appreciate, that everything has worked out as he has said (to Amnon earlier, no less than to David).

28. See 2 Kgs 11:14//2 Chr 23:13; 2 Kgs 22:11, 19//2 Chr 34:19, 27.

29. Ahab in 1 Kgs 21:27.

30. See 2 Kgs 5:7, 8; 6:30.

31. Hezekiah in 2 Kgs 19:1.

32. As in 1 Sam 4:12; 2 Sam 1:2; 13:31; 15:32; 2 Kgs 18:37//Isa 36:22; Jer 41:5.

2 Samuel 13:34–20:19
David and Absalom

Following the lead of the blank sections in CL, this portion of Samuel is presented in five sections. Three of the breaks are shared with the Aleppo Codex. The godlike intuition of the king over the role of Joab in promoting Absalom's cause (14:17) is hardly matched by his readiness to allow the returned prince to pay his vows at Hebron (15:7); but the usurper's end is already signaled when he backs the wrong adviser, even though supported by "all Israel" (17:14).

2 Samuel 13:34–14:7 Absalom Flees

34 And Absalom escaped.
And the lad, the scout, *went up and* raised his eyes,
and he saw
and there was a great people on the move off the *Soraim* way[a] [after him]
on the side of the mountain[b] *on the descent.*
And the scout came
and reported to the king
and said,
"*I have a certain sighting of men from the Soraim/Oronen road*
on the side of the mountain."[c]
35 And [Jonadab] *Jonathan* said to the king,
"Look, the sons of the king have come;
according to the word of your servant,[a] so it has happened."
36 And it came to be as he finished speaking,
and look, the sons of the king did come.
And they raised their voice
and they wept.
Even the king and all his servants, they wept with a very great weeping.[a]
37 And Absalom, he escaped
and went to Talmai son of Amihur, king of Geshur, *in the land of* Helam.[a]
And he was in mourning[b] for his son*s* all the time.

38 And Absalom, he escaped
and went to Geshur;
and he was there three years.
39 And *the spirit of King* David[a] stopped
going out [to] *against*[b] Absalom;
for he was comforted over Amnon,
that he was dead.

14:1 And Joab, son of Zeruiah, knew
that the heart of the king was against Absalom.[a]
2 And Joab sent to Tekoa
and took from there a wise woman;
and he said to her,
"Please go into mourning,
and please dress in mourning clothes
and do not anoint yourself with oil,
and become like a woman in mourning [this] many days for a dead one.
3 And come to the king
and say to him saying— . . ."
and Joab put the words in her mouth.
4 And the Tekoite woman [said] *came* to the king—
and she fell on her face on the ground
and prostrated herself—
and she said,
"Save, O king, *save*."

5 And the king said to her,
"What's with you?"
And she said,
"To be sure,[a] I am a widow
and my husband has died.
6 And your maidservant had two sons,
and the two of them struggled[a] in the field
and there was no [deliverer[b]] *reconciler* between them,
and the one struck [the other] *his brother*
and put him to death.
7 And the whole family[a] has risen up against[b] your maidservant
and has said,
'Give [over] the one who struck down his brother
and let us put him to death for the life of his brother
whom he slew,
and let us destroy[c] even the one who inherits.'

And they will quench the coal
which is left,
not establishing name nor remnant for my husband on the face of the earth."

34a. Mostly *mdrk* is made definite by the cst. relationship of which it is a part; in the poetical line, Job 24:4, it is an implied definite. The only comparable instance is 2 Sam 11:10.

b. The phrase *mṣd hhr* occurs only in 1 Sam 23:26 (2x), there of the relative positions of David and Saul.

c. The GT continues at much greater length than MT, which has suffered from a classic instance of the copyist's eye slipping from one instance of *mṣd hhr* to the next.

35a. The "servant" must be himself in the shortened MT, but could also be the scout.

36a. "Weeping a great weeping" is found elsewhere only in Judg 21:2; 2 Kgs 20:3// Isa 38:3.

37a. The LT's *eis gēn Chalaama* has the support of 4QSam[a] (DJD 150). Codex B supports the plus with *eis tēn Machad.*

b. The *hitpaʿel* of *ʾbl* is used in 1 Sam 6:19; 15:35; 16:1; 2 Sam 13:37 (cf. Gen 37:34); 2 Sam 14:2 (2x); 19:2—and elsewhere in Exod 33:4; Num 14:39; Ezek 7:12, 27; Dan 10:2; Ezra 10:6; Neh 1:4; 8:9; 1 Chr 7:22; 2 Chr 35:24.

39a. "The spirit of the king" (4QSam[a]) is shorter than LT. Driver describes the text of MT as "impossible": a f. vb. *wtkl* followed by m. subj. *dwd*. It is likely that a f. noun has dropped out. Here *rûaḥ* ("spirit") fits the context, and the first letter of *rwḥ* is easily confused with that of *dwd*; but *rûaḥ* is found elsewhere in 2 Samuel only in the two poems at the end.

b. Some MSS, LT, and Tg. attest *ʿl*, presumably of "going out" to war against; *ʾl* in MT and B may suggest compassion.

14:1a. The opening words can also be read neutrally, as in NRSV: "the king's mind was on Absalom" (*epi* [GT] is as ambiguous as Heb. *ʿal*): see below.

5a. With *ʾăbāl*, *DCH* 1:110 compares 2 Kgs 4:14, and possibly Isa 33:9 and Job 34:36. And Mand. lists with Gen 17:19; 42:21; 1 Kgs 1:43; 2 Kgs 4:14; Dan 10:7, 21; Ezra 10:13; 2 Chr 1:4; 19:3; 33:17.

6a. The vb. *nṣh* is found in narrative in Exod 2:13, and in law in Exod 21:22; Deut 25:11.

b. For *mṣyl*, LT uses the very rare *syllysōn* ("helping to settle"), and B the stock rendering *exairoumenos* ("delivering/setting free"). The LT likely has been influenced by the context: nowhere else in HB is *hṣyl* followed by *byn* ("between").

7a. For *mšpḥh*, LT has *phylē* and B has *patria*. There is attractive assonance in MT with the woman's self-description as David's *špḥh*.

b. The whole family has risen up "against" her: *ʿal* again.

c. The GT uses *exairein* ("take out," rather like the contemporary military English usage) for *hišmîd*.

[34–39] Absalom's escape is first mentioned almost in passing (v. 34); but it becomes an accentuated theme in vv. 37–38. He takes refuge in Geshur with his maternal grandfather (3:3). Helam, specified in the plus shared by GT and 4QSam[a] (v. 37), was scene of the encounter reported in 10:16–17 (BTH) between David and Aram.

Within Samuel, it is most often David who is making his escape (*brḥ*), first from Saul (1 Sam 19:12, 18; 20:1; 21:10 [11]; 22:17; 27:4) and then from Absalom (2 Sam 15:14; 19:9 [10]; cf. 1 Kgs 2:7). However, there are different sorts of "flight," or at least different attitudes toward it. The verb *nws* is much commoner in BTH, and throughout HB, and is normally the action of the defeated party. And David is subject of *nws* only in 1 Sam 19:10, where he is fleeing from the actual danger of Saul's throwing his spear at him. By contrast, *brḥ* is used in BTH only once: of Jeroboam's making himself scarce from Solomon (1 Kgs 12:2). Apparently *brḥ* refers to taking evasive action from potential danger. Jacob's flight (*brḥ*) from Esau and Laban (Gen 27:43; 31:20, 21, 22, 27; 35:1, 7) supplies the most distinct resonances. There are few other instances in the Pentateuch or Former Prophets.

Before leaving this Tamar, some comments are appropriate on her links with the other Tamar in Gen 38, and more generally between the David and Jacob stories. When Amnon grabs hold of Tamar, she replies (13:12) in language used in only two of the Jacob stories in Genesis—and both tell of mischief within families relating to women: "It is not done so in Israel" (Gen 34:7) or "in this place" (29:26). The consolation of David (2 Sam 13:39, "was comforted") is reported in an expression found elsewhere only in Gen 24:67 (of Isaac) and 38:12 (of Judah). I have argued elsewhere that much of the detail in the final quarter of the book of Genesis is drawn from these chapters in 2 Samuel. When a significant part of the action in both Tamar stories takes place in connection with a sheep-shearing party, coincidence has to be excluded. The links are particularly densely concentrated in Gen 37–39; yet the rape of Tamar, the only named daughter of David, will also have influenced the telling of the rape of Dinah, the only named daughter of Jacob (and "in Israel" [Gen 34:7] is a clear indication of an import from a later period). Dinah was raped by a foreigner, not a half brother; but Shechem came to love her and wanted to marry her, unlike Amnon, who started by loving Tamar and finished by hating her.

[14:1–4] The beginning of ch. 14 plays some interesting variations on two preceding stories. David's heart is featured at the outset, in the description of his attitude to Absalom. A wise person is again involved (13:3; 14:2); and action that is key to the plot is described in verbs in the *hitpaʿel*. But whereas the wise man devises the scheme for Amnon (13:5), the wise woman is used in a scheme devised by Joab (14:2–3). And while the woman is to assume the clothes and bearing of a mourner, it is unclear how far Amnon was pretending to be sick (13:5) and how far he had really become sick because of his love for Tamar (13:2). This flexibility in the use of the *hitpaʿel* of the verb already nicely added to our difficulty in deciding whether Bathsheba had actually been rendering herself *qdš* or had simply been making herself out to be *qdš* (11:4). Like Jonadab, the woman from Tekoa is wise, though she is prepared to speak lines that are not her own. And like Nathan, who had also been given his words (in his case by Yahweh: 12:1, 7), she engages the king's attention by appealing to him on a matter of justice. However, unlike Nathan, who also presents David with a fictitious case, Joab engages an agent to speak his lines—he appears to be less confident than Nathan of the outcome.

[5–7] Two brothers struggling outside may be an everyday occurrence, but it is infrequently fatal. The story in which Joab coaches the woman from Tekoa is entirely appropriate to the Amnon-Absalom clash to which it is addressed. But the tale also recalls the primordial scene of Cain and Abel (Gen 4), though we cannot know whether our author knew that story. Like Cain, the fratricide should be protected, not executed: to take the life of the killer is to continue, and not to break, the vicious circle of bloodguilt. The family is like a fire (v. 7) in the days before matches and firelighter: as long as there is life in one smoldering ember, it can be blown again into flame.

2 Samuel 14:8–17 An Astute Woman Seizes Her Chance

8 And the king said to the woman,
"Go to your house *in* peace,[a]
and I shall give orders concerning you."
9 And the Tekoite woman said to the king,
"Upon[a] me, my lord king, be the guilt and upon my father's house,
and may the king and his *royal*[b] throne be clear."

10 And the king said,
"Whoever is speaking to you,
bring him to me
and he will not continue further
touching[a] you."
11 And she said,
"Please let *my lord* the king remember Yahweh your God,

for if the blood kinsmen multiply among the neighbors,[a]	not multiplying the blood kinsmen's destroying,
you will not take out my son."	and they will not wipe out[b] my son."

And he said,
"By the life of Yahweh, there shall not fall to the ground any of the hair of your son."
12 And the woman said,
"Please, may your maidservant say a word to my lord king?"

And he said,
"Speak."

13 And the woman said,
"And why have you reckoned like this about the people of [God[a]] *Yahweh*

and from the king's disregarding	—and from the king's saying
this word,	this word—
exercising self-control,	as guilty,

the king's not bringing back his outcast?[b]
14 For *your son is dead* [die we must[a]], and like the waters
that are poured on the ground,
which will not be gathered,

so he cannot take up his life again,	and God will not raise a life[b]
and the king has reckoned reckonings	nor will reckon reckonings
to cast out from him an outcast.	not to cast out from him an outcast.

15 Now then, when I came to speak to my lord king this word,
because the people *will see me* [were making me afraid],[a]
and your maidservant said,
'Please let [me] *your servant* speak to the king;
perhaps the king will do his servant's word.
16 Yes, the king will hearken,
delivering his servant from the hand of the man
seeking to wipe[ing] me out and my son together[a]
from the possession of [God] *Yahweh*.'
17 And your maidservant said,
'Pray let the word of my lord king be as [repose] *an* offering,[a]
for as the messenger of [God] *Yahweh* so is my lord king
in hearing the good and the evil;
and Yahweh your God *will* [—may he] be with you.'"

8a. Both LT and B attest *bšlwm*.

9a. Though she has complained about her family rising "against" her, she says she is content to bear the guilt "upon" her—*ʿal* again!

b. Here 4QSam[c] appears to attest the fuller text of GT.

10a. As in English, *ngʿ* can imply hostile "touching."

11a. The LT's *geiōrais* is nicely assonant with *gēr* ("sojourner, neighbor").

b. Here 4QSam[c] reads *yšmydw* ("they will wipe out") in full, and so is aligned with MT.

13a. Codex B supports MT and 4QSam[c] with "[people of] God," while LT offers "Lord."

b. The nominal use of *niddāḥ* seems to occur only in late texts: Deut 30:4; 2 Sam 14:13, 14; Isa 11:12; 16:3, 4; 27:13; 56:8; Jer 49:36; Ps 147:2; Neh 1:9.

14a. Codex B supports MT's *mwt nmwt*, but LT attests *mt bnk*.

b. Again widely different texts: "and [the] God will take a life/soul, even reckoning to drive out from him the one driven out" (B) is closer to MT, but without either negative; "and no life/soul has hope for it; and the king reckoned a reckoning to drive out from him the one driven out" (LT) does attest *wl'*, but not *lblty* in place of which *hmlk* may have been read.

15a. In MT we read *yr'ny* as (pf.) *pi'el* of *yr'*, found otherwise only in 2 Chr 32:18 and Neh 6:9, 14, 19. The GT has read the *qal* impf. of *r'h*, "will see."

16a. Codex B does not attest "together."

17a. The GT reads not *lmnwḥh* ("for rest") but *lmnḥh*, "for an offering"; several Heb. MSS also lack the *w* but still vocalize the word as "rest."

[8–9] The king's first response is opaque: he will give orders (v. 8). As she persists, the Tekoite woman shows that she might have been trained by Abigail. She starts the appeal she has really come to make (v. 9) just like Abigail (1 Sam 25:24): "On me be the guilt"; and she uses "my lord (the king)" more densely (9x) than any other speaker apart from Abigail (15x). Each has her good sense ("wisdom") proclaimed by the narrator (1 Sam 25:3; 2 Sam 14:2) before she goes on to demonstrate it. And in their readiness to bear "guilt" even where it is far from merited, both offer interesting anticipations of the way David will throw himself on Yahweh's mercy over the counting of his people (2 Sam 24, BTH). But the Tekoite goes beyond Abigail in accepting any guilt: when she echoes David's claim (3:28) that he and his kingdom are innocent of the death of Abner, the wise woman varies this to "the king and his (royal) throne" (v. 9). It is a significant variation because Abner was killed (by Joab!) when trying to "set up the throne of David over Israel and over Judah" (3:10); precisely that unity will be threatened in the emerging hostility between Absalom and David.

[10–12] It is her hope that the king, as God's representative on earth, will remember Yahweh his God and prevent the blood kinsman from indulging in "destruction" (v. 11). She uses two very strong verbs with interesting resonances: *hišmîd* three times (vv. 7, 11, 16), and *šḥt* (also v. 11). The verb *šmd* (both *hip'il* and *nip'al*) is notably prominent in Deuteronomy and Joshua—BTH had used it only once (2 Kgs 21:9//2 Chr 33:9). The threefold use in this passage is all the more noteworthy: it comes between only three other single instances in Samuel: (1) In 1 Sam 24:21 (22), Saul extracts an oath from David not to eliminate his house. (2) In 2 Sam 21:5, the Gibeonites make exactly this charge against Saul. (3) In 2 Sam 22:38, David sings of eliminating his enemies.[1] This theme of 2 Sam 14 may also be linked with the unique instance of the word in Jacob's mouth (Gen 34:30), where (once again during a conflict that started with a rape) the patriarch fears the elimination both of himself *and of his house*.

1. Psalm 18:37 (38) has *w'śygm* instead: "and I shall overtake them." Notice that 1 Sam 30:8 has the same wording as Ps 18:38, not like 2 Sam 22:38.

The verb *šḥt* ("destroy") is also drawn from BTH: what David's forces under Joab do in Ammon (2 Sam 11:1); and what Yahweh is not prepared to do to Jerusalem or Judah (2 Sam 24:16; 2 Kgs 8:19).[2] If as much as this is at stake, David is prepared to guarantee her son's well-being (v. 11b). The Tekoite's response is much more wordy and deferential than Nathan's "You are the man," but the point is the same, and Joab's trap is now sprung. This episode may not simply draw on 2 Sam 24, but may be intended also to throw further light on that seminal narrative. It may be implying that, when David takes the guilt on himself and on his wider family, he is not just exculpating the people whom he shepherds—but also Yahweh, the divine judge and ruler. The divine throne is innocent despite, in the present text of 2 Sam 24:1 at least, having incited the fateful action.

The *gōʾēl*, the responsible kinsman, is mentioned only once each in Samuel and Kings. He is a close male relative, with the duty of righting a wrong experienced by the family. Such a wrong may relate, as in the story told in Ruth, to loss of family property probably connected with the absence of an heir. But it may also, as both here and in 1 Kgs 16:11, relate to violent death and the need for blood vengeance. The totality of Zimri's purge of those associated with King Baasha is underscored by listing all males ("all pissers on the wall"), and his kinsmen, and his associates: Zimri took care to eliminate absolutely everyone who would have had any responsibility for avenging the previous king's death. Here the even more specific technical term is used (v. 11): *gōʾēl haddām* ("blood redeemer"), which is found elsewhere in HB only in legislation.[3] The interplay is interesting between Yahweh as alive and the potential for further death from blood vengeance.

[13–17] Both MT and LT appear confused and confusing in vv. 13–14. It may be that an earlier version of these sentences left the subjects of the verbs unstated; and the actions became variously attributed to God and the king. After the woman's more cautious or deferential start ("perhaps," v. 15b), she appears to gain in confidence, expecting a favorable hearing (v. 16). Elsewhere in Samuel we always find "*Yahweh*'s holding" in both MT and GT (1 Sam 26:19; 2 Sam 20:19; 21:3—and implicitly in 1 Sam 10:1); the first of these instances, where David himself is the fugitive "servant," pleading his case before his "lord" King Saul, offers wider connections with this passage.[4]

Both *mnwḥh* (MT) and *mnḥh* (GT) are puzzling in v. 17. There seems to be no good parallel to MT's "rest" (v. 17), although it may have been suggested to

2. In Samuel as a whole, we find *šḥt piʿel* in 1 Sam 23:10; 2 Sam 1:14; 14:11; 24:16; and *hipʿil* in 1 Sam 6:5; 26:9, 15; 2 Sam 11:1; 20:15, 20; 24:16.

3. See Num 35:12, 19, 21, 24, 25, 27; Deut 19:6, 12; and Josh 20:3, 5, 9 (*hṣyl* is part of the context in Num 35:25; and *byn . . . wbyn* in 35:24).

4. These include the use of *šḥt* ("destroy") in 1 Sam 26:9, 15.

a reader who was thinking of Deut 12:9 ("for you have not yet come to your rest and to your holding") or of 1 Kgs 8:56, which talks of Yahweh's granting *mnwḥh* to his people Israel, who have just been called a "holding" (*nḥlh*). The GT may be recalling David's words in 1 Sam 26:19 about what should placate Yahweh: he speaks there of an "offering" if Yahweh is responsible for his plight, or a curse if humans have driven him from his "holding." And Joab's brother heard David speaking to Saul on that occasion. A gift is often given to the judge, whether king or God, who will decide a case; but according to GT, it is the petitioner who will take a favorable word from the king as a "gift" (*mnḥh*). Another wise women will warn against endangering Yahweh's *nḥlh* in 2 Sam 20:19.

The Tekoite credits David with being like the Deity's "envoy" (*ml'k*, v. 17). Is she saying that the king has wisdom like an "angel" (v. 17)? "Hearing good and evil" is like an abbreviated form of the fuller statement in Solomon's first vision (1 Kgs 3:9): "a hearing heart, . . . understanding the distinction between good and evil." The idea may be that the king, as supreme judge, acts as God's "representative." Solomon's visionary request is immediately tested in the classic judgment between the two prostitutes.

2 Samuel 14:18–15:6 Joab and Absalom

2 Samuel 14:18–23

18 And the king answered
and said to the woman,
"Please do not conceal from me [any] *the* thing
that I am asking you."
And the woman said,
"Let my lord king speak."
19 And the king said,
"Is the hand of Joab with you in all this?"
And the woman answered[a]
and said,
"By your very own life, my lord king, it is impossible[b]
to turn right or left from anything
my lord king has said.
Yes, your servant, Joab, he commanded me;
and he, he placed in the mouth of your servant[c] all these words.
20 In order to turn the face of the matter,
your servant Joab did this thing.
But my lord is wise, like the wisdom of the messenger of the Deity,
knowing everything on the earth."

21 And the king said to Joab,
"Take note please: I do[a] *for you* this thing;
[and] go *and* bring back the lad, Absalom."
22 And Joab fell on his face on the ground
and prostrated himself
and blessed the king.
And Joab said,
"Today your servant knows
that I have found favor in your eyes, my lord king,
in that the king has done the word of [his] *your*[a] servant."
23 And Joab got up
and went to Geshur,
and brought Absalom to Jerusalem.

19a. Codex B lacks "answered."

b. Some authorities read *ʾš* as equivalent to *ʾyš* ("someone") and others as equaling *yš* ("there exists").

c. Here 4QSam[c] reads *ʾmtkh* for *šp̣ḥtk* (MT).

21a. Both B and LT support MT's first-per. *ʿśyty*, though some Heb. sources have second-per. *ʿśyt*; however, both also read *soi* immediately following; next LT renders *dābār* by "word."

22a. At the end of the verse, GT supports K.

[18–20] She has compared him to a divine messenger, and the king now proves her point by discerning Joab's hand in her approach. "Conceal" (*kḥd*) is used only twice more in Samuel, and each of these instances resonates with this one. The next one also involves Joab and Absalom, though the attitudes of Joab and David to Absalom are by then reversed: one of Joab's men notes (18:13) that "nothing is concealed from the king." Then Eli was quite insistent that Samuel should not conceal from him whatever he learned from Yahweh (1 Sam 3:17–18)—Samuel is never actually styled a "messenger" of God; but he was a "seer" and knew what was what. Neither the cattle returning the ark to Israel (1 Sam 6:12) nor Asahel pursuing Abner (2 Sam 2:19, 21) had deviated to right or left. Instructions from an all-knowing David require a similarly direct response (v. 19).

The language of v. 20 also has interesting echoes. The verb *sbb* (its *piʿel* here is unique in HB) will play on the equally unique noun *sbh* (1 Kgs 12:15, BTH): "make a (significant) turn."[5] "The face of the matter" (v. 20) is an unusual phrase; but it presumably conveys much the same as "how the situation looks." "Face" and "appearance" are important terms in what immediately follows, which may

5. The GT has not observed the connection: *sbb* is rendered "move round" in B, and "encircle" in LT.

have influenced the wording here. Followed by a noun, *bʿbwr* ("for the sake of") is a favorite term in Samuel, as already in BTH.[6] But *lbʿbwr* preceding an infinitive is used just once more (17:14). And there, as in 1 Kgs 12:15, it is Yahweh who is exerting influence. Perhaps because here it is Joab who is seeking to turn matters, the woman is more cautious in what she says: Joab is simply seeking to turn how matters appear to be—and Joab, she also carefully insists, is David's servant. Told not to conceal anything, she concludes her answer with another fulsome compliment about the (semi)divine wisdom of her lord king.

[21–23] The Tekoite was introduced to us as a wise woman. Despite that, it is with Joab's scheme that she approaches the king, and she is more than courtly in her praise of the king's wisdom. However, she does show herself well capable to cope with the king's cross-questioning. We are not told whether Joab is at court during the woman's audience with David, or whether he has to be summoned to hear the verdict in his favor (v. 21). David passes in silence over Joab's claim that David's positive response proves that he (Joab) has found royal favor; and Joab departs to fetch Absalom from Geshur, to which he has fled (13:37).

2 Samuel 14:24–27

24 And the king said,
"He shall return to his house,
but my face he shall not see."[a]
And Absalom returned to his house,
and the king's face he did not see.[a]

25 And like Absalom there was no fair[a] man in all Israel
to praise exceedingly.
From the sole of his foot to his crown there was no blemish[b] in him.
26 And when he shaved his head—
and it would be at the [end] *beginning* of each year that he shaved,
for it was heavy on him
and he shaved it—
he would weigh the hair of his head: [two] *one* hundred shekels by the king's stone/weight.
27 And there were born to Absalom three sons and one daughter—
and her name was [Tamar] *Maacha.*
She became a woman *very* lovely [in appearance[a]];
and she became wife to Rehoboam son of Solomon,
and bore him Abia(thar).

6. As in 2 Sam 5:12; 7:21; 10:3 (all BTH) + 1 Sam 1:6; 12:22; 2 Sam 6:12; 9:1, 7; 12:21, 25; 13:2; 18:18.

24a. The LT, as MT, uses the same vb. twice for "see," while B offers *blepetō* first, then *eiden*.

25a. Codex B does not attest *yph*.

b. For *mûm* ("blemish"), GT has *mōmos* ("blame, disgrace"). If one of these words is not in fact a borrowing from the other, at least GT has chosen well.

27a. Here DJD 263 finds enough space to reconstruct both *m'd* ("very") and *mr'h* ("in appearance").

[24–27] As if David is well aware that he has been "turned" by Joab, he chooses another form (*qal*) of the same verb *sbb* to speak of Absalom's (re)turn to his house. Joab may have achieved a turn in the "face" of affairs; but the royal prince is not permitted to see the face of the king. From "the appearance of the matter" (v. 20), we move here to Absalom's (not) appearing before the king (v. 24), and how not only Absalom (vv. 25–26) but also his daughter (v. 27) look. This short paragraph about Absalom's looks and his children, who include a second beautiful Tamar, makes the reader sure that we have not reached the end of this story.

2 Samuel 14:28–30

28 And Absalom lived in Jerusalem for two years;
but the face of the king he did not see.
29 And Absalom sent to Joab
to send him to the king,
but he was not willing
to come to him;
and he sent again a second time,
but he was not willing
to come.
30 And [he] *Absalom* said to his servants,
"See Joab's field beside me
and he has barley there.
Go
and kindle it with fire."
And Absalom's servants kindled the field with fire.
And Joab's servants came to him,
having torn their clothes,
and said,
"*The servants of Absalom have kindled the field with fire*."[a]

30a. Here 4QSam[c] shares the plus in GT. It is easy to see how MT has become accidentally shorter.

[28–30] Absalom has not actually been exiled by David after having Amnon killed, but fled of his own accord. Even so, Joab had to resort to a stratagem to have him brought back. But David has now ruled that he cannot present himself at court; and Joab is clear that his own credit in this matter is now exhausted.

2 Samuel 14:31–33

31 And Joab got up
and came to Absalom at home,
and said to him,
"Why have your servants kindled with fire the field that belongs to me?"
32 And Absalom said to Joab,
"Look, I sent for you, saying,
'Come here
and let me send you to the king, saying,
"Why have I come from Geshur?
It would have been good for me still to be there."'
Well then, I shall see[a] the face of the king;
and if there is guilt in me,
let him put me to death."[b]
33 And Joab came to the king
and informed him;
and he called for Absalom,
and he came to the king
and prostrated to him
and fell on his face on the ground before the king;
and the king kissed Absalom.[a]

32a. After *ʾrʾh*, 4QSam[c] is followed by LT in reading *nʾ*.
b. The LT makes the final expression passive.
33a. Here DJD 263 reconstructs a much shorter verse ending for 4QSam[c]: ". . . to the king and he prostrated himself, and the king kissed Absalom."

[31–33] Under heavier pressure, Joab consents to transmit Absalom's request to the king. In effect he is seeking a judicial appeal: better to be killed if found guilty than remain alive but under a cloud. Absalom's repetition of his father's exact words from 1 Sam 20:8 ("and if there is guilt in me") reminds us of the similarities and the differences in their relationships to the king of the time. David was son-in-law to Saul and commander of his forces; he was both out of favor with the king and, at the same time, expected at the royal table. Saul could see that David was usurping Jonathan's place, and yet Jonathan was the intermediary between David and Saul. We have not yet seen any evidence of Absalom making a bid for power (the first signs follow immediately in ch. 15); but he is David's third-born son, and he has had the eldest eliminated. His intermediary is not a royal prince, but David's commander-in-chief. David was avoiding Saul, and challenged Jonathan as if prince plenipotentiary to act as judge and, if necessary, executioner. Absalom wants to see King David again and assures Joab that he is prepared to face the consequences. Both protest their innocence; both appear to acknowledge that they will not be put to death unless some guilt attaches to them, but neither concedes that he himself has actually done wrong.

When Absalom's wish is finally granted, he does not dare to look at his father but does obeisance before him. Nothing is reported about anything spoken between son and father. However, the king raises him and kisses him—and kissing does of course imply meeting face-to-face. The two precedents in Samuel for such an exchange of greetings are interesting. Samuel kisses Saul when he anoints him (1 Sam 10:1), but he does not relinquish authority; and then there is the ill-fated bond between David and Jonathan (1 Sam 20:41).

2 Samuel 15:1–6

1 Now it came to be further after this;[a]
and Absalom prepared for himself a chariot and horses, and fifty men running before him.
2 And Absalom would rise early
and stand at [the side of] the way to the gate,[a]
and there was[b] every man
who might have a plea
coming to the king for judgment[c]—
and Absalom called to him
and said,
"From whichever city are you?"[d]
And he *would answer*
and say[e] [said],
"Your servant is from one of the tribes/staffs of Israel."
3 And Absalom said to him,
"See, your words are good and straight;[a]
but there is no one hearing[b] for you from the king."
4 And Absalom said,
"Who will set me judge [in] *over* the land *over Israel*,[a]
and to me every man will come
who has a plea [or a judgment],
and I will set him right?"

5 And it came to be at a man approaching
to prostrate to him,
he put out his hand
and grasped him[a]
and kissed him.
6 And Absalom acted like this for all Israel
who would come for judgment to the king,
and Absalom appropriated[a] the heart[b] of the men of Israel.

1a. The clause that opens MT is unique in HB: *wyhy m'ḥry-kn* rather than the normal *wyhy 'ḥry-kn* (most recently in 13:1). While we read the normal *wyhy 'ḥrykn* in 4QSam[c], that text recalls 13:1 in its immediately following disjunctive introduction of Absalom.

2a. The long text of MT is rendered in B; 4QSam[a] has "the way" but not "the gate," while LT does not represent "the side."

b. Both 4QSam[a] and 4QSam[c] include portions of this section, and both largely maintain the series of frequentative *wĕqāṭal* forms begun also in MT in v. 2 and attested throughout in LT by impf. forms.

c. The closest parallel in FP to *lbw' 'l-hmlk lmšpṭ* (cf. also v. 6) is Judg 4:5, of Deborah.

d. Absalom's question is worded exactly as Jonah 1:8.

e. Both 4QSam[c] and LT "add" that the man would "answer [and say]."

3a. For *nkḥym* Codex B offers *eukoloi* ("contented") and LT *kateuthynontes* ("keeping straight").

b. The term *šōmēaʿ* is variously rendered as *akouōn* in B, *ho akousomenos* (middle in same sense as active?) in LT, and "the one who will be hearer" in Armenian.

4a. Here *'l yśr'l*, attested by LT but apparently not read by either 4QSam[a] or 4QSam[c], opens with the same letters as the following *'ly* ("to me").

5a. Here, as in 13:11, MSS vary between the preps. *b*- and *l*- following "grasp."

6a. The translation above follows GT in rendering the emphatic *piʿel* of *gnb* by *idiopoieito*.

b.The *qal* of *gnb* ("steal") is used with *lb* ("heart") in Gen 31:20, 26.

[1–6] Absalom may have taken the initiative in recruiting an armed retinue; however, since he needs to secure the king's permission some years later (v. 7) to go to Hebron, presumably David has given at least tacit approval to such military trappings for a senior royal prince. These symbols of power have proved to Absalom that his restoration in Jerusalem is complete, and to the wider population that he has the full confidence of the king. He makes a point of dealing with everyone coming to seek justice from the king exactly as the king has dealt with him: not only refusing obeisance, but also in fact kissing the suppliant. Is David's justice still operating as it should, but Absalom seeks to disrupt it? Or are people failing to get a hearing?

Absalom's pitch to those coming to Jerusalem for judgment is rich in its associations with a small number of biblical passages:

1. It is likely that, in modern English, to "steal someone's heart" is morally neutral. But the nearest parallel to the Hebrew wording here is Jacob's cheating on his uncle Laban (Gen 31:20, 26): it appears that in HB, stealing a heart is as bad as stealing anything else.

2. A short poem in Prov 24:23–26 offers several parallels to this Absalom, who tells suitors, "Your words are good and direct":

> Partiality in judging is not good.
> Whoever says to the wicked, "You are innocent,"
> peoples will curse him, nations abhor him.
> But for those who reprove, it is well,
> and upon them will come a good blessing.
> He kisses the lips who returns direct words.

The poem warns against partiality in judgment, and itself immediately follows an injunction to fear both Yahweh and the king (24:21–22). If the poem in Proverbs is a meditation on Absalom, then it is more explicit in condemning him than the narrative in Samuel. But if the portrait of Absalom draws on the poem, the poem helps us decode what the Samuel narrator is intending.

3. The only other plaintiff or suitor in the books of Samuel, with a *rîb* (vv. 2, 4), is David himself. He appeals to Yahweh to judge his complaint against Saul of baseless persecution (1 Sam 24:15 [16]), and receives the due verdict from Saul that he (David) is in the "right" rather than the king himself (24:17 [18]). And when Nabal dies, David blesses Yahweh for having taken up his complaint against him.[7]

4. One of the few parts of the David story in BTH to speak of "all Israel" is the interim evaluation of his reign in 2 Sam 8:15, which notes that "David reigned over all Israel, and David was practicing judgment and righteousness for all his people."[8]

5. As so often in Samuel, BTH also helps clarify one of the most puzzling elements of this short narrative: the initial exchange between Absalom and the plaintiffs whom he intercepted. He would ask those he greeted to identify their town of origin; they would reply they were from one of the "tribes" of Israel; and he would assure them they had a good case, if only it could be heard (v. 2b). Are the visitors deliberately correcting Absalom's terminology: pointing out that the basic units of self-identity in Israel are tribes, not towns (see further

7. The term *rîb* is also used in the poems that serve to frame the books of Samuel: 1 Sam 2:10; 2 Sam 22:44.

8. In MT "all Israel" is in 1 Sam 2:14, 22; 3:20; 4:1, 5; 7:5; 11:2; 12:1; 13:4, 20; 14:40; 17:11; 18:16; 19:5; 24:2 (3); 25:1; 28:3, 4; 2 Sam 3:12, 21, 37; 4:1; 5:5; 8:15; 10:17; 11:1; 12:12; 14:25; 15:6; 16:21, 22; 17:10, 11, 13; 18:17; 19:11 (12); and "all *X* of Israel" in 1 Sam 2:28 (2x); 7:2, 3; 8:4; 10:20; 11:3, 7, 15; 13:19; 14:22; 15:6; 17:19, 24; 18:6; 27:1; 2 Sam 5:1, 3; 6:5, 15, 19; 7:6; 15:10, 13; 16:18; 17:4, 14, 24; 19:9, 41 (10, 42); 20:2; 21:5; 24:2.

on v. 10)? Is Absalom waiting to hear this correct answer before offering them any assurance? Whatever may be the answer to these questions, their reply is couched in terms we have found Yahweh himself using in BTH, when speaking to David (7:7): when moving around among the sons of Israel, has Yahweh spoken with "one of the tribes (or tribal leaders) of Israel"? But I suspect that the author of Samuel is using his source (BTH) more cleverly than is immediately apparent. According to the parallel in 1 Chr 17:6, Yahweh does not disclaim having spoken with "one of the tribes [*šbṭy*] of Israel" about building a house, but with "one of the judges [*špṭy*] of Israel." If the Chronicler here, as so often, preserves an older text of 2 Sam 7, then one of the dynamics of the beginning of 2 Sam 15 may be working like this: the plaintiffs "misquote"[9] Yahweh's words as they introduce themselves (v. 2), and in his response (v. 4) Absalom alludes to the "original" when he wishes that he were such a "judge of Israel."

2 Samuel 15:7–17:13 Absalom in Revolt

2 Samuel 15:7–9

7 And it came to be at the end of *four* [forty] years,
and Absalom said to the king,
"Please may I go
and pay my vow*s*[a]
which I vowed to Yahweh in Hebron.
8 For your servant vowed a vow
when I was sitting/living in Geshur in Aram, saying,
'If Yahweh does really bring me back to Jerusalem,
then I shall serve Yahweh *in Hebron*.'"
9 And the king said to him,
"Go in peace."
And he got up
and went to Hebron.

7a. The GT reads *ndry* as pl., MT as sg.

[7–9] To what does "in Hebron" (v. 7) relate? In the translation above, should these words be set in a new line of their own? Is Absalom claiming that one vow or two vows need to be paid? Did he vow when in exile that, on return, he would worship Yahweh in Hebron? Or did he vow in exile that, on return, he would honor an earlier vow made in Hebron?

9. Of course such creative "misquotation" could have been influenced by Ps 122, which sings of *šĕbāṭîm* (tribes/tribal leaders/scepters) of Yah (v. 4) going up to stand in Jerusalem's gates (v. 2), where thrones belonging to the house of David are set for judgment (v. 5).

Only three other biblical contexts link the three words "pay" and "vow" (v. 7) and "sacrifices" (v. 12). Like this passage, 1 Sam 1:21 and Jonah 1:16 may both be drawing on a third text, the great thanksgiving Psalm 116:17–18:

> I will offer you a thanksgiving sacrifice
> and call on the name of Yahweh.
> I will pay my vows to Yahweh
> in the presence of all his people.

Absalom identifies himself as David's "servant," who wishes to offer "service" to Yahweh, David's God. Then "may I pay" (*'šlm*) is an especially natural request for Absalom to make, for this verb sounds like, and is written with some of the letters of, his own name (*'bšlwm*). In giving him permission, David—again doubly appropriately—wishes that he will go "in peace" (*bšlwm*).

2 Samuel 15:10–26

10 And Absalom sent agents[a] into all the tribes/staffs of Israel, saying,
"When you hear the sound of the trumpet,
you shall say
'Absalom has become king in Hebron.'"
11 And with Absalom there went two hundred men from Jerusalem,
invited and going in all innocence/honesty—
they did not know anything.
12 And Absalom sent
and invited Ahithophel[a] the Gil*m*onite, David's counselor, from his city from [Giloh] *Metallaad*
when he was offering sacrifices.
And the conspiracy became strong*er and stronger*;
and the people was becoming bigger and bigger with Absalom.
13 And the informer/herald[a] came to David, saying,
"The heart of [the men of] *all* Israel is behind Absalom."
14 And David said to all his servants
who were with him in Jerusalem,
"Up
and let us slip away,
for there will be no escape for us in face of Absalom.
Make haste
to go,
lest [he] *the people* make haste
and catch up with us
and thrust on us the [disaster] *city*[a]
and strike the city by mouth of the sword."

15 And the servants of the king said to *him* [the king],
"According to anything [my lord] the king may choose,
your servants are here."
16 And the king went out, and all his house, on foot;
and the king left behind ten concubines[a]
to watch the house.
17 And the king went out and all [the] *his* people on foot;
and they stopped
and stood at the Far House.
18 And all his servants were crossing beside him, and all the Creti[a]
and all the Pleti [and all the Gittites] *and stood at the olive in the*
desert, and all the people passed by close to him.[b] *And all the*
powerful and all those round him and all the fighters of the king,
six hundred men who came from Gath on foot passed by in face of
the king.
19 And the king said to Ittai[a] the Gittite,
"Why will you also go with us?
Go back
and live with the king.
For you are a foreigner,
and you are also an exile [to] *from* your place.
20 Only yesterday you were coming;
and today should I make you wander with us,
walking—
and I am walking
wherever I am walking—
Go back
and take your brothers back with you;
and Yahweh will practice with you loyalty and faithfulness."
21 And Ittai answered the king
and said,
"By the life of Yahweh and by [the] *your* life [of] my lord king,
in whatever place my lord *king* is, whether for life or death,
there will be your servant."
22 And David said to Ittai *the Gittite*,
"Walk on
and pass over *with me*."[a]

And Ittai the Gittite passed over	And Ittai the Gittite passed over
and all his children/servants,	and all his men
and the king and all the men	and the children that were
with him.	with him.

23 And all the land were [weeping] *blessing* loudly *and* weeping,[a]
and all the people were crossing over,
and the king was crossing by the Wadi Kidron,
and all the people were crossing

opposite him	Toward
down the way of the olive,[b]	the way
which is in the wilderness.	to the wilderness.

24 And look at Zadok [too] and all the Levites with him
carrying the ark of the covenant of the Deity
from Baithar,

and they set down the ark of the covenant	and they poured out[a] the ark of the Deity,
	and Abiathar came up[b]

till the whole people finished
crossing from the city.

25 And the king said to Zadok,
"Take the ark of the Deity back to the city
and let it dwell in its place.
If I find favor in Yahweh's eyes,
he will bring me back
and will let me see it[a] and its [dwelling place] *beauty.*

26 But if [this is what] he says to me:
'I take no pleasure in you,'
I am here
and he will do to me
whatever is good in his eyes."

10a. Are these "agents" spies, like the only others in Samuel (1 Sam 26:4); or should we compare the use of *rgl* (*piʿel*) in 2 Sam 19:27 (28): "to slander."

12a. In MT, Absalom sends Ahithophel; in B, he sends to him; 4QSam[c] like LT has the fuller "sent and called" but does not join LT in specifying Absalom as subj.

13a. The ptc. *mgyd* with article is unique to 2 Samuel (1:5, 6, 13; 4:10; 15:13; 18:11). The reports come usually to David (but to Joab in 18:11); and the preposition is normally *l-*, but *ʾl* here.

14a. "The city" in LT attests *hʿyr* rather than *hrʿh* of MT and B.

16a. Only here is *nšym plgšym* used and in 20:3, and sg. in Judg 19:1, 27; normally *plgš(ym)* is used alone. The word is probably cognate with Greek *pallax* or *pallakē* but may be neither Greek nor Semitic in origin. Persian has been suggested (cf. the Arabic name for the Queen of Sheba, *Bilqis*).

18a. Both *Chettei* (B) and *Chetthi* (LT) attest *tt*, but not the *rt* in *krty* (MT).

b. The LT concludes the verse at much greater length after *hplty*: *adros* ("powerful") renders *gdwl* in 2 Kgs 10:6, 11. Codex B is even longer, with a conflate reading.

19a. The name *ēthi* (LT) is closer to *ʾty* (MT) than *Seththei* (B). Note the assonance of *ʾty* and *ʾtnw* ("us"), and the repeated *ʾth* ("you").

22a. Here GT's concluding "with me" may have read a second assonant (and in this case also ambiguous) *ʾty*.

23a. The LT, followed by OL, appears to have read a form of *brk* as well as *bwkym*: possibly *mbrkym*, since a *qal* form *bwrkym* is unknown in HB.

b. In v. 18 too, the longer text of LT includes "the olive in the desert."

24a. It has been suggested to read *wyśgw* (< *nśg*? "set down") for *wyṣqw* (< *yṣq*, "poured out"); GT reads *kai estēsan*. And yet GT has *kai ethēkan* for *wyṣqm* in Josh 7:23 of Achan's plunder.

b. Here GT's "from Baithar" looks like a variant of "and Abiathar went up" in MT (B preserves both variants). In vv. 29 and 35 (and implicitly in 27), Zadok and Abiathar function as a pair, as also in the older BTH summary of David's officials (8:17). However, it is only in v. 24 that Levites are mentioned (elsewhere, only in 1 Sam 6:15). Theoretically *wyʿl* could mean "and [Abiathar] offered up."

25a. The LT's *autēn* for *ʾtw* takes "ark" as the antecedent (also OL), while B's *auton* takes it as "Lord"; MT is suitably ambiguous.

[10–11] This chapter's second mention of the "tribes" of Israel (v. 10) makes us suspect that the response by the royal supplicants to Absalom's query about their "town" of origin (v. 2) was less inconsequential than may have first appeared. The three synoptic instances of *šēbeṭ* in 1 Kgs 8:16; 14:21; 2 Kgs 21:7 are found unchanged in 2 Chr 6:5; 12:13; 33:7. The term is also found within three synoptic contexts in 2 Samuel: but as a plus in 5:1; 24:2; and in 7:7 (*šbṭy*) as a variant for "judges" (*špṭy*) in the parallel version in 1 Chr 17:6. The other instances in Samuel are 1 Sam 2:28; 9:21; 10:20; 15:17; 2 Sam 19:9 (10); 20:14. Apart from the textually uncertain 2 Sam 7:7,[10] there are two possible parallels for "one of the tribes of Israel":

> Dan shall judge his people, as one of the tribes of Israel. (Gen 49:16)
> . . . the place Yahweh will choose in one of your tribes. (Deut 12:14)

Each of these suggests that "Your servant is from one of the tribes of Israel" represents a proud boast by the appellants whom Absalom intercepts.

[12] David is reported as offering sacrifice only in connection with the ark (2 Sam 6) and the future temple site (2 Sam 24); and both these instances are drawn from the main source of Samuel in BTH. Absalom's sacrifices in Hebron (v. 12) may be part of his claimed "service" of Yahweh (v. 8); but they also form part of a pattern established in 1 Samuel of sacrifice in connection with the anointing of a new king. David himself (1 Sam 16) and Saul before him (1 Sam 9–10) were anointed by Samuel on the occasion of a sacrificial festival, although each of them in secret. And sacrifice accompanies the self-proclamation of Absalom (2 Sam 15:10, 12), and later of Adonijah (1 Kgs 1:5, 9–10). The many "invited guests" (2 Sam 15:11) from Jerusalem are another part of

10. Apart from the fact that Chronicles has "judges," GT has the sg. "tribe."

the same pattern: the term is used only in 1 Sam 9:13, 22; 1 Kgs 1:41, 49; and here. All three celebrations are associated with a king who will not last: Saul, Absalom, and Adonijah. The point is made explicit here (v. 11), but seems true of the other accession parties as well, that these invitees are simple "extras," unaware of what is going to happen.

[13–17] Absalom's kingship begins where his father's did, in Hebron—where David became king first over Judah and then over all Israel. In terms of textual space, David capitulates remarkably quickly (vv. 13–14). He may know well that he has lost the support of the people at large. And Absalom's two hundred guests from Jerusalem must have accounted for most of the city's citizens of any substance. On hearing how Absalom's movement is progressing, David proposes giving Absalom the slip (*brḥ*); and then, using a term that is unique here within Samuel but at home in late biblical texts, he notes that escape (*plêṭâ*) would not be possible for them if they faced Absalom (v. 14). David's entourage responds in very skillful terms (v. 15) to his proposal. He has proposed a tactical "withdrawal" (*brḥ*); they will fall in with whatever their master chooses (*bḥr*), not excluding flight. Given the other instances of wordplay in this chapter, it may also be significant that David leaves Jerusalem "on his feet" (*brglyw*, vv. 16–17) and with his folks, while Absalom has sent spies/slanderers (*mrglym*, v. 10) through all Israel. In addition to the wordplay, there are other indicators of emphasis in v. 16: the king and his house leave on foot, not on mounts; the king "abandons" women, who are to "watch" the house; these abandoned women should have some status in the house.

[18] Cherethites and Pelethites mostly appear as a pair, as already in BTH (8:18)—a note resumed in 20:23—see 2 Sam 15:18; 20:7; 1 Kgs 1:38, 44.[11] Cherethite appears alone in 1 Sam 30:14, suggesting that the Cherethite Negeb was not far from Ziklag, the town gifted to David by the king of Philistine Gath. And two pieces of prophetic rhetoric link Cherethites explicitly with Philistines:

> Ah, inhabitants of the seacoast,
>   you nation of the Cherethites!
> The word of Yahweh is against you,
>   O Canaan, land of the Philistines.
> (Zeph 2:5)

> I will stretch out my hand against the Philistines,
>   cut off the Cherethites,
>   and destroy the rest of the seacoast.
> (Ezek 25:16)

11. We noted at 8:18 Van Seters's view that these were Greek mercenaries.

It is entirely possible that *plty* (Pelethite) was simply an alternative spelling of *plšty* (Philistine).

[19–22] The brief but poignant exchange of words as David tries to turn Ittai back (vv. 19–22a) has several linguistic echoes. The first group of echoes are located in the second half of Ruth 1 (plus "foreigner" in 2:10); and the resonance is strengthened by the weeping of the whole land (2 Sam 15:23), like that of Naomi and her daughters-in-law (Ruth 1:9, 14). When it forms the second element in a pair, *ʾĕmet* ("faithfulness") most often strengthens *ḥesed* ("loyalty"), as here (v. 20).[12] The words are left hanging in MT, which has clearly lost the words preserved in GT. In Psalms and Proverbs, "loyalty and faithfulness" are most often associated with Yahweh or the king. David wishes Yahweh's "loyalty and faithfulness" for only one other party, when he sends his compliments to the people of Jabesh in Gilead, after he learns that they have buried Saul (2:6).

[23–24] Following echoes of Ruth, a second group echoes Josh 3–4 as well as the phrase "loyalty and faithfulness" in Josh 2:14. Crossing, wilderness, and Levites carrying the ark of (the covenant of) God (vv. 23–24) are all obvious in English translation. But "till the completing of [the whole people crossing]" is the only instance in Samuel of a construction (*ʿd-tm*) more familiar in Joshua (4:10; 5:6; 8:24; 10:20). And the word for "the children" (*hṭp*) in v. 22 is unique here within Samuel–Kings, but is found in later portions within FP in Josh 1:14; 8:35; Judg 18:21; 21:10.[13] The role of the Levites is the giveaway clue that at least their presence in these verses, no less than 1 Sam 6:15, is a late addition. It is attractive to suppose (with NRSV) that MT and GT exhibit different repairs to a damaged text: that the words "and Abiathar went up" originally headed the verse. In that case, Abiathar and Zadok would originally have been responsible for carrying the ark, and the Levites could have been added later. The whole passage was probably drafted in response to a question whether the ark was more closely linked to Jerusalem itself or to David, who had brought it there. However, once introduced in this paragraph (no less than 8x), *ʿbr* ("cross, pass by") and its cognates remain a major element till the end of the campaign (ch. 19).

In the case of most of the links in phraseology or situation between Joshua and Samuel, it seems likely that Joshua has drawn on Samuel rather than the other way around. However, this passage may be the major exception that proves the general rule. The report in 1 Sam 4 of the capture of the ark offers a warning against taking the ark to support even a defensive military campaign.

12. As in Gen 24:49; 47:29; Exod 34:6; Josh 2:14; 2 Sam 2:6; 15:20; Pss 25:10; 61:7 (8); 85:11; 89:14 (15); Prov 3:3; 14:22; 16:6; 20:28.

13. Elsewhere Gen 34:29; 43–50 (7x); Exod 10:10, 24; 12:37; Num (10x); Deut 1:39; 2:34; 3:6, 19; 20:14; 29:11 (10); 31:12; Jer 40:7; 41:16; 43:6; Ezek 9:6; Esth 3:13; 8:11; Ezra 8:21; 2 Chr 20:13; 31:18.

But later readers of Samuel would have known the reports of the ark's leading Joshua's people as they crossed the Jordan and captured Jericho. Despite the involvement of Zadok, David makes a clear distinction between the (non)presence of the ark and the full involvement of Yahweh in the decision on what will happen to him. Ideally, the place of the ark should be Jerusalem. This will bear on the question of whether Uriah's mention of the ark (11:11) implies it has left Jerusalem during the Ammonite campaign.

The third set of echoes—on the question of whether someone from Gath should, as an alien, accompany David on a campaign—takes us back to David in exile in Gath (1 Sam 21; 27–28), and to the debate between Achish and the other Philistine leaders over whether David's loyalty can be counted on (1 Sam 29).

[25–26] When David mentions the possibility that his predicament implies that Yahweh has no pleasure in him (v. 26), we recall Yahweh's fateful displeasure with Eli's sons (1 Sam 2:25) and with Saul (15:22). Given the conjunction of priest and ark and talk of Yahweh's speaking to David, is an oracular consultation implied (2 Sam 15:25–26)?

2 Samuel 15:27–16:13

27	And the king said to Zadok the priest,	
	"See! You[a] go back	"Are you[a] a seer? Go back
	to the city in peace,	
	and *look*, Ahimaaz your son and Jonathan son of Abiathar—both your sons[b]—with you.	
28	See,	
	I am waiting for you	I am lingering[a]
	at the olive in the wilderness,	at the fords[b] of the wilderness,
	till word comes from you	
	to report to me."	
29	And Zadok and Abiathar took back the ark of the Deity to Jerusalem, and lived there.	
30	And David was going up by the olive ascent,	
	and was weeping [more and more]	
	and his head covered[a] and walking barefoot;[a]	
	and all the people who were with him—	
	each had his head covered,	
	and they went up,	
	climbing and weeping.	
31	And they reported to David,	31 Now David reported,
	saying,	
	"Ahithophel is among the conspirators with Absalom."	

And David said,
"Pray make foolish[a] Ahithophel's counsel, Yahweh."
32 Now David was arriving at the summit,[a]
where he would prostrate himself to [the Deity] *Yahweh*;
and see, *there came*[b] to meet him Hushai the Archite,
with his cloak rent and earth on his head.
33 And David said to him,
"If you crossed over with me,
you would be a burden on me.
34 But if you go back to the city,
say to Absalom,
'*Your brothers have passed through,*
and the king your father has passed through after me;[a]
and now I am your servant, O king,
let me live;
I too was the servant of your father from long ago;
and now I too am your servant.'
And you shall cancel for me the counsel of Ahithophel.
35 Will you not have with you there[a] Zadok and Abiathar the priests?
And whatever word you hear from the king['s house],
you will inform Zadok and Abiathar the priests.
36 You will find there with them their two sons, Zadok's Ahimaaz and Abiathar's Jonathan,
and you will send by their hand to me whatever word you hear."[a]
37 And Hushai *the Archite*, David's friend, came to the city,
and Absalom too was coming to Jerusalem *and Ahithophel with him.*
16:1 Now David passed on a little from the summit;[a]
and see, Ziba page of [Mephibosheth] *Memphibaal* meeting him,
and a pair[b] of donkeys saddled
and on them two hundred loaves, one hundred bunches of raisins,
one hundred summer fruit, and a skin[c] of wine.
2 And the king said to Ziba,
"What are these things of yours?"
And Ziba said,
"The donkeys are for the king's house to ride;
and the bread[a] and the summer fruit are for the young men to eat,
and the wine is for the faint[b] in the wilderness to drink."
3 And the king said,
"And where is the son of your master?"
And Ziba said to the king,
"He is in fact sitting on in Jerusalem;
for he has said,

'Today the house of Israel will return to me the kingdom of my father.'"

4 And the king said to Ziba,
"You in fact have everything that is [Mephibosheth's] *Memphibaal's*."
And Ziba said,
"I prostrate myself.
I am finding favor in [your] *the* eyes *of* my lord king."

5 And King David was coming to [Bahurim] *Chorram*;[a]
and see from there a man coming out, from the family of the house[b] of Saul;
and his name was Shimei son of Gera,
and he was coming out and out[c]
and cursing.

6 [And he pelted] *and pelting*[a] David and all [the] *his* servants [of King David] with stones;
and all the people and all the mighty men were to [his] right and to [his] left *of the king*.

7 And thus Shimei said in his cursing:
"Out! Out! man of blood and no-use man!

8 Yahweh has brought back on you all the blood of the house of Saul,
in whose stead you have reigned,
and Yahweh has given the kingdom into the hand of Absalom your son;
and [look at] *has shown* you [in] your evil,
because you are a man of blood."

9 And Abishai son of Zeruiah said to the king,
"Why should this [dead] *accursed* dog curse my lord king?
Please let me cross over
and remove his head."

10 And the king said,
"What I have to do with you, son[s] of Zeruiah.
Let him be.
He curses so,
because Yahweh has said to him,
'Curse David';
and who should say,
'Why have you done so?'"

11 And David said to [Abishai] *Joab* and to all his servants,
"Look at my son,
who came out of my loins,

seeking my life.
How much more the Benjamite.
Let him be
and let him curse,
if Yahweh has told him.
12 Perhaps Yahweh will look [with my eye[a]] *on my distress*,
and Yahweh will return good to me instead of his cursing this day."
13 And David and his men went on their way.

And Shimei was going on the ridge of the hill,
going alongside him,
and he cursed
and he pelted with stones alongside[a] him
and dirtied him with dirt.

27a. In GT *ʾth* ("you") is an emphatic address before the sg. imper. "return"; and David's speech begins with an imper.: sg. in LT (*rʾh*), pl. in B (*rʾw*). But MT links the independent "you" with the previous word "see," reading it as the ptc. with the mark of the question (*hrwʾh*): "Are you seeing?" or "Are you a seer?" And B (*rʾw*) attests a beginning identical to v. 28.

b. The verse has started by addressing Zadok in the sg., then finishes with pl. forms, which assume Zadok and Abiathar together: "your [pl.] sons with you [pl.]."

28a. Here *mhh* (*hitpalpel*), "tarry," is unique to Samuel (see also Gen 43:10); and so the Greek renderings may have been guessing: B offers "take the field," and LT "wait for you."

b. For MT's *ʿbrwt*, B offers the commoner *arabōth*; cf. MT in 17:16. The LT's "olive" is quite different and anticipates v. 30.

30a. Notice the shared consonants between *ḥpwy*, "covered," and *yḥp*, "bare[foot]."[14]

31a. Only here and in Isa 44:25 is the *piʿel* of *skl* used. The *nipʿal* is used in 2 Sam 24:10 (BTH) and also in 1 Sam 13:13; and the *hipʿil* in 1 Sam 26:21.

32a. The GT transliterates *Rōs* (*Roōs* in B), as a proper name but does not represent the article as in MT's "the head" (*hrʾš*).

b. LT with a main verb reads more easily than MT (and B); but it agrees with MT and B in 16:1, where several elements of 15:32 are repeated.

34a. The lengthy omission from MT may be explained by the similarity in Heb. characters between its initial *ʿbrw* ("they have crossed") and *ʿbdk* ("your servant") at the start of the shared material.

35a. In LT this verse opens exactly as does v. 36, as if *hnh-šm ʿmm* had been read in both cases.

36a. At the end of the verse, LT repeats much of (the plus in) v. 34: "and you will say to Absalom, 'Your brothers and the king have passed through after me, your father has passed through, and as for me, I have just arrived, and I am your servant.'"

14. The Arabic cognate *ḥafay* can mean both "reveal" and "conceal" (McKane 318).

16:1a. The GT again takes *Rōs* (*Roōs*) as a name, this time with the article.

b. The noun *ṣemed* ("yoke") is found in two further (Saul [and Jonathan]) contexts in 1 Sam 11:7; 14:14 as well as in 1 Kgs 19:21; 2 Kgs 9:25.

c. In their measures of provisions, both B and LT transliterate *nbl*. All four types of food are represented, and in the same order, in MT, GT, and 4QSam[a]. The LT's *oiphi* is a transliteration of *ʾyph*, which 4QSam[a] also uses, but with a different item in the list. It is over the amounts that the textual witnesses differ most:

	loaves	**raisins**	**summer fruit**	**wine**
MT, B	200	100	100	skin
LT	200	ephah	200	skin
4QSam[a]	{200}	{100}	ephah	skin

2a. The GT agrees with Q in reading only *whlḥm* ("and the bread"); *wlhlḥm* (K) could be read as "and for making war."

b. The LT's *eklelymenō* is sg. like MT *yʿp* ("tired") but B has the participle in the pl. *eklelymenos* means "unstringed/paid off."

5a. Has LT lost the opening consonant of Bahurim?

b. The phrase "family of the house of . . ." is infrequent, and absent from the book of Numbers, where *mšpḥt* (cst.) predominates; cf. only Judg 9:1; Zech 12:12, 13. The term *mšpḥh* itself is rare in Samuel: cf. only 1 Sam 9:21 (2x); 10:21 (2x); 18:18; 20:6, 29; 2 Sam 14:7 (in the parable of the woman of Tekoa).

c. The emphatic resumption of *yṣʾ* ("go out") at the end of this verse draws our attention to a word that plays an important role in this whole chapter.

6a. The GT opens this verse with a further ptc. and may have read *wmsql*, not *wysql*.

12a. The GT attests *bʿnyy* for *bʿyny* (Q) and *bʿwny* (K).

13a. In place of *lʿmtw*, LT attests simply *ʿlyw*.

[27–30] The connections between David—and possibly the ark too—leaving Jerusalem and the arrival of the ark in Jerusalem (2 Sam 6) and the arrival of the ark in the promised land (Josh 3–4) have already been noted. David's departure from Jerusalem is not like his crossing to Rabbah to lead the formal conquest of the Ammonite capital. It is more like a formal quitting of the city of promise. And if the "fords of the wilderness" (v. 28 MT) are in fact the Jordan fords, then the symbolism of this narrative is all the stronger—not just quitting the city of promise, but the land of promise as well. But David will not have the ark leave the city: he hopes to return, and the priests' sons can be his spies.

[31–37] David's (principal?) counselor has accepted Absalom's invitation to join him in Hebron (v. 12). When David hears this (v. 31), he prays to Yahweh that Ahithophel's advice might be rendered foolish. "Ahi-tophel" means "My brother is *tōpel*." Hebrew words very similar to *tōpel* mean "tasteless" and "whitewash": each of these is an effective symbol for folly. David's comment on Ahithophel's defection may be a play on the meaning of his name. No sooner has he voiced this request than he meets a new main agent at the top of the hill

(v. 32): he immediately asks Hushai to act for him in rendering null and void any able counsel Ahithophel might provide to Absalom (v. 34). Hushai is destined to outclass David's former adviser; he is able to slip into Jerusalem from the northeast, just as Absalom is entering from Hebron, to the south.

The story of Ahithophel, Absalom, Hushai, and Yahweh is elaborated below (16:20–17:23), with much use of the technical term "counsel," *ʿēṣâ*. That noun and the related verb occur only there in Samuel, apart from this brief anticipation (vv. 12, 31, 34). But David's crisp instructions to Hushai sum up perfectly what will be at stake in the longer, later scene. The policy advice of Ahithophel is so much trusted that it is effectively binding. As such, it needs to be nothing less than "cancelled" (v. 34), a verb (*prr, hipʿil*) more normally used of setting aside the binding terms of a treaty, pact, or covenant. And the only way to frustrate binding counsel is to make it appear "foolish" (v. 31).

[16:1–4] By leaving Jerusalem toward the northeast, David immediately enters the territory of Benjamin. It is hardly surprising that his next meetings are with members of Saul's house—the first being a very well-provided steward. The provisions he offers David (16:1) are very similar to those Abigail made available to David (1 Sam 25:18). In the case of Ziba, as of Abigail, it is unclear whether from the outset they are seeking to benefit themselves over against master or husband. However, given the opportunity of David's asking him about his master, Ziba uses his generosity with goods that are not his to plant a lie and is rewarded for such "loyalty" (vv. 3–4).

What exactly is Ziba's master doing in Jerusalem, according to his not-very-loyal steward? The combination of the verb *yšb* with "in Jerusalem" (v. 3) is often quite significant. The verb has two main meanings: "sit" and "live"; and when someone who is or would like to be king is being talked about, "sit" often has the sense of "sit enthroned": my master is "on his seat" in Jerusalem waiting to have the kingdom of his father given back to him. And the very similar-sounding verb used for "return" (*yšyb*) serves to concentrate our attention on what this Saulide is doing and hoping for in Jerusalem.[15] Although David has rivals as king, it appears that he has established Jerusalem as the capital city of Israel: Absalom is moving on the city, and Ziba's master is said to have quite independent hopes of what "the house of Israel" will do to restore him and his family to their rightful place.

[5–10] Shimei's "cursing" or "slighting" (*qll piʿel*) is one of the keywords of the passage. It is used no less than seven times in vv. 5–13 (much more densely than in any other context in HB), and is noted again in 19:21 (22). The last person of whom this verb form was used was Goliath (1 Sam 17:43); and he also was hurling verbal abuse at David. The comparison, though strengthened

15. The other subjects in 2 Samuel of "seated in Jerusalem" are Mephibosheth (9:13); David (11:1); Uriah (11:12); Absalom (14:28)—only 11:1 is from BTH.

by talk of dogs (1 Sam 17:43; 2 Sam 16:9) and pelting stones (1 Sam 17:49; 2 Sam 16:6, 13), serves only to heighten the contrast. The very repetitiveness of the reference to Shimei's cursing, over against the single mention of Goliath's, only underscores its inefficacy. And the same must be said of Shimei's many stones thrown at David, over against David's single stone slung at Goliath. "Come/go out" (*yṣ*ʾ) frequently implies challenge (not just in 1 Sam 17–18), as in the case of Shimei (16:5); but when Shimei shouts "Out! Out!" (*ṣ*ʾ *ṣ*ʾ) at David (16:7), it must mean "Get out" rather than "Come out (to meet me)."[16]

The GT translates literally the first nickname that Shimei hurls at David: "man of bloods," *dāmîm* (pl., vv. 7–8), is used in Samuel–Kings, but never in Joshua–Judges. In 1 Sam 25:26, 33, Abigail and Yahweh are praised for saving David from bloodshed; in 2 Sam 3:28, David asserts his innocence of bloodguilt over Abner's death; and in 21:1 Yahweh identifies Saul's house as guilty in respect of the Gibeonites. Compare also 1 Kgs 2:5, 31, 33; 2 Kgs 9:7, 26. Shimei goes on to call David to his face what Abigail called her "foolish" husband behind his back: even if *bĕlîyaʿal* does literally mean "no use," it has come to refer to a particularly pernicious uselessness.

David has also already come close to being stoned by his own men after the sacking of Ziklag by the Amalekites (1 Sam 30:6). A few stones from a single discontent has been of little consequence to a David adequately protected by his loyal followers. And he has already recognized (at least rhetorically) the possibility that behavior hostile to himself by Saul has been divinely instigated (1 Sam 26:19), and so why not also now by a later member of Saul's household? Just as David invokes Yahweh's name four times in his self-defense against Saul (26:19–20), so too now "Yahweh" is four times on his lips (16:10–12): twice (vv. 10–11) he recognizes that Yahweh may have told Shimei to slight him; and correspondingly he hopes ("perhaps," v. 12) that Yahweh will see and that Yahweh will return good to him in place of Shimei's slighting. "Perhaps" (*ʾwly*) recognizes properly and deferentially that an appellant cannot and should not presume on the granting of the appeal. The woman from Tekoa has already addressed David so (14:15). David's own words echo the all-important "perhaps" at the very heart of the book of Amos (5:15): it may be that Yahweh will bring good out of bad.

[11–13] When David refers to Absalom as "my son who has gone out from my loins" (v. 11), he uses the verb Shimei has used in his cursing (v. 7); but even more significantly he refers back to the divine promise mediated by Nathan, which included "seed . . . who would come out from his loins" (7:12). David's response to that promise culminated in the prayer that the house so constituted would continue forever and be blessed forever (7:29). In Shimei's cursing and

16. Is any connection being suggested between *ṣ*ʾ ("Out!") and *ṣʾh* ("dung")?

Absalom's revolt, David can sense the promise unraveling. Earlier in Samuel, "Benjamite" has been used by the narrator (1 Sam 9:1, 4) and by Saul (1 Sam 9:21; 22:7). But here (v. 11) it is David who attaches the label to Shimei. Is that because he knows him or has been reliably informed about him? Or is it a simple deduction from his partisanship toward the house of Saul?[17]

2 Samuel 16:14–19

14 And the king came and all the people,
who with him were tired,
and [he] *they* took breath[a] there.
15 And Absalom and all the people,[a] the men of Israel, came to Jerusalem,
and Ahithophel was with him.
16 Now, as Hushai the Archite, friend of David, came *into the city* to Absalom,
Hushai said to Absalom,
"Long live the king[;
long live the king[a]]."
17 And Absalom said to Hushai,
"This is your loyalty to your friend!
Why have you not gone with your friend?"
18 And Hushai said to Absalom,
"No, rather, whomever Yahweh has chosen and [t]his people and all the men of Israel:
his[a] I shall be
and with him I shall stay.
19 And the second thing:
to whom should I be servant?
Not in face of his son?
As I served in face of your father,
so shall I be in face of you."

14a. For *wynpš*, B has the literal *kai anepsyxan*, but LT *kai anepausanto* ("took rest").
15a. Codex B does not represent "the people."
16a. The GT is supported by two masoretic MSS in not repeating the loyal acclamation.
18a. Here GT supports Q's *lw* for K's *l'*.

[14–19] The main textual witnesses do not specify where the king and his people reached (v. 14). Some versions add "by the Jordan." Elsewhere, weariness is reported of the people (1 Sam 14:28, 31; 2 Sam 17:29) and of the

17. See further below on 19:17–18.

king (2 Sam 21:15). Here both are mentioned, although the grammar of the sentence in MT is a little strange: it is common enough for the opening verb to be singular (in agreement with the principal subject, "the king"); and there is no surprise that the adjective "weary" is plural (*'ypym*), after the introduction of "the people"; but it is more remarkable that the verb "took breath" reverts to the singular (though B and LT use different verbs, both are in the plural). The sentence may have lost more than the location of the stopping place. This verbal form related to *nepeš* appears just twice more in HB: both in Exodus and both in connection with Sabbath refreshment—for one's household staff (23:12), and for the Creator on the first Sabbath (31:17). Contemporaneously—the description using many of the same words—Absalom arrives in Jerusalem (v. 15). David's "all the people that was with him" is trumped by Absalom's "all the people, the men of Israel." If the first "with him" serves to set limits on the people with David, the second serves to emphasize that all the men of Israel with Absalom include Ahithophel.

David's friend Hushai comes well through his first meeting with the new king in Jerusalem. His words are a fine study in courtly ambiguity. Although he may have intended his "May the king live" to refer to David, Absalom seems content to think otherwise. Like many new to power, he may be only too pleased to hear what sounds like the right answers (vv. 16–19).

2 Samuel 16:20–17:13

20 And Absalom said to Ahithophel,
"Give yourselves counsel—
what should we do?"
21 And Ahithophel said to Absalom,
"Go to the concubines of your father
whom he left at rest
to watch the house,
and all Israel will hear
that you have [become vile to] *shamed*[a] your father,
and [the] *your* hands *and those* of all who are with you will become strong."
22 And they pitched for Absalom the tent on the roof,
and Absalom went in to *all* his father's concubines in the eyes of all Israel.
23 And the counsel of Ahithophel,
which he proffered in those days,
it was as if one[a] asked of [the word[b] of] the Deity.
That is how all Ahithophel's counsel was, both for David and for Absalom.

17:1 And Ahithophel said to Absalom,
“Please let me choose *myself* [twelve] *ten* thousand men
that I may rise
and [pursue[a]] *go down* after David tonight;
2 and that I may come upon him while he is tired and relaxed,
and terrify him;
and all the people who are with him will flee,
and I shall strike down the king only.

3 And all the people will return to you,	**3** And I shall return all the people to you,
like the return of the bride to her man;[a]	like the return of the whole;
nothing but the life[b] of one man[a]	the man[a]
you are seeking,	whom you are seeking,

all the people shall be at peace.”
4 And the word was right[a] in Absalom’s eyes, and in the eyes of all the elders of Israel.

5 And Absalom said,
“Please call also for Hushai the Archite,
and let us hear what is in his mouth [—his too].”
6 And Hushai came to Absalom,
and Absalom said to [him] *Hushai*,
“In this fashion has Ahithophel spoken.
Shall we do his word or not?[a]
You speak.”

7 And Hushai spoke to Absalom,
“The advice
that Ahithophel has advised
is not good on this occasion.”
8 And Hushai said *further*,
“You yourself know your father and his men:
that they are mighty men
and they are bitter-spirited like a bear bereft[a] in the open field—
and your father is a man of war
and will not pass the night[b] with the people.
9 Look! Now he is hidden in one of the pits or in one of the places;
and,
supposing [some of them[a]] *the people* fall at first,
whoever hears the report will say,
‘The people following Absalom have suffered a blow.’

10 And he, even the man of valor
whose heart is like the lion's heart,
will melt to liquid,
because all Israel knows
that your father is a mighty man—and *all* the men of valor
with him.
11 [Yes[a]] *Thus* I *myself* advise:
Let there be a complete gathering to you of all Israel
from Dan to Beer-sheba, like the sand that is by the sea for number,
and your face marching in the midst *of them.*
12 And we shall come to him in one of the places
where *we shall find him* [he is found[a]],
and we shall [be on] *amaze* him
like the dew falls on the ground,
and we shall not leave of him and of all the men who are with him
[even] one.
13 And,
if they gather to a city,
all Israel will have ropes carried[a] to that city,
and *they* [we] shall drag[b] *it* [him] to the wadi-bed
till[c] there not be found there even a pebble."[d]

21a. The GT's active *katēschynas* renders not MT's *b'š* (*nip'al*) but apparently *bwš* (*hip'il*).

23a. Here LT and Q add the similar consonants *'yš* after *yš'l*. But B supports the shorter K.

b. The LT does not attest *dbr*; the idiom *š'l b'lhym* is familiar in Judges and Samuel. The MT, supported by B, is unique: the closest analogy may be *nglh yhwh . . . bdbr yhwh* in 1 Sam 3:21. In fact, *dbr* is construed with *'lhym* only in 1 Sam 9:27, while *dbr h'lhym* is unique to 1 Chr 26:32 (both MT).

17:1a. The MT reads *w'rdph* ("and let me pursue"), but LT renders the shorter *w'rdh* ("and let me go down").

3a. The MT lost text between one occurrence of "the man" and the next. Confusion had followed between *klh* ("bride") and *kl* ("all"); and between *'ḥd* ("one") and *'šr* (rel. marker).

b. Fragments of "only the life" are preserved in 4QSam[a] (DJD 162).

4a. This idiom *wyyšr hdbr b'yny* is shared precisely only with 1 Sam 18:20, 26; 1 Chr 13:4; 2 Chr 30:4 (with a different subj., cf. also Num 23:27; Judg 14:3, 7; 1 Kgs 9:12; Jer 18:4; 27:5).

6a. Likewise, *'m-'yn* is used in the sense "if not" in Gen 30:1; Exod 32:32; Judg 9:15, 20; 2 Sam 17:6; 2 Kgs 2:10; Job 33:33; and meaning "or not" in Exod 17:7; Num 13:20. The LT's *ē pōs* is either freer, or has rendered a different text {*'m 'yk*}.

8a. The LT has pl. "bears" and calls them "stubborn" (cf. Hos 4:16) rather than "bereft" (cf. Hos 13:8; Prov 17:12). However, B offers a pair of animal images: "a bear bereft in the field or a savage sow in the plain"; and both *agros* and *pedion* are regular renderings of *śdh* in one and the same book.

b. Here GT has read *ylyn* as *hip'il*, and hence transitive; the following *'t* is ambiguous.

9a. The MT's *bhm* is supported by *autois* in B; but LT's "the people" attests *h'm*.

11a. Codex B attests both *ky* with MT and *kh* or *kn* with LT.

12a. The GT reads *nmṣ'* as *qal* ("we shall find"); MT is more naturally read as *nip'al* ("he is found").

13a. Elsewhere *nś' hip'il* is found only in Lev 22:16.

b. Otherwise *sḥb* ("drag about") is known only in Jer 15:3; 22:19; 49:20; 50:45 (and the pl. of the noun *sḥbh* only in Jer 38:11, 12). These Jeremianic contexts for this vb. are always threatening.

c. The composite *'d 'šr-l'* is compared to *mbly-'šr-l'* in Eccl 3:11.

d. In contrast to v. 12, GT here reads *nms'* as *nip'al*, but I have chosen to render it as *qal*.

e. At the end *ṣrwr* has caused the translators much trouble: *lithos* ("stone," B), *systrophē* ("collection/[morbid] stone," LT), *conversatio* or *cumulus fundamenti* (OL).

[20–23] Hushai's offer of service is not immediately taken up. Absalom turns first to Ahithophel, who has accompanied him into the capital. Absalom speaks grandly in the royal plural (16:20; 17:5) and extends this plural courtesy to his counselor (the "you" is plural, matching the "we"). But those early readers of Samuel who were familiar with the still earlier Book of Two Houses would have had a premonition of disaster looming: there the inexperienced Rehoboam is the only king to "take counsel" with advisers. Admittedly, in his case, he made the mistake of *not* listening to those who had advised his father. Ahithophel has advised David; but in a more important respect, he also resembles Rehoboam's young circle: Ahithophel's description of David's concubines seems contemptuous, whether of David or of them. If the verb *hnyḥ* is used literally, then guards are not normally left at "rest"; and when used in the equally common sense of "place" or "deposit," this verb normally takes a nonpersonal object—the concubines are items.

The advice is acted upon beyond the letter. Ahithophel has specified that all Israel should hear about what Absalom will do. But it is so arranged that "all Israel" will see. Seeing is particularly important. The roof of the king's house, where the tent is erected for this proxy revenge on David, is precisely the locus from which he saw Bathsheba in the first place. Like Israel's insulting the Philistines by defeating one of their posts in Benjamin (1 Sam 13:4), like Hanun's insulting David by abusing David's ambassadors (2 Sam 10:4–6), so now Absalom throws down a gauntlet to his father by deliberately mistreating his womenfolk. In each case the humiliation is deliberately planned. The narrator wryly adds that advice given by this counselor, whether to the old or the new king, has the force of a divine oracle. We may not be sure what the mechanics of the oracle are; but it does apparently settle matters. When David calls for Abiathar and the ephod, that deflects from himself the sore rage of his men (1 Sam 30); and even when his men questioned a first oracular response about tackling the Philistines at Keilah, they were satisfied when confirmation came in a second (1 Sam 23:1–5). Ahithophel's advice has no less force.

[17:1–4] After his first success with Absalom, the sage counselor does not just wait to be consulted but next offers practical help: to lead a force in immediate pursuit of an exhausted David, frighten off his followers, and strike him down alone (vv. 1–3). Interestingly, Ahithophel, though now in Absalom's entourage, is still calling David "the king" (v. 2). To Absalom and the elders, his advice seems right: "to be straight/level/right in someone's eyes" (v. 4) is an expression used in both Samuel–Kings and in Chronicles, but only in portions additional to BTH. "The elders of Israel" (v. 4) featured in BTH at two key points: when David was invited to be their king (2 Sam 5:3), and when the ark was moved into the new temple (1 Kgs 8:1, 3).[18] No role has been ascribed to them in Absalom's coming to power (2 Sam 15–16);[19] now, with David out of his capital, they figure as part of Absalom's council.

[5–6] However, still further advice is taken, now from Hushai (vv. 5–6); and the story develops some resemblance to the account in BTH in which Ahab and Jehoshaphat are also planning a campaign in Transjordan (1 Kgs 22//2 Chr 18). In this variation, we find court favorite Ahithophel in place of the four hundred court prophets ministering the word of Yahweh, and Hushai in place of critical Micaiah.

[7–13] Ahithophel's advice about David's harem effectively scorns the old king as a nonperson; and his proposal for hot pursuit assumes that David's men can be detached from himself. Hushai comes straight to the point and challenges both judgments together. On this occasion the great man's advice has been faulty—David is still too much the old campaigner to be so easily caught: at night he will not even be found among his men. Hushai speaks to Absalom not about "the king," but about "your father" (17:8, 10). "Bitter-spirited" (v. 8) is used just twice more in Samuel: in 1 Sam 1:10, of barren Hannah; and in 1 Sam 22:2, where the first gathering of David's band of desperadoes is described.[20] If "bitter-spirited" reminds us of the origins of David's close followers, "bear" reminds us of his early boast to Saul (1 Sam 17:34–37) that as a shepherd lad he had been more than equal to such a predator. Hushai nicely clashes the normally positive image of the mighty hero with the normally negative one of discontent or bitterness of spirit, illustrated by a she-bear deprived of her cubs, to produce the equivalent of our proverbial danger of an angry or wounded lion (v. 8).

18. The discussion of 2 Sam 5:1–3 noted elders at two further significant points in BTH, but these are not specified as "the elders of Israel."

19. In fact they appear in Samuel only in 1 Sam 4:3; 8:4; 2 Sam 3:17; 5:3; 17:4, 15.

20. For *mar-nepeš* ("bitter-spirited"), cf. Judg 18:25; Isa 38:15; Ezek 27:31; Job 3:20; Prov 31:6—and compare also Job 7:11; 10:1; 21:25.

Here, in fact, even a lion-hearted hero will quail before such a she-bear (v. 10). Nothing less than complete mobilization of all Israel will suffice.

In the broad context of the Former Prophets as a whole, the description of "all Israel" ("like the sand by the sea in multitude," v. 11) is transitional here. Such terms were used previously in FP of enemies: all the nations of the land (Josh 11:4), the camels of the Midianites and Amalekites (Judg 7:12), and the Philistines (1 Sam 13:5). By contrast, in 1 Kings, it will also be used of Israel and Judah at peace (4:20) and of Solomon's understanding (4:29 [5:9]). "From Dan to Beer-sheba" is the measure of the whole land, according to 1 Sam 3:20; 2 Sam 3:10; 24:2,[21] 15; 1 Kgs 4:25 (5:5); 2 Chr 30:5. Is it because of the dangers of a complete "count" of Israel (2 Sam 24:2, BTH) that Hushai recommends here a thorough "gathering" of the people instead—without mention of actually counting them? Perhaps not very auspiciously, the *nipʿal* of *ʾsp* ("gather") was used also of the huge Philistine forces in 1 Sam 13:5, the only other "gathering" in Samuel compared to the sand by the sea; and *bʾš* ("stink") was used in that context too (13:4; cf. 2 Sam 16:21); and there too LT attests a name (*Baithōrōn*) very similar to what it reads here (cf. 1 Sam 13:5; 2 Sam 17:18). Hushai builds up a flattering picture of the support for Absalom relative to his father: his forces will represent the whole of the country (v. 11), while David's will be able to be gathered into one single city (v. 13).

2 Samuel 17:14–20:19 Absalom Outfoxed, David Restored

In MT—or at least in CL, which is widely followed in modern printed editions—the first of the two "paragraphs" (*pĕtûḥôt*) in this section is the longest in all of Samuel. It opens with the joint judgment of Absalom, all Israel—and Yahweh too—in favor of Hushai rather than Ahithophel. The following paragraph opens (19:30) with David's judgment that Saul's grandson and his steward should share the land that David earlier made over to Ziba alone on the basis of his dubious testimony (16:3–4). The first and larger portion reports the undoing of first Ahithophel and then Absalom, and finally the return of David. As usual, the following translation and commentary follows the division into subparagraphs (*sĕtûmôt*) in that same codex.

2 Samuel 17:14–19:28 (29)

14 And Absalom said, and [all] the men of Israel,
"The advice of Hushai the Archite is better than the advice of Ahithophel."
And Yahweh, he had given orders

21. But 1 Chr 21:2 (//2 Sam 24:2) has the reverse order.

to cancel the good advice of Ahithophel *and the advice of Absalom*,
for the purpose of Yahweh's bringing the disaster [to] *on* Absalom.

15 And Hushai said to Zadok and to Abiathar the priests,
"In this way and that, Ahithophel advised Absalom and the elders of Israel;
and in this way [and that], I myself advised.
16 Now then send quickly
and inform [David] *the king*, saying,
'Do not [spend] *journey* tonight in the wilderness plains,[a]
but actually make a complete crossing *of the waters,*[b]
lest there be a swallowing down for the king
and for all the people who are with him.'"
17 Now Jonathan and Ahimaaz were stationed at En-Rogel,
and the maid would go
and inform them,
and they would go
and inform King David,
for they could not let themselves be seen
or come [coming] to the city.
18 And a lad saw them
and informed Absalom,
and [the two of them] *they* went quickly
and came to the house of a man at [Bahurim] *Beth-horon*,
and he had a well in his yard,
and they went down into it.
19 And the woman took
and spread the coverlet over the face of the well
and scattered the grains[a] on it,
and nothing was known.
20 And the servants of Absalom came to the woman at home
and said,
"Where are Ahimaaz and Jonathan?"
And the woman said to [them] *the men*,
"They passed over [the watercourse[a]] *hurrying*."
And they searched
but did not find them;
and they returned to Jerusalem.

21 And it came to be after their going,
and they came up from the well
and went

and informed King David.
And they said to [David] *him*,
"Up
and cross the water quickly;
for thus has Ahithophel advised against you."
22 And David got up, and all [the people] who were with him,
and they crossed the Jordan till morning light,[a]
until not
a thing was left behind. Thus they one was left[b] who had not
crossed the Jordan.
23 And Ahithophel, he saw
that his advice was not practiced;
and he saddled his donkey
and upped
and went to his house, to his town;
and he ordered his house,
and hanged himself;
and he died
and was buried in his father's grave.

24 And David, he came to Mahanaim;[a]
and Absalom, he crossed the Jordan, himself and every man of Israel with him.
25 And Amasa, Absalom placed him over the army instead of Joab.
Now Amasa was son of a man named Ithra the [Israelite/ Ishmaelite] *Jezreelite*
who had "come to" Abigal daughter of [Nahash] *Jesse*, sister of Zeruiah, mother of Joab.
26 And [Israel] *Absalom* encamped, and [Absalom] *every man of Israel*, in the land of Gilead.

27 And it came to be as David came to Mahanaim,
and Shobi[a] son of Nahash from Rabbah of the sons of Ammon and
Machir son of Ammiel from Lo-debar and Barzillai the Gileadite from
Rogelim[a] 28 *brought ten* beds *and rugs* and ten basins and pottery vessels, and wheat and barley and flour and parched grain and beans and
lentils and parched grain, 29 and honey and butter and sheep and curds[a]
from the cattle,
and they presented (them) to David and to [the] *his* people [which was with him] to eat;
for they said,
"The people is hungry and tired and thirsty in the wilderness."

18:1 And David numbered[a] the people which was with him,
and put over them leaders of thousands and leaders of hundreds.
2a And David [dispatched[a]] *thirded* the people: a third under Joab; a third under Abishai son of Zeruiah, Joab's brother; and a third under Ittai the Gittite.

2b And the king said to the people,
"I shall in fact go out—I too—with you."
3 And the people said,
"You shall not go out.
For if we are in fact put to flight,
[they will not set to] *there will not stand in* us any heart;[a]
and if half of us die,
they will not set to us any heart.
But {you}[b] are like ten thousand of us;
so then it is better
that you should be our help [from] *in* the city."

4 And the king said to them,
"What is good in your eyes I shall do."
And the king stood by the side[a] of the gate;
and all the people—they went out by hundreds and by thousands.
5 And the king commanded Joab and Abishai and Ittai, saying,
"Gently for me[a] with the lad, with Absalom."
And all the people listened[b]
to the king commanding all the leaders in the matter of Absalom.
6 And the people went out to the field
to meet Israel,
and the battle was in the forest of [Ephraim] Maainan.[a]
7 And the people of Israel were smitten there before the servants of David;
and the blow there on that day was great: twenty thousand *men*.
8 And the battle [there] was scattered over the face of the whole [land] *forest*;
and the forest was greater in devouring of the people
than the sword devoured on that day.
9 And Absalom [chanced[a]] *was great* before the servants of David,
and [Absalom[b]] *he* was riding on his mule,
and the mule came under the network[c] of the great oak,[d]
and his head was caught[e] in the oak,
and he was [placed[e]] *hung* between the heaven and the earth,
and the mule under him passed on.
10 And a certain man saw
and informed Joab;

and he said,
"Look![a] I saw Absalom hung on the oak."[b]
11 And Joab said to the man
who was informing him,
"And look! you saw—
and why did you not strike him there to the ground?
And it would have been on me
to give you [ten pieces[a]] *fifty shekels* of silver and one belt."
12 And the man said to Joab,
"And supposing [I was] *you yourself*[a] *were* weighing in my [palms] *hands* a thousand pieces of silver,
I would not set my hand*s* on the son of the king,
for in our ears the king commanded you and Abishai and Ittai,
saying,
'Take care [whoever[b]] *for me* of the lad, of Absalom.'
13 Or had I acted falsely[a] at cost of my[b] self
(and no matter is concealed from the king),
you yourself would be positioning yourself at a distance."
14 And Joab said,
"Accordingly[a]
it is I[b] who shall start[c] before you."
"Not so
shall I tarry before you."
And he took three staves[d] in his hand
and thrust them in the heart of Absalom
while he was still alive, in the heart of the tree.
15 And ten lads, Joab's armor-bearers, surrounded him
and struck Absalom
and did him to death.
16 And Joab thrust[a] on the horn,
and the people turned back
from pursuing after Israel,
for Joab held back the people.
17 And [they] *Joab* took Absalom
and threw him in the forest into a big pit;
and they erected over him a very great heap of stones.
And all Israel, they had fled, each to his tent.

18 And Absalom, he had taken
and erected for himself, in his lifetime, a monument in the valley of the king;
for he had said,
"I have no son
to bring my name to remembrance."

And he called the monument by his name,
and [there was a naming of] *they named*[a] it "Pillar of Absalom" to this day.

19 And Ahimaaz son of Zadok, he said *to Joab*:
"Please let me run
and bring news to [the] King *David*
that Yahweh has delivered him from the hand of his enemies."
20 And Joab said [to him],
"You are not a newsman today,
but you will bring news another day.
But this day you shall not bring news, surely [on account {of this}[a]]:
the king's son is dead."
21 And Joab said to the Cushite,
"Go, inform the king
what you have seen."
And the Cushite prostrated himself to Joab,
and ran.
22 And Ahimaaz son of Zadok went on
and said to Joab,
"Be what may,
please let me run, me too, after the Cushite."
And Joab said,
"Whyever are you running, my son,
when you have no {productive}[a] news *as you go*?"[a]
23 *And Ahimaaz said*,
"Be what may,
I'll run."
And he said to him,
"Run."
And Ahimaaz ran by *the appointed* way [of the plain[a]],
and he passed the Cushite.
24 And David was seated between the two gates.
And the lookout went to the roof of the gate, [to] *upon* the wall,
and he raised his eyes
and looked
and could see a man running on his own *before* him.[a]
25 And the lookout called
and informed the king;
and the king said,
"If *he is running* alone,
there's news in his mouth."
And he came on and on, getting nearer.

26 And the lookout saw another man running,
and the lookout called to the gate[keeper],
and said,
"Look a[nother] man running alone."
And the king said,
"This one too is bringing news."
27 And the lookout said,
"I see the running of the first as the running of Ahimaaz son of Zadok."
And the king said,
"He is a good man,
and about a good report will he come."
28a And Ahimaaz [called] *drew near*[a]
and said to the king,
"Peace."
And he prostrated to [the king] *him* on his face to the ground.

28b And he said,
"Blessed is Yahweh your God,
who has delivered up the men
who had raised their hand against my lord the king."
29 And the king said,
"Well for the lad, for Absalom."
And Ahimaaz said,
"I [saw] *heard behind me* the great tumult[a]

at Joab the servant of the king's sending	at Joab's sending the servant of the king and[b]

your servant;
but I did not know what *was there*."
30 And the king said,
"Turn and position yourself so."
And he turned
and stood *behind him*.
31 Now the Cushite comes;
and the Cushite said,
"[Let it be reported] News,[a] my lord king,
that Yahweh has vindicated[b] you today from the hand of all those who rise up against you."

32 And the king said to the Cushite,
"Is it well for the lad, for Absalom?"
And the Cushite said,

"Let them become like the lad—the enemies of my lord the king, and all
who have risen against you—for ill."

33 And the king [shook] *shed tears,*[a]
and went up on top of the gate,
and wept;
and this is what he said as he [went] *wept*:[b]

"My son, Absalom,	"My son, Absalom, my son;
Absalom, my son,	my son, Absalom,
who will grant me death	who will grant my dying,
in place of you,	me in place of you,
Absalom, my son!"[c]	Absalom, my son, my son!"

19:1 And [it was] *they* told Joab, *saying*,
"Look, the king is weeping
and [has gone into] mourning[a] for Absalom."
2 And the deliverance[a] on that day became mourning for all the people,
because the people heard it said on that day,
"The king is grieved[b] over his son."
3 And the people became furtive[a] on that day entering the city,
just as the people shamed at their fleeing [in battle] become furtive.
4 And the king, he concealed[a] his face;
and the king cried with a loud voice,
"My son, Absalom; Absalom, [my son,] my son!"

5 And Joab came to the king, to the house,
and he said:
"You *yourself* have shamed today the face of [all] your servants
who are delivering today your life, and the life of your sons and daughters, and the life of your wives, and the life of your concubines—
6 loving those who hate you and hating those who love you—
for you have declared [today]
that you have *today* no leaders and servants;

For you know	for I know today[a]
that were Absalom alive today,	that were Absalom alive
were all of us dead,	and all of us today dead,
that that one would be acceptable	that then it/he would be right
in your eyes.	in your eyes.

7 Well then, up, [out,]
and speak to your servants' heart;

for by Yahweh [I] *they* have sworn:
Supposing you do not go out,
no man will lodge with you tonight,
and *take cognizance of this*,
that this disaster of yours will be worse than all the disaster*s*
that ha[s]*ve* come upon you from your youth till now."

8 And the king rose,
and sat down at the gate;
and the whole people [they] *was* informed,[a] saying,
"Look, the king is sitting at the gate."
And the whole people came before the king *to the gate*;
and Israel, it fled, each man to his tent[s].

9 And all the people were [disputing[a]] *grumbling* among all the tribes of Israel, saying,
"The king, he delivered us from the hand of *all* our enemies,
and he himself saved us from the hand of the Philistines;
and now he has fled from the land *and from his kingdom* from Absalom.
10 And Absalom,
whom we anointed over us,
he is dead in battle.
Well then, why are you silent
over [bringing back] *returning to* the king?"
And the word of all Israel came to the king.[a]

11 And King David, he sent to Zadok and Abiathar the priests, saying,
"Speak to the elders of Judah, saying,
'Why will you be behind in bringing back the king to his house?

	And the word of all Israel has come to the king, to his house.[a]
12 You are my brothers. You are my bone and my flesh. And why will you be late in bringing back the king to his house? And the word of all Israel came to the king.'	12 You are my brothers. You are my bone and my flesh. And why will you be late in bringing back the king?'

13 And to Amasa you will say,
'Are you not my bone and my flesh?
And now,[a] so will God[b] do to me and so will he continue,

if you will not be army leader [before] *for* me for all time
instead of Joab.'"
14 And [he] *Amasa* turned the heart of every man of Judah as one man;
and they sent to the king:
"Return, you and your servants."
15 And the king returned
and came to the Jordan;
and *the men of* Judah, they came *as far as* to Gilgal
[walking] *coming down* to meet the king,
to bring the king across the Jordan.
16 And Shimei son of Gera the Benjamite who was from [Bahurim] *Chorran* hurried
and went down with the men of Judah
to meet King David—
17 and a thousand men with him from Benjamin,
and Ziba "steward" of the house of Saul,
and [his] fifteen *of his* sons and his twenty servants with him,
and they *dispatched to*[a] [plunged into] the Jordan in face of the king.
18 And [they crossed the crossing] *they served their* service,[a]
bringing across [the house of] the king
and doing what was good in his eyes.
And Shimei son of Gera, he fell in face of the king at his crossing in the Jordan.
19 And he said to the king,
"Let not my lord reckon wrong to me,
and let him not remember
what your servant did wrong on the day
on which my lord king left Jerusalem,
the king taking it to his heart.
20 For *I* your servant know[s]
that I [myself] sinned.
But see, I have come today,
first of all the house of Joseph
in coming down to [meet] my lord the king."

21 And Abishai son of Zeruiah answered
and said,
"Instead of this shall [not] Shimei be put to death:
that he has cursed the anointed of Yahweh?"

22 And David said,
"What have I to do with you, sons of Zeruiah?

For you would become to me today as [adversary] *plotter*?[a]
Shall any man be put to death today in Israel?
For do [I] *you* not know
that today I am king over Israel?"

23 And the king said to Shimei,
"You shall not die."
And the king swore to him.

24 And Mephi[bosheth]*baal, son of Jonathan* son of Saul, he went down
to meet the king;
and he did not [do] *tend*[a] his feet,
and he did not pare his hands,
and he did not do his moustache,
and his clothes he did not wash,
from the day of the king's going
till the day on which he came in peace *to Jerusalem.*
25 And it came to be,
for he came to Jerusalem to meet the king,
and the king said to him,
"Why did you not go with me, Mephi[bosheth]*baal*?"
26 And he said,
"My lord king, my servant—he deceived[a] me;
for your servant said *to him*,
'[I will] saddle[b] me the ass,
and I will ride on it,
and go with the king—
for your servant is lame.'
27 And he slandered your servant to my lord the king;
but my lord the king

as the envoy of God	is as the envoy of God;
did what was good in the eyes of God.	and do what is good in your eyes.

28 For my father's whole house was nothing but sons of death to my lord the king,
and you placed your servant among those-who-eat[a] at your table.

And from whose hand[b] is there still right for me?"	And what right do I have still
And he cried still to the king.	even to cry still to the king?"

16a. Some MSS, supported by B, read *bʿbrwt hmdbr*, "at the wilderness crossings," for *bʿrbwt hmdbr* (MT; cf. 15:28).

b. At David's departure from Jerusalem, it is not always clear whether *ʿbr* is to be rendered "cross over" or "pass on"; the plus in LT anticipates the specification in v. 21.

19a. Here *hrpwt* (defective spelling of a noun known otherwise only in Prov 27:22) is transliterated in B by *araphōth*; LT renders with *palathas* ("cakes of preserved fruit"; cf. 1 Kgdms 25:18); possibly *[p]tisanae*, "pearl barley" or "barley-water."

20a. For *mykl hmym*, B has *mikron tou hydatos* and LT *speudontes*. McCarter (2:383) suggests (1) that *mikron* may turn into standard Greek what had started as a transliteration of the puzzling *mykl*; (2) that *speudontes* renders *mbhlym*, "acting hastily"; and (3) that the original, which also helps to explain LT, was *mybl hmym*, with the first word related to *ybl* ("stream" or "channel") of Isa 30:25; 44:4.

22a. The LT's "till it became light" apparently takes *ʾwr* as an inf., not the noun "light." Of the six instances of *(qal) ʾwr* (Mand.), three are in Samuel (1 Sam 14:27, 29; 29:10), with the others in Gen 44:3; Isa 60:1; Prov 4:18. The expression *ʿd-ʾwr hbqr* ("till the light/lighting of the morning"), as alternative to the simple *ʿd-hbqr*, is found only in Samuel and its immediate neighbors: Judg 16:2; 1 Sam 14:36; 25:(22,) 34, 36; 2 Sam 17:22; 2 Kgs 7:9. The shorter expression is found in Exod 16:23, 24; 29:34; Lev 6:9 (2); Judg 6:31; 19:25; 1 Sam 3:15; 2 Kgs 10:8; Prov 7:18; Ruth 3:13, 14.[22]

b. The idiom *lʾ nʿdr* is found in 1 Sam 30:19; also in Isa 34:16; 40:26; Zeph 3:5. McCarter's translation of his retroversion of the Heb. underlying LT is followed in the translation above. The noun means "flock" or "herd": "not herded" has much the same sense as *lʾ npqd* (1 Sam 25:7, 21), "not counted (as missing)."

24a. Codex B's *Manaeim* takes *mḥnym* as a proper name; LT and OL render it as "camps."

27a. The LT has *Sepheei* (Josephus says *Seiphar*) for *šby*, and *Rakabein* for *rglym*.

29a. The term *špwt* is a hapax: Syr. and Tg. understand it as "cheese/yogurt." Codex B partly transliterates *špwt bqr* as *saphphōth boōn*; but LT offers "suckling calves."

18:1a. The vb. *pqd* is expressly related to counting in 1 Sam 11:8; 13:15; (14:17 [2x];) 15:4; 2 Sam 24:2, 4; and the idea may be present also in 1 Sam 17:18; 20:6; 25:15—in each of the latter, the sense is "count and find missing."

2a. The LT and OL attest *wyšlš* (also *piʿel*, like MT) for *wyšlḥ* (MT and B). "Thirded" fits the immediate context well; but "dispatched" is a key vb. in 2 Sam 10, which may have served as the model for such cooperative division.

3a. The GT supports MT; but OL offers "they will not pursue us with intent heart."

b. Here *ʾth* ("you") is widely attested for *ʿth* ("now"). Yet LT does attest *ky-ʿth*, and then a longer text than MT (supported as regularly by B): "for now the land will remove from us ten thousand" (so translated because here "ten" is used alongside the noun "thousand," or possibly "regiment"; this is not the word "myriad").

4a. The LT's *klitos*, though lit. "slope" or "hillside," is used to render "side" elsewhere in LXX.

5a. In GT *lʾṭ-ly* becomes *pheisasthe moi* or *mou* ("spare me"); GT also uses *pheidomai* to translate *ḥśk* (v. 16).

b. After "all the people," 4QSam[a] has *šmʿym* ("were hearing") for the equally pl. MT *šmʿw* ("heard"); however, GT offers sg.

6a. In place of "Ephraim" in MT and B, the LT offers *Maainan* or *Malinan* (an unknown place). Ephraim in its normal sense is problematic geographically, as Kratz (175) notes but Polzin (1993: 182–87) ignores.

22. "Till the morning" is linked with the vb "lie" (*škb*) only in 1 Sam 3:15 and Ruth 3:13, 14.

9a. In MT *wyqr'* is read as *nip'al* of *qr'* II (= *qrh*), but as *qal* in B ("met"). McCarter's retroversion of *kai ēn megas* (LT) is *wygdl*, but there seems to be no precedent for his interpretation: "and Absalom was greatly in front . . ."

b. The LT agrees with 4QSam^a in not repeating "Absalom" as subj.

c. Here MT *śôbek* is rendered *dasos* ("thicket") in B, and *phyton* ("plant") in LT.[23]

d. The noun *h'lh* is rendered lit. as "oak" in B, but more freely in LT.

e. Codex B uses "hung" in place of both *wyḥzq* and *wytn*; the LT varies between "embraced/entangled" and "hung up"; and the latter shares the reading *wytn* in 4QSam^a; cf. the ptc. *tlwy* in v. 10; also, in LT he is suspended between "earth and heaven," not "heaven and earth."

10a. The LT's *Idou egō* may have read *hnny*. The MT's simple *hnh* before "I have seen" is supported by B (and DJD 163).

b. Again LT locates the accident in an unspecified "tree."

11a. Here MT and B have only "ten of silver," while LT mentions "fifty shekels of silver," apparently in agreement with 4QSam^a.

12a. With *Egō eimi*, Codex B has clearly read *'nky* ("I") of MT, but it then offers *histēmi* ("raise") in place of *šql*; LT uses the same root Gk. vb. but emphasizes the second pers. with *parastēsēs sy* ("present/deliver").

b. The MT is isolated in attesting *my*, not *ly*.

13a. There is considerable diversity over the opening words and how these relate to the previous sentence. The MT's *'w-'śyty* lit. means "or I have acted" or "or had I acted"; "and how shall I act" (LT) would retrovert to *'yk ''śh*; and B's infinitival *mē poiēsai* ("not to act") would retrovert to *blty-'śwt* and continue the previous royal instruction.

b. The LT agrees with Q's "my life," B with "his" in K. The translation above uses "self" rather than "life" for *nepeš* in order to distinguish it from *ḥayyîm*, "life[time]," below (v. 18).

14a. The GT attests *'l-kn* at the beginning for *l'-kn* (MT).

b. The GT attests the emphatic first-person pronoun.

c. Apparently GT reads a form of *ḥll* (*hip'il*); but MT of *ḥyl* = *yḥl* (cf. Judg 3:25).

d. The MT's *šbṭym* are taken to be "splinters/darts" (LT) or "missiles" (B); and NRSV specifies "spears." The idiom with *tq'* ("thrust") has a parallel in Judg 3:21; 4:21.

16a. This verse has Joab doing to the horn (*tq'*) what he has done with staves to Absalom's heart; GT does not or cannot deal with this link.

18a. Here GT's statement of the final clause is simpler. The syntax in MT is reminiscent of 1 Sam 9:9.

20a. Codex B's *hou heineken* ("on account of which") retroverts to *ky-'l-kn*, as in Gen 18:5; 19:8; 38:26; Num 10:31; 14:43 (but not Gen 22:16; Isa 61:1), which Q represents here; in each of these other cases, *ky-'l-kn* occurs within direct speech; that makes it likely here that MT understood this formula as introducing the final words of what Joab says, rather than a comment of the narrator. The LT attests only *ky*.

22a. In place of the short and puzzling *mṣ't* in MT, the GT offers the fuller but hardly less puzzling *eis ōpheleian poreuomenō*. The MT's *mōṣē't* could be understood as "finding" (from *mṣ'*) or "producing" (from *hip'il* of *yṣ'*); McCarter prefers to read *ṣ't* as inf. *qal*,

23. Plato describes humans as *phyton ouranion*, "a plant rooted in the skies"!

"from going out." The GT may conflate two attempts at rendering MT. Neither *ōpheleia* nor the related vb. occurs elsewhere in the historical books: the only other instance of *eis ōpheleian* cited by HRCS renders *lhwʿyl* in Isa 30:5.

23a. Codex B transliterates *hkkr* by *tou Kechar*; LT has *tēn diatetagmenēn* ("appointed/ in battle order," possibly rendering a form of *šmr*).

24a. At the end, GT attests not only *lbdw* but also *lpnyw*.

28a. In place of MT's *wyqrʾ*, the LT attests *wyqrb*.

29a. Here *hāmôn* refers both to a surging throng and to the din it causes; B follows the visual emphasis of MT, while LT exploits the audio possibilities. In 1 Sam 4:14; 14:16, 19 too, it refers to the clamor of defeat (first of Israel by Philistines, then of Philistines by Jonathan and his armor-bearer).

b. The phrase "and [your servant]" is not read in all masoretic MSS; it certainly results in a puzzling statement before the king himself. The LT has the messenger distinguish carefully between Joab, as the king's *pais*, and himself, as his *doulos*.

31a. In place of the pass. vb. (MT), the LT offers the one-word exclamation: *Euangelia*.

b. Codex B repeats *ekrinen* as in v. 19 for *špṭ*, while LT shifts here to *edikase*.

18:33[19:1]a. The LT's opening vb. (rare in LXX) denotes quieter weeping rather than louder crying; however, *rgz* in MT is used of the violent shaking of earthquakes.

b. The LT appears to attest not *blktw* (MT and B) but *bbktw*.

c. Codex B is longer than MT or LT, and seemingly conflate. The added emphasis in MT is probably secondary.

19:1[2]a. Here GT probably attests the ptc. *mtʾbl*, found in Samuel also at 1 Sam 16:1; 2 Sam 14:2; most if not all occurrences of the *hitpaʿel* of *ʾbl* are late.

2[3]a. The noun *tšwʿh* also seems most at home in late contexts.

b. Similarly *nʿṣb* is used elsewhere in Samuel only in 1 Sam 20:3, 34; then also in Gen 45:5; Eccl 10:9; Neh 8:10, 11.

3[4]a. Codex B renders *ytgnb* lit. (the idiom is like the English "steal in"), but LT uses *hypostelletai*, "dissemble, prevaricate."

4[5]a. Here *lʾṭ* here is probably equivalent to *lṭ* (< *lwṭ*), used in 1 Sam 21:9 (10; *qal*) and 1 Kgs 19:13 (*hipʿil*).

6[7]a. The first letters of the second "today" are read at the beginning of a line in 4QSam[a]; that appears to guarantee its position as represented in MT. On the other hand, the editors of the fragments reconstruct "you know" at the end of the previous line and find no place for MT's third "today" in this verse. See further below.

8[9]a. Contrast v. 1 [2]: here MT has "inform" in the active.

9[10]a. In HB *dyn nipʿal* is unique here but is so read by B; the LT attests not *ndwn* but *nlwn*.

10[11]a. The plus in LT (at the end) simply anticipates what is reported in MT and LT in vv. 12–13, though in different positions.

11[12]a. The above rendering of MT assumes that the final "to his house" is all Israel's message to David. However, given the differing placement in LT and MT of the statement about the word of all Israel, it is not unlikely that the second "to his house" simply mechanically recapitulates the first on the insertion of this floating statement. See further below.

13[14]a. The GT attests resumptive *wʿth* after *ʾth*.

b. Here DJD 169 argues that "vertical alignment requires" the shorter *yhwh*, not the longer and normal *ʾlhym*; it notes that the oath formula does have the rarer Yahweh in 1 Sam 20:13 (MT).

17[18]a. Here LT's *apostellousin* attests *wšlḥw* in place of MT's *wṣlḥw*.

18[19]a. The GT attests cognate forms of *ʿbd* rather than *ʿbr* (MT).

22[23]a. Here LT's *epiboulos* renders *śṭn*, as in the only other occurrence in Samuel (1 Sam 29:4).

24[25]a. The LT uses a different vb. with each of four objects. Elsewhere in LXX, *onychizō* is found only in Lev 11 and Deut 14, only in the active and with the cognate obj. The use of *ʿśh* ("do") with *śpm*, though unique, is supported by GT—in any case, *śpm* is uncommon. The much commoner *regel* is nowhere else the obj. of *ʿśh*; equally "feet" is nowhere else the obj. of *therapeuein*. Here DJD (170) supports the mention of attending also to hands in the longer LT.

26[27]a. The vb. *rmh* has been used also of Michal's deceiving Saul (1 Sam 19:17), and Saul's deceiving the bottle-mistress at Endor (28:12).

b. In support of GT, here DJD (171) notes that "the servant, not the lame speaker, is the obvious one to harness the ass."

28[29]a. "Those-who-eat" renders a Hebrew ptc., not a relative clause.

b. Attested at the opening of LT, *wmyd-my*, is found once in MT (at 1 Sam 12:3). The MT attests *yeš* in 1 Sam 9:11, 12; 14:39; 17:46; 20:8; 21:3, 4, 8 (4, 5, 9); 23:23; 2 Sam 9:1; 14:19, 32; 19:28 (29).

[14] Yahweh is relatively seldom mentioned throughout 2 Sam 9–20; where his name is used, it is mostly on the lips of characters in the narrative. The narrator's own reports of Yahweh's displeasure over the death of Uriah and the marriage of David and Bathsheba (11:27) and of his love for their second son (12:24–25) are exceptions to this rule. And the third and only other exception is the report of Yahweh's instruction in the matter of frustrating Ahithophel's counsel (17:14b). "Command" (*ṣwh*) has also a divine subject in 1 Sam 2:29; 13:13, 14 (2x); 25:30; 2 Sam 5:25; 7:7, 11; but in each of these cases the divine command is mediated or reported by another character.

Yahweh's decision both supports and at least apparently negates the decision by Absalom and all Israel. In preferring Hushai, they achieve the right result. And yet their argument is that Hushai's advice is better. But Yahweh's assessment is that Ahithophel's policy is good. Are Absalom and his people doing the right thing but for the wrong reason? Yahweh's own command gives effect to what David has wished when giving Hushai his instructions: that Ahithophel's advice be canceled, or undone (15:34). The terms of David's own earlier wish to Yahweh has been that Yahweh would render foolish his old adviser's counsel (15:31). However, Yahweh demonstrates his own independence and sovereignty. He both recognizes the quality of Ahithophel's advice and, despite that, cancels its effect. It is possible to judge that the one counselor's policy is good, but the other is better; yet there is no question, as far as Yahweh is concerned, that Ahithophel's counsel has been bad or foolish. It is not Ahithophel who has been deluded by divine will, but rather all those who have heard his counsel: both leader and led. Our discussion of Saul at En-dor (1 Sam 28) noted links with the Micaiah story in BTH (1 Kgs 22). That controverted narrative portrays an intriguing (lack of) connection between truth and falsity, on one side, and Yahweh's purposes, on the other. And here we have another much briefer glimpse of similar issues.

[15–20] The narrator reports the divine intention immediately after his note on the first reaction of Absalom and people to Hushai's advice. However, the rival counselors themselves wait to see how things will turn out. Hushai moves immediately (vv. 15–16) to use the secret priestly channel (15:27–28, 35–36) to brief David, his real master, about both sides of the rival advice, and to urge David to act as if Ahithophel's sensible counsel were in the end to prevail. It turns out that there is one further link in the information chain, about which David has not spoken: a female servant communicates between the priests and their sons, who cannot let themselves be seen entering Jerusalem. However, the priests' sons are seen and are aware that they have been seen by someone who might report to Absalom; and they are able to make their escape.

Bahurim (v. 18) occurs in just two other contexts: it is as far as Michal's second husband was allowed to follow her on her return to David (3:16); and it is the home of Shimei (16:5; 19:16 [17]; 1 Kgs 2:8). In all four passages, Bahurim is recognizably transliterated into the Greek preserved in LT. But here LT's *Baithchorrōn* may attest *byt-ḥrwn*, which is also in the small territory of Benjamin. Beth-horon is found in MT of Samuel only in 1 Sam 13:18 (where LT has *Baithōrōn*).[24]

[21–23] David acts quickly at night (v. 21), without waiting to see whether Absalom will in the end take Hushai's advice or Ahithophel's. He is twice identified as the (single) recipient of the lads' warning; yet the content of their warning is given wholly in plural forms (v. 21b). The need for speed is part of what they say, and the crossing is made before morning light (v. 22). David is still acting as if Ahithophel's advice is as good as Yahweh's word (16:23). The totality of the night crossing is a first acted response to the policy of total destruction of any town to which David might resort recommended by Hushai and endorsed by Absalom (17:13–14).

Before David's arrival at Mahanaim is reported (v. 24), the focus shifts back briefly to the failed counselor, who has lost face (v. 23). The parenthesis is marked by placing the name of Hushai's rival first in the Hebrew sentence. Although the word for speed (v. 21b) is not repeated in reporting the consequences for Ahithophel, his many separate actions are reported very crisply. Few words are required to report the fatal consequences of going against David.

24. And that corresponds also to MT's *byt-'wn* ("Beth-aven") in 1 Sam 13:5; 14:23.

The verb *ḥnq* (v. 23) is found once more in HB, in Nah 2:13, where in the *piʿel* it means "strangle." Ahithophel's final action before taking his life has an interesting resonance. It has been by the higher authority of Yahweh's command (v. 14) that his own advice has been passed over. His response is to "command" (*ṣwh*) his own house[hold] before hanging himself: to give instructions in a context where he is still in control, before acting as he is still free to do. The decisiveness of the counselor's actions, his control of his own death, and his burial in the family tomb—all exhibit striking contrasts with the hapless fate of Absalom, still to come (18:9–18).

The way both rival counselors react to the decision-making process is noteworthy. It may be that neither was immediately aware of the policy chosen by Absalom and (all) Israel. Hushai has both sides of the debate communicated to David; and advises him that he should act as if his rival's counsel will be followed. As for Ahithophel, there is no suggestion that he immediately loses face when the decision goes against him: only when he sees for himself that what he advised is not being done does he take personal charge of one of the consequences.

[24–26] David bases himself in Mahanaim (vv. 24, 27), some way up the river Jabbok, which flows into the Jordan at Adam (modern Damiye). Mahanaim ("Twin Camps") was exactly where the remnants of the house of Saul made their home after Saul's death and David's anointing at Hebron over Judah (2:8, 12, 29). Absalom's response is to follow David across the Jordan and "camp" at some location in Gilead. (Gilead is very flexibly used in HB: it could include Mahanaim, or refer to the area only north of the Jabbok.)

Instead of specifying the location of Absalom's camp, the narrator reports the appointment of his choice of army commander to replace Joab, who has remained loyal to David (v. 25). Amasa is a full cousin of the man he follows. The relatedness of his mother and the mother of Joab and his brothers to each other and to the family of David (and Absalom) is more important than the identity of the fathers of these military men. There is considerable textual doubt over the name and associations of Amasa's father; and the statement that he "came to" Amasa's mother suggests sexual liaison rather than marriage (cf. 20:3 below).

The appointment of Amasa is featured, rather than simply reported, between the two parts of the report of Absalom's crossing the Jordan and encampment in Gilead. When Absalom and Israel are repeated (v. 26), GT retains the relative order used in v. 24 (and "every man" before "Israel'), while MT introduces variety by reversing the order and shortening the mention of Israel.

[17:27–18:2a] When we return to the story of David (v. 27), interrupted in vv. 24b–26, we have to reevaluate any impression we may have gained of a refugee king attended by only meager forces. He receives generous provisions from three local contributors. The first is a brother of his erstwhile enemy in Rabbath Ammon (chs. 10–12), higher up the Jabbok from Mahanaim—a further son of King Nahash, with whom he used to have good relations. The second has been host to Mephibosheth in Lo-debar (9:4–5), from where David brought him to Jerusalem. The third, Barzillai, makes his first appearance in the narrative here; and his base of Rogelim (mentioned again in 19:32) is otherwise unknown in HB.

David may now be fleeing from Absalom, as he once was fleeing from Saul. But these three leaders from east of the Jordan treat David much more richly than Nabal had during that earlier flight (1 Sam 25). His successful campaigns against Ammon and Aram have served to encourage respect. Based in one town though he is (remember Ahithophel's boast, 17:13), it appears that his forces are far from insignificant. Divided against Ammon into two armies under Joab and Abishai (10:9–11), they are now to be in three, with Ittai from Gath as third commander. Even if the "companies" and "regiments" described as "hundreds" and "thousands" are below full strength, the description requires that we recognize David's forces, no less than his sources of supply, as not negligible.

[2b–3] As they discuss whether or not David should personally be part of the fight, "the people who were with him" (v. 1) have been abbreviated to "the people" (vv. 2b–3). That reads as more intimate, more connected, than "those with him." Two of their leaders may have been among the king's cousins; but the majority, whether originally outlawed discontents or foreign mercenaries, have become David's "folk," his "people," his "kind," because they have been through thick and thin together. David's insistence that he join the battle ("Go out with you I too most certainly will," v. 2b) is triply underscored linguistically: the verb is doubled by use of the infinitive absolute; the independent pronoun is used to stress the subject; and even that is further emphasized with the added "also" (*gam*). Given all that, his emphatic words might be more convincing if he had taken personal command of one section of his forces. On a previous occasion, he has been almost as emphatic about his need to be at dinner with Saul (1 Sam 20:5)! See below on 24:17.

The opening of his troops' response adapts his own words: his "going out" is simply vetoed (*lōʾ tēṣēʾ* is stated like the briefest of the prohibitions in the Ten Commandments); the emphatic use of the infinitive absolute is transferred from his "go out" to their "flee," as they stress to him that, given the odds, fleeing is a real possibility. David has once and only once been put to flight (*nûs*) by Saul's spear hurled at him (1 Sam 19:10). All his later escapes are described in different language, such as "evade" or "save himself." To have to flee in face of his enemies is one of the three options put to David by Gad after the census (2 Sam 24:13, BTH), the only one he implicitly rejects outright (v. 14). His men demonstrate in their response that they are fully aware of how unthinkable it would be for David to be involved in "flight," in the sense of being put to flight in defeat.

The explicit wishes of David's "folk" are in marked contrast to Hushai's striking advice to Absalom (17:11): "Your face marching in the encounter." Of course Hushai wants Absalom to be hazarded; and so he persuades him to enter the field by using diplomatic speak for "you must be seen to lead." In a related expression, David has allowed Absalom to return to Jerusalem, but not to "see his face" (14:24); and had warned Abner that unless accompanied by Michal, he would not "see his face" (3:13). The people seek to persuade David that they are more expendable than he—who is worth no less than ten regiments!—and that he will be of more help to them in the city than in the field (18:3).

[4–8] Apart from his appointment of three commanders over "the people" (v. 2), David's only reported order of the day concerns Absalom, who should be gently treated. This instruction, though addressed to the commanders, is heard by everyone.

The terms used to identify the rival forces are flexible but only occasionally confusing:

1. Absalom's original appeal is to "the tribes of Israel" (15:2, 10), "all Israel" (15:6, 13 [GT]), "the men of Israel" (15:6, 13 [MT]), or "the people" (15:14 [GT]). As this force approaches Jerusalem, David leaves in the company of his "servants" (15:15, 18), who include the "Creti and Pleti" and Ittai's Gittites (v. 18), and are also termed "the people" (vv. 17, 24). Ziba claims that his master's hopes have their focus on "the house of Israel" (16:3).[25]

2. As Shimei pelts David with stones while he departs with "his men" (16:13), they are also termed "David and the people who were with him" (v. 14). At this point, Absalom's associates are "all the people, the men of Israel" (v. 15) or "this people, all the men of Israel" (v. 18); and it is "all Israel" that should hear of and see what Absalom does with David's concubines (vv. 21–22).

3. Ahithophel's proposed expedition (17:1–4) will restore "all the people" to Absalom and bring peace to "all the people." Interestingly, Ahithophel, though apparently loyal to Absalom, continues to talk about David as "the king" (v. 2). Hushai's advice to Absalom speaks of "your father and his men" (17:8, 10) and "the men who are with him" (v. 12), over against "the people who are behind Absalom" (v. 9) and "all Israel" (vv. 10, 11).

4. Hushai's message talks of his advice to Absalom and "the elders of Israel" (17:15), and the priests' sons are pursued by "the servants of Absalom" (v. 20). On receipt of the message, David and "all [the people, MT] who were with him" cross the river (v. 22); it is to David and "the people who were with him" that the three donors present their gifts of food (v. 29); and it is "the people who

25. Found also in 1 Sam 7:2, 3; 2 Sam 1:12; 6:5, 15; 12:8—but not elsewhere in chs. 13–20.

were with him" that David counts (18:1), who are then identified more briefly as "the people" (vv. 2, 3), or "all the people" (vv. 4–5). Meanwhile, Absalom has also crossed, "and every man of Israel with him" (17:22).

5. Possibly the most striking collocation of these flexible terms comes as "the people" take the field to meet "Israel" (18:6); the result is that "the people of Israel" are smitten in face of "the servants of David" (v. 7). The same terms reappear at the end of the account, as "the people" cease pursuing "Israel," and "all Israel" flee severally to their tents (vv. 16–17). There is no overt surface confusion about who is on which side: presumably "the people" of whom "the forest consumed more than the sword" (v. 8) are Absalom's forces, "the people of Israel," not David's. But how the key clauses in vv. 6–7 should be read is puzzling. One way is simply to note that they quite powerfully evoke the tensions and ambiguities of a civil war situation. Another takes as its starting point the order in which the two parties are mentioned:

The people . . .	attacks . . .	Israel.
The people of Israel . . .	is defeated . . .	before the servants of David.

The "people" before whom the real people (of Israel) has been defeated are but the (mercenary) servants of David. The only other occurrence in Samuel of "the people of Israel" (*ʿam yiśrāʾēl*) follows shortly in 19:41 (see below). Comparison with earlier passages in Samuel offers further vantage points. The only comparator to Joab's holding back (*ḥāśak*, v. 16) the people from their pursuit is David's blessing Yahweh for "smiting" Nabal, and "holding him back" from the "evil" of killing the fool himself (1 Sam 25:38–39). As in the time of Eli, Israel is not defeated by its mortal foe, but is smitten by Yahweh in front of its enemy. Appropriately, the forest consumes more than the sword (v. 8b); even Absalom is only finished off by Joab and his men—his capture has been effected by a tree.

[9–17] DJD reconstructs a paragraph break before v. 9. Absalom's ignominious end in the oak draws ironically together several separate strands in his story. Although at an earlier stage of his royal pretensions he provided himself with chariot and horses (15:1), now after the rout of his army he is seen riding a mule, just like his brothers in fleeing his own assassination of Amnon (13:29). Seeing his head caught in the network of the oak's branches reminds the reader that the narrator has earlier suggested his tallness and drawn attention to the profusion of his hair (14:26). The three other instances in HB of "between earth and heaven" (so LT; the MT is unique with its "between heaven and earth") are all visionary: 2 Sam 24:16 (4QSam^a)//1 Chr 21:16; Ezek 8:3; Zech 5:9.[26] The subsequent use of the verb "hang" (v. 10) aligns Absalom's fate with that of

26. For further discussion of this verse, see below on 24:16.

local kings who were dispatched by Joshua (Josh 8:29; 10:26), if not also the chief baker in the Joseph story (Gen 40:22) and Haman in the book of Esther (7:10).[27] Yet unlike these corpses hung up for display, Absalom is hanging from a tree but not dead. His burial under a great cairn of stones recalls both disobedient Achar/n from within Israel (Josh 7:26) and the hostile kings of Ai and the south (8:29; 10:27); it comes far short of his own intention of burial beside a fine monument in Jerusalem (2 Sam 18:18). We are reminded of the counselor whose advice Absalom did not take: he dispatched himself and was buried with his fathers (17:23). Another set of correspondences is triggered by the report of David's men happening on, chancing on, Absalom. We have not met such language since the Amalekite messenger used it—and used it emphatically—in his report to David of his battlefield encounter with Saul (1:6). Both opponents caused David much trouble. Both were movingly mourned by him on their death. And both were chanced on by witnesses of their predicament who completed—or at least claimed to complete—their killing.

The fellow who reports Absalom's plight to Joab speaks clearly over the centuries for so many in junior positions who are criticized by their seniors for not taking decisive action—and especially action against official "company policy": he would be wrong whatever he does, and he would be held responsible (vv. 12–13). Unlike Jonathan, who was not present when Saul insisted that no one should eat till victory was assured, Joab is left no excuse by the narrator: *all* the people heard what David commanded *all* the officers—nothing else in this paragraph is so total until the flight of "all Israel" at its end. However, Joab himself has no compunction, and with his bodyguards finishes off the upstart king. The king may have ordered otherwise, but Joab has every personal reason to see Absalom dead. He engineered Absalom's recall to Jerusalem (ch. 14), only to have one of his fields torched at his first refusal to tackle David a second time on the prince's behalf. And then this Absalom, for whom he has twice risked his own position, mounts a rebellion against his king.

Joab's chosen tools for Absalom's dispatch are appropriate at several levels. The literal sense of *šēbeṭ* is a wooden rod or staff; and Absalom has become entangled in a tree: more precisely, three wooden staves are put into Absalom's heart while he is in the heart of the tree. The punishment is also stated in terms that correspond not just to the place of execution, but the nature of his original crime as well: those whom he has called out in support of his cause have also been designated by the plural of *šēbeṭ* (15:10), there denoting the "staffs" of tribal office. Then again, we noted it as plausible that a poem in Proverbs provided some of the background to the beginning of Absalom's mischief. In similar spirit, these staves or rods may now be in the heart of Absalom because

27. Although the verb is different, there is some correspondence between what happens to Absalom and the fate of his spurned counselor Ahithophel.

they are too late for the back (Prov 10:13; 26:3) of this spoiled child (13:24; 22:15; 29:15). Proverbs 13:24 is the only other passage in the Bible to link key words of vv. 14, 16 in this narrative: "Who holds back the staff hates his son" (*ḥwśk šbṭw śwnʾ bnw*). Calling off the pursuit compounds Joab's inversion of the gentle treatment commanded by David for Absalom. But the fact that he does not hold back his staves from the badly behaved son, though he does hold back his forces, may again serve to show Joab in a better light than his master (compare his attempted intervention over the census). His treatment of the corpse could, conveniently, be variously interpreted. On the one hand, it is flung unceremoniously into a great pit. On the other, as we shall just learn, Absalom has prepared himself a monument (though in Jerusalem): and now a great cairn is provided for him—in the depths of the forest.

We learn from Deut 21:22–23 that someone hung on a tree is under God's curse, and also that he should be buried before nightfall. This follows provision for the stoning of a rebellious son (vv. 18–21), which in turn follows instruction relating to the inheritance of a firstborn son and another son when these have different mothers (vv. 15–17). The immediately preceding paragraph insists that the beautiful woman you see and fall in love with when you are on a campaign must first complete her mourning before she becomes your wife (vv. 10–14). We cannot fail to hear echoes with how Abigail and Bathsheba became David's wives, with firstborn Amnon and Absalom, and with Absalom's end.

One further set of close correspondences is between this paragraph and the account in ch. 2 of Joab and David's servants in their encounter with Abner and the men of the house of Saul.[28] The broad geographical context is identical: Abner's base is Mahanaim, where the remnants of the house of Saul are in exile; Joab and the servants of David have started from Hebron, where Absalom like his father before him has become king. Only Joab and David's men feature in both stories; but whereas their base in 2 Sam 2 is Hebron while Abner sets out for Gibeon from Mahanaim, in 2 Sam 18 David and his men are pursued to Mahanaim by Absalom who has started his rebellion from Hebron.

2 Sam 18:4–16		**2 Sam 2:17–28**	
7	The people of Israel were smitten before the servants of David.	17	The men of Israel were smitten before the servants of David.
8	The forest devours more than the sword.	26	Will the sword devour forever?
9	Absalom's mule "passed on" (*ʿbr*).	15	The combatants … "crossed over" (*ʿbr*).

28. Very well explored in Polzin 1993: 182–87.

9	Absalom's head was caught (*ḥzq*).	16	Each caught (*ḥzq*) his fellow's head.
14	staves in heart of Absalom	16	sword in side of fellow
16	Turn [*šûb*] from pursuing Israel.	26	Turn [*šûb*] from pursuing Israel.
16	Joab blew the trumpet and . . . the people stopped pursuing Israel.	28	Joab blew the trumpet and all the people stopped pursuing Israel.

It is no accident that the very name Mahanaim ("twin camps") is evocative of civil strife. Similarly, David or his men have good fortune when at Bahurim ("choice"), which occurs in the same two broad contexts (3:16; 16:5; 17:18; 19:16 [17]).

[18] There is an apparent but not a necessary contradiction between this account of Absalom's pillar (v. 18), with his talk of having no son to continue his name, and the earlier report of his offspring (14:27): three sons and his beautiful daughter Tamar. Unlike Tamar, none of the sons born to him is named, so all may have died in infancy. With "in his life[time]" (*bḥyw*), compare Judg 16:30; 2 Sam 1:23; Ps 49:18 (19); Eccl 3:12; 9:3.[29]

Standing stones often have a phallic significance. Appropriate to this connection, the common Hebrew word for arm or hand (*yad*) can be used by extension to denote either phallus or memorial. Very effective play on this is made in Isa 56:5, where eunuchs who have been sexually damaged and hence, because of impaired *yad*, can engender no son to continue their name (*šēm*) are promised a memorial (*yad*) and a name.[30] It may be that 2 Sam 18:18 is the only other text in HB which so suggestively combines some of these associations.

[19–28a] After underscoring that Absalom has no son but only a "hand" (v. 18), attention is drawn (v. 19) to David's eyes and ears (15:35–37). Ahimaaz, Zadok's *son*, wants to be the first to bear the news to David about the failure of the enemies' *hand*, here in the sense of "power." But Joab puts him off with what seems to be a lame excuse: its being the day the king's son has died does not stop Joab from enlisting "the Cushite" for the same task. But Ahimaaz may not know the background of which Joab and we readers are aware: that when Saul and Jonathan died, David wanted no good news sent to the Philistine cities; that David had the Amalekite killed who brought him Saul's crown—and the thugs who later brought him the head of Saul's remaining son. In fact, the verb and noun for "(bearing) good news" (*bśr* and *bśrh*) are used in Samuel only

29. Notice that "life" and "living" are relatively common terms in Ecclesiastes (20x), yet rare in BTH (only 1 Kgs 8:40; 12:6; 22:14//2 Chr 6:31; 10:6; 18:13)—and the vb. *ḥyh* ("live") is used in BTH only in 2 Kgs 11:12; 14:17//2 Chr 23:11; 25:25.

30. Movingly and appropriately, in modern Jerusalem *Yad Vashem* was chosen as the name of the national memorial to the millions whose families were cut off in the twentieth-century Holocaust.

in 1 Sam 4:17; 31:9; 2 Sam 1:20; 4:10; and then in 18:19, 20 (3x), 22, 25, 26, 27, 31. We are given no further information about this Ethiopian. Joab may reckon that it is better to hazard a foreigner to inform the king with his uncertain temper about the death of his son, than send the son of a priest and one of David's trusted messengers. However, after another excuse greets his second attempt, Ahimaaz is lucky the third time in securing permission—and then outruns the Ethiopian. At his second attempt (v. 22a), his request is couched in terms very similar to David's when he is refused leadership in the field (v. 2), but without David's characteristic infinitive absolute.

Ahimaaz had wanted to tell David that Yahweh had found in his favor over against Absalom—had vindicated his cause and delivered him. All of this is implied in the simple Hebrew expression *špṭ myd* (lit., "judge from the hand of"). The phrase has only been used once before in this book (1 Sam 24:15 [16]). There David expresses to Saul his confidence that Yahweh will vindicate him; his statement of the expected verdict is preceded by each of the other key related legal terms: "judge," "rule," and "plead." Does that precedent save Ahimaaz (see below on 19:1–5)?

The tension in the narrative is nicely built up. The delivery of the message is delayed first by the several-stage discussion of who should bear it, then by which runner will arrive first, and then by the interaction of the lookout and the king at the city gate. Like a previous lookout (13:34), this one "raised his eyes and saw" (18:24); and both notes follow soon after reports of Amnon's other brothers (13:29) and now his assassin brother (18:9) making their escape on mule-back. The whole Absalom story is well framed. A further element of tension in this episode—once Ahimaaz is identified as a runner—is provided by David's ambiguous comment that a good fellow like him would bring a good report. Is a report good because it is accurate, or because it tells us what we want to hear?

When Ahimaaz does arrive first, he does not disappoint his king: he reports accurately on great commotion and remains silent on the death of the king's son. Seemingly Joab has had no reason to doubt the youngster's discretion: Ahimaaz avoids a straight answer to David's question about Absalom's fate. The Cushite will also be suitably diplomatic. When David speaks to the first messenger in terms of *šālôm* for Absalom (v. 29), his words are not marked as a question. They may be intended as simply a comment to himself.

[28b–31] The verb *sgr* (v. 28) is used in several contexts throughout Samuel. It is used right at the beginning (1 Sam 1:5, 6) in the *qal*, of Yahweh closing up Hannah's womb. The passive sense is stated in the *nipʿal* (1 Sam 23:7), of David's being "shut up" by entering a city (Keilah) with gates and bars. In *piʿel* and *hipʿil*, the verb has the sense of "[imprison and] hand over." The *piʿel* always has Yahweh as subject and is found in HB only in 1 Sam 17:46; 24:19; 26:8 and here in 2 Sam 18:28. The *hipʿil* is used in 1 Sam 23 (4x) and 30:15, never with

Yahweh as subject; and 14x in the rest of the Hebrew Bible, 8x with Yahweh as subject. David threatens Goliath with decapitation when Yahweh puts him in his hands (1 Sam 17:46), just as Abishai offers to finish off Saul (26:8). But Saul thanks David (24:18 [19]) for not doing the obvious thing.

[32] When David replies to the next messenger, his words are clearly marked as a question. On each occasion, he has been wondering whether or not the expected fate has been meted out to his son. The Cushite, while again suitably diplomatic, says enough for David to understand—and stagger into mourning. The ambiguity whether the final noun "ill" relates to the lad or to the king's enemies may also be part of the Cushite's discretion. I suspect that both are intended.

[18:33–19:4] Through the several paragraphs of ch. 18, all mention of Absalom's death has been doubled: David's command is first issued (18:5) and then referred back to (18:12); he questions first one messenger and then the next (18:29, 32); and now his cry (18:33; 19:4 [19:1, 5]) is also doubled. Just as there could have been no doubt about his orders, so too it is doubly sure that the people have heard his grief. At each stage the repetition helps to mark the transition from *hnʿr* ("the lad") in 18:5, 12, 29, 32 to *bny* ("my son," as many as eight times in 18:33; 19:4 [19:1, 5]).

When David told Saul that he expected to be divinely "judged" or "vindicated" (*špṭ*) from his hand, Saul wept (1 Sam 24:15–16 [16–17]). Now that the Cushite has reported David's vindication from those who have risen against him, it is David himself who weeps. This same David wept while his baby son was ill, but refused to weep once he was dead. The report that David is in mourning for Absalom reminds us of the earlier ambiguous statement that he mourned for "his son" over a long period (13:37). Was David then mourning the dead Amnon, who already caused him disappointment, or the absent Absalom, who may already have caused him disappointment—and if not already, then certainly would? The ambiguity is heightened because Samuel before him went into mourning for the disappointing but still active and mischievous Saul (1 Sam 15:35)—and was criticized for this by Yahweh (16:1).

David's grief leads to one of the most poignant scenes in the book: his victorious men slinking about as if their victory, their defense of their king, should cause them shame (v. 2 [3]). The unique and effective *ytgnb* (v. 3 [4]), meaning "play the thief," "steal about," "act furtively" has interesting resonances. We will encounter literal (but hardly blameworthy) theft only in 2 Sam 21:12. Elsewhere in Samuel, the word occurs only three times: in 2 Sam 15:6 of Absalom's appropriating the people's hearts, in 19:42 of Israel's complaint that Judah has stolen their king, and this passage in between. In its (*hitpaʿel*) verbal form, it also echoes the immediately preceding *ytʾbl* ("go into mourning," v. 1 [2]), which has described David's response, and what has become also their response of *ʾbl* ("mourning," v. 2 [3]). We may wonder whether, when the deliverance becomes mourning, David's men are truly sharing their king's grief despite Joab's claim, or whether they simply dissemble, knowing that they cannot openly celebrate when their king is in mourning. This latter option may underlie the decision in LT to render "act the thief" by "dissemble" or "prevaricate." Yet a more literal understanding of this verb invites closer comparison of how his "people" and David himself are behaving. Like thieves, the people melt into the shadows and disappear from view; and David too covers his face as he grieves.

The verb *l'ṭ/lwṭ*[31] is used again with "face" in 1 Kgs 19:13 (Elijah on Mount Horeb), and also describes Goliath's sword "wrapped up" in the sanctuary at Nob (1 Sam 21:9 [10]). In both cases the concealment is real; and yet in neither case does it appear improper—indeed quite the reverse. The only other instance in HB of this verb occurs in a (late?) passage within Isaiah (25:7–9) where several resonances with this narrative can be detected: Yahweh will swallow "the face of the covering" (*pny hlwṭ*), which is then explained as "death"; Yahweh will then remove the "shame of his people"; and they will rejoice in his deliverance (*byšwʿtw*).

[5–7] David is caught between private grief (although all too publicly displayed) and public responsibility. Joab's scolding speech (vv. 5–7 [6–8]) is powerful: at its climax, tellingly, an appeal to David's self-interest. The word for "mourning" (*'bl*, vv. 1–2 [2–3]) has represented one subset of the Hebrew letters for Absalom (*'bšlwm*); Joab's response to David's "mourning" is cleverly stated (v. 5 [6]) in a word spelled in another subset of the same six Hebrew letters: he charges David that his mourning for Absalom should in fact be understood as a cause of shame (*bwš*). A principal issue here is the relational triangle David—Joab—"the people." The narrator has just called David's men "the people" (vv. 2–3 [3–4]) and will again immediately (8 [9]). But Joab speaks to the king of his "servants" (vv. 5–7 [6–8]). It is Joab's claim that David has let them down in his grief. But how far is that a simply honest report, and how far a self-serving claim by the very man who has struck Absalom down despite being given and then reminded of the king's explicit instructions (18:5, 12)?

The thrice-repeated "today" in 19:6 (7) resumes the previously twice-repeated "today" (v. 5 [6]). Although a keyword of this short speech, in v. 6 [7] it is placed and used differently in GT and MT, and possibly also in 4QSam[a]. The two instances of "today" in GT underscore a contrast between the leaders and servants on the one side (and David, according to Joab, no longer has servants) and Absalom on the other (whom David would still like to have). The first two instances of "today" in MT contrast what David has declared with what Joab knows (in GT the opposition is between what David declares and what he himself knows), while the third underscores Joab's charge that David would not

31. Can there be any connection with *l'ṭ-ly* in 18:5?

mind if all his followers were dead "today." This quite outdoes what his men have said to David: that the enemy would not reckon it as significant if all of them flee, or half of them die (18:3). The very fragmentary Qumran evidence suggests a third (and even primary?) combination of these elements: only two instances of "today" (like GT), but placed like the first two in MT. (See further below, on 19:22 [23].)

The translation above of the end of v. 6 (7) recognizes the formal ambiguity of the Hebrew: "it" or "he." Either Absalom still alive, despite all he has done, would be acceptable to David; or Absalom alive and all of them dead would appear an acceptable balance. However, since Achish's declaration to David ("You are right," 1 Sam 29:6) offers the only close parallel in Samuel to the use of *yāšār* here, LT may well be correct to insist that Joab has Absalom precisely in mind.

Absalom had stolen the heart of the men of Israel (15:6). Now Joab urges David to "speak to the heart" of his own servants (19:7 [8]). This expression is used also in Ruth 2:13 (often understood as "speak tenderly"), and also in 2 Chr 30:22 (where "speak encouragingly" may be more appropriate). Hushai, whether accurately or not, has counseled Absalom that David will not be found among his men at night—but that is when they are being hunted. Joab now threatens the king with the reverse fate: that even after his enemy's rout, his men will not stay with him at night. If that is the worst thing ever to happen to David, his situation must be still far from secure.

[8] David does respond (v. 8 [9]): he presents himself to "all the people" at the city gate. If his men are satisfied by his appearance seated before them, the narrator makes it his business to underscore that "all the people" (2x) are distinct from "Israel," who has fled severally to their tents. By reminding us of the concluding statement of the battle report, he also emphasizes the separate identity of the opposing forces in 18:4–17. There "people" was used of both David's men and Israel (18:6–8), though the final words spoke of "all Israel" in flight (18:17). Here the whole people are emphatically before David, while Israel has fled.

[9–10] If it has been clear up till now who the different parties are, this is no longer the case (vv. 9–10 [10–11]). It is hardly surprising that MT and LT offer different readings. The words "Absalom, whom we anointed over us" are the clearest indicator that at least some of the speakers are from among his defeated followers. They have anointed Absalom, followed him, and been routed with him. They should now return to the old king, who has saved them from their enemies, and in particular from the Philistines. But who are "all the people"? In the immediately previous subparagraph, they are undeniably the David party, "the servants of David." Are they now a subgroup within "all the tribes of Israel," who are grumbling against or disputing with the majority? Especially if (with LT) it is a matter of "grumbling," then it is more likely to be an internal matter within "all the tribes of Israel." If (with MT) a dispute is involved, then it is more natural to think of two parties: and these could be either David's servants and the tribes of Israel, or a minority and a majority within the tribes of Israel. The former already have the king with them; the others should bring him back. Apart from LT's final clause, which is not represented in MT until a few clauses later, the Hebrew text implied by LT differs from MT only in two or three letters.

"Grumbling" (LT) points out the contrast with situations in Exodus and Numbers, where it is against their divine leader that Israel is grumbling. Coming so soon after vv. 2–3, 8 (3–4, 9), the role of "the people" (v. 9) nicely underscores the complexity of this term in 2 Samuel. There they are David's leaders and servants, and clearly contrast with the dispersing "Israel" (v. 8). Here they are active among all Israel's "tribes" or sceptered leaders. The phrase *šbṭy yśr'l* ("tribes of Israel") is used in 1 Sam 2:28; 9:21; 10:20; 15:17; 2 Sam 5:1; 7:7; 15:2, 10; 19:9 (10); 20:14; 24:2 (MT at least). However, *šbṭy* is a Samuel plus in the three synoptic (BTH) passages (2 Sam 5:1; 7:7; 24:2), and there is textual variety in the second and third. It appears that "the people" are in dispute with their local leadership over not supporting the king. The term *mḥryš* ("silent") is used also in 1 Sam 7:8; 10:27; 2 Sam 13:20. In each case the silence is the result of self-restraint.

[11–15] Amid this grumbling, David uses his loyal priests as ambassadors to the leadership in Judah, here described as "the elders of Judah" (11 [12]). Judah's elders appear elsewhere in the books of Samuel only in 1 Sam 30:26. There they are the beneficiaries of his Amalekite booty. Here, where they have exhibited no answering loyalty, they come in for reproach. David's approach first to the men of Judah (12 [13]) and then to Amasa (13 [14]) on the basis of their being his "bone and flesh" takes up the language used to himself by Israel's representatives, when they came to him after Saul's death to make him their king (5:1–3, BTH). He cleverly overstates "the word/talk of all Israel" in his appeal to Judah not to be backward in bringing him home. He also promises them a change of army commander, confirming the appointment made by Absalom and repeating the words that the narrator had used (17:25) when reporting Amasa's promotion "in place of Joab." That is enough to achieve unanimity in Judah (Amasa "turned the heart of every man of Judah as one man"): they issue a welcome not only to David but explicitly to all his (foreign) servants. In tune with the symbolism we detected in his departure (15:23–25), the appointed Jordan crossing for David's return is at Gilgal. And those Benjamites who first met him as he left Jerusalem now hurry to join Judah's representatives in welcoming his westward return across the Jordan.

At the end of v. 10 (11 LT), the floating statement noted above can be read as suggesting that the previous "all the people" was equivalent to "all Israel." But within v. 11 (12), the same statement functions rather to reinforce the plea to Judah not to delay: Israel has already made its response; and it could bear a similar force at the end of v. 12 (13 LT). Here DJD (169) claims that the "fragments . . . require that we follow the Masoretic placement."

[16–20] Shimei, the cursing stone-thrower (from 16:5–8), has pardon to seek. He was introduced as belonging to "the house of Saul," and David later termed him a Benjamite (16:11). Now (19:16 [17]) the narrator styles him "the Benjamite." But Shimei will shortly claim to be the first northerner, the first of all "the house of Joseph" to welcome the king home (v. 20 [21]). "The house of Joseph" will recur within Samuel–Kings only in 1 Kgs 11:28, in connection with Solomon's appointment of Jeroboam "over all the forced labor of the house of Joseph" (NRSV). Shimei knows he has sinned (2 Sam 19:20 [21]) but pleads not to have to bear his guilt (v. 19 [20]). In the Book of Two Houses, David makes an identical approach to Yahweh (24:10).

According to Mandelkern, the relatively uncommon verb *ʿwh* ("do wrong," v. 19 [20]) is used twice each in *qal* and *piʿel*, four times in *nipʿal*, and nine times as here in *hipʿil*. Among these, it appears in BTH in 1 Kgs 8:47//2 Chr 6:37; but in Samuel only in pluses within the synoptic contexts 2 Sam 7:14; 24:17—the unique occurrence in Chronicles of the cognate common noun *ʿwn* is in the synoptic 2 Sam 24:10//1 Chr 21:8; however, the further fourteen instances in Samuel–Kings are all (as here) in nonsynoptic contexts. In both BTH contexts it is used in close proximity to the verb *ḥṭʾ* ("sin"). It is clearly much more important in Samuel than in Chronicles.

[21] Earlier Abishai sought permission to remove Shimei's head when he was cursing (16:9), and he was refused by David: the curses might be Yahweh-inspired. As Abishai now seeks a second opportunity (v. 21 [22]), he shows he has learned from this and also from a still earlier refusal by David. When he offered to dispatch the sleeping Saul, David warned him against moving against Yahweh's anointed (1 Sam 26:8–9). And when he first offered to kill Shimei, David hoped that Yahweh might return good to him "instead of" Shimei's cursing (16:12). His renewed request starts with "instead" and finishes with "Yahweh's anointed."

[22–23] The terms in which David reproaches the sons of Zeruiah (v. 22 [23]) could have been learned from the warning against David himself, which his sponsor Achish had received from the other Philistine leaders (1 Sam 29:4). Their analysis contains the only other use of "satan" in Samuel.[32] When we see David treating the sons of Zeruiah with the sort of visceral suspicion more appropriate to an enemy turncoat, we are conscious of a very different relationship in the books of Samuel from the one sketched more briefly in the Book of Two Houses. In several respects, the relationship of Joab and his brother with David is more complex in 2 Samuel than in BTH. We meet Abishai only

32. The dialogue between Achish and David was cited just above in connection with 19:6 [7].

twice in BTH. He is numbered among David's chiefs (2 Sam 23:18–19); he also has a minor role as leader of part of David's forces against Ammon and Aram (10:10, 14). But there he does not speak, and there is no tension between his king and himself. As for his more prominent elder brother, the Joab of BTH would try to save David from (divine) enticement. We shall see below (on 2 Sam 24:1–3) that the principal source of Samuel (BTH) included "satan," as 1 Chr 21:1 does still. Joab has been trying to save David from being snared by Yahweh—and here David accuses the brothers of instigating his entrapment. It is highly likely that this narrative is exploring one of the several open questions (gaps) in the story of the census. It is only David and Joab, the two named human characters at the beginning of that story, who are ever called "satan" elsewhere in Samuel.

In his concern to protect "Yahweh's anointed" (v. 21 [22]), Abishai demonstrates that he has learned from David's scolding during their nocturnal visit to Saul's camp. On that occasion (1 Sam 26:8) he had claimed a heaven-sent opportunity and requested leave to strike Saul through; but David insisted on protecting "Yahweh's anointed." However, although Abishai has paid attention to the details of what David said to him on two occasions, it appears that Abishai cannot win: now that he is protecting (the reputation of) "Yahweh's anointed," he is scolded again. At the previous encounter with Shimei, David noted that his cursing might be appropriate, even divinely inspired. David's successes since this earlier meeting have shown it unlikely that David has lost Yahweh's favor; however, this time of celebration is not to be spoiled.

Here David's dealings with Shimei represent another anticipation of the final and influential census story. Shimei has just made a confession to his lord (vv. 19–20 [20–21]) in terms that anticipate 2 Sam 24:10: "guilt . . . your servant . . . I have sinned." In his response (v. 23 [24]), David is quite explicit in his assurances to Shimei, reinforcing "You shall not die" with an oath. His treatment of Shimei is, apparently at least, more generous than the treatment he will receive from Yahweh after the census. When David himself needs to admit to a servant's sin and guilt (2 Sam 24), he will long that his divine Lord will match the ready assurance he has offered Shimei. Yet words and the lack of them speak less eloquently in the end than deeds. It will turn out (1 Kgs 2:8–9) that David's assurances are more ready than candid; for in his deathbed advice to Solomon, his "You shall not die, I swear it" is effectively transmuted into "I swear that it is not I who will kill you." Correspondingly, the treatment of David and his house by Yahweh after the census may be more merciful than the lack of explicit divine response immediately suggests.

In our discussion of v. 6 (7) above, we noted evidence of significant editing: partly in the positioning of "today" and partly over whether "I [Joab] know" (MT), or "you [David] know" (GT). The divergence between "I" (David) and "you" (Joab and brothers) as subject of "know" (v. 22 [23]) is similar: in each case MT has the speaker claiming the knowledge, while GT has the speaker claiming that the other party knows full well. Each is a mark of deliberate, even if minimally achieved, editing.

[24–28] Ziba has every reason to demonstrate gratitude. The narrator seems to have taken pleasure (v. 17 [18]) in reminding us of the size of his (parasitic) household (9:12b). But this time it is his "master" who comes to meet David too (vv. 24–28 [25–29]). Mephibosheth's very appearance provides evidence that he has been in mourning for the absent king. Though slandered by his steward, he has no further call on David's generosity: he must simply appeal to the divine scope of the king's wisdom. We have been told what Ziba said to David as he left Jerusalem (16:3), and what his master now says to David as he crosses the Jordan on his way back. But the narrator gives no independent account of what has earlier passed between master and servant. All we do know is how (bad) saddling a donkey for Mephibosheth sounds at this stage in the whole narrative. Ziba presented David with a pair of donkeys saddled—for the use of the royal family (16:1–2). Ahithophel has saddled a donkey to go home, arrange his affairs, and hang himself (17:23). What one onlooker might see as necessary support for a disabled man, another would interpret as a royal pretender from a dispossessed house. His final estimate of his situation is expressed in a formulation that, for all its difference, reminds us of earlier statements by David (1 Sam 20:8) and Absalom (2 Sam 14:32). They both conceded that guilt might have become attached to them, even though they had done nothing wrong. Mephibosheth is aware, though he himself is clear about his innocence, that in the view of the king no innocence has attached itself to him. His whole extended family have become "men of death" to David, as David himself once was to Saul (1 Sam 20:31) and also implicitly to Yahweh, though Nathan assures him he will not die (2 Sam 12:13). Mephibosheth's final protesting question grimly adapts *yeš-ʿôd* ("Does there still exist . . . ?") from David's happier-sounding opening gambit in 2 Sam 9:1: "Does there still exist someone remaining of Saul's house to whom I may act loyally?" has become "What sort of right or innocence still exists for me?"

2 Samuel 19:29 (30)—20:19

29 And the king said to him,
"Why do you further [speak] *multiply*[a] your words?
I have said:
'You and Ziba shall divide the field/land.'"
30 And Mephibosheth said to the king,
"Even the whole let him take,
after my lord the king has come in peace to his house."

31 And Barzillai the Gileadite, he came down from [Rogelim] *Rakabein*,
and crossed the Jordan with the king,
[dispatching him . . .[a]] *to escort him from* the Jordan.
32 Now Barzillai was very old, a man of eighty years,
and he had provided for the king during his residence[a] [at Mahanaim] *in camps*,
for he was a very great man.
33 And the king said to Barzillai,
"*If*[a] You cross with me,
[and] I shall provide for you with me in Jerusalem."
34 And Barzillai said to the king,
"How many
days shall be to me there,[a] are the days of the years of my life,
that I should go up with the king to Jerusalem?
35 I am today a man of eighty years.
Could I distinguish between good and bad,
or could your servant taste
what I would eat
or what I would drink,
or could I [still] listen to the voice of singers, men or women?
And why should your servant still be a burden to my lord the king?
36 *Rather a* [Some] little[a] (way) your servant will cross the Jordan with the king.
And why would the king recompense me this recompense?
37 Let your servant in fact return
that [I] *he* may die in my city
[by] *and I shall be buried in* the tomb[a] of my father and my mother.
But look: your servant [Kimham] *Ahimaam my son* will cross with my lord the king,
and *you will* do to him
what is good [in your eyes[b]] *before you*."

38 And the king said *to him*,
"*Let Ahimaam cross with me* [With me Kimham shall cross];
and I for my part shall do for him what is good in your eyes,
and everything
that you [choose] *enjoin* upon me,
I will do it for you."
39 And the [whole] people crossed the Jordan,
and the king [crossed] stood;[a]
and the king kissed Barzillai

and he blessed him,
and [he] *Barzillai* returned to his place.

40 And the king crossed to Gilgal;
and [Kimhan] *Ahimaan*, he crossed with him.
And the whole people of Judah brought[a] [the king] *him* across,
and [also] half the people of Israel.
41 And look, all the men of Israel were coming to the king,
and they said to the king,
"Wherefore have our brothers stolen you, the men of Judah,
and brought the king and his house across the Jordan,
and all the men of David with him?"

42 And [all] the men of Judah answered the men of Israel,
"Because the king is close(r) to us.
And whyever are you [heated] *despondent*[a] over this matter?
Have we actually eaten from the king?
[Or have we actually been carried?]
Or has he given us a gift or lifted a burden[b] *for us?*"

43 And the men of Israel answered the men of Judah,
and said,
"I have ten hands in the king,
and am I firstborn or you?[a]
And even in David I am over you,
and wherefore have you slighted me?
And was not my word first—mine—to bring back my king?"
But the word of the men of Judah was harder[b] than the word of the men of Israel.

20:1 And there there happened[a] to be a no-good[b] fellow,
and his name was Sheba son of [Bichri, a Benjamite] *Beddadi, an Arachi*[c] *man*;
and he sounded on the horn
and said:
"[We] *I* have no part in David;
[we have] no holding in the son of Jesse.
Each man to his tents, O Israel."
2 And all [the men of] Israel went up, from behind David, behind Sheba son of [Bichri] *Beddadi*;
but the men of Judah, they clung to[a] their king, from the Jordan right to Jerusalem.

3 And David came to his house in Jerusalem;
and the king took [ten women,] *the ten* concubines
whom he had left at rest
to guard the house,
and put them in a guardhouse
and provided for them—
but to them he did not come,
and they were bound till the day of their death—*living widows*[a] [life widowhood].

4 And the king said to Amasa,
"Call out[a] for me the men of Judah in three days—
and you yourself, stand here."
5 And Amasa went
to call out Judah;
and he was late for the appointment
that [he] *David* had appointed him.

6 And David said to [Abishai] *Amasa*,
"Now Sheba son of Bichri is worse for us than Absalom.
[You yourself] *And now*[a] take *with you* the servants of your lord
and chase after him,
in case he find himself fortified cities
and [save his eye[b]] *be sheltered from us*."

7 And Amasa summoned behind him the people,	
and Joab	And Joab's men went out[a] after him
	and the Creti[a]
and the Pleti and all the heroes	and the Pleti and all the heroes,
from Jerusalem,	and they went out[a] from Jerusalem,
and they chased after Sheba	to chase after Sheba
son of [Bichri] *Beddadi*.	

8 They were by the great stone which is [at Gibeon] *on the hill*,
and Amasa, he came before them;
and Joab was girt with a clothing garment *on* him,[a]
and on it a belt with a sword attached to his loins in its sheath—
and [he[b]] *the sword* came out,
and it fell.

9 And Joab said to Amasa,
"Is it well with you, my brother?"
And Joab's right hand took hold of Amasa's beard,

to kiss him.
10 But Amasa did not pay heed to the sword
that was in Joab's hand,
and [he] *Joab*[a] struck him with it to the [belly] *flank*,
and he poured his guts on the ground;
and he did not do it to him a second time,
and he died.

And Joab and Abishai his brother—they pursued after Sheba son of [Bichri] *Beddadi*.
11 And a certain man stood over him, *Amasa,* of Joab's lads,
and he said,
"Whoever has pleasure in Joab, and whoever is for David—after Joab!"
12 And Amasa was [rolled] *dead and sullied*[a] in his blood in the middle of the highway;
and the man saw
that all the people had stood still,
and he [turned] *cast* Amasa from the highway into the field
and cast over him a garment,
as he saw[b] everyone who came up to him would stand still.
13 [As he was "removed"[a]] *And it happened, when he removed Amasa*[b] from the highway,
[every man] *all the people*[c] passed by after Joab,
pursuing after Sheba son of Bichri.
14 And he passed through all the tribes of Israel [to] *and* Abel and Beth Maacah and all the [Berites] cities.[a]

[And they] assembled
and came, [even] after him.
15 And they came
and made seige against him in Abela *and* Beth Maacah,
and [poured an earthwork[a]] *threw a palisade* toward the city,
and it stood on the rampart.
And all the people who were with Joab were [destroying,] *intending*[b] making the wall fall.
16 And a wise woman called from the city,
"Listen for sure, listen.
Say for sure to Joab,
'Come near here,
and [let me] *I shall* speak to [you] *him*.'"

17 And [he] *Joab* came near to her,
and the woman said,
"Are you Joab?"
And he said,
"I am."
And she said [to him],
"Listen *for sure* to the words of your servant."
And he said,
"I am listening. Speak."[a]

18 And she said, saying,
"They used to say and say[a] at first,
'Let them ask and ask at Abel'—
and so they brought to completion.[b]

19 I am of the most peaceful of the [faithful] *foundations* of Israel.
You are seeking
to bring to death a city and a mother in Israel.
Why would you swallow up Yahweh's holding?"[a]

29[30]a. The LT's *plēthyneis* (LT), unless a free translation, attests *trbh*; and that shares three radicals with *tdbr* (MT, supported by B).

31[32]a. The MT is very problematic.

32[33]a. Here B and LT, though differently, both attest *bšbtw*, with some Heb. MSS. The consonants in CL should be read as *bśybtw*: "in his old age."

33[34]a. The LT's *Ei diabēsē* may attest *ʾm tʿbr* instead of MT's *ʾth ʿbr*.

34[35]a. In place of *kmh ymy šny ḥyy* (MT), LT attests *kmh ymym ly šm*.

36[37]a. The LT's *hoti oligon* attests not *kmʿṭ* (MT), but *ky mʿṭ*; yet LT's "because" may have missed the force of *ky* following an implied negative.

37[38]a. Here DJD (172) argues that LT's longer "and I shall be buried in the tomb," though easier, is supported by Tg. and is likely to be original.

b. The variation between "before you" (LT) and "in your eyes" (MT) is found in the opposite direction in 19:6 (7). Here 4QSam[a] agrees with MT.

39[40]a. The LT attests *ʿmd*, not *ʿbr*.

40[41]a. Here LT's *diebibasan* attests *hʿbyrw* of Q.

42[43]a. The LT's *athymein* corresponds to MT's *ḥrh* in 1 Sam 15:11; 2 Sam 6:8; 13:21; 19:42 (43).

b. Here GT appears to make a double attempt on the obscure Hebrew at the end.

43[44]a. The GT adds a rhetorical question between the two claims reported in MT.

b. The term *qšh* is construed with *dbr* only once more, in Deut 1:17; however GT's *esklērynthē* supports the reading.

20:1a. Three of the five/six instances of *qrʾ* II (*nipʿal*, "befall") are in 2 Samuel (also 1:6; 18:9), the others being Exod 5:3; Deut 22:6; and possibly Jer 4:20. Codex B's *epikaloumenos*, however, takes this from *qrʾ* I ("call").

b. Here HRCS notes *loimos* for *blyʿl* in 1 Sam 1:16; 2:12; 10:27; 25:17, 25.

c. The LT's *Arachi* represents *ʾrky* (MT) in 17:5, 14 (Hushai the Archite), while in 15:32 and 16:16 the LT has the shorter *Archi*.

2a. Here LT's "side with" probably interprets *dbqw* of MT.

3a. The LT has read the *-wt* ending of the final two words as *-ôt* (f. pl.), but MT as *-ût* (abstract); MT's *ḥayyût* ("life") is found only here in HB.

4a. The vb. *zʿq* (*nipʿal*) is used in a pass. sense in 1 Sam 14:20. The vb. is a little commoner in Judges, where we find the active *hipʿil* (as here) in 4:10, 13.

6a. The variation between *ʾth* ("you," MT) and *ʿth* ("now," LT) is frequent.

b. Presumably both "will cover/shadow our eyes" (B) and "will be sheltered from us" (LT) represent not MT *whṣyl*, but forms of *ṣll*.[33]

7a. Codex B supports MT; however, LT lacks the Cherethites and attests neither instance of *wyṣʾw*: the opening "(and he) summoned" could be a rendering of the not dissimilar *wyṣʿq*; "from Jerusalem" is attached to "all the mighty men," and the following main vb. is "and they pursued."

8a. Here LT appears to have read *ʿlyw wʿlyw*.

b. "Sword" is f. in both Heb. and Gk.; and so the explicitly stated subjects ("he" and "the sword") are not just removing ambiguity from the verb: a deliberate change has been made in one direction or the other.

10a. The GT specifies that Joab does the striking.

12a. Here GT's *pephyrmenos* means "mixed with/sullied by"; LT adds that Amasa is "dead," perhaps to discount the possibility inherent in the Hebrew ptc. *mtgll* that he is still alive and wallowing in his blood.

b. The subj. of "saw" (*rʾh*) is unclear: for LT it is the still unnamed actor: "for he saw that everyone coming is standing over him."

13a. The unique *hopʿal hōgâ* is rendered *ephthasen* ("arrived") in B. The LT offers an active expression, which makes the agency clear.

b. The longer reading in LT is required also in 4QSam[a] to fill out the line (DJD 174).

c. "All the people" (LT) has the support of the clear reading of 4QSam[a].

14a. In place of the unknown "Berites" of MT (*hbrym*), LT renders *hʿrym*.

15a. "Pour" (*špk*) is the stock vb. used with "earthwork": also 2 Kgs 19:32 (= Isa 37:33); Jer 6:6; Ezek 4:2; 17:17; 21:22 (27); 26:8; Dan 11:15.

b. The GT does not render MT *mšḥytm*, but "intend"—perhaps reading *mtʿštym* (cf. only Jonah 1:6)?

17a. The LT's *lege* at the end of the verse might attest *ʾmry* after the similar *ʾnky*.

18a. Here GT's *logos* reads *dbr* as a noun; MT reads it as inf. abs.

b. The second part of the verse is much fuller in GT and may attest a riddling and assonant text that has become corrupted in MT: "they would ask and ask at Abel and Dan whether they have completed what the faithful of Israel have set down. They would ask and ask at Abel, and so they completed."

GT retroverted	**MT**
lʾmr šʾl yšʾlw bʾbl wbdn	*lʾmr šʾl yšʾlw*
htmw ʾšr śmw ʾmwny yśrʾl	
šʾl yšʾlw bʾbl	*bʾbl*
wkn htmw	*wkn htmw*

33. However, Mand. recognizes *ṣll* III only twice in HB (Ezek 31:3; Neh 13:19), neither in a passive sense. The LXX recognizes an active usage in Jonah 4:6, where MT also reads *lhṣyl*.

19a. On the basis of a final *-m*, DJD (175) reconstructs [*nḥlt ʾlwhy*]*m* for *nḥlt yhwh* in the other witnesses. The MT uses "Yahweh" after *nḥlt* in 1 Sam 26:19, but "God" in 2 Sam 14:16.

[29–30] David is seemingly impatient: "Why do you still speak your speakings?" The verb *dibber* ("speak") and cognate noun *dābār* ("word") are quite frequently combined in Samuel,[34] as elsewhere. The king makes his ruling ("I have said") that Saul's property be divided between Ziba and Mephibosheth. He may have returned as king, but he does not have the last word. Mephibosheth has won the argument; he is the descendant of Saul; he no longer requires personal income; and he has the last, and grandest—and apparently most gracious—word (v. 30): "Your return is enough for me; let Ziba take all."

[31–39] Barzillai has been David's principal host and supplier in Mahanaim (17:27–29). His business at the Jordan crossing is not to "build bridges" by greeting him on his return, but rather to escort him safely to the home side. David offers, not to have him "eat at his table," but—more generously—to provide for him in Jerusalem. The eighty-year-old protests (v. 35) that he is too old to enjoy the lifestyle of the palace; he requests the peace of his own home and family tomb. And he notes, in a neat addition to a king who has himself been recruited to Saul's court as a musician, that he can no longer enjoy the singers. The apparently late verb *gml* (v. 36 [37], "recompense") and noun *gmwlh* (more commonly m. *gmwl*) have been used twice in the exchange between David and Saul in 1 Sam 24:17 (18), and will appear also in 2 Sam 22:21//Ps 18:20 (21). We suppose that Chimham, whom he recommends to David in his place, is his son (v. 37–38 [38–39]). David and Barzillai debate politely on which of them will be the best judge of Chimham's interests.

[40–42] It is far from easy to pinpoint exactly what groups are referred to in the last verses of ch. 19 (vv. 39–43 [40–44]). That is part of the essence of a civil war situation. It is exactly in v. 40 (41) that we meet the phrase "the people of Israel" for the second time (see on 18:7). This time "(half of) the people of Israel" is associated with "the people of Judah"; there the victorious counterparts of "the people of Israel" have been "the servants of David." Given the prominence of both "people" and "Israel" in much of HB, it comes as a surprise to find that this combination of the two occurs only twice more: heading the almost identical lists of returnees in Ezra 2:2 and Neh 7:7. (And there, nicely illustrating the complexity of this terminology, the reference is to groups returning to the lands of Judah and Benjamin.) The surprise is all the greater to readers of modern translations, which often adjust the common

34. As in 2 Sam 7:7, 25 (BTH); and 1 Sam 3:17; 8:21; 11:4; 17:31; 18:23; 20:23; 24:16 (17); 28:21; 2 Sam 11:19; 14:12, 15; 19:30; 22:1.

phrase "the sons of Israel" to the more gender-inclusive "the people of Israel." It is probably no accident that these lists of returnees make special mention of the descendants of this Barzillai: a priest has married one of his daughters and taken his name (Ezra 2:61; Neh 7:63).

[19:43–20:1] As we noted above on 19:8–15 (9–16), David himself seems to have been responsible for the tensions between Judah and Israel: bouncing his own kindred in Judah into not being left at the back of a movement that has in fact hardly yet started. That there is conflict between the claims of the majority (Israel in v. 42 [43]) and those of the activists (Judah) is too familiar in all peoples and all times to need explanation. But the arithmetic proportions have interesting resonances. In v. 43 (44) *ydwt*, plural of *yd* ("hand"), is much less common than the singular or indeed the dual. Although it is found in the (more literal) extended sense of "something projecting," it is also used in statements of proportion: "You shall give a fifth to Pharaoh, and the four *ydwt* shall be yours" (Gen 47:24); "[The king] found them ten *ydwt* over all the magicians" (Dan 1:20). By analogy, Israel has a tenfold greater claim on David than Judah (v. 43 [44]). This ten-to-one ratio is stated and repeated in one other biblical context (1 Kgs 11:31, 35–36), although the ratio is complicated there by being introduced into a prior total of twelve "rents" (pieces) into which the prophet's new garment has been torn (11:30).

The books of Samuel are familiar with such decimal comparisons. Israel contributes 300,000 troops to Saul's campaign for Jabesh, and Judah 30,000 (1 Sam 11:8). Saul is credited with causing thousands of enemy casualties, but David with tens of thousands. Then, more immediately, Joab has claimed he would have rewarded the man who found Absalom with ten pieces of silver if he had finished him off, to which the man retorted that he would not have countered the king's orders for a thousand pieces. But they never in fact speak of "twelve tribes." There is no evidence to suppose that the author of this portion of 2 Sam 19 was familiar with 1 Kgs 11 (which was also not part of BTH), or that Israel made its tenfold claim to precedence on the basis of the twelve-tribe structure familiar elsewhere in HB. Indeed it is much more likely that (the more clumsily drafted) 1 Kgs 11 has been influenced by 2 Sam 19.[35]

There is an alarmingly swift transition in Israel's attitude, from the lavish protestation of their interest in David (19:41–43 [42–44]) to withdrawal from him (20:1–2). Just as Israel's claim of ten shares in David anticipates 1 Kgs 11, so Sheba's call almost precisely anticipates the wording of Israel's rejec-

35. Not only does the combination of twelve pieces with a 10-to-1 ratio appear secondary, but the very different texts of MT and OG may be evidence that the relevant portions of 1 Kgs 11 were drafted late.

tion of Rehoboam on the death of Solomon (1 Kgs 12:16, BTH). As usual, we should understand that Samuel is drawing on BTH (preserved here in Kings). The context here requires a rendering of *nḥlh* more literal than "possession," which we have used till now. A family's *nḥlh* or *ḥlq* ("division") is its share or stake or holding or portion of the whole land of its community. The portions of the whole earth have been allotted by the Most High (Deut 32:8–9); and Yahweh's own *nḥlh* (20:19 below) within them is Jacob/Israel. The fact that (land) holdings are frequently heritable has led, since the Gk. OT, to the rendering "inheritance" or "heritage."

We know nothing of Bichri except for his son Sheba. They are not said to be related to Saul, but they are also from Benjamin. Sheba is the third character in 2 Samuel whose just "happening" on a situation leads quickly to his death. And yet the fate of each does not come as any surprise: the first is an Amalekite (1:6, 8), the second a royal rebel (18:9), and now Sheba is identified at the outset as a scoundrel (20:1). He sounds the trumpet as a rallying call, or at least to call for attention; and shouts out a version of what all Israel say to Rehoboam, according to BTH, when the negotiations at Shechem fail (1 Kgs 12:16//2 Chr 10:16).

[20:2–3] All Israel does follow him, but Judah "sticks by" their king.This "Benjamite" (so MT at least) behaves and fares very differently from the last man to be so introduced, Shimei ben Gera (19:16 [17]). It is not easy to see how the Saul-Benjamin-Israel issues treated in 2 Sam 19 relate to those in 2 Sam 20. Chapter 20 breathes a different atmosphere and also anticipates issues in 21:1–14—and hence may be later than both. And yet, in one respect at least, the third of three instances in 2 Samuel of "chanced" (20:1), as read at least in MT, serves to suggest an alignment of Sheba's opposition to David with those of Saul and Absalom.

David's only reported act on gaining Jerusalem, and before dealing with Sheba, is to provide for his ten concubines who have been defiled by Absalom in the previous revolt (v. 3). The task he has then set for the ten women (15:16) now sees a double reversal: "guards" have been put under guard; women destined for sexual encounter ("concubines") are "widowed." The second element of the wordplay ("guard the house . . . guardhouse") uses (or creates) a combination unique in HB of two common nouns. They are to be under "house arrest" till their death, but apparently made comfortable—the same word "provide" has just been used of the hospitality exchanged between David and Barzillai (19:32–33 [33–34]).[36] And yet there may be more to say. "Till the day of their death" echoes what we earlier read about Michal: "Till the day of her death" (6:23). If a deliberate echo, it may suggest an answer to the

36. But it is used mainly in later biblical passages: Gen 45:11; 47:12; 50:21; 1 Kgs 4:7; 4:27 (5:7); 17:4, 9; 18:4, 13; Zech 11:16; Ps 55:22 (23); Ruth 4:15; Neh 9:21.

question whether David resumes sexual relations with Michal on her return from Palti[el]. Her destiny, as determined by David, is to have no child, just as the ten are to be living widows.

There are not many "tens" in the story; and these ten women reappear just after talk about Israel's ten shares in David. Are these women a symbol of the Israelite majority (temporarily) alienated from the house of David? Is their confined "widowhood" till their death an image that anticipates the view from a Davidic perspective of northern Israel after Solomon: spoiled and fruitless till it exists no more? This verse is completely absent from 4QSam[a], and so its presence in both MT and GT may represent a later interpolation. Be that as it may, its final words make a bitter contrast with Abigail's promise to David himself. First Samuel 25:29 is the only other verse in Samuel to use the passive participle "bound," in Abigail's wish that David's life will be "bound in the bundle of the living." Early or late, this setting aside of the ten women may be parabolic of David's relationship with the northern tribes, following a revolt so soon after their claim of ten shares in David to Judah's one. There are curious echoes of this unusual wording in 1 Kgs 11:26, where Jeroboam is introduced in MT as being from Zeredah (*ṣrdh*), and son of a widow named Zeruah (*ṣrwʿh*)—but in GT as coming from Sarira, and son of a widow (who is not named). Sarira presumably retroverts to *ṣryrh*, closest of these three similar name forms to *ṣrwrh* ("bound") in 2 Sam 20:3.

[4–5] Amasa, the recently appointed army commander (19:13–14), is summoned; but, for some unexplained reason, he delays too long.

[6–8] David entrusts the pursuit of Sheba to Joab's brother, who takes Joab's and David's men (vv. 6–7). But clearly Joab himself is one of the party; for it is he personally who assassinates Amasa at Gibeon, just north of Jerusalem (v. 8). The only other person in these books to miss an appointed meeting (*môʿēd*) was Samuel (1 Sam 13:8, 11)—rather unfairly he claimed to be in the right and Saul in the wrong! But that precedent does not bode well for Amasa. The texts diverge over what happens next. In LT, David reminds (the delayed) Amasa of the need for speed against an enemy who may prove more dangerous than Absalom if he gains control of fortified cities (v. 6). But in MT, David appears to have given up on Amasa and briefs not Joab but his brother Abishai about the urgency of the situation.

The precise location of the encounter between Joab and Amasa is given as "the great stone," which is probably a euphemism, or rather bland description, of a [once] sacred standing stone or altar associated with the "great high place" for which Gibeon was once famous (1 Kgs 3:4; cf. also Josh 24:26; 1 Sam 6:14–15; 14:33–35). Dress (*lbš*, v. 8) appears to feature more prominently in later biblical books, such as Ezekiel, later books among the Twelve, Esther, and Daniel. There are references to garments in 1 Sam 17:5; 28:8; 2 Sam 1:24;

13:18; 14:2; 20:8. The sole instance common to Samuel–Kings and Chronicles is in 1 Kgs 22:30//2 Chr 18:29.

[9–10a] Amasa dies (v. 10) with a single stroke by Joab, described just like brother Abishai's threat to kill Saul for David (1 Sam 26:8). The actual deceit practiced on Amasa by Joab is reinforced by the words used in its description. Even the six instances of kissing in the books of Samuel are part of quite different sorts of interaction: 1 Sam 10:1 (Samuel/Saul); 20:41 (David/Jonathan); 2 Sam 14:33 (David/Absalom); 15:5 (Absalom/suppliants); 19:39 (40, David/Barzillai); 20:9 (Joab/Amasa). But only in this last case is the kiss (reinforced by calling Amasa "my brother') positively deceitful. Here *wtḥz . . . bzqn* ("he seized . . . the beard") reuses the key letters of *whḥzyq* ("he would grasp") from 15:5.[37]

[10b–14a] No matter whether it was Amasa or Abishai that David has urged on against Sheba, it is unsurprisingly Joab who immediately assumes command of the pursuit. Amasa, like Abner before him (3:27), has been felt by Joab as a threat and is struck down. Joab and his brother plunge on after Sheba while Amasa is still in his death throes. But the men of Judah, who have been called out by Amasa, are hesitating. One of Joab's men takes two necessary steps (vv. 11–13): he urges and apparently persuades them that loyalty to Joab and loyalty to David are one and the same thing; and he moves their dying former commander quite literally "out of the way" and covers him up.

[14b–19] Abel, where Sheba is finally besieged, is one of Israel's northern border cities. It is one of the cities listed in 1 Kgs 15:20 (BTH) as captured from Baasha of Israel by the Aramaean king in Damascus on behalf of Asa, king of Judah; and it features again in 2 Kgs 15:29. It is no exaggeration to say that Joab and his men have chased Sheba through "all the tribes of Israel," from Jerusalem to the very north. Strong efforts to reduce the city are being made (v. 15) when Joab is summoned to speak to a wise woman on the walls (vv. 16–17). Abel, he learns from her, used to be a place where matters were brought to conclusion by consultation—she does not say whether consultation of the Deity, or of wise people like herself. She claims to be among "the associates of the faithful in Israel" (v. 19; her terminology here is quite unique in the Bible)—but what he wants to do is destroy and swallow up.

What she says Joab wants to "destroy" is ambiguous: we could translate it either "city and mother in Israel," or "a city—and [one that is] a mother—in Israel." But what is "the heritage of God" that she claims he has in mind to "swallow up"? We met "God's holding" in 2 Sam 14:16 in the mouth of another

37. If the connection is deliberate, it may help to explain why *wtḥz* is spelled defectively (for *wt'ḥz*). However, the reason may be more mundane; for in v. 5 *wywḥr* has also been spelled defectively for *wyw'ḥr*—again without the silent '.

wise woman, that time from Tekoa. She told David of her concern for the life of her son in a family feud—and her words had been put in her mouth by Joab (14:3). Now another wise woman is returning his own words to Joab. The other two contexts in Samuel suggest that the nation's land is "what Yahweh gives as heritage holding" (1 Sam 26:19; 2 Sam 21:3). But from the mouth of a woman and mother, we may expect instead, or as well, to hear an echo of Ps 127. For, in between mention of guarding the city (v. 1) and speaking with one's enemies in the gate (v. 5), it speaks of sons as "Yahweh's holding" (v. 3). This woman reproaches Joab for his will to destroy mothers and children among his people.

2 Samuel 20:20–24:25
Concluding Perspectives

Two powerful and mysterious stories bracket 2 Sam 21–24: Gibeon's revenge against the house of Saul, and David's tragic mistake in counting Israel. Next to them are miscellaneous notes about David's fighting men. And at the heart of these four well-structured chapters are two poems that articulate the royal ideology. The first and fourth of these six elements are unique to Samuel; the longer of the poems (2 Sam 22) is found also as Ps 18; and three (elements 2, 5, 6) are variants of material that Samuel shares with Chronicles. The larger literary or structural grounds for detecting a fresh start and unique shaping from 21:1 appear incontrovertible. However, they are not represented in our ancient witnesses. As presented in DJD (175), the evidence of paragraphing from 4QSam[a] is different from MT in each respect: there is not even a *sĕtûmâ* between 20:19 and 20:20; there is only a *sĕtûmâ* between 20:26 and 21:1; and there is a *pĕtûḥâ* between 21:1 and 21:2. As in 4QSam[a], so in LT there is no space before the start of 20:20, while MT as represented in Aleppo has a major paragraph break, and CL even a blank line.

In 1 Chronicles, what corresponds to 2 Sam 21:18–22 (1 Chr 20:4–8) immediately precedes what corresponds to 2 Sam 24 (1 Chr 21). The final elements of the synoptic material about David in Chronicles are also part of this balanced conclusion to the portrait of David in Samuel. However, the list of David's heroes and some of their exploits (2 Sam 23:8–39) appears much earlier, and no less appropriately, in 1 Chr 11:10–47, right after the report of David's taking and establishing himself in Jerusalem. If the order in Chronicles of these three elements is the more original, 2 Sam 21–24 may have been built as follows:

1. The story of the divine plague associated with David, Gibeon, and Saul was set at the beginning (A) to correspond to the plague following David's census told as the synoptic conclusion (A′).
2. The list and exploits of David's heroes was moved from near the beginning of the synoptic account (1 Chr 11:10–47) to the penultimate position (B′) to correspond to the anti-Philistine exploits of David and some of his servants (B).
3. Two poems were set at the core (C/C′).

2 Samuel 20:20–21:22 Swallowing Up and Destroying

2 Samuel 20:20–26

20 And Joab answered
and said,
"A curse, [a curse[a]] on me
were I to swallow up or were I to destroy.
21 The matter is not so:
rather a man from Mount Ephraim, Sheba son of Bichri [his name[a]],
he has raised his hand against the king, against David.
Give *me* him only,
and let me go from the city."
And the woman said to Joab,
"Look, his head is thrown to you over the wall."
22 And the woman came to all the people
and spoke to all the city[a] in her wisdom;
and they cut off the head of Sheba son of Bichri
and threw it to Joab;
and [he] *Joab* sounded on the horn
and [they] *the people* were scattered from the city each to his tent[s];
and Joab, he returned to Jerusalem to the king.

23 And Joab was over all the army, Israel;
and Benaiah son of Jehoiada was over [the Cre(t)i[a] and over the Pleti]
the brickworks/troopsquares and over the chiefs.
24 And Adoram[a] was over the corvée;
and [Jehoshaphat] *Shaphan* son of Ahilud[b] was the Recorder.
25 And [Shya[a]] *Sousa* was scribe;
and Zadok and Abiathar, priests.
26 And *Jodae*[a] [Ira too, the Jairite,] of Jether became priest to David.

20a. There is space in 4QSam[a] for only one *ḥlylh* ("a curse").

21a. Here DJD 176 finds that 4QSam[a] agrees with the shorter LT, without "his name." At the same time, it notes that *šmw* following a name frequently has demeaning significance and hence is appropriate here.

22a. Codex B also attests the plus in LT after "the people."

23a. Here B has *Cheleththei* for MT's *hkr(t)y*; LT seems to take this and the next word as common nouns, which could retrovert to *ʿl-hmlbn wʿl-hgbrym*. *plinthion* (lit. a small brick) can refer to troops drawn up in a square.

24a. In place of MT's *ʾdrm*, B attests the fuller *ʾdnyrm*, while LT offers the quite different *Iezedran*.

b. It is not clear how far *Achithalaa* (LT) represents an original different from Ahilud (MT).

25a. The scribe is variously the puzzling *šyʾ* (K) or *šwʾ* (Q) in MT, Jesus in B, or Sousa in LT; and other texts exhibit many variations on these. The reconstruction in DJD follows LT and Josephus.

26a. Codex B more or less supports MT over the name of David's priest, while LT may attest *ywdʿʾ* son of Yether.

[20–22] Joab describes Sheba to the wise woman as being "of the hill country of Ephraim" (v. 21). In 20:1 MT has introduced him as a Benjamite, but LT as an Arachite. These pieces of information are less in tension with each other than first appears. According to Josh 16:2, "Archite territory" marks part of the southern border of Joseph (with Benjamin). Elsewhere in Samuel–Kings, "the hill country of Ephraim" describes the area where the hometown of Samuel's father was (1 Sam 1:1); where Saul looked for his father's lost animals (9:4); where men of Israel hid from the Philistines (14:22); the first district in Solomon's Israel (1 Kgs 4:8)—there clearly distinct from Benjamin (4:18); the area that includes Shechem (12:25); and the provenance of two unnamed prophets (2 Kgs 5:22). Abel is much further to the north of Sheba's home territory than Jerusalem is to the south.

When Joab explains that he wants only rebel Sheba, the woman promises his head, confident on negotiating that in the city (vv. 21–22a), despite normal rules of hospitality. We might say, to close a bargain, even ahead of delivery: "You've got your head." The plus in GT represents Hebrew *wtdbr ʾl-kl-hʿyr*, which is shaped like and shares many letters with the preceding *hʾšh ʾel-kl-hʿm*. Such similarity could have led to accidental omission from MT. But it is quite as possible that the second phrase was added to clarify that "all the people" refers this time only to the people in Abel, not to the forces of all northern Israel. The two previous instances of the phrase (20:12, 15) refer to all David's people with Joab. Most of the action in the books of Samuel is located in the central and southern highlands west of the Jordan. But the story of David as king over Israel begins with a friendly embassy to Jabesh in Gilead, in northern Transjordan (2 Sam 2:4–7); and these many chapters of conflict end at Abel in the far north, just west of Dan, among the headwaters of the Jordan. The head is duly thrown down to Joab, who now sounds the trumpet in grim echo of Sheba (v. 1).

[23–26] Mention of Joab's return to the king in Jerusalem (v. 22b) is not followed by any indication of David's reaction to Joab's assumption of command or to his success. But we now read (vv. 23–26) a repetition with some changes of the information transcribed in 8:16–18 from BTH. After what has just been reported, there is no surprise to find that Joab is again mentioned first (v. 23 corresponds to 8:16a, 18a): there is no change in command of the army. The mention of Adoram in charge of the forced labor is new (v. 24a); 20:24b corresponds to 8:16b; 20:25 corresponds to 8:17, but is reordered; and Ira as priest of David in 20:26 replaces 8:18b, which reports David's sons as priests.

2 Samuel 21:1–14

1 And there was a famine *in the land*[a] in the days of David, three years, year after year,
and [David sought the face of Yahweh] *a word was David seeking from* Yahweh.[b]

And Yahweh said:

"Upon Saul and upon his house is the guilt: through his putting the Gibeonites to death by a bloody death."[c]	"For Saul and for the bloody house, because he put the Gibeonites to death."

2 And the king called the Gibeonites
and said to them—
now the Gibeonites were not of the sons of Israel but of the remnant of the Amorites,
and the sons of Israel swore to them
not to destroy them;
and Saul sought[a]
to [strike them down] *finish them off*[b] in his zeal for [the sons of] Israel and of Judah—
3 and David said to the Gibeonites,
"What shall I do for you?
And by what means shall I atone
and you bless Yahweh's holding?"[a]
4 And the Gibeonites said to him,
"It is not silver or gold for us with Saul or with his house,

and it is not for us to put to death a man[a] out of all Israel."	and we have no man[a] to put to death in Israel."

And he said *to them*,
"What are you [saying[b]] *wishing*,
and I shall do (it) for you?"
5 And they said to the king,
"The man who finished us off
and pursued us[a]
and who made plans[b] [for us—we were destroyed[c]] *to destroy us*,
let us make him disappear
so as not to take a stand[d] in all the territory of Israel—
6 let there be given us seven men of his sons,
and let us *be atoned*[a] *in them* [expose them dislocated[a]] for Yahweh at Gibeah of Saul, Yahweh's elect."[b]

And the king said,
"I, I shall give them."
7 And the king took pity on *Memphibaal* [Mephibosheth] son of Jonathan son of Saul,
because of Yahweh's oath
that [was] *they had sworn* between them, between David and Jonathan son of Saul.
8 And the king took the two sons of Rizpah daughter of Aiah,
whom she bore to Saul,
[Armoni] *Akhi* and Mephibosheth,
and the five sons of [Michal] *Merob* daughter of Saul,
whom she bore to [Adriel] *Ezri* son of Barzillai the [Meholathite] *Maathite*.
9 And he put them in the hand*s*[a] of the Gibeonites,
and they dislocated them on the mountain[b] before Yahweh,
and the seven of them fell *there* together.[c]
And they were done to death in the days of harvest, [in the first ones,]
the start of the barley harvest.
10 And Rizpah daughter of Aiah, *the concubine of Saul*, took the sacking
and stretched it out for herself [toward] *on* the rock from harvest start
till water *of God*[a] was poured [on them] from the heavens;
and she did not allow the birds of the heavens to rest on them by day
nor the beasts of the field by night.
And they were set free,
and they were taken down by Dan son of Joash from the offspring of the giants.[b]
11 And it was told David
[what] *all that* Rizpah daughter of Aiah concubine of Saul had done.
12 And David went
and took the bones of Saul and the bones of Jonathan his son
from the [lords] *men* of Jabesh-gilead,
who had stolen them from the [broad space] *wall* at Beth-Shan
where the Philistines[a] had hung them on the day
the Philistines struck down Saul on Gilboa.
13 And he took up from there the bones of Saul and the bones of Jonathan his son,
and *he* [they] collected the bones of the [dislocated] *sunscorched.*[a]
14 And *he* [they] buried the bones of Saul and of Jonathan [his son] *and the bones of the atoned for* in the land of Benjamin in [Zela[a] in] *the side of* the tomb of Kish his father.
And they did all that the king commanded;
and God accepted entreaty[b] for the land after this.

1a. It is unclear to me why, following a substantial (reconstructed) space, it is claimed (DJD 175) that there is no room in 4QSam[a] for LT's "in the land."

b. "And David sought a word from Lord" (LT) may simply interpret MT rather than represent a different underlying text.

c. Codex B shares LT's longer text in v. 1b. Here DJD reconstructs an "original" response close to MT, but one letter shorter: "Upon Saul and upon his house there is (blood)guilt, because he put the Gibeonites to death."

2a. The LT's *estēse* may be an inner-Greek aural mistake for *ezētēse*.

b. Here LT appears to have read not *lhktm* (MT) but *lkltm* (cf. *klnw* in v. 5).

3a. Elsewhere in Samuel *nḥlh* is found in 1 Sam 10:1; 26:19; 2 Sam 14:16 (in connection with *hšmyd*); 20:1, 19.

4a. Codex B renders *ʾyš* by *anēr* (nom.), so taking the "man" to be the executioner; LT renders with *andra* (accus.)—a strict retroversion of LT would require a different word order: *ʾyn-lnw lhmyt ʾyš mkl-yśrʾl*.

b. The LT's attested *ʾwbym* ("wishing") looks very similar to *ʾwmrym* ("saying," MT, B).

5a. Codex B shares "and pursued us" with LT, and 4QSam[a] gives cautious support (DJD 178).

b. The *DCH* supports the sense "intend" for *dmh* I (*piʿel*) with *l-* in the sense "against." But the only other cases of *dmh l-* mean "liken to/compare with."

c. The shorter MT may result from the corruption of the GT-attested *lhšmydnw* into *lnw nšmdnw*. Elsewhere in Samuel *šmd* is found in 1 Sam 24:21 (22); 2 Sam 14:7, 11, 16; 22:38. From the longer variant texts, DJD reconstructs only "to destroy us." The LT's *aphanizō* also renders *šmd* in 1 Sam 24:21 (22); 2 Sam 22:38.

d. In MT it is the Gibeonites who are unable to maintain a position in Israel, whereas in GT it will be Saul.

6a. The practice of dislocation/dismemberment—if that is what is meant by *yqʿ* (*hipʿil*)—is attested only here and at Num 25:4; *yqʿ* (*qal*) is used in Gen 32:25 (26) of the dislocation of Jacob's limb by his divine assailant. Codex B renders by *exēliazō*, "hang in the sun"—Num 25:4 specifies that *hwqʿ* should take place "over against the sun"; while LT offers *kai exilasometha en autois*—also apparently in v. 14, while in vv. 9, 13 it uses the assonant *exēliazō* (*exileasthentōn* appears to be a mixed form: in contemporary Greek, *ē* had become pronounced like *i*).

b. The MT takes Saul to be Yahweh's elect (sg.), but LT—presumably at least—speaks of the seven victims (pl). It is easier to suggest that *tous eklektous* (LT) would retrovert to *bḥyry yhwh*, only minimally different from *bḥyr yhwh* (MT), than to explain why the seven "elect of Yahweh" should appear here in the accus. case rather than nom. or dat. in agreement with either previous mention in the sentence.

9a. Here 4QSam[a] clearly reads sg. *byd* with MT.

b. The LT specifies that the Gibeonites expose them in the sun.

c. In Samuel *yḥd* ("together") is used in 1 Sam 11:11; 17:10; 2 Sam 10:15 (BTH context, but a Samuel plus); 14:16 (links with this passage); 21:9. This form of the word is to be distinguished from *yḥdw* in 1 Sam 30:24; 31:6; 2 Sam 13, 15.

10a. The LT has read *my ʾlhym* ("water of God"), not *mym ʿlyhm* ("water over them") as in MT.

b. The substantial plus in LT anticipates "set free" and "offspring of the giants" in vv. 15–22 below.

12a. Here Q treats *šm hplštym* as misdivided for *šmh plštym*; in MT, unlike 4QSam[a], "Philistines" seldom bears the article.

13a. The LT's *exēliasmenōn* resumes the vb. used in v. 9.

14a. Here *ṣlʿ* ("rib") is rendered by *pleura* (as here) or *pleuron* in 1 Kgs 6–7, as a feature of the Jerusalem temple. However, MT appears to have understood it here as a proper name—presumably as the place specified more precisely as *ṣlʿ hʾlp* in Josh 18:28.

b. The LT returns to the overworked *exilasato* ("successfully entreated") at the end, in place of MT's *wyʿtr* and B's *kai epēkousen* (*ʿtr* and *šmʿ* are linked in 2 Chr 33:13). Notice the variety within the small LT tradition over this key vb.

[1a] The wise peace-seeking words of the woman in Abel ill prepare us for the chilling tragic episode that follows. A three-year famine sets the scene; and famine is always interpreted as a divine punishment. David "sought Yahweh's face" is a rare expression and unique here within Samuel (in 2 Sam 12:16 we read simply "sought Yahweh")—the best parallel is provided by the participial expression in 1 Kgs 10:24 (BTH), which talks of all the [kings of the] earth paying court to Solomon to learn of his [divine] wisdom. The formulation *wybqš dwd ʾt-pny yhwh* may be unique within the Hebrew Bible; but it does not appear to give us less information about David's technique of divination than the more common *wyšʾl dwd byhwh*. The alternative formulation in LT ("and a word was David seeking from Lord") could retrovert to *wdbr mbqš dwd mpny yhwh*, but might simply represent the translator's own avoidance of an even more overtly anthropomorphic expression. Be that as it may, "the word of Yahweh" is the object of "seek" in Amos 8:12—and in connection with famine there too!

[1b–6a] Terming the Gibeonites "the remnant of the Amorites" (v. 2) recalls (or anticipates) the report in BTH about Solomon's pressing former inhabitants of the land into forced labor (1 Kgs 9:20–21//2 Chr 8:7–8). This link is reinforced when the Gibeonites speak to David about the man who "finished" them (v. 5)—2 Chr 8:8 reports (possibly more originally) that Israel "did not finish" this remnant, while 1 Kgs 9:21 reports that they "could not put them to the ban" (we found both expressions used in 1 Sam 15). Saul's putting the Gibeonites to death is not part of the Saul story appearing in 1 Samuel; that omission is now put right (v. 2). It is Josh 9 that tells the part of the story relating to Israel's oath to spare the people of Gibeon; it explains how the Gibeonites become Israel's temple servants. Then 1 Kgs 3 (BTH) describes Gibeon as the great "high place" of the period before Solomon built the Jerusalem temple: Solomon offers vast sacrifices and receives a night vision there (recalled above at 2 Sam 20:8). Given these associations, we might fairly suppose that it is also at Gibeon that David has sought divine wisdom; but the language actually used (v. 1) is of him seeking Yahweh's "face" or "word." Saul has also been "seeking" (v. 2): in his case benefit for Israel and (surprisingly) Judah as well. Saul's attempt to finish off the Gibeonites is attributed to his zeal for Israel; the mention of Judah here anticipates their separate listing in the account of the census, which balances this story (24:9).

In this case, Saul's previously unreported action (against the Gibeonites) has only postmortem significance for himself. Although it has grisly consequences for some of his family, it will result in his own more appropriate burial. However, it is reminiscent of the other incident that is prefaced by a brief report of a death and burial, and of previously unreported action taken by Saul. We learn of his removal of mediums from the land (1 Sam 28:3b) immediately after a reminder of Samuel's death and burial in his home town (28:3a, repeating 25:1). As with the removal of mediums, finishing off earlier inhabitants of the land would be praiseworthy in terms of other biblical norms; but in this case Israel has undertaken a solemn and exceptional vow.

Expiation or appeasement or atonement—the same Hebrew word is translated in each of these ways. The verb *kippēr* (v. 3) is very rare in the narrative books of the Bible: the two occurrences in the books of Samuel put an interesting bracket round the extended preface to the story of Israel's kings provided by these books. We met this term first in 1 Sam 3:14; the bald message given there is that the guilt of Eli's house simply cannot be expiated. But here David puts a question that expects a positive answer, and he himself takes responsibility for achieving it. He is seeking blessing for "Yahweh's holding." In the context of famine, it little matters whether that phrase refers to the land or its people. However, one of the only two mentions of *naḥălâ* in BTH occurs in Solomon's prayer at the dedication of the temple: when there is no rain because of sin, yet the people repent and pray toward "this place," then "grant rain on your land, which you have given to your people as a holding" (1 Kgs 8:35–36).

If these two instances of *kippēr* may make a significant pairing, this instance also suggests an interesting triple relationship. The two outer panels of chs. 21–24 demand to be thought together. Gibeon and the future temple site in Jerusalem will be precisely the locations of Solomon's two visions, before (1 Kgs 3:4–15) and after (9:1–9) the building of the temple. And, while *kippēr* does not feature in ch. 24 itself, it is a key element in the language of Exod 30:11–16, which specifies how potential guilt relating to counting the people can be coped with.

If expiation and appeasement and atonement are all possible translations of one Hebrew word, so too zeal and jealousy of another (*qn'*). The idea that Yahweh's "jealousy" can lead to punishment of an extended family over a few generations, for a crime as serious as idolatry, is familiar from the Ten Commandments (Deut 5:9). Saul's "zeal" (v. 2) for Israel and against the Gibeon enclave was similarly uncompromising—and also their riposte.

The Gibeonites give a somewhat riddling response, which in a few words (v. 4) is both diplomatic and firm. The first element is ambiguous, taken on its own; and it might have meant "There are no financial obligations between us." But when they go on to say they have not the power to put to death in Israel, we realize their meaning that the problem between them and Saul cannot be solved financially. Monetary compensation is out of the question. David's response is to ask them to put their request in all clarity. They repeat the seriousness of their complaint against Saul; then they ask that seven of his male descendants be put to death by some form of exposure—not just anywhere, but at Gibeon for or before Yahweh (vv. 5–6). For the Gibeonites, the case they make to David is stated in all-or-nothing terms. The verb *htyṣb* ("take a stand") is much more important in Samuel (10x) than in the other narrative books in HB (7x).[1] It refers to taking or holding one's position quite deliberately or self-confidently. However, MT and GT read this key infinitive in different ways: MT has the Gibeonites claiming that they have been destroyed and are no longer able to "take their stand" within the confines of Israel; but GT has them wanting Saul's family destroyed and thus no longer able to "take their stand" within the confines of Israel. The GT version provides a very effective echo of the process by which Saul was selected as king (1 Sam 10:17b–24). Samuel first challenged Israel to "take their stand" (*htyṣb*) in their tribal units before Yahweh (v. 19); when Saul was "taken," they had to seek oracular guidance on where he was hidden, and only then did he "take his stand" among the people (v. 23). The adjacent and even rarer phrase "in the territory/borders/confines of Israel" also nicely echoes one of Saul's early exploits, when he sent severed pieces of cattle "in all the territory of Israel" (1 Sam 11:7) to encourage support for Jabesh. In the present story, oracular guidance has again identified Saul—not as the new king, but as a troublesome legacy still to be sorted out.

Until the opening of this story (v. 1a), there has been no talk of David's seeking the will of Yahweh since the early days in Jerusalem (2 Sam 5—in contrast to appealing for the sake of his child [2 Sam 12:6]). Success and failure in consulting Yahweh mark one of the contrasts between David and Saul. Ironically, Saul's only reported success (1 Sam 14:41) provides another grim anticipation. When he learned that the problem lay with Jonathan and himself, and not anyone else within his people, he asked for a divine decision between him and his son. When Jonathan was identified, he was prepared to let him die.

[6b–14] Having heard the second presentation of the Gibeonite case, David has no question about handing over descendants of Saul—for him to lose further members of the house of Saul is hardly inconvenient. But David does exempt Mephibosheth because of his oath to Jonathan.

1. See 1 Sam 3:10; 10:19, 23; 12:7, 16; 17:16; 2 Sam 18:13, 30; 21:5; 23:12 (BTH), as compared with Josh 1:5; 24:1; Judg 20:2; 1 Chr 11:14 (BTH); 2 Chr 11:13; 20:6, 17.

Rizpah is mother to two of the victims (v. 8), all of them guilty only by (family) association. Her vigil over the many hot months from harvest to first rains, protecting the corpses from dismemberment by carrion day and night, recalls Antigone's vigil over her dead brother, which was immortalized by the Athenian tragedian Sophocles (fifth c. BCE). Barley harvest is the earlier of the two grain harvests. Two earlier scenes in 1 Samuel are located at the time of the wheat harvest (6:13; 12:17), several weeks later. Ruth (1:22; 2:23) is the only other biblical book to specify barley harvest, which was celebrated in the festival of (Passover and) Unleavened Bread; but it may be intended in Josh 3:15, since the Jordan crossing was followed immediately by the first Passover in the promised land.[2] Rizpah's piety comes to David's attention and brings to his mind the hazardous care shown by men from Jabesh in Gilead for the corpses of Saul and Jonathan (1 Sam 31:11–13), exposed by the Philistines, though for different reasons. He arranges for them to be (re)buried "in the land of Benjamin," in the family tomb. The stress on Benjamin here completes the story of Saul, which started with the same emphasis (see above on 1 Sam 9:1, 16). The Hebrew puts "after that" at the very end of v. 14. The suggestion may be that Yahweh was moved as much by the due burial of Saul and his family as by the awful price exacted by Gibeon.

The textual variety in v. 10 is interesting. When translating MT, it seems important to render both occurrences of *ʿlyhm* the same way: "on/over them." Yet that simply points up the issue of whether "them" has the same reference in both cases; and if not, why the sentence has been drafted this way. "Water of/from God from heaven" (LT) renders a very similar-looking Hebrew but is somewhat tautologous.

The connections between 2 Sam 21 (esp. v. 12) and 1 Sam 31//1 Chr 10 have been thoroughly explored by Craig Ho. He makes a convincing case for the shorter text in 1 Chr 10 being prior to the more developed 1 Sam 31 at almost every point of difference. His demonstrations that 1 Chr 10 is often more congruous with material elsewhere in 1 Samuel than is 1 Sam 31 provide some of his strongest arguments. The principal exception to this general argument is the agreement between 2 Sam 21:12 and pluses in 1 Sam 31, when that is compared with the shorter 1 Chr 10 (Ho 97–98). All of this suggests (1) that 1 Chr 10 is the better witness to the account of Saul's death in BTH; (2) that this earlier version has influenced the drafting of several elements of 1 Samuel; but (3) that it has been redrafted when, at a later stage in the development of the books of Samuel, 2 Sam 21:1–14 was added.

Campbell (2:184–86) underemphasizes the connectedness at several levels between this story and many others in 1–2 Samuel. He certainly is correct to say that 1 Sam 31 talks of the death of Saul and his three sons, while 2 Sam 21

2. Yet it should be noted that the (unusually) longer Greek text specifies "wheat."

talks only of Saul and Jonathan. And yet this discrepancy is no novelty: David's elegy in 2 Sam 1 also laments only the deaths of the king and the crown prince. As for the nonmention in 2 Sam 21:12 of the burning of Saul's body by the men of Jabesh-Gilead—on the one side, we should not expect every detail to be repeated; and on the other, the burning is one of the features of 1 Sam 31:12 not shared by 1 Chr 10:12.

It is easier to spot the broad correspondences between this narrative and the following census story in 2 Sam 24 than confidently to explain just how they should be compared or contrasted. The most obvious connections are the positioning at beginning and end of the final four chapters, the catastrophic consequences for people and land of a disastrous and impious action of the king, the mention of Judah alongside Israel, the prominence of the numbers three and seven, and the appeasement of Yahweh through a "sacrificial" action. Just before the end of Samuel, we are reminded of Saul as wrongdoer—but the question lingers whether in this he is like or unlike David. It is also easy to notice how conveniently matters turn out for David: more members of Saul's house are killed off; David is portrayed as enabler of the divine will, rather than as selfish instigator of their fate; and David arranges proper burial for Saul and Jonathan. David's rule began (2 Sam 1) with a poignant elegy for the leaders of the rival royal house; it comes to an end with him arranging for their honorable interment. But what of David himself?

2 Samuel 21:15–17

15 And there was still war of the Philistines with Israel;
and David went down and his [servants[a]] *men* with him
and fought with *the* Philistines;
and David was [exhausted[b]] *set free.*
16 And [Yishbi at Nob[a]] *Dadou son of Joash,*
[who was[b]] of the offspring of the [Raphah] *giants,*
and the weight of his spear[c] was three hundred [weight] *shekels* of bronze,
and he was girt [new[d]] *with a girdle,*
and he spoke
of striking David down.
17 And Abishai son of Zeruiah [helped[a] him] *saved David*
and struck down the Philistine
and did him to death.
Then David's men swore [to him], saying,
"You shall not go out again with us to battle,
and you shall not quench the lamp[b] of Israel."

15a. Here 4QSam[a] clearly reads "servants" with MT. "Men" (LT) may be influenced by v. 17.

b. The term *wyʿp* (< *ʿyp*) is used of Saul's battle-weary "people" in 1 Sam 14:28, 31, and of the dying Sisera, between the verbs "fell deep asleep" and "died" (Judg 4:21). An appropriate sense is caught by LT's *exelythē* (this pass. can mean both "be released" and "be made unserviceable"; and so DJD [180] may be wrong to suppose a retroversion to *wyṣʾ*, "and he went out"); however, B has the surprising "went." The new *Índice* notes how in LT *eklyō* corresponds in turn to *yʿp* (2 Sam 16:2); *ʿwp* (1 Sam 14:28; 2 Sam 21:15); *ʿyp* (2 Sam 16:14; 17:29); as well as to *rph* (2 Sam 4:1; 17:2—hands "released" in the sense of relaxed).

16a. Codex B transliterates the name as *Iesbi*, but does not reflect the following *bnb* in MT.[3]

b. The syllable *-ash* at the end of Joash (LT) may also be reflected at the beginning of the relative marker *ʾăšer*, which is unique to MT. Here DJD (180) gives support to LT.

c. The noun *qyn* is a hapax.

d. The MT's *ḥdšh* is puzzling: LT's *parazōnēn* is used to render *ḥg*[*w*]*rh* in 2 Sam 18:11—and in 2 Kgs 3:21 *ḥ*[*w*]*gr ḥg*[*w*]*rh* is used of men ready to be called up for war. The LT probably attests this expression here; and DJD (179–80) gives support: although *ḥwrh* is the clear reading of 4QSam[a], this may be a corruption of either *ḥgrh* or *ḥgwrh*.

17a. Codex B renders "helped" lit., but LT has "saved"—a correspondence unique in Samuel, but found 3x in 2 Chronicles.

b. For *nēr* or *nîr*, see 1 Sam 3:3; 2 Sam 22:29 (diff. from Ps 18:28 [29])—cf. 2 Kgs 8:19//2 Chr 21:7.

2 Samuel 21:18

18 And after this there was still the warring at Gob[a] with the Philistines.
Then Sibbechai the Hushathite struck down Saph,[b]
who was of the children of the Raphah.

18a. The MT's *gôb* is *Geth* in B and *Gazeth* in LT.

b. The LT's *episynēgmenous* ('those gathered together to a place") reflects *ʾsp*; and B's *Seph* reflects MT.

2 Samuel 21:19–22

19 And there was still the warring at Gob[a] with the Philistines,
and Elhanan son of Yaare[b]-Oregim the Bethlehemite struck down Goliath the Gittite;
and the wooden shaft of his spear was like a weavers' beam.

3. Nob (MT) may be a corrupted anticipation of Gob (vv. 18, 19).

20 And there was still warring at Gath *with the Philistines*.[a]
And there was a man of *Madon*[b] [Midian];
and the digits of his hands and the digits of his feet were six and six, twenty-four in number;
and he too was born to the Raphah.[c]
21 And he taunted Israel;
and Jonathan son of Shimei brother of David struck him down.
22 These four were born to the Raphah at Gath;
and they fell at the hand of David and at the hand of his servants.

19a. Again *gôb* is the location in MT; but B has *Rom* and LT has *Rob*.
b. Given the ready interchange of *d* and *r*, we count *Iaddein* as related to *yʿry*.
20a. The LT's "with the Philistines," uniform with earlier verses, is absent from MT and B.
b. Here B's *Madōn* follows Q; the LT's *apo Raazēs* takes the opening *m*- as the prep. "from."
c. This time LT renders the phrase as "offspring of a Titan."

[15–22] At least two sections with a separate history have to be recognized in the remainder of ch. 21. Both (vv. 15–17 and vv. 18–22) deal in all brevity with military struggles between David's men and Philistines—and particularly with vast individual opponents who are said to be descended from giants of an earlier age.

Three of these notes (vv. 18–21) and the conclusion (v. 22) reappear as 1 Chr 20:4–7, 8 with small differences in detail. As we compare this synoptic material, we have to ask whether the first and longest of the four notes in Samuel (vv. 15–17) has been added by the author of Samuel or deleted by the Chronicler. The opening note in Samuel is doubly different from each of the others (the three shared with Chronicles): it is twice as long as those that follow, and it features David as well as one of his men. Within the notes in 1 Chr 20:4–7 actually shared with Samuel, David receives a mention only in the very last word—as brother of one of the heroes; and the shared conclusion (2 Sam 21:22//1 Chr 20:8) attributes these successes against Philistine giants to David and his servants. This joint attribution is perfectly understandable within the shorter version found in Chronicles, but it has been more fully justified in Samuel. What makes it more likely that the shorter version, much as in Chronicles, is also the more original is the introductory formula in 2 Sam 21:18//1 Chr 20:4: "Now it came to be after this . . ." (*wyhy ʾḥry-kn*). This formula belongs to the structure of part of the old source (in BTH), relating to David's wars. And the shaping of that source is still readily visible in the use of the repeated formula in the contiguous 1 Chr 18:1; 19:1; 20:4; but is much less obvious in the more widely separated 2 Sam 8:1; 10:1; 21:18—now much supplemented by the addition of chs. 9, 11–12 (with the exception of the older 11:1 and 12:30–31), 13–20, and 21:1–17. The final one of these supplements is the opening note about David (21:15–17).

If we assume that 21:18–22 comprises the older text,[4] then much of v. 15 has been built from the introductions to vv. 19 and 20 ("there was warring again . . .") together with the conclusion of v. 22 ("David and his servants"). The final part of the introduction "and David was tired" (*wyʿp dwd*) is similar to 1 Sam 14:28, 31 (not drawn from BTH)—the verb is found only in these two contexts in Samuel, and in both cases the exhaustion follows fighting with Philistines. Then the statement that David's assailant is one of the "offspring" or "progeny" (*yldŷ*) of "[the] Raphah" anticipates what is said of Saph at the end of v. 18 (1 Chr 20:4 MT uses the plural "Rephaim").[5] Verses 20 and 22 (cf. 1 Chr 20:6, 8) make the same point about the large man with twenty-four digits and then about the group, but use the related verb "was/were born[6] to the Raphah" (see further below).

I am arguing that these several elements of vv. 15–16, shared with what follows in vv. 18–22 and the parallel passage in 1 Chr 20:4–8, have also been drawn from these synoptic notes. Another key term, *mšql* ("weight"), is shared with the immediately preceding 1 Chr 20:2–3 (//2 Sam 12:30–31).[7] And that adds to the likelihood that a text very similar to 1 Chr 20 as a whole was the source from which 2 Sam 21:15–22 was redrafted, as well as the much more extended 2 Sam 11–12. First Chronicles 20 is no secondary composite of the beginning and end of 2 Sam 11–12 together with the final five verses of 2 Sam 21:15–22.

Abishai plays a relatively minor role in BTH. At each of his appearances there (2 Sam 10:10, 14; 23:18), he is introduced as brother of Joab; that subordinate role is maintained in some of Samuel (1 Sam 26:6; 2 Sam 3:30). But sometimes the brothers are listed more equally together (2 Sam 2:18, 24; 18:5, 12); and here (21:16–17), as in 2 Sam 16:9 and 20:6, he emerges from his brother's shadow and needs to come to the aid of an exhausted David. However, his characterization is not developed: we meet him first (1 Sam 26:6) as the brother of a Joab of whom we have not yet read; and his story is left hanging—no assassination is reported, like that of his more famous brother (1 Kgs 2:5–6, 28–35). "Help" (*ʿzr*) is given once in BTH (2 Sam 8:5) and remains rare in Samuel as a whole (additionally only in 1 Sam 7:12; 2 Sam 18:3; 21:17); the noun is much commoner in late biblical texts. After David's rescue, his men

4. Is the order of writing (1) 18–21, (2) 22, and (3) 15–17?

5. "The valley of the Rephaim" is also part of the shared tradition of the struggle between David and the Philistines: 2 Sam 5:18//1 Chr 14:9; 2 Sam 23:13//1 Chr 11:15.

6. This is *puʿal* of *yld* in Samuel, *nipʿal* in Chronicles.

7. Also in the more extended account of Goliath (1 Sam 17:5), who seems to be something of a composite of the Philistine giants in 2 Sam 21:15–22.

warned him not to join them in battle (such swearing [v. 17b] plays no part in BTH). If he dies, David would thereby "quench the lamp of Israel."

"You shall not put out the lamp of Israel" is reminiscent of two other passages in Samuel: "before the lamp of God went out" (1 Sam 3:3); and "put out my ember which is left" (2 Sam 14:7). There has been discussion as to whether *nîr* in 2 Kgs 8:19 (BTH), and also in 1 Kgs 11:36; 15:4, does in fact mean "lamp." But it is unambiguously clear that the term relates to the dynastic significance of David's house within Yahweh's economy. Whether or not *nēr* ("lamp") is the same word (written simply *nr* rather than *nyr*), it does seem clear here that David's men are using a word that sounds very like, or even exactly like, *nîr* to describe David's importance for Israel and—therefore?—for Yahweh.

A principal interest of vv. 18–22 to readers of Samuel is not the unnamed giant with six digits on hands and feet—some of the (royal) Stuart family had a similar distinction—but rather that Goliath of Gath, killed by David in 1 Sam 17, reappears at the end of 2 Samuel among these giants. Here he is again killed by a Bethlehemite, but this time a townsman called Elhanan. A note in BTH about an individual victory over a Philistine giant has been reattributed to David, as his legend developed; and the end result is the famous story we earlier read. But the source was not simply deleted. And this will be testimony to the high regard in which the traditions of the Book of Two Houses were held.

Both Samuel and Chronicles report the struggles with the Rephaim near beginning and end of their accounts of David as king: in 2 Sam 5 and 21; and in 1 Chr 14 and 20. The "Rephaim" are presumably one and the same as "the offspring of [the] Raphah." The plural form is the more familiar, which leads us to believe that the mysterious Raphah is simply their assumed progenitor.

2 Samuel 22–24 David's Legacy

2 Samuel 22:1–23:7

1 And David spoke to Yahweh
the words of this song,
in the day Yahweh delivered him from the grip[a] of all his enemies
and/especially from the grip[a] of Saul.

2	And he said: I shall love you, Yahweh, my strength.[a] Yahweh is the one rescuing[b] me from my distress[c] and saving me;		Yahweh is my rock and my defense and my rescuer;
3	my God,[a] my fashioner,[b] I shall be sheltered in him.	3	God of my rock[b]—I'll seek refuge in him.

My shield and horn of my salvation,
most unique to me,
my refuge[c] and my savior,
from impious ones he will save me.
4 Praised I call Yahweh
and from my enemies I shall be saved.
5 Crushings of waters[a] encompassed me,
mighty[b] torrents choked me.
6 The cords of Sheol surrounded me;
the snares of death confronted me.
7 In my adversity I called Yahweh,
and to my God I shouted.
And he heard from his holy temple[a] my voice,
and my scream was in his ears.
8 He looked down[a] and the earth shook and quaked,
the foundations of the heavens were excited,
and they gave voice for Yahweh was heated against them.[b]
9 Smoke went up in his anger,
and fire from his mouth would consume the earth;
coals burned from him.
10 And he turned aside the heavens and came down;
and gloom was under his legs.
11 And he rode on cherubim
and flew;
and he was seen on wings
of winds.
12 And he set darkness his secret place,[a]

My shield and horn of my salvation,
my height
and my refuge,[c] my savior,
from violence you will save me.
4 Praised I call Yahweh,
and from my enemies I am saved.[a]
5 For the breakers of death[a] surrounded me;
the torrents of No-Good terrified[c] me.
6 The cords of Sheol surrounded me;
the snares of death confronted me.
7 In my adversity I call Yahweh,
and to my God I call.
And he heard from his palace my voice,
and my appeal was in his ears.[b]
8 And the earth shook and quaked,
the foundations of the heavens were excited,
and they shook for he was heated.
9 Smoke went up in his nostril,[a]
and fire from his mouth would consume;
coals burned from him.
10 And he turned aside the heavens and came down;
and gloom was under his legs.
11 And he rode on a cherub
and flew;
and he was seen on wings
of wind.
12 And he set darkness

around him was his canopy;
and he had consideration for his waters;
clouds of air
13 from brightness; before him
passed hail and coals of fire.
14 Thundered from the heavens did Yahweh,
and the Highest uttered his voice.
15 And he sent out hurled stones,[a]
and scattered them;
and flashed lightning in hail,
and sounded them forth.
16 And the channels of the sea feared;[a]
the foundations of the world were bared
—at Yahweh's threat,
from the wind[b] of his nostril.

17 He sent from on high and[a] he took me;
and drew me up from many waters.
18 He delivered me from the strength of my enemy;
from those that hate me, for they are too mighty for me.
19 They were before me in the day of my calamity;
and Yahweh became my prop.
20 And he brought me out to a broad place;
he drew me out because he took pleasure in me.
21 Yahweh recompensed me according to my righteousness;
the honor[b] of my hands he will make return to me.
22 For I have kept the ways of Yahweh;

around him as canopies;
gatherings[b] of water

as thick clouds.
13 From brightness before him
burned coals of fire.[a]
14 Thundered from the heavens did Yahweh,
and the Highest uttered his voice.
15 And he sent out arrows,
and scattered them;
lightning,[b]
and confused them.
16 And the channels of the sea were seen;
the foundations of the world were bared
—at Yahweh's threat,
from the breath of the wind of his nostril.
17 He sends from on high, he takes me;
and draws me out[b] from many waters.
18 He delivers me from my enemy,[a] the strong one;[b]
from those[a] that hate me, for they are too mighty for me.
19 They were before me in the day of my calamity;[a]
and Yahweh became my prop.
20 And he brought me out to a broad place;
he drew me out because he took pleasure in me.
21 Yahweh recompenses[a] me according to my righteousness;
according to the cleanness[b] of my hands he makes return to me.
22 For I have kept the ways of Yahweh;

and I have not been guilty
before[a] my God.
23 For all his judgments are in front of me,
and his statutes will not keep far from me.
24 And I shall become pure to him,
and I shall keep myself from my wrong.
25 And Yahweh will make
return to me according to my righteousness,
and according to the cleanness of my hands
my reckoning is before his eyes.[a]
26 With the merciful[a] you prepare mercy,
with the pure man you show yourself pure.
27 With the guiltless, guiltless you will be,
And with the select, select you will be;
and with the crooked you shall twist about.
28 For you[a]—the gentle people you will deliver,
but the eyes of the exalted you will bring low.
29 For you, Yahweh, light[a] my lamp;
my Lord,[b] you shine out to me in my darkness.
30 For by you I shall run fenced in;
by my God I shall mount as a bull.
31 The Deity—pure is his way;
the word of Yahweh is mighty—
champion is he of all who pay honor to him.

and I have not been guilty
from[a] my God.
23 For all his judgments are in front of me,
and his statutes—I do not turn from it.
24 And I became perfect to him,
and I kept myself from my wrong.[a]
25 And Yahweh made return
to me according to my righteousness,
according to my cleanness
before his eyes.[b]
26 With the loyal you show yourself loyal,
with the perfect hero you show yourself perfect.
27 With the one that keeps clean,
you show yourself clean,
and with the crooked you show yourself twisted.[a]
28 The humble people you will deliver,
but your eyes are over the exalted—you will bring low.
29 For you, Yahweh, are my lamp;
and Yahweh lightens my darkness.
30 For by you I crush a troop;
by my God I shall mount a wall.[a]
31 The Deity—perfect is his way;
the declaration of Yahweh is refined[a]—
he is a shield to all who take refuge in him.[b]

32 For who is El, other than Yahweh?
And who creator, other than our God?
33 God is the one bestowing[a] on me power
and giving[b] purity to my ways.[c]
34 Establishing my feet as the hind's
and standing me on the heights.
35 Teaching my hands for battle,
and the bow of my arm he did not weaken.
36 And you gave me the shield of my salvation,
and humiliations multiplied for me,
and your right hand laid hold of me,
and your rearing restored me.[c]
37 You made broad my step below me,
I did not weaken in my tracks.
Nonentities[c] displaced me;
and the opponents did not resist me.
38 I ran down my enemies and made them vanish;
and I did not turn back till they left off.
39 And I finished them off
and I dashed them and they would not rise,
and they will fall under my feet.
40 You girded me with strength and exultation to make war on them;
you shattered those rising against me.
41 And my enemies were given to me;

32 For who is El, other than Yahweh?
And who a rock,[a] other than[b] our God?
33 This El is my strong place,[a] power;
and the perfect one set free my way.
34 Making his/my legs like hinds,
and on my[a] heights he stands me.
35 Teaching my hands for battle,
and a bow of bronze presses down[a] my arms.
36 And you gave me the shield of your salvation,[a]
and your lowliness[b] made me great.
37 You made broad my step below me,
and my ankles[a] did not slip.[b]
38 I would pursue my enemies and destroy them;
and I shall not turn back till finishing them off.
39 And I consumed them[a]
and[b] I dashed them and they could not rise,
and they fell under my feet.
40 And you girded[a] me with strength for the battle;
you made those rising against me kneel under me.
41 And my enemies—you gave[a] me their neck;[b]

	the necks[b] of those hating me I trampled down.		those that hate me, and I silenced[c] them.
42	They cried out, but there was no deliverer; God[a] is Lord, and he has not answered them.	42	They will look, but there is no deliverer; to[a] Yahweh, but he has not answered them.
43	And I'll scatter them abroad like down before the wind, like mud in the streets I will grind them.	43	And I'll rub them away like dust of the earth, like mud in the streets I will crush them, I will stamp them.[a]
44	And you delivered me from the powerful[a] of my people, you put me as light of nations;	44	And you delivered me from the arguments[a] of my people, you keep me as head of nations;
45	A people I knew not served me;		a people I knew not—they serve me.
		45	Foreigners act deceitfully to me;
	at the hearing of an ear, they were obedient to me; they disclaimed[b] me at the hearing of an ear.		at the hearing of an ear, they were heard[a] to/of me.
46	Strange sons did foolishly[a] to me, they saved me,[b] they were ransomed from their bonds.[d]	46	Foreigners wither, and they gird[c] [themselves] from their enclosures.[d]
47	May Yahweh live, and blessed be my shaper;[a] and exalted be God[b] my savior.	47	Yahweh is alive, and blessed is my rock;[a] and exalted be the God of the rock[b] of my salvation.
48	Powerful is the Lord, the Deity, the one granting me vengeance, and humbling peoples under me.	48	The Deity, the one granting[a] me vengeance, and bringing down[b] peoples under me.
49	And bringing me out from the wrath of my enemies; and from my place[a] you exalt me —from ungodly men you maintain me.[b]	49	And bringing me out from my enemies; and you exalt me[a] above those rising against me —from a man of much violence you deliver me.
50	Therefore I praise you, Yahweh, among the nations;	50	Therefore I praise you, Yahweh, among the nations;

	and of the name of Yahweh I will make mention.[a]		and to your name I sing praise.[a]
51	Extolling the deliverance of his king,	51	Increasing the deliverances of his king,
	and performing compassion to his anointed		and performing loyalty to his anointed
	—to David for a family[a] and to his seed		—to David and to his seed
	forever.		forever.[b]
23:1	And these are the final words of David:		
	Faithful[a] is David son of Jesse,		The utterance[a] of David son of Jesse,
	faithful the man		and the utterance of the man
	whom Yahweh raised up,[b]		raised on high,
	anointed,[c] the God of Jacob;		the anointed of the God of Jacob,
	and delightful is the song of Israel.		and the delight of the songs of Israel.
2	The spirit of Yahweh has spoken by me, and his word is on my tongue.		
3	The God of Jacob has declared,	3	The God of Israel has declared,
	the rock of Israel speaking[a] in me,		to me has spoken the rock of Israel,
	rule[b] among humans justly;		ruling among humans, just;
	rule by the fear of God.		ruling (by) the fear of God.
4	Like morning light,	4	And like morning light
	and the sun will rise		the sun will gleam,
	in the morning,[a] and will not darken[b]		a morning not cloudy.
	from light, like rain,		From brightness and from rain
	like grass from the earth.		there is grass from the earth.
5	For is my house not so with El? For he has set for me an eternal covenant		
	to save me[a] till this time in everything,		arranged in everything
	and he will keep it.		and guarded.
	For all that is opposed to me,		For all my salvation and all pleasure
	he shall not will.		will he not make sprout?
6	For all that rise up are like thorns,	6	And no good, as chased thorns

	and the rest like a lamp blown,		—all of them,[a]
	all,		
	for they do not take (them)		for they do not take (them)
	by hand.		by hand.
7	And a man shall squeeze	7	When a man touches them,
	in them		
	unless[a] iron		he is filled[a] with iron
	and wood cut through[b] them.		and the wood(en shaft) of a
			spear.[b]
	And all by fire are utterly		And by fire they are utterly
	burned		burned
	in their shame.[c]		as they sit.

1a. The term *kap* (lit., "palm") is the part of the limb that grips. Thus the Ps 18 superscription (18:1) uses *yad* in place of repeated *kap*.

2a. The LT opens like Ps 18:1 (18:2 MT = 17:2 GT) with *ʾrḥmk yhwh ḥzqy*; and *rḥm* corresponds to *agapan* also in Isa 60:10; Hos 2:23 (25); Zech 10:6; Prov 28:13—i.e., normally the *rḥm* is Yahweh's, as in 2 Sam 24:14.

b. The LT reads *stereōn mou*. Psalm 18:1 (17:2 GT) has *stereōma mou*, although *stereōma* normally corresponds to *rqyʿ*.

c. The LT attests *mṣrty* ("from my distress") for *mṣdty* (MT).

3a. "My god" (LT) reads *ʾlhy* differently from MT ("god of").

b. "Rock" (*ṣwr*) is linked with "seek refuge in" also in Deut 32:37; however, "my fashioner" (LT) relates *ṣwry* to *ṣwr/yṣr* (cf. v. 32 below).

c. The LT may attest the same reading as MT (*ʾḥsh*): *skepazomai* is used also in 1 Sam 23:26, where it corresponds to *ḥpz nipʿal*; however, it renders *ʾḥsh* in Ps 61:4 (5).

4a. The grammatical balances in MT are noteworthy: ptc./impf./ptc./impf.; and also pass./act./act./pass.

5a. The LT appears to have read not *mwt* (MT), but *mym*.

b. The LT's *biaios* is hapax.

c. The vb. *bʿt (piʿel)* is used mostly in Job (8x), but also in Isa 21:4; Ps 18:4 (5); esp. notice 1 Sam 16:14, 15, Saul terrified by the evil spirit from the Deity.

7a. The LT is reminiscent of *hykl qdšk* in Jonah 2:4, 7 (5, 8).

b. Here LT agrees with MT against the longer Ps 18:6b (7b), which reads "before him will come" between "my cry" and "in his ears."

8a. The LT's *epeblepsen* is not reflected in Ps 18; the most likely retroversions would be *wypn* and *wybṭ*.

b. Here LT may attest not *ḥrh lw* (MT = Ps 18) but *ḥrh lhm yhwh*.

9a. "Fire from his mouth" gives encouragement to use the literal "nose/nostril" for *ʾp* rather than the derived "anger."

12a. The LT like Ps 18 attests *strw* after "darkness," and both read not *skwt* but *sktw*.

b. Psalm 18 offers not *ḥšrt* (a hapax often explained on the basis of Akkadian *ašaru*, "collect"), but *ḥškt* (f. poetic variant of *ḥšk*, "darkness"). The testimony of LT may point to a similar consonantal text: *pheidesthai* corresponds in 2 Sam 18:16 and 2 Kgs 5:20 to *ḥśk*.

13a. The fuller *mngh ngdw ʿbyw ʿbrw brd wgḥly-ʾš* (Ps 18) is of a more normal length and may underlie both LT and MT here: LT does not attest *ʿbyw* ("his clouds"), which differs by only one letter from the following "passed"; MT has only *bʿrw* ("burned") in place of *ʿbyw ʿbrw brd*.

15a. The LT may interpret *ḥṣym* ("arrows," MT), but it agrees with MT in not representing a possessive suf., while Ps 18 reads *ḥṣyw* ("his arrows").

b. Psalm 18 offers the fuller *wbrqym rb* for *brq* (MT); LT here is even longer.

16a. The LT reads *wyrʾw* as if from *yrʾ* (*qal*), not *rʾh* (*nipʿal*).

b. The LT's *pneumatos* apparently attests only either "breath" or "wind."

17a. Unlike LT, here 4QSam[a] is held to have read no "and" before "he took me." A lengthy note (DJD 182) reports substantial divergence (in both directions) between Ps 18 and 2 Sam 22 over the presence or absence of the connective at the beginning of a colon (but not in this verse).

b. Here and in Ps 18:16 (17), *ymšny* is pointed *hipʿil*—the only other attestation of the vb. is in Exod 2:10, where in *qal* it explains Moses's name: "from the waters you drew him."

18a. Note the shift from sg. "enemy" to pl. "haters," reminiscent (though in reverse order: "enemies . . . Saul") of the title verse.

b. "The strong one" (ʿz) may be either the subj. of the vb. or in apposition to "my enemy."

19a. Often *ʾyd* ("calamity") with suf. is construed with "day": Deut 32:35; Jer 18:17; 46:21; Obad 13 (3x); Prov 27:10; and with "time" in Ezek 35:5.

21a. The term *ygmlny* is used also in 19:37, there of David.

b. The LT reads not *k* + *br* ("cleanness"), but *kb[w]d*.

22a. Nowhere else is *ršʿ* used with *mn* ("from"); however Ps 18 = MT. The LT either interprets, or renders something like *lpny*.

24a. Psalm 18 offers a shorter form in both vbs.: *wʾhy* and *wʾštmr*. Both there and in MT here, *w-* has a strong pointing, while LT renders with future tenses, as if following simple connectives.

25a. The printed edition of LT treats as a separate sentence "My reckoning is before his eyes."

b. This verse both resumes vv. 21 and 23 while "his eyes" (*ʿynyw*) at the end uses the same consonants as "my wrong" (*ʿwny*), which ends v. 24.

26a. In the Psalms, *hosios* is the stock rendering of *ḥsyd*, not of *tmym*. The meaning of these terms is discussed below.

27a. The terms *ʿqš* and the rare *ptl* (Ps 18:26 [27] and LT here read *ttptl*) are linked also in Deut 32:5 and Prov 8:8; in Gen 30:8 the latter is used to explain Naphtali's name. There is no satisfactory explanation of *ttpl* (MT) from a conjectural *tpl*.

28a. The LT renders not *wʾt* (MT) at the beginning of this line, but *ky-ʾth*, as in v. 29 (MT and LT).

29a. Here LT attests the vb. *tʾyr* ("light"), as in Ps 18:28 (29).

b. "My Lord" (LT) is intermediate between "Yahweh" (MT) and "my God" (Ps 18:28 [29]).

30a. The rare word *šûr* for "wall" is found (beyond Ps 18:29([30] and Job 24:11) in Gen 49:22, Jacob's blessing of Joseph, shortly after (49:19) the only occurrence in

Pentateuch of *gdwd* ("troop"), playing on the name of Gad. The LT has read *šwr* as the more common *šôr*.

31a. Once *ṣrwp* is used of *ksp* (Ps 12:6 [7]); however, *ṣrwph* (f.) is used only (as here) of the divine *ʾmrh* ("word")—cf. also Ps 105:19.

b. The final clause is found exactly in Prov 30:5.

32a. For "rock"/"creator," cf. v. 3 above and v. 47 below.

b. The version of the poem in MT repeats *mblʿdy* in both cola, while Ps 18:31b (32b) reads *zwlty* (see above on 2 Sam 7:22). Here DJD (188) reconstructs *zlty*.

33a. The LT's *ho perititheis moi* may have read not *mʿwzy* (MT) but *hmʾzrny* (as in Ps 18:32 [33]); cf. v. 40 below; 4QSam[a] preserves the whole of *mʾzrny* but without article.

b. Here LT's *kai didous* seems to read *wytn* (with Ps 18), not *wytr*.

c. The LT's *tais hodois mou* agrees with the suf. in the Q (K has "his way") but takes the noun as pl.

34a. Here LT does not attest the suf. on *bmwty*; the fact that the following word begins with *y-* has contributed to the shift (in whichever direction).

35a. In this verse and in Ps 18, *nḥt* (*piʿel*) is unique; the *nipʿal* is attested once (Ps 38:2 [3]) in connection with arrows!

36a. Here 4QSam[a] reads "your salvation" (*yšʿk*) with MT.

b. The phrase *wʿzrtk* ("and your aid"), read uniquely by 4QSam[a], was already conjectured by Wellhausen in place of *wʿntk* (MT).

c. The LT has two further half lines.

37a. In this verse and in Ps 18, *qrsl* is unique.

b. Over the words reconstructed in DJD (183) as *wl[ʾ ʿmdy qmy]*, the scribe of 4QSam[a] has written *wlʾ m[ʿdw qrsly]* (2d colon in MT). The resultant tricolon is accepted as original and rendered: "You enlarged my step(s); (and) my ankles did not wobble; (and) my enemies did not stand." The LT's *hyphistanai* corresponds in 1 Sam 30:10 to *ʿmd*. The third colon in LT may retrovert to *ṣʿyrym ḥttwny*, a corruption of *ṣʿdy tḥtny* within the first colon in MT.

c. The LT's *oligotētes* is hapax.

39a. Here 4QSam[a] agrees with Ps 18 in not repeating the vb. *wʾklm* after *klwtm*.

b. Again 4QSam[a] agrees with Ps 18 in lacking a connective before *ʾmḥṣm*.

40a. Here *wtzrny* is written defectively: we find *wtʾzrny* in 4QSam[a] and Ps 18.

41a. Also, *tth* appears to be a defectively written form of *ntth*, read in Ps 18.

b. Psalm 18 divides the line as does MT, while LT attributes *ʿrp* ("neck") to the second bicolon.

c. The vb. *ṣmt hipʿil* belongs otherwise only to the Psalms, mostly with the Deity as subj. (54:5 [7]; 73:27; 94:23; 143:12) but the king in 101:5, 8.

42a. The MT reads *ʾl* as the prep "to," but LT as "El" or "God."

43a. At the end of the line, MT appears to have preserved two of at least three ancient variants: given the similarity of *d* and *r* in Hebrew, *ʾdqm* (*dqq hipʿil*) and *ʾrqʿm* (< *rqʿ*) are easily confused. Here 4QSam[a] reads simply *ʾrqʿm*. However, *ʾryqm* ("I'll pour them out") in Ps 18 is different again.

44a. Here *dynastōn* ("powerful") might retrovert to *ndyby* (cf. 1 Sam 2:8), similarly easily confused with *mryby* (MT).

45a. The vb. *šmʿ nipʿal* is used in 1 Sam 1:13; 17:31. There seems to be no parallel in HB for a following *l-*.

b. Psalm 18 reads "foreigners act . . ." after rather than before "at the hearing of an ear . . ." as in MT; but LT is different from both. In LT, *diapseudesthai* ("disclaim") is found nowhere else in the historical books.

46a. Has "did foolishly" (LT) misunderstood the vb. *nbl*, which underlies *yblw* (MT), or was *yhblw* written defectively?

b. "They saved me" is an LT plus.

c. In place of *wyḥgrw* (MT), Ps 18 reads (the otherwise unknown) *wyḥrgw*.

d. The LT appears to have *mmsrwtm*, like 4QSam[a], not *mmsgrwtm* (MT).

47a. As in vv. 3 and 32, LT renders a form of *yṣr*, not *ṣwr*.

b. The LT attests simply *ʾlhym*, while Ps 18 has *ʾlwhy* and MT has *ʾlhy ṣwr*, with repeated *ṣwr*.

48a. Here 4QSam[a] has *ntn* ("granting"), without the article.

b. Psalm 18 reads not *wmwryd* (MT) but *wydbr* ("and he drove back"). The LT used *tapeinoun* in v. 28, where MT read *špl hipʿil*. However, 4QSam[a] reads the rarer *wmrdd*, which may well underlie LT.

49a. The LT's *kai ek tou topou mou* appears to attest *wmmqwmy*. The MT reads *wmqmy*; and Ps 18 has *ʾp mn-qmy*.

b. Here DJD (180) conjectures *tṣrny* at the end of the verse, as the assumed text underlying LT.

50a. The LT's *mnēsthēsomai* appears to attest not *ʾzmr* (MT; cf. *ʾzmrh* in Ps 18) but *ʾzkr*.

51a. The phrase *eis genean* after "David" attests *ldr* or, more likely, *ldwr*—a duplicate of *ldwd*.

b. The final "forever" is set on its own new line in CL.

23:1a. The LT's *pistos* apparently attests not *nʾm* but *ʾmn* or *nʾmn*.

b. Here LT = 4QSam[a]: *hqym ʿl*. It appears (DJD 186) that the much-discussed "raised on high" has resulted from the confusion, so frequently observed, between the consonants *ʾālep* and *ʿayin*.

c. The LT's *christon* reads *mšyḥ* as complement of the previous clause, rather than parallel to *hgbr*.

3a. Here LT's *en emoi lalēsai* reads *dbr* as inf.

b. The LT reads both instances of *mšl* as imperative; the first is aorist, the second present.

4a. Here LT makes the pause after the second "morning" (*bqr*), then reads *lʾ ʿbwt mngh* together.

b. The LT's *skotasei* may attest *yʿwb*—only *hipʿil yʿyb* is attested once in HB, in Lam 2:1.

5a. "To save me" (LT) is plus: "till this" (LT) has read *ʿd-kh*, not *ʿrwkh* (MT).

6a. Here *klhm* is a unique pausal form ("all of them"). The GT apparently does not represent the suf.; does it represent a different text?

7a. In place of the one word *ymlʾ* (MT), here LT renders two words, *ʾm lʾ* ("if not").

b. It is not easy to retrovert the vb. *diekopsen* (LT) to anything like *ḥnyt* (MT).

c. The LT has read the final word not as *bšbt* (MT), but as *bbšt* (see also on v. 8).

The text of LT + 4QSam[a] seems similarly close to Ps 18 here as to Josephus and Chronicles elsewhere. Either there has been (mutual) adjustment between these texts or this was the form of text at the point of original linkage. In that (more likely) case, LT + 4QSam[a] is a much earlier textual witness than proto-MT. At several points, LT prefers active, dynamic images, while MT's language is more concrete and solid—as "shaper" over against "rock."

The Song of David (2 Sam 22) is the first and longer of two poems close to the end of the books of Samuel. It has to be read as a poem in its own right and also as a part of the whole work. And realizing each of these aims is more interesting than we might at first expect—or more problematic, if one's taste is more anxious. As poetry it is distinctive in its context: it has to be read in its own right, as in a sense discontinuous with the prose context. Both the Aleppo and the Leningrad codices accord this song special treatment. It is transcribed not in three columns, like the rest of Samuel, but with the half lines justified to right and left margins of the whole page. This generous layout leaves more unused space on the precious page than elsewhere and presumably says something about the importance that tradition accorded to David's extended poetic words. The final lines of the second page are occupied by the beginning of 2 Sam 23, written right across the page and without spaces between half lines.

Yet what does it mean to accord this poem "its own right"? It is only one version of the poem—another, very similar, version can be found as Ps 18. Then, in what sense is it part of Samuel? How far is it like the shorter songs we have already discussed, the Song of Hannah (1 Sam 2) and the lament of David over Saul and Jonathan (2 Sam 1), which seem more immediately tied to their context? There are other long poems positioned just before the end of Genesis and of Deuteronomy. In what sense do Gen 49 and Deut 32–33 and 2 Sam 22 and 23:1–7 belong to the individual books, and how far do they represent wider structures in the biblical canon? Of all these poems near the end of books, only our chapter is preserved in the book of Psalms.

[1] Second Samuel 22 and Ps 18 share the same prose introduction to this praise for victory. It is hardly insignificant that only Saul is named here out of all David's many enemies: for the books of Samuel, he is the principal foe. Twenty chapters have passed since David lamented Saul's death and that of his eldest son (2 Sam 1). But here he has only just buried that same Saul and Jonathan, only just given his permission for the elimination of most of the survivors of his house (ch. 21). In the Book of Two Houses, in this case faithfully preserved in 1 Chr 10, Saul, like Elhanan and Goliath, has simply a walk-on part: he was killed, "and his three sons, and his whole house together" (v. 6). But the authors of Samuel first build him into a major and tragic character, then prolong the death agonies of his house. Many other psalms have a heading that ties the poem to a particular point in David's career. A group of four (52; 54; 57; and 59) introduce (what purport to be) cries of David for divine help when under pressure from Saul. Psalm 18 is in different mode: it celebrates the stage at which David recognizes that he has been given victory over all his enemies, not least Saul.

[2–51] The song opens with repeated talk of God as rock, refuge, stronghold—and of the singer as delivered or saved (vv. 2–4). It is death that has threatened to entrammel the singer (vv. 5–6). The distress call was quickly answered—note how briefly that point is made (v. 7). Yahweh's display is in the form of a terrifying storm of thunder and lightning (vv. 8–16). He acts to deliver, because of his delight in the singer (vv. 17–20). The delight is explained in terms of the singer's activity (vv. 21–25) and of God's nature (vv. 26–31). Some of the language of the opening section reappears in vv. 32–43, which make plain that the form of defense used was attack. The opponents also cried to Yahweh but were not helped (v. 42). Explicit mention of the response of foreign nations (vv. 44–46) makes it possible, even likely, that the psalmist's enemies of the long previous section were from within. The final verses (vv. 47–51) return to language used at the beginning; but they now specify that, as deliverance was provided from foes that included outsiders, so praise for this rocklike God will be offered among the nations.

We have to wait till the very last words of the song to have the beneficiaries of the divine love identified as "David and his descendants forever." Historically speaking, the language of the song is very general. Indeed, on internal evidence, the only safe conclusion would be that it was composed for the use of a member or members of the Davidic house at some stage in its long history. Only the prose heading (v. 1) ties it to David himself and specifies the (principal) internal enemy as Saul. The book of Psalms as a whole, like the Book of Two Houses, is unconcerned with Saul: Saul in the headings of Psalms is in fact like Saul in the books of Samuel—a secondary narrative development.

The poem is readily comprehensible as an official hymn for use by or in the royal household on an occasion of special thanksgiving for deliverance. It is a feature of the royal ideology to portray the Deity and his royal representative as sharing similar or overlapping characteristics. A keyword here is *tāmîm*: just as in Ps 18, it appears 4x in MT. That he himself is *tāmîm* is part of the king's claim (24). He expects Yahweh to show himself *tāmîm* with a heroic figure (like the singer) who is *tāmîm* (26). After all, God's own "way" is *tāmîm* (31). And he has made "my" way *tāmîm* (33). It is easier to observe how this word functions in comparisons between the royal singer and Yahweh than to translate it both consistently and accurately. And this difficulty has been felt since ancient times. LT uses the adj. *hosios* or its cognate noun in all four verses; but in B we find *amōmos* ("unblemished") in vv. 24, 31, 33, but *hosios* ("pure") in v. 26. *amōmos* is quite the commonest rendering of *tāmîm* throughout the Gk. OT; and that is hardly surprising: it is used frequently in Leviticus and Numbers where the need for unblemished animals for sacrifice is often noted; and the five books of Moses were the first to be translated. But *tāmîm* is often used in an ethical sense: Noah is so described (Gen 6:9), and Abraham is instructed by God to be such (17:1).

Although the commonest Gk. translation is normally by a negative term ("without blemish"), the Heb. word has a positive connotation: "complete." Forms of the related verb (used three times in Samuel) illustrate the sense: "till the whole people completed crossing" (2 Sam 15:24); "and so they brought (matters) to completion" (2 Sam 20:18); and "are the lads complete (all present)?" (1 Sam 16:11). This gives support to the choice of the positive *hosios* in LT: pure, or pious, or devout. Of these, the most suitable for both God and human is "pure."

That is a straightforward matter of report. But it is not easy to square the claims of the central sections (vv. 21–31) with the David about whom we have been reading in much of Samuel. "I was perfect before him, and I kept myself from guilt" (v. 24) reads strangely after David's confession of sin before Nathan (12:13). Did Yahweh's immediate removal of the sin restore David's perfection, or is there a tension here? There are other interesting connections and echoes. Yahweh as the psalmist's "lamp" (v. 29) corresponds to David as "the lamp of Israel" (21:17). More overt, the proportionality of 22:26–27 contrasts with Joab's complaint against his king: "loving those who hate you and hating those who love you" (19:6).

The introduction to the Song (v. 1) serves both to anticipate one of its key themes and to suggest the appropriateness of its location: immediately following a catalog of successes (21:15–22) and the near extinction of the family of Saul (21:1–14). Campbell (2010: 353) finds that "the emphasis [in the Song] on deliverance seems quite out of place for David; the affirmation of dominance over foreign nations receives more verses in the song than it does in the sweep of Davidic traditions." "More verses," perhaps; but "quite out of place," no. Deliverance from other nations and domination over those of his neighbors who challenge him—this is the topic of 2 Sam 5:17–25; 8:1–14; 10:1–19. Yahweh is subject of the verb *hwšyʿ* ("save/deliver") in 2 Sam 8:6, 14 just as in 22:3, 28. The cringing fear of the king's enemies at the end of the "song" (vv. 45–46) is explicit in 10:19;[8] and the way David treated his prisoners in 2 Sam 8:2 and 12:31 makes their fear entirely credible. It seems to me that Campbell is more confident than he should be that he knows what David was really like when he writes: "The poetic texts do not apply particularly well to David; their emphasis sits better with the ideal for kingship in ancient Israel" (2010: 357) Yet we have to ask, Just what can a modern historian "know" of the "historical reality" of David?

Each of the examples cited just above demonstrates the convergence of 2 Sam 22 with the synoptic traditions about David. But there also are significant links between the poetry and the material special to Samuel:

8. The synoptic 1 Chr 19:19 states only that "they were not willing."

1. "Just," *ṣdyq* (23:3), is used also in 1 Sam 24:17 (18) and 2 Sam 4:11.
2. "Righteousness," *ṣdqh* (22:21, 25), reappears in 1 Sam 12:7; 26:23; 2 Sam 19:29.
3. "Judgment," *mšpṭ* (22:23), occurs in 1 Sam 2:13; 8:3, 9, 11; 10:25; 27:11; 30:25; 2 Sam 15:2, 4, 6.
4. "Recompense," *gml* (22:21), is used twice in 1 Sam 24:17 (18).

Items 1, 2, and 4 are part of the defense in 1 Sam 24 and 26 of David's innocence over against Saul—important chapters for Campbell (2010: 347) when he describes the material on David's rise as a first and more favorable wave of tradition. But one of the occurrences of *mšpṭ* is placed strategically nearby. The defense of David is quickly subverted when we learn in 1 Sam 27:11 that the *mšpṭ* (item 3) that characterizes his leadership in the south, from his base in Ziklag, consists in keeping alive neither man nor woman among those whom he encounters. This is just one of the details making me skeptical about Campbell's suggestion that the traditions of David's rise (in the first wave) are more favorable to him.

It can be urged in the opposite direction that *mšpṭ* commonly does not carry its principal sense of "judgment" or "justice," but means simply "custom" or "manner"—and that it is commonly and properly so rendered here. However, two counterarguments are appropriate: (1) The matter could have been described another way—the presence of *mšpṭ* so close to *ṣdyq* and *ṣdqh* does seem deliberately provocative. (2) A disregard for human life, so regular as to be described as customary, is quite as prejudicial to David's reputation for acting according to "right." Fokkelman (2010: 22) well observes how an important feature of the end of this long poem echoes the end of Hannah's Song: the rhyming word pair "his king" and "his anointed," *mlkw* and *mšyḥw*.

[23:1–7] At the "chapter" division, 4QSam[a] has a space. However, there is no *pĕtûḥâ* ("open" sign, פ) in MT. This might suggest that the MT wished both poems to be read together. On the other hand, "David's Last Words" (2 Sam 23:1–7) are not laid out on the page by the scribe like his "Song"—and in this they are no different from the Song of Hannah or David's lament over Saul and Jonathan. The scroll 4QSam[a] also has a space at the beginning of 23:6. The LT largely makes good sense; but that need not imply that the underlying Hebrew is always superior to MT's.

This second and much shorter "concluding" poem (23:1–7) also encapsulates the official royal ideology, but is much more unusual. The surprise is not that the narrative introduction presents it briefly as "David's last words" (v. 1), while there is still a major episode to follow in ch. 24—the location of the blessings in Gen 49 and Deut 33 is similar. The strangeness consists more in a series of features that can be matched across the HB only in two oracles of the seer Balaam, reported in Num 24:3–9, 15–19. The first of these utters a rich blessing of Jacob/Israel; the second foresees distantly a star/scepter rising from Jacob/Israel that will dominate the various peoples of Transjordan. In this third and far separated oracle, David claims by the authority of the God of Jacob/Israel to be that long foreseen king. Seven formal correspondences between these three poems can be readily noted.

1. The introductory *nĕʾum* refers to inspired human rather than divine speech.
2. They introduce the speaker's name with his father's in the same unusual formula:

   nĕʾum dāwid ben-yišay, "the utterance of David son of Jesse," 2 Sam 23:1
   nĕʾum bilʿām bĕnô bĕʿōr, "the utterance of Balaam son of Beor," Num 24:3, 15.

3. The resumptive phrase uses the same rare word for "male" followed by a passive ptc. and noun:

   nĕʾum haggeber huqam ʿāl, "the utterance of the man raised on high," 2 Sam 23:1
   nĕʾum haggeber šĕtum hāʿāyin, "the utterance of the man 'sealed' of eye," Num 24:3, 15

4. A line with "Jacob" and "Israel" in parallel follows shortly afterward.
5. The divine name El (*ʾēl*) is used in 23:5a, and frequently in all four poetic oracles of Balaam (Num 23:8, 19, 22, 23; 24:4, 8, 16, 23).
6. If we follow MT in 23:1 (see above), *ʿāl* ("Highest") will correspond to the more usual, longer *ʿelyôn* in Num 24:16.
7. David claims that Yahweh's spirit has spoken by him (23:2a), while the narrator says of Balaam that the divine spirit comes on him when he views Israel (Num 24:2).

Quite apart from the several striking links with Balaam in Numbers, this short poem has other quite distinctive features. Jacob has been named only once before in Samuel: it was "Jacob" who went down to Egypt (1 Sam 12:8) and was rescued by Moses and Aaron. It is only here (2 Sam 23:5) in the books of Samuel that there is talk of David and the deity (here "El") as linked in "covenant."[9] And it is this biblical oracle that establishes the important post-

9. The unusual phrase "Yahweh's covenant" in 1 Sam 20:8 was discussed above.

biblical tradition of David's status as prophet, whereby many of the psalms became understood as prophetic oracles. And the suggestion it makes at the end of 2 Samuel of a prophetic role for David corresponds in an interesting way to the presentation in the early chapters of 1 Samuel of Samuel the prophet as something of a royal figure.

2 Samuel 23:8–39

8 These are the names of the *chief*[a] *of the* heroes [who[a] were] of David.
Yeshbaal[b] *son of Tekemani* [Yosheb-Bashebet[b] Tahkemoni], head of the *Three* [Third],
he *regulated their performance* [. . .] over *nine* [eight] hundred pierced at once.

9 And, after him, Eleazar son of Dodo [son of Ahohi] in the three heroes:
with David *in Serram* [when they were reviling, among] *and* the Philistines, they gathered there for battle
and the men of Israel went up [before them].
10 He rose
and struck down [among] the Philistines
till his hand was weary
and his hand stuck to his sword.
And Yahweh achieved a great deliverance on that day;
and the people, they turned back after him,
[even] for the stripping.

11 And after him Shamma son of *Ela the Arachite* [Age Harari];
and Philistines gathered to *Jawbone* [Lehi],
and there was there[a] the plot of ground full of lentils;
and the people, they fled before Philistines.
12 And he took his stand in the midst of the plot,
and he delivered it
and he struck down Philistines,
and Yahweh performed[a] a great deliverance *on that day*.[b]

13 And there went down three of the thirty heads,
and they came [toward harvest] *to the rock,*[a] to David to the cave of Adullam,
and the Philistine beast was camping in the valley of Rephaim.
14 And David was then in the stronghold,
and a Philistine post was then in Bethlehem.

15 And David longed,
and said:
"Who will draw me water from the well of Bethlehem
which is at the gate?"
And the Philistine post was then in Bethlehem.[a]
16 And the three men broke through the Philistine camp
and drew water from the well of Bethlehem,
which is at the gate,
and bore it
and [brought[a] it] *came* to David;
but he was not willing
to drink it,
and poured it out to Yahweh.
17 And he said,
"Far be it from me, Yahweh, that I do this.

The blood of the men who went	Is it (not) the blood of the men who went
at (the cost of) their lives shall I drink?"[a]	at (the cost of) their lives?"

And he was not willing to drink it.
These things did the three heroes.

18 And Abishai, brother of Joab, [son of Zeruiah,[a] was] head of the Three, *withstood in his fight* [and he brandished his spear[b]] over [three[c]] *six* hundred pierced,
and he had[d] a name among the Three.
19 [From the Three[a]] *Above the two*[b] he was [much[c]] honored
and he became their chief,
but up to the Three he did not come.

20 And Benaiah, son of Jehoiada, son of *Jesse*[a] [a man of valor[a]], great in deeds *above Gabasael* [from Kabzeel]:
he struck down two *sons of*[b] Ariel of Moab;
and he went down
and struck down the lion in the middle of the cistern on the day of the snow.
21 And he struck down an Egyptian man, a man of looks,[a]
and in the hand of the Egyptian a spear *like a ladder*-beam,[b]
and *the Egyptian* [he] went down to him with his [staff[c]] *spear*,
and he robbed the spear from the hand of the Egyptian
and he slew him with his spear.

22 These things Benaiah son of Jehoiada did,
and he had a name among the three heroes.
23 Over the [Thirty[a]] *Three* he was honored,
but up to the Three he did not come.
And David set him [to] *over*[b] his [subordinates[c]] guard.[c]

24 And *these are the names of the heroes of King David*:
Asahel, brother of Joab, was in the Thirty;

	Elhanan son of Dodo, in Bethlehem;		Elhanan son of Dodo, Bethlehem;
25	Shamma the Adarite;	25	Shamma the Harodite; Eliqah[a] the Harodite;
26	Helez the Palmonite; Idae, son of Iqqesh, the Tekoite;	26	Helez the Paltite; Ira,[a] son of Iqqesh, the Tekoite;
27	Abiezer the Anathothite; Sabeni[a] the Hittite;	27	Abiezer the Anathothite; Mebunnay[a] the Hushathite;
28	Eliman[a] the Akachite; Maharnan[b] the one of Phatia;	28	Zalmon[a] the Ahohite; Mahray[b] the Netophathite;
29	Allan son of Baanah the Netophathite; Ittai son of Eriba, from Gibeah of Benjamin;	29	Heleb[a] son of Baanah the Netophathite; Ittai son of Ribai, from Gibeah of the sons[b] of Benjamin;
30	 Hiddai from Nachabai;	30	Benaiah Pirathonite;[a] Hiddai[b] from the wadis of Gaash;[c]
31	Talsabees the Saraibathite; Azelmon the Abarnite;	31	Abi-Albon[a] the Arabathite; Azmaveth[b] the Barhumite;
32	Salabath the Shaalbonite; Yassai the Gounite;[b] Jonathan, son[c] of	32	Elyahba[a] the Shaalbonite; sons of Yashen,[b] Jonathan;[d]
33	Shamaa; Arachi son of Saracho, Ararima;	33	Shammah the Hararite; Ahiam[a] son of Sharar the Ararite;
34	The Phellite, son of Assaia; Makarthi,[b] the Thalaam; Ahithophel, the Galaad;	34	Eliphelet,[a] son of Ahasbay, son of the Maachathite; Eliam son of Ahithophel the Gilonite;[c]
35	Dami the Hezrite; Carmali the Apharite;	35	Hezraw the Carmelite;[a] Paaray the Arbite;[b]
36	Yoel[a] brother of Nathan; Massaba,	36	Yigal son of Nathan from Zobah;

son of Ageri;[b]
37 Salaad the Anamin;
Araia[b] the Berathite, bearers of the weapons of Joab son of Zeruiah;
38 Oiad the Jithrite;
Gaber the Jethem;
39 Uriah the Hittite.
All: thirty-seven.

Bani the Gadite;
37 Zeleq the Ammonite;[a]
Nahray[b] the Beerothite, bearer of the weapons of Joab son of Zeruiah;
38 Ira the Jithrite;[a]
Gareb the Jithrite;[b]
39 Uriah the Hittite.
All: thirty-seven.

8a. The LT's *archēs* is not noted in the *Índice*; it has rendered *rʾš* of which *ʾšr* (MT) is a variant.

b. The original *-baal* (LT) was distorted, as often, into *-bšt* ("shame"), and that in turn has corrupted into *-šbt* (MT).

11a. Here GT reproduces the Heb. idiom.

12a. In the synoptic 1 Chr 11:14, *wywšʿ* ("delivered") is cognate with the obj.; but *wyʿś* ("made, performed") is supported by OG here, represents the normal idiom, and is very likely to be original.

b. The GT's plus may reflect 1 Sam 14:45, which in turn has drawn on this verse.

13a. The GT has read *ʿl-ḥṣwr* ("to the rock"), as in 1 Chr 11:15; but MT has *ʾl-qṣyr*.

15a. The absence from 4QSam[a] as well as from 1 Chr 11:17 of the repeated note in GT confirms that it is secondary.

16a. Here the LT reads *wybʾw* as *qal*, MT as *hipʿil*.

17a. The GT and Vulg. attest the somewhat similar-looking *ʾšth* ("shall I drink?") after *bnpšwtm* ("with their lives"). Yet 1 Chr 11:19 has a still fuller text: "Shall I drink the blood of these men with their lives?—for with their lives they brought it [the water]." The linkage of blood and life is reminiscent of Gen 9:4: *ʾk-bśr bnpšw dmw lʾ tʾklw*.

18a. Here LT = 1 Chr 11:20.

b. The MT = Chronicles.

c. Again MT = Chronicles.

d. Chronicles reads not *lw* but the negative *lʾ*: "There was no name among the three."

19a. The synoptic 1 Chr 11:21 opens with "From the Three, in the Two," apparently combining something like the readings of MT and LT.

b. In LT, "above the two" is more naturally read as the end of v. 18.

c. Here LT = Chronicles.

20a. *Iessai* (LT) is the normal Gk. transliteration of the name of David's father, *yšy*. The MT has the odd consonantal text *ʾyš ḥy* ("a living man"); but it requires the reading *ʾyš ḥyl*, as written in 1 Chr 11:22.

b. The shorter MT = Chronicles; but *bny*, as attested in LT, could easily have been omitted after *šny*.

21a. Here MT = LT, but Chronicles reads not *mrʾh* but *mdh*: "a man of size," a giant.

b. The LT = Chronicles, which uses the same phrase as is used of Goliath's weapon at the end of 2 Sam 21:19 (but the Gk. is different in each verse).

c. Here MT = Chronicles.

23a. Again MT = Chronicles.

b. The LT = Chronicles.

c. Here MT = Chronicles. "Guard" (LT) could attest *mšmrt*; however, *mšmʿt* always appears to have the sense of bodyguard, perhaps because their hearing is attuned to his wishes, or they never allow him out of their hearing.

25a. Eliqah is also absent from 1 Chr 11:27—has the eye jumped from one Harodite to the next?

26a. Here 1 Chr 11:28 also has *ʿyrʾ*—the *d/r* interchange is common.

27a. For *mbny* (MT) and presumably *sbny* (LT), 1 Chr 11:29 has *sbky*. The LT provides a mediating reading; but *sbky* appears also in 2 Sam 21:18//1 Chr 20:4.

28a. For *ṣlmwn* (MT) and presumably *ʿlymn* (LT), 1 Chr 11:29 has *ʿyly*. Again LT provides a link.

b. The MT = Chronicles.

29a. Here 1 Chr 11:30 has *ḥld*.

b. Again MT = Chronicles.

30a. Yet again MT = Chronicles.

b. Here 1 Chr 11:32 has *ḥwry*.

c. The MT = Chronicles.

31a. Here 1 Chr 11:32 has *ʾbyʾl*.

b. Again MT = Chronicles.

32a. Yet again MT = Chronicles.

b. Here *bny hšm hgzwny* (1 Chr 11:34) has elements of both MT and LT.

32cd. Similarly *ywntn bn-šgh hhrry* (1 Chr 11:34) has elements of both MT and LT in vv. 32–33. Also, MT = Chronicles.

33a. See previous note.

34a. Here *ʾlypl bn-ʾwr* (1 Chr 11:35) differs from both MT and LT.

b. The phrase *ḥpr hmkrty* (1 Chr 11:36) gives some support to LT. But in vv. 34b–35, the first and second elements of the names in MT and LT no longer match.

c. Here 1 Chr 11:36 has *ʾḥyh hplny*.

35a. The MT = Chronicles.

b. Here 1 Chr 11:37 has *nʿry bn ʾzby*.

36a. The LT = Chronicles.

b. Here *mbḥr bn-hgry* (1 Chr 11:38) gives support at least to "son of Ageri" (LT).

37a. The MT = Chronicles.

b. Again MT = Chronicles. An *n* has moved between the two names in this verse; cf. *mhry hn- / mhrnn h-* (see note 28b).

38a. Yet again MT = Chronicles.

b. Also here, MT = Chronicles.

[8–12] The remainder of this chapter offers a list of David's principal military men. Most of the material in Samuel is found also in 1 Chr 11, just after the report in that book of David's takeover of Jerusalem.

[13–17] The most famous and very poignant story in this section is set immediately after the three superheroes have been introduced (vv. 13–17). Yet the account is not attributed to them but to three heroes among the thirty. Since these remain unnamed, the matter of their relationship to the surrounding lists cannot be settled. In any case the action is more striking than the actors. David is in the cave of Adullam. This mention of the cave in a story drawn from the Book of Two Houses may be the source on which 1 Sam 22:1–2 draws. Though Bethlehem is not many miles (about 13) above Adullam, David is prevented from entering his hometown by a Philistine garrison. Like many an exile, he longs for nothing more than the familiar water of home; and he is incautious enough to say so in the presence of daring and devoted heroes. When his dream actually materializes, he does not even drink the water but pours it out as a solemn libation. It is not for drinking: it is men's blood—and all blood needs to be poured on the soil. Water that is men's blood is powerfully suggestive of bread that is a man's body and wine that is his blood (Mark 14:22–24).

[18–19] Campbell (2010: 354) observes rather strangely that "both the Three and the Thirty come as a shock to us; despite all the material on David's early guerrilla years, prior to this we have never heard of them." And yet we have long been aware that David is far from being a lone *gibbôr*. He sent off Joab with "all the army [of] the *gibbōrîm*" (2 Sam 10:7); he had *gibbōrîm* on his right hand and on his left when Shimei was stoning him (2 Sam 16:6); and Hushai warned Absalom, reminding him that his father was himself a *gibbôr* and had *gibbōrîm* around him (2 Sam 17:8, 10). The other repeated keywords of 2 Sam 23:8–39 are *rōʾš* ("head") and *šlš/šlšy/šlšym* ("three, third/s"). As for "head" and "three" in a military context, we should remember that David divided the force he mustered against Absalom under three *rāʾšîm* ("heads"; 2 Sam 18:2), just like Saul (1 Sam 11:11) and the Philistines (1 Sam 13:17) before him. It seems rather unfair of Campbell to say that "the extensive traditions supporting David failed to mention that his military success owed a great deal to a well-developed command structure and highly respected warriors." We have noted elsewhere that it is very difficult to decide whether the books of Samuel are for or against David. They do suggest that David gets more credit (or blame) for some actions than was the case in the inherited material (BTH). We have argued that these lists of his many heroes were moved from being near the report of (David and) Joab's taking Jerusalem to their present position in the chiastically organized coda (2 Sam 21–24). It is much harder to determine whether such a relocation resulted in a greater or lesser role for the heroes themselves.

[20–39] The Chronicler reports sixteen further names in 1 Chr 11:41b–47. This longer list is immediately followed by a long account, not represented at all in Samuel, of support that David received in men and supplies from each of the tribes while he was still in Ziklag. There is an excellent discussion of 1 Chr 11–12 in Klein 2006: 296–97, 306–10.[10] Here and there 1 Chr 11:11–41a

10. Klein notes the Transjordanian links of many of the additional names in Chronicles. But can 1 Chr 11–12 be a chiasm if 11:5–9 is not included (possibly an oversight; cf. 313)? See also Williamson 168–70.

may have preserved a name better than Samuel, although mostly its names are close to either MT or LT in Samuel. And the Chronicler's position for this list may be more original. However, we do well to prefer the shorter version of the list here in Samuel. It is sometimes hard to keep control of the arithmetic; but the text broadly keeps a distinction between three superheroes, of whom some exploits are mentioned (vv. 8–12), and thirty heroes simply listed (vv. 24–39). Yet exploits are also reported of Abishai and Benaiah, who though leaders of the thirty did not attain to the three (vv. 19, 23). We should note that the list begins with Asahel (featured in 2 Sam 2) and ends in Samuel with Uriah the Hittite (featured in 2 Sam 11). As with Goliath and Saul, who are also only briefly mentioned in BTH, theirs are names we know much better from the much fuller story we have earlier read: all of them have met violent deaths. One result of placing (possibly as a result of reshaping) the old source material (BTH) within 2 Samuel is that we are reminded of the name of Uriah immediately before the account of David's final great sin.

Lists of proper names, mostly unremembered in the larger narrative, are notoriously unstable. A remarkable number of the names in LT are obvious transcriptions of the names as preserved in MT. In some cases a pair of consonants has been transposed; in other cases the Hebrew name attested in LT differs from MT by only one Hebrew consonant. Despite the fact that LT also reports the total of 37 names given in MT (v. 39), it is easier to read its list as one of 30 names. The CL scribe copied the MT list in twos, with a space between each pair. That suggests a total of 31 names; but it is hard to have any confidence in the unusual "sons of Yashen, Jonathan" (v. 32) as a single name. Since it has not been derived from the characters of the larger narrative, the list itself is probably of only archival interest. If so, it may seem of little concern to this commentary which form of each name is the more original. Nonetheless, if this list (as part of BTH) was one of the sources available to the author of the narratives in Samuel, it will be interesting to follow up interconnections from this point of view.

2 Samuel 24:1–11a

1 And [Yahweh's[a]] *God*'s anger continued
to burn on Israel,
and he enticed David against them, saying,
"Go tally[b] Israel and Judah."

2 And the king said to Joab, [leader of the army who was] *and to the leaders of the armies that were* with him *in Jerusalem*,
"Roam[a] now among[b] all [the tribes of] Israel *and Judah* from Dan to Beer-sheba
and number the people

and bring to me
that I may know the count[c] of the people."

3 And Joab said to the king,
"And may Yahweh [your] *their*[a] God add to the people like these [and like these] a hundred times,
and the eyes of my lord the king seeing it.
But, my lord king, why has he taken pleasure in this matter?"
4 But the word of the king was firm on Joab and upon the leaders of the army;[a]
and Joab went out, and the leaders of the army from [before] the king,
to number the people, Israel.
5 And they crossed the Jordan;
and they [camped at] *began from* Aroer [to the south of] *and from* the city that is in the midst of the ravine (the Gad*dite* and [toward] Jaazer).[a]
6 And they came to Gilead[a] and to the land of [Tahtim Hodshi] *Hittiim Kadesh*;
and they came to Dan [Yaan],
and *went* round [about to] Sidon *the Great*.
7 And they came to the fortress of Tyre, and all the cities of the Hivites and the Canaanites,
and they came out to the south of Judah, to Beer-sheba.
8 And they roamed[a] in all the land,
and came at the end of nine months and twenty days to Jerusalem.
9 And Joab gave the count of the number of the people to the king;
and Israel was [eight] *nine* hundred thousand army men drawing a sword,
and the men of Judah [five] *four* hundred thousand men.[a]
10 And the heart of David struck[a] him afterward;
because[b] he had counted the people.

And David said to Yahweh,
"I have sinned greatly in what I have done.
And now, Yahweh, make [I beg you] the guilt[c] of your servant pass:
I have indeed been very foolish."
11a And David rose in the morning.

1a. Syntactically LT is close to MT, but B takes Yahweh as subj. and "anger" as obj. of the vb "add."

b. The term *mnh* is the first of three more or less equivalent words in this story. In BTH, it is used only in this opening verse of the census story and then in 1 Kgs 8:5//2 Chr 5:6—of the people that cannot be tallied.

2a. Apparently B has read not *bkl* but simply *kl*.

b. Here B's *dierchesthai* is a unique rendering of *šwṭ*; GT uses it in 1 Chr 21:4 for *hthlk*.

c. The GT's *arithmon* for *mspr* (also v. 9) is cognate with its *arithmēson* for *mnh* in v. 1.

3a. Here LT attests *'lhyhm*, not *'lhyk* (MT), while B attests *'lhym*.

4a. The LT uses forms of *dynamis* throughout for *ḥyl*, as in v. 2. Codex B varies between forms of *ischys* and of *dynamis*.

5a. Most of GT and many Heb. MSS read the same consonants as in MT as "and Eliezer"; LT supports MT in recognizing *y'zr* as the basic name at the end, but without the prep. *'l*.

6a. Only at beginning and end is B recognizably a rendering of (the very difficult) MT; LT is closer to MT.

8a. Codex B's *kai periōdeusan* for *wyšṭw* is used elsewhere only in Zechariah (5x)—there rendering *hthlk*, the vb. that MT uses in the parallel 1 Chr 21:4 (see note 2b above); LT has *periēlthon*.

9a. Codex B specifies that the men of Judah counted are also "army" men.

10a. Both *lb* and *hkh* (*hip'il* of *nkh*) are common words; but "heart" is subj. of "strike" only once more in HB. In 1 Sam 24:5 (6), *wyk lb-dwd 'tw* is the central element in a more idiomatic verse: "and it came to be after this, and David's heart smote him, because he had cut . . ."

b. The LT may attest *ky* before *spr*; or it may simply interpret a logical link, although none is preserved in MT. The nice French rendering of MT in Caquot and de Robert (627) could be translated: "After that, David felt his heart thump: he had counted the people!"

c. Codex B has *anomian* for *'wn*; but the majority tradition in GT has *adikian*.

The books of Samuel close with a chapter that is enigmatic and at the same time very rich in its wider biblical associations and in its links throughout Samuel. The synoptic account in 1 Chr 21 of David's census of the people and its aftermath is both shorter and longer at several points. I find it best to suppose that the original report in the Book of Two Houses was shorter than each of the successor accounts and was differently expanded and developed in Samuel and Chronicles. A wide range of different readings are immediately observable from a comparative reading of the opening scene, the count itself. In addition to many smaller variations, the motivation for the census is differently expressed at the outset; only 2 Sam 24:4b–7 specifies the route taken by Joab and his party; and only 1 Chr 21:6–7 excludes two tribes from the count.[11]

[1–2] Our problems as readers begin at the beginning: Yahweh's anger has "burned against Israel" only once before in Samuel—of Yahweh's bursting out on the wretched Uzzah (6:7). Is Samuel deliberately linking these rather distant

11. A fuller comparison of 2 Sam 24 and 1 Chr 21 can be found in Auld 2011 in press.

episodes? No indication is offered as to why there should be renewed divine anger now. And yet it is always a puzzle to know just why Yahweh burst out on Uzzah. If we set aside this unusual linkage in wording and concentrate instead on the balanced structure of chs. 21–24, this renewal of wrath will resume the more recently reported divine displeasure manifested in the three-year famine (21:1) and its outworking. Israel is again for some reason in the divine sights, and incitement of David to conduct a census is the means of achieving what is being aimed at.

The Chronicler starts the story differently: "The satan/accuser took his stand against Israel . . ."; and two immediate reasons persuade me that the Chronicler is following the original text of BTH here and/or an earlier text of Samuel. The first is that, in both Samuel and Chronicles, there is a small cluster of neighboring and uncommon words that share the first two consonants of *s-t-n*. The satan may have been suppressed in the versions of this portion of Samuel that have survived;[12] but the evidence of his earlier presence is still there. The other is the terms in which the short scene involving Shimei, David, and the sons of Zeruiah (19:18b–23 [19b–24]) is played out. Shimei confesses to David in the language that David will use to Yahweh in 24:10. When Abishai's response is to ask permission to put him to death, David rounds on him, calling him and his brother a satan to him—apparently unfairly, since Joab tries to talk David out of the divine enticement (whether by a satan or an angry Yahweh). The author of 2 Sam 19 (esp. v. 22 [23]) still seems to have been aware of the earlier version of the census story's start.

It has long been commonplace to argue that the issue between Samuel and Chronicles here is theological. The later Chronicler (so the case goes) was offended by the boldness of attributing to Yahweh the initiative over a failed test for which Israel would pay so heavily; hence it diverted the blame from Yahweh to satan. It has been objected that, since this satan is a member of the divine court, Yahweh must still have been ultimately responsible; yet we have already seen something of an analogy at the end of 1 Sam 16: the spirit of Yahweh coming on David, and an evil spirit from Yahweh tormenting Saul.

However, Knoppers has strongly revived the argument that *śāṭān* without the article (in 1 Chr 21:1 and 2 Sam 19:22 [23]) is not the divine agent. Granting his case certainly makes it easier to argue the connections with 2 Sam 19; but in Samuel we are still dealing with a theological issue. Did our author recognize that an unnamed agent provocateur was an inadequate prompt to a narrative dealing with such big themes as the sin and folly of the king, devastating plague on Israel, the status of Jerusalem, and the site for Yahweh's temple? It may be wiser to take a more nuanced view of this unarticulated *śāṭān*. Without the

12. The MT and GT—we can only speculate as to how 4QSam[a] introduces this narrative: it shares readings with Chronicles against MT and GT later in the story (esp. v. 16).

article, he may not be specified at the outset as the divine agent. And yet Yahweh's (divine) emissary who plays a role in the second paragraph of this narrative is identified as *mal'ak yhwh* (v. 16); and "Yahweh's messenger" and *śāṭān* are sometimes identified elsewhere in HB, or at least associated as colleagues or opponents. And the verb associated with the *śāṭān* at the outset (*ʿāmad*, 1 Chr 21:1) reappears later (21:16, 17)—and precisely with *mal'ak yhwh* as subject.

There is less theological distance between these two forms of the introduction to this narrative than most commentators suggest. It is widely supposed that the Chronicler has altered the earlier form of the story he found in Samuel, that he was concerned to remove responsibility from Yahweh himself for upsetting David, and that he instead blamed a partly independent divine figure (the satan). When I argue that the textual change was made in the opposite direction, I am in no sense arguing for the opposite theological move: that the divine "anger" we meet in Samuel has suppressed a partly independent divine figure. If the satan in the census story is a divine figure, he is no more independent of Yahweh than the "evil spirit from Yahweh" that afflicted Saul (1 Sam 16:14), or the "lying spirit" that Yahweh sent to deceive Jehoshaphat and the king of Israel (1 Kgs 22:19–23, BTH). Theologically, Yahweh's anger and his satan are but the two sides of the same coin. And if the change in 2 Sam 24:1 was not made after all to safeguard a theological point, then it was probably made to encourage exegetical comparison between David and Uzzah.

Although David and his actions and his responses bulk very large in this extended narrative, it is important to note that the final word of the very different introductory clauses of 2 Sam 24:1 and 1 Chr 21:1 is the same. The prior prepositions may be different, but the name is the same. The story is about "Israel": it is the people that is in focus. The Chronicler's *ʿal* is more overtly hostile: a satan takes a stand (over) against Israel; but we do not have positive expectations of a satan in any case. In Samuel *bĕyiśrā'ēl* is more neutral and is rendered in Greek by the equally overworked *en*; but the anger of Yahweh is all the more menacing because its cause is not made clear, and it matters little whether its continuation is within or against Israel. In both texts, a separate total for Judah will be brought to David (see below); but in Chronicles, the instruction is to count "Israel," while in Samuel (more typically) it is to count "Israel and Judah."

As David proceeds to give instructions to Joab (v. 2), there are several small but significant differences between these texts:

1. Samuel (MT) calls him leader (*śar*) of the army (*ḥayil*), while Samuel (LT) has David instructing Joab and the leaders of the army/ies; but in Chronicles Joab is leader of the people (*ʿam*). The use of *ḥayil* to mean the "army" or the "forces" appears to belong to later Hebrew and is commoner in Chronicles (in nonsynoptic

passages)—correspondingly, Samuel often uses *ʿam* where Chronicles reads "Israel."

2. Samuel varies between "Israel" (Chronicles) and "all the tribes of Israel," as in 2 Sam 5:1.
3. Samuel describes the totality of the land as from north (Dan) to south (Beer-sheba), while Chronicles has the coordinates in reverse order.
4. Both vary the term for "count" from *mnh* (v. 1); but while Chronicles uses the cognate *spr* for the act and *mspr* for the result, Samuel varies between *pqd* and *mspr*—so introducing the third synonym (*pqd*, 2 Sam 24: 2, 4) earlier than does 1 Chr 21:5.

It is easy to concede priority to Chronicles over points 1 and 2; if Samuel has rebuilt expansively a narrative that includes many threes, it is hardly surprising that it made the triad of number words more explicit at the outset (v. 4.). Beer-sheba to Dan (point 3) will be discussed below.

[3–10a] It is Joab rather than David who questions the initiative: the king's interest in numbers is proper, but there is still something wrong about his instructions. Samuel's Joab may not be distancing himself from Yahweh when he calls him David's God; but he hopes rather ominously that, if there is an increase, David will still be able to see it (anticipating a phrase from 1 Kgs 1:48). Solomon in his vision more circumspectly states that he is among a people who cannot be counted or numbered (1 Kgs 3:8). We have never met Joab so hesitant in the face of action. However, he comes under strict orders, and the count goes ahead throughout the whole land. We [modern] readers only learn at the end (v. 9) what David and Joab know at the outset, that the count is of men of military age.

Quite the largest "plus" in Samuel's version of the opening scene reports the itinerary of Joab's mission. Dan and Beer-sheba (v. 2) had been stipulated briefly in BTH as limits of the count; and these two cities are more naturally understood as marking the northern and southern extent of territory west of the Jordan and Dead Sea valley (the Arabah). "From Dan to Beer-sheba" is the more familiar form of the territorial formula; and there are at least two reasons for this: it is the direction always used in Judges, Samuel, and Kings; and it is used seven times in these books (Judg 20:1; 1 Sam 3:20; 2 Sam 3:10; 17:11; 24:2, 15; 1 Kgs 4:25 [5:5]), over against only 1 Chr 21:2 and 2 Chr 30:5. The only synoptic passage is 2 Sam 24:2//1 Chr 21:2. We may fairly suppose that the expression was original to that context; and that it was from there that it was copied four times in Samuel and twice nearby and once in Chronicles. But is the more familiar form also the more original?

The longer text in Samuel specifies a route starting east of the Jordan (vv. 5–6a), moving (possibly significantly) northward from the south, then via Dan to the Phoenician coast (vv. 6b–7a), before heading to Beer-sheba in the south of Judah (v. 7b). Does this added itinerary take its southern starting point from the Chronicler's version of the "Beer-sheba to Dan" formula? Or does it end up in Beer-sheba because the formula ran "from Dan to Beer-sheba"?

Various descriptions of territory in Deuteronomy, Joshua, and Judges start from Aroer, by the wadi Arnon. "The city that is in the midst of the wadi" (v. 5) is exactly so described only in Josh 13:9, 16 (but cf. also Deut 3:16; Josh 12:2). The Hivvites (v. 7) are located "under Hermon" in Josh 11:3 and as living "in Mount Lebanon" (Judg 3:3). Only here in HB are they paired with the Canaanites. This route in Samuel may draw on the book of Joshua and its neighbors.[13] Given that Samuel is one of the longest books in the Bible, it is remarkable that it is only here (v. 7) that there is any mention of "Canaanites"—in Samuel it is the Philistines who are the principal "other."

The more detailed version of the count in Samuel specifies the time taken. Nine months and twenty days (v. 8) is a curious and curiously specific period, though quite close to the length of human gestation. When Joab returns to Jerusalem, he brings two tallies, the larger one for Israel, the smaller for Judah. The text does not make plain whether the Judah total is intended to be additional to the Israel total, or to represent a subset of the Israel count. As so often, MT and GT within Samuel, and also Samuel and Chronicles, disagree over the component figures. If it is correct to compute their totals together, MT and GT do agree on an overall total of thirteen hundred thousand. The Chronicler goes about reporting the totals in a way that is both similar and different: "all Israel" is eleven hundred thousand, and Judah is four hundred and seventy thousand. Since he goes on to state that Joab has not included Levi and Benjamin in the count (1 Chr 21:6), we may suppose that Judah too is a subset representing close to half of "all Israel."

[10b–11a] The authors of Samuel and of Chronicles have substantially rebuilt the openings of their reports of this census. But when it comes to David's triple confession (v. 10b), the version in 1 Chr 21:8 is almost identical. The main question here for interpretation is just how the three elements of the evaluation relate to each other. David first admits that he has sinned (*ḥṭ'ty*) greatly. He then asks that his guilt (*'wn*) be removed—he does not say where to. As for the final phrase by which David describes his action as "folly" (*ky nsklty m'd*), we might ask whether he is seeking to reinforce or to lessen the impact of the other two terms. Was his enumeration of the people simply a case of careless and unintentional "folly" (as stated in Adam 2010: 149)? Or in addition to amounting to sin and guilt, was it a case of gross and culpable "folly"? The *ky* that introduces the statement about folly has to be interpreted from the context. "For" is often appropriate; and the clause might mean "for I have (simply)

13. Links between Joshua and Samuel are explored in Auld 2011b.

been foolish." However, the final *m'd* puts a different complexion on the issue: whatever "foolish" means exactly, being "very" foolish is hardly a venial matter for a king. Accordingly, the translation above assumes that this *kî* marks a strong assertion and introduces here a powerful climax to the triple royal admission: great sin, . . . guilt, . . . and (in fact) gross folly. None of the other verbal forms of this word in Samuel is strengthened by "very." However, as we have already noticed when discussing these others, they do tend to support the view that *skl* normally means culpable folly. The charge that Samuel makes against Saul, and that includes "folly," is sufficient to justify the noncontinuation of his royal line (1 Sam 13:13–14).[14] When Ahithophel realizes that his advice has been deemed "foolish" (2 Sam 15:31), he takes himself home and hangs himself (17:23). In each case it is apparent that David or Samuel or Ahithophel (or Laban) has faced the facts as they are. The exceptional case is Saul. When he uses a unique (*hip'il*, not *nip'al*) form of this verb (1 Sam 26:21) to explain his actions to David, he immediately follows it—and in so doing makes its sense more precise—with the verb for unintentional error; and it is to that latter verb that Saul attaches not just "very" (*m'd*) but also the superlative "a very great deal" (*hrbh m'd*). Saul's use of the term *skl* tells us less about its (proper) meaning, less about how it is used by others in this same book, and more about his own self-serving misuse of it.

The three terms that have described the census action ("tally," "number," and "count") are matched by three terms that evaluate its significance ("sin," "folly," and "guilt"). In fact, while the confessional triad (v. 10) is original to BTH, the enumerating triad of verbs has been created by the author of Samuel for the start of the narrative (vv. 1–2). The fact of enumeration is made more prominent by the more immediate grouping of "tally," "number," and "count." When we compare the versions of the story in 2 Sam 24 and 1 Chr 21, we find that *pqd* ("number") is a variant in 2 Sam 24:2 and a plus in 24:4. In its earlier version of the story, BTH used only the related noun *mpqd*, and a few verses later (2 Sam 24:9//1 Chr 21:5).[15] Further editorial preferences can be readily noted. Just as in the opening verses of 2 Sam 7, we find several examples in this narrative of the preference of the author of Samuel for "the king" instead of "David." The title "the king" is used in 24:2, 9, and 20, contexts where the synoptic 1 Chr 21:2, 5, and 21 preserve his personal name. The fact that the author of Samuel uses "the king" in 24:2, 3, 4, 21, and 23, within his own additions to the older version of the story, confirms this preference.

Presumably David understands Joab's reservations when he overrules him (vv. 3–4); but it is only after the census is complete that he takes his error to

14. The charges made by Laban against Jacob, and culminating in "foolish action" (Gen 31:26–28), are of similar severity.

15. Also, *pqd* is used in a Chronicles plus (1 Chr 21:6).

heart. As noted above, the clause *wyk lb-dwd ʾtw* has a parallel only in 1 Sam 24:5; it is quite clear there that David's conscience troubled him because he had cut part of the king's robe. Yet the wording of this whole short report (2 Sam 24:10a) is unusual from several perspectives: (1) It has already been noted that the MT is clumsy as it stands: "And David's heart smote him afterward he counted the people." And this is true whether "afterward" is read as the end of the first clause or the start of the second. (2) LXX[B] and LXX[L] are more logical and illustrate both of these readings: "And David's heart struck him after counting the people" (B) and "And David's heart struck him after this, because he counted the people" (LT); but neither is a straightforward rendering of the Hebrew text in MT. The LT might attest that *ky* ("because") has been omitted after *ʾḥry-kn* ("after this"). (3) The beginning and end of v. 10a (*wyk . . . ʾt-hʿm*) reappear in the synoptic 1 Chr 21:7b as the brief clause "and he struck Israel" (*wyk ʾt-yśrʾl*); but the striker there is Yahweh and not the heart of David.

According to Chronicles, David's confession is a response to Yahweh's striking Israel after the count. According to Samuel, David realizes that he has done wrong in advance of a divine reaction. We may do well to suspect a two-way relationship between the stories of the census and of David and Saul in the cave (1 Sam 24). David's men urging him to take action against Saul anticipates the older story of a satan enticing David to count Israel. But in the newer story of David in the cave, he takes only symbolic action against the king; his heart then warns him against doing more substantial damage to Yahweh's anointed. The language of heart striking is then rather clumsily copied into the retelling within Samuel of the census story.

David confesses to sin and folly; he asks Yahweh to take away his guilt (v. 10b). We have found the terms of the confession, drawn here from BTH, anticipated by the authors of Samuel in the confessions of Saul to David (1 Sam 26:21), David to Nathan (2 Sam 12:13), and Shimei to David (2 Sam 19:19–20 [20–21]). But what was wrong with counting? Why was it sin and folly for a leader to know how large a force he could muster? Why did David fall for a proposal that Joab found immediately problematic and continue in the action despite his principal lieutenant's advice? Does divine entrapment simply blind one to normal reason? Several campaign stories in the Bible make it plain that the armies of Israel are simply human "extras" to a divine fighting force. Their number does not matter: indeed, the story of Gideon and the Midianites suggests that the fewer the better (Judg 7). To count Israel is to lack trust in divine promises.

Additional material by the Chronicler (1 Chr 27:23–24) develops and explores this issue, after a listing of monthly divisions of labor, with an odd reversal of roles from what we read in 1 Chr 21:1–4a (as also in 2 Sam 24:1–4a): "David did not count those below twenty years of age, for Yahweh had promised to make Israel as numerous as the stars of heaven. Joab . . . began to count them but did not finish; yet wrath came upon Israel for this." David's reputation is protected: a wrong start is made by Joab, and Israel suffers for it. This author has given a similar "spin" to the beginning of the census story as the author of 2 Sam 19:22 (23) did. Although loyal Joab tried to save David from a disastrous mistake, both fresh passages turn him instead into part of the problem.

The final three Hebrew words of the opening main paragraph (v. 11a) are Samuel plus. The stock expression in HB for making an early morning start is *wyškm bbqr* (as in 1 Sam 1:19; 5:4; 15:12; 17:20; 29:10–11—and also 2 Chr 20:20). The very common verb *qûm* is construed with "in the morning" within FP only twice at the end of Judges (19:27; 20:19), in Solomon's judgment of the women (1 Kgs 3:21), and here—and elsewhere in HB only in the Balaam story (Num 22:13, 21). The implication may be that David's remorse is expressed to Yahweh at night, and possibly in a dream. See further below, on 11b.

2 Samuel 24:11b–17

11b And Yahweh's word, it came to Gad [the prophet[a]], David's seer, saying,
12 "Go and speak to David,[a]
'This Yahweh has said:
"Three things am I [laying[b]] *speaking* upon/against you.
Choose yourself one of them[c]
and I will do to you."'"
13 And Gad came to David
and informed[a] him,
and said to him
"[Shall there] *Choose for yourself that there* come [to you]
three[b] [seven] years famine on [your] *the* land,
or three months of your fleeing before your adversaries
and [his[c]] *their* pursuing you,
or three days' plague being on [your] the land.[?]
Now know
and see
what word I should return my sender."

14 And David said to Gad,
"[It is] *Even the three are* very adverse[a] to me:
let [us] *me* fall, I beg, into/by Yahweh's hand
for *very* great are his mercies,
but by/into man's hand let me not fall."
And David chose for himself the plague.
And days of reaping of wheat . . .[b]

15 And Yahweh put a plague on Israel from the morrow till an appointed time;[a]
and the plague began in the people,[b]
and there died of the people from Dan to Beer-sheba seventy thousand men.
16 And the envoy directed his hand to Jerusalem
to destroy it;
and Yahweh regretted[a] the ill
and said to the envoy[b] who was destroying among the people,
"It is much.
[Now[c]] slacken your hand *now*."
And Yahweh's envoy, he had come to be *standing*[d] by the threshing floor of [Araunah[e]] *Orna* the Jebusite.

(And David raised his eyes,
and saw the envoy of Yahweh
standing between earth and heaven,
and his sword drawn in his hand,
stretched out over Jerusalem,
and the elders fell on their faces covered in sacking.[f])
17 And David said to Yahweh,
on his seeing the envoy
who was striking down among the people,
and he said,
"Look, I myself sinned[a]
and I [myself was guilty] *the shepherd did ill*;
but these—the sheep—what have they done?
Let your hand, I beg, be on me and on my father's house."

11a. Here LT = Chronicles.

12a. Codex B attests "saying" after David, found also in MT of 1 Chr 21:10.

b. Codex B's *airō*, of which *erō* (LT) is a corruption, corresponds to "I am laying."

c. Notice varying genders in *šlš . . . 'ḥt-mhm* (m., f.-m.).

13a. The phrase *wygd lw* ("and reported to him") is a Samuel plus. Does it intend a play on Gad's name?

b. The GT like Chronicles has 3 years, not 7. What is the force of 7 in MT?

c. In MT only, notice the interesting shift from flight before pl. foes to a sg. pursuer (GT again agrees with Chronicles here): that this is not simply accidental may be suggested by the fact that the ptc. *rdp* is used with pronominal suf. only once more in MT—in Ps 35:5 (6), where the subj. of *rdpm* is none other than *ml'k yhwh*.

14a. The phrase *ṣr ly* is language familiar from the Psalms (e.g., Ps 18:6 [7]//2 Sam 22:7); however, the way in which it resonates here with *ṣryk* (v. 13) is hardly accidental.

b. The GT has a long plus between vv. 14 and 15 (MT): the first clause retroverts to straightforward Heb., as rendered above; however, the following words, *kai hēmerai therismou pyrōn*, hardly grammatical in Greek, make hardly more sense when retroverted (*wymy qṣyr ḥṭym*): as it stands, the phrase ("and days of reaping wheat") seems fragmentary and is difficult to construe with either the clause that precedes or the one that follows—but see below. The closest parallels are in Gen 30:14; Josh 3:15 (GT); Judg 15:1.

15a. In place of *mwʿd* (MT), the GT has *aristou*, "breakfast." The term is seldom used in LXX books with Heb. counterparts; but it corresponds to *leḥem* in Gen 43:25 and 1 Kgs 4:22 (5:2). See below on the sense of *mwʿd* here.

b. The plus in LT corresponds to the concluding phrases in vv. 21 and 25.

16a. The vb. *wynḥm* occurs shortly after the assonant noun *rḥmw* (v. 14): the related vb. *wyrḥm* is twice attested in HB, both times with a personal suf. (2 Kgs 13:23; Isa 55:7).

b. Codex B attests "envoy of God."

c. Here B reads "much" and "now" together: *Poly nyn*; however, LT accentuates the break between them by delaying *nyn* till the end of the command. The terms *rb ʿth* appear together only in the parallel 1 Chr 21:15. The MT appears to pause at *rb* in both Samuel and Chronicles. An alternative rendering would be "destroying among the people greatly."

d. With B, the scroll 4QSam[a] is without *hyh*, but it reads *ʿwmd*, with 1 Chr 21:15. In LT, *ēn hestēkōs* appears to attest both.

e. Here *hʾwrnh* (K) reverses middle consonants—but both forms start with definite art.; 1 Chr 21 offers *ʾrnn*; and GT has indeclinable *Orna* in both; cf. *ʾrnʾ* in 4QSam[a] (2 Sam 24:20).

f. The extended plus, rendered above (in parentheses) as reconstructed in DJD, is preserved in 4QSam[a], as also in 1 Chr 21:16 (where David and the elders fall on their faces).

17a. Codex B's *Idou egō eimi ēdikēsa* suggests that it has read simply *hnh ʾnky ʿwyty*; 4QSam[a] like MT does attest two verbs of confession, but apparently[16] agrees with 1 Chr 21:17 over the second: *hrʿh hrʿty*. The LT attests the same text but reads *hrʿh* not as the strengthening inf. abs. of *rʿʿ hipʿil*, but as ptc. of *rʿh qal* ("the shepherd"). (The only other biblical instance of inf. *hrʿ* with the finite vb. occurs within Samuel's warning to Israel in 1 Sam 12:25.)

[11b–13] The divine answer comes through Gad, David's seer. He is called "prophet" as well as "seer" in 2 Sam 24:11b (MT and B), but just "seer" in LT and 1 Chr 21:9. Some scholars seek to make an original distinction between the "seer" (*ḥōzeh*) as a court official and the more independent "prophet" (*nābîʾ*), who was answerable to the Deity. But the evidential base is too slim. The BTH may preserve our oldest biblical testimony; and there, paradoxically, David consults "Nathan the prophet" about housing the ark (2 Sam 7), while his own "seer" Gad is sent to him and bears a divine choice. Yahweh's response to David's confession is introduced unremarkably in 1 Chr 21:9—"And Yahweh

16. Only apparently, because all 3 instances in HB (i.e., MT) of inf. abs. of *rʿʿ hipʿil* are spelled *hrʿ*, not *hrʿh*.

spoke to Gad, David's seer, saying . . ."; and this may well have been the original text. The divine response has been delayed in 2 Sam 24:11b by the introduction of the oddly worded and oddly placed report (v. 11a) about David's rising in the morning. Either because of this interruption, or for another reason, greater emphasis has been given in Samuel to the divine "word": *wydbr yhwh ʾl-gd* has become *wdbr yhwh hyh ʾl-gd*. Perhaps Yahweh's speaking to Gad was not felt to be a straightforward response to David's rising in the morning, such as would be marked by the normal narrative *wayyiqṭōl* sequence. If the prophetic formula "word of Yahweh" had been original, it would hardly have been altered by the Chronicler. The rendering in NRSV ("When David rose in the morning, the word of the LORD came . . .") does violence to the syntax, in addition to setting aside the masoretic paragraphing. The CEV pays closer attention to the disjunctive syntax: "Before David even got up the next morning, the Lord had told . . . ," but this freer rendering does not recognize *dbr yhwh* as a technical term. And in MT, though not in LXX, Gad has become "the prophet" as well as "David's seer."

This response gives barely a partial answer to the questions stated and implied in David's request (v. 10): will David's guilt be "transferred," and, if so, whereto? There is no explicit divine response to the terms of his confession, simply the declaration of a choice between famine, war, and plague as punishment. David's people will certainly pay, but he has the choice of how they will pay. David's people will pay, but all the massed second-person forms throughout vv. 12–13 are singular: "Choose for yourself, and I will do it to you." Has David's guilt been transferred? Has it been transferred to his people? Or is there no discernible connection at all between royal admission and divine demand to choose? In the discussion of ch. 12 above, we suggested that this aching question is offered an answer there: guilt can be transferred to another—in that case the child. If we had only MT available, we might suppose that David opts for the first or third choice, hoping desperately for greater mercy from God than from a human foe, almost as if "better the devil you know." But we must note that the plus represented in GT has him narrow the choice to the third of the divine options.

Apparently MT, which has given Gad a new title ("prophet"), has also altered three years to seven years of famine (v. 13). "Three" (with related "thirty") is the key number through much of chs. 21–24. But seven victims were chosen from Saul's family (21:6); and those who will succumb to the divine plague are seventy thousand (24:15)—and Yahweh has struck down seventy men at Beth-shemesh (1 Sam 6:19). In place of "your fleeing," the parallel in 1 Chr 21:12 has "being taken/swept away" (textual confusion between *nskh* and *nsph* was easy). In whichever direction, there is presumably a link between the unique use of the verb *sph* here in Chronicles and its use three times in 1 Samuel (12:25; 26:10; 27:1)—the commentary on each of these passages has suggested that they should all be understood as anticipations of the census narrative. The idiom "return someone a word" (2 Sam 24:13) is used again in 1 Kgs 12:6, 9 and 2 Kgs 22:9, 20 (all BTH), as also in 2 Sam 3:11 and 1 Sam 17:30 (MT plus). Normally *dābār* is placed, as here, at the end of the clause (in 1 Kgs 12:9 an added relative clause leads to reordering). Here the delayed *dbr*, at the end of a subparagraph, is all the more effective because it plays on *deber* ("plague"), used only a few words earlier and selected for Yahweh to "send."

[14–16] David's response to the seer (v. 14) appropriately begins and ends in language we find in several psalms. He is celebrated as the quintessential psalmist and ch. 22 has provided a large demonstration of his art. But his opening and closing words are only once found together in our Psalter. His opening gambit, "It is very adverse to me," echoes *ṣr* in Pss 31:9 (10); 59:16 (17); 69:17 (18); 102:2 (3); it is anticipated by Israel collectively (1 Sam 13:6), by Saul (1 Sam 28:15), and by himself when mourning Saul and Jonathan (2 Sam 1:26). And his concluding appeal to Yahweh's many mercies (*raḥămîm*) is shared with Pss 51:1 (3); 69:16 (17); 119:156; and prayers in two late books (Dan 9:18; Neh 9:19, 27, 31); but has never been voiced in so many words within Samuel, although David has claimed such a visceral love for Yahweh in the opening words of one version of his Song (2 Sam 22:2 [LT] = Ps 18:2). In Ps 69:16–17 (17–18), where the psalmist is appealing to Yahweh for deliverance from his enemies, the two elements are in reverse order:

> Answer me, Yahweh; for good is your loyalty.
> As the multitude of your mercies, turn to me.
> And do not turn your face from your servant;
> for I am distressed—hurry, answer me.

Here in 2 Sam 24, however, Yahweh is the immediate source of the coming "distress."

The beginning and end of David's answer may be familiar, yet the central element is quite unique: no one else in HB ever asks to "fall." This very uniqueness makes it all the harder to determine whether *bĕyad* after "fall" is intended to mean "by the hand of" (as most recently in 21:22) or "in the hand of" (as most recently in 21:9). The ambiguity may be deliberate.

David has excluded human agency, and pestilence is Yahweh's choice from the remaining options (v. 15), and it claims some 5 percent of those counted. First Chronicles 21:14 is much briefer and may represent the older version: "And Yahweh put a plague among Israel; and there died from Israel seventy thousand men." The two pluses in Samuel specify time and place more precisely and are stated in the same form: "from . . . and up to . . ." The spatial definition simply repeats the terms of David's instruction to Joab (v. 2): the plague is to cover the same territory as the census. The punishment appears appropriate to the offense: David has gloried in the number of his people and is punished by losing many of them. "From the morrow/morning till an appointed time" (MT) is a formulation never repeated in HB; and in fact it has only one close comparator—"from the morning and up to the noon" (1 Kgs 18:26)—although there the second element of the phrase is definite like the first. "An appointed time" is less specific than the threatened three days (v. 13); and Yahweh does interrupt his agent in the course of his destructive work (v. 16). The unusual wording may allude to Ps 102:13 (14): "You yourself shall arise, shall show mercy to Zion; for it is time [*ʿēt*] to favor her, for an appointed time [*môʿēd*] has come."

Here GT's puzzling plus (vv. 14/15), though apparently fragmentary, does have some relevant contextual links. Rizpah's vigil over the seven victims from her family began at harvest, though the earlier barley harvest (21:9–10). In the more detailed conclusion to the census story in 1 Chr 21, the Jebusite is threshing wheat on his threshing floor (21:20) and volunteers to give David wheat for his grain offering (21:23). And wheat harvest also provided the occasion for the return of the ark to Beth-shemesh (1 Sam 6:13). There too (6:14) the wood associated with the cattle was used in their sacrifice; and there too (6:19) many of the townsfolk died because of looking into the ark (6:19).

When the messenger of death reaches Jerusalem (v. 16a), Yahweh for his part relents and calls a halt. The verb "be sorry" or "repent" or "relent" (*nipʿal* of *nḥm*) is used only here in BTH, though it is anticipated in one further context in Samuel—1 Sam 15:11, 29 (MT), 35. It is associated with the assonant *rḥm* only twice more in HB, in the almost identical Jonah 4:2 and Joel 2:13, where the "mercy" word is an adjective (*raḥûm*):

> You are a gracious and merciful God, slow to anger,
> abounding in loyalty, and relenting from disaster.

[17] The narrator (according to LT and 1 Chr 21:15) reports the divine messenger "positioned/stationed [*ʿwmd*] by the threshing floor" (v. 16b); and David (in the longer version shared by 4QSam[a] and 1 Chr 21) sees the messenger "positioned/stationed between earth and heaven." The use of *ʿmd* a second time, in adjacent sentences and both within a description of the position of the divine envoy, invites the reader to coordinate the two descriptions. In the next paragraph we will learn that this threshing floor is to become the site of an altar. A temple, where a god resides, is regarded as a small portion of heaven on earth; thus the significance of this threshing floor is nicely anticipated in the statements that the envoy is both "in position by the threshing floor" and "in position between earth and heaven." In MT the loss of *ʿmd* before *ʿm*, like the loss in both

MT and GT of the longer following text, may have been accidental; but a very suggestive earlier text was lost with them.[17]

The fact that the Chronicler reports the use of sackcloth only this once (21:16), and in a synoptic context, increases the likelihood that he is following his source. Sacking is found surprisingly seldom in the Psalms (only 30:11 [12]; 35:13; 69:11 [12]). But Ps 69:11 [12] appears to form part of a pattern with the intercessory practices commended in Joel 1:8, 13 and Jonah 3:5, 6, 8. Sacking is mentioned in v. 11 (12) of Ps 69, whose close links to 2 Sam 24:16a were noted above (elsewhere only 2 Sam 21:9 [Rizpah] and 2 Sam 3:31); and sacking is also prominent in Joel 2:13 and Jonah 4:2 (mentioned just above, along with Ps 69:17–18, in the discussion of vv. 16a, 14).

Reading the longer ending of v. 16, attested both in 4QSam[a] and in 1 Chr 21:16, together with the account of the fleeing Absalom (18:9), raises interesting questions. If the longer ending is part of an older text of the census story, and if 2 Sam 24 (as part of BTH) is part of the oldest main source of the books of Samuel, then the precise terms used to describe Absalom with his head caught in the oak tree are likely to have been chosen in order to suggest a connection. Absalom, no less than the divine messenger, was a divinely appointed destroyer sent to punish David for his sin. Like the divine messenger, Absalom was seen in midair after bringing destruction to a substantial part of the land. Thus 2 Sam 18:9, no less than 19:20–24, draws on the older census story.

The reading shared by LT and 4QSam[a] as the middle element of David's second triple confession (v. 17) starts with the longer first-person singular pronoun *ʾnky* and moves to the assonant "shepherd" and "did wrong"; in the synoptic passage, Chronicles doubles "did wrong" with the infinitive absolute (also assonant). Perhaps the wording in Samuel was intended to be ambiguous: the independent pronoun followed by doubled verb was used by David in earlier protestations (1 Sam 20:5; 2 Sam 18:2).

2 Samuel 24:18–25

18 And Gad came to David on that day,
and said to him,[a]
"Go up
and raise to Yahweh an altar on the threshing floor of [Araunah] *Orna* the Jebusite."
19 And David went up according to the word of Gad the prophet,[a]
which [just as[b]] Yahweh had commanded.

17. The preservation in 1 Chr 21 of elements of an older text that had influenced other portions of Samuel is reminiscent of Ho's discussion of 1 Chr 10 and 1 Sam 31, discussed above in relation to 2 Sam 21:1–14.

20 And [Araunah] *Orna* looked down[a]
and saw the king and his servants
passing toward him;
and [Araunah] *Orna* went out
and prostrated himself to the king on his face on the ground.
21 And [Araunah] *Orna* said,[a]
"Wherefore did my lord the king come to his servant?"
And David said to him,
"To get from you the threshing floor,
and to build an altar to Yahweh,
that the plague be restrained from upon the people."
22 And [Araunah] *Orna* said to David,

"Take,[a] and let my lord the king do for Yahweh what is good in his eyes.	"Let my lord the king take and raise up what is good in his eyes.

See the cattle for the holocaust and the [threshing sledges] *plows*[b]
and the cattle harness for wood.
23 Everything *Orna* [Araunah, the king/O king] has granted to the king."

And [Araunah] *Orna* said to the king,
"[May] Yahweh your God [take pleasure in] *will expect*[a] *of* you."
24 And the king said to [Araunah] *Orna*,
"No. Rather must I in fact get it from you [for a price] *by an exchange*.
I shall not raise to Yahweh my God holocausts gratis."
And David got the threshing floor *by an exchange* and the cattle for fifty shekels of silver.
25 And David built there an altar to Yahweh
and raised holocausts and peace-offerings.
And Solomon added to the altar at last,
because it was small at first.[a]
And Yahweh [was besought for] *became favorable*[b] *to* the land;
and the plague was restrained from upon Israel.

18a. "To him" (MT) is supported by B but not read in LT or 4QSam[a].

19a. Here LT, but not B, has added the title "prophet."

b. The clause "just as Yahweh commanded" is attested in 4QSam[a]. The conjunction of Yahweh's command with *kdbr* of a human may be unique.

20a. The scroll 4QSam[a], exactly as the end of 1 Chr 21:20, notes that Orna is threshing wheat. Yet 4QSam[a] preserves only the last word of the preceding clause, "in sacking" (*bśqym*), while Chronicles reads "hiding themselves" (*mtḥb'ym*). Here DJD 192 harmonizes the two endings, but "hiding themselves in sacking" is a unique combination.

21a. Here 4QSam[a] uniquely specifies that Orna speaks "to the king."

22a. "Take" (LT) may attest simply *qḥ*, not *yqḥ*.

b. The LT here, as GT in 1 Chr 21:23, has *ta arotra* for *hmrgym*; B's *trochos* ("wheel") for *mwrg* is attested elsewhere only in Isa 41:15.

23a. The LT's *prosdexetai* renders *rṣh* more than all other vbs., though *para sou* is surprising for the pron. suf. Codex B's *eulogēsai se* is a surprising rendering of *yrṣk* since *eulogein* is the stock rendering of *brk*, but *eudokein* of *rṣh*; however, in Pss 49:13 (49:14 MT; 48:14 LXX) and 119 (118 LXX):108, B has *eulogein* where Codex A and others have the expected *eudokein*.

25a. A retroversion of the long plus in GT following *wšlmym* includes *mʿṭ* and *hwsyp*, and these appear in reverse order within Nathan's second oracle (2 Sam 12:8).

b. The LT's *ileōs egeneto* corresponds once each in OT to all of *nḥm*, *nśʾ*, *slḥ*, and *kpr*, but never elsewhere to *nʿṣr*. The construction of *ʿṣr* (*nipʿal*) with *mgph*, as in the final clause, is found also in Num 17:13, 15; 25:8;[18] and Ps 106:30. The BTH also uses the vb. in 1 Kgs 8:35//2 Chr 6:26, with *šmym* ("heaven") as subj.

[18–25] David asks that the (innocent) people be spared and only he (the guilty party) bear the guilt (v. 17). The divine response, again implicit, comes through Gad: erect an altar on Araunah's threshing floor (v. 18). Both altar and the means for sacrifice are offered free, but David refuses the Jebusite's offer: he holds that sacrifice should cost the worshiper (v. 24). His purchase of the threshing floor and building of the altar are described in assonant verbs (*wyqn . . . wybn . . .*). Yahweh duly responds to the offer of sacrifice; and the plague is not just halted, but decisively averted. The first of the two final statements in v. 25b ("Yahweh . . . for/to the land") is not shared with 1 Chr 21, but it does recapitulate the conclusion in 21:14 of the story of the Gibeonite curse; the second confirms as report what BTH stated (2 Sam 24:21//1 Chr 21:22) as intention (to restrain the plague). Already in BTH, the verb *ʿlh* is prominent in this final paragraph: twice (vv. 18, 19) in *qal* ("go up"), and twice (vv. 24, 25) in *hipʿil* ("raise up"). The recurring force of this word is underscored (vv. 22, 24, 25) by the cognate *ʿlwt* ("holocaust sacrifices") and by the expected removal (v. 21) of the divine blow *mʿl hʿm* ("from upon the people").

Samuel and Chronicles stress different details of the negotiations between David and the Jebusite. Samuel reports two short speeches not in Chronicles: "Why is my lord king coming to his servant?" (v. 21a), and "Yahweh, your God, will be pleased with you" (v. 23b). In the first of these, the Jebusite addresses David in a formula used widely (34x) in Samuel: "my lord king."[19] In 2 Samuel (30x) it is only used in address to David; and in 1 Samuel (4x) it is used

18. Num 25:4 uses *neged hašāmeš* as in 2 Sam 12:12; cf. "expose in the sun" in 2 Sam 21:1–14 (GT) for *hwqʿ* ("impale/hang," 21:9; also Num 25:4).

19. See 1 Sam 24:8 (9); 26:17, 19; 29:8; 2 Sam 3:21; 4:8; 9:11; 13:33; 14:9, 12, 17, 18, 19, 22; 15:15, 21; 16:4, 9; 18:28, 31, 32; 19:19, 20, 26, 27 (2x), 28, 30, 35, 37 (20, 21, 27, 28 [2x], 29, 31, 36, 38); 24:3 (2x), 21, 22.

only by David—to Saul (3x) and to Achish (1x). In all of the synoptic royal story (BTH), we find it only twice: in 2 Sam 24:3//1 Chr 21:3 and in 2 Sam 24:22//1 Chr 21:23. It is used nowhere else in Chronicles and rarely in Kings. In the census story, it is Joab (24:3) and the Jebusite (v. 22) who address David this way; it may not be unrelated that the Jebusite is the only character in BTH to prostrate himself before a human. The first time David addresses Saul this way (1 Sam 24:8 [9]) is part of a narrative in which we have already noted significant links with the census story (see on v. 10 above). The lordship of the king, and especially of King David, appears to have been less a regular feature of the historical court etiquette of ancient Israel and Judah, and more a key theme of the book of Samuel.

The fragments preserved in 4QSam[a] of this paragraph have a puzzling relationship with MT and LT and with Chronicles as well. There are two unique mentions of "sacking": the main Samuel texts have no sackcloth in 2 Sam 24, while Chronicles agrees with 4QSam[a] only over sackcloth in 1 Chr 21:16//2 Sam 24:16. This may be part of a wider phenomenon. We noted above (on 2 Sam 12:16) that LT and much of the Greek tradition agree with 4QSam[a] in portraying David as lying on the ground in sacking—and 4QSam[a] reports the scene by using standard *wayyiqṭōl* verbal forms, while MT appears suspiciously stilted: MT may have written sackcloth out of its account of the king's intercession for his child. But now in this case, the triple agreement of MT + GT against 4QSam[a], and even more the double agreement of Chronicles against 4QSam[a] (which shares the plus including sacking in 1 Chr 21:16), combine to make it very likely that the return of 4QSam[a] in 2 Sam 24:20 to the sackcloth theme is secondary.[20]

The Chronicler makes explicit (1 Chr 22:1) what many readers of Samuel–Kings find implicit there: that this threshing floor is the site of the temple and altar that Solomon constructed. In addition to occupying the city for Israel, David is credited with both the moving there of the ark and the acquisition of the site of the temple where it will be lodged. The first resulted in the dread death of Uzzah, the second was associated with a terrible plague. We should not be surprised that the Samuel version of the census may allude to the earlier story when it warns us at the outset that we will find in 2 Sam 24 another kindling of divine anger.

The book of Samuel in its Hebrew canonical form (MT) comes to its end exactly at the conclusion of the more ancient David story told in BTH. To judge from the very sparse shared material in 1 Kgs 1–2 and 1 Chr 22–29, the death and burial of David and the transition to Solomon was only briefly reported there. The culminating *ʿlh* theme of the final paragraph of 2 Sam 24, together with the *pqd* ("take [ac]count of") theme of the opening paragraph (vv. 2, 4, 9) of the census report, is anticipated at the opening of the book of Samuel. Hannah

20. Herbert (2) issues a careful warning about the relationship of 4QSam[a] and Chronicles.

and her husband repeatedly "go up" to the sanctuary (1:3, 7, 21, 22; 2:19); and Hannah "brings up" first her son (1:24) as the promised once-for-all offering and then a regular offering of a (priestly?) garment for him (2:19). Yahweh, on his side, "took account of Hannah" (2:21), giving her five further children. As the book of Samuel opens, this may or may not be a deft suggestion that Yahweh, and not David, is the appropriate subject of the verb *pqd*. Be that as it may in 1 Sam 2, this point is emphatically made twice over in the closing words of Genesis: "God will assuredly take note [*pqd ypqd*] of you and will bring you up [*ʿlh hipʿil*] from this land" (50:24). "God will assuredly take note [*pqd ypqd*] of you, and you will bring up [*ʿlh hipʿil*] my bones from here" (50:25). And the next and final verse of Genesis simply reports that Joseph died, and they embalmed him and placed him in a casket." In 2 Sam 24, *pqd* and *ʿlh* are the keywords of the beginning and end of the census story; only that narrative in all of the David story in BTH employs the strengthening infinitive absolute (*qnw ʾqnh* in v. 24, like *pqd ypqd*).

Excursus 6: Afterword on 2 Samuel 24

There are many other interesting echoes of this narrative in biblical story. It shares a whole cluster of rare Hebrew words with the prose prologue to Job (1–2), and not just the common theme of the testing of the hero. The testing of the hero, with consequences for the whole nation, is reminiscent of the divine instruction to Abraham to sacrifice Isaac (Gen 22); and in all of the Hebrew Bible, the negotiation over the purchase of the threshing floor has no closer comparator than Abraham's buying the plot of land for Sarah's tomb (Gen 23). Still more immediately, and read now within the coda to the book of Samuel (2 Sam 21–24), Polzin (1993: 211) observes how Saul's error costs (only) seven of his own family and yet final extinction, while David's error costs seventy thousand of Israel yet his family endures.

The verb *qnh* ("acquire, purchase") itself has interesting echoes (2 Sam 24:21, 24). It is used once more in BTH—in 2 Kgs 22:6//2 Chr 34:11, of purchase of supplies for repairing the temple that would be built on this site by Solomon.[21] Although not actually a part of the narrative in Gen 23, it is used in the recollections of Abraham's purchase in Gen 25:10; 49:30; 50:13. The one occurrence in Joshua (24:32) is linked with Jacob's parallel purchase of land in Shechem (Gen 33:19). The only other instance in Samuel is in 2 Sam 12:3—part of a narrative with many links to the census story.

This whole chapter is distinctive in several respects within the synoptic narrative about David. It includes more dialogue; the role of the divine messenger is unique; and as noted above, the infinitive absolute (in v. 24, and perhaps originally also in v. 17) is not found elsewhere in that narrative. Though shared, even if also rewritten, in both Samuel and Chronicles, and though influential on the drafting of many portions of Samuel, the older report of the census may have had a different origin from much of the rest of BTH.

21. Dr. Lydie Kucová (International Baptist Theological Seminary, Prague) cogently argues (private communication) that 2 Kgs 12:13 is a secondary anticipation of 2 Kgs 22.

But the more immediate resonances in the books of Kings and Chronicles, and so originally in the Book of Two Houses, may be more relevant for eliciting the earlier significance of this episode within its own larger narrative. The divine plague, like the revolt of Israel and Jeroboam on the death of Solomon (1 Kgs 12), and like the Assyrian army in the time of Hezekiah (2 Kgs 18–20), did stop short of destroying Jerusalem and the house of David in Jerusalem. Even the threat in the time of Josiah was delayed (2 Kgs 22–23). Divine incitement to disastrous behavior is mirrored in the intervening story of the king of Israel and Jehoshaphat of Judah and their campaign in Transjordan (1 Kgs 22). Read against these contexts, the threat against Jerusalem that David "saw" in the divine messenger came closer and closer over the generations—and the altar he built and the sacrifices he offered did not in the end stop the destruction of Israel.

This somewhat parabolic reading of the census and its aftermath, as presaging the grim—even if long delayed—fate of Israel and Jerusalem, helps to explain one of its details that is otherwise unique within the David chapters of BTH. David orders a count to be made of Israel; but the results of that census come back to him in totals for Judah as well as for Israel. That divided nation is not the Israel he has known, at least in the pages of BTH; but it is the Israel and Judah that will be—and will begin no later than the death of his own son. And it is the Israel that authors of Samuel import into their new story: making David king of Judah before he becomes king of Israel; and even having Saul count his people as Israel and Judah.

Excursus 7: Prospect to 1 Kings 1–2

The book of Samuel in its Hebrew canonical form (MT) ends with the final major portion of the David section of BTH. However, in at least one major element of the Greek tradition (LT), the book of 2 Kingdoms/Reigns ends only with Solomon firmly established on David's throne (1 Kgs 2:12 in MT). The material in 1 Kgs 1–2 is very closely related to what we have read in 2 Sam 11–20. David's powers are failing (1 Kgs 1:1–4); and Adonijah, his eldest surviving son, claims the succession but does not include Nathan or Solomon among his guests (1:5–10). Nathan and Bathsheba visit David in his bedchamber and "remind" him that he has promised the succession to Solomon (1:11–27). David confirms from his deathbed that this is his will and has his trusted men anoint Solomon (1:28–40). Adonijah's celebrations come to a quick end, and he himself seeks safety by the altar (1:41–53). David advises Solomon to keep faith with Yahweh (2:1–4) and makes specific recommendations about the fate of three men: Joab and Shimei should be put to death, but Barzillai's family should enjoy Solomon's hospitality (2:5–9). David's death and burial, the length of his reign, and Solomon's settled succession are briefly noted (2:10–12). The remainder of 1 Kgs 2 describes how Solomon gives effect to David's advice. Adonijah plays into his hands and is struck down (vv. 13–25), and Abiathar is banished (vv. 26–27). Finally Joab and Shimei are both struck down by the same Benaiah who has killed Adonijah, and he duly succeeds Joab as army chief (vv. 28–46).

All of these characters and most of the locations are familiar from (at least a mention in) Samuel. Adonijah (so MT, but GT knows him as Ornia)[22] had been listed in 2 Sam

22. The GT has read not *ʾdnyh* but *ʾrnyh*.

3:4 as the fourth son of David born at Hebron, but was otherwise unknown. He had the support of Joab, the army chief, and of Abiathar the priest. En-rogel (1:9), site of his accession party, is where the sons of Abiathar and Zadok waited for intelligence from Absalom's Jerusalem (2 Sam 17:17). Just a few elements of the story are new. We have not previously met the young Abishag, recruited to warm the aged David (1:1–4) and then foolishly claimed by Adonijah (2:13–25); but she hails from Shunem, which served as the Philistine base before the battle at Gilboa (1 Sam 28:4). Gihon, the location of Solomon's anointing (1:33, 38, 45), reappears in HB only in reports of building operations by Hezekiah and Manasseh (2 Chr 32:30; 33:14). And we are told (2:26) that Abiathar has his land at Anathoth—when we first met him (1 Sam 22:20), he was the sole survivor of the slaughter of the priests from (nearby) Nob. At least some sections of 1 Kgs 1–2 are familiar with what we have identified as some of the latest sections of Samuel. Part of the charge against Joab (2:5, 32) is that he struck down Amasa (2 Sam 20); and the listing of David's Hebron-born sons as well as Joab's earlier elimination of Abner are part of 2 Sam 1–4. Benaiah has a role in the oldest David story (BTH): he was "over the Cherethites and the Pelethites" (2 Sam 8:18) and personally valiant in protecting David (23:20–23); but his role is never developed or further explored in Samuel. However, in this transitional period, Kings has him head the army and become chief executioner.

Excursus 8: Themes and Growth of the Book of Samuel

Historical and theological reflections on Samuel both develop naturally from our discussion of 2 Sam 24. Throughout this commentary I argue that we have to reckon with at least three major phases in the development of this book. The earliest of these is relatively easy to define in outline: it is simply the material shared with the Chronicler. There are small though significant differences between Samuel and Chronicles in textual detail; and there are two differences over the ordering of episodes. I hold Chronicles as the more conservative version of the story held in common.

In this oldest connected account of David (BTH), the reader meets David for the first time when the new king is approached by Israel's leaders, who invite him to succeed Saul. He is introduced as an already-established leader of men; and he is quickly pictured with his men around him. Joab, his chief commander, has a prominent role in the taking of Jerusalem. Several daring episodes are recounted, some anonymous, some naming his chief warriors, several of them with names from outside Israel. Philistines are the only enemy named at the outset. Much of the remainder of the story reports first steps toward building the national shrine that David's son Solomon will complete in Jerusalem. The divine ark is brought to Jerusalem from a Philistine border area, and the averting of a divine threat defines the location in Jerusalem where the future temple will be built. Yahweh declares to David that his concern is more to build David's house(hold) than to have David build a house for Yahweh—but only after David has brought into Jerusalem the symbol of divine presence and power (the ark). The rest of the story is taken up with a few more campaigns, against neighbors to the east of the Jordan and more Philistines. There is always a prominent position in this older story for David's lieutenants, whether in leadership or deeds of individual prowess. The final episode is distinctive in both language and theme. It shows David as making a serious error of judgment, against the advice of loyal Joab. And the divine response to his wholesale confession is quite opaque. At least a strong hint is given that David himself is responsible for the end as well as for the beginning of his long line.

The new story of David, which we read within 1 Sam 9 and onward, retains all this material, except that it has reordered and rewritten some of the episodes to make David more prominent, although not necessarily to his advantage. However, it has a great deal to tell the reader about David before Israel comes to make him king. He has been anointed king long before, youngest of eight brothers, by divine emissary Samuel. He has dispatched a heavily armed Philistine champion with a stone from a slingshot, like a shepherd dealing with a lion or bear, and become immediately ten times more popular than the king. Saul has taken him onto his staff but become immediately suspicious of his success and popularity. David has married Saul's daughter, after paying the bride-price by circumcising an improbably large number of (dead) Philistines. These are all legendary deeds of individual prowess. A long report follows about Saul and David's falling out. Finally, while David is on the run, Saul has accidentally come into the power of the "outlaw"—and been spared. At one level, Saul certainly could not die in any way other than the older story had told—in battle with the Philistines. But two other factors were also important to the new storyteller. One was negative: the new king could not be responsible for his death. And the other was positive: the already anointed king-to-be should foster the mystique of anointedness. All that the older shorter version had told about David's predecessor was that he had died with his sons while fighting the Philistines.

The older story of David had in fact opened with a report of Saul's death. This new version of the story begins at 1 Sam 9 and introduces us to the future King Saul as a young man sent by his father to look for lost donkeys. When he asks help of Samuel, a local seer or man of God, he receives much more than he expected and finds himself anointed as king—as well as being told that, in his absence, the donkeys have been found. At much the same stage, a new narrative was also contributed about David and his family after the second king became established in Jerusalem. This paints a mostly bleak picture of dysfunctional relationships. The opening story of David and Bathsheba and Uriah and the prophet Nathan both anticipates and interprets key features of the census climax of the older David narrative. David is the wrongdoer, and his own family will pay. His guilt can be "removed," but only in the sense of being transferred: it cannot vanish into nothing. First the baby born of the adulterous union dies; then David's eldest son replicates his father's crime by raping a half sister and is killed by her brother. That son (Absalom) goes into exile; but after restoration to Jerusalem, he mounts a rebellion against his father that ends in his death. Tensions emerge between different parts of the kingdom.

The final stages of major extension and of rewriting may belong together. The one is represented by the latest new beginning (in 1 Sam 1–8). This crafts a fresh introduction to the Samuel who will anoint both Saul and David king, and to the prophetic movement as a whole. The other involves a substantial return to several previous scenes, such as Saul among the prophets, the rejection of Saul, Saul's life spared by David, David and the Philistine king of Gath, and the deaths of Samuel and of Saul. New themes make an appearance among these returnees, such as Amalek as major enemy, and also the distinction between Judah and Israel as present and not just future reality. This material is concentrated in 1 Sam 15; 25–30; 2 Sam 1–4; 20; and it includes 1 Sam 19:20–24 and possibly all of 1 Sam 20. The distinction between the second and the third is admittedly much easier to draw in some parts of the book than others. Which themes are present throughout, even if modified? Are any important earlier themes dropped later? And which themes emerge only at later stages? Being aware of possible connections does not prove anything, but it does encourage us to heighten our expectations as we read.

The narratives are brilliantly crafted. Their repeated ambiguity makes it all the harder to pin down their themes. When we read from beginning to end, we are attracted to the story of the legendary young hero, adored by the populace and suspected by the jealous king. Forced into hiding, we see him recruit a rabble of discontents and forge a coherent fighting force. When we read from the end, when we read with prior knowledge of the older story, we notice how often in the newer material David is featured as the solitary hero, able to succeed on his own; we notice how Joab and Abishai his brother have come to irritate him: he uses them, but also curses them; we notice how the heroes of Adullam have become traduced as bitter-spirited outlaws. Our broad proposals about the writing and rewriting of Samuel—each time with a still earlier introduction, as well as additions within the existing story—help us to understand better the changing way some topics and characters are portrayed than just by reading from beginning to end and by continuing to suppose that the Chronicler has rewritten the David story he found in Samuel. Following are some chief characters and themes of Samuel.

1. Joab and his brother Abishai, the sons of Zeruiah, make a good starting point. In Chronicles (and, I have claimed, in BTH too) Joab is simply David's right-hand man, with Abishai giving occasional support. Joab wins his position by his prowess at the taking of Jerusalem. Both brothers have honorable mention in the lists of heroes. Abishai has success in Edom. Both lead sections of the army against the Aramaeans. Joab effectively captures Ammon. After failing to stop David's counting his people, he leads the expedition that carries out David's tragic wishes. As a first author of Samuel makes this inherited material his own, he writes Joab out of the capture of Jerusalem, gives David the credit against Edom, and moves the brothers with his many other named heroes to the very end of the book. Despite these moves, which heighten David's own role, the presentation of Joab in the new material in 2 Sam 11; 12; 14; 18 remains positive. His open critique of David in 2 Sam 19:1, 5 (2, 6) leads to his replacement in 19:13 (14). It is only in what we have identified as among the latest chapters in Samuel that we find Joab taking quite independent action. After David's move to Hebron and his dealings with Jabesh-gilead (2 Sam 2:1–7), this new king of Judah plays no role in the remainder of ch. 2. Instead, it is two apparently independently acting strong men, Abner and Joab and their forces, who meet and struggle at Gibeon; and it is after another expedition from Hebron that Joab has his revenge on Abner for the death of his brother Asahel. Just as he frustrates David's dealings with Abner (ch. 3), so too he sweeps aside Amasa (ch. 20), whom David has made army commander in his place. Abishai's position between David and his brother (19:21 [22]; 20:6, 10) is somewhat ambivalent. An early author of Samuel may have raised David's profile by removing the brothers from his script; but it is only a later successor who has David curse his loyal lieutenant early in the story (3:29, 39)—and advise Solomon at the end to have him killed (1 Kgs 2:5–6). The David

who labels Zeruiah's sons (his own cousins) as harder men than he (2 Sam 3:39) seems to speak for this author: they are part of what he has inherited, and he has to cope with them. Abishai's end remains unreported.[23]

2. None of the women in the book of Samuel plays as large a role as Joab. However, women become increasingly important as the book develops; and the change is actually quite dramatic. There is only one woman in the David story shared with Chronicles—in fact only one woman in BTH till the Queen of Sheba—and she is Michal daughter of Saul. In BTH, we have but a tantalizing glimpse of her (2 Sam 6:16), after her father and brothers are dead, looking through a window and despising David's dancing as the ark is brought into Jerusalem. Her introduction in the central strata of the book is quite the opposite: she is enamored of the young hero who has killed the Philistine giant, is married to him, and helps him to escape from her father. In a new conclusion to 2 Sam 6, David rejects her contempt, and she remains childless: the daughter of Saul will produce no claimant to her father's throne. And in the final drafts of the book, at some point after she has assisted David's escape, her father remarries her to Palti[el] (1 Sam 25:44), but David insists on her return to him as part of Abner's negotiations to deliver all Israel to him (2 Sam 3:12–16). Michal is the only woman whose depiction is developed over all the rewritings of the book. At least part of what each new author is doing is answering questions that a previous version has left open. Why did the daughter of Saul despise the new king of Israel? After all, she had once been in love with him and had married him. What happened after she helped her new husband to escape from her father? Saul married her to another man. Then what was their formal relationship when she saw David from the window and despised him? After Saul's death, David had insisted that she return to his house: he did not want any rivals from the family of Saul.

The other women in the central strata of the book, apart from the swooning crowds who shared Michal's admiration for Goliath's nemesis, are Bathsheba, Tamar, and the wise woman from Tekoa. Bathsheba is very beautiful and is seen and taken by David. She sends a message to David announcing her pregnancy; and we are told that she laments her dead husband, Uriah. But any speaking she does is offstage; and even that is simply to give instructions for the delivery of a two-word message: "I'm pregnant." We see the lovely Bathsheba, who has fascinated artists over the generations, but we barely hear her till 1 Kgs 1–2. Tamar has more to say, both before she is raped and as she is being thrown out of Amnon's house; we are left wondering whether she should have spoken out earlier, when David sent her to make heart-cakes for her half brother. Like Tamar, the unnamed woman from Tekoa is recruited to do a task. Unlike Bathsheba and Tamar, she is not simply acted upon: though Joab had given her a role to play and words to speak, she demonstrates her personal wisdom by holding her own in debate with the king.

In the final strata of Samuel, the Tekoite's role is twice resumed, though by others. The first is the similarly anonymous wise woman from Abel. This woman takes the initiative herself, when her town is under siege by Joab. She urges Joab to prefer a

23. This sketch of the development of the material leads to a very different reading from the "literary" account of the same material in Eschelbach.

peaceful outcome and then persuades her fellow townsfolk to cut off just the one head necessary to save the whole town. Then Abigail too anticipates important elements of the Tekoite more fully. She also acts decisively and successfully, when tipped off by her husband's men. Her wisdom makes a striking contrast with her husband's folly; and it is well demonstrated in one of the longest speeches in the book. David is more than impressed: he marries her immediately on her husband's sudden death—a death that, by her words and by her excellent sense of timing, she may herself have precipitated.

If Abigail is a major character in the narrative that opens the second main block of late material in the book, the other major female character starts off the whole story at the beginning of the first block. Hannah takes responsibility for her own life and becomes nothing less than the mother of prophecy. Many later characters in the book, not least David, will use the phrase "find favor in the eyes" of someone or other. Hannah is the first (or last?) of these, and her very name means "favored." Like Abigail and the unnamed wise women of Tekoa and Abel, she is recognized as able to hold her own in a man's world: with her husband and also with the priest Eli, who is in addition the power in the land. She not only dedicates to divine service the son she may bear, but also anticipates Samuel's prophetic office by her praying and in her poetic foresight.

The roles of Bathsheba, Tamar, and the Tekoite at the beginning (2 Sam 11–14) of one major block of material in the central strata, and of Hannah and Abigail at the beginning of each of the major blocks in the later strata (1 Sam 1–8; 1 Sam 25–2 Sam 4) can hardly be accidental. The only woman, apart from his daughter(s), to feature in the story of Saul is his unwilling medium and then attentive hostess on the last night of his life (1 Sam 28). As we have seen, she is presented in a remarkably sympathetic manner, given what the rest of the Hebrew Bible has to say about mediums and diviners. Several other women have a minor role to play, of whom the last is certainly one of the most tragic. Rizpah says not a word and is not raped; but her silent vigil all hot-summer-long over seven mutilated family victims speaks volumes about the different worlds of men and women.

3. Jonathan, rather like his father, is never properly introduced to us in BTH. In that core of the David story, he is mentioned only in his death: the Philistines kill him and two younger brothers when they catch up with Saul, and so he dies before his father. Similarly, there is no formal introduction in the central strata of 1 Samuel: he is simply there as a major character in 1 Sam 13–14, both alongside his father and as a (perceived) threat to him. Despite his earlier deeds of prowess, he is not mentioned in the long struggle with Goliath. We meet him just twice more at this middle stage of the book's development: he warns his father against doing harm to a young man who has behaved only correctly toward him (19:1–7); then, when his father is pursuing David in the southern desert, he meets the fugitive and secures a covenant with him. The terms of that bargain recognize that David will be king and that Jonathan's own role will become that of the second son (23:15–18). David in flight, Jonathan's speaking up for him with Saul, and Jonathan and David's making a covenant—these themes are integrated in a major new narrative within the third strata of the book (1 Sam 20). Saul's eldest son was never a threat to David's kingship: in BTH, he was dead before Israel's leaders approached David to be their king. In stratum 2, and even earlier in stratum 3, he recognized David's

claim to the throne by covenant. And in a final addition to the longer Hebrew version of the book, he recognized it immediately after David's defeat of Goliath (18:1–4): by coming to love him, refusing to let him return home, making a covenant, and (like his father before him [17:38]) passing over to him clothing and armor that presumably identified him as crown prince.

4. The act of anointing (the verb) features at all levels of the book, but "the anointed of Yahweh" (the noun *māšîaḥ*, "messiah") belongs only to the central and later layers. The verb that the first authors of Samuel inherit has a human and plural subject in BTH: it is Israel and in particular its elders who anoint David at Hebron (2 Sam 5:3, 17). And the same may be inferred from Absalom's followers who admit (2 Sam 19:10 [11]) that "we anointed Absalom over ourselves"; and it survives in the final stages of the book, where the "men" or "house" of Judah anoint David still earlier at Hebron (2 Sam 2:4, 7). But the subject of "anoint" in 1 Samuel is either Yahweh (10:1; 15:17) or Samuel at Yahweh's behest (9:16; 16:3, 12, 13). Nathan also declares (2 Sam 12:7) that Yahweh has anointed David and saved him from the hand of Saul.[24] On this view of the growth of the book, the noun "messiah" makes its first appearance in Samuel within the central strata of that book. The earliest use of the noun, in 1 Sam 24:6, 10 (7, 11; at the end of the first draft of the Saul-David story), corresponds to the several instances of the verb at the beginning of that block. We find the noun also in several poems (1 Sam 2:10; 2 Sam 1:21; 22:51; 23:1), as also in several passages among the later strata (1 Sam 2:35; 12:3, 5; 26 (4x); 2 Sam 1:14, 16; 19:21 [22]).[25] One of the larger issues raised by these observations is the relationship between the poems and the third main prose stratum. The moral compromises and naked power of "real" kingship are more fully displayed in the third stratum than earlier in the depiction of Saul and David, while the poems are an embodiment of the royal "ideal."

5. Issues of guilt and forgiveness span all of Samuel, and all levels of development of Samuel. David's comprehensive and repeated confession comes at the very end of his story as first told. He has been very sinful and very stupid, and he asks for his guilt to be removed (2 Sam 24:10). When the king sees the punishment he has selected being meted out on his people, he asks that he and his wider family bear the weight of the divine hand, and not his people: it is he who has sinned and he who has done very wrong (24:17). The divine response to this second declaration of guilt seems pregnant with the distant exilic future: an altar should be built and sacrifice offered, leading to favorable divine response toward the land and Israel—but not a word about David and his own house having to bear his guilt. Will the house of David share the divine favor toward Israel and her land? Or will the renewal of divine favor for land and people come at the cost of the shepherd's, and not his sheep's, carrying his guilt?

These words of David are anticipated—and the silence of Yahweh is pondered—many times throughout the book. "Folly" alone, in not keeping an appointment with

24. The term *hṣyl* ("deliverance") belongs mostly to the latest strata and links the statement of 2 Sam 12:7 to 1 Sam 15:17.

25. The last of these passages is linked through Abishai with 1 Sam 26.

Samuel, is enough to cost Saul's rejection as king; and the turning to folly of a royal counselor's advice causes him to take his own life. Thus *skl* ("act foolishly") reappears twice in the middle layer (1 Sam 13:13; 2 Sam 15:31). Although the word occurs most often in the late book Ecclesiastes, it is also used earlier, in Jeremiah's poetry (4:22; 5:21). "Sin" is prevalent throughout the book of Samuel. In the middle layer, there is talk of Saul and David's sinning or not sinning against each other (1 Sam 19:4, 5; 24:11). David denies he has sinned against Saul and refuses the idea that he might lift his hand against the anointed of Yahweh (24:9–11 [10–12]); but later he needs to admit to sin against Yahweh (2 Sam 12:13). And sin against Yahweh by the people is also reported (1 Sam 14:33–34). The woman of Tekoa takes on herself any guilt relating to her approach to David, and she absolves the king in advance (2 Sam 14:9); Absalom is prepared to die if his father finds *ʿāwôn* in him (14:32).

In the final layers, "sin" is mostly against Yahweh. Eli states the general problem (1 Sam 2:25): for sins between humans, there is a remedy—but what about sins against God? The people's sin against Yahweh consists in following other gods (7:6; 12:10); Saul's sin consists either in disobeying instructions from Yahweh and Samuel (15:24, 30) or in pursuing David (26:21); Saul underscores his declaration to David by framing a tripartite anticipation of David's confession to Yahweh, linking his "sin" to "folly" and very considerable "error." In these later chapters, there is greater diversity over how "guilt" is used. The guilt of Eli's own house (1 Sam 3:13–14) is an acute example of the problem he has already voiced about sin against Yahweh (2:25). The guilt that David feels shadowing him from Saul is left unspecified (20:1, 8). When Abigail as suppliant takes on herself any guilt, she is anticipating the Tekoite's role (25:24). And when Saul absolves the medium from En-dor of any guilt (28:10), he speaks as king and judge (though she does not know it yet), in respect of an earlier ruling he himself has made. Abner details his loyalty to the house of Saul and rebukes his new king for counting against him guilt in a case concerning a woman (2 Sam 3:8).

6. The "father's house" theme also spans the book of Samuel from beginning (1 Sam 2:27–31) to end (2 Sam 24:17), and that also means from early in the tradition to late. We have seen some reason to consider that the census story may have been an early supplement to the rest of the David story in BTH. The theme that David introduces there is taken up in the central strata of the book. It helps to form a bracket round the older account of Saul's kingship: Samuel notes that Israel's desire is for Saul and his father's house (1 Sam 9:20); then Saul, once he has told David that he knows David will be king, begs him to swear that he will not destroy Saul's name from his father's house (24:21 [22]). He will be well aware that what does happen in the end (2 Sam 21:1–14) corresponds to well-established practice. And later within these central strata, the wise woman of Tekoa anticipates several elements of the census story. David, after hearing her case, tells her to go to her house (an unremarkable expression) till he decides what to do in response. When she remains in his presence, she takes up the "house" cue and introduces what she has to say by adapting David's own words to the destroying divine messenger at the end of the older story: "The guilt is on me, my lord king, and on my father's house—the king and his throne are innocent" (2 Sam 14:9). But she presses

on to note that David is like a "messenger" of God (14:17) and is "reckoning" (another counting verb, though not one of the three used in the census story) something against the people of God (14:13): he should not keep someone banished forever (14:14). A still later author has David curse Joab and his whole father's house with a range of physical disabilities to prevent them from exercising rule (2 Sam 3:29): a list more detailed, even if more briefly stated, than the judgment against Eli and his father's house (1 Sam 2:30–36).[26] The comprehensive statement by Solomon when condemning Joab (1 Kgs 2:31–33) resumes elements from both 2 Sam 3:29 and 2 Sam 14:9. And finally, "father's house" features among the substantial pluses in the longer Hebrew version of the Goliath story: David is told that whoever kills the Philistine will receive from the king riches and the king's daughter in marriage and freedom for his father's house (1 Sam 17:25); but when he has duly killed Goliath, "Saul took him . . . and would not let him return to his father's house" (18:2).

The critique of Joab in later strata of Samuel also employs *dāmîm*, the plural of the common noun for "blood," which has the sense of "bloodguilt" (2 Sam 3:28; 1 Kgs 2:5, 31, 33). The same term is used to identify the bloodguilt on Saul for what he has done to Gibeon (2 Sam 21:1) and on Jezebel for her actions against both Yahweh's prophets and Naboth (2 Kgs 9:7, 26). At this later stage in the tradition, we meet *dāmîm* first in a double disclaimer: Abigail tells David that Yahweh has restrained him from incurring such guilt by killing Nabal, and David replies that it is she who has held him back (1 Sam 25:26, 33). It seems to have been necessary for this later author to make an early response to the charge attributed by an earlier author to Shimei as he met David leaving Jerusalem: that David was "a man of bloods," and Yahweh had brought back on him all the bloodguilt for the house of Saul in whose place he had become king. Saul and his sons have certainly died bloodily, and David has become king in their place. But Shimei seems to be speaking wildly in making David the cause of the fall of Saul's house. However, he had said it; and his statement needed to be countered. Later authors would make three points in response: (1) The violence to Abner, Saul's kinsman and chief of staff, was perpetrated by Joab, who would be dealt with. (2) David had been held back from lashing out at Nabal and had (similarly) spared Saul twice in the same period. And (3) even if servants of the house of Saul had died at Gibeon, and Abner later as part of the same affair, Saul himself had tried to wipe out Gibeon and its people altogether.

Toward the end of the narrative, "sin" and "guilt" are brought together by Shimei in a very significant combination: he admits that he sinned at the time when David was leaving Jerusalem, but asks David not to reckon his guilt to him or remember it (2 Sam 19:19, 20).[27] Abishai counters that Shimei deserves death because it was Yahweh's anointed he cursed. Shimei's pleading his case before David might be a parable for David's pleading his case before Yahweh—but if so, then it is a rather bleak parable. David does not

26. The clustering of the expression "father's house" in 1 Sam 2:27–31 finds a parallel in (the similarly priestly context of) 1 Sam 22:11–23.

27. In one of the three ancient readings of David's response to Shimei's original cursing, he may have been hoping that Yahweh would look on his "guilt" (which led to Absalom's revolt), but repay him with good for Shimei's curses (2 Sam 16:12).

"reckon" Shimei's guilt that day and swears that he will not die (19:22–23); but equally he does not forget it and advises Solomon to have Shimei killed (1 Kgs 2:8–9). Should we hear the author as suggesting that the house of David was spared at the time, but that Yahweh would wait for his own moment to punish David's sin?

7. Prophets have roles to play in all strata of the book, but they differ in each layer. In BTH, Nathan is consulted by David and offers a response as his adviser before he receives a different divine response to transmit (2 Sam 7). And we may presume a similar role for Gad (2 Sam 24), since he is called "David's seer." The earliest stories about Samuel (from the middle layers of the book) depict a somewhat similar situation. He is not a court prophet or seer, for there is no king; but he is a seer or man of God available for consultation (1 Sam 9); like Nathan, he may also transmit a message from God that has not been sought (1 Sam 9–10). Divine undertakings to kings, announced by Samuel and Nathan, may also be radically revised by them (1 Sam 13; 2 Sam 12). Samuel, unlike anything reported of Nathan or Gad, has a relationship with a band of prophets (1 Sam 10). In this layer of the book, there is no role for prophets in 1 Sam 17–24 except for the report of Samuel's death (25:1). In later strata, Samuel is given a much expanded and extended role (1 Sam 1–3; 7–8; 15; 19:20–24; 28). Like Jeremiah, he is called before he is born. Like Elisha, he has a role to play after his death. Part of his developed role is as judge (1 Sam 7). And, like Elijah and Elisha, he both raises kings up and puts them down.

INDEX OF SCRIPTURE AND OTHER ANCIENT SOURCES

INDEX OF SUBJECTS AND AUTHORS